GROWING UP IN ENGLAND

Anthony Fletcher has been professor of history at the Universities of Sheffield, Durham and Essex, and director of the Victoria County History at London University. His previous books include *Gender, Sex, and Subordination in England, 1500–1800* (1995), published by Yale University Press.

ANTHONY FLETCHER

GROWING UP
IN ENGLAND

The Experience of Childhood
1600–1914

YALE UNIVERSITY PRESS
NEW HAVEN AND LONDON

Published with assistance from the Annie Burr Lewis Fund

First printed in paperback 2010

For information about this and other Yale University Press publications please contact:

U.S. Office: sales.press@yale.edu   www.yalebooks.com
Europe Office: sales@yaleup.co.uk   www.yalebooks.co.uk

Set in Caslon by J&L Composition Ltd, Filey, North Yorkshire
Printed in Great Britain by Hobbs the Printers Ltd, Totton, Hampshire

Library of Congress Cataloguing-in-Publication Data

Fletcher, Anthony
    Growing up in England: the experience of Childhood, 1600–1914 / Anthony Fletcher.
        p. cm.
    Includes bibliographical references and index.
    ISBN 978–0–300–11850–6 (alk. paper)
    1. Children—England—History. 2. Children and adults—England—History.
    3. England—Social conditions I. Title.
    HQ792.E54F54 2008
    306.8740942—dc22

                                                                              2007030910

A catalogue record for this book is available from the British Library

ISBN 978–0–300–16396–4 (pbk)

10 9 8 7 6 5 4 3 2 1

Contents

For Brenda

Plates

I have chosen images to illustrate several themes central to this book, including the artistic representation of Georgian family life, the education of boys at public schools, the domestic role of the governess in English country houses and the schooling of girls.

I have selected from my family's archives images of some of its members which, showing them as parents or children, are informative and arresting. Melesina Trench, my great-great-great grandmother, too little known for her educational thought, set out, some two hundred years ago, strikingly liberal and modern ideas about and precepts for the upbringing of children. Charlotte Bloomfield's well documented and tragically short life is movingly commemorated in a small portrait which is reproduced here and was painted by the leading child portraitist of Regency England. The family life of the Trenchs of Cangort Park in County Offaly, captured in their photograph albums, is redolent of the mores of the Anglo-Irish Protestant Ascendancy. The Howards, of Bark Hart at Orpington in Kent, expressed to the full the values of Victorian domesticity as the goal of the good life.

Tom Isham, Lucy Lyttelton and Louisa Bowater are three of the most spirited of the teenagers who, through their diary accounts, stride through the later pages of the book. The portraits of them here were commissioned during their young adulthood. Lucy Lyttelton's diary entry, about meeting her new governess, written in 1855 when she was fifteen years old, is a single teenager's authentic testimony to just one of thousands of encounters between children and adults over more than three hundred years. These formative relationships are the crux of this book. It is through myriad such relationships that I have sought to understand and explore how children grew up in England between 1600 and 1914.

1. George Romney, *Melesina Trench*, *c*. 1798, engraving by Francis Stoll. Trench Archive.

2. William Hogarth, *The Graham Children*, 1742. Reproduced by permission of the National Gallery, London.

3. Enoch Seeman, *Lady Anne Cust with her Children*, 1743–4. Reproduced by permission of the National Trust, Belton House.

4. Sir Joshua Reynolds, *Lady Cockburn and her Three Eldest Sons*, 1773. Reproduced by permission of the National Gallery.

5. Sir Joshua Reynolds, *Mrs Thrale and her Daughter Queenie*, 1781. Reproduced by permission of Beaverbrook Art Gallery, Fredericton.

6. The Trench family at Cangort Park, *c*. 1860. Trench Archive.

7. The governess at Cangort Park and the Trench girls, *c*. 1864. Trench Archive.

8. Mrs Mee, *Charlotte Bloomfield*, *c*. 1826. Trench Archive.

9. John Hassall, *Bark Hart House Academy*, 1780. Trench Archive.

10. Rayner, *Bark Hart*, *c*. 1900. Trench Archive.

11. Ellen Howard with her daughters and the governess at Bark Hart, *c*. 1902. Trench Archive.

12. The Howard girls at Bark Hart, *c*. 1900. Trench Archive.

13. Amy and Clare Howard, *c*. 1899. Trench Archive.

14. Clare and Amy Howard, *c*. 1900. Trench Archive.

15. Pigne D'Arolla, Switzerland, 1910. Trench Archive.

16. Ellen Howard, 1897. Trench Archive.

Preface and Acknowledgements

I have been a long time working on this book, begun while teaching at the University of Essex and completed several years into retirement. Looking back on the process of research and writing, I have substantial debts to record.

I was granted financial support by the University of Essex's Research Promotion Fund in 1995, to employ a Research Assistant who would identify relevant material, through a comprehensive postal enquiry to local record offices and bibliographical investigations. The enormous benefit of the work which Dr Helen Berry carried out so admirably has struck me time and again during the book's prolonged gestation. The History Department at Essex provided a lively research environment during the years from 1995 to 2000. I am particularly grateful to Catherine Crawford, Alison Rowlands and John Walter, among my colleagues there, for their company.

In 1998, the Leverhulme Trust granted me a Research Fellowship, which provided for replacement teaching at Essex during the academic year 1998 to 1999. This enabled me to travel widely seeking primary source material, and to work extensively in the Bodleian Library. I am grateful to the staff of the numerous record offices listed in the bibliography for their ready assistance. Our dependence on the dedicated support of the national archive profession is often taken for granted. I must record particular gratitude to the archivists at Chatsworth House, the Northamptonshire Record Office and the West Sussex Record Office, who assisted me on my visits to read three incomparable teenage diaries, deposited in these archives, which are fundamental to the arguments I set out and to the story I tell.

Over the period from 1996 to 2007, I have given seminar papers on aspects of my work for this book at various universities. Numerous discussions have informed and advanced my thinking. I am grateful to all the colleagues and friends who have participated on these occasions. I especially enjoyed the

Royal Historical Society's conference at the Huntington Library, San Marino, California, in September 2001, on 'English Politeness: Conduct, Social Rank and Moral Virtue, *c.* 1400–1900', which I organised with John Tosh. This was where I was able to introduce to the academic world three fascinating teenagers, Sophia Baker, Lucy Lyttelton and Louisa Bowater, key figures in this book, whose upbringings are related much more fully here.

I have made extensive use of my own family's archives. I am grateful to my mother, Delle Fletcher, for her meticulous care, over many years, in preserving and annotating the Bloomfield and Trench archives. Saive Coffey has kindly given me access to the Coffey Archive and Dr James Reilly to the Loughton Archive. I would also like to thank friends who have given much time and patience to reading material in draft and to discussing issues arising from the book. At Essex, Carole Williams was a highly stimulating and dedicated research student, whose important PhD thesis I draw upon extensively in these pages. Three previous students at Durham, Joanne Bailey, Helen Berry and Elizabeth Foyster, all of whom now hold senior academic posts in England, have kindly offered constant support, commentaries and many suggestions. Roger Highfield commented helpfully on chapter fourteen and Caroline Wells on chapter fifteen.

This is the third substantial monograph of mine that Robert Baldock has published. He is the most sympathetic of publishers. The completion and final form of this book owes much to his trust, enthusiasm and meticulous care.

My mother and family have been loyally supportive of my research and writing. Mary Dawkes has become a constantly perceptive counsellor and friend. The dedication records my most profound debt during the twelve years this book has been in preparation.

A.J.F., South Newington, June 2007

Introduction

This book presents an entirely fresh view of the upbringing of English children between 1600 and 1914, constructed on the basis of a very wide range of sources. There is consensus among historians that throughout this period England was essentially a hierarchical society. Keith Wrightson has explored the language of 'sorts' of people in the seventeenth century, when a descriptive terminology of the 'better', the 'meaner' and the 'middle sort of people' became familiar.[1] England was then still essentially a society ruled by landlords. Under the transforming impact of urbanisation and the Industrial Revolution, much non-landed wealth was created.[2] The power of the aristocracy declined, a powerful, numerous and ambitious middle class emerged and the professional and business classes became strongly established. Yet class as hierarchy remained the ruling principle, before the cataclysmic years of the First World War with which this book closes.[3] The focus here upon the upper class, including professional families, reflects the availability of vivid personal documentation of parental upbringing and of the experience of childhood.

Great landed families inevitably dominate the analysis. These pages provide a roll-call of parents and children from such families, from every county and district of England and from Ireland as well: Bacons of Redgrave, Bankeses of Kingston Lacy, Custs of Belton, Drydens of Canons Ashby, Flemings of Rydal, Fitzherberts of Tissington, Harleys of Brampton Bryan, Ishams of Lamport, Oglanders of Nunwell, Rothschilds of Aston Clinton, Sitwells of Renishaw, Smyths of Ashton Court, Trenchs of Bursledon and of Cangort Park and Verneys of Claydon. The aristocracy features too, with particular attention to the Bloomfields of Loughton, the Hattons of Kirby, the Lytteltons of Hagley, the Richmonds of Goodwood and the Stanleys of Alderley. What all these families had in common was land. Much of the growing up discussed here took place in country houses and on landed estates, miniature worlds teeming with servants.

Paul Langford has stressed the unity of polite society in Georgian England, the extent to which, despite intense competitiveness and fine gradations separating one stratum from the next, 'the pursuit of politeness submerged rather than exposed distinctions'.[4] This pattern of social coherence among the upper ranks, and the divide at some point which separated them from the mass of the people, is well expressed by the eleven-year-old Emily Shore at the opening of her diary in 1831. 'Papa takes pupils' she began, summarising his station as a writer and educator. She continued by enumerating 'the nearest gentlemen's places' to Potton, where the Shore family lived, and by explicating the realities of social leadership in this little Bedfordshire town. The 'principal persons', besides Papa and the vicar, were two surgeons, a wool merchant and a rich farmer. 'Potton contains no less than thirteen public houses besides beer shops', Emily continued, leaving its polite world behind her.[5]

However, there are also many fathers, mothers and children in this book whose families, like Emily's 'principal persons' in Potton, had not inherited land, yet who had substantial status. Some, like the Orpington barrister and quintessential commuter Henry Howard, acquired land or a mansion by lease. He lived the life of Victorian domesticity after the walk from the station. A good many never dreamed of having land. Thus the book is almost as much about professional attitudes and practice in the upbringing of children as about landed practice. The peripatetic Philip Francis, the Oakes family of Bury St Edmonds and the Gurneys of Norwich were all business people. Ralph Josselin, Giles Moore and John Taylor were clerical fathers. Admiral Edward Boscawen and Thomas Freemantle were naval men. William Rowe was a civil servant. Matthew Flinders was an apothecary and surgeon.

There is no difficulty in assimilating such families to the story, or families that took the national political stage, like the Foxs of Holland House and the mercantile Gladstones of Liverpool. They all absorbed and made what they could of the same precepts and prescriptions as the landed men. There was no fundamental divide in attitudes to upbringing within the upper and genteel strands of society.

Class is important because, as Leonore Davidoff and Catherine Hall have put it, 'gender and class always operate together' and 'consciousness of class always takes a gendered form'.[6] English upbringing, at the social level which is discussed here, was always pervasively gendered. The practice of parenting, equally, was gendered. Parents between 1600 and 1914, born to the assumption of gender roles and gender identity themselves, trained children to see themselves as functionally and essentially different, according to their sex. Boys and girls, they believed, had separate and distinct destinies.

Joan Scott's essay in the *American Historical Review* in 1986 'Gender: A Useful Category of Historical Analysis' was something of a trumpet blast to the historical profession. Historians needed, she declared, to examine the ways in which 'gendered identities are substantively constructed', since gender is a cultural construction. She described it as a social category, that, in numerous societies, has been imposed upon a sexed body. Gender, she argued powerfully, demands the attention of historians, since it has to be seen as a normal 'constitutive element of social relationships'. It is, she asserted in a famous phrase, a 'primary way of signifying relationships of power'.[7] Gender studies have come a long way since 1986: a brief review in relation to the English family will put this book in its context.

The first fruits of Scott's call for action were two studies with an explicit gender perspective, published respectively in 1987 and 1991: Leonore Davidoff and Catherine Hall's *Family Fortunes*, dealing with 'men and women of the English middle class 1780–1850', and Michael Roper and John Tosh's edited collection of essays, *Manful Assertions*. Since then, works on masculinity across the period have been more numerous than on femininity. Michele Cohen's *Fashioning Masculinity* (1996), focusing on the eighteenth century, was followed by Tim Hitchcock and Michele Cohen's edited collection *English Masculinities 1660–1800* (1999), then by Philip Carter's *Men and the Emergence of Polite Society, Britain 1660–1800* (2001). John Tosh's *A Man's Place* (1999) was the most substantial and important of this group of books, with its original and persuasive argument about the connection between masculinity and the concept of domesticity in the middle-class Victorian home. This was the only one of these studies explicitly to address boyhood.

The comparative void in studies of women after 1700 is grandly compensated for by Amanda Vickery's splendid study of genteel women's lives in Georgian England, *The Gentleman's Daughter* (1998). Sara Mendelson and Patricia Crawford's deeply-researched account of the lives of women in the Tudor and Stuart period, *Women in Early Modern England* (1998) is an impressive exercise in popular history. But none of these books, whether on men or women, set out, as a principle objective, to address the formative impact of childhood and upbringing from a gender perspective.

There has been some other perceptive work on the family and childhood, which has not been approached through gender. Hugh Cunningham's *Children and Childhood in Western Society* (1995) is a useful and important introductory text, stronger on prescription than on the practice of upbringing. John Gillis's entertaining *A World of their Own Making* (1997) focuses upon myth and ritual in the family life of the past. Leonore Davidoff, Megan Doolittle, Janet Fink and Katherine Holden offer many new insights, in retelling the history of the English family between 1830 and 1960, in *The Family Story* (1999). In *Forgotten Children* (1983), Linda Pollock offered a broad survey of parent-child relations, innocent of a gender approach, over a longer period than this book, using diaries and autobiographies as her source material. Her *A Lasting Relationship* (1987) is a superb anthology of primary source material relating to parents and children. Lawrence Stone's *The Family, Sex and Marriage in England 1500–1800* (1977) proposed a schematic model of change in family relationships. My own *Gender, Sex and Subordination in England 1500–1800* (1995) contained short chapters on educating boys and girls, which can be seen as sketches for the fuller arguments about boys and girls that are developed in this book.

The three sections of the book are based on different kinds of source material and conceived as distinct yet complementary. Ideally, they should be read in a logical progression. There is no reason why a reader who wishes to do so should not go directly to section two or section three, yet the book is best read as a single connected argument.

The first section of the book deals with three hundred years of prescriptive literature, which set out a developing ideology of childhood. This ideology moved from a Calvinistic and repressive mode to John Locke's blank sheet of paper, then to Romanticism and the Victorian sentimentalisation of childhood. At the prescriptive level, childhood certainly changed during these three hundred years, but it is an open question how far the basic objectives of parents and the practice of upbringing were affected by the changing concept.

Notions of formative masculinity and femininity were elaborated and refined in conduct book advice that was published in spate from 1660 onwards. The conduct of parenthood itself became the subject of a torrent of advice, which has lasted until the present day. The danger with all the material presented in part I of the book is of falling into the trap of thinking that parental behaviour at particular times followed closely upon current advice. Modes of upbringing were always various, numerous and subject to complex pressures. In a sense, no two sets of parents brought up their children identically during these centuries. At best, the prescriptive advice establishes themes in upbringing. There is no question that it was much read and absorbed, but how it was enforced is only revealed by the particular stories told in part II. Parenting was never a question of deliberate and unhurried reference to the manual: it was a day-to-day effort to do the sincere best that adults could for their children.

The second, by far the longest, section of the book amasses a large range of detailed evidence to delineate the modes of English parenting. A much wider range of sources is brought to bear at this point. Letters and memoirs form the centrepiece, illustrating the breadth and scope of parental activity in bringing up the young. The argument starts with the issue of care and affection, indicating that this was always seen as the core of the responsibility of parenthood. A review of parents as partners, in the responsible business of raising their children and in securing their health and strength, is provided, setting the scene for an account of growing up in the past. The searing impact of grief when children died indicates the depth of parental love and devotion. Throughout these chapters the emphasis is more on continuity than on change.

Chapters 8 to 17 treat the gendering of both parenting and of children's upbringing thematically, distinguishing the roles of fathers and mothers and the courses pursued by boys and girls. The overriding notion in this analysis, as they became increasingly self-conscious about how they were doing, is parental performance. At the domestic level, this was largely straightforward, though, as chapter 15 shows, the presence in the house of a governess could complicate parental care and authority, unless clear rules were laid down and boundaries were observed. With regard to the education of boys at school and university, chapters 11 to 14 indicate that marital partnership was more fraught, as fathers and mothers often had different priorities. Yet the relationship was constrained by patriarchal assumptions about male initiative. Schooling of girls, when it was adopted, was relatively uncontentious, since it could be seen as contributory to overall objectives in female training that were agreed between parents. Chapter 17 shows how girls were trained for society, whereas boys, through schooling, were trained for work and for the world.

In the final section of the book, children, largely silent until this point, previously objects rather than subjects, speak for themselves. A small sample of English children who grew up in these centuries kept diaries. These diaries are used to bring alive the responses of these children to the upbringings that parents provided. The meanings that children brought to key aspects of their lives, before they were adults, are explored through vivid and spontaneous notes and reflections made in private.

Chapter 18 seeks to establish the validity and authenticity of the personal testimony of these witnesses, who necessarily are largely drawn from the latter decades of the period covered by the book. Something of the realities of their lives is then told in accounts, in successive chapters, of their homes, schools and their travels in England and abroad. In chapter 22, rare material is used to penetrate the emotional lives of a very few teenagers, who lived in the later decades of the period. The concluding chapter treats the central issue of personal identity. The focus is upon three outstandingly detailed private diaries, a matchless kind of source material, diaries kept daily across several years by teenage girls. It is here that the experience of childhood comes alive, in the recorded experience of a few particular children.

In certain respects, early Stuart children in the upper class and Edwardian or late Victorian children in the same class lived very different kinds of lives. The material conditions of children's lives changed out of all recognition over three hundred years. Wooden cradles and baby walkers stand in museums and country houses in mute testimony to the simplicity of children's nursery furnishings in the seventeenth century. The contrast with the kind of nursery wing designed by Queen Victoria for Osborne House, to ensure that the royal parents climbed only one flight of stairs to visit children, could hardly be greater. Secluded from the adult world, the royal children nevertheless inhabited a well-furnished and well-equipped world of their own. The nursery wing at Lanhydrock in Cornwall, built in 1882 and restored by the National Trust, where nine children of the Robartes family were brought up, is the best place to appreciate this world. It ran round a courtyard to the side of the house with all rooms facing south to catch the maximum light. Night and day nurseries, Nanny's bedroom, bathroom and the schoolroom were linked, to servants' bedrooms above and the kitchen below, by the servants' stairs. Yet, at the same time, the children were within easy reach of Lord and Lady Robartes's private rooms.[8]

The nurseries of grand Victorian houses were full of toys and reading matter; schoolrooms boasted globes, rocking horses and numerous books. Toys, commercially available since at least the early seventeenth century, had only recently become abundant. Ben Jonson had Lanthorn Leatherhead, the puppet master, selling toys, probably imported ones, at *Bartholomew Fair*. He mentions hobby horses, drums and 'babies', in other words dolls. In 1726, there is a reference to a London toyshop, with furnishings for a dolls' house on sale.[9] By the 1780s, toy shops were numerous. But it was after 1850 that toys invaded country houses. More than 1800 toymakers were listed in the 1850s, a decade when at least 1,500 rocking horses were made for the upper- and middle-class market. 'On Saturdays and Sundays only we played with our Noah's Ark which during the rest of the week stood high and unheeded on the inaccessible Ararat of the very top bookshelf', wrote Eleanor Acland.[10]

Bought toys now competed with the numerous constructions of deferential estate carpenters. The sheer range of nursery and schoolroom facilities was revealed when the National Trust took over and unpacked a treasure-trove of children's playthings at Calke Abbey in Derbyshire. These were the belongings of Sir Vauncey Harpur Crewe, who inherited the house in 1886. There were dozens of dolls wrapped up in drawers, sets of lead soldiers in mint condition, books, games and tin trams on a wooden track.[11]

The highlight of a well-furnished Victorian nursery was the dolls' house. The spectacular one at Uppark, made for Sarah Lethieullier about 1735, has the arms of the family in the central pediment. Its nine rooms show all the domestic arrangements of the period in miniature, with pictures individually painted in oils down to the hall-marked silver. The dolls' house at

Nostell Priory in Yorkshire was made for the children of Sir Rowland and Susanna Winn, who married in 1729. Dolls representing the family are made of wax, the servants of wood. All the domestic world which awaited them when they grew up was arrayed here for the edification of the Winn children. The dolls' house was a formidable educational tool, designed to inculcate notions of privilege and hierarchy. The massive collection of dolls' houses at Wallington Hall in Northumberland includes one with 36 rooms, populated by 77 porcelain-faced dolls representing family and servants. It has all the modern conveniences of the 1880s, including electric light, a working lift and running water in the single bathroom.[12]

Until the 1740s, children's books consisted mostly of ephemeral chapbooks and ballads.[13] Then, in the middle years of the century, three publishers, Thomas Boreman, Mary Cooper and John Newberry, firmly established children's books as a separate branch of the trade. Newberry, the most prolific of them, published *Giles Gingerbread*, *Goody Two-Shoes* and *Mother Goose's Melody*. 'Duly purified', wrote Mary Jackson, 'Tom Thumb and Jack-the-Giant-Killer are his little people, and the giants they outwit and tame are his specially tailored foes – ignorance, sloth and profligacy.'[14] Victoria's reign was the golden age of books for children. Routledge published more than a hundred titles over twenty years in their New Sixpenny Toy Books series, started in 1866. Some of the most enchanting were those of the Arts and Crafts artist Walter Crane, recounting tales like 'This Little Pig went to Market' and 'Sing a Song of Sixpence'. A new genre of children's adventure stories began with Johann Wyss's *The Swiss Family Robinson* in 1814, followed by Frederick Marryat's *Children of the New Forest* in the 1840s. It would reach its Edwardian apogee with the incomparable and empowering children's books by Rudyard Kipling: *The Jungle Book*, *Just So Stories*, *Puck of Pook's Hill* and *Rewards and Fairies*.[15]

Swaddling very young children to stop them moving about was only gradually abandoned in the eighteenth century. In the highly formal portrait of four children of Sir Thomas Lucy in 1619, the little boy wears a biggin over his coif and an apron with a bib over his bodice.[16] Children were dressed without distinction of sex in frocks, waisted garments down to the feet, until boys were breeched at about six years old. Three group portraits of children, dated 1742, 1803 and 1885 respectively, illustrate the gradual liberation of children from tight and restrictive clothing, as fashion took over. The old conventions of control of the infant body became relics of the past.

The portrait of the Lucy children, set beside those of the Graham children, the Croft children and the Robartes children, marks the scale of change in this aspect of children's lives. In the 1742 Graham family portrait, the boy plays on his musical box and the canary sings, while the household cat peers over the chair, at the girls displaying their pretty frocks and the baby, given mobility by his wooden carriage, with his sister holding his hand.[17]

Sixty years later, in John James Halls's 1803 portrait of the four sons of Sir Richard Croft, the eldest boy, Herbert, wears a coat, breeches and an unbuttoned waistcoat over his frilled shirt. Jean-Jacques Rousseau's advocacy of comfortable, loose-fitting clothes, which give a boy liberty, has made its mark here. Herbert's brother, Thomas, sports the latest eminently practical fashion in boyswear: the skeleton suit. His trousers are cut to come above the waist and fastened to the bottom of a short jacket with buttons. His red jacket is turned back to the shoulders, revealing his frilled shirt collar. Herbert's three-year-old brother Francis, not yet breeched, is dressed traditionally, in a white dress, with a lace-edged muslin cap trimmed with blue ribbon. While Herbert, who in fact had recently died of smallpox at Westminster School, sadly holds a book, Thomas entertains his younger brothers by blowing bubbles.[18]

A rather sentimental group portrait of the eldest children of Lord Robartes of Lanhydrock, painted by Anna Lea Merrit in 1885, is designed to demonstrate sibling devotion and affection in a sylvan setting by much linking of arms. Thomas wears a kind of black cavalier suit; his twin sister Eva has decorative detail, then all the rage, in the smocking on her white dress.

The last decades of the nineteenth century witnessed the commercial availability of nursery furnishings, wallpapers and friezes and a new fashion for decorated crockery for nursery teas. Fashion had entirely taken over the market in children's clothes. Girls went from boned bodices and skirts to frocks and sashes in the 1770s, to Regency muslin chemise dresses and then crinolines with long pantalettes in the 1850s. Breeching of boys came forward in the nineteenth century, with skirts exchanged for tunic-style dresses at two, then knickerbockers with a matching jacket at around six. After 1846, when the Prince of Wales first wore one, the sailor suit became all the rage from around five years' old onwards. For girls, meanwhile, the pinafore dress and blouse became the standard uniform in the late Victorian period. Childhood was being celebrated: mothers showed off their children, having them photographed in fetching poses, in a competitive manner.[19]

Children dressed differently in Victorian England from how they had done earlier; they enjoyed many more toys. They could reach for nursery rhymes or even for adventure stories off the schoolroom shelf. So there were many respects in which the experience of childhood changed in the period from 1600 to 1914. The conventions through which children expressed deference and obedience to their elders changed too. But the research for this book has not revealed any grounds for supposing that anything of fundamental importance changed, between 1600 and 1914, in the dynamic of the relationships between English parents and their children.

This book seeks to be sparing with assertion. Family relationships were often full of tension and ambivalence. They defy easy generalisation. Along with demonstrative affection and passionate love, went argument and quarrelling, distrust and defiance. The documentation presented here, about growing up and the experience of children, is often left to speak for itself and for the reader to interpret.

PART I

PRESCRIPTION

1

Childhood

The core of seventeenth-century thinking about the child was that it lacked self-control and self-discipline. The crux of the argument about parental and school training, put didactically by the puritan clergy who held the field of advice literature before 1660, was that children should therefore have their original sin beaten out of them. Commentators drew upon animal similes from the Old Testament: children were like 'wild asses and wild heifers'. Parents should regard their child as 'like a young colt, wanton and foolish, till he be broken by education and correction'.[1] The word 'correction', dominating this prescriptive literature, always referred to the use of the birch rod or another instrument, used by someone in authority to beat a child at home or at school.

In Thomas Becon's *Catechism*, the father asks the boy whether it was right that children be beaten. 'Yes,' replies the model son, 'most lawfully. For moderate correction is as necessary for children as meat and drink.' The buttocks, according to one writer, were specifically created by God in human beings so that they might receive the blows of childhood correction, without serious bodily injury.[2] Citing three chapters from Proverbs, William Gouge described beating children as 'physick to purge out much corruption that lurketh in children and as a salve to heal many wounds and sores made by their folly'.[3]

The unanimity of this period about the necessity for domestic physical punishment of young children is attested by a survey of 22 printed advice sources, ranging from conduct books to commentaries on biblical passages, sermons and catechisms, published between 1560 and 1640. These writers were clear, and consistent with each other, about the rules of household discipline. There is no sign of gender distinction: girls and boys were equally subject to parental authority; the disciplinary powers of mothers equalled those of fathers, though, in recognition of motherly doubts and hesitance, it was expected that fathers would normally take the initiative. Beating should only follow failure of verbal reproof; its rigour should be judged against age, temperament and stages of moral development. Where God's express commandment was broken, as in swearing, lying and stealing, this should be made clear beforehand. Levin Schucking saw the ritual as pietistic in character.[4]

Puritan anxiety concerned the child's salvation. Ways to address this were summarised by three instruments in the battle against original sin: books of advice to parents on upbringing written by puritan clerics, a torrent of printed catechisms and school ordinances.[5] Occasionally a father's imbibing of advice can be documented. Thus Henry Newcome wrote in his diary in 1661, 'I read in Mr White his manual for parents and children and I was hugely I thought concerned in several passages in it'. He was probably referring to Josias White's *A Plain and Familiar Exposition upon the Creed, Ten Commandments*, which had been published in 1632.[6] The fundamental premise was put starkly by Sir Simonds D'Ewes in a commonplace book entry: 'Parents are especially bound to instruct the children, pray for them and train them up in fear of God because they drew original corruption from their loins.'[7]

Correction was to be used as the last resort. Christopher Hill argued that the spiritualisation of the household, the fount of godly upbringing, was a key feature of the Protestant Reformation. 'Parents and masters of families are in God's stead to their children and servants', declared John Mayne in 1623.[8] Writers like John Dod, William Cleaver, and William Gouge set out a programme of parental duty in taking provident care for their children's spiritual and material good. They demanded outward marks of deference and obedience: silence before elders, bending the knee, bowing as appropriate. Inculcation of bible reading and church attendance, as soon as children could 'sit reverently and fruitfully', were both seen as essential. Children were expected regularly to ask a blessing of their parents. 'Give me I pray thee', ran a prayer by Gouge 'for a child to use', 'a mind pliable to my parents will being ready to obey their commandments . . . and willingly also not only to hearken to but also obediently to observe my parents instruction and patiently to bear all their reproofs and corrections.'[9] 'As they increased in understanding', it was said of Gouge's children, their mother 'wisely ordered her authority over them, as with a child-like fear they much reverenced her.'[10] Printed catechisms, which provided question and answer sessions between parent and child, flooded the market. Gouge berated parents who neglected catechising and did not even teach their children the Lord's Prayer, the Creed and the Ten Commandments.[11]

The new grammar schools, which burgeoned in market towns across the country between 1560 and 1700, built on this teaching.[12] They were religious foundations, with ordinances which required for boys inculcation of morality besides a classical curriculum. There were specifications about regular church attendance accompanied by the master. At the same time, these schools were, in a very real sense, instruments of discipline. The schoolmaster taught social behaviour as well as Latin. His precepts were punctuality, care of basic possessions like inkhorn, pen and book, neat attire, quietness and steady application. School statutes did nothing to limit their powers beyond, in some cases, cautions against excessive severity with the birch rod. Most made ample use of this deterrent. 'Your points untie', were the schoolmaster's dreaded words, indicating submission before their fellows with their breeches down.[13] 'At country schools your masters drive you on by fear', noted Richard Baxter.[14]

There are two important respects in which the schooling of the seventeenth century set the pattern of educational practice to 1914 and beyond: it was gender segregated and it was based on a remote classical tongue, which held no intrinsic interest for most boys and which there was no good reason for them to learn. Yet Latin became the badge of class privilege. Walter Ong suggested that Latin was in fact a puberty rite, intended to provide a difficult and painful initiation into an exclusive adult society. Latin beaten into boys was becoming, by 1660, the crucial foundation of a whole class and gender system that provided a revised basis for English patriarchy. It was the male elite's secret language, a language that could be displayed as a mark of learning, of superiority and of difference. As a select group of old grammar schools established the cachet of public schools, these were monopolised by the national governing elite.[15] Boys were set on an entirely different path from girls by their schooling. The notion of educating both sexes in the same school did not enter anyone's head in England before the First World War. In this sense it is difficult to talk about prescriptions for bringing up English children as opposed to those for English boys and English girls.

A prescriptive tradition treating male upbringing began before the civil war with translations of courtesy books like Baldassare Castiglione's *The Book of the Courtier*, published in Italy in 1528. Works like Francis Segar's *School of Virtue* and William Fiston's *School of Good Manners* were based on Erasmian texts and intended for schoolboys in a pedagogic context. The influences were the Italian courtly tradition and writings from France. The stress was on categorisation of behaviour and manners through the pattern of the day. A text like De Courtin's *Rules of Civility* in 1671 treats practical issues in a way that overlaps with more obviously child-centred works.

It was Richard Allestree, Regius Professor of Divinity at Oxford and then a Restoration bishop, who became the prince of a new literary genre. He published, successively, *The Whole Duty of Man* in 1659, *The Gentleman's Calling* in 1660 and *The Ladies Calling* in 1673. Allestree established the point that upper-class upbringing was decisively gendered in prescription and principle. The first of these books went through 64 editions by 1842 and the

third at least twelve by 1787. Allestree's highly-organised tracts gave gender
training systematic treatment. In many respects he was highly traditional, in
his obeisance to the basis of masculinity in honour and virtue for example, and
in his assumptions about womankind.

Allestree set out to mould male and female personalities on a clearly pred-
icated class basis. Thus, in the case of women, he wrote first about their
'general qualifications, duties and ornaments', then about the 'respective
duties' and 'peculiar cautions' of the three stages of a woman's life. The female
conduct literature of the next 80 or so years was deeply influenced by his
words and views.[16] There is less obvious and opaque derivation in the case of
the male literature but here again he was the first of a line. His overall
achievement was that he fixed upon a concept of breeding or civility which
held manners and demeanour to be an outward manifestation of religious and
moral principles. Style and behaviour, in Allestree's terms, reflected the inner
man or woman.[17]

The publication of John Locke's *Some Thoughts Concerning Education*, in
1693, was a signal moment in the development of the positive ideology of
childhood. For Locke, experienced as a tutor to gentlemen's sons, wrote with
lucidity and authority. His work, cast in the format of a traditional conduct
book, answered a hunger for advice on the upbringing of the male child, based
upon intelligence and common sense. Gone were the fierce religious imperatives. Locke's work was radical in many respects. In the first place, it was
highly secular in tone. 'There ought very early to be imprinted on his mind',
he allowed, 'a true notion of God, as of the independent Supreme Being,
author and maker of all things, from whom we receive all our good, who loves
us, and gives us all things.' But children should learn about God and imbibe
the Lord's Prayer, Creed and Ten Commandments simply to provide 'easy and
plain moral rules . . . ready at hand in the whole conduct of life'.

Secondly, there was the entirely novel idea of habit formation. Locke applied
this to the development of the mind, envisaging habit formation in terms of the
gradual applicability of reason, as the child became more capable of thinking for
himself and therefore eventually of subduing his will to his own reason.
Convinced that a child must first become used to submitting 'his will to the
reason of others', he allowed that there might be a place for beating him for
'obstinacy' or 'rebellion'. But he condemned the emphasis of the century just
ending on beating children: 'I am very apt to think that great severity of punishment does very little good; nay, great harm in education.' Submission of the will
was seen by Locke, as Hugh Cunningham has put it, as 'a process whose
internalisation was the key to the creation of a successful and moral adult'.

But habit formation also applied to the body, with a tough regime recommended. Thus Locke advocated giving the child leaky shoes, so he did not

catch cold through wetting his feet and experiencing cold baths, so he would always be warm.[18] Underlying this notion of habit formation, was Locke's radical break with old assumptions about inherent childhood evil. The child was to be 'considered only as white paper or wax to be moulded and fashioned as one pleases', for 'nine parts of ten are what they are, good or evil, useful or not, by their education'.

The implication was that upbringing required skill and subtlety, since every child had his or her own abilities and temperament. Parents should hearken to their children's nature, not seek simply to bend the twig. The task of rearing them required 'great sobriety, temperance, tenderness, diligence and discretion'.[19] Parental responsibility towards the child, as an individual bundle of attributes and potentialities, was profound. No two children were alike: they had 'various tempers, different inclinations and particular defaults'. A proper system of upbringing had to fit their 'natural genius and constitution'. Children's curiosity should be encouraged; their questions should be carefully answered. This was Locke's startling new message.[20]

Locke's educational programme was a self-consciously snobbish one, designed implicitly for males from the upper social groups. His book was undoubtedly read widely, though, among the middling sort as well as the gentry. Locke taught parents to see education and upbringing as a training of the moral and social man. Under his influence, a whole range of positions previously taken for granted, including swaddling, corporal punishment and the complete centrality of the classics, became issues for debate, visible in the polite literature of Samuel Richardson, Oliver Goldsmith and others. Education, Locke implied, should above all fit a boy for daily life and its various challenges by developing and strengthening his personality.

The clear implication was that childhood was a definite stage apart. Hugh Cunningham sees an 'incipient child-centredness' in Locke's argument, which was blunted by his overriding purpose of producing conformable adults. Yet it is the radicalism of Locke's new reading of the nature of the child which is most striking. The central image, and it is an expansive one, was the child as a plant: this gave rise to a complex range of images surrounding the notion of cultivating a child's nature. It placed responsibility for the character of the adult that emerged, as never before, fairly and squarely on parents.[21] In America, Locke was the standard authority on child rearing in the second half of the eighteenth century and many copied from him without crediting the source. As in England, parents often quoted him in correspondence.[22]

Locke's impact on parental attitudes can be related to the series of liberating developments in the conditions of children's lives. These include changes in the clothes children wore, as has been mentioned, as well as the new practice of giving them more toys and encouraging them to play, and the burgeoning of a children's literature of nursery tales. Kate Retford has shown how portraits like Johann Zoffany's 'The Blunt Children' exhibit a mixture of relaxed insouciance and innocent gravity. In the celebrated family groups painted by Arthur Devis, children are included and given individuality, yet at the same time they are demarcated from adults.[23]

For some while Locke's thinking held the field. Then Jean-Jacques Rousseau's *Emile*, published in England in 1762, drastically challenged all previous thinking about childhood. He called for the child to be allowed to discover the secret of true happiness for himself, for, he asserted, 'childhood has its own ways of seeing, thinking and feeling'. 'Leave childhood to ripen in your children ... beware of giving anything they need today if it can be deferred without danger to tomorrow.' Childhood, Rousseau argued, against Locke, was 'the sleep of reason'. Locke's stress on developing the mind by practising reasoning with a child should be abandoned.[24]

At least two hundred treatises on education were published in England before 1800 which were in some way influenced by *Emile*.[25] Yet Rousseau's impact on the English side of the Channel should not be exaggerated. Certainly, there was much parental support, in the late eighteenth century, for less authoritarian upbringing but, as Paul Langford notes, it was Locke's psychology that remained the basis of educational theory. 'Little of substance' was added.[26]

Just as *Emile* was available to confuse them, parents also found themselves faced with the tension between different English publications. The free flow of fancy and imagination, represented by John Newberry's successful nursery publishing trade in the 1750s, was controverted by a revived moral didacticism, strongly led by Anna Barbauld's series *Lessons for Children*, which was available from 1778. Barbauld's graded readers were aimed at obedient youngsters, strictly guided by mothers who had their eyes on producing useful adults. They were in fact highly Lockean in style, adopting his notion of appropriate learning stages. Other writers followed – for instance Sarah Trimmer and Ellenor Fenn – who built on Barbauld's notion of dutiful submissiveness, with children learning virtue and sensibility.[27]

Rousseau's *Emile* clashed with English thinking. In the first place, the evangelical tradition was still alive and in fact vigorously reborn. Hannah More challenged the new prevalence towards treating children as if they were innocent, claiming that education's chief end was to rectify their 'corrupt nature and evil disposition'.[28] Rousseau had attempted to abolish the notion that children should be taught or trained, whereas the English gentry and middle class believed it to be their duty, through instruction, to perpetuate social and gender order and to create moral adults. In so far as Rousseau made an impact, he was seen as encouraging an excess expenditure on children and indulgence of them by their parents, and attempting to make them into objects of status and social gratification.[29]

Not all the major writers of a series of manuals informed by religious and moral concerns were actually evangelicals, though most of them moved in evangelical circles. *An Enquiry into the Duties of Men* by Thomas Gisborne, an Anglican clergyman, appeared in multiple editions between 1794 and 1811. Hester Chapone's *Letters on the Improvement of the Mind*, which has been characterised as 'perhaps the least flaccid' of these works, was regularly reissued between 1773 and 1851. The nonconformist minister James Fordyce, whose pulpit performances were much admired by his female congregations, published *Sermons to Young Women* in 1766. He followed this with more in the same moral and sentimental vein in his 1777 tract *Addresses to Young Men*.[30]

The hallmark of these conduct books was their subordination of manners to morality. They were aimed at, and avidly purchased by, many middle-class, as well as upper-class, families. A first edition of Chapone's *Letters* cost six shillings in 1773; Gisborne's *Enquiry* and John Gregory's celebrated *Father's Legacy to His Daughters* cost fourteen shillings and three shillings respectively in 1810.[31] They were not cheap. But their influence on the thinking of schoolmasters, governesses, parents and guardians – all those concerned with moulding youth – was enormous. The personal and confiding tone of a book like Gregory's *Father's Legacy* accounted for much of its appeal. This was a society aware of political disorder and intent on social hierarchy, which was seeking comprehensive and encyclopaedic advice about how to rear the next generation. It was a society clinging to universalism in moral principles and proper behaviour, intent on the firmly gendered upbringing of children.

From around 1800, the printed literature which purveyed ideas about gender and upbringing was in effect going in two directions. The domestic novel became established as a genre which reiterated the newly established notion of women's moral influence within the home. The argument found its apogee in Coventry Patmore's poem 'The Angel in the House', which was written in the 1850s. But even by Jane Austen's time, the early modern obsession with women as disorderly and lustful was long gone.[32] Writing as a moderate feminist, Austen emphasised women's complexity, celebrating their capabilities and the feminine virtues of perceptiveness and flexibility. Alison Sulloway has stressed Austen's influence on the progressive novels of women writers such as Fanny Burney and Maria Edgeworth. Charlotte Bronte's *Jane Eyre*, published in 1847 under a male pseudonym, portrayed a strong, passionate and self-conscious heroine, accentuating, as others did, much that was positive and forceful in the new model of womanhood. Representations of the kind of women that girls might become were now more positive and less totally confining.[33]

Henry Mackenzie's novel, *The Man of Feeling*, published in 1771, had promoted feeling as a guide to virtue, yet it sought to retain a degree of fortitude in the making of masculinity.[34] Boys were coming to be expected to be less boorish and lead more disciplined lives. Patmore's poem, while idealising feminine passivity, criticised male aggression, particularly in the sexual sphere. The cult of chivalry, associated with the novels of Walter Scott, confirmed the notion that husbands were protectors of wives and children. Works by Thomas Hughes and Charles Kingsley made much of manly virtues founded on Christian purpose.[35]

William Wordsworth and the romantic poets gave Rousseau's thinking a further twist by their exposition of a concept of nature as the foundation of moral virtue and beauty. They shared with Locke attachment to the mind as a *tabula rasa* and with Rousseau an instinctive trust in experience as against reason. Wordsworth's *Ode on Intimations of Immortality* made a huge impact:

> But trailing clouds of glory do we come
> From God who is our home
> Heaven lies about us in our infancy.

The Romantics would have happily consigned Mrs Barbauld and her improving tales to oblivion, seeking to recover for children their own freedom of imagination. Where Wordsworth differed from Rousseau was in finding in nature foundations for moral life as well as for beauty. Early years, in the thinking of the Romantics, became the spring of the whole of life; the adult was bound to keep those years alive within his soul.

Childhood became a special time, the best of times, a time that was sanctified. Thus the Romantics, with their emphasis upon the child as 'father to the man', extended selfhood backwards into childhood. We must attribute to them the creation of the modern notion of an inner self, that could be seen as having experienced innocence and as having a personal history which could be told through autobiography. During childhood, they believed, the unique self that created the particular individual was being constructed. In the mature adult this inner child remained, as a repository of feelings, creating a personal reading of the world, of social life and of relationships.[36]

Romanticism offered no programme of upbringing, but many children were reared in its spirit. This, in turn, contributed a great deal to the sentimentalisation of childhood in the Victorian period. The commercialisation of the accoutrements of childhood, from clothes to toys, were the predictable outcomes, in an industrialising society, of these ideas. Ritual and order pervaded households in which children, much under the control of

nursemaids and governesses, learnt their place. Yet, as we have seen, they were given their own spaces in the home.

Attitudes about convention and proper behaviour hardened in Victorian England along fiercely polarised gendered lines. The socially inexperienced Evelina, in Fanny Burney's novel of 1778, longed for advice when she was swept up in the London season: something like 'a book of laws and customs à-la-mode'.[37] The word 'etiquette' appeared in an English dictionary for the first time in 1791, defined as 'the polite form or manner of doing anything'. Etiquette acknowledged social difference and carried it through into a maze of detail. Books with the word in the title had appeared since the 1770s – for example, the *Fine Gentleman's Etiquette* in 1776. But it was not until the 1830s that they appeared in any quantity. They then at once established themselves as a lucrative market: the rules hardly altered between the 1830s and 1914 and these books for the young and uninitiated were much reissued.

Victorian and Edwardian etiquette books were impersonal and thin on intellectual and moral substance. In format, many were small pocket-books, which could be conveniently carried about and easily digested. They set out precise prescriptions about how to behave in particular social situations: what a lady or gentleman should do or not do. The inner self that they should cultivate had been forgotten.[38] Yet, as has been pointed out, there was a central and underlying moral principle behind this genre of literature. Tact, capacity for self-sacrifice and sensitivity to the feelings for others were seen as essential, not just useful, personal attributes.[39]

Childhood had become commercialised. Yet the advice that parents imbibed about upbringing had not changed fundamentally since Locke's writings. The common ground in parental aspirations remained the need to produce orderly, self-controlled adults. Despite the cross currents of evangelicalism and Romanticism, Locke's thinking about the child as *tabula rasa* held sway over two hundred years and more, inspiring the serious and dedicated upbringing provided by Victorian and Edwardian parents. What these parents hoped was that their children would turn out to be some kind of reflection of their best efforts to mould and educate them for responsible adulthood.

2

Boyhood

Masculinity, Michael Roper and John Tosh have argued, 'is never fully possessed but must be perpetually achieved, asserted and renegotiated'.[1] It can be argued that there were core notions, across the three hundred years this book explores, about the nature of manhood and about the potential for channelling boyhood energies. Sir Thomas Elyot's statement, in 1531, about what constituted man's 'natural perfection', that he was 'fierce, hardy, strong in opinion, covetous of glory, desirous of knowledge', represents an enduring view.[2] Men were seen as the more assertive and aggressive sex, but there was also much agreement about the male tendencies to haughtiness and rigour, to thinking too much of their own importance, to obstinacy, irritability or impatience.[3] Male intellectual powers, however, were seen as superior to women's and therein lay the boy's potential, it was believed, to exercise the command and authority over others which his patriarchal role demanded.

So far as sexual experience was concerned, this was not so much prohibited in youth as directed away from the respectable girls whom an upper-class boy might seek to marry. In his 1596 tract, *The Haven of Health*, Thomas Cogan proposed the moderate use of teenage orgasm: 'it maketh the body more light and nimble; it opens the pores and conduits . . . quickeneth the mind, stirreth up the wit'.[4] A young man was expected to sow his wild oats, but with servant girls or, as they became available with increasing urbanisation, with prostitutes. Simple fornication, as one of the Elizabethan Homilies put it, was widely seen as 'no sin at all but rather a pastime, a dalliance and but a touch of youth'.[5] Sexual initiation fed into manly confidence. Laura Gowing found that, reading church court defamation cases from the early seventeenth century, men were inclined to brag about sex, talking of it freely, pleasurably and without self-consciousness.[6]

Across this whole period, fathers by and large encouraged a man-of-the-world approach to early sex. The exceptions were those in the evangelical tradition, especially in the Victorian period, who warned against sexual experience before marriage in terms of moral danger and degeneration.[7] Some mothers, it is clear too, could be insistent in this respect, especially if they feared this rite of passage was not going smoothly in a conventional direction. Hence the frantic programme of sexual redemption planned for young Sir George Saville in 1750, when his mother, the dowager Lady Saville, discovered that, let out of her sight, he had begun 'a new score in a stable yard with a waiter at Mount's coffee house'. Within three months, it was reported that she 'had taken her young twig of Sodom into the country and, by way of weaning him from that unnatural vice, taken great pains to cocker him with every Abigail in her house and all the milkmaid cunts in the neighbourhood'.[8]

Female servants were certainly often seen as fair game, though it is apparent that, when they became pregnant, it was more likely that this was because of frequent sexual activity with men from their own class than from bouts with the gentry.[9] Thomas Parry revelled in his son's precociousness at home at Llidiadom in Cardiganshire just after 1800: 'George is a noble fellow . . . he is even at this age a very naughty boy. I am afraid he is often found in bed with little Penelope's nurse.'[10]

If sexual appetite in boys and young men could, by and large, be allowed to run free, violence was seen rather differently. Boyhood and aggression were closely identified in early modern England. 'Anything that looks like fighting is delicious to an Englishman', wrote a French visitor in 1719, when he had observed large crowds gathering in the London streets to watch boys fighting. James Clegg recalled, from his Derbyshire childhood, how 'being a clear moonlight night I was engaged with other boys in a mock fight'.[11] Alexandra Shepard's study of Cambridge youth between the 1580s and 1640 has shown that English youth were little different from Augsburg youth, who Lyndal Roper found plaguing the town with their drinking, whoring and gorging.[12]

The path to adult acceptance and respect in male company was often pursued through acts of bravado. The legacy of the chivalric tradition enshrined much of this physicality in a haze of adventure and glory. Thus the chapbook literature fed boys' minds at all social levels.[13] Fathers at the start of our period stressed courage as the source of male honour. John Temple advised his son to practise 'horsemanship and vaulting especially of all bodily exercise'.[14] The Earl of Northumberland, instructing his son in 1609, suggested the selection of physical exercises with attention to 'managing of all sorts of arms'. 'I like it as a commendable way of breeding for a young gentleman', mused Henry Slingsby, on six weeks of campaigning during the war against the Scots in 1639. He saw the military life as enabling the 'body to labour' and the 'mind to watchfulness'.[15] In many respects, this was a society in which male aggression was channelled rather than checked.

Susan Amussen has argued persuasively that, if the use of violence was a key component of the traditional model of masculinity, this model was nevertheless being challenged.[16] The upbringing of young males was coming to be seen as a process of taming their wildness. We have seen how they were regarded as like 'asses and wild heifers'.[17] It was generally recognised that self-control could best be taught by a pattern of intellectual and moral inculcation. Richard Allestree was writing at a time, in 1660, when it was possible to be challengingly original about constructing gender in something like a modern form. As a traditionalist he spoke of infant passions being 'checked and bridled', through a form of discipline which broke children's 'natural rudeness and stubbornness'; yet at the same time he was advocating instruction to 'mould them into some form of civility'.[18]

During youth, Elizabeth Foyster has argued, the passions were seen as able to undermine manhood and it was the passion of anger which was most threatening to boys. Children could be taught directly how to handle this. Ian Watts, in his *Discourse on the Education of Children and Youth*, published in 1809, argued that 'children should be instructed in the art of self-government, which meant them learning to keep the lower powers of nature under the command of their reason'.[19] Watts was writing in a long tradition which saw a classical education, together with inculcation of Christian principles, as the foundation of male self-mastery. Locke, we should note, put virtue first; learning, he allowed, was 'necessary but not the chief business'.[20]

The conduct writers who came just before Locke – men like Richard Braithwaite, James Cleland, Richard Allestree and Clement Ellis – all made godliness an indispensable qualification for gentility.[21] Thus the seventeenth-century ideology of manhood, founded on strong class consciousness, integrated religion, morality and learning. Its basis was a coherent argument about the use and development of the male's capacity for reason and the integral relationship between this and his moral sense. Ellis spoke of a boy learning to make his 'will and affection' the instruments and servants, not 'the guides and mistresses', of his soul. 'When in men passions are exalted above reason', wrote Jean Gailhard, 'nothing follows but disorders, mischiefs and unavoidable ruin both within and without.' For Locke himself, self-control from infancy was the key: boys 'should be used to submit their desires and go without their longings, even from their very cradles'.[22]

It is worth noting how specifically fathers' instructions to their sons in the seventeenth and eighteenth centuries purvey this ideology. William Martyn, writing for his son Nicholas at Oxford in 1613, put an equal stress on religion and knowledge, emphasising their complementarity. Declaring that 'an ignorant man without learning is altogether barren and dry', Martyn insisted that his son's study should be 'moderate not violent, more pleasing than painful'.

At the same time, he stressed the intellectual application of religious under-standing, which 'maketh a man warily and carefully to look into his ways and wisely to govern and to rule himself'. Martyn, like others, clearly saw classical learning as a means to virtue. His son should make 'the improvement of your manners' the test of what he applied himself to, learning 'what virtue is and how to study it'.[23]

Pursuing the same argument, the Earl of Warrington, in 1696, saw the end of male upbringing as 'justice and moderation in public proceedings' and a firmness of resolution against 'rash or hotheaded actions'.[24] Thomas Scott, in an eighteenth-century set of *Father's Instructions,* began with the impor-tance of prayer, self-examination and public worship, proceeding to warn against extremes such as drink, gaming and strife. The notion of the English gentleman's necessary reserve, the expression of his good judgement, was by then well entrenched. The rational youth learnt, and demonstrated in adulthood, that his public role was pursuit of the good of others:

> Thy soul, thy sovereign and thy native land
> Their tax of duty and of love demand.[25]

A key issue for the parents of boys was achieving an upbringing that guarded against effeminacy, slippage, that is, into the weakness, softness and delicacy of womankind. It was Jean Gailhard who handled this most fully. 'It is a great matter,' he asserted, 'when boys were hardened from their childhood for it makes their constitution strong and lucky': exercise would 'dissipate bad humours', and make them 'nimble and stronger'. Hunting, riding and walking were all activities that prepared boys for adulthood, 'for 'tis well to be fitted to wrestle against what difficulties we shall meet withal'. 'Some', Gailhard regretted, 'are brought up in so tender and effeminate a way . . . so that if ever they be put upon any inconvenience they are not able to hold out but sink under any hardship and are soon swept away.'[26] Locke's programme began, as we have seen, with exposure to the elements. He advocated plenty of riding for young gentlemen, supplemented by tuition in wrestling. He invented the enduring notion of a sound mind in a sound body.[27]

Central to the making of manhood was the notion of male independence. This began with the ceremonial of breeching at around five or six, which marked escape from the female and maternal world.[28] Into the late nineteenth century, upper-class boys wore petticoats in their first years. Yet, as John Tosh has noted, the symbolic meaning of breeching had by then been lost, since gender was coming to be seen not as an identity acquired over time but as something based upon innate sexual difference.[29] Learning to 'shift for oneself', acquiring independence, was crucial to boyhood destiny in the world.[30] Adult men were expected, to varying degrees, to acquire, hold and fulfil public responsibility: a whole series of notions of hospitality, philanthropy and patriotism surrounded this core requirement.[31] At the very least, they could expect to have to exercise domestic responsibility.

For the apprentice or professional man the groundwork was independence. Edward Herford, the son of a prosperous Unitarian liquor merchant in Manchester, training to be an attorney, reflected on what this independence meant, in his diary on 9 July 1832, at the age of sixteen. It was not 'vulgar low-born independence', that he sought, but 'a tolerable opinion of yourself, hidden under a very modest demeanour and not the least sense of shame or fear of doing that which is not morally wrong'. Herford captured the sense that independence involved both learning a way of behaving and finding an interior strength and confidence.[32] A boy's work at eighteen, declared Gilbert Burnet in his *Thoughts on Education*, 'should be to know the world . . . now should he be much abroad and in all company'. Through exposure to the social world, a youth from the upper ranks, the Earl of Chesterfield told his son Philip, would 'learn life and discover on what hinges it turns; he will detect the arts and follies of mankind, observe the genius of affairs'.[33]

If manhood was represented by a whole set of proper behaviours, civility was the very essence of proper manhood. For manners, as Anna Bryson has remarked, 'expressed, perhaps even enforced' the distinctions of class and gender which are central to the argument of this book.[34] The prescriptive literature about civility, good breeding and politeness insisted that all this was the mark and prerogative of society's upper ranks. There was an assumption that the children born at this level would be taught the kind of control of natural bodily functions, together with a containment of appetite and aggression, which would enable them to be marked out by their civility.[35]

The concept of civility became familiar to English readers through works like *Youth's Behaviour*, translated from the French by Francis Hawkins, which went through eleven editions between the 1640s and 1872; Antoine de Courtin's *Rules of Civility* of 1671; and Obadiah Walker's *Of Education*, published in 1673.[36] James Cleland set the tone in *The Institution of a Young Nobleman* in 1607 with a broad treatment of social behaviour and virtues, listing the recommended learning and recreations for a young gentleman. His central message was that a boy must not be bashful, by showing 'foolish shamefastness in hanging down his head and blushing at every light word' or by 'affectation in his speech, countenance or behaviour'.[37]

The emphasis in all these books was on rules of social form and technique. Civility was narrowed down to good manners and then given an overall gloss through the notion of affability. 'Be courteous, affable, gentle and familiar in all your carriage and behaviour unto all such as do either keep you company or crave your help', William Martyn advised his son.[38] Allestree summarised the behaviour to be expected of a young gentleman as 'affable and civil'.[39] Clothes and demeanour should alike be neither slovenly nor vain, insisted Clement Ellis in his 1660 tract *The Gentle Sinner*: 'such a gravity as becomes a Christian' should be matched by 'such a decency as becomes a gentleman'.[40]

Manner of speech was seen as the essence of affability. Advice about this complemented words on physical demeanour. Bryson noted a new preoccupation, in the sixteenth and seventeenth centuries, with the implications of language, as the notion of male conversation as a sociable and polite discourse took hold. Thus Obadiah Walker's separate chapter 'Of Conversation and Discourse' enumerates appropriate subjects and kinds of discussion, turning conversation into an established issue worthy of systematic conduct book analysis.[41]

A number of central points were constantly reiterated. Enunciation should be smooth, clear and distinct: a man should 'not speak too fast or too loud but softly and gently', declared Gailhard.[42] William Martyn censured volubility.[43] There was much condemnation of scatalogical, scurrilous, lewd and blasphemous talk. The ideal writers usually set out was one of verbal tact and adjustment of vocabularies and subjects to the company a man was in, and to time and place. What men spoke about and how they did so was seen as revealing of their inner character and morality.[44] A man's words, insisted Allestree, should be temperate and decent, 'the product of judgement not of rage'.[45] He should 'not brag of himself or anything of his', cautioned Gailhard in 1678, 'despise or speak amiss of others'.[46]

There was also much specific advice about verbal deference and appropriate modes of salutation. Essentially, a boy should learn a manner of speech which showed natural elegance without pedantry.[47] The emphasis was on gravity, put well by the Earl of Warrington in his advice to his boys in 1696: 'deep and weighty notions . . . will touch the reasons and convince the understanding many degrees beyond light and frothy thoughts'.[48] Clement Ellis provides a succinct summary. The expression of civility, he declared, was found in a discourse 'neither flashy nor flat, neither boyish nor effeminate, neither rude nor pedantic . . . sober yet ingenious, virile, strong and masculine yet sweet and winning'.[49]

Upper-class boys were to be educated for their responsible adult roles. As members of both a 'politic body' and a 'civil society', declared Jean Gailhard, 'I wish they were fitted to keep the bond of it and therefore taught the practice of meekness, humility, civility, etc, which qualities breeding a mutual respect and affection, do much contribute to keep peace in families, amongst neighbours and through whole nations'.[50] Gailhard here enunciated a fundamental ideological principle to which the English social elite clung firmly.

National society and order was seen to rest upon a social hegemony which was preserved by the gentry.

Although there was much continuity in this construction of masculinity between the seventeenth and nineteenth centuries, the context nevertheless altered. For thinking about gender was transformed in a mental world that became emphatically one of two sexes, not one. Thomas Laqueur's chronology of the move from a humoral model of the body to one in which women and men were anatomical opposites, has been qualified by several historians.[51] Karen Harvey's reading of sexual difference in the eighteenth century has integrated thinking about the body.[52] There is now no question that a notion of incommensurability between masculinity and femininity, previously no more than incipient, had emerged by 1800. David Hume captured the new atmosphere, writing in 1751 about decency: 'an effeminate behaviour in a man, a rough manner in a woman; these are ugly because unsuitable to each character and different from the qualities we expect in the sexes'.[53] As men and women came to be seen as wholly different and distinct in body, temperament and mind, they also started to be expected to socialise together, complementing each other in the principal areas of polite society.

The discourse of male civility was rewritten in the language of gendered politeness. This process has been well mapped by Laurence Klein and its implications have been drawn out for the history of masculinity by Michelle Cohen.[54] Politeness was, as Cohen puts it, 'the intricate play of manners, language, self-display, sociability and *je ne sais quoi* that was central to the self-fashioning of the gentleman.[55] Gendered behaviour became endlessly discussed. It was not simply that didactic conduct literature burgeoned, as we have seen, or that the novel, from *Clarissa* to the *Man of Feeling*, made gender a focal issue. A novelist like Henry Fielding could turn to writing a courtesy guide.[56] The popular periodicals the *Tatler* and the *Spectator* included papers discussing male conversation.[57] Moreover, the Earl of Chesterfield's advocacy of male dissimulation, in his letters to his son Philip Stanhope, published in 1774, provoked vigorous debate.[58] Many vilified his presentation of politeness as a fake form of behaviour.[59]

The ideology of politeness had a huge impact upon thinking about boyhood and manhood. On the one hand, the precepts of classical and traditional manliness – physique, self-control and independence – were still much reiterated. On the other, the proponents of a new, refined masculinity emerged.[60] The debate was conducted in an atmosphere of anxiety about patriotism and national character. Cohen has seen the protagonists here as Chesterfield, on the one hand, with his constant admiration for French breeding and David Fordyce on the other, arguing in his *Dialogues Concerning Education* that the frivolity of French politeness was undermining

English gentility. For Fordyce, gentility rested on plain food, exercise and manly enthusiasm, taking the form of a patriotic spirit.[61]

A deeper and even more crucial polarity at the heart of the debate, explored by Philip Carter, was that between the integrity and ease of the true Englishman and the degeneracy of the fop. He has shown how fops were painted as exhibitionist social actors who took politeness to excess. They showed so much refinement that their conduct became false. The behaviour of the fop was ceremonious to the point of absurdity. The acceptable face of sociability – a genuine, relaxed and measured demeanour – was thus entirely lost. The negative stereotype, argues Carter, proved effective. The fop functioned to promote the development of new standards of male conduct by providing a conspicuous and forceful image of failed masculinity.[62]

The real test for boys as they became young men was now their ease and social performance, not only with other men, but with women as well. For while womankind was still believed to be powerful, women's company had come to be seen as beneficial. As William Alexander put it in 1779, 'of all the various causes which tend to influence our conduct and form our manners, none operate so powerfully as the society of the other sex'.[63] Men recognised that they needed women, to refine them out of their roughness. Yet it also remained accepted that too much female company could emasculate a man and make him effeminate. Thomas Gisborne feared the effects of a woman's witty tongue in this respect.[64] Men were taught to grow up requiring private space, in balance with their opportunities, in mixed social circles, to display social refinement and gallantry. The problem was getting the balance right.[65]

Criticism of the more brutal and arrogant aspects of men's behaviour, by feminists from Mary Astell in the early eighteenth century to Mary Wollstonecraft at its end, had its impact on the formation of the reformed ideal of manhood in which boys were reared. The cults of sensibility and tender-heartedness and the power of evangelicalism made themselves strongly felt. Henry Mackenzie's *Man of Feeling* in 1771 was received with rapture.[66] James Fordyce's *Addresses to Young Men*, three years later, was redolent with idealism about male upbringing. Youngsters reaching adult manhood should be expected to show, Fordyce insisted, 'a lively fancy, a ready understanding, a retentive memory, a warm temper, and tender affections, a quick sense of humour and disgrace, an irresistible love of action and enterprise, an ambition to be admired and praised, especially for their probity, manhood, generosity, friendship, good nature and other virtues'. Fordyce's paragon, in other words, combined a traditional mastery of reason and desire for action with the sensitivity of temperament and character which characterised the man of feeling.[67]

Fordyce's account foreshadowed the emergence of muscular Christianity, with its emphasis on moral courage, earnestness and responsible piety. His new man might be capable of enactment of the evangelical manhood described by Leonore Davidoff and Catherine Hall, with its twin pillars of work as a calling and domestic piety as the focus of non-working life.[68] Civility as a set of outward behaviours was here replaced by character. The old argument about the virtue boys should learn as the essence of manhood had been revived in a new form. 'Manliness is superiority and power certainly', declared Isaac Taylor in his 1820 advice book for the male teenager, 'but it is power and superiority of character not of vociferation.' Not something to shout about, this new manhood was based upon the inner resources of the heart.[69]

In his sermons and writings as headmaster of Rugby School in the 1830s, Thomas Arnold set out unequivocal goals. He intended to make the school a 'place of Christian education' that would 'form Christian men'. Arnold believed that males developed in three stages: childhood, boyhood and manhood. Boyhood was marked by great temptations to evil, but, through the Christian values of the school, he intended that his pupils should be taught to resist them. In the meanwhile, like the puritan clerics of the seventeenth century, he was convinced it was proper and not degrading for a boy to be beaten regularly. Exemption from flogging was earned by the display of 'manly conduct and a manly sense of duty', expected of the higher forms in the school, Arnold argued in an article in the *Quarterly Journal of Education* for 1835. Arnold was entirely traditional in seeing classical education as an instrument of moral training, insisting that Latin and Greek gave boys a framework for dealing with good and evil.

In setting out his idealistic concept of Christian manliness, Thomas Arnold emphasised certain personal qualities. His boys would learn self-denial, self-mastery and self-restraint; their characters would be moulded as 'regular and amiable, abstaining from evil, and for evil in its lower and grosser forms having a real abhorrence'. What should be looked for at Rugby, Arnold told his prefects, was, in the first place, 'religious and moral principles', in the second 'gentlemanly conduct' and in the third 'intellectual ability'.

The first biography of Arnold, by his devoted pupil Arthur Stanley, which was published in 1881, asserted that he had 'changed the face of education all through the public schools of England'. A work of fiction seemed to give credence to this claim. Its author, Thomas Hughes, entered Rugby in 1834. Stanley testified to the accuracy of *Tom Brown's Schooldays*, writing that 'the general tone of that charming book' provided a vivid picture of Arnold's career. Other Rugby boys agreed. Albert Pell spoke of its 'complete picture' of life at the school: 'I and many others lived just the life therein depicted', declared Richard Temple. Hughes's decent fantasy of public school life was given a rapturous reception in 1857, quickly becoming a classic. Tom Brown, the muscular Christian, became a heroic figure. As the *Spectator* put it, he was a 'thoroughly English boy': 'full of kindness, courage, vigour and fun – no great adept at Greek or Latin, but a first rate cricketer, climber and swimmer, fearless and skilful at football and by no means adverse to a good stand-up fight in a good cause'.[70]

Generations of headmasters spoke with conviction and unanimity about the products of public schools as boys who were muscular, moral and manly. Three who testified to the *Strand Magazine* in 1905, Joseph Wood of Harrow, Charles Hancock of Tonbridge and H.W. Moss of Shrewsbury, can be seen as representing many others. 'In courage and kindliness and frankness of character English public schoolboys seem as good as they ever were', wrote Wood. Taken in the mass, the Edwardian generation was, Hancock insisted, 'far more sensible, obedient and manly than schoolboys of, say, fifty years ago'. The Edwardian public schoolboy, according to Moss, was 'as devoted a lover of justice and fair play . . . as honourable and straightforward as those who have gone before him'. This was the rhetoric. These statements summarised the ideology of boyhood education just after the Boer War.[71]

There is no question that, by the early nineteenth century, evangelicalism had done much to remodel the overall standards set before English boyhood. But at the same time as they 'adjusted their image to make it acceptable to middle-class morality', Mark Girouard has argued, the upper classes were elaborating a way of living which expressed a notion of gender polarity more forcefully than any previous domestic and social arrangements. The fashion for an architecture redolent, through the gothic revival, of old-fashioned hospitality, gave precise expression to the dichotomous Victorian notion of male and female minds and temperaments.

The drawing room acquired new functions in the nineteenth century, which stressed its femininity, as the venue for morning calls and afternoon tea. Smoking rooms became a male safety-valve and, since smoking after dinner was often combined with billiards, billiard rooms and smoking rooms were often found side by side. The logical conclusion, evident, for example, at Abbeystead Hall in Lancashire by the 1880s, was separate male and female domains indoors, with a study at one end of the house and a lady's boudoir at the other.[72] Upper-class boys, when they were not away at boarding school, spent their first years in an environment that spelt out gender polarity. Gender permeated their domestic world.

Public schooling, creating the stiff upper lip, sought the building of the inner strength, based upon systematic denial of emotional life, that made the kind of gender construction that has been outlined here possible. This conduct book material, in its stress on male reserve, built upon a long tradition of male taciturnity. Public school education fed into the professions, the civil service and the Empire. Male prescriptive ideology in Victorian and Edwardian England was rigid and sharply demarcated. In no sense did it put emphasis upon self-expression, creativity or the realisation of emotional and spiritual identity. On the contrary, all of its governing assumptions were about repression and self-control. Manliness, indeed, throughout this period, was about checking the will, the imagination, passion, impulse and self-indulgence.

The sheer resilience of the scheme of male gender training discussed here can be related to continuity both in men's psychic needs and in attachment to the patriarchal social arrangements that upper-class men imposed on women, children and servants. It was a training that fulfilled the demands of a 'hegemonic masculinity', carefully preserved and handed on from generation to generation. We should not be expecting, John Tosh has suggested, to find transformative change in the early modern and modern history of English masculinity. It is the impermeability, immutability and durability of English patriarchy that is striking.

Men, as fathers, clung to their allotted role in this scheme, with no questioning or even debate. Their boys had no choice in the matter. The victory in the eighteenth century of the idea of a sexual dichotomy between the male and female body produced, in Tosh's words, 'an increasingly dichotomised notion of mind and temperament'.[73] This gender polarisation in turn highlighted the need to set boys firmly apart from their sisters, training them in a manhood that was entirely distinct from everything feminine and providing them with wholly different life goals.

In the longer term, a fundamental shift in the concept of masculinity has wrenched it from its early modern roots as social reputation and created it as an aspect of modern subjectivity.[74] The hallmark of masculinity has become for many an interiority not previously dreamed about.[75] This was not on the Victorian or Edwardian horizon. What gives the period from 1600 to 1914 unity is the requirement for boys to live out a male social role, rather than to realise their personal individuality and destiny, in the way that has been prized more recently.

Girlhood

The construction of femininity was an insistent preoccupation for men throughout the three hundred years covered by this book, since patriarchal society was seen to rest most crucially on the ideological subordination of women. Although the understanding and interpretation of the female body, mind and temperament changed very considerably during the period from 1600 to 1914, men's basic approach to the nature of womanhood remained constant. Men's bodies, ideally, were never a social obstacle, but rather gave them potentiality and capability; women's, on the other hand, were consistently read in medical terms, which justified restrictions on what they could achieve, and in domestic terms that stressed their mothering role. This was where subordination rested.

A girl's prime obligation was always obedience to her parents and principally to her father; an adult woman's was obedience, if she married, to her husband. It was only in widowhood that a woman might, in theory, escape dependence, but in practice male relatives often managed to secure its continuance. The ideology of subordination was constantly reiterated, first by puritan clerics and then by conduct book writers. The print of government, declared William Whateley in 1623, appeared in man's 'very face which is more stern and delicate than the woman's'. Men should 'not suffer this order of nature to be inverted'.[1] Men's superiority in body and mind, announced William Fleetwood, an Anglican bishop, in 1705, was 'established by God and acknowledged by custom'. Women, following the curse of Eve, should live subject, 'in chaste conversation coupled with fear'. For women in any respect to attempt to equal men, argued James Burgh in 1754, was 'opposing nature': 'if we appeal either to reason, scripture or universal consent, we shall find a degree of submission to the male sex to be an indispensable part of the female character'.[2]

The legacy of the past was strong. On the one hand there was the Christian story of gender, told in the book of Genesis; on the other there was ancient medical teaching about the biological differences between men and women.[3] In humoral physiology women were painted as weak and passive, because they were cooler and moister than men. They were governed by their reproductive parts: the uterus was seen as so powerful it could cause hysteria, loquacity and lust. They were fundamentally irrational, lacking the interior heat to drive blood to their heads and create strong minds.[4] They were not actually capable therefore, as even so bold a philosophical writer as Margaret Cavendish in the seventeenth century confessed, of rigorous thought.[5]

All of this gradually changed with the emergence, in the late seventeenth century, of a new sensational physiology based on the workings of the nervous system. This, from the start, carried a basic assumption about gender difference. Women's nerves were seen as thinner, finer and more delicate than those of men.[6] The gaze, which the medical profession turned on the Georgian and Victorian woman, drew heavily on traditional thinking. A pyramid of powerful images led to a series of assumptions about female nervous instability. Meanwhile, the study of sexual differences by gynaecologists became inextricably bound up with debates on the social functions of the sexes. Science was seen as the means of providing conclusive evidence for allocating gender roles.[7]

There was a wide currency in Victorian literature of the notion that the female was predisposed to hysteria. In the early stages of psychiatry, characteristically female mental illnesses were identified and distinctive forms of female insanity, linked to menstruation, pregnancy, parturition and lactation, were diagnosed. The work of gynaecologists and psychiatrists in effect provided a biological rationale for gender differentiation. But, in a society which was based upon blatant class discrimination, working-class women were entirely excluded from the subject-matter of this medical debate; on the other hand, women and their daughters from the upper class were central to it.[8] The medicalisation of upper- and middle-class females is thus a process of fundamental importance to an investigation of female upbringing. This medicalisation was, in a sense, the logical outcome of a dichotomous notion of culture versus nature, which, from the eighteenth century, was used to drive forward the male ideological work of gender.[9]

The argument about women's weakness was pursued logically, coherently and insistently between 1600 and 1914. In the early seventeenth century, an abiding European misogynist tradition remained dominant in English drama, ballads and proverbial utterance. Sexually, women were seen as insatiable, lascivious and predatory. Literary men were obsessed, between 1600 and 1660, with the link that they posited between shrewish or scolding female behaviour and sexual infidelity. Women's tongues were the tongues of serpents; their pride and vanity constantly threatened men with undoing.[10]

Men could only defend themselves at this time through a fierce didactic literature, which stressed women's oppression by their passions and emotions. It taught chastity, silence and obedience.[11] In educational practice, it harped upon subjugation of the self.[12]

Women, incapable of taking responsibility for themselves, had to expect to 'live under obedience'.[13] Yet, after the Restoration, this entirely negative view of women began to shift. As more precise knowledge about women's nature became established, it was never allowed to divert men from their ruling conviction that women's supposed weakness debilitated them. We can trace an evolving gender ideology between 1660 and 1800 which, while it took women's weakness as read, created for them a positive private and public social role. Girls were to become men's partners in the business of life. This involved inventing for them a set of attributes which provided their lives with meaning and their persons with respect. Men gave young women, it can be shown, a complementary and distinct yet, at the same time, a managed and controlled role in their world.

Seven tracts written between the 1570s and the 1640s seemed to foreshadow aspects of a new and gradually developed ideology of femininity. Nine key texts, including Richard Allestree's *The Ladies Calling* and John Gregory's *A Father's Legacy*, published between 1673 and 1780, indicate how it was fully elaborated.[14] It seems incontrovertible that it was from the 1670s that a fully fledged prescriptive literature, constructing adult womanhood in positive terms, emerged; that its basic terms of reference remained constant until the Edwardian period and that its enforcement was highly effective. A quotation from the Marquess of Halifax's *The Lady's New Year Gift or Advice to a Daughter*, of 1688, may be seen as the starting point: 'we are made of differing tempers that our defects may the better be mutually supplied: your sex wanteth our reason for your conduct and our strength for your protection, ours wanteth your gentleness to soften and entertain us'.[15]

Complementarity and mutuality were the key principles; the argument, entirely secular in tone, was conducted in terms of the positive aspects of both men's and women's natures. For example, Allestree found in women a generosity of mind which gave rise to their affability. According to Wetenhall Wilkes, compassion was 'so natural an ornament to your sex, whose soft breasts are made and disposed to entertain tenderness and pity'. In his sermon to young women on female piety, James Fordyce talked of their propensity to 'tender affection'.[16] The strength overall of this ideology lay in its sheer plausibility. Self-discipline came first and foremost.

The fundamental principle of patriarchal society was that a girl should prize and preserve her virginity until her father handed her over to her husband. Her chastity then symbolised her loyalty to him. This was the crux of living under obedience. 'A young lady of refined education', wrote Bernard de Mandeville in 1714, 'keeps a strict guard over her looks, as well as actions, and in her eyes we may read a consciousness that she has a treasure about her not out of danger of being lost, and which yet she is resolved not to part with at any terms.'[17]

The huge importance men gave to the issue shows in Fielding's *Tom Jones*, in Squire Allworthy's portentous reprimand of Jenny Jones for her confessed loss of chastity:

> How bare and mean must that woman be, how void of that dignity of mind and decent pride, without which we are not worth the name of human creatures, who can bear to level herself with the lowest animal and to sacrifice all that is great and noble in her, all her heavenly part.[18]

Whereas it was taken for granted that a boy would soon learn about masturbation, the assumption was that anything so privately pleasuring was totally out of bounds for girls. The subject is frequently hinted at in discussions of female modesty. Wetenhall Wilkes is one of the few to be explicit: modesty, in his reading, was 'a suppression of all irregular desires, voluntary pollutions, sinful concupiscence and of an immoderate use of all sensual and carnal pleasures'.[19]

The prescriptive arguments about female chastity always rested on the notion that it was a woman's own responsibility to protect it. Upper-class girls never talked of their sexuality in this period. Repression was complete, yet all the evidence about sublimation is there, in the passion for reading novels, in the effusive excitement about the balls and social gatherings at which young people from selected families mixed freely. Chastity, the record suggests, was very thoroughly internalised.

The stress was on teaching girls to protect themselves against their own sinful ways. Dorothy Leigh's posthumous *The Mother's Blessing*, available in 1616, stressed innate female sinfulness, foregrounding chastity, 'without which we are mere beasts and no women'. Elizabeth Joceline, at much the same time, proposed the standard remedies for female weakness: 'remember thou art a maid and such ought thy modesty to be that thou shouldest scarce speak but when thou answereth'. Allestree, taking modesty to be the core of self-discipline, underlined its inward importance, besides its value as one of what he called the 'outworks' of chastity: 'it . . . does not only ballast the mind with sober and humble thoughts of one's self but also steers every part of the outward frame'.[20]

The relevance of women's pleasure in intercourse to conception was increasingly questioned in the eighteenth century, as the notion of their sexual passivity replaced the stress on their lustfulness. In parallel, male sexual drive and rapacity came to be more heavily emphasised.[21] Samuel Richardson's portrait of Mr Lovelace in *Clarissa* was much pondered in this respect.[22] *Clarissa*'s prolonged impact is indicated by the clergyman James Fordyce's cloying sermon reference to it, eighteen years after its publication. Her 'beauty, sweetness and artlessness', he declared, was never equalled; her delicacy provided 'the most exalted standard of female excellence that was ever held up'.[23] But what his young hearers must have recalled, above all, was the brutality of Lovelace's seduction and of his rape of Clarissa. As Lovelace himself remarked in the novel, 'the whole of their education is caution and warning against our attempts'.[24]

Successful resistance to men, the conduct book writers of the early eighteenth century taught, was an exercise in inner moulding of the whole personality in virtuous terms. It was shining virtue, the argument went, that held men off. Body language and decorum in public situations were seen as carrying huge meaning: even a kiss of the cheek, declared William Kenrick, could inflame a man's desire. Wetenhall Wilkes reflected on the dynamic of gender relations, noting that 'the double temptation of vanity and desire is so prevalent in our sex that we are apt to interpret every obliging look, gesture, smile or sentence of a female we like on the hopeful side'.

The female is painted in such writings as object not subject. Wilkes gave his female readers a tantalising glimpse into masculinity: by his prurience, fascination with female innocence and affected fatherly concern about female vulnerability, he saturated every social exchange in which a young girl was involved with sexuality and its dangers. For the message was that it was she who must judge between the rake and libertine on the one hand and the respectable, well-intentioned man of feeling on the other. Writing of this kind made girls themselves focus their own efforts upon reading men for signs of libertine behaviour. In doing this they could not but be aware of sexual desire: the possibilities for fantasy were released and active and passive sexual roles were blurred. Was a girl to fall or to rescue her tempter? This was Clarissa's battle.

If there was the possibility that every man was at heart a rake, how mocking was Wilkes's idealised depiction of internalised chastity, as 'a kind of quick and delicate feeling in the soul which makes her shrink and withdraw herself from everything that is wanton or has danger in it'.[25] Self-restraint, denial, inhibition of the personality: these were to be a girl's maxims. The prescriptive ideology imposed on girls was cruel; to live it out was arduous and the silence of diaries and letters conceals the weight of female sublimation.

Everything else in the male strategy for genteel womanhood can be seen as following from the requirement for chastity of mind and body. Piety was chastity's foundation and, together with the rationality developed by appropriate learning, this was intended to give a woman the strength to master herself. Politeness involved a gendered manner which encapsulated and expressed female innocence. The active roles of emotional support to others and moral leadership were the positive expressions of a girl or woman's purity of heart. The appeal of the argument from nature, rather than from scripture, was that it could be used to give the whole programme of gender construction a positive gloss.

A girl's upbringing had, above all, to be a moral one, which implied that it should be a religious one. John Evelyn, eulogising his daughter at her marriage in 1693, shows how firmly this was established. She is 'a good child', he wrote first, 'religious and discreet'; then he went on to her ingenuity in 'all the ornaments of her sex'.[26] Sir Justinian Isham, in 1642, was one of the first to posit a particular kind of religious education as appropriate for girls, when he wrote a code of conduct for his four daughters. They should avoid 'knotty disputes' and concentrate instead upon 'prayers, meditations and such like treatises', learning 'to keep your hearts upright and your affections to God unfeigned'. Allestree, predictably, developed the argument, maintaining that piety engaged girls' eminent passions of fear and love. It was 'their greatest ornament and advantage', since their temper, more than men's, predisposed them towards religion.[27]

The instruction to engage in acts of piety became a standard item in female conduct books.[28] Richard Steele found devotion in women not 'only more excellent in them, in regard to its effects' but 'more necessary in respect of their obligation'. God gave them, he avowed, more free time, 'so expected a greater diligence in spiritual employments'.[29] John Gregory believed that it was 'the natural softness of their dispositions', along with 'the natural warmth of their imaginations', which made females especially susceptible to feelings of piety. But he repeated Isham's warning against their meddling in theological debate.[30]

'There is an empire which belongs to you', James Fordyce's female readers were told, 'I mean what has the heart for its object, and is secured by meekness and modesty, by soft attraction and virtuous love'. Paul Langford, questioning whether many daughters wanted to hear his message, has declared that 'no doubt to parents he was balm itself'.[31] Sarah Pennington went into some detail about a girl's religious duties, holding that the sincere practice of these led to the proper discharge of her social ones.[32] Thomas Gisborne reiterated, in 1798, that the whole of a girl's education should be directed towards engaging 'the understanding and affections of the pupil in favour of piety and virtue'.[33]

One of the outcomes of the evangelical movement was the assertion that women were potentially more virtuous and moral than men. Thus Sarah Ellis, author of several immensely popular works, could maintain, in 1850, that 'the noblest passions, the deepest feelings and the highest aspirations of humanity may be found within the brooding quiet of an English woman's heart'.[34] Female religiosity was given full reign in Victorian England: schoolroom instruction and family prayers were taken very seriously and churchgoing on Sundays provided a pattern and routine to country house life.[35]

In the child care advice of the time, the imperative of religious instruction of girls was pervasive. Through this, girls were expected to discover the essence of self-abnegation and self-sacrifice. But the danger, as Mrs Sandford warned in her advice book of 1831, was that they might become inured to a dry routine of religious instruction, come to see the Bible as a class book and then throw all this off, when they grew up, with 'the schoolroom trammels'. It was no good religion being 'learnt, repeated and then thrown aside'. Her piety 'should be the star to gild the young child's path and to give zest even to her little pleasures'.[36] Deborah Gorham has noted the paradox that, in Victorian England, a form of belief was inculcated that sanctioned women's inferiority in their daily lives, yet supported the idea of spiritual equality between the sexes.[37]

The public upbringing of girls, from the late seventeenth century onwards, was conducted in the newly established venues of the polite world.[38] Whereas prolonged schooling was necessary for boys, a girl's testing introduction to social life, in the eyes of many parents, could not begin too soon. After all, if the objective of the whole exercise was an advantageous and satisfactory marriage, there was no time to be wasted. The debate about the best pattern of training was wide-ranging. What was inescapable and pervaded the conduct books was the requirement for social training to add polish to a girl's essential inner purity. Her conduct in company should exemplify her goodness, commending her as genteel and making plain her accomplishments.

In early Stuart drama, male nervousness about women's 'gadding' from home and its implications was exemplified by relentless satire. Pretended visits to distant churches and mourning widows were painted as excuses for gatherings of boozing gossips.[39] Richard Braithwaite, in his 1631 tract *The English Gentlewoman*, pronounced that the appearance of women at stage plays, wakes and solemn feasts was indecent.[40] In his 1667 tract *The Virtuous Wife is the Glory of her Husband*, Laurence Price was still harping on neglect of the home: 'wantons and careless housewives are gadding abroad and wantonising among their companions'.[41]

But things changed dramatically in the more socially mobile world of Hanoverian England. Wives, now it was believed more firmly subordinated by the internal construction of gender, were expected to be out and about. 'Women not only shared fully in the literary and recreational life of the day but seemed positively to dominate it', Paul Langford has argued.[42] Whereas didactic writers sought to trivialise the socialising activities of genteel women as 'idle time wasting in otherwise empty lives', Ingrid Tague has argued that in fact the centrality of female domination of Georgian socialising was crucial to that society's gendered structure.[43]

Amanda Vickery found the social life of Georgian women, portrayed by their letters and diaries, brimming with comment on an array of public diversions. This correspondence celebrated an exciting cultural life, opened to their daughters, in many cases, at an early age. The rise of assembly rooms in provincial towns, as a forum for social and sexual mixing, was a crucial step, providing a protected and respectable indoor venue, where young girls paraded under parental tutelage. In London, the famous pleasure gardens at Vauxhall, Ranelagh, Marylebone and Kensington dominated the social round.[44] Custom-built walks were laid out for the fashionable evening promenade in provincial towns. Peter Borsay links these, in his study of the urban renaissance, with the theatres, musical societies and festivals, assemblies and horse racing meetings that punctuated a dynamic social calendar.[45] There was also the whole new world of the spas and seaside resorts. Conduct book advice took it for granted that polite women would be introducing their daughters to this whole social scene, seeking to guide their choice of activities and to check any excessive indulgence.

The scope of public entertainment, where the chaperone ruled, remained remarkably constant between the 1720s and the 1820s. But Queen Victoria's long reign saw much change in the patterns of fashionable socialising. At the opera house, for example, it has been found that the pit was a respectable choice by the 1840s, though the boxes remained ultra-fashionable. In London in the 1880s, galleries, tea shops, concerts and plays were all social venues open to accompanied young girls. Though, by then, the London pleasure gardens had all closed, the seaside promenade was in full swing. By 1900, new initiatives like tennis clubs and garden parties had established themselves.[46]

Victorian daughters were brought up to forms of feminine sociability which were more introverted than previously. Pleasure gardens closed because they lost social cachet and then custom. The stress was on privacy and controlled social interaction. Hence the country house party, redolent with hierarchy, as armies of servants waited upon privileged guests. Leonore Davidoff has characterised Victorian society as 'one of the most effective instruments for social control ever devised'. Its hallmark was 'control of individual behaviour and face-to-face interaction through a rigidly applied mode of personal behaviour'.[47]

Schoolboys, too immature to appear in public, were banished from the domestic social arena. Girls, by contrast, were always on the edge of society, even if at first it was only furtively glimpsed from the top of a staircase. The schoolroom kept them apart from social functions, but it did not entirely isolate them. They gradually emerged in their teens, making calls with mothers in the carriage, appearing at lunches with neighbours and visiting hospitable relatives. Then, by coming out, a girl put her footsteps on the path to society and thereby to the marriage market.

A mother's role and her closeness to her daughter became critical. It was she who did the work of preparing the debutante, work ranging from instruction in the elaborate rules of court procedure, for those about to be presented, to learning how to fill in dance cards, or to enter the dining room. This process of maternal initiation was exhaustive.[48] For, as Sarah Ellis remarked in a celebrated advice book, 'society is to the daughters of a family, what business is to the man'.[49] Paying calls in company with her mother was just a beginning for a girl: cards were reprinted with a daughter's name appearing beneath her mother's, to signal, when these were left on a hall table, that she had now arrived as a member of society.[50]

This upper-class ritualisation of social behaviour can be seen as the logical development of the unrelenting gendering of the upbringing of upper-class girls. It began with personal decorum and body language. Its apogee, in Victorian England, was a whole way of life ruled by convention, correct procedure and etiquette. 'For your carriage', opined Richard Brathwaite, writing a class-conscious passage in 1631, 'it should neither be too precise nor loose. The simpering made faces partake more of chambermaid than gentlewoman.'[51] Facial expression and style of movement were seen to matter equally.

Training by a dancing master was critical. John Essex, Richard Steele and Wettenhall Wilkes all accompanied their approval of eighteenth-century dancing masters with strong warnings against girls being carried away with vanity in their movement and dancing. But dancing should be started young, advised Essex, for it 'strengthens the fibres' and 'fashions the whole body to a graceful and becoming carriage'. It was an absolutely necessary accomplishment, claimed Wilkes, which 'tends to perfect graceful carriage and to give a freedom and easiness to all the motions of the body'.

The dancing master's work was concerned as much with general deportment as performance at the children's balls, which launched young girls on to their local social scene. Writers of advice books treated this in increasing detail. Essex dealt with how to enter and leave a room, when to sit down, how to sit at dinner and so on. How a woman walked was a grave test of politeness:

Nothing sets you off better than a modest, free and graceful motion in walking; your air, your shape, your choice in dress are here agreeably expressed . . . the fine turn of the head and neck, the uprightness of the body and the decorum of the feet at once point out to us good sense, symmetry and regular education.[52]

Wilkes was vehement about young girls who sat cross-legged before strangers.[53]

The conduct writers set out the programme of accomplishments which could win a girl a husband. This curriculum of female politeness was already well-established in the early seventeenth century. Ann Fanshaw and Anne Halkett reflected on the typical training they received in the 1620s and 1630s, which included tuition in French, needlework and music, besides dancing. Replying to his eight-year-old daughter's request that she should master the art of Japanning boxes in 1682, Sir Edmund Verney wrote: 'I approve of it; and so I shall of anything that is good and virtuous . . . for I admire all accomplishments that will render you considerable and lovely in the sight of God and man'.[54]

Verney shared the consensual view in his social circle that, above all, girls should not be idle.[55] This concern became almost obsessive. Sarah Pennington, in 1761, firmly structured the day, proposing half an hour before or after breakfast for pious authors or the Bible, a morning devoted to 'improvement', and the afternoon for what she called 'diversions'. These could include socialisation, reading, needlework, cards and visits to plays, and balls.[56] Conduct writers came to take it as read that girls would follow some kind of programme like this. But some, like the evangelical James Fordyce, began to deride the products of fashionable boarding schools, where politeness was most systematically inculcated. They had learnt 'to prattle much nonsense', he thought, and 'to practise I know not how many pert conceited airs and in consequence of all to conclude themselves accomplished women'.[57] Soan Jenyns's biting satire of 1717, *The Modern Fine Lady*, coruscated the fall, 'by friends, cards, lovers crossed', of Lady Harriott, who had been launched into society 'skilled in each art that can adorn'.[58]

In time a deeper and more lasting reaction set in against some aspects of the female curriculum. Dancing and French, acknowledged Hester Chapone in 1773, were 'now so universal that they cannot be dispensed with', but, so far as music and drawing were concerned, she would only wish, she advised, 'you to follow as genius leads'. These were agreeable enough pursuits for women who found time hanging on their hands.[59] The point was made more forcefully by Elizabeth Sandford in 1831, who argued that 'constrained studies are seldom successful'. Her vignette of the poor girl, 'doomed to symphonize three or four hours every day, to play without an ear and to sing without a voice' was acute. So was her account of the artistic displays 'of some laboured studio the only event of which is its painful execution'. A woman, Mrs Sandford was quite convinced, 'may be very good, very clever, very pleasing', without all these accomplishments.[60]

Girls, as we have seen, were believed at the start of this period to be weak in mind, incapable of learning rationality. Yet, though they were given no encouragement to develop intellectual interests, there were some who did so and earned the applause of fathers. Lucy Hutchinson was a prodigy as a Latinist. She recorded her father's pleasure at the progress she made.[61] Lady Judith Barrington was described in a funeral sermon as 'in the very upper form of female scholars'.[62] The daughters of Christopher, Viscount Hatton, were reported, around 1698, to be 'good Latin scholars'.[63] Such examples denied the stereotype of incapacity.

Yet there was a strong and persistent tradition of distrust of girlish intellectuality. Gentlewomen, avowed Richard Braithwaite, excoriating 'she-clerks', preferred to be approved by their 'living than learning'.[64] Sir Ralph Verney disapproved strongly of his godchild Nancy Denton learning Latin, explaining in a letter of 1687 to her father how he esteemed it a vice for a girl to do so. 'Good sweet heart be not so covetous', he wrote to her, telling her that 'a bible and good plain catechism' were 'much more suitable to your sex'.[65]

Negative views of this kind were challenged by early feminists like Hannah Woolley and Mary Astell between the 1670s and 1690s. But the impact of the first arguments for educational equality was muted by the generally conservative tone in which they were put. Nor did others who advocated female education thereafter, like Aphra Benn and Eliza Heywood, present an overall case for reinterpreting women's position. When that case was powerfully put by Mary Wollstonecraft in the 1790s, its impact was limited by public perception of the author's political radicalism and advanced views on female chastity.[66] The political atmosphere was such that the views of the evangelical Thomas Gisborne, for the present, got a better hearing than those of Wollstonecraft.[67]

Yet some learning was seen more generally to have a place for girls in the eighteenth century. It was a source of inner strength, a bulwark for modesty and chastity, a defence against fashion and triviality. The issue was the kind of learning that was appropriate. 'Nature has given them as good talents as men have', declared Richard Steele as early as 1714, 'and if they are still called the weaker sex, 'tis because the other, which assumes the name of the wiser, hinders them of improving their knowledge by accustoming them to the practice of vanity and trifles'. The objective of the education of girls, as he saw it, was a 'well informed and discerning mind'. A woman should seek a balanced understanding of herself, through a self-respect that erred on the side of humility.[68] John Essex, in 1722, set out his conviction that 'the fair sex . . .

have as good a taste of reason . . . as the proudest man can boast'. 'Reading valuable books', he declared, 'would improve those faculties of sense and reason which God and nature hath given them.' This would turn them away from the social round of frippery and tea drinking.[69]

Wetenhall Wilkes took up the argument in 1740, asserting that cultivation of learning was more worthy of attention than external graces, since the reading of moral and religious authors amounted to an 'enquiry into such truths as will fix you in your duty'.[70] Hester Chapone's tract in 1773 made the issue explicit with its ringing title: *Letters on the Improvement of the Mind Addressed to a Young Lady*. Her work took the form of a letter to a niece, who was told 'it is high time to store your mind with those principles which must direct your conduct and fix your character'. Chastity, piety, politeness, were all founded, in Chapone's view, on intellectual exercise which was coherent and systematic. Betsy Francis, who we shall encounter more closely later, and who was busy with bringing up five little girls, bought a copy in 1774.[71]

James Fordyce explained, in a sermon which explored 'Female Virtue with Intellectual Accomplishments', that it was not the 'argumentative but the sentimental talents' which a girl should master, through her reading and study. History taught about human virtues and vices; voyages and travels were a cure for too much national pride; geography was useful in conversation; astronomy, fables, allegory, drama and poetry were all 'improving'.[72] Sarah Pennington's proposed academic curriculum, similarly, consisted of the English and French languages, history, geography and the study of nature.[73] Education should 'call forth the reasoning powers of girls into action', declared Thomas Gisborne in 1798, 'and enrich the mind with useful and interesting knowledge suitable to their sex'.[74]

There were two overriding issues at the heart of this construction of femininity: the emotional support a woman should show her husband and her moral influence in the home and beyond it. The keynote of Richard Allestree's treatment of the role of the wife and mother was the exercise of emotional strength. 'She is to endeavour', as Steele put it, 'to bring him as much assistance, comfort of life as is possible, that so she may answer that special end of the woman's creation, the being a help to her husband.' Essex took the argument further. A woman's 'patience, courtesy and fortitude' enabled her 'to soften and divert those troubles and cares which ruffle the tempers of mankind'. In the writings of Fordyce and Chapone, the sentimentalisation of women reached its apogee in a vision of united domestic bliss. Writing of women's 'strong propensity to a union of hearts, their unutterable fondness', Fordyce saw wives as destined to disarm men's fierceness and appease their wrath. Chapone contemplated the weary husband returning to domestic serenity: 'let your cheerful complacency restore his good humour and quiet every uneasy passion'.[75]

Above all, a girl's destiny was to be a mother. This was how she would exercise significant power. Presenting herself as an example to her offspring, attending to her children's physical and emotional needs, she would, in effect, 'diffuse virtue and happiness through the human race'. In his *Sermons to Young Women*, Kate Retford argues, Fordyce stresses the 'affecting qualities of maternity' so forcefully that his female reader 'attains an ideological pedestal that surpasses even that allotted to the virtuous wife'.[76]

In one sense, all a girl's training was about adult moral leadership as mistress of a household, but this was made far more explicit in the late eighteenth and nineteenth centuries than earlier. The role she was being trained for involved household administration, the management of servants, guardianship of material culture, oversight of the nursery and training of daughters right through their adolescence until marriage.[77] Whether she was at the head of her dinner table or dispensing charity to the village poor, social polish would be the mantle that the accomplished woman wore. Propriety would be her watchword.

The first full statement of what this meant in terms of moral practice comes in Thomas Marriott's 1759 tract, which he called an 'essay on the art of pleasing' directed at 'the fair sex before and after marriage'. Beginning with conventional statements about women's 'soft mould' and 'various graces', Marriott went on to deplore the influence of dancing masters and excoriate the neglect of the proper education of girls. If this could be remedied, he believed, they might be the standard bearers of both domestic and public morality: they 'have it very much in their power by their exemplary behaviour to render virtue fashionable and discountenance vice among men'.[78]

It was in the home, above all, that a woman might wield her moral influence. This idea, developing in Georgian England, reached its culmination in the Victorian period. An ideology of moral womanhood then came to unite the aristocracy with the middle class. The redemptive power of the home came, as John Tosh notes, to be 'the subject of a vast quantity of prescription'. 'At once caring and authoritative', writes Kate Flint, Victorian novels were texts which 'implicitly claimed for themselves something of the ideological role of the mother which was constructed within their own covers, bonding the reader . . . into a framework of categorical self-definition.'[79] John Ruskin summarised the role of a wife as the linchpin of a static community: 'The woman's power is not for rule, not for battle . . . but for sweet ordering, management and decision. She sees the qualities of things, their class, their places.'[80]

Courtship and marriage were overwhelmingly what teenage girls were thinking about and preparing themselves for. So how far was conduct book

advice hegemonic? What did young girls come to believe about their subordination? It has been argued that the conduct books were effectively repressive.[81] Yet there is very strong evidence that girls, like adult women, were
active, not passive, in their reading, that their appropriation of what they read
was subtle, that their self-fashioning involved borrowing and reshaping
prescriptive notions rather than simply letting themselves be moulded
by them. Elaine Hobby has made the point that women made 'a virtue of
necessity'. The patriarchal framework was constantly being challenged in
detail and renegotiated.[82]

Among the striking and relevant vignettes in the literature, in Jane
Austen's *Pride and Prejudice*, published in 1813, is Mr Collins reading
aloud to his cousins Kitty and Lydia. He is offered a novel and then,
when he protests about this, other books, including Fordyce's *Sermons to
Young Women*, first published 48 years previously. Lydia interrupts him after
three pages of this, causing Mr Collins to reprove the girls for their lack of
interest in a serious book, 'so advantageous to them as instruction'. Vivien
Jones has commented upon how this episode 'plays with the familiar generic
opposition between fiction's dangerous pleasures and the irreproachable
programme of self-improvement provided by sermons and other forms of
advice literature'.[83]

A girl could choose to read a conduct manual, but responding to its advice
was a demanding exercise. Kitty and Lydia, Austen acutely implies, know
what they felt about the contents of their bookshelf. At the same time, they
might suspect that multiple and subversive readings of conduct books are
possible. It has been noted that while the works, for example, of Sarah Ellis
could be taken at their face value, as advocating supportiveness and meek
domesticity, they could also be seen as empowering, leading women into a
manipulative role towards their menfolk.[84]

Yet most upper-class girls probably never actually read a conduct book.
They were anyway primarily intended for parents. There is good reason to
think, judging by the many reprintings of items like Halifax's *Advice*, that it
was they who absorbed this kind of advice most avidly. Parents had available
to them, in an increasing torrent over three centuries, a mass of prescriptive
writing about their children's upbringing, advice couched in broad terms
about the nature of childhood, of boyhood and of girlhood. This was complemented by advice about the duties and responsibilities of parenthood. We
must take account finally of this genre of advice literature before turning to
the practice of parenting in England.

4

Parenthood

If prescriptions about the kind of values and behaviour that should be inculcated in children were numerous, direct advice on the conduct of parenthood was thin until the 1670s. Puritan clerical writers simply excoriated both mothers and fathers for pampering and 'cockering' their children.[1] Fathers' advice to sons, like William Martyn's *Youth's Instructions*, occasionally appeared in print in the seventeenth century with an apparent didactic purpose.[2] There were a few fathers, like John Temple, who left written instructions to their sons that have survived in manuscript, but these cannot be seen as having a prescriptive impact outside that family.[3]

Three very well-circulated printed tracts relating to motherhood were composed before 1660 for particular reasons. Dorothy Leigh's *A Mother's Blessing* was a guide to Christian living, given emotional thrust by its posthumous publication 'lest my children should not find the right way to heaven'.[4] Elizabeth Joceline's *A Mother's Legacy to her Unborn Child* acquired the same potency through her death in childbed. If she had a son, she hoped he might be ordained; if a daughter she desired her 'bringing up to be learning the bible . . . good housewifery, writing and good works'.[5] The Countess of Lincoln's specific purpose was to persuade mothers to breastfeed their children at a time when many were sent to wet nurses.[6]

Published autobiography offered occasional incidental advice on parenting. Thomas Tryon wrote about feeding and teaching children to read and write from his family experience. 'When your children are of dull capacities and hard to learn', he insisted, 'reproach them not, nor expose them, but taking them alone, talk to them familiarly, and give them sweet and soft words, show them the advantages of learning, and how much it will tend to their advancements.'[7]

In the absence of a genre of advice on parenting, there was reliance on common sense and traditional roles. Children, a source of happiness and pleasure, were born to be loved and cared for. 'The peevishness of a child's infancy is quite forgot when he begins to prattle', declared Thomas Heywood in 1637, 'what comfort their toward youth breeds and what consolation their more staid years beget, I leave to their consideration who have been the fruitful parents of a fortunate progeny.'[8] The Marquis of Halifax's bald statement about motherhood, in his advice to his daughter, that 'the first part of our life is a good deal subjected to you in the nursery where you reign supreme' was an accepted truism.[9] Fathers were expected to provide economic support, authority and discipline, then to take the lead in seeing a child into the world, either through finding a boy work or through involvement in a girl's marriage.

It was predictable that Richard Allestree should have turned his attention in 1673 to motherhood. It was generally accepted, he noted, that motherly care lasted till around six or seven for boys, when they went to school, and until marriage for upper- and middle-class girls. Allestree began by stating that motherhood was natural, but that this did not mean that all mothers hit the right balance in exercising it. Whereas some were too rugged, others were too selfish and others, again, were too doting. But a mother's love, he believed, 'by strength of feminine passion', usually exceeded a father's. Her care, he argued, should be characterised by 'prudent severity'. This meant inuring children's bodies to 'moderate hardships' and providing an early beginning in moral training: 'we may see early dawning of reason in infants which would sooner come to a brightness if we would betimes set to scattering of those passions which eclipse and darken it'.

Mothers should beat their boys and girls as necessary, rather than subject them to 'infinite and invisible affrightments, the beloved methods of nurses and servants', such as 'the menacing of sprights and leaving in the dark'. For the child's will was 'supple and pliant'. With 'native stubbornness subdued', Allestree was convinced, 'the yoke will fit easy'. All this, besides instruction in what Allestree called 'useful knowledge', was a mother's personal responsibility. Her close company was the best security against the debasement of minds and corruption of manners that would follow from allowing servants to exert influence on her children.[10]

Allestree's sane and balanced, if highly class conscious, account of parenthood breathes the gentry's consensus in Restoration England about a hierarchical society. There is a striking contrast here with the brutal and excessively demanding advice of the puritan clerics, like William Gouge and John Dod and Robert Cleaver, before the civil war. They, as we have seen, made much of nurture in religion, which structured their whole philosophy of the child.[11] There was undoubtedly deeply-felt terror at that time of parental indulgence, which was traced principally to mothers. Gouge reported scornfully that he knew of mothers who, neglecting their duty of correction, were offended with their husbands for beating their children. They would not commit them to a tutor or schoolmaster, without 'a straight charge that they correct them not'.[12]

Too much pampering and cherishing, said Dod and Cleaver, would 'utterly spoil and mar their children'. Parents, mothers especially, needed to be taught 'not to love them too much'.[13]

Men differed about whether boys or girls were more trouble. 'There is more trouble', reflected Unton Dering, writing to a relative in 1647, 'with girls than boys.'[14] Thomas Marriott, in his *Female Conduct* of 1759, took the opposite view, finding girls 'by nature of a more docile and tractable turn, more apt to receive and retain impressions than the other sex'. He noted boys' 'more stubborn genius but inflexible self sufficiency and pride'.[15] Yet fathers generally accepted that maternal influence on boys, once beyond the cradle, was often inappropriate and could be pernicious.[16] Boys, 'bred like fondlings at home', warned John Locke, often developed a 'sheepish softness'. Maternal tuition, argued John Costaker in 1732, produced 'a complete fop'. Daniel Defoe and Jonathan Swift early in the century, and James Fordyce towards its end, all took the same line.[17]

Two supremely influential works, Allestree's *Ladies Calling* and Halifax's *The Lady's New Year Gift or Advice to a Daughter*, Toni Bowers has argued, outlined standards of maternal behaviour that became 'part of eighteenth-century Britain's cultural consciousness'. A 'Mother', insisted Allestree, was 'a title of so much tenderness'. Almost all the Augustan conduct literature of motherhood abridged, conflated or repeated this seventeenth-century precept. Mothers were urged to give constant personal attendance to their children and to educate them themselves. They must neither spoil and indulge nor love too little. Breastfeeding became the touchstone of maternal virtue.[18]

Writers about female conduct assumed it was mothers who formed their most attentive readership. John Essex included a summary of 28 instructions for those in charge of girls 'for their future conduct of life'. These included preserving them against the superstitious talk of servants, cultivating 'the little seeds of reason', achieving a balance between commendation and criticism, giving proper advice about diet, exercise and adequate sleep. Predictable items were the need for moral instruction and the inculcation of politeness.[19] William Kenrick warned against doting: 'when the dawn of reason appears learn thy child obedience'. He saw the young child in a mother's hands as the young osier growing as it was bent. Indulgence should not hold a mother back from chastisement, but spankings should model severity to 'temper and capacity'.[20] Gisborne, likewise, called for a deep parental involvement in 'modelling the human mind during the early stages of growth'.[21] What all these writers stated or implied, following Locke, was that each child was an individual, with their own 'constitution and genius'. A mother's task was to study and understand this, directing the style of her upbringing appropriately within general limits.[22]

Kate Retford has shown how between 1750 and 1800 portraiture of the art of motherhood burgeoned. Mothers and infants were detached from the household unit and 'placed close to the picture plane, conveying a sense of immediacy and infancy'. In a Sir Joshua Reynolds portrait of 1763, Susanna Hoare gazes into the face of her daughter, who, returning her gaze, reaches up with one hand to caress her mother's face. Portraits confirm the new idealisation and glamorisation of motherhood at this time. They often made direct reference to old masters and to Renaissance portraits of the Holy Family. Yet their message was directly contemporary, stressing a mother's role as the instructor of her young children. In Reynolds's account of the Countess of Pembroke and her son George, the breeched boy holds an open book.[23]

From around 1750, a new more focused genre of parenthood tracts, with variations in format, began to appear. Henry Wotton's *Essay on the Education of Children in the First Rudiments of Learning* was the prolonged encomium of a child prodigy, who read Homer at six and whose learning was set out to present him as a paragon that others might be taught to equal.[24] Sarah Pennington's 1761 tract, *An Unfortunate Mother's Advice*, was detailed and specific about the kind of motherly regime which set an 'example of regularity'. In her *Letters on Different Subjects*, written to Miss Louisa, which followed in 1770, she was didactic about diet: 'plain and simple kinds' of food were 'certainly best'. She was horrified that 'the barbarous custom of swaddling is not yet universally exploded', recommending for an infant's 'first habit' simply 'shirt, a robe and a cap', the last two quilted for sufficient warmth.[25]

James Nelson's *Essay on the Government of Children*, published in 1763, was the most comprehensive treatment of the subject to date. It dealt with aspects of exercise suitable to a healthy physical development. This was followed by a thoughtful discussion of discipline. Milder methods should be tried before spanking a child, which was obviously bad practice in excess, since the observable result was fermenting the child's blood and inflaming the skin on the buttocks. In forming a child's manners, parental attitudes should show balance. When a father felt he had to show severity, 'let the mother put in an equal share of lenity and compassion mixed with grief' and vice versa. Nelson demanded that boys and girls should have separate rooms, so they were 'not exposed naked to one another'. A firm routine should structure their day. Boys, he concluded, 'stand in need of every help to make them diligent' and should be carefully watched by parents since they were 'naturally giddy'.[26]

A series of prescriptive genres concur in their new emphasis, after 1750, on fathering that freely displayed emotion in situations of family intimacy. Philip Carter has explored the developing advice literature about men's behaviour at home. Samuel Johnson, he argues, identified manliness as a truly refined form of domestic conduct in the *Rambler*: 'only as a loving rather than a disciplinarian husband or father was a man able to show that his heart is pure'. Similarly, James Fordyce painted father and son as 'bosom friends' and wrote of the 'mild and noble feelings' that could be created across the parent and child divide. Men started to be seen as caring guides to their offspring in the transition to adulthood. Thus Thomas Gisborne highlighted help with the start of apprenticeship or university life.[27]

Thomas Percival's *A Father's Instructions Consisting of Moral Tales, Fables and Reflections* in 1781, written under the impetus of Romanticism, was intended to 'refine the feelings of the heart' among the young. Percival believed that boys, in particular, found didactic education irksome but that they would be responsive to the tales he extracted from classical literature. These were concerned with such subjects as cruelty to animals, compassion for the poor, circumspection, pride and pedantry. This was a novel and intriguing model of parenthood.[28] The watchwords proposed in bringing up girls, by J. Moir, in 1800, were diligence, activity and economy. She wanted mothers to remember just how important it was to make a 'proper beginning'. If they could make simplicity prevail among their offspring, 'all the smiling and benevolent virtues' would flourish.[29]

Yet, with Hannah More in 1799, evangelicalism found a strident voice. She sought to persuade mothers that, so far from innocence, children exhibited 'a corrupt nature and evil disposition which it should be the great end of education to rectify'. She painted a graphic picture of how obsession with teaching girls politeness could lead them astray. Children's balls, she suggested, were peopled by 'lilliputian coquettes ... their little hearts beating with hopes about partners ... their fresh cheeks pale after the midnight supper, their aching heads and unbraced nerves'. Thus, she argued, did some parents simply beguile their offspring.[30]

Melesina Trench, born in 1768, belonged to the bluestocking circle of women who published anonymously during the 1790s.[31] A particular governess had a formative impact on this remarkable woman's mind in her early childhood. Melesina recalled her very long face and waist 'and a stocking in her hand, which she knitted so perseveringly it seemed a part of herself; and a determination to rule by rigour, to pass nothing, to correct seldom but then to do it with effect'. She would not dwell 'on the cruelties I suffered', but, she confessed, they had 'impressed me with a deep horror of unkindness to the young and of all that is fierce and despotic in every shape'. She had lacked 'the smallest disposition to falsehood or mischief', Melesina was convinced, 'and I sympathised with every being that felt'. Despite 'restraint, fear and inflictions of every kind', she herself was 'the best child possible'. 'I was obedient and loving, docile and lively, although timid.'

The loss of a son at two years old in 1806 led Melesina to abandon her career in Regency society. She wrote in her journal of this as 'the misfortune from which I date my second life, as different, certainly, from the former as two separate modes of being'.[32] Bringing up four more boys between 1806 and her death in 1827, Melesina dedicated her middle age to motherhood, writing and correcting a tract on parenting that sprung both from experience and her battles to improve the lot of her sons when they attended Harrow.[33] She wrote her manual for parents, which was published after her death in 1837, in the conviction that if a child was treated properly, all would be well.[34]

Melesina believed that it was of crucial importance to breastfeed her own children and spend much time with them in their early years.[35] By 1816, when she wrote a deep-felt letter of thanks to Charles, her adult son from her first marriage, for some pieces of china he had sent her, her younger boys were at Twyford, the well-known prep school not far from her home at Bursledon in Hampshire. 'These beautiful specimens of art will often furnish me with an occasion of conversing about "my son" – and as love is the same in all ages, I shall be able to say "'tis a present from him".'[36]

Melesina was emphatic that the first objective of motherhood was 'to train up of an immortal soul'; the 'second (but second at an immeasurable distance) is to do this in a manner most conducive to earthly happiness'. She was scathing about friends who were obsessed with promoting their daughters and with their accomplishments. Finding children's 'differences of temper' observable from birth, she resisted schemes of upbringing which, ignoring this, were too unbending and systematic. A mother's influence could begin to be felt in the nursery, when, Melesina insisted, 'education of the heart' should begin. Unless correct principles were planted then, they would prove 'too weak to operate as restraints during the perilous and impassioned hours of youth'.

The choice of a nurse was critical. She needed a severe temperament but her character should show 'mildness, patience, truth and self denial'. 'Noisy loquacious dames' were entirely unsuitable. Mother and nurse both needed to find their way between injudicious fondling on the one hand and severity on the other. She had seen governesses who quickly resorted to spanking, 'to the utter extinction of health and firmness in her pupil but without gaining her point'. All concerned should meet the demands of a young child by 'gravity, sweet, austere composure' with, when this was needed, 'an effort to divert his attention'.[37]

This beginning set the tone of Melesina Trench's book. She went on, in six chapters, to treat at length the issues of instilling religion, forming manners, teaching humanity to animals, learning courage, imposing punishment and encouraging play. This was the most powerful statement of the case for liberal parenthood in England to date when it was published. Deeply read in the advice literature, she had absorbed, but was not governed by, Rousseau's principles.

A mother's spiritual role, Melesina declared, went way beyond teaching prayers and a desire to read the Bible: 'I shall tell them of a Being all powerful – all wise – all good, who sees us in every moment of our lives and reads every thought of our hearts.' She never doubted that the good would be rewarded and the wicked punished, but she saw it as inappropriate to cloud a child's mind with such matters, which should be passed over lightly. The child should grow in knowledge of the delights showered by God, from fruits and flowers, sun, moon and stars to the joys of family affection. Biblical stories should be carefully explained in accessible language, with regular reference to exemplars: the firmness of Moses, the resignation of Isaac, the magnanimity of David and so on.

Manners, in Melesina's argument, should not be taught as a code, but by example. 'In ameliorating hearts', she wrote, 'you polish manners', inculcating 'good nature, good humour, gentleness, the habit of respecting oneself soberly and of attending to the feelings of others without the formality of precept'. A child's bow, the manner of entering or leaving a room, were not matters to be studied but the fruit of general self-possession and good breeding. Parents should inspire 'kindly feelings for the weak and helpless, respect for old age, due deference for rank and station'. Prudent and affectionate parents would feel 'the incalculable advantage of being the companions of their children'. Hers was consciously an upbringing for a high responsibility and, as it happened, one of her sons went on to become Archbishop of Dublin.[38] Parents should teach how to relate easily and naturally to servants and lead them in visiting estate cottages and inspecting workshops.[39]

Melesina cited Locke, Milton and Addison in treating the issue of childish sensitivity, relating this to kindness to animals. She saw that as a starting point in the formation of benevolence in a child's character: 'the seeds of kindness or cruelty may be cherished by the conduct they are taught to observe to the fly in the window'. She took her approach to reading matter, graded for the developing but vulnerable childish mind, from three writers who were in the forefront of the movement from the 1770s to promote children's literature: Sarah Trimmer, Anna Barbould and Maria Edgeworth.[40]

The cultivation of courage in the child was one of her central concerns. Melesina warned against the effects of sudden noise, dazzling light or violent motion on infant mentality. Matching stories to stages of confidence was crucial. Reading should never be indiscriminate: there was a time for *Red Riding Hood* and *Blue Beard*, then for *Macbeth* and *Richard III*, as the mind grew stronger. Ghost stories, she feared, were often told when children were far too young and terrified them accordingly. The correct diet of reading should be matched by a programme of air and exercise, including cold bathing, to strengthen the body. Both Maria Edgeworth and Rousseau, Melesina believed, were too partial to play, but there was a place for this as well.[41]

There was no subject on which Melesina was more eloquent than corporal punishment. Beating children at home, she noted, had been 'losing ground for many years but by very slow degrees'. 'As soon as a child can comprehend why it is being punished by physical pain, it has intelligence enough', she asserted vigorously, 'to be restrained by milder measures.' Melesina Trench believed that attachment to spanking children was proof of 'a disposition to cruelty which is the darkest stain of our fallen nation'.

Beating children produced 'pusilanimity or hardness, cruelty, obstinacy'. Tutors or governesses who did it should be dismissed. Chastisement, she believed, however applied, whether spanking, 'caning, slapping, ear-pulling, hair-dragging or any other uncouth and barbarous shape', would never 'produce good'. 'Many of the wise', she added, 'are doubtful of its having a favourable effect even in public schools.'[42] She favoured a small pocket money fine, or a word or look of displeasure, as the means by which an effective mother could retain discipline. Summarising her precepts, Melesina concluded that parents were 'too anxious their pupils should be wise, good and happy exactly their way', forgetting 'the infinite variety of existence and diversity of excellence this world affords'.[43]

There was a strong tradition in Quaker circles of mothers recording and reflecting upon their experience of bringing up their children. In several cases, these reflections were published in the nineteenth century with prescriptive and didactic intent. Three of these works were by Margaret Woods in 1829, Priscilla Johnston, a Norfolk Quaker and niece of Elizabeth Fry in 1862, and Mary Sewell, the daughter of a Suffolk gentleman farmer and mother of the author of *Black Beauty*, in 1889. They shared attitudes about the importance of their role, about their responsibility for the characters of their children and about the need to find assurance that their style and methods of upbringing were proper and correct.[44]

Margaret Woods, sitting introspectively in 1777 'with my dear little cares', reflected upon how they might 'be deemed uncertain blessings, their lives are very precarious and their future conduct proving, as one could wish, not less doubtful'. 'I already often look forward with anxiety', she realised, 'and the most ardent wishes for their welfare'. It was the understanding that each of her children was an individual in his or her own right that informed the commitment to teach and train them with all the sensitivity she could muster.

In two passages, written in 1799 and 1815, Margaret pondered the crux of upbringing: how far to indulge her children's desire for independence and when to impose her authority:

> Little benefit can arise from mere compulsion, either in doing or forbearing, further than as it may gain time for the understanding and judgement to ripen and if they can be kept in the practice of good and preserved from evil, till that time, it will be a great point gained. The body acquires strength and the power of its movements but by slow degrees and the mind more slowly.

Sixteen years later, wiser by experience, Margaret Woods wrote, 'I have always wished that they should be afraid of doing wrong but not afraid of me'. If she erred, she reflected on this occasion, she would rather it was on the lenient side: 'fear and force will, no doubt, govern children while little, but having a strong hold on their affections will have most influence over them in their progress through life'. Margaret Woods believed strongly that cultivating obedience was indispensable in educating a child, but it was imprudent, she reflected, 'to call it forth too frequently on trivial occasions'. Above all, her children must feel equals in her sight. It was pernicious to 'exalt one with the view of either lowering or stimulating another'.[45]

Mary Sewell, writing in about 1830, based all her thinking on the issue of character: 'the metal of a child's character must be formed early. The soul must be trained to govern the body and not to be its slave.' She was convinced that the benefits of providing regularity in a child's day were invaluable. 'The child should be set up at the table to amuse itself quietly', she declared, 'without any assistance except being furnished with its amusements for the time.' Nor should these be too various: habits of perfection could be learnt by repeated play with stringing beads, drawing or cutting. 'Perfect play', she believed, 'is the anticipation of perfect work.'

Mary put strong emphasis on training in observation and curiosity. There was no end to lessons through which 'a child obtains the power of using his own mind and learns the value of current language and description'. Exploring her children's capacities gave her both encouragement and surprise. Weighting and measuring, she found, were 'quite within the compass of a child under eight years old'. The objective throughout was to make her children less troublesome, more interesting and more independent. Yet she kept them on a tight rein.

Anna and Philip Sewell received annual parental reports on their birthdays, which provided chiding, instruction and encouragement. 'Anna Sewell', one of these ran, in 1829, 'has this day completed her ninth year and is in many respects a delight and comfort to her mother.' Yet she was at that time 'much disposed to be idle over lessons and work'. Philip was told he was 'a nice little boy', even though he 'can neither sit nor stand still'; he was 'more persevering in play than in work' and had 'an awkward habit of repeating what other people say'.[46]

Priscilla Johnson felt her inadequacy 'to convey any idea of the almost ceaseless engrossment of my heart, mind and time' about her children. She found herself preoccupied day by day, in 1844, with her 'precious, anxious treasures', revealing, in a passage when her eldest son was ten, the depths of her absorption and delight:

> I often think that as children in the charms and fascinations of their first years are like the blossoms, so they go through the state of unripe fruit, their infantile charms are gone, and the full fruit is far from being come; yet this is not true fully; for though unripeness and hope for the future may predominate, yet how large a measure of enjoyment is there from them in all stages.

Priscilla had imbibed the new thinking about teaching the Bible through scripture illustrations, as well as the Romantic absorption, which she hoped to pass on to her children, in every aspect of nature. She made Sundays, she recorded in 1838, 'very much of a treat: the cake, clean clothes, a large picture bible, walks with Papa and Mama in the garden'.[47]

The ultimate test of motherhood came to be seen as leaving a record that a child could review happily in the teenage years or adulthood. The novelist Elizabeth Gaskell began a diary for her daughter, charting her development, in 1835, when the child was six months, admitting how the moulding of her character weighed upon her:

> there have been many little indications of disposition etcetera already, which I cannot now remember clearly . . . In general she is so good that I feel as if I could hardly be sufficiently thankful that the materials put into my hands are so excellent and beautiful, and yet it seems to increase the responsibility.

She worried about the mistakes she expected to be making: 'if when you read this you trace back any evil or unhappy feeling to my mismanagement in your childhood, forgive me, love!' she wrote.[48]

The period from 1800 to 1850 saw the elaboration of the cult of domesticity. A man's place in the Victorian home has been defined and explored by John Tosh. Domesticity denotes, he has written, 'not just a pattern of residence or a web of obligations, but a profound attachment'. Its defining attributes were 'privacy and comfort, separation from the workplace, and the merging of domestic space and family members into a single commanding concept'. This, he argues, became 'the goal of the conventional good life; home came to be identified with childhood, innocence and roots – indeed with authenticity itself'.[49]

Leonore Davidoff's examination of this domestic idyll is illuminating. Home, she explains, 'was seen as a living entity, inevitably compared to the functional organs of a body, harmoniously related parts of a mutually beneficial division of labour'. The husband, father, master linked the home to society as both an individual and citizen; his dependants gave him 'love, obedience, service and loyalty'. Legitimate relationships in this world were vertical only. Wives, servants and children never left the estate, 'except under the closest scrutiny and control'. 'The idea of domesticity as a general good', writes Davidoff, 'was intimately tied to the powerful symbol of the house as a physical place'.[50]

So powerful was this domestic ideology that inculcation of gender attitudes appropriate to its fulfilment was begun early in childhood. Little girls were always potentially managers within the home, setting an example to younger brothers, keeping them quiet and orderly by demonstration of their own lady-like behaviour. Little boys, by contrast, as Davidoff puts it, 'were to be manly, to observe the etiquette of doffing caps, opening doors, offering chairs to ladies'. They were quickly sent into the rough and tumble of boarding schools. In the holidays they were leaders, taking coy sisters on expeditions and into scrapes. At the same time, they expected to protect them from insult and physical harm.[51]

With motherhood on a pinnacle, boys were taught to idealise their mothers. Isaac Taylor's *Advice to the Teens* in 1818 had tackled the issue. Starting from the principle that 'home is the grand nursery for virtues and admirably adapted for the purposes', he instructed boys that 'all the tenderness and delicacy which belong to the sex plead in behalf of your mother', who always deserved 'polite and affectionate attention'.[52] Yet the patriarchal imperative led boys, glimpsing the future, to claim a privileged position in the household.

C.M. Howard was thoughtful about the stresses and strains of trying to be a good mother, stressing the importance of rituals like her games before and after dinner, and Sunday dinner with the 'nursery party'. She saw transition from the nursery to the schoolroom as a key moment, more simply managed for a girl than for a boy. Well aware of incipient gender privilege, she noted how easy it was to let an heir apparent get above himself, with sisters fetching and carrying for him from an early age. Howard flattered herself that she had avoided this: that her boy was rescued from selfishness of character yet 'considerably and affectionately looked up to'.[53]

Whereas close responsibility for boys ended early, mothers expected to remain, as we have seen, close confidants of their daughters, giving them firm practical, moral and spiritual advice. They had to hold their child fast from danger on every side: from becoming a hoyden on the one hand, from slipping into the impurity of heart that, it was believed, novels, fasting and masturbation could prompt on the other. Puberty was a dangerous, but also a demanding, time in the mother–daughter relationship. Little girls, Victorian doctors held, though they were as hardy as their brothers beforehand, became delicate and fragile in adolescence, easily losing their emotional bearing through excitement and pleasure, the mental strain of excessive study or the thrills of travel.

There were plenty of advice books available by the 1850s about how mothers should handle female diet, dress, exercise and hygiene, both in early childhood and in adolescence. There was insistent advice, in the cause of fashion, on corsets and stays which put a limit upon vigorous physical activity. Yet at the same time air and exercise continued to be taken very seriously: 'it is well not to acquire the habit of coddling', wrote Mrs Pullan in 1855, 'as in a climate as changeable as ours it is impossible wholly to escape draughts and damp'.

From the 1860s, new physical activities for girls, such as bicycling, hockey and tennis came into fashion. These accompanied a gradual alteration in the way that the developing female body was perceived.[54] In the 1880s, it has been argued by Sally Mitchell, a culture of the 'new girl' was apparent in juvenile literature, suggesting models of active independence that were just beginning to be seen as acceptable for the teenager and young woman.[55]

The central Victorian preoccupation was with competing and less desirable influences than parental ones, which, disturbing class cohesion, could make an impact on the minds of daughters. Was the governess sufficiently alert to conversations between teenagers 'upon subjects it is not fitting they should discuss'? This was a question that Elizabeth Sewell posed for the attention of the diligent mother. Whereas boys were expected to encounter sexual talk and perhaps even sexual experience at school, girls were to be shielded from every hint of the existence of the sexual act. Mothers and governesses, Sewell advised, should develop the tactics of deferring answers to awkward questions and hurrying past risqué passages in history. Elizabeth Sewell had no time for girls' boarding schools, with their lack of personal privacy, their low tone and their atmosphere of irreverence.[56]

In the nineteenth century, fathers were seen as somewhat out of their depth in parenthood, because they lacked the moral resources called for in the job.

'As in infancy a mother is the best nurse, so in childhood she is the best guardian and instructress', declared Elizabeth Sandford confidently. It was women's expertise in affairs of 'individual feeling', fathers lacking 'the nicety and tact' to manage these, which enabled women to excel in training children, Sarah Ellis believed.[57] A changing philosophy of child-rearing was leaving upper-class men ideologically high and dry. Few, it has been suggested, would lower their dignity by doing more than visit the nursery, where, in wealthier families, infants were increasingly segregated and placed under the charge of nannies and governesses.[58]

John Tosh has noted how many commentators regarded performance of the central function of work, which provided economically for the family, as effectively disbarring Victorian fathers from other aspects of parenting. By 1830, Kathryn Hughes argues, the middle-class home was a female domain: 'a power-house of moral virtue, the chief purpose of which was to absolve the capitalist world beyond the front door from the sins of greed, envy and lust'.[59] It was increasingly expected that fatherhood should be exhibited intermittently. Yet the sentimentalisation of the home extended to the father as its protector, who, in the words of Sarah Ellis, folds a daughter 'tenderly in his arms, toils for her subsistence and comfort and watches over her expanding beauty that he may shield it from all blight'.[60]

Victorian mothers had a clearly-depicted role and a set of duties in which they were supposed to advise their girls; fathers, by contrast, were made constantly aware of the ideals of manliness that their society held dear, yet were offered no guidance as to how to inculcate these in their sons. The practice of fatherhood became a striking vacuum in the mass of prescriptive material available. This perhaps reflected a pervasive sense that the matter was fraught with difficulty. Mothers, colluding in an experience that deprived men of the emotional resources to be effective partners in their own homes, were themselves stormtroopers of the stiff Victorian ideology of manliness, taught by sending boys away to school.

The public schools offered, as John Tosh has put it, a 'crash course in manliness', relieving fathers of the dilemmas of home discipline. Fathers felt comfortable in the knowledge that their boys were growing up in an environment that was far from domestic, that banned all female terms of reference and played down the emotional aspects of life, yet which held the respect of their upper- and middle-class society.[61] They expected their boys to be beaten at school, to learn, through fagging and then being prefects, the ways of hierarchy and subordination and to mimic the stringencies of adult male life. Writing in 1988, F.M.L.Thompson accounted for this as an internal arrangement within the class, a matter of an older generation imposing upon and moulding the younger in the cause of the self perpetuation of class identity.

Public schools conditioned boys, he argued, into 'becoming upright manly characters who did not cheat, sneak or whine and who could lead without being needlessly cruel to animals or servants'.[62]

For domestic upbringing had become, for most fathers, a conundrum. The gender polarisation of Victorian England left parents sharply divided about whose business parenting really was. Mothers were soft, warm and affectionate; fathers were left with bread winning, discipline they often shrank from, rigid values and plenty of anxiety.[63] We shall see how this played out in practice and how, although strict evangelical fathers were rare, the tyrannical Victorian father did exist.[64]

For all men who had imbibed the Romantic notion of childhood, it was at least disturbing, if not abhorrent, to train their sons, which could mean beating them at home, supposedly a haven of love and devotion. Breaking the will had anyway gone out of fashion; moulding the individual was becoming a new orthodoxy for which public schools were exactly designed. Domestic punishment, in this respect, became an integral aspect of women's child management, a finely-calculated process at which mothers were seen to have the potential to excel with very little boys and with girls of all ages.

There was little prescriptive material about how fathers should relate to daughters. But in practice men found themselves able to be more relaxed, more openly affectionate, and have more fun at home, with them than they could with their sons. A father, we have seen, provided for and protected a daughter; at the same time he could claim some part of the responsibility for her moral training. Given these demands, the Victorian domestic ideology gave him leave to bask in the atmosphere of redemption which, through an idealisation of girlhood, teenage femininity was expected to bring to the home. As her father's daughter, a girl was expected to be learning a role for her later performance as another man's wife. She adorned the home with her skills in music, painting or needlework; she was a sunbeam providing distraction, rest and amusement for a father who bore the cares of the world.[65]

The ideology of parenthood, it is argued here, was developed slowly, under the influence of thinkers and writers whose account of the nature of childhood went through specific stages. Puritan harshness was replaced, over two hundred years, by Victorian sentiment. Yet there was consistency from 1600 to 1914 in the teaching that parental responsibility was basically about training and preparation for manhood and womanhood. Parents understood and grasped the potential that Locke first made explicit, for adults to form and mould the child.

But these were not, as the present so stridently is, child-centred ages. No parent before 1914 believed that his or her task was simply to enable a child to 'find' himself or herself. Rather, parents aimed to help the child fit into the society of their time along prescribed lines. There were tight gender rules in this period which held sway within ruling class assumptions. Reviewing the whole period from 1500 to the present day, Hugh Cunningham is surely right to suggest that it was in the twentieth century that change became most rapid in the conceptualisation of childhood. The same must apply in the case of the conceptualisation of parenthood.[66]

PART II

PARENTING

5

Care and Affection

The foundation of upbringing throughout the period covered by this book was parental care and affection for children, in the intimate and private world of family life. Parents, Keith Wrightson has argued, made a huge material and emotional investment in their children and expected little in return. Family relationships were already warm and loving in the seventeenth century, long before John Locke's positive thinking about childhood gave impetus to recording incidents in the upbringing of particular children. Thus the fulminations of authoritarian puritan clerics against mothers who spoilt or cockered their children can be read as indicating a critical view of the lavish cuddling and attention that most enjoyed.[1]

There is no reason to think that the broad pattern of thinking within which they brought up their children changed in any linear fashion between 1600 and 1914. This chapter and the ones that follow on marital partnership and on children who died will focus upon this broad pattern of family relationships, before we investigate in more depth the ways in which parenting was gendered. Gendered parenting, we shall see, produced gendered children.

Sometimes the evidence that parents loved their children dearly between 1600 and 1700 emerges incidentally in the accounts of serious puritan parents, who were wont to record the providences from which they were delivered.[2] Nehemiah Wallington, recounting how his daughter Sarah almost fell into the fire one day in 1630, described her typical behaviour. This suggests the child's security in a halo of parental love: 'my sweet child being very merry all that day and prattling to me prettily the next day, it could not but make me call to mind God's great love and mercy in preserving and delivering us'.[3] Diaries and autobiographies testify to the notion that parents hoped their children would become 'comforts'. Ralph Josselin found his first daughter 'a pleasant comfort'. He was 'sweet company to his poor mother in my absence and a refreshing to me [*sic*] at my return', wrote Adam Martindale about his baby son. Henry Newcome recorded a conversation with a

Warrington gentleman, Samuel Leech, at a fair on 6 November 1680: 'his children are all comforts', he noted, whereas poor Richard Nichol's were 'all discomforts'. 'If most of mine be comforts', he reflected, 'how kindly I am dealt withall'.[4]

Occasionally a parent testified to the bonding that a child needed in a manner that seems remarkably modern. An explicit comment by Lady Willoughby, in 1635, shows her spontaneously seeking emotional contact with her infant, giving and expecting love:

> Even at my child's tender age, he is sensibly affected by the feelings apparent in the faces of those around him. Yesterday it happened as I nursed him that, being vexed by some trifling matters that were not done as I had desired, the disturbed expression of my countenance so distressed him that he uttered a complaining cry. Made happy by a smile and more serene aspect that affection called forth, he nestled his little face against my bosom.

The child's grandmother, Lady Willoughby noted, had visited a few weeks before, taking the baby in her arms and looking fondly on him. That summer he was growing finely and 'sheweth already a masterful spirit', but the next month, sadly, he died.[5]

There are many scraps of information which give insight into a largely hidden world, before 1700, of domestic affection. Worrying about her daughter at ten months in 1614, when she was teething and not putting on much weight, Anne Clifford told her mother that though Margaret was small, 'a livelier and merrier thing was never yet seen'.[6] 'Kiss all my little boys for me', wrote Endymion Porter to his wife unselfconsciously on 28 February 1628.[7] Sir Richard Newdigate's diary for 1683 notes his reading with his children and time spent with them in his garden at Arbury in Warwickshire. On 2 May, he watched Amphilis, his fourteen-year old, 'dance and play' and fenced with his boy Stephen. Other days that summer he ate 'too much fruit' in the garden with his boy Dick and walked there with his girls.[8]

'You cannot imagine how pleased I am with the children', John Churchill told his wife Sarah around 1687, while his little girl pulled him by the arm. 'They are so fond of me', he went on, 'that when I am at home they will always be with me, kissing and hugging me'.[9] 'I feel the same love to thee', a Quaker woman wrote to her child, 'as I did when I dangled thee upon my knees and sweetly hugged thee in my bosom'.[10] Lady Elizabeth Smyth, writing to her sister-in-law in 1711, compared her boisterous nursery with her studious boy Jack away at school. His master said he would be 'an extraordinary scholar and I hope will make a very good man but I believe will never be so merry as his brothers, which are the maddest brisk boys that can be, they do sing and holler about the house like little wild things'.[11]

There is no reason to think that fathers were less fond of their children than mothers, although they had less day-to-day responsibility for childcare. Endymion Porter sent home 'little glass bottles with silver chains', expecting his boy George to 'keep a terrible stir with them'.[12] Sir Thomas Pelham bought presents in London in the 1630s and 1640s to take down to his children in Sussex, including a bonnet and drum for Henry, a muff for Ben and a 'looking glass' for Nan.[13] Nicknames and shortenings were normal. In early Stuart Warwickshire, Anne Newdigate's letters to her husband, making constant reference to her large brood, normally used their pet names of Mal, Jack, Dick, Letti and Nan.[14]

Their knowledge of the enormous range of dangers that threatened children's lives in pre-industrial society prompted parents' protectiveness. Correspondence and diaries are packed with references to children's illnesses, to the dangers that they faced and to the accidents they sustained. Even coughs and colds, and certainly agues, were not taken lightly. Lady Anne Clifford recorded in her diary in 1617 that, 'in so much I was fearful of her, I could hardly sleep all night', when her daughter Margaret had 'a bitter fit of her ague'.[15] When Mary Josselin suffered a 'great cold' at three years old, her parents sought help from the Earls Colne lady of the manor, Lady Honeywood, 'who gave us divers things for her'. Jane Josselin was frightened that her baby Thomas was 'even at death's door' with a cold in 1644.[16]

There was never any hesitation in rushing to doctors and apothecaries where they were available, but the worst scourges of children's health were not at this time susceptible to cure.[17] It was a matter of watching, retaining faith and acknowledging deliverance if this came. Parents lived through their children's illnesses together, largely without outside support. Henry Newcome sent his daughter into the country, attempting to cure her of rickets and later visited her: 'she met us on her feet which was a great rejoicing to us'.[18] Thomas Josselin contracted smallpox, two weeks after being sent to London as an apprentice in 1659. He returned home to be nursed: it 'came out after a treacle posset' and within a few days, he was able first to sit up, then to come down into the hall.[19] Katherine Thornton's smallpox in 1666 began after three days of shrill crying, sleeplessness and no food. Her mother, having 'used many cordials to save her life', had to hand over her care to two maids and retreat 'into the scarlet chamber for want of rest'. 'The Lord give me a thankful heart and that she may live to his glory', Alice Thornton concluded as the girl passed the danger of death.[20]

Parents recorded their gratitude for numerous deliverances. The strength of the Protestant doctrine of God's providence during the seventeenth century made the interpretation of such day-to-day incidents a principal feature of diary and journal accounts of family life.[21] Yet, as late as 1843, we find a mother listing 'mercies received' at the end of her diary, in a manner that echoed an earlier age that had been obsessed with God's providence. Ann Bramfill recorded the survival that year of her boy Bridges, shot by an air gun, of her girl Leila, who was thrown by a horse and of her boy John, who had his head pierced by a heavy rake which fell from a tree.[22] Fire was a particular danger. In the Josselin household, Jane fell into the fire twice and both Mary and Anne once.[23] William Coe's daughter Judith, at five, had a spit narrowly miss her head; on another occasion, his wife caught a boiler of fat hanging over the fire where little Henry was sitting just in time, so there was minimal damage to his frock; a candle caught young William's cap alight but he escaped burning.[24]

Children were always falling dangerously but often survived largely unscathed. Documented falls obviously represent the tip of an iceberg, and there were many of them. Tom Josselin fell from a chair, narrowly escaping scalding in 1646 and fell into the pond the same year; Jane Josselin fell down the stairs in 1647, when her father was going up and was able to catch her; Daniel Newcome had a narrow escape from drowning while fishing at a weir in 1657; Robin Thornton just missed a boulder when, at play with a sister and cousin, he fell from a hay barn in 1668; William Coe fell into a creek at six years' old in 1700 and then from a mare the following year; and James Coe fell down the kitchen stairs in 1714.[25]

There were also mishaps with animals. The wording of diary accounts of such incidents indicates the fears that parents had undergone. In 1650, Tom Josselin 'escaped a great danger from a great mastiff bitch who run mad and snapped at him'; in 1658, Daniel Newcome was pulled down by a dog while out snowballing which 'frighted the child sadly'; in 1705, William Coe's great bitch Surly 'flew upon my daughter Sarah and bit a hole under her right eye', but 'I thank God', he noted, 'she had no further mischief'; six years later his little Thomas, playing in the courtyard, had a cow run its horn into his mouth and hurt the inside of his cheek.[26]

Adventurous play often ran children into danger. Arthur Dee's nose was hurt by a friend playing with a razor, 'not in anger, but by chance wantonly'; Jane Josselin ran a pair of scissors into her brother Tom's eyebrow.[27] Alice Thornton was fearful that when Kate, 'being very full of spirit and play', leapt upon her sister Alice from a window seat, thrusting her against a wall, she had hurt 'the inner rind of her belly' so badly 'she had broken it'. Choking fits were also often recorded. John Evelyn wrote a long account of how his son Richard got a mutton bone stuck in his windpipe and nearly expired before he removed it and treated his throat with balsam.[28]

At a time when health care regimes were primitive, such accidents posed immediate and heavy parental responsibilities. Gentlewomen, like Lady Honeywood at Earls Colne, exchanged advice, kept recipe books of remedies and preventatives and in many cases ministered to the neighbourhood besides their families.[29] There was much traditional medical lore, which parents absorbed, digested and practised. The determination with which they did this shows their dedication to their children. 'I hope you will let him go bare-headed', wrote Endymion Porter, fussing about his two-year old to his wife while away from home in 1623, 'otherwise he will be so tender that upon every occasion you will have him sick'.[30]

Of all these trials, of course, life-threatening illness was the most dangerous and the most heart rending. Defences against the epidemics that scourged eighteenth-century towns and the countryside remained weak. 'Witnessing the acute suffering of one's children', Amanda Vickery has noted, writing about the Georgian period, 'was a virtually universal ordeal'. Illness in the family was 'one of the monumental concerns of adult life'.[31] James Boswell was 'tortured with apprehension' when he thought his two-and-a-half-year-old daughter had measles. Mary Fletcher wrote, 'I felt it as a knife in my heart, she is my earthly all' when her adult daughter was seriously ill.[32]

These attitudes reflect a mental world in which sickness and health were seen in entirely different terms from today. With the finger of providence dominating the minds of parents, 'sickness', Roy Porter wrote, 'became one of many ways God revealed His will to man ... the medical culture of pre-industrial England was thus centred upon the individual and God's purposes for him, more than upon disease or the might of medicine'. This meant, Porter stressed, that people pondered their children's symptoms and attempted diagnosis within the home. There was no notion that children might be treated any differently from the adults of this time when they were unwell.[33]

There was a tendency to try anything, faced with a suffering child. Nicholas Blundell began with sea bathing, when his daughter Mally had a skin eruption in 1707 and, only when that failed, agreed to the doctor making an incision in her arm.[34] Mary Lovett, watching her failing boy Verney in desperation in 1723, accepted his being put on asses' milk and being bled every month for six months. Charlotte Papendiek was sent by her father back and forth to 'take sea water' at nine, when he was at a loss to cure an inflammation in her eyes. Charlotte Oakes, with tuberculosis, was rushed from Suffolk to Bristol for treatment as a last desperate measure, after doctors in Bury, Norwich and Yarmouth had failed to cure her.[35]

Many clung to home remedies. Claver Morris, himself a doctor, gave his ten-year-old son purges, believing, since they made him sick, that they 'worked with him'; he followed them up with spoonfuls of cordial mixture. Fanny Boscawen, with three children ill at once in 1748, tried customary family remedies like water with a roast apple and jelly. Some were simply sceptical about the doctor's wares. John Byron's letters provide much insight into the attitudes of a fussy but attentive father in the 1720s. 'The diet of children', he kept insisting, 'is the only thing to look for.' He told his wife he favoured bleeding his little girl, who was much subject to a cough, on 7 December 1729, adding that 'when the children have tea they had better drink it while it is good and not the last dregs of it only'. They should be kept out of the sun, he had advised earlier that year, and have their ears washed often. On no account should vomits or blisters be used: 'I should think all sorts of herbage and grass were good for children as well as grass for young animals'.[36] Occasionally we find parents falling out about a child's illness. Johnny Stedman's wife, for example, blaming the boy himself for his measles in 1787, was for putting him in 'the cold garret' as a cure.[37]

The stirrings of infection were never far away. Smallpox, in particular, was cataclysmic and incomprehensible. Low down the social scale, it was seen in entirely superstitious terms. 'The boggard has touched me', cried out John Armstrong's child at Chapel-en-le-Frith in 1730, when the disease was taking hold as he lay at night in his parents' bed.[38] The large number of fond epitaphs to children who died of smallpox found in parish churches from the late seventeenth and eighteenth centuries is instructive.[39] No wonder that, when inoculation against the disease was introduced into England in 1718, it was much discussed and a good many gentry families took it up. 'I think the smallpox can never come at a better age than theirs', wrote Lady Cave, recommending to her brother Ralph Verney, Viscount Fermanagh, inoculation of his healthy brood in 1721.[40]

Inoculation, though, was seen as an uncertain business. Margaret Woods noted in 1782 that, though she was quite clear about the propriety of doing it, she felt 'deeply anxious for the event'. She went ahead with it 'in the fear of the Lord', having all her four children inoculated on the same day. After Fanny Burney had her son Alexander inoculated in 1797, she wrote about the relief she felt 'at length from a terror that almost from the birth of my darling has hung upon my mind'. Elizabeth Fry was concerned at the principle of giving a child one disease to avoid another, but decided, after taking the doctor's advice in 1801, that 'so trifling a complaint as the cow-pox, being likely to prevent so dreadful a disease as the smallpox, at least it appears justifiable to try it'.[41]

Mothers wrote emotional accounts of the actual event. Fanny Boscawen sought to reassure her husband, at sea in 1755, that their trusted doctor had convinced her that their boy Billy, at three years' old, was 'in the most desirable state for inoculation that can be'. She had been instructed to give him no bleeding or purging in advance but just a little rhubarb. But Billy retched and this caught at her heart, 'the little stomach heaving all the while'. 'I must have had a heart of flint to torment him any more', she declared to her husband.[42] This was one of the severe trials of motherhood. However, Fanny Boscawen exulted, three days after the rhubarb incident, that it was over with 'no fuss, no rout, no assistance': 'I held the child myself and so effectually employed his eyes and attentions that he never was sensible of the first arm. For the second, he pretended to wince a little, but I had a sugar plum ready which stopped the whimper before it was well formed.'

Fanny Burney used a barley sugar with her boy Alexander in 1797, who was just over three when he had his inoculation. While the maid attracted his attention with a toy, she 'began a little history of the misfortunes of the toy we chose which was a drummer'. Alexander screamed at the incision, then gave his mother a look of astonishment, turning an appealing eye to her, 'as if demanding at once explanation and protection'.[43] Burney's account here unselfconsciously uses a language of sentiment which had only recently become familiar in describing family relationships.[44]

There are numerous accounts by parents of their emotions, and often of their sense of helplessness, in caring for suffering children. Sydney Smith and his wife were alarmed when their three-year old, Noel, coughed up blood and developed fits in 1802, explaining in a letter, when he thought the boy had recovered, how he had 'sat up with him for two nights, expecting every moment to be his last'. When Noel died six weeks later, Sydney reflected sadly to his correspondent that 'children are horribly insecure'. He had found the life of a parent to be 'the life of a gambler'. The actor William Macready felt 'struck down' when his two-year-old son William was taken ill in 1833. 'If it be the will of God to try my spirits by the illness of these dear babes, may he give me power of mind and body to support it', he wrote in his diary. In 1840, after caring for his ill toddler Henry for several months, he set down his feelings when he seemed to have turned a corner: 'whilst trying to divert the dear boy he smiled twice. No sunshine was ever brighter or more cheering to the earth than those dear smiles to my heart.'[45]

Fearing their children might be taken ill or even die, parents put tremendous emphasis on the development of the physical strength which acted as reassurance that disaster would not befall them. Moreover, looks, health and strength held the promise of effective manhood in boys and an appealing beauty was likely to bring about favourable marriages for girls. 'My brother Hatton will tell you what a fine girl Susanna is', Frances Hatton assured her husband, away from home in 1677. But her report the next year compared her less favourably with the new-born Betty, who 'grows a very fine child': 'she is most likely to make a handsomer woman than Susanna; she has the finest eyes'. Admiral Thomas Freemantle warned his wife in 1803 against too much care of their three boys when they were three, four and five:

> Believe me nothing tends more to health than exercise and air, and that the more they are out of the house the better . . . consider what your boys must undergo before they arrive even at manhood, and I am sure you will agree with me that it is not wise to bring them up too tenderly.[46]

The love and affection revealed in seventeenth-century sources is even more bountifully evident in the two centuries that followed. The impact of Locke's hugely important and influential tract, *Some Thoughts Concerning Education*, the principal formative work, as we have seen, on the practice of eighteenth-century upbringing, was, in this sense, entirely predictable. The stage was set for the construction of an ideology of motherhood. It became a matter of principle quite early in the eighteenth century that, in the well-established upper- and middle-class pattern of privatised marriage, wives did not work. Motherhood, Ruth Perry has argued, was 'increasingly desexualised as it was sentimentalised: evolving expectations suffused the roles of wife and mother with new meaning'.[47] John Locke's creation of the notion of the child as blank paper released parents from their bondage to fierce puritan teaching about discipline. Purging children of original sin, it gave them a positive role in child-rearing, which they readily embraced.[48]

But the visual representation of English family life was slow to catch up with the realities, from 1600 and earlier, of children's experience of growing up in loving and caring homes. Domestic affection was celebrated in Italian art two hundred years before it became apparent in English portraits. Paolo Veronese painted portraits of Paolo and Iseppo da Porto clasping their little boy and girl in warm embraces in 1551.[49] It was not simply that the dire negative effects of puritan ideology were prolonged in England, inhibiting celebration of affection and caring. Art was relatively undeveloped; sixteenth- and seventeenth-century England was dependent on visiting foreigners like Holbein and Van Dyke for artistic innovation. Easel painting hardly entered into the gentry's aesthetic values when our period begins: 'the well-to-do lived surrounded by carved panelling, tapestry and elaborately decorated plasterwork in rooms that were essentially total works of art', Keith Thomas has noted.[50] Further ornamentation through the display of family portraiture had hardly begun. It was the rise of consumption, already fuelling Italian Renaissance art two centuries before this, which created the demand for luxury furnishing and decoration in England after 1700. This paved the way for the art of domestic life.

The 'striking shift' in family portraiture which did finally occur in England in the middle decades of the eighteenth century, and which has been documented by Kate Retford, has seriously misled social and literary historians into supposing something new was happening in family life.[51] A group portrait, like Gawen Hamilton's *Harley Family* in 1736, still 'presented diminutive, stiffly posed figures ranged against backdrops that evidenced the family's status, wealth and their tasteful dissemination of that wealth'. Relationships were still being indicated by token hand gestures. Children were demarcated by their smaller scale and their toys and pets, in miniaturised versions of adult dress.

Marital Partnership

Marital partnership meant shared attitudes and mutual commitment. It never occurred to most parents, during the period considered in this book, that fathers and mothers should relate to, show affection for, or discipline their children, in exactly the same way as one another. But they did believe that their roles were complementary. In this sense, partnership was the keynote of children's upbringing, as of marriage more generally, throughout these centuries.[1] Parents did not have to be together all the time to approach parenting as a shared endeavour. So letters between them often exemplify parenting in action very sharply indeed. The case studies of marital partnership in rearing children presented here, from across the puritan to royalist spectrum, illustrate a Stuart familial world. Further case studies, it is argued, indicate continuity in the fundamental aspects of marital partnership, as notions of domesticity were elaborated in the Georgian and Victorian periods.

The affectionate letters of Nathaniel Bacon, from Redgrave in Suffolk, to his wife Jane, who was detained for some weeks in London on occasions from 1623 to 1624, show how much they were enjoying their two children, Nick and Jane, who he sometimes called Nan. 'Our children are well', he assured his wife in 1623. Nick, at four, had 'cast his coat and seemeth metamorphosed into a grasshopper'. Jane was 'a very modest maiden', at eighteen months, 'wholly taken up with travelling by herself, which she performeth very handsomely and will be ready to run at your command when you return'. He wrote several times in 1624: the children, he declared on 15 May, 'have since your departure (thanks be to God) suffered little in my breast'. 'Nick sends you word of a brood of young chickens', he wrote a few weeks later, retailing an incident at table as, 'a disaster he escaped at my being with him; for he ate so much milk porridge at supper that he cried out "Oh Lord I think I have almost broke my gut"; and I was fain to walk him a turn or two about the chamber to digest it.' On 13 June 1624, Nathaniel gave his wife another account of his childminding at Redgrave. Nick had 'well recovered his ague'. 'Miss Mop', he continued, 'is a much finer girl than ever and more familiar with me and I hope before strawberries go out I shall win her heart for ever.' That summer, the Bacons started Jane on reading at three. In October, Nathaniel, himself in London this time, sent word he had bought her a new gown, adding 'I shall expect a great forwardness in her book at my return.' Pressing for news of his daughter, on another trip from home in 1626, Nathaniel wrote, 'I should have been glad to have understood some of her new language.' Delayed by illness on his way home in June that year, he requested that the coach be sent for him, ending 'bless ours and kiss little Jane from me and so I rest in all true affection only yours'.[2]

The Puritan zealot Sir Robert Harley was a friend of William Gouge, author of the most famous tract on patriarchal marriage in the early seventeenth century, yet he himself fell into a love match, after twice becoming a widower, in 1623. A relative teased him with the quip that he wanted to know his new spouse, the 23-year-old Brilliana Conway, better 'for men in love are always held to be not their own men'. The Harleys lived in an old-fashioned castle at Brampton Bryan in Herefordshire. Passionate in her love for him, Brilliana had difficulty early on in drawing him out of his conventional male reserve, but their marriage was blessed with seven children. Their mutual puritan faith was a durable bond.

Lady Brilliana's letters provide intimate detail about the growth of their young family under a halo of close and affectionate care. She sought to create partnership by showering her husband with information. They named their first-born Edward, after Brilliana's father, Sir Edward Conway, then, in 1624, Secretary of State. When a second son came along in 1626, Sir Robert, busy in parliament, urged her to have him christened rather than await his return. 'Because you said nothing of the name', Brilliana wrote on 21 April, 'I chose the name I love the best it being yours.' She longed to have him home and sent news of their toddler. 'For Ned and Robin I beg your blessing', declared Brilliana, making reference to traditional patriarchal lore, 'and let me have your prayers and love.'

Brilliana, following gentry custom at this time, did not breastfeed her boys, but the historian Jacqueline Eales notes the deep concern for the development and welfare of her children evident in her correspondence. Her delight in their doings showed constantly in the bulletins she sent Sir Robert in London. Thomas, Brill, Dorothy, Margaret and Elizabeth followed Robin between 1628 and 1634. Ned took his first steps and went through teething, Robin grew 'fat and big', Brill's first two teeth arrived. Brilliana made touching references to the joy that the children brought to an ageing grandfather, at home in Herefordshire, who was especially besotted with their first-born, Ned. Lady Brilliana had an excellent relationship with her father-in-law, telling her husband that, when it came to young Ned, he 'will not yield that any should be loved like him, he must be the finest boy in his eyes'.

Brilliana took the initial education of her boys in hand. 'He begins now to delight in reading', she wrote of Ned, just turned five, requesting Sir Robert to send down a Bible for him: 'that is the book I would have him place his delight in'. Finding good tutors for her growing brood in the 1630s turned out to be problematic, since the Harleys were determined that their boys should be brought up by ministers of approved godliness, acting as household tutors, who they expected to pay well. Thomas Pierson and Richard Symonds were two of the men who worked for them. Brilliana sometimes stood in, supervising study herself. The local grammar schools in the Welsh marches were poor and the Harleys were far too dedicated parents to opt systematically for one of the nation's brutish great schools, though Ned did put in time at Shrewsbury in preparation for Oxford, where he went to study in 1638 just before he was fourteen.[3]

Thomas Froysell, preaching Sir Robert's funeral sermon in 1656, emphasised that he was both a strict and a kind father who 'loved his children most tenderly'. 'I think no man in the world', he declared, 'carried more of a father's dearness in him than he did; yet he would never bear with any evil in any of his children: he would often say to them, I desire nothing of you but your love and that you keep from sin.' Ned had testified six years before this, as an adult looking back on his upbringing, to what his parents, 'noble wise and above all godly', meant to him. He was thankful 'that they instructed me in the fear of God and never cockered me in any evil but always corrected it'; that God had given his parents 'hearts to give me liberal education and inclined their affection to be very tender to me'; that his was a family in which his 'brethren and sisters and I love one another . . . as becomes Christians'.[4]

Sir Ralph Verney's behaviour towards his child bride Mary Blackhall exhibited the fussy direction of a crusty patriarch, Yet, over 21 years, from 1629 to 1650, she grew in maturity, replacing meek subservience with an insistence upon spirited partnership. He was inconsolable about her early death at age 34, and remained a widower for more than 40 years thereafter. Their correspondence, while he was a royalist exile in France between 1646 and 1648, illuminates the heartaches of their parenting. Only two of their six children survived to adulthood, the infant Ralph and the much favoured Peg dying within a week of one another in 1647.

Little Mun and Peg travelled with their parents to France in early 1644, both suffering from smallpox at the time. Mary returned pregnant to England to seek to recover their sequestrated estates in early 1647. Ralph, born there, died at a few weeks old from convulsion fits. Sir Ralph's friend Dr Denton retailed this news, finding Mary 'in bed lamenting and as my wife told very inquisitive also how her children did, expressing that you had sent her no word of them for a month or longer'.

Sir Ralph had been caring for his eight-year-old Peg through what proved her last illness and was distraught, writing to Denton about how the news of the girl's death could be broken to his wife. He should try to 'break it to her by degrees, finding 'the best way you can devise'. If she was not 'too virtuous' for heaven, he believed, she was 'too good for me'. He knew his wife 'loved her tenderly and the child deserved it, for there was never a better natured, more obedient, nor more patient creature born'.

The Verneys had left their first-born, Jack, in the care of the servants at Claydon when they went into exile. So coming home to handle the sequestration business also brought Mary a reunion with her boy after three years. Jack was now nearly seven. Mary told her husband at once that, 'as far as I can tell by candlelight', he was a 'brave lucky boy'. A few days later, she made the best of what she had discovered by daylight, describing Jack now as 'a very fine child all but his legs'. These, she confessed, were 'crooked as ever I saw any child's'. It was not much consolation that he was 'a very ready witted child'. Yet, finding Sir Ralph devastated at this news of Jack's physical imperfection, she piled on the reassurance. Jack was a 'very gallant boy' and 'extreme witty'.[5] There was further bad news for Sir Ralph in August, when Mary announced 'an imperfection' in Jack's speech. Their good friend Dr Denton consoled the boy's parents with his view that what Jack 'will want in rhetoric I dare say he will have in craft'.[6]

Despite their straitened financial circumstances as royalists in exile, the Verneys were discussing an ambitious programme of accomplishments for their children at this time. Mary responded positively to her husband's musings, in March 1647, about their son Mun, who was, at eleven, learning 'to sing and play on the guitar': 'now for Mun he hath a good voice which will do well upon the guitar . . . therefore I prithee let him begin it and to sing'. Peg could well start on the lute at eight, 'but it may be she is of the youngest to do that'. Sir Ralph, in a rapid reply to his wife's opinions, said that Mun's dancing lessons were going well and that he favoured the guitar, which he could manage without neglecting his Latin. He was emphatic that, at eight, Peg should be starting on some needlework. He worried that 'she grows a great girl and will be spoiled for want of breeding'. Until his wife came back to France, there was no one 'to look to her', as her parents launched her into society. In fact, her early death intervened.[7]

Ralph Josselin, Vicar of Earls Colne in Essex from 1641 to 1683, kept a diary which provides the best account we have of the upbringing of the

children of a puritan clergyman in the seventeenth century. Entries indicate
his tender and loving relationship with his wife Jane, in a marriage that developed deep emotional bonds but that was also marked by periods of discord.
They loved their ten children deeply. There were sleepless nights, his little
ones 'a great grief', he wrote one October, by their 'sudden cryings out in the
forepart of the night'. As the village schoolmaster, Josselin supervised his own
children's first steps in reading. Anne started just before she was four years old
and Mary at just over four, quickly showing 'an aptness to her book'. At
almost six, Josselin described Thomas as 'of a good memory, a good speller,
apt to learn and attain the hardest words in his bible or accidence in which he
reads.'

Josselin took the education of his girls very seriously. Jane was sent off to
Mrs Piggott's school in Colchester at ten in 1656, residing with a cousin in
the town. 'The Lord bestow his blessing in mercy on her there, his prudence
was very visible in her going', he wrote in his diary. Mary went to school at
White Colne aged ten in 1668 and Elizabeth at Bury St Edmunds in 1674,
when she was thirteen.[8] When Anne, at fourteen, went to London to be
bound as a servant, her parents kept in close touch with her. Alan Macfarlane
described relationships 'of great warmth and intimacy' between both parents
and their daughters.

Josselin's eldest son Thomas died at 29, after some years in which his father
had been highly supportive, setting him up in business. His younger son John
caused him much anxiety, through a wayward and spendthrift course of life
that brought Ralph close to disowning him. 'My soul yearned over John' was
how he put it.[9] Despite admonitions and prayer sessions, John remained
undutiful for many years. Yet in his old age, when John finally left home,
Ralph wrote 'John went to his house, God bless him.'[10]

The letters received by Thomas Brockbank, while he was studying at
Queen's College, Oxford between 1687 and 1692, reveal the strains his
absence caused his parents far away in Westmoreland. These were heightened
by his brother's death from smallpox, soon after Thomas had left home. This
family of four was evidently very close. Thomas had shone at Kendal
grammar school: there were 'none of your age that did excel you in learning'
his father reminded him, clutching at himself at the sacrifice he, a scholar and
schoolmaster himself, and his wife had made in sending the boy to Oxford.
The evidence of their devotion lies in their persistent fussing and badgering
about Thomas's health. They heaped presents on him, sent via the Kendal
carrier. The gifts were multifarious: cash, books, shirts, stockings, linen sheets,
towels, gloves, 'a good suit of clothes', a map of the world, a bundle of quills
contributed by old schoolfellows, and, feelingly, 'your dear brother's buckskin
breeches which will last very long'.

Eat and drink enough, urged his father the first winter; avoid too much study which 'cannot be serviceable'; 'put on two pairs of stockings to keep you from cold for fuel with you is dear'; 'take recreation . . . that your body may be better able to endure study'. Was his cough better? his father enquired later in the winter. 'Make yourself a vest, get shoes', he urged. His father was proud to have heard from a friend visiting Oxford 'that you are a noted student all the college over', but he was dismayed at the story that he was studying much by candlelight. 'Be moderate in study', he implored, 'lest you do yourself harm.'

With no other children to replace his lost brother, Thomas's parents missed him more and more. By August 1688, they were pressing him to return home: the tension in the relationship reflected the wish to be unselfish on both sides. If he was 'fully resolved to continue', his father wrote that month, they would still maintain him. Thomas, desperate to cling to his newly found academic world, declared in reply his reluctance to leave, yet 'with all submission and willingness' he was 'to be commanded'. His mother, he soon heard, had a troubled heart at the loss of his grandmother, besides a son; his father mean-while declared his sorrow, 'having but one child in the world and being so far from him'. News of the landing of William of Orange and of political uncer-tainty in the south of England increased their concern. The correspondence shows how Thomas's ageing parents went downhill, yet continued their unstinting support, before he, after more persuasions, finally bought a mare for six pounds and rode home in the summer of 1692. The parental joy, unrecorded, was evidently profound.[11]

Sir John Mordaunt and his wife Penelope, who lived at Walton in Warwickshire, both had to spend time away from home between 1698 and 1704. They indicate, by their affectionate dialogue in letters, their mutual involvement in bringing up their children. They delegated a good deal of day-to-day care to nursemaids and a governess, yet remained fully in charge them-selves. In October 1698, Sir John, away on business, fretted about colds clinging to the children at home. Assured that his eldest, Charles, who he was told was 'brisk', blew his nose stoutly, he suspected 'Miss can do it better'. He was pleased to know that the toddler Pen had cut two large teeth. Details of physical progress like this were a staple of such correspondence, when the susceptibility of children to disease and fear of losing them was a constant preoccupation.

The following summer it was Sir John who was sending his wife news, keeping closely in touch at home with the nursemaid. Pen was recovering from a bout of illness, which had kept her upstairs: 'I think her stomach doth mend for she eats more this day at dinner than I have seen her since she came down and they tell me she sleeps very well, which she may likely do for she is running about all day long.' 'I find her cold is wearing off', he noted. Returning from a night away, he found both his babes very well and 'very diverting'. This domestic bliss was only incomplete since, he wrote to Penelope, 'all the pleasure I have here I enjoy but by halves for want of your company'.

Later in 1699, Penelope related the story of a disastrous dinner party, when she had sought to show off her children in adult company. Little Pen, encouraged to role play, was given a swaddled wax doll to amuse her: 'there was to have been a great christening of it and Pen was to have been the godmother, but the life was short'. Pen dropped the doll; it broke in pieces; she cried. 'Your daughter did fall a stowing and squealing that then baby was broke; that you would have laughed to have seen her, but her uncle asking her who she was angry at she was quiet, but would not endure to see the baby.' Charles, she feared, was beginning to get above himself. He 'would call for a glass of claret as Papa did and did not drink water'. Sir John saw the need to take him in hand. His wife's accounts portrayed Pen as 'the most orderly'. 'I hope that you will bring Charles to be so and make him learn his book or else I shall not be pleased with him', he told her.

Tensions began to show as Charles demandingly asked for a periwig around his sixth birthday. His mother flapped about the price of them locally. He 'desires his duty', Penelope informed Sir John, 'and says he wants to see you and to talk with you about breeches and his periwig'. He was soon off to boarding school. But Sir John's daughter was at home for her father to bask in. 'I look to see my pretty girl', Sir John wrote, which brought the immediate response, via her mother, 'Pen bids me tell you she thinks the house very melancholy without you.' [12]

The contrast between the Mordaunts' rural Warwickshire world at the very start of the eighteenth century and the domesticity of Holland House in the 1740s and 1750s is immediate. Henry Fox's London home was on the political stage. He and Caroline Lennox, married in 1744, quickly produced a son, Stephen, always known as Ste. 'They fell in love all over again, with their child and with one another', Stella Tillyard has written, noting that they thought Ste 'the most beautiful, most intelligent, most charming child ever born and they never tired of telling one another so'.[13] Henry Fox was an exceptional father on two counts, for his indulgence to his children and for his insistence, living round the corner from his political stamping ground, on spending so much time with them.

Caroline Fox became obsessive about Ste's health and well being. She took him to Bath at eighteen months, leaving Henry immersed in London political business. Henry found plenty of time for his boy Charles James Fox in the early 1750s, as his duties as Secretary of War declined. Beginning as a weakling, by the time he was a year old, his father found him handsome. 'Charles is playing by me and surprises me with the eclat of his beauty every time he looks me in the face', he told Hanbury Williams, the friend who had provided the setting in Conduit Street for his secret love match with Caroline Lennox in May 1744.[14]

The Foxes had lost their second son as an infant in 1746, replacing him in 1755. Henry revelled in them all as little ones. 'Charles is very pert and very argumentative', Henry wrote to his wife in 1756. 'I rode to Holland House this morning and found Harry . . . in the park, looking cold but very well. I called him Squeaker and he looked at me and laughed, but upon the whole seemed to like my horse better than me.'[15] There was nothing surprising about visitors to great houses noticing children everywhere in the 1750s. The Victorian seclusion of them in the nursery and schoolroom, under the eye of the governess, was in the future. At Holland House, though, visitors encountered a father's sentimentality over his boys and an obsessive concern for them that could thrust politics aside altogether. 'I drank claret at Holland House into the morning with Henry', noted Richard Rigby, but he could not 'wash away the sorrow he is in' at Ste's shocking condition with St Vitus dance, convulsions it was then expected would kill him.

The lenience of Henry and Caroline Fox with their boys Ste, Charles and Harry was legendary. It scandalised London. Pitt derided Fox as a disastrous example to the nation, educating his children 'without the least regard to morality and with such extravagant vulgar indulgence'. But they were thoughtful and entirely sincere parents, well aware of what they were doing and constantly discussing their children with each other. When Caroline reminded her sister Emily that Holland House was 'reckoned such a house of liberty for children', she did it nonchalantly, knowing her own mind. This, we should note, was formed by Locke, not by Rousseau, whose *Emile* was published in 1762, when her elder boys were already teenagers.

Caroline encouraged her boys to read widely and to go to the theatre at an early age. Charles was reading plays at five, graduating to novels and poetry at six, when Caroline started teaching him Roman history. Indulgence ruled: when Charles wanted to take apart a fob watch, his father stood by, murmuring, 'well, if you must, you must'. The most famous and notorious incident had occurred while he was still in petticoats. Brought in for dessert, as children often were then, he wanted to bathe in the huge bowl of cream on the table, so Henry had it put on the floor for him to slop about in, to his heart's content. 'Let nothing be done to break his spirit', said Henry Fox of Charles; 'the world will do that business fast enough'. [16]

Caroline would not have it that Ste was spoilt. Unless boys were ill and needed medical attention, she declared, they must be given the opportunity to show high spirits, and be 'lively and merry'. Ste had 'grown what people call very naughty and unlucky', she confessed, when he was with her at five years' old in Bath in 1750, 'but it's such a sort of naughtiness I should be very sorry if he had not . . . as to his being most exceedingly rude, unlucky and full of mischief . . . I own I like it in a child.' Her method, when her three became boisterous, Caroline explained to her sister Emily, was to ask them 'to go into the garden or hall or some proper place to riot in'.

Rousseau's anti-intellectualism was not for her. She took the education of her boys in hand in the nursery, teaching them the alphabet before they were two. By five, all of them could read fluently and had learnt to write. The library at Holland House afforded abundance of teaching materials. There were Hogarth prints, which Harry took to as young as three, and there were maps for a start on geography. When Harry was seven, Caroline was using jigsaw puzzles, recently invented for the purpose, to teach him geographical knowledge. She did not neglect air and exercise. Her summary of Harry's regime at the family's seaside home in Kent in 1762, in a letter to her sister Emily, illustrates a mother picking and choosing shrewdly from the advice literature available to her:

> Dear little Harry is a pleasant child to have here; he really works very hard all day out of doors, which is very wholesome and quite according to Monsieur Rousseau's system. He eats quantities of fish and is so happy and pleased all day. At night we depart a little from Monsieur Rousseau's plan, for he reads fairy-tales and learns geography on the Beaumont wooden maps . . . he is vastly quick at learning that or anything else.[17]

Yet Caroline's overall judgement about Rousseau was scathing: 'there is certainly a small objection to putting his scheme of education into practice, viz, that it's impossible – there are also a number of contradictions in his book, but it is immensely pretty'.[18]

Fox permissiveness remained blatant when the boys were at Eton. 'I much wanted to see your hair cut', Henry wrote to Ste there, 'to a reasonable and gentlemanlike shortness. You and some Eton boys wear it as no other people in the world do. It is effeminate; it is ugly; and it must be inconvenient.' Ste had made some sort of gesture when his father had raised the matter previously. He would now be 'much obliged' if Ste did cut his hair.[19]

There is no question about how bountiful in affection Henry and Caroline Fox were to their boys. Charles, in adulthood, told his mother just how much the deep emotional attachment of his parents meant to him: 'to be loved by you and him has always been the first desire of my life . . . no son ever felt more duty, respect, gratitude or love than I do for both of you'. Yet, sadly, in the 1770s Ste and Charles, notorious at Newmarket and in St James's as insouciant losers, gambled away much of the Fox fortune. 'Never let Charles know how excessively he afflicts me', wrote Henry Holland to Ste in 1772. Caroline was less detached, regarding, Stella Tillyard has suggested, 'her sons' indulgence as an unfavourable verdict on her motherhood'.[20]

Emotional, evangelical and dependent, William Jones, an impecunious rector and schoolmaster at Broxbourne in Hertfordshire, kept a deeply revealing diary of his family life. He married Theodosia Jessup in 1781, when he was 26 years old. He was a man who felt constantly wracked and almost defeated by life. His wife's pain in childbirth sent him into agonies.[21] He lived on a switchback with her, one moment exulting in her, the next reflecting 'with respect to the training up of children and the management of other parts of our family how distinctly opposite must our sentiments be'. Early in the marriage, he was upset when he and his wife seemed 'to be disputing about the mastery'. This was a rollercoaster partnership with an undercurrent of tension which marred cooperative endeavour.

In due course William accepted that he was the weaker partner, arranging that Theodosia should take on the managing of the income of his imprudent boy Augustus, 'my sage wife being well assured that she not only plays at cards and stirs a fire but does everything else better than her dear husband'. Earlier, when they quarrelled about household finances with a meagre income and nine children to feed, he acknowledged that she was extremely frugal, even if she lacked mildness and gentleness towards him.[22]

'I seem overpowered by the largeness of my family and am continually drained by my wife's complaints of the dearness of the times and the absolute impossibility of living on our present income', William wrote in 1797. Yet he clung to a vision of domestic bliss rooted in evangelical seriousness. A diary entry on 30 December 1798 reads as follows:

> I have never spent a more happy evening than the present! It has been with my dear, dear children! They read to me and I exhorted them to early seriousness and to devote themselves without delay to their God and saviour. We were so affected that we were at length all of us in tears.

William drove himself relentlessly to be a good father. His state of mind was summarised by what he wrote one day in 1794, when money problems oppressed him:

> My poor dear children little know what passes in my mind and I am truly glad of it. May they ever rejoice with me when I rejoice but never

weep when I weep! . . . May no impatience or fretfulness arising from my painful feelings ever check their sweet smiles or interfere with their innocent cheerfulness.[23]

Dire financial straits meant placing children as soon and as best William could. He sent his boy William to sea in 1799, following a failed apprentice-ship with a stationer in St Paul's churchyard: 'I spent almost every day of last week with him', he recorded, before seeing him aboard the *William and Mary*. The strain of their parting was considerable. 'His behaviour on this occasion was manly', William noted, 'I felt very severely (Heaven Knows) but I strug-gled with my feelings and resisted them: so did he evidently'. A few weeks later, he confided in his diary that he 'knew not the strength of my love and attachment to the dear fellow till I parted with him'.

On his son Henry's eleventh birthday, William declared 'he and I are very good friends . . . he is a very docile, even-tempered, good fellow'. Five years later, he launched him in a post in the Register Office of the Land Tax, congratulating himself on an outcome 'as favourable as I could wish for a lad not fifteen'. The next year, his son George was placed in the navy, with fatherly advice about the 'pliancy of temper' which would secure his good understanding with the ship's captain. George was, his father noted, a 'most active and undaunted fellow'.

Then there were the girls. Having lost two babes in infancy, William grew close to, and dependent upon, those remaining. In 1807, now in his mid-40s, William took stock of his needs and those of his family:

My sons, all those who show any attention and duty to me, I truly love and will do everything in my power to assist them . . . but my daughters seem more than ever endeared to me since the loss of my poor Caroline . . . for they cannot defend themselves and bustle through the wicked world as boys can. To leave them in something like independence will be to me an inexpressible comfort.[24]

Children's letters to their parents in the papers of the Fitzherbert family of Tissington in Derbyshire, over two generations between 1788 and 1824, convey the warmth and security of domestic happiness based on the mutual care demonstrated by parents. George related his aunt's treat, in July 1788, when his mother was away from home, staying with her brother in London. 'There was such a plumb pudding that I never saw before it was so full of plumbs', he wrote, describing an expedition in the chaise to Ashbourne. He hoped his mother would take him fishing when she came home. The artichokes in the garden meanwhile were being well cherished for his Papa's house guests.

Henry and Fanny, his younger siblings, 'join with me in duty', George Fitzherbert told his mother in 1791. 'I have rode out every day which I much enjoy', was his news; 'we have begun to make a garden and intend to get some peas and radish seed'. In the next letter on 25 March, George wrote reassuringly about having 'wrote out my old copy book and begun a new one', reported that his sister Fanny's 'stays came by the cart' and nurse thought them 'a very pretty pair' and announced that the peas and radishes had arrived and been sown 'before rain came'. Trees 'come out remarkable for the time of year' at their Derbyshire home, George noted on 8 April, regretting his having been kept from riding by poor weather. He was a little anxious about no letter having come from his mother, but he wrote again, knowing that she expected one each week. 'Our little cats are well and we are as fond of them as ever', scrawled George's baby brother Henry on the back of one of these bulletins. 'Papa thinks Fanny grown and is wilder than ever we think', George declared in a letter to his mother. The peas and radishes 'come up very well', he related on 29 April, saying a letter from her would 'add much to our happiness', though they were all well.[25]

Nearly 30 years later, Sir Henry, George's surviving little brother, had succeeded to the Tissington estate. His boys William and Richard, born in 1808 and 1809, now at Charterhouse, were writing to his wife Lady Agnes Fitzherbert. Richard's letter on 20 October 1819 was a typical schoolboy epistle. The apples sent from home were very good; the calendar showed seven weeks and five days until the Christmas holiday; they were rising at 8.15 but did at least have a fire in their room. William's cheerful letter in January 1820 explained that he had cured his sore throat 'by tying my stocking round it and next morning it was quite well'. 'We thank you and Papa very much', he wrote, 'for your trouble' in assisting them with their holiday tasks. When these were looked over, 'some were turned down but we managed well'.

In 1822 William wrote of victory in another playground battle and two years later sent his mother a letter in accomplished French. By then his brother Alleyn had joined the older two at Charterhouse. The boys used to return home from London using coaches like *The Defiance* and *The Regulation*, which served Ashbourne in Derbyshire. The cohesiveness and affection of this family is evident in the boys' fondness for their sister Selina, often mentioned in their letters, and for Judith, the baby of the family.[26]

Between 1800 and 1850, the context of marital partnership in children's upbringing was subtly transformed, at the gentry and professional level of society, by the elaboration of the cult of domesticity which has been discussed above. Exceptional documentation of the family life of the Lytteltons of Hagley in Worcestershire, in the 1850s, comes from the papers of Lucy, the eldest child but one in the household. 'My childhood was a bright, unruffled river, and I would not lose any of its memories', she wrote, in a memoir of the years before she entered her teens.[27] Mary Lyttelton bore her husband twelve children between 1839 and 1857. When Lucy, born in 1841, reflected on her family life about 1854, everything about it took its tone from living in a crowd. For this was a great house, teeming with servants both indoors and out. The Lytteltons were typical of those aristocratic and gentry families who ruled Victorian England from great parks and mansions. Like many of the wealthiest of them, they had a London house too and spent time there regularly. But, as her brother Nevy put it later, '"we dwelt among our own people", we entertained our neighbours in rather a formal fashion, we knew most of the villagers, played cricket with the boys, and all our interests were local'.[28]

George Fourth Lord Lyttelton was poor as noblemen went, only worth £7,000 per annum when he married in 1837. Yet, as he claimed on one occasion to his brother-in-law William Gladstone, his estate was 'of very great antiquity'. His great uncle, the first Lord Lyttelton, had built one of the great Palladian houses of England at Hagley between 1756 and 1760, an austere mansion with corner towers and rich interior Rococo decoration, in a fine and extensive park. An eager huntsman, Lyttelton was earnest and serious-minded, tackling his duties as Lord Lieutenant of Worcestershire assiduously. He worked to promote schooling locally for the children of the poor. His son Edward remembered him as 'a strong, righteous man, incessantly busied in work for others'. Besides his paternalism, high church piety was the centre of his life, leading him to improve the interior of the parish church on the estate, which the family attended twice each Sunday. Lucy was very devout but she also revelled in her father's uproarious sense of fun.[29]

There was a clear framework, in Lucy's account, to the lives of the four Lyttelton girls. The boys' holidays punctuated the pattern: 'seeing the dear boys' faces again', rejoicing over prizes won at prep school or Eton, a holiday from schoolroom work begged by them to celebrate their coming, 'the wild scampers over the place with them'. Travel to London or to visit relatives broke the schoolroom routine. Lucy caught her breath at thinking of 'the astonishing excitement of packing and journey days . . . when my imagination woke into song!'

This was a particular sort of domesticity, for Hagley's scale as a home required a full-time manager. This was the role that Mary Lyttelton fulfilled, besides her endless childbearing. George Lord Lyttelton lived a busy public life. Together, they stood over the children, somewhat remote but a powerful spiritual and moral presence. Lucy's resume put it neatly. 'Mama taught us our bible when we were little and Papa as we grew older and we had them always to help by their example as well as training.'

The Hagley schoolroom was brilliantly placed. Time there, 'where day after day we went through the well known routine', was enlivened by its being the passage between the rooms where their parents habitually worked. 'It was seldom', Lucy explained, 'that either took any notice of us, beyond a smile from Mama and "You little pigs" or "Absurd monkeys" from Papa.' But it gave her, she confessed, 'a happy feeling when I heard Mama's little cough outside the door, or saw her tall and graceful figure passing through the room and it was nice to feel that they were so close to us'. Lord and Lady Lyttelton had the added bonus of keeping their succession of governesses closely under their eye and well up to the mark.

Mary Lyttelton often took one or more of the girls with her when she took an afternoon drive in the pony carriage. Moreover, routinely, as in many Georgian and Victorian country houses, the children joined their parents for dessert before bedtime, in the grandeur of the Hagley dining room, festooned then, as now, with its carefree Rococo plasterwork. 'High and cool' was how Lucy thought of it. Sometimes, on fine summer evenings, the older children then accompanied their parents on the flight of steps to the garden, 'till the first stars came out, while everything slept in still beauty, and Malvern and Aberleigh rose deeply blue against the sky'.[30]

With the death of Mary Lyttelton in 1857, three daughters in turn took up her reins, as Mistress of Hagley, until each left to be married. Meriel, the eldest, took this role from 1857 to 1860, Lucy from 1860 to 1864 and Lavinia from 1864 to 1867. The younger Etonian Lyttelton boys thus experienced something of the same security at home as the older ones had done, while school hardened them to the realities of the male adult world. These girls were mothers before their time.[31]

Hagley was aristocratic and grand. Bark Hart at Orpington in Kent, on a long lease, from the 1870s to 1918, to Henry Howard, a London barrister, was impeccably bourgeois. The Howards' home and estate, with its lovely walled garden and farm, expressed the sentiments of Victorian domesticity exactly. The house had been named by Queen Elizabeth, when she visited the Hart family there in 1573, so legend went, and had been enlarged in the eighteenth century. Henry Howard, squire of a small Kentish village recently connected to London by the railway, improved it, adding a billiard room and a conservatory.[32] His wife Ellen, prematurely aged, as Mary Lyttelton was, by endless childbearing, bore him ten children.

The censuses of 1891 and 1901 provide snapshots of the Howard household. In 1891, there were seven indoor servants and a gardener and coachmen living in cottages on the estate, each with a family of their own. There were then four girls in the charge of Helen Tobin, the governess, in the schoolroom: they were Edith, Maud, Ida and Violet, aged from thirteen down to five. The two youngest children, Walter and Amy, were still in the nursery. Three boys, Hal, Stanley and Edgar, were at boarding schools. Henry Howard presided over his home while his wife managed it. Servants attended morning prayers, that epitome of respectable domesticity, led by Ellen if Henry had left for the train to his chambers in the Middle Temple.

Bark Hart was very well organised, running to a precise and invariable schedule. Ellen set the schoolroom lesson routine. She managed the work of the cook, parlour maid, housemaid and nurse. The kitchen maid, Sarah Reid, who in 1901 was aged nineteen, answered to the cook, Fanny Davidge, who was 24; the nursemaid answered to the family's nurse; the schoolroom maid, Jane Roberts, who was twenty, answered to the governess. Ellen had little day-to-day contact with the children, though the older girls sometimes accompanied her in the carriage, when she paid calls in the village and neighbourhood.

Nothing much had changed in 1911 except, predictably, for a complete turnover of the seven staff.[33] The nurse, nursemaid and schoolroom maid had been replaced by under-parlour maids and a sewing maid, to take account of the needs of three adult daughters living at home, besides the schoolroom children, who were now Violet, Amy and Clare. There was a new governess, Edith Wall. Maids who came to serve at Bark Hart and who were unfortunate enough to bear the name of a girl in the household, like Edith Edwards in 1911, were simply renamed for day-to-day purposes by Ellen when she hired them.[34] Formal and paternalistic, built on deference and fixed codes of behaviour, this was a typically benevolent Victorian upper-class establishment.[35]

The partnership of Henry and Ellen Howard was built upon a formal structure of life, lived in a community of about twenty, including the servants. Ellen inscribed her life as Mother in a small leather-bound notebook, where she entered its vital statistics: the time, as well as date of each birth, weights, infant illnesses, teeth and progress. She noted specific incidents. At twelve, Edith's schoolroom lessons were halted when her mother judged her to be suffering from nerves. Ida had her lip 'torn and sown up under chloroform' at six. Stanley broke his collarbone playing football at his Brighton prep school at thirteen and had his appendix removed on the kitchen table by the Orpington general practitioner at fifteen, when he was back from Eton. Walter's lessons were stopped in view of 'twitches and stammering' at seven years old. Clare was stitched under chloroform, when she cut her forehead against her cot at two years old.[36]

In the early years, Ellen Howard matched her household management with the role of local society hostess, holding dinner parties and organising events which coloured the North Kent social round. The printed programme for a concert, in the drawing room at Bark Hart in July 1889, reveals that five vocalists sang a selection of airs, quartets and madrigals. Ellen, in her paternalistic role, sent soup to poor families that attended church but not to those that went to chapel.[37]

Encouraged by their governess, the older girls, Edith, Maud and Ida, were imaginative and energetic in their summer activities, besides the round of tennis parties and participation in village fêtes and jumble sales. In 1890, they organised a musical entertainment of their own for invited guests, persuading Stanley, who was only seven, to play a solo piano piece. The family newspaper that August recorded Hal's arrival home from prep school, met at Victoria by Ellen and then by others in the carriage at Orpington. He came bearing a school prize, won 'much to the satisfaction of his family'.[38]

In 1893, the new governess, Miss Jacob, organised an Opening of the fantasy Ivy Castle, created by the children in the Bark Hart grounds. Edith, as the eldest, made a formal speech of welcome to Ellen, who took the role of guest of honour and was sung a welcome chorus by the children. A scrawled note from Edith to Maud in 1896, teasing her with goodbye wishes to 'silly sixteen' and 'cartloads of love, kisses, congratulations' on her birthday, indicates the relaxed and affectionate atmosphere, within its rigid routines, of the Bark Hart upbringing.[39]

Clare Howard's first diary, in a tiny notebook made at ten years old in 1903, indicates how, for the baby of the family, this was a life in which parents hardly featured and the comings and goings of elder siblings structured daily existence. The exception was Christmas Day, when 'all of us', but not Mother and a couple of the boys, went for the traditional long walk with Father 'after luncheon' across the local fields.[40] Ellen Howard, portly and ageing visibly after this time, made regular visits to the Belvedere Mansion Hotel at Brighton for sea air in the years 1904 to 1909, where Clare wrote to her faithfully. She spoke of walking in the hotel garden and of doing occasional shopping on her own. 'Mother spends a good deal of the evenings in a shawl', wrote Maud on 25 September 1905.[41]

Ellen had as good as handed Amy, at fifteen, and Clare, at thirteen, over to their bossy and nagging elder sister. 'I hope you take all that Maud orders you like an estimable child and that Amy is not ill', she wrote in one letter signed 'your loving mother Ellen Howard'. 'As there are several business things to be said you will see that somebody does them please', Maud instructed Clare at this time, listing errands and things to be posted to the boys, who were at school and away finding a living.[42] As at Hagley, elder sisters at Bark Hart served an apprenticeship for the motherhood to which they themselves aspired by looking after and controlling the little ones.

This chapter has described a series of different social and domestic worlds. From the Harley, Verney, Josselin and Brockbank families in the seventeenth century to the Howards in the late nineteenth and twentieth, marital partnership remained the crux of most children's upbringing. But not all. Some children, we should remember, lost both parents at a young age and yet were provided with the security of a loving home by grandparents or relatives. One example is Melesina Chenevix, who we encountered above when she wrote about the education of children as a parent herself. Born in Dublin in 1768, both her parents, remembered by her for their warm affection, were dead before she was four years old. She was looked after until she was eleven by her paternal grandfather, the Bishop of Waterford: 'one of those guileless, humble, benevolent, firm, affectionate and pious characters rarely seen and never duly appreciated'. She was often miserable, under the day-to-day charge of a fearsome governess. So the bishop, she confessed, good, kind and doting though he was, 'had not made me happy, though he had tried to do so . . . but I felt he loved me more than all the world'. At his death in 1779, 'without knowing the value of deep and exclusive love, I regretted him, both from gratitude and from affection'.[43]

A letter from Melesina, at nine years old in January 1778 to her maternal Grandmama, is remarkable for its maturity, its neat hand and the thoughtfulness of a child who, in her own account, was 'obedient and loving, docile and lively, although timid'. She was pleased to hear that her grandmother, who she knew had been ill and had not been in touch, was 'rather better'. She postponed an invitation to dine out, 'as my Grandpapa thinks it dangerous for me to be out late at this time of the year'. With duty and affection, Melesina sent 'many happy returns of this season' to those in her nearby Irish grandmother's household.[44]

This harping on children's duty was constant. Attitudes to upbringing developed, without changing fundamentally, across three hundred years. In the seventeenth century, there was considerable dissonance between prescription and practice, with the harsher prescriptions about patriarchal discipline being largely rejected in many homes. All along, parents drew from the advice literature what made sense to them, taking it more seriously in the eighteenth century as it came into line with their own instincts. By and large they then adopted a broadly Lockean philosophy, which gave them full responsibility for moulding their children's characters.

Social assumptions changed, but the realities and demands of childhood did not. The chapters which follow outline how parental dedication provided a solid and constructive foundation for day-to-day upbringing. Day by day and month by month, children's own gender identity was being created, as a reflection of parental gender models and behaviour.

7

Children Who Died

The death of a child represents the loss of all hope at the start of life: it is the most bewildering, distressing and incapacitating kind of death.[1] Hence the strong belief in the seventeenth century that a mother's grief could be such that her own death would follow.[2] Elizabeth Holland wrote of this maternal anguish as a 'species of savage despair'. When Mary Cary wrote a description of her ideal society in 1657, her first item was that in this society 'no infant of days shall die when they are young ... they [parents] shall not be afflicted for the loss of their children'.[3] The seventeenth-century physician Richard Napier recorded treating 134 cases of disturbing grief and attributed 58 of these to the death of a child.[4]

There is no other subject which provides us with such heartfelt outpouring of the emotions of parenthood as the death of children. Cumulatively, this evidence, in diaries, journals and correspondence, is the bedrock of the argument that parental love and affection was constant, powerful and virtually invariable from 1600 to 1914.[5] 'God grant', wrote Charles Hutton to his brother Christopher, when Charles's son, Robin, died in 1672, that you may not 'know what the loss of a child is'.[6] By exploring how parents handled grief, we can appreciate what their children meant to them in their, too often, very short lives.

The circumstances of a child's death – its age, its place in the family and its health record – were always important influences on the degree and intensity of parental grief. Sir Simonds D'Ewes commented, losing his son Clopton in 1636 at the age of two, after the loss of three boys soon after their birth, that those infants were 'not so endeared to us'. But Clopton was one on whom 'we had bestowed so much care and affection'. His father wrote feelingly of his 'delicate favour and bright grey eye', which were 'so deeply imprinted on our hearts'.[7]

With a son and daughter already, Matthew Flinders was philosophical in 1775, when his second son died at six weeks old. It was a merciful dispensation, he reflected, to lose the youngest, always a sickly child, since 'to have parted with either of the other two would have afflicted us much more and, as we have naught in a natural sense but my industry in business to depend on, we ought to welcome the non increase of our family as a blessing'. His view of God's providence in the matter emerges more fully the following year, when twins were still born: 'the two we have living, if agreeable to divine wisdom, I would gladly keep but by no means wish an increase, however, let that happen as it may, I hope we shall acquiesce to the good will of God'. In 1778, when two more twins died within 24 hours, Matthew again thanked the divine mercy which had not burdened him 'with the additional care of more children'.[8]

But faced with the languishing of her boy Frederick, aged nine, in the summer of 1806, Melesina Trench avowed that her earlier loss of an infant daughter 'shrinks into nothing when compared with this': 'she was merely a little bud; he was a heavenly blossom which had safely passed all the earliest dangers and gave clearest promise of delicious fruit'.[9]

If, in general, parents found it easier to accept the loss of infants than older children, this should not cause us to underestimate how every mother grieved on seeing the care and devotion stored up in the months of pregnancy come to naught. Sara Coleridge, commenting on the death of her eleven-day-old daughter in 1840, speaks for all mothers: 'strange as it may seem, these little speechless creatures, with their wandering, unspeaking eyes, do twine themselves around a parent's heart from the hour of their birth'.[10]

Yet seventeenth-century parents, especially those reared in the godly puritan tradition, were also wont to interpret how a child fared in health or sickness as signs of God's intentions towards it. Ralph Josselin's diary entries with regard to the ten days that his second son Ralph, born in 1648, lived are revealing. The references lack any sense of the child as an individual, with prospects in life: 'my infant', 'our babe', 'it', as well as 'he'. On 17 February came the first mention of the infant's sickliness: 'we sent for the physician, he gave it syrup of roses . . . my wife persuaded herself that it would die'. It was the child's quietness that struck his parents during the following days, as they watched him, full of anxiety. On 19 February he was 'very still and quiet'; on 20 February, 'he had a little froth in his mouth continually . . . he cheered up very sweetly at night and in the night was very still, what God will do I know not, but it becommeth me to submit to his will'; the next day, 'my dear babe Ralph quietly fell asleep and is at rest with the Lord'.

A strict puritan, Ralph was bound to see God's dealings with him, regarding the boy who bore his own name, as a 'correction' and 'chastisement' that he should seek to profit from. His summary mixes the bitterness of loss with spiritual calm:

> The Lord gave us time to bury it in our thoughts, we looked on it as a dying child three or four days, then it dies quietly without screeches or sobs or groans, it breathed out the soul with nine gasps and died, it was the youngest and our affections not so wonted unto it.

Two years later, when Jane Josselin gave birth to another son, she and Ralph decided on the name Ralph again. They were grasping, not uncommonly in this period, at the notion of replacement. They did not think in terms of interchangeability, rather of memorialising their earlier babe. This Ralph lived longer, but also sickened and died, at a year old. Josselin, probably seeing this second rejection of his Christian name as decisive, let the name Ralph go now, firm in faith and without too much difficulty: 'my dear Ralph before midnight fell asleep whose body Jesus shall awaken, his life was continual sorry and trouble, happy he who is at rest in the Lord'.[11]

Men found it particularly hard to bear the loss of a first son. Alice Thornton was thrilled at giving her husband a son in 1660, reportedly 'exceeding like' him in looks. After a fortnight, William sickened. She took the child in her arms, noting how he 'would sweetly lift up his eyes to heaven and smile, as if the old saying was true in this infant, that he saw angels in heaven'. She believed her husband took his early death more heavily than she did, 'being a son'.[12]

As personality blossomed, parents found grief at the loss of children more and more difficult to bear. Isaac Archer, deprived of his daughter just short of a year in 1670, after she had been ill for five months, contorted himself over the attempt to resign himself to God. 'Oh what grief it was to me to hear it groan, to see its sprightly eyes turn to me for help in vain', he wrote in his diary. Nursing his child, he came to believe in her, before she died, as a person in her own right: ''Twas as pretty and knowing a child as they had ever seen that came to see it', he recorded. 'We have lost our darling child', wrote Charles Lemon to Mary Talbot in November 1812, 'he had latterly acquired so many little engaging ways of interesting anybody who took notice of him, and had occupied so much of our time and happiness, that his loss has made us feel very desolate'.[13]

Elizabeth Egerton, Countess of Bridgewater, idealised her little Katy, who she lost around 1660 at under two. The poignancy of her account rests on the readiness she showed to admit and delight in the mutuality of their love for each other. Katy had been one who would 'make her mind known at any time and was kind to all, even to strangers and had no anger in her'; nor did she sleep or play 'at sermon or prayers'. Katy, her mother said, 'took delight in nothing but me': 'never was there so fond a child of a mother'.[14] The death of his toddler Edward in 1788 inspired the most deep felt entry in William Roe's memorandum book. 'Constant and unremitting affectionate parental care gave the boy two years, six months and nineteen days of life', he noted, whereas surgeons had warned that a congenital spinal injury would make his life very short. They had 'loved him to excess': he was 'the most noble, lovely and interesting child I ever saw . . . his mind was sweet, sensible, touching and very advanced in all ways for his age'.[15]

Nehemiah Wallington and his wife Grace lost three children in succession, over the seven years from 1625 to 1632. Nehemiah recorded the death of his dear Elizabeth at just under three with graphic detail. Her loveliness was the joy of his life. On her last day, she teased her mother at the washing of the dishes: 'Elizabeth, then being merry, went unto her mother and said unto her, What do you here my wife?' Later, in bed with her parents, she declared: 'Father I go abroad tomorrow and buy you a plum pie'. But the pangs of death seized her, we are told, overnight, and the recorded promise 'were the last words that I did hear my sweet child speak'.[16]

Deaths from the age of three onwards were usually felt very deeply. Peg Verney in 1647, Mary Josselin in 1650 and Ann Fanshaw in 1654 are signal examples. The striking feature, in each case, is the parental sense of joy and promise cut off in full bud.

Ralph and Mary Verney were not newcomers to bereavement, when their eight-year-old Peg died in the autumn of 1647. Mary had just given birth to a boy, called Ralph after his father, at Claydon, having been sent by her husband back to Buckinghamshire to settle the family's estate. She returned from her legal business in London to discover her baby dead from convulsion fits. What made the Verneys' grief so searing was the loss of two of their children within days of each other. If Ralph as an infant had hardly developed a distinctive personality and had in any case spent his short life with a wet nurse rather than his mother, Peg was the apple, at eight years' old, of both of their eyes. 'She spake idly for two nights and did not know her friends', reported Dr Denton in an account on 17 October 1647 of how Mary Verney's double bereavement 'did much afflict and distract her'. Her postscript to her husband, when she heard about Peg's death, is perhaps the most moving of many testimonies of seventeenth-century parental grief: 'since I writ this I have received the sad news of two of our dear children's death, which affliction joined with being absent from thee is – without God's great mercy to me – a heavier burden than can be born by thy unhappy M.'.[17]

In this case, it was the husband who found strength to sustain the wife. Ralph Verney's view of the children's deaths was, as he told Mary, that 'they are the most unspeakable gainers by this change; and since 'tis so . . . we should rather rejoice at their happiness'. He was much helped, it is clear, by the exemplary way that Peg had died, which he took as guidance about how, as parents, they should submit to God's pleasure:

> had you but seen with what unparalleled patience poor Peg bore all her pains and with what discretion and affection she disposed of her wearing clothes, unto her maid that tended her, and lastly with what admirable cheerfulness and courage, desiring prayers to be made for her, she peaceably resigned her soul into the hands of him that gave it.

Mary had none of the benefit of all this.

Yet, on 4 November, 'so weak I am scarce able to go up and down my chamber', Mary told Ralph of her emerging faith: 'my trust is in my good God'. Desolation heightened her dependence on him: 'until I am with thee I cannot take any content in anything in this world'. Searing grief brought the couple together. A favouritism concealed and, he believed, shared between them could now be made open. As he explained, 'no creature knew how much you loved that poor child, I ever concealed what passion I had for her and rather appeared to neglect her lest our overfondness should spoil her or make the other jealous'. The depth of integrity in this Verney marriage shines out from their correspondence.[18]

In daily entries, Ralph Josselin recorded the loss of his Mary, also aged eight: on 24 June 1650, he woke in the night 'with the dolour . . . that Mary was dying'. Two days later, the diary shows, she rested 'free from much pain', making her parents 'willing she should be out of her pain'. The entry on the next day, when Mary died, is the most deeply heartfelt in Josselin's whole enormous diary:

> My soul had abundant cause to bless God for her, who was our first fruits . . . it was a precious child, a bundle of myrrh, a bundle of sweetness . . . it was a box of sweet ointment . . . it lived desired and died lamented, thy memory is and will be sweet to me.

Josselin later reflected, as Verney had done, on the qualities of character that he had recognised in his daughter. It was his belief that the 'soberness, towardliness in obedience, spiritualness of her conversation' were the things which argued 'the real impression of the image of God' upon Mary. Earlier losses paled before this one: 'till now I never knew what a grief it was to part with a child'.[19] When Lady Ann Fanshawe lost her Ann, another eight-year old, in 1654, she found herself robbed of one whose beauty and wit, she believed, exceeded any other child of that age she had known.[20]

The loss of teenagers and children in young adulthood was perhaps harder still. Sir John Oglander lamented that most of his earthly comforts had died with his son, when his heir George died at the age of 23 while travelling in France, so close had they been. When smallpox carried off Bulstrode Whitelocke's daughter Frances in 1654, he felt deprived of 'much of the joy and comfort of her, to whom she was a companion in his widowers estate and refreshed him by the music of her voice and discourse'. The seventeenth-century divine Jeremy Taylor took the view that some parents, who could bear the death of infants, were broken in spirit when they lost older children, who might have yielded them comfort in old age.[21]

Thomas Moore has left a full account of the last weeks of the life of his daughter Anastasia, who, after serious illness on and off for two years, died in 1829, at the age of eighteen. As she grew weaker, there were evenings when her parents looked over books and talked with her, played games or draughts or sat with her, as she dressed and undressed a little doll in which she took great delight. She would say 'I can't talk but do you and Mama go on talking for I like to hear you'. Her voice grew hollow and gained a distant softness.

When she told her mother that she would die, there were prayers together and reassurances: 'I am sure God must love you for you have always been a good girl.' 'Have I', she replied, 'I thought I was a very naughty girl but I am glad to hear you say I have been good.' The last moments were with her mother alone. When she came and told him that Anastasia was gone, Thomas recorded, 'I could no longer restrain myself; the feelings I had been so long suppressing found vent and a fit of loud sobbing seized me in which I felt as if my chest was coming asunder'. At her burial, her parents laid cowslips on her bosom.[22]

From the seventeenth century to the nineteenth, the correspondence of those bereaved of children is pervaded by a language of resignation. Parents struggled to accept God's will.[23] Relatives and friends exhorted them to do so with every argument they could master. Thus, in 1638, when Juliana Newdigate lost her first son at 22 months, a friend, Sir Ranulph Crewe, sought to comfort her in the 'great loss of your sweet boy', with the encouragement that 'God will send you more sons', since 'his hand is not so short to such as serve him and no doubt he will graciously look upon you'.[24] In 1756 Walter Stanhope praised his wife for her fortitude, after losing three of her four children in infancy. 'I am glad', he wrote, 'to find you have behaved with prudence in these melancholy schemes, so as not to throw yourself down'.[25]

Some learnt to put total confidence in salvation and resurrection. We might expect this of the celebrated puritan minister of Blackfriars, William Gouge.

prehensive.

A passage in a letter to his friend and patron Sir Robert Harley, in 1613, provides unusual insight into communication from man to man about the loss of a child. The language is conventional, if laden with grief: 'the Lord is wise in ordering the manifold afflictions of his children: I have had my part and among other crosses an heavy hath now lately, even this last week, been inflicted on me. My sweetest child, mine only daughter, is gone.' The words that follow speak volumes about the control that Gouge was having to impose upon himself. 'I can say no more of her', he wrote, 'she is at rest'.[26]

The monument erected in Astley church in Warwickshire by Sir Richard and Lady Newdigate to their three-month-old son Francis in 1670 was a statement of conviction:

The morning of the resurrection
Will see him raised again, and will restore
His parent's joys, then to be lost no more.[27]

Journals are not short of statements in which a parent clings to faith. The Methodist Elizabeth Macall, obsessive about her children's sinfulness, sought to comfort herself in 1743 on the news that her son Russell had died of a fever in New Guinea: 'I will not look upon my child as lost; he is I trust gone where I hope shortly to arrive'. Thomas Moore appears to have achieved some inner calm, when he concluded the account cited above of the death of Anastasia in 1829: 'And such is the end of so many years of fondness and hope and nothing is now left us but the dream that we shall see our pure child again in a world more worthy of her.'[28] Elizabeth Wynne, by contrast, mourning her Louisa, who had died in the agonies of a fever at five years old, was not resigned. She wrote in 1810 that 'my affliction almost overpowers me at the loss of such a darling and lovely child'.[29]

Grief tried and sometimes strengthened the relationship between a husband and wife, as we have seen with the Verneys. Nehemiah Wallington, that quintessential London puritan artisan, was not strong in faith when he and his wife Grace had children die. Grace, as his biographer Paul Seaver has remarked, was in no sense the clinging vine. It was rather she who brought realism and spiritual comfort to the family in its crises. Nehemiah was inconsolable at the loss, related above, of Elizabeth. He confessed in his journal that he wholly forgot himself, to the extent that he broke all his 'purposes, promises and covenants' with God, refusing all comfort from men. He records his wife's reprimands:

Husband, I am persuaded you offend God in grieving for this child so much. Do but consider . . . what a deal of trouble and sorrow she is gone out of and what abundance of joy she is gone into. And do but consider, it is your daughter's wedding day and will you grieve to see your daughter go home to her husband Christ Jesus, where she shall never want, but have the fullness of joy for ever more?

Nehemiah, nonplussed, tried hard to learn from his wife's resourcefulness and certainty. He faced another lesson in Christian resignation less than two years later, when their only son, not yet three, sickened and died. This time, his response was more positive. 'God doth intend us more good than we are aware of', he told Grace, 'for where a man's treasure is, there is his heart: now our child is gone to heaven our heart will be there.'[30]

Nineteenth-century parents prayed earnestly that God would spare their children and equally, Carole Williams found reading their diaries, 'to give them faith and forbearance if the child's time for entry into Heaven had arrived'. The death of Edward Bramfill at eighteen months, in 1831, left his devout parents 'wonderfully supported though sadly cast down'. Anna Acton-Broke wept so heartbrokenly at the funeral of her child in 1856 that those remaining 'in perfect agony screamed out "Oh Mama do not, do not cry" – dear Janey saying "Mama's heart is broken but I will give her my little heart"'. To Anna, in anguish, 'it seemed the very tearing away of my life'. In her excessive grief she found inestimable comfort from her other children.[31]

Victorian churchmen sought to bolster each other with the assurance faith could offer. 'My dearest friend', wrote Archdeacon Samuel Wilberforce to Richard Chenevix Trench, then a curate, in the early stages of his ministry, 'I know that the dark and rough way in which He is leading you now is that which has ever been trodden the most constantly by all great saints.' He commended him, his wife and child dying at seven years old in 1841, 'to the merciful care of our Heavenly Father'.[32]

But just as the religiosity of the seventeenth century puritan was no absolute shield from doubt in this kind of crisis, nor was that of an eminent Victorian churchman. Martin Benson, a precocious schoolboy, was the apple of his father's eye. His father, Edward White Benson, was Bishop of Truro at the time, in 1878, that Martin died at seventeen from tubercular meningitis. Attempting to come to terms with his loss, Benson wrote a 34-page diary account of it in which, among much else, he recorded how differently he and his wife Mary were handling their grief. 'My dearest wife understood it all more quickly – better – more sweetly than I', the bishop affirmed.

At once Mary knew she had never cared for anything but her boy's happiness. Whereas Benson was shattered and never entirely recovered, Mary was severe with herself. The day after Martin died, she wrote to the family nurse that 'he is in perfect peace, in wonderful joy, far happier than we could ever have made him . . . free from fear, free from pain, from anxiety for ever more'. For Edward Benson, his son's death remained 'inconceivable'. At 60 it was still, he could confess, the 'inexplicable grief' of his life: 'to see into that will be worth dying'.[33]

If there were many occasions when a bereavement brought parents closer together, as they discovered each other's strengths and weaknesses, there is ample evidence, too, of the impact of early death on broader family cohesion. The Capel family bore the death of baby Priscilla at seven weeks in 1815 with fortitude and courage. Lady Caroline Capel and her husband were in Brussels at the time, with six of their children around them. The eldest, Muzzy, at seventeen, gave their grandmother a full account of the child's sudden illness, the hurried consultations with a doctor and the loving circle in which the child died. She related the cloying atmosphere of her passing and laying out:

> The little angel expired with her face on Mama's breast . . . so peaceably that we did not perceive it till several minutes had passed . . . we removed the child, and laid it out, washed and dressed it ourselves. Since that, Mama has never left its side . . . I sat up with it last night, for I loved it so much and held its little cold hand all the time. Oh! my dearest Grandmama, you can have no idea of anything so lovely as she looks . . . she was the admiration of the town and we were so proud of her. We have had her picture taken.

Strikingly, Muzzy emphasised Priscilla's lack of tactile contact beyond the family: 'it has been a great consolation to us all and particularly to Mama that our baby since she was born has never been touched but by those who loved her'. Baby Priscilla Capel's short life was entirely a family affair. At the funeral, her sisters Muzzy and Georgy were pall bearers, while Harriet and Louisa walked before the coffin.[34]

An even better documented family death in the same period is that of Charlotte Bloomfield, at the age of almost thirteen, in 1828. Her illness began at ten and, in the interim, she was trained for death by an evangelical and devoted father, Benjamin Lord Bloomfield. He bought her a tiny leather-bound book, in which he entered suitable prayers for her to say, from 1825 onwards. The first one, entitled 'When very ill', began 'Oh God who hast ordained that I should be a helpless suffering child, make me, I pray thee, perfectly resigned to thy will.' After his daughter died on 29 February 1828, Bloomfield noted, in his own hand (see overleaf), that: 'This little book of prayers was in constant daily use by my angelic Charlotte from the day I composed the first . . . up to the week preceding her death.'[35]

This little book of Prayers was in constant daily use by my Angelic Charlotte from the day I composed the first, about April 1825 up to the week preceding her death. March 8th 1828.

In her last years, Charlotte had lived with her governess in England, while her elder sisters Harriott and Georgiana were with their father, who was ambassador at the court of King Charles XIII of Sweden in Stockholm. She engaged in regular and playful correspondence with them.[36] It was they, with her mother Harriott Bloomfield, and her governess, Miss Ridout, who orchestrated little Charlotte's deathbed at The Stud House, Bloomfield's grace and favour residence at Hampton Court. Georgiana's memoir of Charlotte's last days shows their management of the process of her death, making the leave-taking revelatory for both sides and suffusing it with piety. Lord Bloomfield, called home from Stockholm, found the women of the household displaying the emotional resourcefulness that turned this death into a positive and even uplifting experience for the whole family.

On the Friday of the first week in Georgiana's account, Charlotte 'spoke of the Rock of Ages to Miss Ridout'; the following Monday Georgiana wrote 'I gave her this text to think of at night: "my flesh and my heart faileth but God is the strength of my heart and my portion for ever".' She 'certainly knew Mama and testified her fondness', Georgiana noted. Her father did not arrive from Sweden until Charlotte was failing fast. But 'she knew him, embraced him fondly and afterwards she attended to a prayer I said to her and kissed my hand'. The dying girl 'showed kindness to everyone' and 'understood several texts which at intervals were said to her'.

The day before she died, we are told, Charlotte bid Georgiana 'say again a text she liked, "Cast all thy care"'. There were several texts to which she 'uniformly gave a smile' during her last days, including 'The Lord is very pitiful' and 'The Lord loveth whom he chasteneth'. After her death, Georgiana found the leaf turned down in her prayer book at the 'Meditation on Death', which was 'apparently much read because the book opened there'. She cut a lock from her dead sister's auburn hair and tied it, to memorialise her, with a ribbon, inside a copy of this meditation.[37]

The preservation of hair as a tangible reminder of the deceased, often in a ring or brooch, was a common practice at this time. The memoir of the death of her stepdaughter Caroline at eight years old in the Warwickshire Record Office by Lady Emma Penant, written in 1832, has with it a piece of her hair in a wrapper inscribed 'Dear little Caroline's hair'.[38] Artefacts of this kind must be understood in the context of the mourning customs of the period and of the contemporary experience of family grief.[39]

Parental grief was not incompatible with a realistic appreciation of the hazards of infancy between the seventeenth and nineteenth centuries. As we have seen, when a child's survival was short-lived or marked by persistent ill health, parents could accept the loss of one who had not yet taken a deep place in their hearts. It is possible, also, in certain circumstances, to detect a matter of factness about loss through infectious disease during later childhood. Sir John Smyth, informed from Taunton that his boy Samuel had smallpox in 1719 at school, neither attempted to visit him nor attended his funeral and burial arrangements, but he did stipulate the costs. It was left to Hugh, Samuel's brother, to represent the family, his schoolmaster having bought him a mourning cloak. The journey from the family home was not long or hazardous. Why did Smyth not go himself? In the absence of further evidence, we cannot interpret his not doing so as showing lack of feeling for his son.[40]

Yet it is inescapable that ideological change about the nature of childhood and changing attitudes towards death brought some change in the ways that parents sought comfort in this kind of grief over three centuries. The seventeenth-century puritan diarists stressed the communal experience of a child's burial. This community support is less explicit in Nehemiah Wallington's account of the burial of 'our sweet son' Samuel on a 'very wet and doleful day' in 1632, than in Ralph Josselin's rendering of the narrative of little Ralph's burial in 1648. 'The boy was buried with the tears and sorrow of many of my neighbours', he wrote, 'the gravest matrons in our town laid his tomb into the earth, which I esteem not only a testimony of their love to me but of their respect to my babe.'[41]

A considerable degree of secularisation in the eighteenth century shifted the focus on to the family's own handling of their grief. When Charlotte Oakes died as a young adult in 1798, her parents were so grieved at her loss that they kept her body at home for a week, first on her bed, then in an open coffin in her bedroom, until 'an evident change had taken place'. They did not go out, other than with immediate family, for ten weeks. Jane Fiske, editor of James Oakes's diaries, has noted the impact on him of the deaths of several grandchildren. There was no mourning for Edward's death at eight months in 1795, James recording that he was always weakly, and 'by other people not thought a living child'. Yet he was much upset four years later in 1799 by the almost continuous illness of his grandson Charles, leading to his death at two months. James recorded the child's progress daily, noting the anguish of his parents at the boy's 'dying by inches and suffering in the most dreadful manner'. He used the family carriage to take the body to the burial in the family vault in St Mary's Church at Bury St Edmunds.[42]

Arthur Young's loss of his fourteen-year-old daughter Bobbin in 1797 nearly brought on a complete breakdown and led to a dramatic conversion to evangelicalism. 'I was on my knees at her bedside', he recorded, noting the last words exchanged between them: 'thank God of his mercy she expired without a groan, or her face being the least agitated . . . at last she went off like a bird'. Three days later he was struggling with his grief. 'Every room, every spot is full of her, and it sinks my very heart to see them', he wrote. Young sought pardon 'for allowing any earthly object thus to engross my feelings and over-power my very soul'. He could not help dwelling on his little girl and arranged things so he could continue to do so. His decision to bury her in his pew, 'fixing the coffin so that when I kneel it will be between her head and my dear heart', was a means of 'preserving the grief I feel and hope to feel while breath is in my body'.[43]

The morbidity evident in Young's case became more established in the nineteenth century. Melesina Trench found herself still held in almost total thrall to her son Frederick in 1806, three months after he was gone. She paced his room: 'I involuntarily turn towards the glass which reflected his last looks and expect to find some outline, some trace, some shade of him.' There was nothing but 'a solitary lock of shining hair'.[44] When her child died in 1812, Lady Fleming spent weeks in the room where her daughter had been. 'Yet where can I go', she asked her niece, 'that I shall not be reminded of my lost darling: every object is so associated with her idea that to forget her is impossible.'[45]

Lady Caroline Capel, mourning her Priscilla in 1815, noted that, from the window of her rampart room, she could 'see at a distance the wall of the place where she lies and, extraordinary as it may appear, I feel a sense of comfort in knowing I can see it when I please and a dread of deserting it'. She kept the picture painted of the child in death close to her 'to gaze upon'. When William Macready went into the room where his lifeless infant daughter was laid out in 1840, he recorded his emotions in these terms: 'how beautiful, how like a thing of heaven the blessed creature looked'.[46]

'I see her in every corner of the room – in every part of the house – her dolly – her couch – Oh the agony of pain which these remembrances excite', noted Benjamin Goodwin when his young daughter died in 1849.[47] 'Don't quarrel . . . you might be happy', was the teenage Caroline Jones's final admonition to her parents in 1807. William Jones treasured his last conversations with her, which would 'never be erased from his fond memory', characterising her as 'an angel of peace both at her entrance into and departure out of this wicked troublous world'.[48] A Birmingham banker desperately missed his daughter's feminine attentions, recording that he was 'so overwhelmed with the sudden loss of my precious child that I scarcely know how to write . . . how joyfully she met me on my return from Town in the omnibus, was the first to open the door and come to meet me'.[49] These instances suggest a new dwelling upon the death of children, when religious conviction, though earnest, brought less complete comfort and sustenance than it once had done.

By the nineteenth century, while Protestant Christianity still provided a dominant belief system to offer consolation, mourning was pursued much more elaborately than previously within the family and household. Actions like Georgiana Bloomfield's preservation of a lock of her little sister's hair became common. A widely read consolation literature emerged. Letters of gratitude poured in from bereaved parents, who were helped by Archbishop Tait's memorial volume on the catastrophic death of five of his seven children, when scarlet fever ravaged Carlisle in 1856. This was published 23 years later, in 1879. Many, too, found their faith strengthened by reading Catherine Tait's record of her loving resignation more than twenty years before to God's will.[50]

It has been suggested that Victorian mourning rituals, both at home and beyond it, allowed the expression of sorrow in a constructive manner. They clearly provided therapeutic benefits and met psychological needs, making the grieving experience easier to endure and complete.[51] Simple belief in God's providence was no longer enough. Fortunately, since secularisation has proceeded apace, the death of a child is now much less common than it was before 1914.

8

Maternity

Maternity was seen as the essence of the role of a wife. Those rare seventeenth-century gentlewomen who published testified to a view of it that their Victorian successors would readily have echoed. 'There is no love so forcible as the love of an affectionate mother to her natural child', wrote Elizabeth Grymeston, in the preface to her prayers and meditations for her son. A mother's love was beyond the bounds of reason, insisted Dorothy Leigh in a book of maternal advice. 'I am unwilling my children should think I neglected either prayers or advice to make them both happy here or hereafter', wrote the Countess of Westmorland, bequeathing to them a manuscript book of instructions for life.[1] The vast majority of women expected to bear children soon after marriage. The genteel Victorian tradition of spending an entire month on honeymoon, Carole Williams has suggested, may have reflected an unspoken design to maximise the possibility of early conception.[2]

Children were always welcomed, even well down a large family. 'I began to have some hopes of my wife breeding', wrote Ralph Josselin in his diary in July 1641, ten months after his marriage, 'which proved so to our great joy and comfort.' The next April he recorded expenditure of six pounds, thirteen shillings and fourpence on his daughter's christening celebrations.[3] 'I remember how she used to have us all in her room when she was dressing', wrote Frederica Orlebar, born early in the nineteenth century, of her mother, 'and how she used to take me on her knee to play with her hair while it was being done and what a pet she used to make of me, instead of considering me, being the ninth child, as a nuisance.' Despite her heavy workload and ill health, Ann Bramfill was delighted with her fifth baby in 1829. He was 'healthy, fat and everything I could desire . . . altogether a finer child than any I ever had'.[4]

Linda Pollock, discussing the experience of pregnancy in early modern England, quoted a tract of 1668, which conjured a vivid image of what women were seen to suffer:

Going with child is as it were a rough sea on which a big bellied woman and her infant floats the space of nine months: and labour, which is the only port, is so full of dangerous rocks, that very often both the one and the other, after they are arrived and disembarked, have yet need of much help to defend them against divers inconveniences, which usually follow the pains and travail they have undergone in it.

Women expected pain and sickness during pregnancy, but did not all suffer discomfort. Amanda Vickery noted Bessy Ramsden's refusal, in November 1767, though incommoded by her sheer size, to forgo visiting, shopping and card playing, until the 'fatal moment', as she called her labour. But some women read feelings of good health negatively. 'I am very well and never was as fat in my life, makes me fear that my child does not thrive I do so much', wrote Frances Hatton in 1678. On the other hand, there was the pleasure of pleasing a husband by this proof of fertility.[5] 'My husband is extreme fond of me', wrote Susan Alport to her brother Sir Ralph Verney in 1647, 'he was ever a very kind husband to me, but much more so since I was with child.'[6]

Expectant mothers feared the birth and relatives worried for them. 'I hope you will do well yet none can foresee how it may please the Lord to deal with you', Lady Massingberd counselled her daughter in 1700, 'your safe delivery in childbirth is God's own work. Pray spare as much time as you can for meditation and prayer to acquaint yourself with God.' Giving birth successfully once did not allay misgivings the next time. 'Let not this melancholy prevail with you', the Countess of Bedford told her friend Lady Cornwallis in 1623, five months pregnant with her fourth child, 'it hath pleased God to carry you so safely through, and so I doubt not will again, though you may do yourself and yours much harm by those doubtings.'[7]

Childbirth throughout this period was a family event, with relatives and friends rallying round. 'In a sense', wrote Adrian Wilson, 'a woman's whole life revolved around the act of giving birth.' This was the female rite of passage *par excellence*. A gentlewoman, knowing that what mattered was an heir to inherit the family name, title and estates, expected to go on with as many pregnancies as it took to deliver the goods. 'This child, though a daughter, was very welcome both to her and her husband', wrote Sir Simonds D'Ewes, stating a seventeenth-century attitude that persisted, 'because it gave them hope of further issue.' 'Although it be a girl that God has sent', Thomas Chichely told his daughter in 1671, 'yet it is a very great blessing.' He remembered 'a saying of your Grandfather Russell, who said "in time it would turn to a boy"'.[8]

The more patriarchal a man's cast of mind the more likely he was to be dismissive about female births: 'the having of another girl, I thought so little considerable, that I made no haste in acquainting you with it', the Earl of

Northumberland told the Countess of Leicester in 1636. William Blundell
was sardonic about the immediate death of his sixth daughter and ninth child
in 1653: 'my wife has much disappointed my hopes in bringing forth a
daughter, which, finding herself not so welcome in this world as a son, hath
made already a discreet choice of a better'. Some women were wracked by
failure to fulfil the requirement of producing a male to order. Lady Frances
Hatton, giving birth to a daughter in 1678, assured her husband she would
gladly have laid down her life to procure him a son.[9]

Amanda Vickery found that northern women in the Georgian period
seldom committed details of their labour to paper. But she stressed the fortitude and resignation with which the whole female business of childbearing
was faced, citing the 'grotesque ordeal' of Anne Gossip in 1739, recorded by
a devoted husband. The agony of her labour lasted for over 49 hours: 'with a
stoicism barely imaginable' she 'suffered her dead baby to be torn apart within
her and removed in pieces'.[10] Carole Williams, using nineteenth-century
diaries, found that references to childbirth normally emphasised thanks to
God for safe delivery of mother and child, rather than the undignified
specifics of physical experience. 'Sent for Mr Foaker at 2 and at 9 on 30th',
noted Clarissa Bramston in October 1833, 'baby did come . . . our blessed-
ness is complete.' There was sometimes pride in the courage that had been
shown, which may have been seen increasingly as a mark of upper-class self-
control.[11] Frederica Orlebar was pleased with herself in May 1862: 'I did . . .
get through it without more noise than one small shriek which nobody
acknowledged to hearing – I consider that very creditable.'

'The gift of a healthy baby represented the apex of earthly happiness',
Carole Williams has written. Melesina Trench remembered the birth of her
first child, at nineteen, in 1787, as a moment which counterbalanced an
unhappy childhood. 'When I looked in my boy's face, when I heard him
breathe, when I felt the pressure of his little fingers, I understood the full force
of Voltaire's declaration "the core of love is a mother's heart".'[12] Diaries show
the delirious joy of Victorian women after delivery. 'May God be praised for
his great mercy in having so richly blest us', wrote Clarissa Bramston in 1841,
on the birth of a second daughter, 'for having made us so very happy in each
other, for having given us our most precious children . . . our cup is indeed
full.' 'No wonder will describe the feelings of those first few minutes and of
all those hours', concluded Frederica Orlebar in her account of her baby's
birth in 1863, 'it is too holy and tender a piece of feeling for any but a mother
to understand . . . how utterly happy it makes her and how she thanks it for
coming into the world.'[13]

There were growing expectations, in the period from 1650 to 1850, that the
good mother would breastfeed her own baby.[14] Amanda Vickery found

women, well up with expert opinion on suckling and weaning, who in many cases did breastfeed rather than resort to wet nurses. They discussed the issues avidly in their correspondence.[15] Carole Williams found that the majority of Victorian mothers successfully fed their babies, arguing that 'the capability to breastfeed was the first opportunity for mothers to exhibit their maternal capacity to the outside world and to contribute to establishing inner confidence and a maternal bond'.[16] It was through regular feeding that mothers made intimate contact with their babies, internalising the notion that they were the most important person in the baby's life, however far the menial tasks of motherhood were carried by their staff.

Building on the notion that breast milk was the child's best nourishment, Kate Retford explains, suckling became fashionable in Georgian England, 'reconfigured as a satisfying task that would not only benefit the child and the parental relationship but also provide a source of unlimited satisfaction'. At the same time, the subject brought the clash between idealised womanhood and sexuality to the fore. Portraitists could do no more than hint at this motherly duty, as Sir Joshua Reynolds did with superb aplomb in his 1773 work *Lady Cockburn and her Three Eldest Sons*. Lady Cockburn's youngest boy is portrayed at the breast, her creamy white dress blending smoothly into her skin and concealing her nipple. This portrait made a powerful impact as prescriptive propaganda entirely by implication. Mothers took the message to heart.[17]

Thus inability to feed a child could depress a mother. Frederica Orlebar was frank in her diary about feeling wretched, 'when the wet nurse came and gradually I watched the child's opening mouth turn towards her'. She worried that the maternal bond was much stronger with her second boy, Beauchamp, born in May 1863, who she did nurse, than with her first, Rouse, who she did not: 'how could I help loving him best when I nursed him and so had to fondle the little creature for hours on my arm'. Beauchamp basked in Frederica's immediate and enduring love. But she nearly wore herself out with feeding this little boy five times a day. She had to retreat from her husband to the sea, with boys and nurses, to convalesce in August 1863. When, the next month, she reluctantly agreed to wean Beauchamp, her health improved at once.[18]

Women's diaries show the very great pressures on their time that leisured women were under, given their expected roles of mistress of the household, social companion to a husband and visitor to the local poor. Even if blessed, as under the circumstances of multiple pregnancies many were not, with good health, they simply could not fulfil their obligations without adequate help.[19] Reviewing the lives of three Lancashire women, Elizabeth Parker, Jane Scrimshire and Bessy Ramsden, between 1753 and 1775, Amanda Vickery concluded that 'motherhood devoured almost all reserves of physical and emotional energy for at the very least a decade of a fertile woman's life'. 'Mrs Ramsden was called up to her nursery or she would not have left off so abruptly', pleaded her husband William, completing a half-finished letter in the 1760s. Jane Scrimshire and Elizabeth Parker accepted postponement of longed-for cross-country visits to each other in Lancashire, while they were nursing their infants.[20]

There was huge diversity of practice in the employment of nursery servants. Mothers had the matter constantly under review. In Lancashire in the 1780s, Betty Parker employed a full-time nurse for round the clock care of her infant, enabling her to pursue a comparatively lively social life. Ellen Parker found her nursemaids a chronic source of anxiety in the 1820s, when she doubted the strength of mind of some of them to manage her increasingly turbulent brood of five, suspecting neglect or outright cruelty when her back was turned.[21]

In Queen Victoria's reign, it became common to employ a nanny and under-nurse once there was more than one child. Mothers entrusted their treasured children to untried staff with trepidation, even when they came with sound references. 'It is an awful and a solemn moment when one entrusts one's child to the tuition and guidance of a stranger', wrote Clarissa Bramston in 1841.[22] Mothers resorted to intensive direction and supervision of nurse-maids, as they sought to ensure their children's care, yet to give themselves some scope for a life outside the nursery. They always risked transfer of emotional dependence. 'I don't love you Mummy, I'm sure I don't', insisted Tom Bosworth, when his nurse Clare cried 'very sadly', tucking the children up for the last time.[23]

Some did achieve a good balance between the roles of mother, mistress of the household and wife. Between 1878 and 1882, for example, Freda Lorraine produced, nursed and cared for four children, while keeping up her own busy social schedule. She was supported by relatively high numbers of nursery staff and an exceedingly participant husband. She was a fully caring mother, regu-larly taking an unwell child into her bed to sleep, despite the extra tiredness this involved. This pride, enjoyment and interest in their babies among mothers pervaded the Victorian period.[24]

The ultimate control and management of the nursery, as well as of the schoolroom, rested with the mother. This was common ground from the seventeenth century to the twentieth. Nurseries were often mentioned in country house inventories from around 1600.[25] Sir John Mordaunt extended the nursery at Walton around 1700, enabling Penelope to put this aspect of the household on a proper basis, with staff to manage the children day-to-day. Her memorandum for her nursery maid, on the routine for Pen and Kate, is a highly illuminating, possibly a unique, document from this period:

As soon as they are up and their cots laid, to say their prayers, then hear them their catechism and after to eat their breakfast; then dress their heads and when that is done bring them down to ask blessing; three times a week hear them their psalms, Kate her creed every Saturday to get them perfect; every Monday cut their nails; when you have dined come into the parlour for them to go up to their books; hear them both read and then you are to get their tasks that their Mistress sets them until 6 o'clock; then you may play but not daly themselves; Kate to go to bed at 8 o'clock and Pen at 9.

If there was time when the governess had finished with the children before dinner, the nursery maid should do needlework with them. Penelope Mordaunt's stress on regularity and structure became a standard motherly tactic.[26]

Mothers dedicated themselves to the moral and spiritual education of their children. Kenneth Charlton amassed massive evidence of this commitment, the very essence of their maternity, from seventeenth-century papers and there is much more for the eighteenth century. Lucy Thornton of Little Wratling in Suffolk was portrayed, at her funeral in 1619, in the tract 'A Pattern for Women', as having instructed her children through morning and evening prayers, psalm singing and reading from the scriptures. Oliver Heywood, born in 1630, recalling his early years, spoke of how his mother 'was continually putting us upon reading the scriptures and good books and instructed us how to pray'. 'It was her constant concern when my father was gone to London to make all her children pray'. Sir Henry Slingsby recorded that his wife taught their daughter Barbara so carefully, before she was five years old, that she was then, in 1638, 'able already to say all her prayers, answer her catechism, read and write a little'.

Sir John Bramston explained that his wife Alice, who died in 1647, 'a most careful and indulgent mother to her children, instructed them in the church catechism, teaching them the Lord's Prayer, the Ten Commandments and the Creed, which she heard them say constantly every morning'. Lady Alice Lucy, the preacher of her funeral sermon the following year related, normally had had one of her children read a passage of the Bible to the others before supper, 'frequently taking occasion of instilling into them some sweet and profitable instructions'. 'She had the bowels of a tender mother', declared the preacher when Anne Terry died in 1693, 'with the souls as well as the bodies of her dear children and did endeavour by counsel and instruction to instil in them the principles of true godliness.' Lady Rachel Russell, writing to her children aged eleven to seventeen in 1701, commended the Bible as their daily vade mecum: 'be constant in reading of it, and use yourself to make some use of what you read; before you lay away the book, consider what virtue is recommended or what vice is forbid or what doctrines taught in that chapter you have there read'.

Mothers were equally sedulous in teaching their little ones to read, the *sine qua non* of their spiritual progress. Margaret Boate was so successful in this with her daughter, born in 1646, that 'in a few weeks the child had perfectly learned all her letters and the spelling of all single syllables, with a good progress towards the spelling of more compounded ones'. Lady Elizabeth Delaval, born in 1649, and the presbyterian divine Edmund Calamy, born in 1671, were among many who testified to their mother's pains with their reading. Susanna Wesley, who married Samuel Wesley in 1690, detailed the procedure with her children:

> Samuel the first taught, learned the alphabet in a few hours . . . and as soon as he knew the letters began at the first chapter of Genesis. He was taught to spell the first verse then to read it over and over till he could read it offhand and without any hesitation and so on the second verse . . . the same method was used by them all.

Many mothers read stories to their children to show, as Roger North put it, recalling his childhood, 'how virtue may be mixed with delight'. When he and his siblings begged their mother for a story on Sundays, she complied, with the insistence that 'it must be a Sunday one as she called it'. They found her scriptural tales 'more pleasing to us because more admirable and extraordinary than others'.[27]

The overwhelming sense of the seventeenth century's intensive maternal upbringing is of religiosity, duty and seriousness. Roger North's account of his upbringing, taken as a whole, is paradigmatic. 'The government of us was in general severe but tender: our mother maintained her authority and yet condescended to entertain us.' He stresses, because the memory of it remained strong, how she could be 'fluent and pungent' in reproof, as well as demonstrably affectionate. He and his brothers tested the boundaries. He characterised their naughtiness in terms of their 'stubborn spirits': 'we would often set ourselves up and try the experiment but she would reduce us to terms by the smart of correction'. The humiliation of being made to stop crying and ritualistically thank 'the good rail' remained a vivid memory.[28]

Once Lockean teaching balanced the dire precepts of Protestantism, by inculcating respect for human pliability and potential, a new world of mothering was opened. Mothers came to believe that they were expected, and allowed, to revel in the joy of their children. They now saw it as entirely acceptable to show them off. In Glamorgan in the 1730s, Julia Mackworth was 'content to play with them all day long, for though it be ninny, 'tis very natural and quite in her character'.[29]

Lady Maria Stanley enjoyed her children at Alderley Hall in the first years of the nineteenth century. Lucy was 'always in motion', she wrote to her cousin Serena on 6 April 1800, 'and wanting to be where she is not and as complete a little Stanley as you can imagine in eyes, eyebrows and complexion'. She was 'the liveliest looking animal you ever saw', Lady Maria declared that November. But, at two and three, respectively, she was finding Lucy and her sister Rianette exhausting. 'I am not equal to having them all day with me', she confessed, 'nor have I patience to teach.' But the next January she told her sister Louisa that 'Rianette and I get on tolerably well considering my want of patience and her want of application.' She had acquired 'a delightful new-invented spelling book', which made their studies easier.

Within another year the demands upon Maria grew, her twin boys Edward and William coming along to join the nursery. Basking in the success of rearing boys as well as girls, she told Serena in 1804 that the twins were 'the greatest darlings possible', adding that 'had they had the misfortune to be girls they would be thought nice clever babies'. More girls did follow and Maria revelled in them: Alethea born in 1805 was 'a very nice little thing' and Maude, born in 1806, was 'quite a beauty'. Yet Lady Maria knew that, in her husband's eyes, it was the boys, and above all the heir, who counted. 'My lord was much pleased with Teddy's manliness and spirit', she wrote on 29 October 1807. 'The chicks fight, kick and cuff', she confessed next April. 'The future hero Edward is a troublesome boy as needs be.'[30]

'Alfie is such a bright little sunbeam', Caroline Head told her mother in 1879, 'I think he is one of those children that will always be good.' He loved his toddler games: 'being a lamplighter, or engine driver, or coal man or man with organ and monkey'. She enjoyed his imaginative mind and his being a 'chatterbox'.[31]

Motherly pride flowed from genteel women's letters. 'Little Tom is a wonderful favourite and most excessively admired', wrote Eugenia Freemantle in self-congratulation in 1801, after taking him to Stowe: 'he is a good little boy and much more sensible and cleverer than Lord Cobham'.[32] Tom had 'said his prayers and lessons daily to nurse, taken his chalybeate regularly, he does not eat like a ploughboy', Anastasia Fletcher told her sister around 1818. She was thrilled at how his eyes had sparkled on spying, coming through the hall, a hat dripping with rain: expecting his Papa, he 'looked up at me with a most enquiring countenance'.[33] It became common on social occasions for mothers to boost their own self-esteem by showing children off.

But mothers also risked losing face by misbehaviour. 'I am so grieved at his shyness and naughtiness before strangers', declared Matilda Bosworth, as she told of her Tom being sent out of the room in disgrace at just under two in 1884. 'I fear people must think him a most objectionable and badly trained child.'[34]

Less obsessed, after 1700, with the notion of original sin, mothers believed that constant vigilance, within a deeply loving relationship, was the core of their duty in inculcating sound moral values. With both boys and girls, they were constantly having to judge when to be mild and when authoritative. Some women thought girls less preferred, 'for fear of the disgrace which attends their misbehaviour and ill conduct, whereas boys could scarce do anything the world esteemed a fault'.[35]

A mother knew that quite soon she would send a son off into the world. Many stood in some degree of awe of the little person who was heir to the estate. They were often particularly besotted with the first son. In this sense, the most unfortunate child was the female first-born on a great estate, whose displacement when a boy came along was especially rancorous. This was the experience of Viola Bankes in Dorset. She had a vague and bitter intimation of her own future at two years old, when, with oxen roasted, bonfires lit and fireworks exploded, her brother Ralph was welcomed into the world, and excitement at his birth flooded the estate at Kingston Lacy. Nanny slept with Ralph; nursery maids looked after the girls.

Viola quickly learnt her place: 'we watched him grow out of the domineering vulnerability of babyhood, when he was corrected, pampered and protected into a self sufficient strong little toddler, solid and very masculine, despite his golden curls'. Viola recalled her childhood as a saga of the dissatisfaction that she caused her mother, while Ralph could do no wrong. 'I was continually being scolded for being in a hurry, running and upsetting food instead of acting with dignity and decorum.' At seventeen, the effect of her mother's presence had become daunting and her expectations at balls fearsome.[36]

Yet, in those early years, boys were often especially difficult. Mothers had to allow a boy to test his strength, to be assertive, even, up to a point, to run wild. At the same time, she had to cope with his high spirits, control and manage him, with few weapons beyond the strength of her personality at her command. Carole Williams found 'maternal desire not to crush a child's will but to mould, channel and direct'. There was very little reference to spanking by her diarists. Linda Pollock believed, analysing numerous diaries, that many parents sought a middle way between severity and lenience. Though she concluded that more parents beat their children at home in the nineteenth century than in the eighteenth, she adduced little specific evidence of actual corporal punishment, rather than threats about it, in either century.[37] Mary Carberry remembered the birch rod that hung as an ornament in her nursery in the 1870s: 'if Harry shows signs of being a young turk Nanny had only to glance at it'. It was never used.[38]

Henry Crabb Robinson, growing up in the 1770s and 1780s, was grateful to his mother for his happy childhood. Its only real trial was chapel twice on Sundays with the problem, for a small bored youngster, of sitting still for an age. 'I was often sent to bed without supper for bad behaviour at Meeting', he recalled. The only spanking his mother gave him was for naughtiness there. But this was trivial in comparison to the way he benefited from her instruction. 'Henry, don't take any more, do you not suppose the maids like to have some?' she would say, when there was a particularly nice pudding or pie on the table. Ascribing 'every good moral or religious feeling' he had in childhood to her, he explained: 'A respect and attention to servants and inferiors was a constant lesson, and if I have any kindness and humanity in my ordinary feelings I ascribe it all to her, and very much to this particular lesson.'[39]

May Williams, born in 1803, the sixth child of Sir John Williams of Boddlewyddan in North Wales, wrote an account of her life in her 80s, which included testimony to her mother's wise handling of her. She remembered her as 'the most perfect character, not to be bettered and hardly to be equalled'. 'She had us every morning to read the psalms', she recalled, explaining the schoolroom routine with her younger sister. 'She was always instilling good in us', May declared: 'when she had occasion to reprove us she did it in so sweet and gentle a manner you could not help (at least I could not) putting your arms round her neck and kissing her with your eyes full of tears and your heart full of repentance'.[40]

A Colchester mother, Maria Marsh, regarded the moral training of her children as a sacred duty. When a child was disobedient, she would take the offender into her own room and point out the sin committed, 'how grievous it was in the sight of God and how painful to her'. They then knelt and prayed together.[41] When Edward Allen hit his brother Stanny in 1846, his mother called him upstairs 'to me in my room and, whilst wondering how best I could bring home the grief I felt, I was touched by the penitent look on his face . . . and when tears ran down his cheeks and he seemed repentant I knelt with him and sought forgiveness'. Downstairs again, the boys kissed and she was glad she had not taken 'severer measures'.[42]

Lucy Lyttelton recalled the kind of naughtiness, acts like pilfering plum pudding and cutting off a front lock of her hair saying her brother had done it, for which her mother reserved a special ritual of humiliation in the 1840s. This was 'taking us into Papa's room and putting our small tender hands under a thing for pressing letters together; a bronze hand it was which pinched us slightly, leaving the dents of the fingers on the back of one's hand'. Lucy felt the disgrace of this procedure deeply, 'it being performed very solemnly, Mama shaking her head at us all the time'. Its impact can be judged by her conviction, each time, that 'I should never lose the marks'.[43]

Frederica Orlebar was another mother who was as ingenious as Mary Lyttleton in exerting control without resorting to spanking. She used kisses to soften maternal discipline. If her child was in a rage, she noted, 'I threatened very decidedly to punish him if he were not good in a few minutes and then I set him with his back towards the room to recover, always taking the precaution of kissing him first.' Then 'his voice and face changed' and the fit of temper passed. She sometimes tied her boy Beauchamp to a tree with a rope and left him with his gardening tools in a defined space. She checked on him from a window and was gratified by the obedience he displayed.[44]

A single crucial event was overwhelmingly important in the development of boyhood, a moment of pride that was regularly recorded for this reason. This was the ceremonial abandonment of female dress with the ritual of breeching. Ann North's account of the breeching of her grandson Frank in 1639 is paradigmatic: 'You cannot believe the great concern that was in the whole family here last Wednesday, it being the day the tailor was to help dress little Frank in his breeches . . . When he was quite dressed he acted his part as well as any of them.' Henry Slingsby's breeching in 1641 was pushed forward after his father, at his mother's prompting, had sent for the clothes, including a doublet, from his London tailor. He was seen as fully young for it, at five years old, but she had 'a desire to see him in them, how proper a man he would be'.[45] In London, at much this time, John Greene sent his son to school at five and had him in breeches the same year.[46] John Josselin was 'put in breeches' in 1657 just after his sixth birthday: 'I never saw two sons so clad before', Ralph exclaimed, with his older boy in mind.[47]

Breeching continued into the nineteenth century. But in the Victorian period it was a conservative hangover from the past, carrying much less symbolic significance than it had done before. Yet mothers still thought it worth recording. Eugenia Freemantle commented, in 1801, when Tom was three, that he had 'changed his dress today and looks very pretty in his Nankeen jacket and trousers'.[48] But so did fathers. Phil Holt was described by his father in 1882, when he was six, as 'looking very sturdy and well: he struts about in his knickerbockers and speaks in a deep important voice and gives himself such airs that he constantly makes us laugh'.[49]

Motherhood was a social, moral, religious and academic role which required intelligence as well as good sense. Mary Wollstonecraft, noting that 'the formation of the mind' lay in a mother's power, argued that this motherly duty afforded 'many forcible arguments for strengthening female understanding'. She campaigned for improved education for women, since this would lead in turn to improved children, reared by properly educated women.[50]

Anna Larpent, a cosmopolitan figure married to a successful civil servant, was a pious Anglican who brought up two children of her own and a stepson in London. She devised 'stated times' for her children's regular study, even in infancy. She was almost a model mother, setting her own standards and disagreeing with some fashionable educational theory, always ready to hear her children read and spell. In the 1790s, Amanda Vickery notes her spending 'countless afternoons escorting them round educational exhibitions and panoramas'. 'I never found my children troublesome', she boasted, 'I always tried to feed their minds as well as their bodies . . . by encouraging observation and interest in what they see and by early giving them an idea of getting information.'[51]

The prescriptive requirement for mothers to teach their children was expressed in portraits of breeched boys in the eighteenth century, such as that of the Countess of Pembroke with her son George. Here we have an upright six-year old, with his book open in his hand, while his mother protectively clasps his shoulder.[52] Even more vivid evidence of the dedication of a mother to her children's learning lies in the remarkable 438-piece nursery library made by Jane Johnson, wife of the vicar of Olney in Buckinghamshire, as she reared her four children, Barbara, George, Robert and Charles during the 1740s and 1750s. The centrepiece of this collection is 24 hand-made sets of instructional materials.

Jane's collection includes alphabet cards, with illustrations based in the child's world of play and work in familiar surroundings. There are word cards, merging shape and colour in invitations to children to create their own vocabulary and word-building games. There are lesson cards with paraphrases of bible verses. Jane's children had their learning made into fun by her ingenuity. But her didactic intent is entirely explicit. Her children learnt the perils of lying, stealing and being lazy. Her strong values, in a firm Lockean mode, were ones of industry and good behaviour.[53]

The pocket book schoolroom diaries kept by the mother of Henry Pease of Darlington, when he was five, shows how entirely traditional the basic maternal curriculum still was in mid-Victorian England. Henry practised writing, repeated psalms, pointed out English counties and towns learnt by rote and attempted to make sentences to show his understanding of the parts of speech. His mother made him repeat the Commandments, write to his Papa and his grandfather and begin French prose. Making a scrapbook and dressing the Noah's Ark were diversions from this taxing programme. Starting a new round of lessons at seven in January 1846, she noted that it was Henry's wish 'such a book may be kept' recording their progress and hoping 'it will be better than the old one'.[54]

Many mothers, interested in contemporary theories about children's education, read very widely indeed. They were often eclectic about their own practice. Thus Mary Talbot was keen on the one hand on Rousseau's teaching about bringing children up in the country but also, on the other, on Hannah More's evangelical and academic ambitions for them. She discussed upbringing at length with her governess Agnes Porter, who early in her career, had copied a passage from More into her extract book. This downplayed fashionable accomplishments: 'the end of a good education is not that they become dancers, singers, players or painters, but to make them good daughters, good wives, good Christians'.[55]

From the middle of the eighteenth century onwards, when the modern ideology of motherhood was fully established, genteel mothers across the land were self-conscious about their performance, feeding husbands and relatives with accounts of their children's 'improvement'. Lady Sarah Lennox was one of the new generation of mothers, who showed confidence in the adults their children would become. She studied as they became older, she told a daughter-in-law, in 1820 'to become their friend': 'in me they trusted to find sympathy, kindness, my opinion or advice if they sought it'. Left to decide on their own actions, she believed, they were 'somewhat of the hue of what they had just heard'.[56]

Yet mothers often found it hard not to be clinging. Her little Tom, aged three, wrote Mrs Powys in 1771, 'at the distance he now is from me makes me feel for him each moment, lest he should not be well as I left him'. Georgiana, Duchess of Devonshire, living a hectic social life, spoke in 1793 about getting up early 'to see the children sooner'. 'I have been interrupted', she noted in 1796, 'by the dear children saying "hear my prayers" with their dear little touching voices.'[57]

The insistent theme of this mothering was often loss, as little ones grew up and flew the nest, hardened by schooling and the world, or accepting the imperative to marry and beget their own children. However, as Melesina Trench mused in 1823, grown children at a distance brought their parents new pleasures of the highest order: 'an unexpected letter, the conversation of a stranger who has seen one's child within a short space of time, the know-ledge of their progress in virtue, intellect and even in worldly prosperity . . . and the rapture of reunion'.[58] 'Alfie is in high frocks and wishing for cloth trousers and I miss the soft bare arms, the last relic of babyhood' wrote Hannah Allen in a letter in 1862.[59] Mary Brabazon reflected in 1882 on her son Normy's final discarding of childish clothing and putting on 'manly attire' at thirteen: 'it made me realise . . . that I must very soon bid him farewell. It is sad to feel his childhood is passing away.'[60]

Given the sparse documentation of motherly practice, fuller assessment of performance has to be impressionistic. This is why the next chapter is devoted to twelve case studies, between 1750 and 1900, which illustrate the particularities of domestic life for women bringing up children. Overall, the story of maternity becomes one of remarkable and consistent dedication by thousands of women, who felt deeply its ideals, daily experienced its strivings, and dedicated themselves to the pursuit of their maternal love.

9

Motherly Performance

Mothers thought about the work of bringing up children as performance. From early in the eighteenth century, inspired by the notion
of a blank sheet on which they could inscribe the makings of adulthood, they began to write about their performance in letters and diaries. They
were measuring their own efforts against orthodox notions of a proper
upbringing, imbibed from the conduct books that they often pondered over
and from their social converse. They were seeking to reassure themselves that
the long-lasting influence of their care and tuition would prove beneficial.
They were seeking solace in difficulties or over their disappointments. They
believed that their own status in the community, besides their self-esteem,
depended on the demonstration of effective motherhood. The task of
mothering, they found, needed constant reassessment, as children grew in
years.

Lady Anne Cust was left with a brood of nine, ranging in age from two to
sixteen, at her husband's death in 1734. She had been brought up at Belton
House, moving to a town house in Grantham when her brother inherited the
family home. A fascinating and instructive family group by Enoch Seeman is
still at Belton. It exemplifies dynastic progression, showing Anne, with her
brother and eldest son, who as Sir John Cust, was Speaker of the House of
Commons, beside her, and all her children looking self-consciously adult. It
was probably painted in about 1744, when Lucy, the youngest, was twelve. In
a further dynastic touch, as Kate Retford has noted, Anne Cust's deceased
husband, Sir Richard, appears in the guise of a head and shoulders portrait of
him as a boy, based upon the full length portrait of him in infancy which is
also at Belton.[1]

The Cust letters exemplify mid-eighteenth-century domesticity: a strong
woman, with the help and advice of her first-born, now thrust into adulthood,
oversees the education and progress of her children into the world,
supporting, encouraging, reflecting on her pride in them. An eldest son here

took up the parenting partnership previously established by husband and wife. The depth of Anne's caring and concern is palpable. The test of the family's bonding came in 1748, with the loss of Billy, shown in the recent group portrait, in battle abroad. His brother Percy wrote home about his discussions with Jenny about plans regarding rings in remembrance. In another letter, Jenny, aged 22 by then and staying, as unmarried girls did so often, with cousins, reflected upon the family's cohesion, showing deep affection and concern for Lady Anne at this bereavement:

> knowing how good and tender a parent your Ladyship is to us all made our fears the greater for you; had we not had so much of your good instruction we should not have been so happy one with another and therefore most naturally feel with one another in our distress.

It was natural that Lady Anne should lean on her eldest son Jacky, who was still at Eton when his father died. Two years later, settled in at Cambridge, he was running the family's affairs, urging his mother to build and improve at their Grantham home. Lady Anne, forging a new kind of relationship with him, responded in March 1736. 'Indeed, my dear child', she wrote:

> I have had nothing but trouble and fatigue upon my mind and spirits this last two years; the seeing you take so right a turn in life and your endearing behaviour to me are indeed real comforts and I hope God will reward you for being so good to me, who am, with real love and friendship, your most affectionate mother and sincere friend.

Jacky was steadily drawn into a responsible role towards his younger brothers and sisters. They treated him with considerable deference. At twenty, Lady Anne marked his coming maturity by abandoning the nickname: briefly he was addressed by her simply as 'My Dear', then, of age in 1739, her letters began 'Dear Sir John'. That December he was in chambers studying for the bar. She expressed her pleasure that he was happily settled: 'the credit and comfort you are really to me is more than I can express'. Moving on eleven years, we find Sir John Cust, married, MP for Grantham and making progress in a distinguished political career. Lady Anne has become the besotted grandmother, requesting the 'pretty company' of his boy Brownlow, now, though only five, at boarding school near her in the Midlands.

With four sons, and a grandson by her dutiful eldest, Lady Anne had good cause for confidence in the future of the Cust dynasty. Her pleasure also rested in seeing sons into the world and daughters achieving the social poise that would assure them husbands. Billy, who as we have seen she lost when he was 28, was good at writing home. In 1736 she mentioned a recent letter of his to Jacky, saying that he 'writes like a seaman downright and honest'. The following year she reported 'an exceeding pretty letter from Billy', with 'a great deal of humanity and good nature expressed in a few words' about his uncle's recent death. Franky was cleverer. His mother revelled in his academic success. His progress at Eton and the promise of a place at King's, Cambridge, she reflected in 1736, were 'the charmingst thing we could wish for'. 'He can have no hardship I think to go through', she told Jacky, 'indeed it rejoices me mightily, for if he takes to anything of good ways, he can't now fail of making a good figure in the world.' Later, Franky urged his mother to make his young brother Dicky, then twelve, also 'fit for Eton'. She found this 'good, natural and affectionate of him'.

All the boys had started at the grammar school in Grantham. At fifteen, Percy was apprenticed to a London linen draper. At first, his mother had qualms about this. His letters confirmed how well he ate and drank; if he supported this, she mused, by 'care and industry', he would 'make himself and his friends happy, but many parents were disappointed when they think they have done well for their children'. A couple of months later, she was writing more confidently about Percy's entry 'on a new way of life'. She need not have worried. Jacky kept an eye on him and in 1741 she sent a message via him: 'tell him I do not at all think much to pay postage for his letters for I like them mightily and the last made us laugh heartily'. At his majority, she declared that 'there is no fear of his doing otherwise than well'. These expectations were soon fulfilled, when Percy became a partner in a firm trading with the Continent. Dicky trailed the rest: home for the holidays from Eton in 1744, Lady Anne found him 'quite a comfort to me, he behaves so prettily'. He stood in for Jacky, showing the Cust flag locally, at a male evening at the Grantham tavern; a few days later he was off again, riding his horse south for Eton.

The girls – Betty, Jenny, Dolly and Lucy – of course spent much more time at home. Lady Anne's letters were full of them. Betty – conventionally as the eldest referred to in letters as 'Miss Cust' – was the only one whose health seems to have given concern. In 1745, Lady Anne decided to send her to take the waters at Bath, worrying to her eldest son: 'I never think of her now but my heart aches about her'. But reports from there did not encourage her, so she had her home again, where she was soon 'better and fatter': 'I do really think being here with her sisters and using exercise every fine day is the best chance of recovery.' She believed Betty needed to relax and arranged a visit to relatives, where 'they say she will ride out, walk out and play at shuttlecock just as she pleases'. The substance of Lady Anne's concern about her eldest daughter is indicated by an introspective letter of Betty's in 1742, which made reference to frequent feelings of 'oppression upon my spirits'. At the time of this letter she was back in Lincolnshire, after a period of instruction in polite behaviour in London. Riding and 'airing' most days, she related, had made her 'not a little happy'.[2]

Ten lengthy letters from Selina, Countess of Huntingdon to her husband, the ninth Earl, in May 1743, testify to parental togetherness at a time of exceptional stress. The warmth of her relations with her boys at school shows that Selina was a very good mother. But she had just lost two of these boys, George and Ferdinando, to smallpox, which often ran like wildfire through boarding schools. On 7 May, two of the children had just reached the home where she was staying: 'the little jewels came about an hour ago . . . I was so affected by seeing my dear little Selina'. She was impressed by her improved 'looks and spirits'. Dear Henry, she continued, 'is the charmingest that I beheld, such health and spirits I never saw and so sensible that no admiration can be enough for him'.

But Henry soon fell ill and Selina appeared to be sickening too, causing terror in their mother's heart that she would shortly lose more of her children. 'I wait every moment expecting an appearance of the smallpox', she told her husband on 17 May. Three days later, the Countess was rejoicing at Selina's recovery, this instance of God's 'mercy towards us', and Henry's illness ended in a fever, leaving him 'in high spirits but weak'. 'I beg my jewel will tell my dear little boys', she told the Earl on 20 May 'that I have been so hurried by their brother and sister's illness that they must excuse me for not having wrote to them.' She was 'wearied out with trials', she confessed on 31 May, missing her husband desperately in this crisis. The pain of their being apart when their family was unwell, 'I think no one can conceive'. 'My heart is so set upon you that I have not one happy hour', she reflected after so much distress born away from him, on her own.[3]

The children 'shall be my sole care and study', Frances Boscawen wrote to her husband, Admiral Edward Boscawen: 'my chief purpose and the business of my life shall be to take care of them and to procure for them a sound mind in a healthful body'. He spent only short periods at their home at Hatchlands in Surrey during the years, from 1747 to 1758, when their children were at their most demanding. Edward Boscawen was an absentee father, but kept abreast of the children's progress in a stream of letters from his wife. She had time to write, being well served with nursemaids and hiring a governess for the girls Fanny and Bess and for her little Billy, when her eldest, Ned, went to Eton at the age of nine.[4]

Frances was as good as her word, yet she managed to combine an active social life with her lone parenting. For instance, she enjoyed supping with her two eldest during 1748, 'before I go abroad'. 'Two immense pieces of bread', she explained, 'being sopped in very weak tea are put into different plates for Ned and Fanny.' Ned fed himself 'with great seriousness and solemnity'; Fanny 'jumps and skips and sings'. Then, 'after they are satisfied, *c'est l'etiquette* to have a great game of romps, in the height of which I escape and gain my coach'.[5]

Frances Boscawen presents herself to her husband in terms of the rigour with which she handles her motherly responsibilities. Outings aside, she was totally sincere about this dedication. 'Have no anxious thoughts for the children', she told him in 1747. 'God give me success', she declared.[6] Edward Boscawen was then Commander-in-Chief of the British forces in the East Indies. He rose to be a Lord Commissioner of the Admiralty in 1751, Vice-Admiral in 1755 and Admiral in 1758.[7] Frances saw herself as the devoted spouse of a public-spirited man playing a national role, who could bring him, as she put it in 1748, 'the comfort of three healthful, beautiful and tractable children' each time that he returned from the sea.[8]

Her 1748 formulation of her objectives was accurately reflected in the practice of her motherhood, as Frances Boscawen related this in her letters. The children's health was a constant preoccupation. 'You can imagine the state I was in', she wrote, describing a time when all three children were ill at once, Ned at three, Fanny at 22 months and Bess at nine months, in 1748. 'We had decreed them for the measles', she explained in view of their coughs and fevers. 'For poor Fanny I trembled, her breath and lungs being already so oppressed that 'twas pain to hear her, and the slut would not drink anything, though she was dying of thirst.' '"No, no, no, can't"' was Fanny's cry, as Frances tried in turn tea, 'water with a roast apple mingled with a drop of wine in warm water, milk, jelly'.

Ned, 'the dear boy', took whatever she brought him, 'but then I dreaded a bleeding which would have been necessary in the measles'. He had promised to submit to this if need be. But she doubted whether she could have born this 'and the least signs of fear in me would have inspired and justified his'. Frances wrote all this, declaring 'I have endured a great deal', when the children were better. She thanked 'the gracious providence which has comforted me and cured them'. Ned and Bess had 'now come downstairs'. All three children had been purged 'and tomorrow the two eldest begin asses' milk'.[9]

Frances ensured that her children, following conventional wisdom, had plenty of air and exercise. She excused herself from taking them out in Hyde Park during a stay in London in 1748, deciding ''tis not necessary in this airy Audley Street'. But she was very conscientious about having Fanny called at six o'clock by Nanny Humphries and sent out early, as the doctor ordered: 'he bid me send her out every morning in the early dew that she might outgrow the difference (not inconsiderable) that there is between her two collar bones'.[10]

Frances Boscawen believed that her children were exceptionally beautiful. Her concern, from the start, was with seeing that they were equally well behaved. 'The boy is a most beautiful sleeping cupid', she told Edward in 1747, when Ned was two years old. She accepted that it 'savoured of vanity' to insist that their children were entirely different from his brother George's, but her conclusion rested 'upon so true a foundation that it ought to excite your gratitude'. George's little girl was 'as far from an agreeable child as she is from a pretty one'.

But everyone admired their Ned. When the Marsham boys, a neighbouring family, visited that year, she recognised that they set a standard for the little Boscawens. Charles Marsham had been breeched early, at three, and Frances found herself embarrassed that her Ned was still 'in petticoats'.[11] The Marshams were 'fine children and the best behaved I ever saw, doing everything at a word – and, indeed, at a look – of their father's'. The lesson was not lost on Frances, who redoubled her efforts to do as well, on her own, as the Marsham parents did together.[12]

The fierce competitiveness of Georgian society, where children were concerned, quickly fastened itself on Frances. Her appraisal, for the benefit of her husband, on 11 January 1748 was excessively self-regarding: 'your son maintains his superiority over Neddy Meadows, than whom he is taller by two inches, though the latter is turned five and our jewel is three and a quarter. Bess too is a jewel that has not its fellow – there never was such a girl.' Fanny, not to be left out, even if less blest with looks, was 'a charming little, plump, blue-eyed maid that would pass for a beauty in any house but this'. [13]

By the summer of 1748, the besotted Frances had become triumphalist. After visiting the Mason family, said to boast a tall boy, she found 'this tall boy proved to be half a head shorter than mine to the great astonishment of his father'. Frances noted the contrast between them 'as well in figure as behaviour': 'he did nothing bid, nor minded father nor mother, would not speak to your son nor play with him, whereas mine obeyed my very looks, was very talkative and civil'. Frances's confidence in Ned was undimmed at Lord Romney's in October. 'Your son beats them all to nothing', she announced, towering over the children who were his hosts, older than him, 'in height and learning'. He had 'also been to church every Sunday and has behaved extremely well'.

It was excusable, in her eyes, that Ned should be set back at dancing a 'hornpike', as he called it, before visitors: 'Mama, I'm ashamed, don't ask me to dance.' But he 'loves you excessively and remembers you perfectly', she assured her husband, recalling a spanking when Ned was 'a naughty baby in coats' and sure that, 'now he is a man', his father would not need to beat him. When a colleague of the Admiral's brought them a black boy as a present, clothed in the Boscawen livery 'most handsomely', acting the grown-up in advance, Ned adopted him as his own servant. His page Tom, Frances recounted, 'walks out in the garden with him, plays up in the nursery, waits upon him at table'.

Frances had instituted a strict nursery regime early on. The routine with Ned, at four, was a walk before breakfast and lessons with her after it, 'by which means he has made a considerable progress since we came into the country, and, if he had but half as much application as he has genius and capacity, he would read soon. But this same application is an ingredient seldom found in such a sprightly cub.' Ned's fantasy play was naturally naval. 'Dear dear Papa, pray come home, I have made you a great many ships to come in and Mama says you will bring me something pretty', he wrote to his father at almost four. By nine years old, Frances accepted that he needed the exterior discipline of Eton. His holiday play now focused upon flags and flagstaffs, building castles and 'a battery of eight brass canon mounted on wooden carriages'.

The gender imperatives of Georgian society predictably dominated the Boscawen upbringings. While the boys' play was all action, the girls learnt their needlework, under tuition from the governess. At that moment, wrote Frances to Edward on one occasion, they were sitting by her, 'hemming pocket handkerchiefs for Mr Billy's coat pocket'. Budding femininity in the girls was commented upon beside the masculinity of her boys. 'If you hum a tune instantly she seizes her frock at each side and falls a-dancing', Frances wrote of Bess. She was well pleased with the regime she and the governess managed, in tandem, for her daughters Fanny and Bess in 1755. The girls were 'much improved both in persons, manners, speech, behaviour', she assured her husband in 1756. Two years later, at twelve and ten, they were still at home under her eye and there was still a governess in residence.[14]

Frances Boscawen was undoubtedly an effective mother, consistent in her efforts to make all her children 'tractable'. Once, with Billy, she did show signs of an iron hand in a velvet glove. She had been soft on him over the period of his inoculation, she wrote to her husband in June 1755, but now it was a case of purging discipline: 'how perverse and saucy we are and how much we deal in the words won't, can't, shan't etcetera . . . the rod and I went to breakfast with him and though we did not come into action . . . the bottom of the porringer was very fairly revealed'.[15]

Hester Thrale was brought up precociously, 'taught to read and speak and think and translate from the French till I was half a prodigy'. She made herself very unhappy trying to reproduce this in her children, when she married a wealthy brewer in 1763. She became an inveterate chronicler of her motherly performance. Reflecting in 1778 upon her own character as a mother, her temper, she explained, was 'warm even to irascibility, affectionate and tender, but claiming such returns to her tenderness and affection as busy people have no time to pay . . . by nature a rancorous and revengeful enemy'.[16] These busy people, to her mind, included her own children, who should have known better. Twelve times between 1764 and 1778 she gave birth, but five of her children lived for less than two years.

From 1766 to 1778, Hester Thrale kept her Children's Book, the fullest and most intimate record of family life in the eighteenth century that we have but, at the same time, the most depressing.[17] Linda Pollock called her an intrusive mother. Lawrence Stone reflected upon 'her selfish ambition to make her children exceptional in their learning and achievements', which alienated them from her. Hester's obsessive documentation reflected almost entirely upon her incessant demands as a parent and hardly at all upon display of the affection that she claimed to have in her heart.[18] Deprived of support by a husband who followed his business and his own fine social life, literature, she declared, was her only resource, so 'no wonder if I loved my books and my children'.[19]

Hester Thrale set her first-born, christened Hester but always called Queenie, a hectic pace in rote learning: at two it was letters and little words, arithmetic, the Pater Noster and signs of the Zodiac; at three she was thrown into geography; at four she was reading, repeating her catechism and starting on her Latin grammar. And so it went on. On her ninth birthday, her mother noted that Queenie's knowledge of English literature was 'clear and compendious'. But the impact of this pressure on the relationship of mother and daughter was catastrophic. Treating her like a show animal and setting herself to create a child prodigy, Hester Thrale found herself faced with a child who she found thoroughly disagreeable. The relationship between mother and daughter became impossibly competitive.

The girl had become, Hester noted on Queenie's sixth birthday, 'reserved and shy with a considerable share of obstinacy'. No punishment, she concluded, reflecting on the spankings she regularly delivered, 'except severe smart can prevail upon her to beg pardon if she has offended'. By the time she was ten, things were worse. Voluble behind her back as she knew, Hester now characterised her eldest daughter as 'sullen, malicious and perverse, desirous of tormenting me even by hurting herself and resolute to utter nothing in my hearing that might give credit to either of us'. Four years later, surveying her life and how she was valued, Hester had become convinced that Queenie 'would doubtless consider her mother's death as a riddance from company she cannot like but is obliged to keep some hours every day'. She had always praised her for her elegance and looks. She declared that, even now, she respected her eldest girl's sincerity. Yet, she wrote plaintively, 'she does not even pretend to love me'.[20]

There was more spontaneity in Hester's pride in her son Harry, the apple of her eye until his early death at nine. He was breeched at two-and-a-quarter, his mother admiring his strength, proportions and 'sweet temper'. He showed, she believed, 'charity, piety, benevolence', even 'a desire for knowledge'. A note on his fourth birthday enthused about his Latin and his reading of the psalms, 'quite smartly, seldom stopping to spell his way'. She revelled in his masculinity, at that time, finding him:

> manly to a most uncommon degree, with regard to general power of self assistance; he lies all alone, bare-headed, buttons his own clothes on and needs no help either at eating or emptying any more than his father does. He bids fair with God's blessing to be a noble fellow.

She asked him that day 'if he remembered ever wearing petticoats and he said no, not the least'. Harry's childhood was systematically abolished, as his mother drove him along the road to manhood.

At six and seven, Harry's lead was lengthened at home but, at the same time, he was still regularly spanked for naughtiness, which meant boyish exploits like jumping ditches and climbing trees. At seven, now under magisterial care at school in Southwark, his mother boasted that he was perpetually passing by in learning boys of ten years old. She alleged that he was adored for his qualities of character. But she soon decided school was putting the precocious boy above himself, recording when he was eight: 'I have heard of my son's naughtiness: it consisted in telling his school fellows a staring story about what was done at a bawdy house, for which conversation Old Penny very wisely flogged him well and I hope we shall hear no more of it.' About that time she heard, to her horror, that, without her prompting, Harry had been reading, and had enjoyed, *Tom Jones* and *Joseph Andrews*.[21]

Hester Thrale was a pessimist about her children surviving as toddlers, let alone into adulthood. She was caustic about sickliness, noting that she had never hoped to rear Anna, when she died at just under two. Her mother had taken charge of the sickly infant being, she confessed, 'well inclined to spoil her and make her think herself something extraordinary'. At three, she found Susanna's colour 'like that of a clorotic virgin at fifteen': 'her temper is so peevish and her person so displeasing that I do not love to converse with her'. The next year Susanna, nicknamed at home 'the little crab', was sent off at the age of four to a fashionable boarding school in Kensington, her mother expecting academic improvement. In fact, whereas at home the girl was 'not exceedingly admired' and would not learn 'because she must not be fretted', Susanna flowered at school. By her ninth birthday, she had won praise from

Hester, for reading French comedies 'to divert herself' and for her knowledge of poetry, arithmetic and geography.

Sophie had an easier time than the older girls. She was healthy, which helped a good deal. She managed to please her mother, at under four, by learning Italian words inculcated by a tutor, by her multiplication and by her knowledge of the catechism. Queenie, seven years her senior, was hauled in to teach her and she was soon learning 'long strings of stuff by heart'. But Hester was now wearied by the pace she had set both herself and her children. Within a year, in 1776, she lost three of her six children. Her Lucy, 'so lively one cannot resist her coaxing', died at four and Harry, her talented and amiable only son and heir, at nine. She was thoroughly disillusioned: 'I have really listened to babies learning till I am, half stupefied – and all my pains have answered so poorly.' 'At present', she felt, 'I cannot begin battling with babies; I have already spent my whole youth at it and lost my reward at last.' Two of her surviving daughters were sullen and hostile to their mother. Sophie, she believed, 'would probably learn very well, if I had the spirit of teaching I once had'.

Defeated, Hester Thrale now pushed the survivors off to school and turned to her literary pursuits in the bluestocking coterie of London. Her tempestuous and exacting mothering had hardly been a success, yet Sophie remained an undoubted source of joy. 'She has a sweetness of disposition', Hester saw, 'which no child of mine ever had but my lovely Lucy'. By 1777, worn down by motherhood, Hester Thrale may have wished she could find in herself the same sweetness of temperament that she recognised in two of her children. She had been quite extraordinarily demanding. For more than a dozen years, she tried almost too hard. Ambitious for their academic prowess and strict over discipline, her expectations of her children had simply been excessive.[22]

The marriage of Philip Francis and Betsy Mackrabie in 1761 was a love match. Their affectionate family life between 1763 and 1772 centred upon their son and five daughters. But Philip then abandoned a boring job in the War Office and went off on a trip to Europe. Here was a man who was openly caring to his family, writing 'love to the chickens' from Europe in 1773, yet who became taken up with ambition and a career abroad. Travelling in England on his return, he sent love 'to the bairns', begging his wife to 'kiss them in my name repeatedly'. But then, in 1774, he set sail more permanently, with an appointment on the Council of India, leaving a desolate wife, whose letters provide an incomparable record of motherly devotion against the odds. 'If it was possible, I love you more than ever', Betsy Francis wrote to Philip in 1777, after three years of his absence, dedicating herself to the lone parenthood she found to be her lot. 'I wept for four hours', she recorded on 30 March 1781, the seventh anniversary of his departure from England.[23]

Before leaving home, Philip Francis settled his son Philip, then only six, in a small London school run by Mr Ribouville. His attitude towards discipline was exceptionally enlightened for this time. 'Since it is my purpose to make him a gentleman, which includes the idea of a liberal character and sentiment', he wrote, 'I cannot think it consistent with that purpose to have him brought up under the servile discipline of the rod. I absolutely forbid the use of blows.' She should see their son frequently, Philip directed his wife, and tell 'Mr Ribouville freely anything you think amiss'. Betsy Francis established a good relationship with Ribouville, finding Philip, much as she loved him, a handful in the holidays. He was reading 'pretty well', though, she reported in the first holiday. Ribouville and his female assistant were 'worthy good people and if they have a fault 'tis being too indulgent'. Philip danced well, was a good French scholar and improved in every way in 1775. 'I keep him very genteel', Betsy Francis wrote in 1776, with two new suits a year.

Philip Francis left his wife very firm instructions about the social training of his five girls, aged from one to eleven in 1774, at home in Fulham. His precepts are interesting and paradigmatic:

> Let the girls be taught a grave, modest, reserved carriage. I dislike hoydens. Keep them constantly in your company when from school and observe everything they do. Let them have exercise abroad and constant occupation at home. Take care what books they read and if you take them to a play, which not above once a winter, let it be some ridiculous comedy or pantomime, at which they may laugh, but nothing sentimental or that borders upon indecorous. Above all things never suffer them to be idle. The older they grow the more necessary you will find this rule to be.[24]

Betsy Francis sought to fulfil this exacting agenda precisely, sending Philip instalments of a journal of the family's life over the next seven years. She created a happy and relaxed domestic atmosphere. Since, during her husband's absence from 1774 to 1781, the family moved to Harley Street, the correspondence provides a full account of their standard of living. The new accommodation included hall, parlour, dining room, drawing room, a servants' hall, housekeeper's room and butler's pantry; there was also stabling for five horses. Betsy ran this home, as she had done the more modest Fulham one, with confidence, though she acknowledged that it was hard work. There was no time for card parties, she told her husband: 'my girls are enough employment for me'. When she was on a visit to Tonbridge Wells in the summer of 1774, little Kitty was brought down by her maid to visit. 'The child talks for ever', she related, 'her joy was so great at seeing me she could hardly express it. Kissed and hugged me all over.'

On 11 January 1775, Betsy recorded that the girls were 'well and good': 'we read, work, dance and play in turn and are very happy'. Tom the cat, she noted another day, 'mews his duty'. Predictably, with five girls moving into and through adolescence, there were some health worries. Sally, for example, was prescribed salt water bathing in 1778. But there were no crises. Betsy accepted childish rumbustiousness. With her son Philip home at Whitsun in 1774, she noted 'a constant noise with the six, but if I am not very well I keep upstairs in my room'. Servants were expected to take the brunt of it, yet she was relieved when Philip returned to school: 'he was beginning to be rather too much for us and I thought a fortnight was quite enough holidays at a time'. Overall, Betsy flattered herself that her husband would think 'no man ever blessed with six finer children in every respect'.[25] Sadly this untiring devotion did not reap its reward. Home in 1781, now a rich man, Philip Francis was soon off again on a tour of Europe. The marriage relentlessly cooled over twenty years.[26]

Frank Palgrave, born in 1824, enjoyed many advantages as a child: he had doting parents and lived in rambling family houses with much scope for adventure, in Hampstead and at Yarmouth in Norfolk. The context was eminent parental piety in the Tractarian tradition, with very regular church attendance on weekdays as well as Sundays. Frank went to Charterhouse at fourteen; until then he and his brother Giffy were under his mother's close eye. She enthused about him in her journal, just before he was two, in 1826: 'he has continued to improve in appearance', she wrote, 'he is fair, rosy and fat, with yellow curling hair and pretty small features'. She could not avoid a note of self-congratulation, noting how, when she was away with him at the seaside, the boy's beauty was 'much admired at Yarmouth: people tell me he is a handsome child'.[27]

Intent and dedicated, Elizabeth Palgrave encouraged the boy's curiosity from an early age: at two, she recorded in her journal, 'mills, clocks and wheels are his great favourites'. At three, he was learning short poems by heart, but he was having some difficulties 'in his book'. At four-and-a-half, she was relieved to find him taking pleasure in learning Latin words, in geography and in reading the first chapter of Genesis by himself. He had learnt by then to be very good and quiet in church. At eight, things were more of a struggle: 'he is disposed to argue and strive for his own will, often tyrannical and obstinate'. As so often, a mother found a son harder to manage as the male assertiveness women were expected to tolerate and indeed even to develop became a mark of his character.

But the answer was found in a resident tutor rather than in strict schooling. Elizabeth told her own father how successful his parenting had been, how he had made her aware of the idlenesses and follies of her own childhood and of the trying ways he had suffered with her. This insight prompted her to urge her boys to 'greater application and zeal'. At eleven years old, what really thrilled Frank were models and 'inventions', attempted at home. The tutorial regime of Homer and Horace had by then become the basic chore of his life. Frank Palgrave's poem 'Recollection of Childhood', written as an adult, traces ecstatic memories. These support the impression that his mother Elizabeth was a woman of great calmness and strength, who had the grace and ability to send sons schooled gently at home towards maturity in the wider world.[28]

Clarissa Bramston, married at 31 in 1832 to the Vicar of Great Baddow in Essex and an adult convert to evangelical Christianity, articulated the intense emotions of her mothering in a regular diary. She looked forward, she wrote on 28 July 1833, to her forthcoming confinement with 'mingled feelings of dread and hope and joy', trusting in 'that mercy which has never yet failed me in the hour of need'. She had previously miscarried. Her daughter Clara was born on 30 October that year, then, during Clara's childhood, she lost three other children, two of whom died within weeks of one another and one who was still born. No wonder she treated Clara as a very special gift.

Clarissa had the support of a 'faithful and valuable' nurse, Foreman, and a valued housekeeper, as she struggled to balance parish duties with Clara's upbringing. 'We are indeed blessed in our servants and I feel their good qualities', she wrote on 12 April 1834. John Bramston was her comfort and love; Clara her 'precious little treasure'.[29] From the time Clara was two years old, Clarissa's involvement in her developing character is evident in her diary. But she was not a confident mother. 'Clara certainly begins to love me and every little word she says becomes more delicious to my heart', she noted in October 1835. By 1836 she had identified the traits she felt she needed to watch in her as 'a strong tendency to self approbation and vanity'. She felt awed by her task and dependent on John's guidance in fulfilling it, writing in April:

> Clara becomes every day a greater treasure and increasing source of heart stirring interest . . . What an awful and sobering and yet what a delightful conviction is this. I do indeed feel that in my own strength I am unfitted and unequal to the glorious charge with which God has been pleased to entrust me.

Clarissa's anxiety about her motherly performance increased with time. She tried to cure Clara by constant reminders of her tendency to vanity. But Clara, a bright child, subjected Clarissa to persisting scrutiny, developing a wicked talent for mimicry. Clarissa's enjoyment of Clara became undercut by her self-analysis and failing self-esteem. In February 1838, she confessed her spirits were depressed 'by being obliged to study so much what I say and do as Clara never allows a look, a word or even a thought of mine to pass by unquestioned'. 'Her little mind', she had noticed as early as December 1837 when Clara was just four, 'is always at work and my poor shattered brains will soon be emptied of their small contents if she continues to ask questions and remember answers as she has hitherto done . . . she has the materials of being a very superior creature.'

Clarissa Bramston had believed from the start that her daughter's education was her own special responsibility, but Clara began to outstrip her. Yet she craved understanding and companionship with the child who had survived while she lost others. The tactic of taking the pressure off herself by employing a personal friend as a governess for Clara proved no solution. In October 1841, she decided to dispense with Miss Matson, because she could not handle the relationship between them: 'observing the improvement which has certainly taken place in Clara's mind and manners under your care', she explained, 'we feel that it is difficult to unite with perfect comfort the relative positions in which you and I are placed'. She would look for a younger governess, who would relieve her 'from the positive fatigue of giving her lessons', without acting independently, and would work more clearly under her guidance and direction.

But Clarissa never found the kind of governess she wanted. With the birth of a second daughter in August 1841 and a son in February 1843, she reluctantly concluded that Clara was too much for her. She sent her to school at the age of nine. Mary, now two, replaced her as the child to be tutored in the nursery. She blamed herself for the faults that, as she saw it, marred Clara's developing character:

> Her strong temptation is to be self-conceited and mine to be too easily offended by her forwardness – her faults are such as could scarcely fail to be those of an only child which she was for some years . . . with the blessing of God she will derive benefit from mixing with other children . . . with a few years maidenly timidity may replace the childish forwardness and confidence which are painful for me to observe because I attribute them, perhaps unjustly, to her consciousness of my infirmity. Clara is too forward and I am 'too suspicious'.

The test was combining the stern approach needed to exert effective discipline with warm affection. Clarissa Bramston's mothering was basically insecure. So she blamed others, such as Clara's doting grandfather, for spoiling Clara and her friend Anty for indulging her, while also suffering anguish about her own inadequacy. All this she set out with quite remarkable candour and honesty in her diary.[30]

Sara Coleridge, daughter of Samuel Taylor Coleridge, was a thoughtful and devoted mother to her son Herby. She took his early academic training, started in 1835, very seriously. Beginning at around three, she believed in 'short instructions at a time and thorough cross-examination of those given', realising that children would not listen to lectures 'either in learning or morality'. She used play to inculcate observations and curiosity, in effect turning it 'to a certain degree into lessons'. Herby certainly was precocious. His mother attributed this to 'a show of Coleridgian quickness, and bookishness and liveliness of mind'.

But Sara worried about Herby's tendency to regale people he met, when he was five years old, with abstruse learning. She suspected this made them think she was practising 'pushing, cramming and over refining'. On the contrary, she was careful to leave the impetus with him: so how, she asked, could it strain his intellect if he wanted to hear stories 'about Troy and other antiquities over and over again' or if 'he is actually fond of poring over maps and tracing the course of rivers'? Sara Coleridge deliberately prepared Herby for the course of his future life, 'the mental labour required in a public school' and gaining 'his bread by head-work'.

She had thought hard about discipline. She aimed, she told a friend, beyond 'extorting obedience in particular instances'. Beating the boy would be to employ external force, which 'does not touch the heart'. 'For the improvement of our children's moral nature', she declared, 'I put my trust in no methods of discipline ... I do not strictly put my faith in anything but the power of grace in the heart.'[31] Sara saw the upbringing of her son as a whole. By teaching Herby writing, for instance, she sought to keep him sitting still. Habits of regularity and submission taught early, to her mind, were the foundations of a strong character in adult life.[32]

The correspondence of Henrietta Stanley, wife of Edward Stanley, the second Lord Alderley, throws shafts of light on a mother hardly coping with her brood, with no husband at home to help, during the 1840s. Nine of Henrietta's twelve children, coming thick and fast between 1827 and 1844, had survived infancy. She was socially gifted, intelligent and able, later a public pioneer of women's education and a promoter of Girton College. She was wrapped up in her children and unwilling to join her husband, a politician and man-about-town, who left her to her country life for much of the year.[33] With maids but no governess and six children at home over five, she struggled at Alderley.

Maria Lady Stanley, writing to her daughter-in-law almost every day, advised and hectored. Henrietta needed a 'moderately accomplished person' as governess in her schoolroom and should 'trust to masters when you can get them as well', she declared in 1844. For the estate gave 'naughty boys a wonderful field for their activities'. By 1841, Johnny, at four, was already obstreperous. Five years later, things had gone from bad to worse. Little Algernon, at three, was an angel with a 'most lovely curly head', Lyulph, the next youngest, was a 'very good boy', but Johnny had become a terror: 'much more selfish and naughty', Henrietta wrote, 'than I ever saw him before', treating the little ones 'as if they were dogs'. Her husband retailed the disciplinary precepts he believed in but was too permanently absent to apply. 'With regard to your male cubs', he advised, 'I should recommend a wholesome application of the birch'. Henrietta shrank from this, plaintively complaining that he had all the fun in London. Worn down by Johnny's behaviour, she was unhappy at being left to act the part of disciplinarian, nurse and housekeeper, 'without meeting any help or sympathy'.

In 1848 Johnny's behaviour broke all bounds, in an incident while his mother was away from home. Leading the quiet and academic Lyulph astray, he ran riot, finding a spear 'with which he had torn the housemaids' gowns in hunting them upstairs'. The gamekeeper, *in loco parentis* and protective towards junior female servants, was incensed, but his lack of parental authority left him in a quandary. He was so alarmed by these 'riotous unruly boys', he told his mistress, 'that he was obliged to be master', taking power into his own hands. He could 'not succeed in being so until he had flogged them both', he told Henrietta. 'I suppose', she remarked, shocked at the impropriety of this initiative by a servant, when she reported the incident to her husband, 'he meant a few thumps'. Her overall conclusion was despairing: 'Johnny is the torment of everybody in the house; they say Lyulph imitates everything the other does'. She saw the departure of both of them, at thirteen and eleven, to Eton, soon after this, as a merciful deliverance.[34]

Henrietta Stanley's experience illustrates strikingly how mothering a large family, with inadequate fatherly support and a single difficult child, could simply run out of control. Yet she was basically a good mother. She did well with her fourth boy Algernon, writing when he was three, 'he never asks a foolish question but finds out things for himself and has so much observation and never shows the least unwillingness that other children should approach his playthings.' Her clever third boy, Lyulph, was reported as the 'brightest prospect' on his entry to Eton at eleven in 1850. He later won high praise for his writing and his Latin hexameters from Benjamin Jowett, the Master of Balliol.[35] Of the girls, Kate turned out especially well, knuckling down to her upper-class female destiny, close to and dependent on Lyulph but also close to her mother in the 1850s.[36] It was only Johnny that Henrietta failed with.

The widowed Georgina Grenfell showed unusual artifice in how she recorded and celebrated the mothering of her six children in the 1860s. She compiled a family scrapbook in an impressive leather-bound volume, which she called The Children's Journal. It contained drawings and photographs by and of her children. Yet she actually wrote it, in their voices, as a collective story of their doings. She deliberately highlighted their characters. Thus, chronicling the bigger boys' game of cricket on holiday at Penmanmawr in 1864, she explained that the five-year-old Algy 'did not care about playing so he walked about the field gathering flowers which he always likes better than anything else'.

There was much proud delight in the virility her boys began to display. When the older ones made an ascent of Snowdon, her eldest Willy, at eight, 'despised a pony and was not the worse for rough walking'. His ninth birthday, back home at Taplow, was a day of races for Willy and Charles on their ponies, followed by a great game of leap frog for everyone. When Mama fell in the Thames the next summer, it was Willy who quickly fastened the boat while Uncle Henry pulled her out. Everyone did 'drilling', as physical exercises were called, that summer. Returning to his prep school, Willy 'has had very happy holidays', Georgina wrote in self-congratulation.

Aunts and uncles supported Georgina in giving the children a traditional Christmas in 1865, with Caroline, the eldest child, who was now almost twelve, acting the grown-up in her father's absence: she 'looked very dignified at the end of the table'. Next August, Georgina made a fuss of Algy, who, on his seventh birthday, steered the boat on the river while his older four siblings rowed. At a special 'children's dinner', 'we had lovely little dishes with real entrees and seven tiny candles burning on the table'.

Grandpapa acted the senior Grenfell family figure, hearing Charles and Claud's Latin in March 1868. When he died suddenly just after this, Georgina wrote in The Children's Journal of his 'tenderness and love to us', which 'will be always one of the most precious recollections of our childhood'. Noting a Twelfth Night afternoon dance at Taplow Court in January 1868, Georgina summarised on the children's behalf, 'we all enjoyed it very much'.

In April 1868, expecting much of her eldest boy, now into his teens, Willy deputised for his father by accompanying Georgina to a major local event, a fete with some 4,000 guests: 'they invite everybody, their friends, volunteers, tradespeople and poor people'. That July, the family's reputation was at stake when Willy sat his exams for entry to Harrow. Georgina described his pluck: all day he was 'running back to the Inn occasionally to say he was doing very badly'. Yet, triumphantly, he ended in fourth place, exactly what 'Mama and Uncle Henry hoped as they only wanted him to work and to take a good place at Harrow'. She regarded Willy's delight, back for the holidays in July 1869, in having 'a foxhound puppy besides two other dogs' as symptomatic of his budding manliness.[37]

Isabel Gurney was a formidable, but sensitive, Victorian mother. She brought up her boys in their early years, and her girls throughout their teens, largely, it seems, unaided. She had eight children between 1873 and 1885, taking pride in their physical appearance and good health. 'What a splendid face', she recorded with regard to Sybil at three: 'much like the pictures of the old Gurneys, marked eyebrows, a small expressive mouth. Her hair is flaxen, her cheeks very rosy and fat'. She found this child's 'chief beauty in her large true blue eyes which look out at you intensely and fearlessly'. But Isabel Gurney appreciated her others as well. There was Nigel, 'tall for his age', Laura, 'her features perfectly formed', Eustace with 'good features and large light blue eyes', and Hugh, a 'lovely fat boy'.[38]

Isabel ruminated in her later years about her approach to discipline at home in one of her presidential addresses to the local Mothers' Union:

> Is it not a good thing to win the confidence of our children whilst they are young? . . . Children are so sensitive, even to a harsh or hard word, and know in a moment by the undulations of a voice whether the person is impatient or not . . . I always believe in the good instincts in children and have tried to cultivate their natural truthfulness, which is really innate in children unless they are frightened or deceived by their elders.

Isabel Gurney felt that she knew from her experience that her philosophy worked. Her children always had masses to do: painting and drawing, 'observation of plants, flowers, insects . . . we had a small workshop arranged for the boys as they grew old enough to play with tools . . . and do everything they liked free of notice from their elders'. 'I had a strong notion', she recalled:

> that one could not trust one's children too much . . . I tried to treat them as if they were grown up people and not as little children and it is certain they rose to the trust placed in them and their opinions became of value as their powers of body and mind increased.

Isabel's mother congratulated her on the inner discipline that she inculcated, noting 'the power of overcoming herself which that blessed child Sybil has acquired'. All this was the fruit of a firm and regular routine. Isabel's typical Sunday began with reading the Bible and prayers with the children, painting with them in the schoolroom, then church and reading to the elder ones after lunch. A rest was followed by a walk until tea, followed by hymns and more reading from the bible, before the children's bedtime. She encountered no resentment: 'the children are wild with delight', Isabel Gurney was quite clear in her own mind, 'at the bible stories which I cannot repeat too often'.[39]

The sometimes agonised dynamic of the mother and toddler relationship is brought out by Matilda Bosworth's diary in the 1880s. At a year and eight months, she found Tommy 'such a little beauty physically' but a 'little Turk morally'. Unable to reason with him, she felt driven into spanking him:

> Poor pet how recklessly he bangs his little body about, clashes his head against anything ... and cries and screams so loudly ... and then perhaps when I have been obliged ... and it is all over ... he comes so sweetly round my neck and the dear little voice is so entreating and so reproachful ... yes, certainly ... it hurts me more than it hurts him.

At three, Matilda found Tommy clever and passionate but selfish and masterful. 'He looks very manly and pretty', she noted in 1885, during his first days in trousers. Tommy began his schooling with his mother, writing on tiny slates, saying texts and poetry, learning from pictures of animals on her lap. Then, when he was four, Matilda put Tommy and his brother under a school-room routine. She found it hard at first to adapt to only seeing her boys from six till seven in the evening, when they 'come down to us'. She knew there was something stilted about this family time, when she and her husband had the children to themselves: 'we generally try to entertain them pleasantly for that hour'.[40] Thousands of Victorian children grew up under these conditions of daily brief encounters with a mother, and sometimes a father too, who were often rather remote figures in their lives.

Unusually, in the case of the Trench family, the springs of besotted moth-erhood and the tireless performance which reflected this can be traced over two generations and across the long period from 1839 to 1900. Benjamin Lord Bloomfield, favourite of the Prince Regent, sent as an ambassador to Sweden in 1822, came under the influence there of a Wesleyan minister, George Scott. He converted Bloomfield to a strong evangelical spirituality, which suffused the remaining 24 years of his life.[41] His daughter Georgiana, a teenager in the 1820s, absorbed this piety, which guided her in her married life to Henry Trench of Cangort Park, a substantial landlord from an Irish Protestant Ascendancy family. Letters between father and daughter, when Georgiana was a young adult, breathe an air of close spiritual companion-ship.[42] Massive correspondence between Georgiana and her children, and then in the next generation more letters between her daughter Isabel and her own daughters, show how the power of this evangelical tradition persisted.

Georgiana Trench's family consisted of three boys and five girls, born between 1839 and 1852. She lived for her children and their spiritual welfare, inculcating her ideals most firmly in Haddie, her eldest. We can observe in Haddie, the first-born daughter, a child trained for substitute motherhood, in the same kind of way as Lucy Lyttelton was at Hagley at much the same time. Haddie was left, in her early twenties, to care for an ailing father and the younger children, when Georgiana took the younger girl, Georgy, to school in England in 1863. One of her mother's letters from this journey poured out her feelings for her:

> It was such a comfort to get your letter last night and to hear something of those sweet little forlorn faces that we left behind. I know that you will succeed, my darling, in making them happy . . . what a comfort you are to me no one knows my child except Him who gave you to me and made you what you are – kiss my darlings for me.

Georgiana went on to enquire after 'dear Isabel', whose caught nail she hoped was 'not turning black' and 'dear Benny', who she hoped was 'not taking too many liberties'.[43] 'Do you remember', she wrote to Haddie years later in her widowhood, 'your dear father saying you were the guiding star of the family – truly he knew you well when he said it.'[44]

In 1864, Georgiana entrusted Henry to Haddie's care, sending her brother Benny along, too, to learn German, on a trip to take the waters for his health on the continent. Her letters, left at home that summer, were touching. 'My darling child', she wrote,

> I wish I could put my arms round you and kiss you – and say how I love you – and wish that I could be a better and wiser mother to you – but I thank God that his gracious hand holds you – so I trust He will keep you from the evil of any sins and ignorances.

Haddie's place in the family carried great responsibility for care of the little ones. 'Happiness is alone to be found in doing our duty', Georgiana wrote, echoing teachings of her father's, 'because it is pleasing in the sight of Him who died for us'.[45]

Letters from her youngest daughter but one, Isabel, indicate just how close this stay-at-home girl was to her mother. Isabel contented herself with the Sunday school and good works in the neighbourhood of her parents' home at Cangort Park during her twenties, when her sisters were married or longed to travel. 'My own darling precious mother, I should so love to kiss your sweet cheek my own pet', Isabel began, writing unusually from Dresden, where she and her sister were hastening to buy mourning clothes on the news of her grandmother's death. She was 'wishing we were near to you to be of use to you darling'. Sending love to relatives in another letter at this time, she added 'and a heap for yourself my own chicken, ever your fond child Tib'.[46]

When, after marrying her cousin Frank Chenevix Trench in her 30s, Isabel's own family came along, she carried over Georgiana's high principles, becoming an obsessively devoted mother to her five children who survived infancy. When she spent time with her husband, who was ailing with consumption, on a long Mediterranean holiday in 1897 and 1898, Isabel terribly missed her little ones at home, Margot at eight, Cesca at seven and Herbert at five. Thanking Haddie for 'your goodness to my pets', Isabel explained how she was trying to feel about being away in a letter on 27 January 1898: 'I am not really in a fuss about my chicks at all.' 'When I came away', she recalled, 'I settled to be quite calm and I have been wonderfully good about keeping to it all the time'.

She had wondered, obsessed as mothers were then about sea air, whether to telegraph 'go to the sea'. But the paper indicated how cold it was in England, so Easter would be a more satisfactory time, if Haddie could persuade friends to take them to St Leonard's then. She would gladly 'defray expenses', reflecting her view that for 'my precious children, I did not think any money could be better spent than in securing for them as good health as we possibly can – but I must leave details to those who are nearer the darlings than I am'.[47]

The next autumn, 1899, when Isabel was away from home again with Frank, still desperately seeking a cure for him, she sent Margot, the eldest of the three who were at a local school together in Kent, a serious letter about their academic and spiritual progress. They should try to be 'very good at school', making her and their father 'happy by hearing that you are trying your best'. The girls should encourage Herbert, now seven, 'to be a good boy and to give up being idle'. She sent a book of devotions, urging the girls to use the prayers: 'some of the hymns are lovely to read over even if you cannot learn them all'.[48]

Usually aided by nursemaids in the day-to-day management of child rearing, mothers bore the brunt of responsibility for children in the first years. The continuities in this story of motherly performance are remarkable across nearly two hundred years. The dilemmas mothers faced remained the same. Whether or not they had help, these mothers threw themselves tirelessly into the task which they believed they were uniquely fitted to perform. Some, like Hester Thrale or Clarissa Bramston, suffered self-doubt or anxiety. Some faced disappointment. But, for many, there was rich fulfilment in their sense that their performance in some way matched public and prescriptive expectations about their motherhood.

Fatherly Performance

Fatherhood was about combining the exercise of guidance and authority with the expression of the affection that fathers felt for sons and daughters. There could be tension between these two things and fathers were always more stiff with boys than girls. In the seventeenth century, gentry fathers normally quite sincerely acted out the patriarchal role that the conduct writers delineated. The authoritarian aspect of their fathering was emphasised in didactic memoirs of their household government, as it was bound to be given that these memoirs told a story of their pursuit of piety and true religion in their families. The hallmarks of sound fatherly performance were described as leading household prayers, catechising children, exaction of deference and obedience, and resorting to beating their children if need be. Yet, as we have seen, in the case of families like the Harleys and Josselins, this high seriousness was complemented by the real love and affection that only emerges incidentally in private letters. If fatherly severity, especially in the decades before 1660, has dominated this historiography so far, there is a need to put it in proportion. The context is the evident joy of fathers in their growing and developing little ones, which is so poorly documented before 1750.

Sir Simonds D'Ewes undoubtedly pursued the precept he entered in his commonplace book, having carefully read his copy of Gouge's *Domestical Duties*, that 'parents are especially bound to instruct their children, pray for them and train them up in the fear of God, because they drew original corruption from their loins'. Thomas Scott's family exercises, in Kent in the 1630s, included bible readings with the assembled family before supper. In Sir Christopher Wandesford's household during that decade, there were family prayers three times a day at six o'clock in the morning, ten o'clock and nine o'clock at night. Later, his widow used to conduct the family devotions of prayer and bible reading before breakfast, after which each child knelt to receive her blessing. John Bruen, at Stapleford in Cheshire, rang a bell to waken the family and summon them to morning devotions. Sir James Harrington's *A Holy Oil and a Sweet Perfume*, published in 1669, included a letter to his wife and children which refers to his habit, at Ridlington over twenty years, of weekly catechising, expounding the scriptures 'and praying with you, besides my constant repetition of sermons'. Sir Nathaniel Barnardiston, his biographer stressed, 'towards his children executed the office of an heavenly father to their souls'. He 'would take them into his closet and there pray over them and for them'.[1]

But there is no reason to think that these men were long-faced patriarchs from morning till dusk, any more than Sir Robert Harley or Sir Ralph Verney were. The warm, intimate and caring aspects of those men's fathering has already been discussed. In some cases, there is explicit evidence that these men, too, were warmly benign in their pious household government. When his children displeased him, it was noted of Barnardiston, in moderation and wisdom, 'he would never correct them, nay, not so much as reprove them in his displeasure, but still waited the most cool and convenient time, wherein they seldom discovered that he was angry by any other effect but his silence'. 'For his conversation in his family', it was said of the Northamptonshire puritan lawyer Sir Thomas Crewe, 'he was very mild and gentle at all times.' He was not 'as some who being sweetened with a fee are wonderful mild and calm to their clients but are lions in their own houses'.

Evangelisers successful in inculcating the practice of exacting spiritual exercises in gentry households were not, it seems, by and large, able to persuade fathers to beat their children. References to fathers who did so in the seventeenth and eighteenth centuries are remarkably sparse. According to his daughter, Sir John Holland was one of these. When she failed to learn her catechism, she related, he 'debarred me from my meat, and if I remembered not the sermons I was made to write them down'. She was a wayward child, she confessed, and often chastised.[2] William Hinde, in the encomium of the patriarch of Stapleford in Cheshire, John Bruen, in 1641 approved his not having spared 'the rod of correction as God's healing medicine to cure the corruptions of children and to heal their souls of their sins by the same'.[3]

Another father who confessed to not sparing the rod with his several children though he was clear that his 'correction has always been moderate', wrote to the *Athenian Mercury* in 1695, troubled at the criticism he was encountering from friends and neighbours. 'My accusers argue', he related, that spanking or 'keeping a child in any awe destroys their natural courage, dulls their understanding and robs them of that presence of mind which is necessary for all to have.' He was told, in reply, that it was perfectly acceptable to continue beating his children, but that correction should be appropriate to the 'tempers of children'. They needed encouragement besides severity.[4]

In two paradigmatic accounts of domestic beating, from the seventeenth and nineteenth centuries, one can sense the anguish of a father who adopted biblical prescription by conviction. 'I discharged my duty of correction to my poor child', Henry Newcome wrote in his autobiography covering the years 1661 to 1663, on the day he beat his twelve-year-old son, and 'prayed with him after, entreating the Lord that it might be the last correction (if it were his will) that he should need'. Around 1856, at six years old, Edmond Gosse, caught by his fiercely evangelical father in an act of deliberate disobedience, received 'several cuts with a cane', after a solemn sermon making reference to scriptural precept. His dear father, he wrote much later, in *Father and Son*, chastised him sacrificially, 'not very severely, without ill temper and with a genuine desire to improve me'.[5]

It is hard to be certain how far insistence on marks of deference remained standard in English gentry families throughout the seventeenth century. Sir Dudley North's characterisation of his crusty patriarchal father sounds authentic. Well into middle age, he declared, he 'would never put on his hat or sit down before his father unless enjoined to it'. Elizabeth, Countess of Falkland, said she always knelt in her mother's presence, sometimes for an hour at a time. 'Gentleman of thirty and forty years old', alleged John Aubrey, 'were to stand like mutes and fools bareheaded before their parents.'[6]

Roger North, born in 1653, grew up, as we have seen, under strong maternal authority. This included respect for the patriarch, who dispensed blessings, 'observed as sacred', in his closet 'as a reward of what was to be encouraged and denied when demerited'. His father was a model and example: 'We were taught to reverence our father whose care for us then consisted chiefly in the gravity and decorum of his deportment, order and sobriety of life, whereby no indecent or mischievous impressions took place with us from his example.' There was nothing over-indulgent about the North household that Roger himself later ruled over. He approved denial to the children of wine or 'strong drink'; he required a diet which was 'very plain and rather short than plentiful'. He imbibed the sober principles that his father had inculcated, insisting, in adulthood, that feeding children 'dainties' depressed appetite and 'makes children grow mere fops in eating'.[7]

Kate Mordaunt's childish defiance in 1701 is a specific documented instance of the dynamic between a wayward daughter and her father, in a family attached to the traditional ritual of asking the patriarch's blessing. Penelope told her husband about the child's overeating, 'if let alone to eat what she will', and gave her a generally bad character: 'she is still very naughty in her old faults'. Meanwhile, Sir John's sister, Katherine, was speaking up for the child, attempting to pour oil on troubled waters. 'She hath committed a few faults, the rest have done the same, but love hides a multitude', she pleaded with her brother. If only, as her aunt, she could inculcate proper deference: 'I would fain teach poor Kate to ask your blessing without being told every word as she doth it but fear I shall not make her remember to do it.' Sir John, it seems, took his sister's chidings, that both parents should treat Kate better, to heart. He wrote on one of her letters: 'enquire after Kate as much as any of them and love her as well'.[8]

With the removal of the puritan disciplinary imperative and with the permeating impact of Locke's teaching after 1700, fathering undoubtedly became more informal. After 1750, through the impact of sensibility and Romanticism, its tone and emotional content softened further. Joanne Bailey has shown, in her examination of the Ettrick divorce case in the 1760s, how by then current ideals of fatherly tenderness could be used against an erring spouse, who had lacked interest in and affection for his children as infants and beaten them severely as children. The case shows how far thinking had moved against unreasoning authoritarian behaviour by a father in the home, which might earlier have escaped censure.[9] The force of evangelicalism reinforced the older pattern between 1750 and 1850 in some families. But doting fatherly affection becomes very easy to document between 1750 and 1914.

So far as art was concerned, it is the same story as with mothering. Historical practice had run well ahead of representation. Children were being painted with their parents from quite early in the seventeenth century. The families of Sir Thomas Burdett, Sir John Curzon and Sir Matthew Boynton are early examples of the new fashion for family groups. Sir John, in the 1633 portrait at Kedleston Hall, is shown holding the hand of one of his children in a gesture of family cohesion.[10] The Saltonstall family, around 1637, appears in an intimate domestic scene, which includes his wife in childbed and two little girls holding their father's hand and each other's. This Tate Gallery image might be said to epitomise patriarchal dominance.[11]

Family portraiture in the second half of the eighteenth century still carried these explicit messages about patriarchal authority. When Sir Joshua Reynolds painted Lady Cockburn with her three eldest sons in 1773, she directed her gaze at the heir to the family's estates, making the point that she had produced two spares in case an accident deprived the eldest of his maturity. The patriarch was still usually present, even if that presence was subtly conveyed. Reynolds, painting Sarah Otway with her daughter Jane and Joseph Wright of Derby's account of Sarah Carver with her daughter Sarah, both include images of their husbands as miniatures on the ladies' wrists. Alternatively, in both *Elizabeth, Countess of Bristol with her Children* by Antonio di Bittio and *Elizabeth Howland, Duchess of Bedford and her Children* by Charles Jervas, the husband appears as head and shoulders in an oval frame on the wall.

Kate Retford notes how, at a time when the conduct writers were continuing to stress the supervisory role and power of the paterfamilias, group portraits of families often used a triangular composition, 'which expressed his dominance and authority, matching conceptual hierarchy with pictorial order'. A striking example of this pyramidal composition, dated about 1766, is Johan Zoffany's *Lord Willoughby de Broke and his Family*. He observes the family at breakfast, ultimately responsible for their behaviour, leaning on a chair behind them to emphasise his dominant position.[12]

Yet portraiture, like didactic literature, now did much to promote the new self-conscious enjoyment of fatherhood. Fathers came to be shown as engrossed and absorbed in their children's play and leisure activities. Sir William Pepperrell, in John Singleton Copley's composition of 1778, gazes attentively at his youngest, who stretches an arm towards him, while two of his girls play with wooden toys at the table by his wife's side. Family portraits began to give visual meaning to Thomas Gisborne's prescription that the good father should be a companion to his children, leading them 'not as a father merely, but likewise as a friend'. This was in no way incompatible with the patriarchal role. 'If his conduct be steady, temperate and judicious', wrote Gisborne, 'their fondness for him will never be impaired even by a strict exercise of needful authority.'[13]

Explicit evidence that fathers regarded being affectionate to their children as central to their parental performance is bountiful between 1750 and 1914. James Boswell painted himself as a child-oriented father, with plenty of time at home to devote to his children. He recorded their lisping efforts as they learned to speak in the 1770s in his diary. He revelled in the emotions of family life, delighted when, leaving for a trip, his five-year-old Veronica 'cried very much and clasped her little arms around my neck, calling out "O Papa"'. He was as pleased on his return: 'the children were quite overjoyed to see me again. Effie and Sandie actually cried. This was very fine.' There was fun in this home as well as Sunday seriousness. Boswell took the children on outings, but also spent time on Sundays listening to them reciting psalms and the Lord's Prayer.[14]

Equally ecstatic evidence of fatherly joy in children, from just the period when these prescriptive norms were making their impact, comes from Lancashire, where Amanda Vickery found two effusively affectionate fathers between the 1740s and 1760s. William Ramsden told a friend how much he enjoyed simply being with his wife and children in the nursery. He was happy to take over in the evenings, when his wife went out to play cards. 'You are always bringing your brats in the way; that I cannot settle to anything for them', was his playful tease, when she charged him about an overdue letter. He patently liked being distracted. William Gossip's letters to his children flowed with tenderness. Willy was his 'dear jewel' and Jack was his 'poor rogue'. 'He does provoke me sometimes', he declared of the latter, 'yet I think I love him too.' He too took infantile distraction in good part, writing to a relative in 1746, 'Fathy is by me and keeps such a perpetual clack that you must excuse me if I blunder. I can't get her to hold her tongue.'[15]

When James Oakes began his diaries in 1778, his children ranged in age from eight to thirteen. Over the next years, his largely unreflective but detailed record shows him to be a fond father, grandfather and great-grandfather. He clearly loved having children about him. He took every opportunity, by invitations and arranging parties for them, to see much of his progeny. He enjoyed their birthdays and noted their ailments anxiously. Jane Fiske, editor of the Oakes diaries, concludes that in this family, so far from their being cloistered away and despite the presence of a living-in governess, attitudes to young children were accommodating and happy.

The Oakes children early learnt how to behave in adult company. James's daughter-in-law Betsy brought her sons to dine at two and a daughter at only eighteen months, while his grandson Henry went out visiting with James and his wife Elizabeth when he was four years old. At nine years old, he was a guest at a tea, supper and a card party. Soon after, he attended a full-scale dinner party. The same pattern had applied in the earlier generation. Thus, at thirteen, Orbell Oakes, father to Henry, had gone to dine with his father at the home of the Duke of Grafton. In summer, the nearby resorts of Yarmouth, Aldeburgh, Cromer and Southwold, which were just emerging, allowed James Oakes to abandon himself to seaside frolics and recreations with his family.[16]

Letters from Sir Thomas Fletcher of Betley Court in Staffordshire to his children, in 1798, both encouraged accomplishment and enfolded them with affection. He hoped Anastasia's music lessons would make her 'a source of amusement to all who play well', but he was deferring buying John the fiddle he wanted, in view of his 'small progress' in his lessons. Thanking his two girls for their 'two very nice written letters', he underlined the words to emphasise his gratitude.[17]

Leonore Davidoff and Catherine Hall found plenty of middle-class men in both Birmingham and Essex, between 1780 and 1850, who revelled in their role as fathers. 'Bosco and myself exhibit a picture of domestic happiness', reported a Birmingham banker, left in charge when his wife was away in 1824, 'for we discourse not wrangle, whilst the weighty subjects which we discuss are rather relieved than interrupted by the prattle of Rosabel'. He had been to church with Bosco and had been gathering acorns with Rosabel, 'so there is nothing among us but love and health and happiness and peace'. 'My children are my treasure and my delight', wrote a Birmingham bookseller in his autobiography in 1841; 'the world would only exhibit a barren desert without them'.[18]

Occasionally, the mode of a parent's child-rearing is wholly explicit and transparent. Thus Samuel Taylor Coleridge's account of his children, one at seven years and the other some months old, catches exactly the mood we might expect of a poet and philosopher in the midst of the Romantic movement. Of Hartley he wrote, in 1803, 'like the moon among thin clouds, he moves in a circle of light of his own making . . . he has no vanity, no pride, no resentments and, though very passionate, I never yet saw him angry with anybody'. As for little Sara, 'a remarkably interesting baby', she 'smiles as if she were basking in a sunshine, as mild as moonlight, of her own quiet happiness'.[19]

Richard Chenevix Trench wrote with all the affection we would expect of a son of the remarkable Melesina, on 1 October 1848, to his boys Charlie and Arthur, who were not yet at boarding school at ages nine and eight. He mentioned their little sister Edy's fourth birthday a few days before, joking 'I hope you had a goose upon that day; at any rate you had a gosling Miss Edy herself'. He sent kisses to Mama and all his brood of six daughters.[20] Five years later, writing to his seventeen-year-old Richard, due from Rugby for Easter 1853, he enthused about all his boys coming home from various schools. As vicar of Itchenstoke, in the delectable Itchen valley, the spring promised family expeditions in the Hampshire countryside he loved: 'the boat has been gotten down to the water . . . it was cracking and drying up . . . now however it is more watertight and will ferry over with safety any happy souls to the Elysian fields of Ovington or elsewhere'.

Francie later recalled the simplicities of this Hampshire upbringing in the 1850s. She and her sisters 'never saw a cake', until the French governess made them one. Breakfast was 'bread and scrape the top slices, dry bread the others'. The vicar made the girls 'wear cotton stockings only knee high' in the depth of winter. 'If they succeeded in running round the garden without crying with cold' he would 'give them each a sugar-plum'.[21]

Robert Southey, congratulating his friend, the London publisher, Joseph Conder, on the birth of his child in 1857, enthused about fatherhood: 'when they begin to know you, and you can handle their soft frames without fear, they very soon lay fast hold upon a father's heart'.[22] 'My father was the most vital personality in my life', recalled Angela Forbes, in reminiscence about a father she lost at fourteen. He could seem imperious and impetuous, but it was 'the charm and gentleness in his character which made him lovable'. He was 'kind hearted to a degree', encouraging her to develop and express her own opinions.[23]

It became usual in the nineteenth century, as it had not been earlier, for fathers to be present to give support to their wives in labour and share in the happiness of birth. William Gladstone stayed at home whenever possible through his wife Catherine's labours and Lord Burlington was 'the greatest comfort' to his Blanche. Close bonding with their babies began to become a normal part of fathering.[24] Thereafter, many Victorian fathers felt licensed to let affection and sentiment flow.

The effusive and romantic correspondence of Sir Lambton and Lady Freda Lorraine used love symbols, such as a circle, from their courtship onwards. This developed as their family increased. 'And give such kisses to my babies', Sir Lambton wrote on 2 June 1883, following this with a large circle for his first son Eustace, a slightly smaller one for his second boy Percy and a smaller one again for his daughter Ji.[25] Many late Victorian fathers felt licensed to play. William Gaskill found release in flying kites and playing pranks with his daughters. Austin Harrison liked his father best 'when he roared', releasing his repressed high spirits in a rampage or piece of acting. John Heaton, the Leeds physician, adored his youngest child Bob, born in 1868, who sang nursery rhymes in his study. The house resounded with shrieks when father and son chased each other from room to room.[26]

The tenor of fathering varied with the characters of the men concerned. Some took their children lightly, some rather heavily. The traditional expectation was that fathers should prepare sons to take their place in society as mature and able adults. This meant inculcating proper manliness of bearing and of character, before seeing younger sons into the world through apprenticeship or other means.[27] The keynote, overall, of fatherly performance, as men represented this in letters and memoirs, and children experienced it, was thus responsibility. The academic and moral education of their children was usually seen by fathers as their special concern.

It is the seriousness with which many fathers took the responsibilities of their allotted role that often emerges strikingly. Seventeen letters from Christopher Lowther to his father Sir John, between July 1656 and March 1658, tell of the difficult first months of his London apprenticeship. In his first letter, at sixteen years old, after the search for a master had been set up, he reported, 'I am at the writing school continuing in writing and ciphering till such time as a master can be got.' Mr Buckworth soon took him on, at £300 paid down by Sir John with a promise he could 'get me any preferment as to make me factor'.

In regular bulletins, through a year that was bad for overseas trade, Christopher obsequiously talked up his prospects and his father shelled out substantial sums for his expenses. 'Son Christopher his hopes of improvement of money' was his dry annotation, on a long enthusiastic account of the trading situation in August 1657. Sir John temporarily lost patience with his boy, but, by 1658, when he relapsed into the annotation 'Kitt's letter', he had recovered it, as Christopher was able to relate various successful dealings. In March, having failed so far to acquire clover grass seed 'that is fresh and good', which Sir John hankered for in Westmoreland, he promised some by the next Kendal carrier. They were now on confident, friendly terms. The story has a happy ending, because Christopher pursued a successful career as a merchant, trading at Constantinople from 1660 to 1663, then setting himself up as a Turkey merchant in London. His father reckoned that establishing him in the trade cost him £5,000 overall.[28]

The piety of her father, in business as a hatter, hosier and glover in York, gave Faith Hopwood, who was born there in 1751, she believed, a structure of meaning for her young life. A diary kept from when she was thirteen into her twenties reveals her as an intent and introspective girl. 'My father's attention to the service of God impressed me with its importance', she testified in a note of 'recollections of her infancy':

> Being taught to read at a very early age, I was required to repeat the catechism, collects and portions of scripture, and these occasionally led to serious examination whether I loved God with all my heart, and what would become of me if I died in my present state; what would be my plea when called to account? Here between judgement and mercy I was at a loss for an answer.

The Hopwood household followed a strict sabbatarian regime, seldom receiving visitors on that day of church attendance, but practising catechising and bible reading instead. Her father, on Saturday evenings, 'read something of a religious nature to prepare the mind for Sunday'.[29]

John Gabriel Stedman learnt his own manhood as a soldier and then kept a journal of his parenting, when he settled into civilian life in Devon in the 1770s. He sent his eldest boy Johnny, the apple of his eye, to boarding school. When he ran wild in his holidays at twelve, he recorded Johnny 'terribly leathered for picking apples' from a neighbour's garden. He read the Bible with him sedulously, then sent him to sea at thirteen in 1787, sailing to Honduras on a new vessel the *Amity Hall*. At not quite sixteen in 1790, he went to Portsmouth to see him: 'Johnny appears for the first time as midshipman of the *Southampton*.' Then Johnny's career faltered, earning him fatherly ire in early 1791. He made him beg his pardon on his knees, noting 'I thought proper to give him a severe lecture and keep him on a shorter allowance.'

Restored to favour, Johnny then sailed as midshipman on a frigate, the *Lizard*, on 17 March 1791. 'Dressed in full uniform and gold laced hat, Johnny goes and takes farewell from his friends in Tiverton' was John

Stedman's entry the previous day. He parted, his father noted, from a first love at nearby Halberton 'with a heavy heart'. In November there came news that Johnny was back on the *Amity Hall*, sailing to Jamaica 'before the mast for twenty pounds a month'. When he died at sea at 21 in 1795, John Stedman composed an elegy for 'my lovely boy, thy shipmates' darling and thy father's joy':

> O agonising pain never felt before,
> My manly boy, my John, my sailor is no more.
> No more thy tender frame, thy blooming age,
> Shall be the sport of ocean's turbulent rage.[30]

Matthew Flinders, an apothecary and surgeon living at Donington in Lincolnshire, was a highly methodical man, who kept a family journal and account book between 1775 and 1802. This shows the realities of making ends meet in a prolific family. But concern for placing his children and devotion to their welfare is palpable. He was hard-headed, certainly, counting the cost of their education and placement. Thus in 1790, when young Matthew was apprenticed to a physician at Boston, he noted 'I shall now be obliged to hire a lad and must make Betsy as useful in the shop as I can'. But then Matthew decided on the sea. His letters from Tenerife, New South Wales and other distant lands show a devoted son. Matthew, soon a petty officer, made such a success of the navy that he inspired a younger brother, Samuel, to follow him when he was twelve years old. Their father acquiesced, his eldest 'lamenting he did not go sooner and would have been promoted to a lieutenancy'.

Matthew Flinders was bold in seeing his children, girls as well as boys, take their chances. In 1797, Susanna moved from an apprenticeship in Boston to Dartford in Kent, where she was apprenticed to a milliner. When she was home, two years later, he recorded his pride in her: 'I am happy to note that she is a very good girl, with a very good understanding and high sense of religion and its duties . . . I have hope of her making a valuable woman and of being a comfort to us.'

Only his second son, John, let Flinders down. The way his father wrote about him brings out the stress of love and care unrewarded. An apprenticeship to a druggist in Boston in 1795 did not work out well. In 1800, Matthew concluded that John was 'the greatest misfortune I have ever met with and what course to take with him I am totally at a loss'. 'His simplicity we might bear with', he noted, but his mind seemed 'debased and vicious'. Finally, more harshly, Flinders wrote, 'may God change his disposition and make him know his interest and duty or otherwise take him to his mercy'. Yet three months later, more mildly, recognising mental illness, he spoke of John as an 'unhappy youth', regretting his 'want of capacity and indolence'. That autumn, he was seen as deranged; next year he was in York lunatic asylum, his parents despairing of his recovery. But, this misfortune with John aside, Matthew Flinders moved into middle age believing, as he told his boy then at sea in 1800, that he had done his best for all his family.[31]

The sober memorandum book of William Roe, a successful civil servant, records his family life between 1779 and 1802. There is little about his daughter Louisa, born in 1778, but much more about William, born in 1776, and Frederick, born in 1787. Father and eldest son became close companions during holidays at Brighton, in William's teens, making trips on their own to towns and country houses. They went to Arundel, Goodwood, Cowdray and Petworth for instance. In 1794, William Roe bought an estate at Withdean, near Brighton. He and his eldest son then became much involved together in its management, including the planning of new plantations. Meanwhile, the boy's academic career prospered: third place in the Westminster entry exam was followed by Christchurch and, in 1799, young William's first appearance on circuit as a barrister, where he 'acquitted himself with much credit'. The sense of William Roe's deep fulfilment in his eldest son runs through a matter-of-fact account.

Frederick was more of a worry. In 1797, 'in the greatest doubt and anxiety about him', William sent him to the spa at Tunbridge Wells. He then extended his holiday at Brighton, convinced that Frederick 'found great benefit from the air'. If there is a stronger emotional content in Roe's journal than in that kept by Matthew Flinders, his affection, nevertheless, is still read by inference. When, at nine years old, young William's horse bolted, throwing him in the ditch and kicking his head, his father was thoroughly alarmed. He had him bled at once, noting William had behaved 'vastly well', not losing 'his courage nor his observation'. 'My sensations in this scene are no way to be described', he wrote, 'we were miserable about him for some days.'[32]

The historian Helen Berry found 'considerable affection' for his children in the letters of Thomas Stutterd to his wife, about their children in the 1780s. Yet he also presents himself as an intensely serious father, with strong commitment to the high ideals he sought to inculcate. 'I sometimes think as I ride along', he wrote once, 'what two fine lads I have in Jabez and John and hope they will be good and great men sometime.' His presents to them, besides Banbury cakes, included the instructive book *A Young Man's Companion*. He bought a copy of Rapin de Thoyras's *History of England*, for both himself and his boys, recalling how his father had commended it very much, as 'the most impartial History of England'. A sense of a responsibility to transmit knowledge through the generations exemplified his concerned fathering.[33]

Anxiety often focused on children's prospects as adults. The Reverend John Breay was preoccupied with the formation of strength of character in his boys, seeing that they 'must eventually mix with a variety of characters'. 'When I look upon my seven boys', noted William Lucas, in 1847, 'I feel an inexpressible anxiety that they may turn out well.'[34] Partings were often difficult. 'He is now nineteen and five months', noted Sylvester Douglas when his son Fred went off on the Grand Tour in 1809, 'and will probably not return till he is of age.' This was 'an epoch in his life and in ours'. His mother would keep a day-to-day journal and forward it weekly. Fred was urged to write 'in the same chronological way'.[35]

As he cogitated upon his duties as a father, the late eighteenth-century Baptist minister John Taylor recalled, he gave attention to New Testament precepts and thought about his own childhood relationship with his father, seeing both his 'imperfections' and his 'excellencies'. His principles were carefully worked out: he sought to preserve his children's 'love, esteem and affection'; he sought not to 'overburden them with work' and was sympathetic when they were in difficulties; he tried to keep them from bad company; he found time to teach them to read, knowing 'the honour and benefit' of this learning when young, rather than scolding or beating them; he talked with his children 'to instruct them and impress their minds'. Finally, he made a daily practice of praying with them, having them kneel with him as soon as they were able, as well as praying for them.[36]

Middle-class fathers, burdened by the responsibility of seeing boys into a secure adulthood, felt bound to practise some formality with them, as they sought to convey something of the harder adult world.[37] A letter from Thomas Freemantle, aboard the *Ganges* in 1803, writing home to his five-year-old Thomas, is conditional. He is aware of the training the boy should be undergoing. Little Thomas's letter showed he had been attentive to his mother's lessons in writing, yet his father felt the need to urge him on: 'be a good boy and obey all your Mama's instructions and then I shall love you very much when I come home'. Thomas was lenient by contrast to his daughter: 'Give Emma three peepers for me and tell Emma to give you three for me', he told his son. 'Peepers' sounds like family slang. Fatherly kisses came to Thomas Freemantle's little boy only second-hand and in the female line.[38]

James King Hall showered his boy William with advice when he volunteered for the Navy in 1829, at not quite fourteen. Encouraged by a letter from his captain, who had formed a high opinion of him in his first months at sea, his father emphasised, in 1830, how easy it would be to lose 'what you have acquired either by industry or good behaviour'. He should read over his letters 'and weigh well all the advice they contain'. He was thrilled that William was serving on 'so fine a Brig'. He and his wife had watched the departure at Sheerness:

> Exert yourself as if your father were dead and the road of glory was open to you ... by strict economy, civility to all, kindness to your inferiors, respect to your superiors, a never ceasing obedience to all orders; a promptitude not to be excelled by anyone, a fearlessness of danger ... these things will make your men respect you, your companions court you, and your Captain will be proud ...

James had reared a young officer who he hoped to see maintain the honour of the British flag. The family had a letter from him, sent from Malta in May 1831, and saw him on his return to Sheerness that July. James then promised another allowance of ten pounds a quarter, saying it was given 'with difficulty': 'whilst you have so much your sister cannot go to school'. He was rewarded by seeing his son's career prosper, with promotion before he was sixteen, from HMS *Ganges* to HMS *Scylla* and HMS *Rapid*.[39]

The leather-bound diary of Sidney Pusey, nine and ten years old in 1849 and 1850, is a rather sad record of a boy sorely tied by the academic demands of an overbearing father, who insisted that he make regular entries in his journal to practise his writing. The family occupied Pusey House, a fine Georgian mansion in Berkshire. 'I neglected my journal', Sidney confided to it after a three-day gap in writing it on 17 April 1849; 'that was very wrong'. Though not apparently beaten or much punished, he survived a fierce and intensive tutorial household regime, in which his sisters Edith and Clara were subjected to at least a good deal of the same pressure as he was.

Sidney's schoolroom routine was based on endless reading from Virgil, learning passages by heart, construing and versification. He lived in terror of his father's discovery of blunders in his work. Two mistakes, he found with relief on 14 April, were 'not irritating to Papa'. 'I did a bad exercise and slunk away from Mama's room because I thought that perhaps Papa was there', he noted on 19 April. Since Papa never saw his work that day, he was miserable about it: not checked, his verses 'are not of a decided character in my eyes'. Moreover, the verses his father did look over three days later were 'full of blunders'. When, soon after this, he was excused versification and instead 'Papa gave me seven lines of Virgil to learn by heart', he commented, 'how mild'.

It was almost impossible for Sidney Pusey to live up to parental expectations. 'I was naughty and cried and went into a passion and was (extremely naughtily) angry' was his summary of a bad day. 'I by mistake read an unsacred book today', Sidney confessed after relaxing with some light reading one Sunday. His Mama contributed to the exacting conscience he developed, by reading him sermons, on subjects like not wasting anything, excessive luxury and sudden death. She specialised, under her husband's direction, in 'serious conversation' with her fraught little boy. It felt to him like a triumph when 'Mama thought I behaved better at prayers'.

Yet it was not all quite so dire at Pusey House. Papa sometimes 'proclaimed a holiday'. When he reached the last pages, reading to them Sir Walter Scott's *Kenilworth*, Sidney marvelled at 'that magnificent production of human prose'. He was excited by a book he read himself about the Albigensians, 'which interested me very much'. There were games of trapball, strolls in the garden with his father, family walks and expeditions to places like the Zoo, Kew Gardens and Hampton Court, where he was thrilled by the maze. Papa sometimes drove the children out in the phaeton. On 14 April 1850, Sidney was seen as sufficiently grown up to join Papa and Mama at dinner. It was a red-letter day, which was duly chronicled. This diary brings alive the seriously exacting but wholly caring style of such Victorian fatherhoods.[40]

Robert Cole Bowen of County Cork, a demanding but caring paterfamilias, was superbly portrayed by his granddaughter, Elizabeth Bowen, in her evocative *Bowen's Court*. Between 1862 and 1877, he had a family of nine children that survived infancy. He 'was a great believer in education and believed education ought to be strenuous':

> It was his habit, at the mellow end of dessert, to have a selection of children in from the schoolroom and put them through the lessons they had learned all day. His cold undivided attention, his handsome torrid presence, pushed back from the table and veering round in his chair, made some wits work desperately, paralysed others. Yes they were afraid of him.[41]

John Russell's fathering, by contrast, was down-to-earth. In 1872, he explained to his wife Kate about how he was seeking to control his demanding and recalcitrant seven-year-old Frank, when they were staying away with friends. A tug-of-war developed over helping him to spell in a letter to his mother, as his father was talking to another adult in the room. When Frank tore up his letter, Russell made an issue of his doing his copybook instead before dinner, which would be replaced by dry bread if he disobeyed. This worked: 'I find the best way is to leave him alone to think over things, till he gets it right', Russell noted.[42]

Thomas Cobden-Sanderson fathered about this time in the same mode. In a narrative written of his son Dickie's 'temper tantrums' at eighteen months, he referred to Locke's advice about making a child's will supple. Meeting crying after bedtime with smacks, then a cuddle and a little talk, Cobden-Sanderson found something that was apparently effective. But 'what a responsibility!' he mused, reflecting on the recurring balance between firmness and affection that he needed to pursue. The scheme he set out in his diary for educating Dickie at home was distinctly Lockean, in its emphasis on the boy learning about himself through a multitude of tasks: 'Hammering nails into board to make a pattern . . . making windmills and teaching him to make them for himself . . . Brickbuilding. Balancing . . . Tracing letters and outlines . . . Knotmaking. Needlethreading. Buckling.' Thomas read to his son and taught him to act out 'stories with pictures, parables and fables'. He listed the eight particular qualities that he sought to inculcate, including obedience, unselfishness, patience and modesty.[43]

Sometimes the combination of warm affection and highly-principled training for life shines out of an archival collection. Henry Trench, landlord of Cangort Park in County Offaly, from 1849 to 1881, was a man of the deepest principles. His wife, Georgiana, was steeped in evangelical piety. In a posed family group in 1861, he was at the centre of an Ascendancy family self-consciously on parade. His three Etonian boys in frock coats and his five girls, from Haddie at 22 to Blanche at nine, dressed according to age and status, were deliberately placed in a linking of hands in hands and on shoulders.[44] He gazed directly at the camera; everyone else looked directly towards him.

For three decades, the life of the Trench family at Cangort Park, in its quiet Irish situation looking to the Sieve Bloom mountains, came close to the model of Victorian domesticity. Boys came and went to their Sussex prep school, to Eton and Cambridge. The girls inhabited the schoolroom under a succession of governesses. It was hard for them all to believe it, when it all ended with Henry Trench's death in March 1881. 'Billy, Benny and I met here again yesterday', wrote the estate steward David McCready sadly to Haddie, 'in the old room – but without the grey hair, the keen intellect and sound judgement – the loved face to which we have for so many years looked up to for guidance and advice.'[45] Georgiana Trench, all her happiness gone, left in revulsion to live in England, even discouraging the girls from going back: 'dear sweet Cangort Park', she sighed to Haddie two months after her husband died, 'so happy a home once – all that happiness left it with your darling father'.[46]

Henry Trench sent his boys to private schools in England, where they mixed with boys of like background, because he believed in the hereditary rule of the gentry and in their responsibility to the poor. His father had opened a soup kitchen in Shinrone parish during the Irish potato famine.[47] His eldest boys, Henry, Billy and Benny, were trained to be landlords. Why was young Billy, after Eton, 'spending the prime of his life in ordinary country pursuits'? McCready once asked his master. He could not be better employed, Henry Trench responded. As a country gentleman, he could 'give a high moral tone to his equals, satisfying the poorer classes that a gentleman could be superior to jobbery and petty influences and showing a good example to all orders of men around him'.[48]

The essence of fatherly performance was always creating manliness in sons. In rural England between 1600 and 1914, field sports were the bond which drew teenage boys and fathers together. They learnt their manhood then by his side, with guns, dogs and horses. Amanda Vickery found that sport was 'a recurring theme, if not the dominant theme of the letters men exchanged with men in Georgian Lancashire', just as it had been in Stuart Sussex. In the north, shooting grouse, woodcocks and partridges, as well as hunting foxes, hares and otters, were central features of this masculine culture.[49] Thus male coming of age focused upon the ritual of initiation, in school holidays and then back from university and the Grand Tour, into the sporting round of local society.

Once into his teens, for instance, correspondence between Charles Lennox and his father became dominated by the family obsessions: riding and shooting. There is no doubt about the closeness of their male companionship in the 1740s. 'After very good sport', Charles reported at fifteen, he had 'killed a hare': 'Goodwood', he told his father during another holiday, 'considering your absence from it, has been tolerably pleasant'.[50] Francis Seymour, son of the fourth Marquis of Hertford, a courtier who became Master of the Robes to William IV, entered Harrow at twelve, left at fifteen and saw service in the Guards before his accident out shooting at seventeen. It occurred when, moving easily under his father's patronage in aristocratic circles, he was staying at Firle Park in Sussex, the estate of Lord Gage. 'My gun went off while loading', he recorded in a journal, 'and blew off two fingers of my right hand.'[51]

John Oxley Parker, in appearance, as one of his sons put it, 'a typical country squire in all his ways', filled his letters to his son, Christopher, with accounts of the field and of the chase in Essex. 'A deer was turned out at Latchingdon with Mr Gale's harriers', he wrote on 24 March 1867, 'the hounds went so fast that few could really live with them, but your pony went capitally and kept a good place all through the run.'[52]

Field sports, for generations of young Englishmen, provided a crucial course in youthful manliness. 'I suppose it would be true to say', reflected L.E. Jones, writing in 1955 of his boyhood experience in Victorian Norfolk, 'that I have more enjoyment, a more vivid sense of the delight of living, with every faculty at full stretch, when pursuing and killing birds and beasts than in any other activity'.[53]

But not every father took the responsibility of their role in upbringing deeply seriously. There were absent and distracted fathers throughout these centuries, as well as caring and engaged ones, especially where girls were concerned. 'I cannot think why he did it', noted Evelyn Pocklington of her grandfather's treat, her first memory, of watching the illuminations on the marriage of the Duke of York, later King George V, and Princess Mary, 'for he really took very little interest in me once I had committed the irretrievable error of being a girl.' Her father, a military man in the same mould, found a role for Evelyn, as she approached her teens, as a supernumerary in the field sports which dominated his life: 'he took a small shoot for which', redeeming her femininity, 'my services were required as under-keeper'.

Yet, despite this treatment, Evelyn's mother was always in the background. Her father filled all the foreground, in terms of her worship of someone on a pedestal:

> To me he was a glorious, heroic figure . . . a fine horseman, he could not afford expensive hunters, but followed hounds dangerously on young horses which he schooled . . . an expert fisherman, he cast a dry fly with exquisite lightness and accuracy . . . he was a gun good enough to find a place regularly in famous shoots . . . he played cricket for the MCC and the Free Foresters. I suppose he also found time for the Fifteenth Hussars.

Evelyn Pocklington could not find it in her heart to blame her father for years of studied neglect, seeing it as 'just the way he, and many another, was brought up'. 'Dazzled by his charm and glamour', she pondered, 'I never realised how entirely self-centred he was, spending on his own amusements all the money which should have gone towards my education and an occasional jaunt to London or the Continent for my mother.'[54]

In an affectionate word portrait of her father, Mary Carberry recalled his 'fine speaking and reading voice', and what a good shot he had been. She grew up in the 1870s and 1880s. 'Papa loves children but he doesn't understand them', was her matter-of-fact summary, 'so he leaves our bringing up to Mama.'[55] David Roberts, in his study of Victorian fathers, found a good many who were apparently indifferent to their children. But few took distraction to the level of the Reverend Sabine Baring-Gould, the Victorian translator of 'Through the night of doubt and sorrow'. The father of sixteen, at a parish Christmas party, he said to a child, 'And whose little girl are you?', to be met by tears and the reply 'I am yours, Daddy.' Even if this story is apocryphal, it makes a poignant point.[56]

Absent fatherhood could be compensated for by engagement from a distance, as we saw with Admiral Boscawen, or it could be studied and deliberate. Isabel Gurney's account of family life with eight children at Sprowston Hall in Norfolk in the 1870s and 1880s indicates how her husband, a banker in Norwich, was a commuting father who managed to integrate himself into family life. 'Even with children's voices, music and other sounds, he could absorb himself so entirely in his books that he never observed what was going on around him', she noted. Yet John Gurney, setting the rhythm of the home, also accepted that family time was important. The children always wanted to go out with him when he got home. 'If he stays home for a holiday, I give up the children's lessons and they have lunch with us', Isabel recorded.[57]

Some men away from home simply did not bother, leaving their wives to bring up the children. 'My father spent little time with us as business filled nearly all his waking hours.' This pained comment came from the daughter of the publisher J.M. Dent, who praised his wife for taking a burden from his shoulders in a manner that was self-sacrificing and self-forgetting. Remoteness, of course, was not incompatible with stern authority. 'The raising of the corner of the tablecloth', remembered the son of Sir Sydney Parry-Jones, after a childhood of formal dinners, 'meant silence.'[58] John Tosh's portrait of the indolent and abstracted father Daniel Meinertzhagen is paradigmatic. A London banker, he spent much more time apart from his family than with them, effectively abdicating responsibility for his children. When not in his office, he was often on extended shooting and fishing holidays with male friends. He appeared at home to hand out treats. His son Richard could not recall either an admonishment or a kiss.[59]

Some found spontaneity difficult, if not impossible. For, as John Tosh has stressed, fathers who feared about the security of their own manhood might worry about the manhood of their sons. 'In the more polarised view of sexual difference which was current by the 1830s', he has written, 'the emotional warmth and physical tenderness which young children so easily elicited from adults were confused with feminine softness and sensitivity.' Thus distance was much more usual than oppression, tyranny or complete absence. It is epitomised by W.P. Frith's 1854 painting *Many Happy Returns of the Day*, where the father is the only one not engrossed in the birthday party. Feeling the onerous responsibility of parenting, anxious about forming character, many a Victorian father, like some eighteenth-century ones, stood somewhat apart. Edward Benson, the formidable first Master of Wellington College, was always moralising to his children. So his boys were frightened of him: 'we sat on the edge of our chairs and were glad to be gone', remembered his son Fred.[60]

Yet widowers could feel drawn closer to children, especially daughters. Henry Howard had a holiday at the Tregenna Castle Hotel at St Ives in August 1909, following his wife Ellen's early death at age 54. Four of his children were a comfort to him, visiting from Perranporth. Clare recorded his 'presiding at the top and a most excellent luncheon and a real Cornish junket, specially ordered by Father'.

A day out at Land's End thrust Henry and his youngest child, Clare, now sixteen, together. It was almost unprecedented for them to spend time alone. When he took her round the stables on Sunday mornings, 'with the appropriate lumps of sugar for the horses', her sister Amy normally went too. Clare left her mackintosh and lunch sandwiches with the others by mistake at Penzance that day, when she joined her father in an open car for the drive across the Penwith peninsular. She was self-conscious and coy about his insisting on her sharing his mackintosh when rain came on: 'we put a newspaper over our knees'. Others were following on bicycles. 'I was on tenterhooks that they would not turn up and that Father would make me have some of his luncheon', Clare wrote in her holiday diary, describing their stroll together over the Land's End cliffs. She enjoyed his comment that the gorse and heather 'looked just like a Turkey carpet'. Her lack of confidence in Henry Howard's company reflected the fact that, as the youngest of ten, she really did not know him very well, though she appreciated his somewhat stiff affection.[61]

George V's coronation brought a great demand for large carriage horses. So, moving with the times, Henry Howard decided to sell his whole stable of horses which served the landau, brougham and wagonette. He invested in a 1909 Armstrong Siddeley landaulette, sending Hammond the coachman off to learn his new job as chauffeur. Clare began to accompany her father on Sunday mornings to inspect the engine of the car: 'the hinged flaps of the bonnet would be ready lifted, exposing the gleaming copper and brass of the engine, as spotless as the bodywork of the car'. All the grown-up children who wanted to, learnt to drive under Hammond's tutelage. 'His pride in his pupils was immense', recorded Clare. The scope for Howard family picnics, with their widower father, was increased, once Hammond could drive them into the Sussex Weald, Clare reminisced in 1978, although 'all this world came to an end with the Great War in 1914'.[62]

For a man like Henry Howard, a Victorian through and through, the outbreak of war with Germany, in August 1914, was a very great shock. He felt a dawning realisation that his whole world was dissolving. 'Father is making recruiting arrangements', Clare wrote to her fiancé on 7 October 1914, 'and is delighted with some striking posters he has had printed in red and black.' They were putting one on the landaulette.[63] His sons Hal and

Edgar were joining up, while Violet, Amy and Clare had trained for the Voluntary Aid Detachment nursing service.

Then suddenly Edith, Henry's eldest daughter, who had long suffered from diabetes, went into a coma and died, with her father and sisters at her bedside, on 12 October. Two days later, more than fifty wounded Belgian and French soldiers started arriving at Orpington. The girls rushed off to prepare the hospital, which was planned in the village hall. These double shocks were too much for the paterfamilias. Henry Howard went to bed, with a morphia injection to calm him before his daughter's funeral, but himself died quietly in his sleep on 15 October.[64]

The double funeral of Henry Howard and his eldest daughter, on 16 October 1914, was a signal and traumatic moment for this family. 'Everything seems in a dream and unreal', wrote Clare to her fiancé Reggie that morning, when her brother Edgar came to her room, as she was dressing, to tell her that their father had died in his bedroom down the corridor.[65] Her Reggie formed a foursome with the three sons at home as pallbearers. The vicar enumerated Henry Howard's good works for Orpington over 30 years, revealing his gift of £250 to improve the recreation ground and allotments. In his will, besides time-honoured legacies to servants of the house, he left 50 pounds to Hammond, his 'chauffeur and former coachman'.[66] 'We all have each other in a closer sense', wrote Clare Howard to Reggie the day after the funeral.[67] This was the sense of cohesion that is felt when a family closes in its grief around a lost parent.

In a curious way, Henry Howard's death at Bark Hart in October 1914, this single death, can be seen as symbolising the end of a long era in English parenting, an era when parental love and affection for children was consistently at the heart of a multitude of varying household arrangements. Lady Muriel Beckwith, born a Lennox and growing up, during the 1880s, in the 'remoteness and secret wildness' of a Sussex Downland estate, was one of many who testified to the immense security of that ordered world, before the cataclysm of the Great War. That war, she wrote in 1936, devastated 'customs we knew as children which can never be restored'.[68] Nowhere was this more true than in the society of the English country house. The post-war world was simply not, and was never going to be, the same.[69]

11

Fathers and Educating Boys

Extracting their boys from maternal influence was a long-established issue upon which fathers were united and determined. 'After a child is come to seven years of age, I hold it expedient that he be taken from the company of women', wrote Sir Thomas Elyot in the *Book Named the Governor* in 1531. Encouraging his wife to lavish care on their girls in 1597, Sir Robert Sidney went on 'for the boys you must resolve to let me have my will for I know better what belongs to a man than you do'. 'Indeed', he wrote regarding his seven-year-old son, 'I will have him from his nurse for it is time and now no more to be in the nursery among women.'

In a paper of advice to his descendants written around 1650, Sir John Oglander, of Nunwell on the Isle of Wight, castigated 'foolish mothers', who reared children 'in such a height of pride and laziness that they are good for nothing ever afterwards'. Fathers who neglected to train boys for a vocation, whether sending them to Winchester College or 'to London to be merchants', exhibited the height of irresponsibility: 'nothing undoeth children more than the fondness of parents when they are young, breeding them so tenderly and keeping them from the hardness and labour that they seldom prove good for anything . . . I conclude when I see a child cockered in his youth in silks that certainly he will live in want in his age'.[1]

'His mightiness', wrote Lord Coleridge of his six-year-old son in 1827, 'was getting out of hand and evidently required stricter discipline.'[2] It was very unusual for an upper-class boy to challenge his father's insistence that he be sent to boarding school. One who did so was John Evelyn, who recalled that, when it was intended he should go to Eton in the 1630s, he was 'so terrified at the report of the severe discipline there' that he refused to go.[3] In the eighteenth century, fears that boys' manhood might be permanently destroyed by excessive female influence became hysterical. In David Fordyce's *Dialogues Concerning Education* published in 1745, the figure of Cleora was used to argue the benefits of upbringing by a male guardian instead of a mother.

Mothers' influence was represented as pernicious, with training in polite social accomplishments standing in for more solid masculine ones.[4]

Novels and conduct books alike berated the too-indulgent mother. Lovelace in *Clarissa* blamed his indulgent mother for his villainy; the physician William Cadogan portrayed the 'puny insect' of a man who was the victim of the mistaken tenderness of a fond mother; James Nelson criticised the interfering mother, with her 'blind fondness', in confrontation with a father exerting his authority.[5]

A few fathers, dedicated to high standards of classical learning as preparation for time at one of the ancient universities, hired private tutors for their sons. Tom Isham's diary, kept when he was fourteen, with its remarkable silence on the role of his mother in his life, shows that this could be an effective means of cutting the apron strings. It provides insights into the regime of his tutor, Richard Richardson, at home. Richardson was a Cambridge man, who, in the 1670s, combined responsibility for the learning of both the heir to the family estate and his brother, with the rectorship of Lamport in Northamptonshire. Sir Justinian Isham also took a personal hand in the education of his boys.[6]

But it was Richardson who was in day-to-day charge of the steady progress through Euclid's *Propositions* and his *Elements of Geometry*. The second of these volumes is still in the Lamport library, in mute testimony to the grind the Isham boys went through. Tom and Justinian were exceptionally well-schooled in Latin by their tutor, as Tom's detailed Latin diary for 1671 testifies. Sir Gyles Isham, the meticulous editor of the family papers, believed that the Virgilian model, adopted by both boys in accounts they wrote, in Latin, in 1671, of the local Rowell horse races, shows clear evidence of Richardson's inspiration as a classical scholar and teacher.[7]

There was no better way of preserving a family's classical tradition than private tuition. Mr Denison, tutor to Frank Dryden at Canons Ashby in the early nineteenth century, was expected by the boy's father to undertake five hours of instruction – 7 to 9, 10 to 1 – each day with him. The stress was on Greek prose and Latin verse, together with mathematics, logic, French and history. Evening homework from four to six invariably consisted of composition, on themes set alternately in Latin and English. There is no question that exceptional tutorial regimes of this kind, matched to a boy's capacity and concentration, were models which offered considerable potential for scholarly attainment.[8]

Sir John Stanley of Alderley in Cheshire wrote an autobiographical account of his upbringing, stressing the dedication of both his parents to a decent and civilised education. Westminster was mooted at fourteen but rejected at his mother's prompting. His boarding years, ignoring the great schools, were spent in small, friendly establishments. He started, with 70 other boys, at Loughborough House in 1771, at five years old, where the fee was £52 for a year's tuition. At ten years old, he was learning French, geography and history, as well, predictably, as a great deal of Latin. He moved to Mr James's school at Greenwich, from the age of eleven until he was aged four-teen, where he enjoyed keeping a garden with the master's son but claimed that he learnt little.

From 1780, with his own tutor, Mr Six, John Stanley's education, now under his mother's tight hold, was taken seriously in hand. She brought in masters to teach him French and the harpsichord. In 1781, at fifteen, he trav-elled with his father on the Continent, learning languages, dancing, fencing, riding and continuing his musical education. Mr Six, travelling with them, instructed him in religious and moral subjects. His father took him to Bath at sixteen, introducing him to balls, concerts and plays. Then, in 1783, he trav-elled to Switzerland, Paris and Turin with Mr Six, working with the violin, Italian and drawing masters. John Stanley's education was a thoroughly untypical way of training English boyhood. It is no surprise that he became a liberal Cheshire landlord, a dignified, high-minded intellectual, who stood apart from his foxhunting neighbours.[9]

A small local school was often seen as a suitable starting point and boarding could thus be delayed. Willie Morris started at the grammar school at Wells as a day scholar at eight in 1709, reading Ovid and Erasmus there, before moving to Sherborne at fourteen. Matthew Flinders started his son Matthew at Mr Whitehead's at five in 1780, where he moved from reading only, in his first year, to writing in his second, when he also began Latin homework in the evenings.[10] William Roe remained sufficiently satisfied with Mr Fountaine's, near the family home at Eltham, where his eldest son William started at five, for him to stay there until be entered Westminster at fourteen, in 1790. In the 1820s, Mary Cowden-Clarke recalled, while living in Oxford Street, how her little brothers went off to school nearby, trundling their hoops with them along Baker Street.[11]

The higher a boy's family was up the social scale, the more likely it was that, sooner or later, he would face spending a large part of his boyhood living away from his family. The issue was the claim to be training a son for membership of a national gentry and noble community, bred in a particular patrician manner. Three gentlemen, living in Cumberland, Somerset and Kent, illustrate this kind of ambitious fathering, setting their sights on Oxford for their sons. Sir Daniel Fleming had left Queen's College, Oxford in 1652 and the next year, on the death of his father, found himself, at nine-teen, the head of a family with extensive estates centred on Rydal in the Lake District. His male brood later consisted of George, Richard, Roger, James and

Fletcher Fleming. Four of them eventually went to Oxford. There were toler-able grammar schools in the 1670s within easy reach of home at Rydal, but not within daily walking or riding distance, so the boys began their schooling, 'tabled out', at Hawkshead and Kendal.

But the finest and best-reputed school of the North-West district was Sedbergh, where the formidable Posthumous Wharton, an expert with Oxford entrants, ruled as master for more than 30 years, between 1674 and 1706. All the Fleming boys passed through Wharton's hands: it is docu-mented how hard they all found his classical regime; how invariably they longed for 'the sight of horses' on the road from Kendal, brought by servants to ride home when it was holiday time. Wharton drove them hard, insisting, in a 'short vacation' afforded Roger and James in 1691, on constant diligence in the exercises and reading that he had assigned them.[12]

Sir John Smyth at Long Aston in Somerset put his trust in the Taunton schoolmaster James Upton, after sending his eldest son to Winchester, a sure route to Oxford. Upton wrote reassuringly in May 1718 about Hugh's 'very considerable advance in learning' and Samuel's being hampered by deafness from a cold. In November, Hugh still flourished, Upton insisting that he had 'scarce known his superior' in either 'morals or learning'. Samuel, meanwhile, had sickened with smallpox and died in December. Hugh, himself stricken but not in danger, was 'tolerably cheerful considering the great loss he hath sustained', a friend of Sir John's informed him on 5 December. His terror now was that he would lose both his younger boys. Upton promised that Hugh would not be allowed out of the town until his recovery was entirely secure. In February 1720, thanking him for a gratuity, Upton, sensing the ambitions placed on Hugh, suggested that Sir John should now write to encourage him in his learning and 'to enforce application with the love of letters'.

Deferential, yet confident in his professional advice, Upton broached the question of Hugh's university prospects in March 1720. He was a good scholar but he needed to enlarge 'the compass of his studies'. So Upton suggested that he needed at least the full year to finish his schooling. In December, Hugh received an excellent end of term report: 'He can express his thoughts with great facility and clearness either in prose or verse, whichever language you shall please to put him in and has a full insight into the beauties of those authors which we call the classics and are suitable to his years.' On the edge of a university career, Hugh Smyth had won the full approbation of his schoolmaster. His elder brother welcomed him when he achieved Oxford entry in 1720, reporting him 'well settled': 'I have seen some performances of his which in my opinion are very good.'[12]

Sir Edward Filmer, resident at East Sutton in Kent, opted for Eton for his first-born. He was there in the 1720s. But he was not sufficiently satisfied with the school to pursue this. In 1727, he and his wife believed it was time to send the next three, who were marking time at a local school, off together. He set his sights on Oxford for his second eldest, Jack, and opened negotiations with an old college friend, John Harris, who had Winchester connections and who offered to take the three Filmer boys, Jack, Robert and Edward under his wing as a tutor, get Jack put on the Foundation and see him from Winchester into New College.

Correspondence between Harris and the Filmer parents over the years 1727 to 1733, documents Jack's successful academic progress. In November 1727, Harris was reporting the boys' efforts to make up lost time in their learning: their tutor gave a good account of their behaviour and diligence. Sir Edward and Lady Filmer were thrilled at their return home that Christmas: 'they bore the journey so well', commented Sir Edward, 'they came galloping into the yard'.[13]

During 1728, Harris's confidence in the Filmer boys increased, as he took over much of their tuition at Winchester himself. They had 'made a very visible progress in their study as I hope upon enquiry you will find', he claimed in a letter, asking for the horses to be sent for them. Dr Burton, the headmaster, himself expressed his satisfaction in the boys, noting 'the disadvantage of former methods'. His usher concurred, commenting upon 'an almost invincible bashfulness contracted by a private education', locally in Kent. By December that year, it was being suggested that Jack would 'probably be at the top of the school' early enough to set his sights on New College. 'Jack pitched upon for the Foundation', was Sir Edward's annotation of the letter about this.

But the bills mounted and what about the other two? Harris was persuasive that Robert, with two or three more years at Winchester behind him, might become an attorney: 'the better they understand Latin, the better they are qualified for that business'. In any case, he pointed out, Sir Edward had acquired such a favourable deal for the three of them that the savings would be minimal by removing one at this stage. By May 1729, the usher was able to report that the boys, still working hard, were 'in a good degree victorious over their excess of modesty'. But the following year Robert died of smallpox. Jack, meanwhile, was said to be speaking out in a manner that, given more confidence, might allow him to be 'a fine speaker in the Commons'. The loss of Robert intensified Sir Edward's ambition regarding Jack. Correspondence with the Winchester authorities and with his brother, Beversham Filmer, became intense, as his son reached for and seized the prize. He made his way to Oxford in 1734, entering as a gentleman commoner at University College.[14]

The saga of the schooling of Sir Edward's sons continued through two further stages. With four more boys reaching school age, he retreated from the costs of Winchester, opting, in 1740, for the school at Cranbrook, a nearby market town. The experiment was a disaster. Perhaps Filmer, a demanding parent, expected too much of a simple country school, for he quickly fell out with the master, Mr Browne, about his management of the school. A schedule of Sir Edward's queries indicates the grounds of his dissatisfaction. Were any proper plans in hand in case of a smallpox outbreak? Sir Edward wanted ten weeks holiday for the boys in all, with a full month in the summer and at Easter instead of three weeks, but only a week at Christmas.

Filmer was willing to pay sixteen pounds a year for each boy for board and tuition, but he found Mr Browne thoroughly disagreeable. After entertaining him at East Sutton, he complained about 'the great coldness and indifference you showed . . . towards my sons' return to your school'. He took seriously his boys' complaints: they were confined 'within too narrow bounds for their health'; they were expected to sleep three to a bed; in his teaching Browne teased and tormented rather than encouraged them. It was the schoolmaster's arbitrary and supercilious manner to the boys that Sir Edward found intolerable. Such severity could so 'dispirit a youth so as never to get the better of it all his lifetime'.

In 1743, the Filmer boys were moved to Maidstone school. Deudatus Bye, the master there, was much more the kind of man Sir Edward felt happy to work with. He quickly brought Edmund on well, reporting that he expected to have him ready to attempt Oxford entry in 1744. That summer, he was keeping his nose to the grindstone, as this account of the school day shows:

> Master Edmund every morning construes one chapter of Tully's offices and at the same time hears another chapter construed by one of the same class. After breakfast, the lesson is in the Hebrew psalter or in Genesis . . . In the afternoon, the first lesson is in Greek, one week in Homer, another in Xenophon . . . Sunday in the evening they construe a chapter in the epistles of the Greek Testament . . . every night in the week exercise is made either Latin, theme or verse.

To Filmer's disappointment, Edmund failed to gain a scholarship to University College. Deudatus Bye said he not only 'came up to my expectations but exceeded them', hinting at a competitor's 'prior application strongly enforced with circumstances for compassion', which had lost him the day. Correspondence in the papers of the ageing Sir Edward, his eyesight now failing, with the school and with Oxford contacts shows the vigour with which he sought to advance his younger boy. Edmund prepared himself to sit a closed scholarship for a pupil of Maidstone school in 1745, under his father's direction at home. Mr Bye had advised against his being sent to continue his studies, prior to this, at Oxford itself, in view of 'the strong temptations of the place and company to a new entered gentleman', which might take him from his books. A series of well-penned Latin prose and verse compositions and translations, in the Filmer papers, stand as testimony to both parental ambition and boyish effort at home.[15]

Gentry and professional fathers had various motives in arranging the education of their boys. They were, in many cases, less ambitious than Fleming, Smyth or Filmer. They watched their purses, considered curriculum issues and listened to the local gossip in their circles. The puritan squires of Stuart England, Trevor Cliffe has noted, 'were usually careful to choose schoolmasters whose religious sympathies were basically in accord with their own'.[16] What united them was the imperative to launch their boys, to accustom them to bustling in the world. The rite of Latin, learnt in a disciplined environment with others of their own generation, was said to be the best and only kind of learning for males. The absorbing business of gathering information about the repute of masters, about costs and about local variations in the curriculum, was treated very seriously.

Fathers did not baulk at sending boys some distance, if it meant finding a sound education at a reasonable cost. Thomas Whale, resident in Cambridgeshire in the 1770s, noted in his diary how enormously school fees varied and how important it was to take into account whether board was included. He had heard of a school at Reigate which offered 'short and compendious finishing of youth', with board, at sixteen guineas a year; but he had also been told of schools in the north offering to educate boys at ten to twelve pounds a year.[17]

Decisions on schooling and expeditions to settle boys were the small change of gentry correspondence. 'We have been at Kegworth', wrote John Newton to his brother in October 1659, 'whither we carried our two younger sons and have left them there at school.' 'I have placed my two boys at Laughton', Francis Stranger told his brother-in-law in 1687. 'William Sacheverell intends the same'.[18] There was often intense scrutiny of what others, especially leading families of the locality, were doing.

When Thomas Oxinden had just started at Wye grammar school in the 1640s, the master there, Henry Bradshaw, explained to his father that, in Latin, 'his learning to make a verse of it will be the first work he must fall upon, those of his form having now some time made an entrance upon it'. Correct pronunciation of the spoken language would follow, for those who showed 'a natural genius' for it, which he hoped to find 'in some measure' in young Thomas. His father later played with the idea of moving Thomas to Westminster where, he was told, 'if any gentleman have a desire his son shall learn to dance or play upon any music', that could be arranged for extra fees. Yet, in the end, he decided to pass by these social accomplishments, leaving Thomas to his solid diet of Latin at Wye.[19]

John Collier, as town clerk of Hastings in Sussex, was a man who had made his own way in the world. He was anxious to advance his boys in their turn. He started Jacky at Mrs Thorpe's school in Battle in the summer of 1728, at just eight; Jemmy, a year younger, followed the next spring. Mrs Thorpe had assistance in teaching her boys from her daughters Nelly and Molly. The idea was that this female tuition should prepare them in reading and writing and they would subsequently go out to masters in the town for their Latin. Letters to Jacky from his father, between November 1728 and March 1729, show a mixture of paternal support and admonition. He would buy the books Jacky requested, 'as long as you continue a good boy and mind your learning'; he had sent a prayer book and some marbles; his mother was sending him raisins. He hoped his boy had 'left off picking your nails'; his writing required attention, bringing his hand down to the size in which his father wrote to him.

Jemmy's respectable hand, even before he came under Mrs Thorpe's tuition, is evident in a letter of early 1729, to his brother from his home in Hastings. With two boys at Mrs Thorpe's, fatherly advice turned to insistence about their minding their books, not quarrelling and assisting one another. Their uncle wrote with a message for Jemmy that he hoped 'he has learned the eight parts of speech'. Inevitably, pranks followed putting the boys in school together: Jemmy was rebuked for his failure to beg pardon 'for being so naughty a boy at market day' in Battle, 'drinking and getting out of The George balcony'.

John Collier requested a special week's holiday for his boys in September 1729, with the condition that they bring their school books, 'that I may see how you go forward'. The correspondence contains constant reiterations about diligence and the boys saying their prayers. Early in 1731, John Collier congratulated Jacky on his writing, whereas he told Jemmy his was not up to scratch. Jacky's deference to his father's wish for them to acquire a polite education showed in a letter to his mother, happy about his new breeches and a new hat. He wrote, 'I did not intend to go dancing any longer but since it is my Papa's desire I should go I will and learn as soon as I can.'

In 1732 the Collier boys moved together to Westminster. One of their mother's letters catches the sense of the grandeur, to her mind, of this new experience in the metropolis. She felt her local news was paltry, yet related the local gossip. She wondered that Jemmy did not enquire after his poultry, which he had left behind. The boys were lodging with the Reverend Carleton in Dean's Yard: 'carry yourselves very civilly in the house', their father wrote, 'and do not go anywhere without leave, nor be drawn into ill practices by other boys'. John Collier spoilt them both by buying them watches.

Then Jacky was swept away by smallpox and it was Jemmy who, after a gradual recovery himself, became the apple of his father's eye. In February 1733, John Collier, in London on business, took him out in a coach to dine in the country. Jemmy was in high spirits about his Westminster life, telling his father, 'I have a whole digest of new tricks and stories to show and tell my sisters when I see them'. The purposeful Collier correspondence, between 1728 and 1733, is suffused with mutual concern between parents and sons, with their care and affection for each other.[20]

Another case, in which a relaxed relationship between father and son enabled a more prolonged course of schooling far from home, was John Grimston's scheme for his son Thomas. During his stay at Cheam and then Harrow from 1762 to 1771, Grimston employed his friend William Whateley, resident near Cheam, to act as Thomas's guardian in the south. Writing to his father in June 1763, when Thomas was ten, Whateley reassured him;

> Your brat at Cheam is well. He dined with us yesterday and paid his repeated compliments to a cold goose in a way that seemed to foretell he would one day be a great man. His finances are indeed much lower than the Nation's notwithstanding the late ruinous and expensive war.

Visiting 'the young monkey', always short of cash, at Cheam a few months later, Whateley found himself inveigled into supporting his plan for buying a garden, 'dung and a glass and mat to put over the hotbed and some seeds'. The boys were encouraged to keep pets and Thomas specialised in hens. He also charmed his uncle, Sir Digby Legard, into buying him a hat and gloves, maps, and a Hunter watch.

Thomas Grimston's brother Harry soon joined him. Both won the plaudits of Cheam's headmaster, William Gilpin, who wrote, 'I am happy to tell you that both your young men have made I understand great improvements ... they seem both to have mild tempers and I hope are both boys of good principle.' Gilpin took seriously his joint scholastic endeavour with the boys' father, which he saw as inculcating piety and morality, besides the traditional classical learning needed for Harrow. 'The sooner', he insisted, echoing Locke, 'the parent makes a rational companion of his son, by reading and conversing with him, the better.'

Their schooling, with the hazardous travel on the Great North Road that it involved, clearly made self-reliant men of the world of the Grimston boys. Whateley oversaw Thomas's transition to Harrow at sixteen in 1769. He boarded with Mrs Crampton, who cared for him when his first term was marred by illness, depriving him of his Christmas holiday. When a serious epidemic of diptheria struck the school in 1771, he took refuge, with Whateley's assistance, in Soho, having a whale of a time meanwhile at the Vauxhall and Ranelagh pleasure gardens.[21]

That October, Thomas was implicated in the riot at Harrow, when the boys did much damage to the coaches of several school governors, in protest at the imposition of a new headmaster, who had been hired from Eton. He gave his father a blow-by-blow account, confessing that he quite expected to be told they had carried their resentment 'a great deal too far'. Yet John Grimston's response, while reprimanding him severely in view of his tender paternal regard and 'desire of your doing right', was also affectionate and trusting.[22]

The annotated account book kept by Matthew Flinders, the Lincolnshire surgeon, provides insight into his thinking about his son Matthew's academic progress. The boy seems to have remained in full accord with him as his father shifted his plans. In 1785, with Matthew nearly twelve, he wrote as follows:

> I have not yet sent him to grammar school, though I thank God he improves in his Latin very much under my own tuition. He goes only half days to Mr Whitehead, keeping close to his Latin each afternoon and, while he continues so to improve and I can teach him, I think I shall not send him.

At twelve, Flinders decided to give his son two years 'at the best neighbouring school I can'. To his delight, as he was always careful with money and concerned about his household costs, Mr Shinglar opened a school at the small village of Horbling, a mere five miles off, the following year:

> They seem genteel people . . . it will be expensive the terms being eighteen guineas per annum . . . he has seven boys . . . the convenience of the situation was a principal inducement . . . indeed it was quite time he was from home . . . he has begun in the Greek and I hope with a blessing will make a good progress in the literature.

But Flinders felt the cost in his pocket and he soon ended Matthew's schooling, taking him away at only age thirteen. 'I mean him to assist me in my business; he has made a proficiency in learning exceeding any hope I could reasonably form. I hope he will be comfort and blessing to us.'[23] Professional men often had a very different perspective from leading country gentry, as they weighed the benefits of continuing a boy's schooling through the teens.

The letters home written by schoolboys were generally formal and placatory narratives of school life. The most childish letters in this collection, written from a prep school at Wandsworth in 1744, by Charles Lennox at ten years old to the Duke of Richmond, are short and in large copperplate. They are clearly guided productions, intended by a schoolmaster, who was looking over the shoulder, to please. At Westminster, in 1747, with the help of his tutor, whose report took up the opposite page, Charles Lennox sought to subdue his father's wrath about the standard of his script. He was 'very sorry I gave occasion to you to caution me about my writing well, which was in some measure owing to my not having good pens, but chiefly to my own negligence concerning which I shall take greater care for the future'.[24]

A letter from William Rugeley, at school in Baldock in 1794, is a fine piece of copperplate writing, designed to ensure approval of his schoolmaster's efforts. William hoped that 'my improvement this half year will meet with your approbation'.[25] Rudolf Fielding's letter to his father from Cheam in 1831, in the same mode, is a classic expression of boyish deference. At eight years old, his need to answer the Earl of Denbigh's expectations of him is palpable. He thanked for the toffee and barley sugar, requesting cricket stumps and a ball. 'I am very glad', he wrote, 'to say indeed that I have a great many friends at school', underlining the words 'indeed' and 'great' for emphasis. Sending his love to his Mama and his Aunt Charlotte and asking after his Aunt Cathy, Rudolf insisted that his manliness was in full bud: 'I am a great deal stronger than I was when I first came to school and I can run a great deal faster.'[26]

Letters of this kind were a good tactic, when the escape home was very much a matter of negotiation between boys and parents. James and William Wiggett regularly tackled the issue, at prep school in Hampshire between 1807 and 1811, emphasising their progress in Latin as an argument for their being collected on time. The best tactic of all was a few weeks' warning of the first official days of freedom and the information that 'my schoolfellows all expect to go on one of those days'. The Wiggett boys were also sensible to emphasise their love for sisters at home and the burgeoning desire to see them again.[27]

Correspondence between the Trench boys and their parents at Cangort Park exemplifies their ready response to the emotional and financial invest-ment in their education that Henry Trench had made. We have seen how he sent three boys, Henry, Billy and Benny, across the Irish Sea to prep school and Eton. Both parents wrote to them regularly and expected a steady stream of news in return. Henry Trench's tone was consistently warmly affectionate; the boys were both deferential and caring about their father's often uncertain health. Henry delighted in their sporting interests. 'I was out with the beagles today', Billy passed on, writing to Georgiana on 30 January 1861, 'and intend going again tomorrow when we are to have a fox turned out.'[28]

The following month Billy was perturbed at the news, communicated by his dame, that his father intended he should go on from Eton to Cambridge that October. The last thing he wanted was to leave just as he was reaching the peak of his career there. He was working hard, he implored, and in academic terms saw no advantage in entry to Cambridge in 1861, rather than 1862. His rowing and football careers were propitious. 'If I stay till next football half I shall be Captain of my House eleven and in the school eleven', Billy promised. If his father had settled on it, he hoped to persuade him to change his mind, hoping for discussion of the matter in the holidays.[29] Five days later, Billy, openly anxious about his plea, sent news Henry would be 'glad to hear': that he had 'got into the Victory which is the most honourable boat one can be in'.[30]

So the Trench boys struggled to please, to live up to fatherly expectations. Benny's prep school letters from Mr Wace's school at Wadhust mixed requests for money with the claims of achievement.[31] His father was concerned when he sustained an injury to his finger. He should follow the advice, he urged, of the Headmaster's wife, the school matron, adding 'you got your bat I hope'.[32] 'My dear Ben', he wrote in July 1859, 'I am delighted that you are likely to have a good place at the end of the half – this is first rate news for Papa'.[33]

When Benny pleaded for a boat on the lake at home, his father responded, indulgent but wary, teasing him, now he was fourteen and just off to Eton, with 'I fear an "Eton Man" would think very little of such an article.' Etonians were 'very swell', he reminded Benny, stressing their portrayal in *The Eton Block*, a book about the school which took its title from the school's notorious flogging block. This letter mixed tales of Benny's favourite dog, Rockwood, chasing hares and news of preparations for harvest with stern admonition about his Eton entrance: 'you are aware that Mr Wace gives you the work which he knows you will require . . . and to say truth I am not a little sanguine that you will get in with a credit for a good examination'. That would depend, he warned Benny, 'on your present determined work'. Having wished him well with his cricket, Henry Trench added, in a postscript, that Wace had told him that Benny was second in the class. 'This is something very near the mark', he declared, 'and cheers up the old gentleman.'[34]

His Eton tutor wrote warmly about his first term that December, finding Benny 'excessively correct', both in construing Latin and in his composition. It was heart-warming for the Trenchs that their youngest boy had so evidently won approval. 'I only trust he will not fall off in industry', wrote his tutor, 'if he goes on as he is now doing I think his career at Eton will be a very honourable one.' Benny was undoubtedly the brightest of these Trench boys, as his subsequent impressive career as a land agent in Ireland and a partner in a firm on the London stock exchange showed.

But what mattered to Henry and Georgiana Trench was Benny's generally appreciated 'gentle and affectionate disposition' and the family's unity, which ensured that his brother Billy saw him into Eton ways with thoughtful care.[35] Whichever of their parents the boys wrote to, the letter was passed between the library and the drawing room at Cangort Park. Thus we find Henry annotating a bulletin from Benny at sixteen about a shooting sweepstake in Windsor Great Park. He came in fifth in the 500 yards competition, but first at 200 yards, his final sentence revealed. Henry liked the humility of that: 'this comes last please observe Mama, H.T.', he scrawled before passing the letter on.[36]

Noblemen could expect a highly deferential attitude from schoolmasters who were favoured by their patronage. Samuel Devis, the master, hastened to assure Lord Bruce in 1768 that a bed would be 'put up and properly aired' for his boy's arrival at his Wandsworth school. After he had spent two years there, Devis, alarmed by a sore throat, moved the boy temporarily to Clapham. He quickly had him back, reporting to Lord Bruce that he was 'very well and healthy'. Devis added, by way of reassurance, that he had appointed a new school apothecary, who was keeping an eye on his young heir.[37]

In due course there were those among the gentry and aristocracy who, instead of opting safely for Eton or Harrow, became more adventurous. General Francis Seymour took advice about Mr Ford's school at Honfleur, which came to his notice when he was thinking about placing his son Hugh in 1856. He was impressed by what he heard about Mrs Ford's care for the health of her boys and about Mr Ford's skill in inculcating French and German. His papers include the annotated reports he received from Mr Ford about Hugh's progress at the school abroad between 1857 and 1859.[38]

The general, unusually, had set considerations of training in English class solidarity aside with Hugh. When he opted for a traditional school, Wellington, in the 1860s for his son Ernest, who was destined for the navy, he was quickly dissatisfied. Reports spoke of the boy's poor examination performances, related to want of industry, and of his nervousness. He discovered that Ernest had forgotten everything 'he had learnt in sacred history and geography from his mother, who has had great success in teaching these subjects in the schoolroom'. So, writing to his tutor, he mounted an attack on the way the public schools were still 'grinding on at Latin and Greek', neglecting important subjects like arithmetic. This letter to the boy's tutor was answered in person by the Master, E.W. Benson, who confessed that there had been cases of boys being taken away, but this was only, he insisted, because of the school food. Benson, living in something of a fantasy world, sought to rebut Seymour's complaint, by a defence of the school's academic record and of its training of character. 'Every day', he wrote, 'brings me some new proof of the high tone and manliness of the boys and of their gentlemanly feelings.'[39]

The case is an interesting one, because it shows why the general, not to be deterred from his objective of achieving Ernest's entry into Dartmouth, removed him from Wellington and sought to have him prepared for the navy's exams by attendance at a small school at Fareham, which quickly confirmed the 'good character of Ernest'. The boy also worked with a private tutor, where his life was worlds away from Wellington's rough and tumble: 'Mrs Domville will be pleased to have him', the tutor's wife wrote, 'and see that he is properly tucked into bed.'[40] The general's pleasure with the good job done with Hugh by the Fords at Honfleur had encouraged him to stand up to Benson at Wellington. He smoothed Ernest's path to Dartmouth by adopting an unorthodox course of action.

As the traditionalist Sydney Smith put it, writing to a friend for advice in 1817 about placing his son Douglas at twelve, 'the great consideration is the ultimate result'. Do they learn to construe Homer, Herodotus and the narrative part of Thucydides and write decent Latin prose and verse?, were the kind of questions he wished to ask. Thomas More, setting his mind on Harrow for his boy, started asking people's advice in 1828 about the best age for entry. Since Tom was then nine, he was told that he should wait about a year.[41]

Getting it right, fathers were by and large sensible enough to appreciate, was a matter of sensing the nature of a boy and the culture of a prospective school. John Grimston opted for Harrow for his son Thomas in 1769, despite his friend William Whateley's warning that drawing – 'your favourite accomplishment' – was not taught there at all, indeed that the only item outside the standard curriculum available was dancing.[42] William Roe had roughed it successfully at Westminster and gone on to Christchurch, Oxford in 1794. It was the Dean there who recommended to his father, who was looking, two years later, for a smaller and gentler establishment for his brother Frederick, 'a boy of slim delicate texture and of much sensibility', that Dr Horne's school at Chiswick might be a better bet than Westminster. It was close to the family home and there were only a hundred boys in the school. William Roe took comfort from the fact that the Dean's recommendation was backed 'by other friends whose judgement I respected'.[43]

John Pryor, a Hertfordshire brewer, sought to fit his son Alfred for a mercantile career, starting with apprenticeship, by placing him in a school in Cambridge. Settling his account with the master, he declared that he wished that attention be given to maths, mensuration, merchants' accounts, surveying and the use of globes. Alfred should also resume his dancing. But Pryor believed a tough regime was appropriate for his brighter second son Fred, who he was more ambitious for. In 1830, he sent him at eight years old across country to the very well-known prep school at Twyford in Hampshire. 'We left dear Fred very comfortable', he recorded in his diary after settling him in, noting the master's precepts and the penalties set out for the boys to read on the school wall. These were headed *ineptus*, *tardus* and *inurbanus*, the last – impoliteness – carrying the heaviest penalty, a public beating in front of the school. Pryor did not quail at the regime his eight-year old faced. It was time for him to take his own chances.[44]

Yet seeing boys off to school was something some fathers found traumatic. A number wrote feelingly about it. His father worried about how Frederick Roe would cope when he started at Chiswick in 1796, yet was much relieved at the outcome:

> He behaved with uncommon spirit and resolution before he went and when his mother, sister and myself left him at Doctor Horne's, he ran up to bed with the utmost fortitude and indeed, through the whole of this wretched process of first going to school and afterwards, he surprised us by his firmness.[45]

Sylvester Douglas, resident in London, reflected upon his feelings when his boy Fred started as a day boy at Westminster in 1801. He approved of how the school managed the boys, he doubted the excessive stress, as he saw it, on Latin and Greek but he believed in the training overall that the school offered. He felt, he noted in his diary, 'as if I should have liked to have entered myself at the same time in order to accompany him in his daily progress'. He recorded that 'Fred went off with considerable emotion but he kept it under very well . . . though if he had perceived my agitation I doubt if he would have done quite so well.'

That first week, he collected Fred each day and walked home with him across St James's Park. Within weeks, the boy had found his feet and his aspirations increased accordingly. 'He improves in looks, health and manliness', noted Douglas, now well satisfied, 'and is become a true schoolboy, but fully conscious that his knowledge is much beyond the Upper Third where he has been placed.' Fred grumbled and pouted at home about where he had been placed. His father, without influence in the matter, would try to change the subject.[46]

John Gisborne had taught his son Frederick himself in the boy's early years and found his departure, in 1807, a considerable wrench: 'when I reflect on the many hours which we have pleasantly spent together, I cannot refrain from tears at the loss of his company and his empty chair in my study touches me more sensibly than perhaps it ought to do'. He recalled that first departure ten years later when, as a proud scholarship boy, Frederick moved on from this local school: 'how I watched him as he turned out of the avenue . . . he had been a most dutiful pupil and I had never observed a sullen look upon his clear countenance'.[47]

Lord John Russell, concerned about how his fifteen-year-old son John was settling into Harrow in 1857, after he had spoken of how hard he found the work expected of him, wrote to his housemaster. 'A very kind nice letter from Mr Bradby', wrote Russell's daughter Victoria to her sister on 19 May. He assured Lord Russell that John was doing well and, though the boy felt burdened by the quantity of work demanded, it was 'not at all above his powers'. He had already risen from thirty-third to sixteenth in his form. But John Russell was patently an anxious Harrovian in the letters he wrote to his sister during 1858.[48]

John Oxley Parker started his son Cris at Mr Wickham's prep school in Worthing when he was nine years old in 1863, travelling with him himself from Essex. 'Cris behaved very well', he wrote in his diary, penning his boy a letter straight away, praising his composure:

> Considering that it was your first separation from home you behaved manfully. I could plainly see that your heart was full, but you bore yourself bravely throughout, and a little overflow at the last was only to be expected. When we parted I think Papa shed nearly as many tears as you did, but he was glad to feel that you were left in kind hands and that you would soon forget your troubles in the bustle of unpacking your things . . .

His father sought to spur Cris on in the next weeks, by holding out the prospect of his coming home: 'go to work like a man and keep at the top of the class and bring home a good steady working character'.

He was ready with reproof the following summer when, although top of the form, Cris was seen as slipping in one respect:

> There is one flaw in the report and it seems to come like an old story of an old fault in the schoolroom at home, you ought to be reminded of it, and the sooner you get rid of it the better. Mr Wickham says that you would do better with more attention at your desk.

'Play hours for play and school hours for school', admonished Papa sternly, reminding Cris of how his governess, Miss Brunswick, 'used to call it silly, and so do I, and so, you see, does Mr Wickham', whenever Cris thought lesson time was still play time.[49]

Fathers placing their boys in one of the major schools were often sensitive to how young they should be subjected to its rigours. Thus Richard Chenevix Trench decided to leave it until almost their fourteenth birthday, the limit the school placed on admittance, before moving his younger boys Alfred and Frank from Twyford prep school to Eton in the early 1860s. He remembered the intellectual thrill of his own maturer years at Harrow, when his mother, Melesina Trench, spoke of his 'craving for books'. He wanted his boys to have gained the confidence and strength of character to survive Victorian public school initiation before he threw them into it.[50]

Schoolboys, across these centuries, were of course bombarded with advice, which was moral, spiritual, academic and social. It was infinite in its variety and emphases. But the common ground lay in the assumption, shared by parents, grandparents, uncles and aunts alike, that schooldays were testing, that this was, in the broadest sense, the training ground for male public adulthood. Sir Henry Sidney, writing to his boy Philip at school early in the seventeenth century, urged him to 'be humble and obedient to your master, for unless you frame yourself to obey others, yea, and feel in yourself what obedience is, you shall never be able to teach others how to obey you'. He should work the hours he was set, 'be courteous of gesture and affable to all', giving reverence where it was due, never swear, and above all, 'tell no untruth'. [51]

Peter Sterry's letter of advice to his son, who started at Eton in the 1650s, is paradigmatic. He began with the grief he felt at leaving him there and his 'fear for the time to come'. The boy was told he must 'hold fast the precepts and rules of scripture, of your father, of your governors and elders'; not go into the town or adopt 'the company of any womankind'; tell his tutor about his 'temptations, dangers and troubles' and be advised. Sterry was not confident about his decision to settle his son at Eton, aware of its snares. If his son was too much tempted into moral degeneration, 'I am resolved', he wrote, 'to remove you before the devil have prevailed too far over you'.[52]

Nicholas Blundell received a firm reprimand at seventeen from his aged grandfather, William Blundell. 'I am sorry to perceive that the characters of your letters', he wrote in 1686, 'do still grow worse and worse.' His sister Mary was four years younger 'and yet she writes a very laudable hand'. Young Nicholas, his grandfather believed, did not lack wit and 'could show diligence as much as you please'. He should not blame his lack of progress in school on having a bad memory. He could still 'come off with credit'. His grandfather enclosed ten shillings and a book for learning his flageolet in encouragement.[53]

Ralph Verney started in 1695 at a small and closeted boarding school kept by Mrs Moreland at Hackney. His uncle sent him a copy of Richard Allestree's *Works*, avowing, 'I know you will make the best use of them.' 'You give your friends such extraordinary hopes of your making a fine gentleman, as well by your early induction to goodness as your industrious progress in learning', Ralph was told, that he deserved 'the greatest encouragement'.[54]

The tone of such advice remained essentially admonitory throughout the eighteenth and nineteenth centuries. Reginald Heber, rector of Hodnet in Yorkshire, wrote to his nine-year-old son in 1783. He was quite sure his boy's intelligence was such that learning was 'much easier to you than to many'. So 'it would be very ungrateful and culpable . . . not to cultivate and improve' his talents: 'I make no doubt you have many clever boys in your class and I doubt not you will feel and be incited by an honest emulation to keep pace with the best of them in running the race of honour and improvement in learning that is set before you.' He reiterated his belief in his son's 'honest and good heart', urging him not to omit his prayers morning and evening.[55]

A.F. Hudleston's father, writing to him at Haileybury in 1808, was an openly affectionate parent: 'we both love you very much and are sorry we are so far off'. The boy was reprimanded, though, for being involved in a recent school riot. He was told to write fortnightly, concentrate on shaping his letters and to 'keep up good habits'. It was 'wholesome' for him, his father made clear, to be under firm discipline.[56] Henry Alford's father was equally caring. He raised him to be a pious and introspective boy, beginning him in Latin himself at eight years old. 'Bring your mind to view things through a more sober medium', was his advice when his son was fifteen in 1825, 'and lower your expectations of happiness from earthly objects.' He was then boarding at Ilminster Grammar School.[57]

Sylvester Douglas's diary tells of his continuing close involvement with his boy Fred at Westminster. In April 1801, Fred went to a ball with two other Westminster boys. They dined at his own home first. The daughters of the host were 'very kind to our little dancer who enjoyed himself very much'. In October, Fred was 'a very subaltern personage' in a major rebellion at Westminster. His father's considered judgement was approval that 'he stood by the rest of the school', for the riot was almost universal: 'I should be very sorry if he were ever to be a ringleader in such a business, but, on the other hand, to stand off from a general act of the school would argue qualities I should dislike to see in him.' The following January, Sylvester was rejoicing in Fred's secure place at the head of the upper fourth form, at almost twelve years old. 'He seems to enjoy a much happier state of existence since he became an upper school boy', he noted.[58]

John Pryor recorded his pride and pleasure at his boy Fred's integration into the Winchester school community in 1835. Dining in hall on a visit, he noted, 'I was much gratified with seeing the whole ceremony which took place and partaking of the good cheer.' In 1838, he celebrated the boy's budding manliness, mentioning that, out with the hounds, he was 'in at the death'. The following year he congratulated Fred on his being made a prefect in chapel, in consequence of his 'application to his studies' and 'good behaviour'.[59]

Richard Chenevix Trench, vicar of Itchenstoke, asked his boy Charles to be 'very kind' to the son of a friend of his from Cambridge days, when they started their public school education together in the 1840s. Eager for news of his new world, he wanted to hear 'what boys you like best, and what games you play', besides where he was in his class. He trusted Charles was happy 'and what is a great deal more important' good: 'striving to please your masters, to be diligent in your work and truthful in all things and also that you maintain what is right and true among your playfellows'.[60]

There was already tension between Edmund Holland, aged sixteen, and his Harrow housemaster, Mr Davidson, over complaints about his behaviour sent in by colleagues, when an unfortunate incident provoked Davidson to lose all patience with him and seek his expulsion. Edmund banged the table, 'to express and convey satisfaction' that Davidson left the hall during a house singing event. His fellows applauded Edmund's audacity, but the housemaster overheard the applause. He withdrew the expulsion on 11 November 1892, after Edmund promised never to be rude to him again. His mother had achieved this lenience by pleading that his not being allowed to shoot all through the Christmas holiday was 'the greatest punishment we can inflict', since 'he likes his gun better than anything'. But his father's letter about the affair, on 24 November, reflects traditional thinking about hierarchy and obedience to superiors in striking terms:

> My dear boy – I was so sorry to hear about your row about your miscon- duct . . . a gentleman always yields to the ideas of right which are really most important and which others universally hold to be true . . . to obey those acting in authority and to respect them is certainly the right and gentlemanly course and one which in afterlife we all look back upon as the wise and just thing to have done.[61]

Things, of course, did not always go well at school. Extensive correspon- dence about George Hastings, between June and November 1692, shows an Eton boy apparently going off the rails, a deeply concerned tutor and a father sufficiently alarmed to agree to have the boy home and see him educated in the neighbourhood. A nobleman's son, George was under the constant eye of a personal tutor, Mr Hope, who took him to and from Eton. In June, Mr Hope reported to the Earl of Huntingdon that George seemed 'discontented and not at all reconciled to school'. A boy who, as his earlier letters home show, was placid and deferential had suddenly showed emotional imbalance.

Mr Hope's next letter reported him to be in 'sullen fits', refusing his breakfast and lolling on his bed: 'though I believe he means no harm to himself yet I have prevented all means by securing his sword'. Then the boy disappeared. His Eton tutor, Mr Newburgh, was fraught, assuring the Earl that 'all enquiry imaginable' was being made of him and that the story of another scholar recently drowning himself was false.

George was sighted tearing and throwing away Latin books. He returned to the school after a week's absence. Newburgh was full of protestations of his plans 'to bring him to his right mind again'. Yet he had to confess that the young nobleman scorned him, having 'an utter aversion to me, so his spirit raises him above any fear of me and where there is no regard either of love or fear, the pupil will have little advantage from such a tutor'. Fulminating against those who had been complicit in George's escape, Newburgh accepted defeat, initiating a move from 'a great to a country school'. By early July 1692, George had started at Tamworth, where he was examined and found 'fit for the second form'. Mr Hope, still watching the boy's progress on his father's behalf, told the Earl that he was 'well pleased with his lodgings and diet and observant to the method of the school'. George himself vowed that he 'followed his book closely' and was in 'active obedience' to his father's commands, in a letter home that November.[62]

There undoubtedly were boys who found the rigours of boarding school almost too hard to accept. Moreover, when a father simply put all his trust in a harsh master, the writing could be on the wall. There is little sign of sympathy or leniency in Thomas Knipe's story, as Master of Westminster in 1696, of how he sought to drag Lord Herbert's son Henry out of childishness. A defensive account, it pleads for patience from a prestigious parent, who has paid ten pounds extra a year for his son to have a chamber to himself. Knipe replied to a letter from Herbert, who had alleged that the school was to blame for the boy's unruly behaviour. He began with a reminder that he had complained before of his 'insufferable negligence and unwillingness to apply his mind to his business'. He had already threatened to send him home as a hopeless case. This was a boy who, 'when he had been called from his play to his studies, he had stood in the yard, crying and blubbering and roaring . . . because he might not play longer'.

Knipe was plausible, declaring that Henry 'can make both true Latin and true verse if he pleases'. He suggested, if his father were to 'propose him some reward he were very fond of', he might expect him to demonstrate the same academic competence at home as he did before his tutor and Knipe himself. He declared his determination and persistence: 'I imputed his carelessness to his childishness which, though it has remained longer with him than others of his age, I expected would go off by degrees . . . if this infirmity of his leaves him, I don't doubt but, upon his continuance with me, to finish him.'[63]

Sir Justinian Isham's boys were more fortunate in the sympathetic care and lenience they experienced from their Rugby headmaster, the Reverend Henry Holyoake, between 1702 and 1707. His cousin Judith kept house for him and looked after the boarders. Many Northamptonshire gentry had begun to patronise Rugby, approving Holyoake's regime, from the 1690s. John Isham was fourteen years old when they started and Edmund was aged twelve. Holyoake's letters chart their progress over five years. 'The little gentlemen will undoubtedly prove scholars', he wrote in an initial letter in May 1700, 'you have been pleased to send me good materials.' He promised to call upon Sir Justinian soon. A sober account of how hard John found his Greek, confessing also that Edmund was 'not so forward as I thought to have advanced him', followed in December. He had them both 'altogether at present under my own care', declaring that he would not part with Edmund 'till I have improved him so as to be able to lead the next class above him which I know I can effect'. Next April, he was promising 'all imaginable care' of John, when he was ill with a fever.

Rugby, escaping the complete tyranny of the classics, was offering what Sir Justinian, by the standards of the day, must have judged a rounded education. There was a resident Frenchman teaching the language: the Isham boys were keeping up a regular correspondence in French with their sister Vere, who was being taught it at home. By June 1702, Holyoake was confident that both boys would 'prove extraordinary scholars'. The writing master, he confessed, 'seems something slow' and the dancing master had not 'performed his part well', but he would do what he could 'to quicken them both'. At Christmas, there was another good report. John was showing 'ingenuity' in his Latin prose and verse compositions; Edmund also had 'made very great improvements'. Their morals bore 'proportion with their learning', their behaviour was 'always civil and decently modest' and their recreations were 'innocent'.

Then something went wrong. In June 1703, Holyoake explained in a letter on 23 July that both had 'strangely fallen from their former diligence and good humour, especially John who has not composed me one exercise well'. When one day he caught John 'cutting and mangling the covers of his new lexicon', Holyoake 'gave him a gentle correction upon the hand'. 'Mr John', he wrote, 'I also corrected in the same manner for his verses, which were intolerably bad, both in the meanness of the sense and quantity.' These beatings, though mild beside standard floggings at this time, caused both boys to run away. They were five miles or so from Rugby when messengers, followed by the headmaster's brother on horseback, found them and brought them back. Instead of the expected thorough flogging, Holyoake now chose a milder course, distressed that 'they who were of so great hopes should frustrate at last the expectations of their parents and master'. He hoped a 'chiding line or two to each of them' would have good effects. He explained the plan to Sir Justinian. 'I have not punished them for this their fault, but make this complaint their punishment, knowing that your frown will produce much greater effects than all the master's rods.' Paternal admonition worked, Holyoake writing:

> The young gentlemen are extremely altered for the better and go cheer-fully on with their business. Mr John was never more diligent than now and seems to make his study his pleasure. Mr Edmund also has effec-tively reconciled himself to school and I am not a little rejoiced to think that I took the right method in giving speedy notice and return my humble thanks, sir, for your so reasonable assistance.

The relationship between Holyoake and Sir Justinian brought mutual satisfaction. John went on from Rugby to Christ Church at age seventeen in 1705. Returning him 'with my humble thanks for the favour of his education', Holyoake told his father, 'I know he'll gain both himself and me no mean credit and am confident will shine with a particular figure in the University.' He took his MA in 1713, the year that he was also elected a Fellow of All Souls. In 1707, Holyoake agreed that Edmund was ripe for university: he was qualified 'both as to age and learning', having made himself 'a good substan-tial scholar'. Holyoake suggested Balliol or Magdalen. He expected Edmund to 'prove diligent and endeavour to please so kind a father, by that means in some measure to answer your great care and expense in his education'. His was actually the more distinguished subsequent career. After a fellowship at Magdalen, he became a judge advocate of the Court of Admiralty from 1731 to 1741, inheriting his father's title and estate as the sixth Baronet in 1737.[64]

Issues of discipline and academic progress were often intertwined. Pedagogic method was based on the assumption, persistent across this period, that learning could be beaten into boys. This did not mean, however, that every father went along with fierce use of the birch. Claver Morris's long-running debate with Mr Wilding at Sherborne School, over his treatment of his son Willie, illustrates this. Morris's tactic was to visit the school. After Wilding had conducted an examination of the boy's classical learning in his presence, he remonstrated with him about the excessive flogging being imposed upon him. He managed to establish that three lashes, not fourteen as previously, should be Wilding's limit.

On another visit in 1724, Wilding was full of promises that he would make Willie an 'incomparable scholar', yet regular use of the birch, he insisted, was still needed to check his idleness. Calling his father's bluff, he declared that Morris could, if he wished, go home and tell the boy's mother he would be whipped no more. No, Morris replied, 'all would be spoiled that way'. He desired 'only moderate correction ... which to him a good-natured and flexible, though lazy, boy I hoped would be effectual'.[65]

The reactions of fathers to how their sons were treated at school depended partly on the intensity of their ambitions for them. Posthumous Wharton knew, in corresponding with Sir Daniel Fleming, that the boys in his charge had a fierce disciplinarian for a father. Roger, in trouble for his football and scrapping with other boys, was threatened with expulsion. He only escaped this because Sir Daniel explicitly gave Wharton a free hand with the birch. When James had been the ringleader in visiting Sedbergh town alehouses and had already been beaten, Wharton, reporting this flogging, followed it up by urging his father to send the boy a sharp letter.[66]

Edward Lord Stanley, exasperated with his obstreperous son Johnny before he went to Harrow, had no sympathy with him at all when, predictably, he soon got into trouble. He had been both flogged and expelled for, as his wife explained to him, 'being up all night and also for jumping over the dinner table when Dr Vaughan was there, which is considered a great breach of discipline'. Vaughan, a formidable Victorian headmaster, was not to be trifled with by this kind of defiance. But Lord Stanley took Vaughan on. His son's expulsion was an unacceptable confession to the school's failure. He blamed Harrow, reflecting, as he paid the school's account, that the 'amount is large and the profits seem to have been small'. The headmaster, he asserted, had not made the school 'the place of education and correction that it should be'. He had nothing to offer, except orders that his boy 'be shut up in his room and deprived of his dog' at home at Alderley. At seventeen, Johnny was sent off to the army.[67]

Thomas More, a reasonable man, informed by Tom's schoolmaster that he had given him an over-severe beating for a fault now confessed by another, reflected with pride that his son was 'very manly and sensible about it'. He took no action.[68] He struck the note which summarises all these interactions between schoolmasters and fathers. Schooling was a training for the knocks in the world. 'My knees are raw with praying, for my master being a priest he makes me pray three or four times daily', wrote Thomas Bishop to his cousin, having been settled at Mr Canton's school in Hammersmith.[69] Fathers, almost but not quite universally, in these centuries, believed in what was meted out to their boys. They took immense trouble to ensure that they were placed in the best school they could afford. They were determined that, in the long run, their sons would benefit from taking the rough with the smooth. Pushing them out of the home young, their sights were set on the independence of their boys and their achievement of strong and effective manhood.

Mothers and Educating Boys

As thousands of boys during these three hundred years tackled the tough and demanding trials of schooldays away from home, thousands of mothers missed them and grieved for their boys undergoing these rigours. The desire that their boys become loving and considerate adults, who displayed gentleness of character, clashed with the kind of masculinity and the emphasis on physical prowess taught in boarding schools. This is a subject that is little documented, because mothers by and large bit their lips and remained silent. They wrote letters to their boys, of course, and, once they were settled in, many boys sent them news regularly, taking care about what they told and what they kept to themselves. The letters of school news that mothers received often brought them solace and encouragement.

The schooling of boys was perhaps the supreme test of a marital relationship. There were men ready to ride roughshod over their wives, in their determination to make a man of their boys, dismissing their concerns out of hand. Others listened and proceeded with patience. With three sons entering and approaching their teens, we have seen how, in 1727, Sir Edward Filmer believed that the time was right to embark on the training that Winchester could give them, as a preparation for entry to its sister foundation of New College. But his wife dragged her heels. In correspondence that summer with her, John Harris wore down her resistance. He assured her that there were men in Oxford who would be glad to give 'friendship to his children'. The prospect, if his advice was followed, of getting a boy on to the foundation was strong. Then came the dose of realism: 'As to the hardships they go through, I do assure you they are no more than what all boys must go through that are bred out of a nursery and it must be a very tender mother that would desire them to be less than they are.'

Lady Filmer argued for delay over Winchester, but Harris urged that, with John thirteen, there was no more time to be wasted on the inadequate teaching of local schools. As for her fears about travelling the notorious

Wealden roads, his home at Chiddingfold in Surrey could be a staging post. He would assist with their ride to Winchester from there onwards. She was mollified. It was reassuring, at Christmas, to see how Winchester air seemed to suit her boys, but Sir Edward had to tell Harris that, under their mother's close questioning, they confessed how hard they were finding the demands of the curriculum and the school's regime. She worried that her boys lacked the 'good memories' that some of the rote learning required of them.

Revealing correspondence with Mr Browne, the master of Cranbrook School, indicates the assertiveness that Lady Filmer learnt later, when the younger members of her brood boarded more locally in the 1740s. He was not the only one writing home about ill usage, her boy Edward confessed to her. Instead of an afternoon holiday, he had been set '100 lines, 30 by heart, 70 to translate from Ovid, for nothing else but beginning our repetition aloud 10 lines too little'. In a strongly worded letter, she accused Browne of 'inspiring slavish awe' in her younger boys. She was particularly incensed by his reading of a letter that she had sent to Edward and his general threat to open letters sent to boys. 'I will never entrust a child', she declared, 'where I may not have the privilege of writing or receiving letters from him without their being exposed, whether I like it or not.'

Georgiana Trench had none of these problems in Ireland in the 1850s. She went along with Eton, such a long way from County Offaly, because her boys were prepared for it, in their tender years, at a small family establishment, remotely situated in the Sussex Weald. Attending the Reverend Richard Wace's prep school, Hill House at Wadhurst, involved a two-day train journey six times a year, crossing the Irish sea and Wales, to London and the south east. A boy who was there with the Trenchs later recalled the school's intimate atmosphere: 'there were only nine or ten boys and we were treated by Mr and Mrs Wace as if we were members of a large family'. Latin and Greek was the basis of the curriculum, but boys were also coached in arithmetic, algebra and Euclid. This commentator testified both to Wace's good influence, as 'a devout old evangelical', and to the 'excellent moral tone' of the school.[1]

The Trench boys were clearly happy at Wadhurst. Georgiana had total confidence in the Waces. 'I feel so thankful, darling Ben', she wrote in his last term, 'that Papa was directed to send you there. I think that good must result from such pains as are taken with the boys and such anxious concern – dearest Ben – for their souls.' Easily emotional, Georgiana wrote from the heart: it was her children's souls that she dreaded losing most. 'We never shall know', she declared, 'the extent of the value of such friends as will care for our souls, till Eternity opens before us and we then see that is [sic] a real thing'.[2]

Apprehension about starting boys at boarding school was entirely normal. Mothers were loath for them to go any sooner than was absolutely necessary.

Jack Verney, the heir to Claydon House, born in 1711, was a big boy but a delicate one. At three-and-a-half, his mother, Catherine Verney, sent for some leading strings, of 'a stuff made on purpose that is very strong, for he is so heavy I dare not venture him with a common ribbon'. Taught by the rector at Claydon, Mr Butterfield, he was something of a handful. 'I heard Jack read yesterday', wrote Catherine to her husband despairingly in 1721, 'and 'tis so bad that I believe I shall have another bout very soon.' It was her further report, that she did not think either of her boys improved 'one bit', that led to their father's decision to send Jack, now nine, to school in Fulham. Catherine had found him 'mighty brisk' outside his lessons that spring.[3]

Around 1800, Lady Elizabeth Holland worried, with her son just off to Eton, that 'the world of a public school he will find very different from that of the world seen from under the parental roof'. Charlotte Guest, similarly, in 1845, visiting Eton which she knew by repute, confided to the privacy of her journal her feelings about her ten-year-old Ivor starting there. Moreover, she faced the prospect of others of her boys following: 'when I thought of all the sorrow and temptation my poor boys would have to go through in that place I quite shuddered'. She found the whole business 'a sad prospect', reflecting that 'everybody says it is the only way to bring up boys; and what is to be done? How can I, a poor weak woman, judge against all the world?'[4]

Despite her own ill heath and growing difficulties in the nursery, Lady Freda Lorraine did not jump at her husband's proposal that her Eustace should go to prep school at seven. It was another three years before he left home at ten, in 1890, when his brother, too, was seen as ready to go, now he was nine years old. Freda's influence on her boys in those extra years was substantial. She was proud of this and was then very proactive, with Sir Lambton Lorraine, in the choice of school for them.[5]

Mothers were deeply involved in the schooling of their sons, whether they were missing them, anticipating their return or just reading their letters. Six letters from the Wiltshire gentlewoman Frances Lake to her son Robert, at school in Salisbury around 1740, exemplify the kind of concerns that exercised them. Her husband had talked of sending for him and his brother, she wrote, but, with the weather 'like to be bad for riding', she preferred them to defer their journey home. Meanwhile, 'we want to have you get this art of keeping money without spending more than is proper', she admonished, sending extra pocket money and some Golden Pippin apples.

'I desire you will not engage in any dangerous exploits on the King's birthday', Frances declared, knowing the temptation there would be in the city for Robert to join others in 'bonfires, squibs, riots'. She urged him to ensure that the new breeches he was ordering were 'made with a sound good skin'. Although she considered them 'ugly', she agreed to his request for a 'shag coat', suggesting that 'a warm lining in your everyday waistcoat' would be better. His parents, she assured him, were determined 'not to deny your moderate requests whilst you so well study your duty to us'.

Robert's father later returned from Salisbury with news that Robert had made a good recovery from a mild attack of smallpox. This reassured Frances a great deal: 'I was mightily pleased yesterday when your Papa came home and told me that he had seen you and how pure, stout and well you do look.' 'Don't scratch your face', she insisted, 'nor bite your nails for I fancy that will keep the infection longer.' It was a pity to spoil his fingers 'now Papa says they be very handsome'.

Despite her longing 'that we may be all together again', she was dismayed, soon after this, when Robert appeared with some friends at their home, Lake House in Wilsford near Amesbury, without warning them. 'There was surely such a decency to be paid to your father', she chided, 'as to believe that no other company could be agreeable to him till you had notice.' Moreover, the virulence of the smallpox in Salisbury made this visit ill-timed. 'The smallpox is such a terror to me that I couldn't think myself safe to be with any one that I knew went where it was.'[6]

We have to infer the emotions behind Mary Woodforde's diary entry about 'my dear little Willie' going off 'to board at Mr Wallace, to go to school' at Winchester in 1687.[7] But Frances Boscawen let slip her excitement, in 1755, about going home to Hatchlands in Surrey, 'where I shall see my dear little fellow', who had just started at Eton.[8] When the Dickensons, of Taxal in Derbyshire, decided to send their boy Jack south to a Northampton school, they asked their friends the Hamiltons, resident there, to keep an eye on him. Mrs Dickenson explained the situation to Mary Hamilton in January 1771: 'he has had great disadvantages by being brought up at a country school, but I hope your fine town will polish him . . . I am under a good deal of anxiety upon parting with my dear boy'. A few weeks later, after Jack had been home, Mrs Dickenson spoke of 'how obliging' the Hamiltons had been to her dear boy, 'which he is perpetually talking of'. 'We think him much grown and improved', she declared, 'and I hope he is good.'[9]

A strong relationship formed between a boy and his mother before he went away could pay dividends. Dorothy Hodges wrote regularly to her son Tom at Harrow and received affectionate and intimate letters in return between 1788 and 1793. She inured herself to his immersion in a brutal society. When Tom often wrote of his longing for the holidays, it consoled his mother to supply his wants meanwhile: a new 'waistcoat with sleeves as some of the boys have them', and a mallet, plane and saw when he took up woodwork. It pleased her that he was diverting himself, first with a share in a rabbit partnership, then by keeping a dog that he 'took out twice a day and sometimes thrice', then with a bantam cock. She lived out his worries with him: 'you can't think how I tremble at the thought of it', Tom wrote when his trial for the fifth form was coming up. 'I hope I shall get in', he declared. He ended with his 'duty to Papa' and love to his sister Eliza.

Finally, well-settled in at Harrow after more than a year, Tom announced that it was a 'pleasure to tell you I never was happier at school than I am'. Dorothy Hodges saw him become serious and responsible. If there were early brushes with authority, he kept them to himself. About to enter the sixth form in 1791, thanking Eliza for her long unanswered letter, he reflected on the prospect of becoming a monitor himself 'and then there is no step higher to be obtained except my further studies and improvement which can only be obtained through my own means'. His confidence burgeoning, Tom wrote to his father about plans for work on the family's estate. Meanwhile, it was his monitor's week. 'I certainly plan to have some noisy youth flogged', he boasted. He had come through the system, which he took at face value, while seeking to allay his mother's anxiety about how his brothers Harry and Frank, coming along behind him, were faring.

Dorothy Hodges realised that the first terms were the dangerous ones at Harrow. So when Harry settled in, trusting that Tom would be honest, she asked for a factual and impartial report on his progress. 'You may I think cease to be alarmed on the flogging head for if he keeps on as he is now he has no sort of chance of suffering.' Tom found his brother's temper more even every day, announcing that he was 'more manly and resolute in his conduct'. Harry, he reckoned, had made it like he had done. 'In short', he concluded, 'if ever any boy was benefited by a public school he has been most essentially.'

Tom was at this time in high spirits. His dancing lessons, 'where we dance country dances and cotillons', gave him, he felt, physical poise; his health was good and he felt himself 'very strong'; he was regular in 'the calls of nature'; he slept well and ate particularly well. His only regret, he told his mother, was his small stature. Yet if school was good for him, Tom kept his heart open for home. His mother's letters, he declared, gave him 'infinite pleasure', making him 'a while forget I am at school'. Holidays in a loving home represented release from privations and challenges: 'when I come I shall bring death to the sparrows with my bows ... every day seems a month, every hour a day'.[10] Dorothy Hodges clearly managed to cope with her own anxiety about her boys being some way from home at an unreformed public school, known before 1800 for its fierce discipline, because they themselves adapted to it so well.[11]

By contrast, Elizabeth Warriner's correspondence with her son George, between 1796 and 1798, reveals a mother in considerable distress, as she tried to hold on to the affections of a boy who she felt was slipping away from her.

She poured out her maternal emotions to him, having settled him into Mr and Mrs Brooks's Brighton prep school in September 1796:

> I could not feel quite comfortable after parting from you, as I know your heart went with us but, bless you, you behaved like a man. We saw you at the end of the Steane and poor Sophia's tears flowed afresh, but, my dear love, we know it is all for your good, both for your health and for the improvement of your mind . . . so I hope and trust in a few days you will find yourself quite reconciled and very comfortable, which will give me very great pleasure to hear . . . I hope you will look upon it as your duty to be happy, in the situation you are in, as you know how ready your father and I are to indulge you in any little matters that may make you so.

She would send him 'your wine', with 'two more pocket handkerchiefs and your other two cravats', the next week. She urged him to write, sending the 'kind love' of his sisters. She reminded him of her prayers daily for his 'health and happiness'.[12]

Her letter on 4 February 1797 shows Elizabeth was distraught about a lump on George's body, which the attentions of her doctor in Warwickshire had not cured in the holidays. She was glad to know that he had arrived safely in Brighton, was sending things he needed and hoped he was 'happy and comfortable'. His Papa was blaming George for not taking the treatment prescribed for him seriously enough. She believed the 'cold sea water' he was now to use would do the trick, so she planned not to mention to Papa that the cure was incomplete. Elizabeth wrote again the next week saying they wanted George to do 'one quarter more dancing'; then again sending mince pies; then again on 2 March, fearing an invasion and directing that, if a foreign landing was attempted at Brighton, he should 'come home directly'.

In her letter on 11 February Elizabeth had pleaded for George's friendship, confessing the turmoil that she had been in over Christmas:

> I sometimes felt myself a little hurt when I thought you did not show so much regard for me as you used to do and I was much afraid your being so long from me had lessened your affection, but I hope and trust it was not so only your being so full of spirits at being at home and my health being so indifferent.

When George replied uneasily but warmly, she realised that she needed to adapt to her boarding school boy's new life, telling him she was 'quite satisfied of your regard' and to 'think no more about it'.

Elizabeth understood that she had to respect her husband's commitment to Mr and Mrs Brooks's school. He urged his son on to 'best endeavours and improvement' in March 1797. In 1798, George moved to a school at Wokingham in Berkshire. Elizabeth fussed about his being out in the rain and joined her husband in again urging 'improvement' that November. She sent cash for him 'to give the servants when you dine out', longing, she said, for his return home. 'We begin to want to see you very much', she wrote on 29 December that year, 'and hope it will not be long.'[13]

Even day school tested motherly protectiveness. Sylvester Douglas was an acute commentator on his wife's distress, when his son started as a day boy at Westminster in 1801. She saw him leave their home in Bruton Street 'like a heroine'. He reflected that this was 'a new epoch and though the relation of mother and son will I am sure remain equally tender and affectionate between them, its mode and form will be different and till the new habit is formed must seem somehow less endearing'. He believed strongly in parental duty to 'resist the softening tendency of such feelings' as those his wife was mastering. 'I know', he noted in his diary, 'she will not fail in this part of her duty.'[14]

Elizabeth Wynne sent her Tom away to boarding school at seven in 1805, recounting to her husband how things were going twice in the first weeks. 'He went to school in tolerable spirits on Saturday', she wrote on 18 September, 'but seemed much affected when his uncle and aunt left him. He however behaved remarkably well . . . I felt extremely low and out of spirits all day, thinking of the boy, though Mr Morgan assures me he was perfectly reconciled to school and his companions.' Four days later, she was more cheerful, after receiving Tom's first letter saying he liked school: 'I hope, poor fellow, he will make himself tolerably happy and comfortable.'[15]

An undated early nineteenth-century letter from William Beal's mother purveyed standard advice to homesick offspring. She had been told he cried very much after she left: 'you know that your mother always loves you . . . be a good boy my dear . . . make haste and learn your tasks and the time will soon come when your father will come and fetch you home again'.[16]

The hardest part for mothers was coming to terms with sons who took to school like a duck to water. 'It has cost me a great deal to part with my boys', wrote Hannah Allen in her diary in 1848. She recounted her Stanny's high glee, his coming back down the street for one more kiss, before he ran off again and his immediate wish to board, so that he could spend evenings at play with other boys. Did he not want to play with his little brother and sister at home, she asked unavailingly.[17]

What could a besotted mother do except write incessantly when a son was far away? The Duchess of Cambridge was separated from her boy George, a nephew of William IV, in 1830, when his father insisted on moving him, at eleven, from their home in Hanover, to begin a rigorous course of training in manliness and polite behaviour at the English court. A private tutor was appointed to take overall control of his work. Her instructions, the day she said goodbye, were intended to preserve as much as possible of what she found precious in her mothering:

> Did I not, my angel boy, well keep my promise to you to make the parting quick and short? God grant that you have not grieved too much and had no return of your severe bad headache . . . You must write to me very fully – all details, my dear good George! . . . No secrets from me . . . Make plenty of time to write, it is my only consolation . . . Your tutors I do not wish should read either my letters to you or yours to me . . . I kiss you in thought. Alas! that I cannot myself really do so.

Reiterating the hopes of the salve his letters might bring, she told him the next day to write to her 'quite alone, as your heart dictates, not stiff and formal'. The Duchess wrote to George every day from Hanover, but it is clear that he wrote to her much less frequently, once he was immersed in lessons, the court round and visits with the King to the Royal Pavilion at Brighton.[18]

The favourite motherly tactic for bereft and unhappy schoolboys was to send regular parcels and treats. John Ramsden, only eleven and missing his mother at prep school in 1842, sent an extensive list of needs: big marbles, biscuits, brown bread loaf with currants, raisins and citron. 'Are not you delighted', he added hopefully and plaintively, 'it is so near the holidays: you will soon have the pleasure of seeing me again very very soon.' He wished 'the day was come for me to go'.[19]

After his rough passage with his housemaster in 1892, Edmund Holland inured himself to his Harrow years, writing chattily to his mother when she sent him things. 'I like the goslings very much', he declared, thanking her belatedly for a hamper in July 1894, which he was sorry not to have acknowledged. A remark that December, near his leaving day, summarised his schooldays: 'nothing has happened here at all and it is awful rot'.[20]

Much of the pressure boys felt under was often created by themselves, as an unconscious response to parental expectation. Writing to Meriel Lyttelton in 1856, Catherine Talbot related how her Edward had fared 'in that awful crisis of life, his debut at a public school'. He was a day boy at Charterhouse, setting out by cab from his home in Westminster and returning by omnibus or penny steamer. At first he was so nervous he could not eat his breakfast. But soon the trouble was that he worked too hard. Her husband had 'preached to him that he is over particular but he says he cannot bear to show up such papers as he sees others do, so he pores over every word till I can hardly get him to bed'.[21]

Mothers needed their boys to write to them. Boys were often not simply conscientious about doing so, but they actually fulfilled their own emotional needs by regaling their news. The letters that the Hastings boys wrote from their Marylebone prep school to their Mama, Selina Countess of Huntingdon, at Donington Park in Leicestershire between 1739 and 1743, were usually cheerful and engaging. She, we have already seen, was an affectionate and dedicated mother. George returned to school after some illness, travelling with an aunt, at about nine years old, in July 1739. He told his mother how she had praised him for behaving himself 'very well'. He now hoped to catch up with work missed towards the task set by his teacher. His youngest brother Ferdinando, at the same school, 'seems to be perfectly easy', George confirmed the next week.

George's letters then became a little frantic when he heard nothing for a while from home. 'I suppose you have been hindered by company', he mused on 6 September. There were some issues that month about the clothes he would need for the winter. When his Mama did eventually write in October, he protested deferentially that his pleasure in making her happy, 'besides duty', drove on his performance: 'That of yours made me very happy as indeed I always am and shall be when I think you and Papa are pleased with my behaviour. I shall often think of and endeavour to put in practice the good instructions you give me.' By December, George was pining for his home. His words 'I long to see you, Papa and my sisters' on the fifteenth were heartfelt. He was grateful for the half crown that his mother had sent and enclosed, as proof of his endeavour, 'an exercise book which I can assure you I did myself and that it has not been looked over by anybody'.

All three Hastings boys at Marylebone found the winter tough. They pleaded for a parental visit to the family home in Enfield Chase near London. 'I think it is very long since I parted with you', wrote George on 25 January 1740. He had expected a letter from his sister for a while, remonstrated Francis in February. Had she forgotten about it? He was keeping an eye on his little brother Ferdy, who, he explained, in September had worn out his black clothes: 'he is obliged to wear his grey every day which are in a fine pickle'. Francis, as he grew older and went on to Westminster, tended to write to his Papa but George, who was thrilled with a visit to Ranelagh gardens in April 1742, remained a good letter writer to his Mama. He was concerned again about Ferdy's clothes at that time. Letters from Ferdy himself, before he died of smallpox in 1743, if they were sent, do not survive. When George, as we have seen, died of smallpox in the same year, Selina was left with two boys only, comforts in an uncertain world.[22]

Her serious-minded eldest son and heir Edward kept up an informative and contented correspondence with Lady Maria Stanley, during his prep school and Eton years from 1813 to 1820. He had not been in much trouble, he reported at eleven years old: 'one imposition for talking and one for being late in the morning'. He went on to Eton before his twin brother William, who he helped through its initial rigours by having him to breakfast and tea each day, when he was getting settled in April 1817. He was thrilled with the kaleidoscope he had been sent at that time. He was trying to make another one but having difficulty 'in getting small bits of coloured glass'. Meanwhile, he was working hard for the trials for his remove.

A year later in 1818, Edward expressed concern about 'poor Papa', immobile after an operation. He assured his mother that William was still 'very well and happy', messing with him every day. 'I have been in very good pax with my tutor the whole of the half year as yet', he wrote. In early May, he passed on thanks to his sister Emmeline, then nine, for a letter he had liked very much. William had 'taken to his old trade of fishing', having acquired a new rod. Edward himself was struggling hard to climb Eton's greasy pole, hoping to achieve a place in the fifth form and escape fagging the next month. He had not played much cricket that summer, 'as I am still a lower boy and liable to be fagged'. Dr Keate was keeping him 'plentifully supplied' with academic demands, he announced later that month. Yet he had been swimming and fishing too. This was all exactly the kind of news a mother wanted to hear, as her eldest ran the course which would fit him for life as a Cheshire landlord.

Edward was at Eton in the years that rebellion against the officious flogging head Dr Keate was at its height. In October 1818, Keate introduced an earlier lock-up and roll call, at five instead of six in winter, which one boy, Marriott, a popular figure, defied. Refusing a flogging, Marriott was expelled and became a martyr. Keate was hissed and jeered in prayers and a posse, all of them later expelled for the act, smashed the headmaster's stately desk of office, raised on a podium, to pieces with a sledge-hammer.[23] Edward knew that news of the latest rebellion would have reached his mother at Alderley. So he hastened to assure her that he had not had 'any concern whatever with the rioting', yet, sharing the general hatred of Keate at that time, he was 'vastly inclined that way'.

Edward Stanley, a studious boy always asking his mother to send him more books to read, was by no means a typical Etonian. The critique he confided to his mother of the school's procedure for confirmation in the Regency period, after he was one of two hundred massed for the service in the chapel, decried it as an empty and conventional piece of ritual: 'I do not think that Eton is the properest place in the world for serious thoughts, neither do I think the ceremony itself sufficiently impressive – the bishop lays hands on two or three at once – says the prayer for about every twenty. It looks altogether too much hurried over.'

By the end of April 1819, Edward and William, at seventeen, were reaching the level plains of seniority. 'All the summer amusements are in full force', ran Edward's report home, 'I have taken up cricket and played a good deal. William has a boat of his own for the season and goes out often.' His work, now stressing Greek exercises, was going well. The following July, he was writing a long poem and a commentary on the New Testament for his tutor in his last fortnight at Eton. Edward berated his elder sister Lucy, via his mother, for failing to write to him. He reflected as follows on the investment his parents had made in his education: 'I really do not know whether I am glad or sorry to leave Eton; it seems like losing an old friend and changing one's entire shell. Certainly for this time it makes me feel older, whether I may be happier or not remains to be proved.' Her eldest son, Lady Stanley could appreciate, having started at Eton as a boy, was now a man. The world beckoned him.[24]

Eton masters and above all the headmaster, John Chandos has written, 'accepted tips from boys in much the same spirit as hotel staff taking tips from departing guests'. Edward Stanley was just one of those who acquiesced in such transactions, conducted by the authorities with 'magnificent shamelessness'. Lady Stanley, the wife of a peer of the realm, was expected to give more than most. He knew she would growl, Edward wrote plausibly, 'at what expense boys are at Eton', but he and William had 'as few debts I think as any'. He enumerated the final expenses that were due: fifteen pounds for Keate, twenty pounds for the tutor with whom they had boarded, a guinea each for the cook there, their manservant and their 'own maid'. Who was Lady Stanley to baulk at time-honoured aristocratic patronage of this kind?[25]

Unusually, the survival of letters home to both his parents written by Rudolf Fielding, a Cheam prep school boy, in 1831, allow comparison of the styles of writing that he employed. Predictably, the one to Mama is easier, less stiff and formal than his missive to his father, which has been discussed above.[26] A remark about whether the family estate at Newnham Paddox in Warwickshire was looking 'very pretty' in its autumn colouring represented conventional politeness, but, taken overall, the letter to his mother showed some emotions and listed his needs. 'Please to tell me whether my little kitchen garden and rabbit are going on quite well', Rudolf asked. He wanted his mother to send 'another straight taper', sealing wax and a 'good bundle of pens'. 'A hasty answer is required', ran the assertive postscript.[27]

Letters from both John Ramsden and from his Eton tutors, Mr Johnson and Mr Norris, to his mother, Lady Ramsden of Bulstrode Park, Gerrards Cross, between 1844 and 1848 illuminate the dynamic and complex web of relationships which sometimes governed a school career in the Victorian period. Quite a timid boy, John felt his way carefully. He had a nice room, his dame gave him 'decent food', he had begun football, he reported in his first year. He pleaded for five pounds more pocket money, raising it to a sum he claimed was normal 'in the part of the school in which I am'. He purchased two goldfinches with the cash, which he kept in a cage in his room.

John explained that he had decided to pass by the tempting prospect of Windsor Fair, with 'all masters up there watching for us'. If caught, he would be 'switched' and lose his remove into the fifth form. He quickly learnt to avoid football as far as possible: 'broken arms and broken collarbones are things of every day occurrence and I know that my collarbone would not stand anything'. The year 1845, marked by his fourteenth birthday, saw John Ramsden's confidence and daring increase. He related a scrape out of bounds, when he 'with another fellow saw two masters coming'. He concentrated on his swimming, winning himself privilege by passing a test. Now he could be on the river whenever he wanted: 'no master can jaw me'.

Letters home in the autumn of 1846 suggest that John was still making the best of things. Homer, Virgil, Horace and Cicero, 'and other vile productions of the ancients', dominated his, as all schoolboys' lives, at this time, but there was consolation in three full cages of birds. He was looking for a handsome parakeet to add to this aviary. Football was getting rougher and had landed him with a broken arm and sprained wrist. He was tense over the Albert Prize: 'I should not object to a ham and other marks of affection', he declared, with the stress of that competition coming up. By December he was broke: 'not to mince it will you send me some money?'.

Lady Ramsden, meanwhile, concerned about her son's progress, was in regular contact with his tutor, Mr Johnson, who was driving John relentlessly. 'You could not wish him to go on better', was his 1846 report. The Eton medicine, he insisted, was working: 'he has taken to football in earnest and in general is becoming less childish and more manly every day'. But, in 1848, John became engaged, at seventeen, in a struggle of wills with Mr Norris, his new tutor. Trouble began when, now rather above himself, he clashed with his dame, who reported him for talking during prayers and insubordination at dinner. Norris punished John for irregularities, like failure to be down for prayers, by demanding extra work on the history of Greece. There was nothing Eton boys prized more than private breakfasting with special friends, a privilege of good behaviour and academic effort, which his tutor now decided John should be denied. He was angry and defiant, seeking to bring his mother into the quarrel, which simply annoyed his tutor.

As the conflict escalated, the prospect of 'school discipline' for insubordination loomed into John's life. Flogging on the bare buttocks at the block remained the ultimate Eton sanction in the 1840s. John Ramsden's attitude to it combined fear of the degradation of removing his breeches with fear of the birchrod itself. If he went on arguing and failed to convince Norris of his case for private breakfasting, he told his mother, 'why I shall be flogged!!!' 'Certainly there is nothing I have such an utter horror of', he declared, yet he felt exasperated by Norris's 'tyranny'.

Norris, meanwhile, told Lady Ramsden of her boy's 'headstrong temper'. He narrated their final confrontation. A lecture on 'the impropriety and unworthiness of all this conduct' brought 'a profusion of tears' from the boy, Norris requiring 'prompt recognition of my authority'. The only alternative was that 'school discipline should take its course'. When John agreed to turn over a new leaf, he thought 'we might do without the extreme punishment'. 'I remember', he told Lady Ramsden, 'what you said about his undemonstrativeness and give him credit for more purpose of amendment than he expressed.' She had effectively helped to save him from the flogging, since it was hard to subject him to it in face of her motherly care.[28]

Inheriting Alderley and the Stanley peerage in 1850, the Etonian Lord Edward naturally sent his boys to the old school. The one who shone most brightly there was clever Lyulph, earlier led astray by his impossible older brother Johnny. Lyulph's academic achievement both there, and later at Balliol, brought gratification to him and his wife Lady Henrietta Stanley. At fifteen, on 29 November 1854, Lyulph was pleading with her for peace and quiet over Christmas at Alderley, since he would come home with much academic work in hand. The next March, enjoying the diversion of skating on the Thames in a hard winter, his principal news was about progress in German and his work on Thucydides, having decided to enter for the Newcastle Prize. He hastened to tell Mama when his tutor gave him an alpha, 'the best mark one can get'.

Lyulph revelled in Eton. When he gave a speech in French in February 1856, he confessed he had spoken 'much too low', but he was pleased that he 'did not feel the least anxious or frightened though I expected to be so'. 'I have got three fags', he announced that April. Lyulph had been horrified to hear a story that fagging was going to be abolished at Harrow, expostulating that this would never happen at Eton. He was enjoying every minute of ruling the roost. Highly competitive in both work and sport, he gloried in a room 'three times bigger than the old one'. Jubilant about a victory in the sculling competition on the Thames, he had 'let off each of my fags a week's fagging' he told his mother. In December 1856, the prize, grasped with ease after eleven written papers and a viva, despite warnings of 'no hope', was the Balliol scholarship on which he had set his sights.[29]

Starting at public school was a severe test of a boy's composure and spirit. John Pratt's letter to his Mama on 26 September 1855, his first day at Eton, is an example of a good stab at immediate survival. He confessed to some anxiety about work that could possibly prove beyond him but had two pieces of positive news: 'as much as I have seen fellows are very nice' and he had begun with Latin prose at 7.30 a.m. 'which I think I managed pretty well'.[30]

Letters from Benny Trench to his mother in 1859 to 1860, his last year before joining his brother at Eton, were well-written accounts of his boyish enthusiasms. He had more than 400 stamps in his collection, he reported on 2 March 1859. He had a scheme to buy 'a small plate electrifying machine', with pocket money he had saved: 'I could do a good many jolly little things with it.' He had sent his brother Billy 'an exercise and verses', he related in October, when he enquired after the family's dogs Mindful, Rockwood, Nettle and Rose. He had a parakeet which kissed him, took seed out of his mouth and crawled up his face.

Yet Benny's last sentence in early November, 'I have not a letter from you for some time', marks the pining of a twelve-year old so far away from home.[31] When his birthday came round that month, Georgiana orchestrated the shower of letters and presents, sent by his sisters at home across the Irish sea. 'I am very much obliged to Georgy for the cuffs and to all the others', Benny wrote on 28 November 1859. His sisters Haddie and Isabel had done him pictures. A brief remark he allowed himself, 'it is getting near the holidays now', in his letter the following week subsumed the homesickness never far below the surface of his mind.[32]

The summer of 1860 saw Benny longing for the Cangort Park holidays, when he hoped Papa would 'get us the little boat he was speaking of' for the valley lake. He wanted to put up an island there 'for the swans to build on'. Georgiana thanked him for this 'nice letter', 'so well written and perfectly spelt'. She regaled Benny with a long story of Rockwood's latest escapade and his 'narrow escape from the Keeper's gun'. He could bring the parrot he had now acquired back home, especially if it was a grey one that talked, which would make it 'very welcome'. Had he thought of a leaving present for Mr Wace?[33] Later that term, preparing the ground for his future, Georgiana sent on letters from Billy at Eton. He could bring them back, she instructed, 'when we have the happiness of seeing you at home again – how delightful to think of its being, DV, so near'. Yet, she reflected, she was sorry to think 'that the return involves leaving Wadhurst finally'.[34]

Mothers could be useful intermediaries when a boy feared his father's wrath. Writing to his Mama from his Wandsworth prep school in 1746, Charles Lennox was much more relaxed than in his epistles to his father. His Latin, he confessed, was 'forging work'. But the main objective of this letter was to ensure that an incident still unknown to his Papa was passed over without heavy patriarchal intervention:

> I have reflected with great concern upon the uneasiness I gave you at dinner by a behaviour which I am extremely ashamed of and sorry for. I scarce know with what face to ask your pardon, after having had occasion to desire it so often, but shall esteem it as a particular favour if you would so far oblige me as not to mention my ill behaviour to Papa, but forgive your most penitent and obedient son.[35]

Anxious one term that 'Papa will think I'm squandering', Tom Hodges explained to his mother, Dorothy Hodges, that he was keeping a full account of his pocket money, which he would bring home. She also was clearly a good buffer.[36]

Examples of mothers who actually stood up to their husbands about boys being sent to board are unusual. Sir William Chaytor was suffering imprisonment for debt in London when his wife Peregrina objected, on behalf of her little boy Harry and his brother, to his plan to send them from their home at Croft, on the Tees, to board in Richmond. Her compromise was that Nanny Peacock should go with them into lodgings there, 'for Harry has declared so much against Richmond unless he have Nanny with him'. Baulking him would 'make him too melancholy'. 'For God's sake what do you intend to make of them?' Sir William expostulated from London, 'I was sent to Danby Wisk school at ten years old and I lived without the Pap there and if you make them too fond of you they will be good for nothing . . . you must prepare and encourage them to part with one another for their advantage.'[37] But Peregrina, on the spot, held the whip hand.

When there was collective riot and rebellion at public schools, such as occurred at intervals until the late-eighteenth century, making an example of ringleaders and culprits with the birchrod was seen as a necessary defence of the whole system. Fathers generally colluded in this. But it was the tales of these riots and of the floggings which followed, as much as anything, which created the widespread and persistent female alarm about places like Eton. Mary Woodforde's documented passivity in a family crisis of this kind in 1687 is striking testimony to the sheer helplessness of mothers. Her diary entry on 6 March 1687 records 'the cutting news' that her son Jack was one of those 'in rebellion' at Winchester, where 'he and all his companions resolved not to make any verses and being called to be whipped for it several of them refused to be punished, mine amongst the rest'.

A cousin of hers had submitted and been flogged. Her boy, with others, was threatened with expulsion. Her husband hurried to Winchester to insist on

Jack's submission. 'God, I beseech thee', Mary wrote, 'subdue their stubborn hearts and give them grace to repent and accept of their punishment, due to their fault and let them not run on to ruin for Christ's sake.' She heard from Jack himself two days later, a letter which gave her hope that 'he has now humbled himself for which I from the bottom of my heart give most humble thanks'.[38] But Mary's younger son Willie remained a worry to her. He had begun to board in January at Mr Wallace's in Winchester. He was very well, returning from his prep school for Christmas in December, but had been in serious trouble: 'Of late he has been guilty of some great faults which he confesses, and seems to be very sorry for, and promises never to commit the same again, which I humbly beg of Almighty God he may not.'

Betsy Francis was somewhat stronger. Her husband Philip, as we have seen, settled his eldest son Philip, then not six, in a small London school with no corporal punishment, run by Mr Ribouville in 1774. So Betsy was much distressed, in 1779, when her husband arranged, behind her back, for Philip to go on to Harrow: 'Mr Ribouville's grief will be great', she protested. The decision for Harrow followed his taking male advice and hearing a favourable report on its headmaster, beside less favourable ones on Westminster and Eton. Betsy Francis, terrified of Harrow's reputation for immorality, spoke out and was not easily mollified: 'I insist on his lying alone. His learning may take its fate. He will always have enough for an honest man. But his health and morals require all our care.'[39] A single bed at this time was an extra charge to parents, one that she believed well worth the money.[40] She won the concession she wanted.

In Betsy's account, little Philip's entry to Harrow at ten was composed. Seventy-two pounds a year covered French, writing, drawing, dancing and fencing, besides his classical tuition. The master in whose charge he was put was 'very severe', but she confessed she thought this 'an advantage'. 'Philip behaved as well and as nobly as a boy could do on such an occasion, he never shed a tear, I was near it', she wrote. Philip Francis went to stay with his kind ex-teacher Mr Ribouville in his summer holiday in 1779. 'He does not think him improved in any branch of learning but the Latin and that not much', Betsy explained to her distant husband, 'everything else is neglected.'

'What I fear the most for is the bad examples from many bad boys', she wrote unhappily. Yet, Betsy confessed, 'Philip seems to have more courage than ever.' Seeing him growing away from her, she feared his learning 'bad language, swearing etc.'. She had consulted widely with her female friends but none had seen any escape from this downhill path: 'I must not move him as you have ordered him to be placed there yourself.' Caught in the patriarchal trap, she could only 'trust he will not be worse off than other boys'. But Philip emerged with strength of character. In 1787 he was doing well at Cambridge, telling his sister that he could now convince his father, if he doubted it on account of 'former follies' at school, that he had not actually idled his time.[41]

Melesina Trench, as we have seen, was transported by the birth of her first son, Charles St George, in 1787, at nineteen. She lost her second boy after nine days, before she was 21, and her husband soon after this. Her happy second marriage to Richard Trench, of Woodlawn County Galway, brought her five more boys and finally a girl between 1805 and 1812. The couple settled in 1803 at Bursledon on the Hamble estuary in Hampshire. Their mansion and parkland were superbly situated, in rolling wooded country, looking across Southampton Water to Cowes on the Isle of Wight. Richard, a kindly and affectionate father, was 'too fond of his family' to do more than the 'semblance of a little occasional business' in the neighbourhood.[42] He was away at times but, it was noted in 1816, 'liked to be with his boys when at home', because he 'enjoyed their prattle'.[43] It was typical of Melesina that, when a close friend of the family, Miss Agar, died young in 1821, she wrote to their school asking that the boys should be told personally of this loss, since she did not want to impart the news by a letter.[44]

This was a refined and intellectual, as well as an affectionate, home. Making Latin verses was seen as appropriate homework for these boys. Thus Melesina encouraged little Richard, not yet twelve and on holiday from Twyford School, in this pursuit. He wrote, in clean copperplate, to his adult half-brother Charles, on 25 July 1819, enclosing Latin verses modelled on the poem 'The Despairing Shepherd', which 'Mama wished me to send you'. He had just won a volume by Lucretius as a prize; his brother Francis, he reported, had won a prize at Harrow 'for having had three copies of verses read over'.[45]

The contrast between the refined culture of family life, under Melesina's eye, at Bursledon Lodge and the world of the public schools in the Regency period is a startling reminder of how gendered upbringings then pulled society in half. Both parents were entirely committed to their boys studying at Harrow. Her boys were hard workers and good classical scholars, favourites with masters for this reason, Melesina noted in her diary. Their work was often read over and given prizes. 'To write good verses is a most graceful accomplishment', Melesina told Francis in September 1819, saying how precious those he sent, whether in Latin or English, were to her. 'Your complete success', she assured him early in his second year, 'gives us at home much pleasure.' Over the years from 1819 to 1823 his Harrow career went from academic strength to strength.[46]

It was her privilege, Melesina reckoned, to fuss over her boys a little when they were away from home. A servant announcing 'Mr Trench, a parcel', as Francis struggled with 'a crabbed and tough passage of a Greek tragedy' on

21 January 1823, brought up Twyford remembrances 'of sundry good things – chickens, apples, jams etc.'. He hoped his mother was not anxious about him in this 'soft' winter weather. 'I wear a flannel waistcoat, I use worsted stockings, I have four blankets, I have a carpet to my study, I have a curtain which lets down over my door', he wrote.[47] There was much to be thankful for, as Francis, and Richard after him, proceeded to Oxford and Cambridge respectively. Cambridge had been in mind for Francis too, but Melesina decided to remove him from the bad influence of certain Harrow friends who had gone there ahead of him.[48] She was every inch the hands-on parent. Francis left Harrow in a blaze of glory in July 1824, pocketing the two school prize poems that year. He penned a poem, with five verses, 'Farewell to Harrow', declaring that Melesina's pleasure in it would be ample return for her love and support:

> Where'er my wandering course I bend, still, Harrow I am thine
> Thine image through the vale of life shall lead me
> And with worldly strife a tranquil charm entwine.[49]

If Melesina was a satisfied parent on the academic front, she was a highly critical one in the matter of discipline. She took a courageous stand when she heard about how Francis, in delicate health, was fareing at Harrow in 1818. He had entered the boarding house run by Mrs Leith, next to Harrow churchyard. The next January, Richard agreed, despite his wife's trepidation, to Mrs Leith's proposal that Francis be made night fag for this house. The account Francis gave of what this involved horrified Melesina. She persuaded Richard to threaten to fetch him home, unless something was done to stop the practice of employing a junior boy as a virtual slave to the community. 'I am full of fears as to what may happen in the interval', she wrote in her diary on 23 January.

'To act as night fag', Melesina noted:

> is neither more or less than to be waiter, footman, porter and messenger to near thirty boys – who pass their evenings in separate studies – in the open air, and have the right to command the service in any way they please of this unfortunate boy from dusk till past ten, and sometimes eleven at night.

Over several weeks, she uncovered more and, through sheer determination, achieved a victory, or so she thought. The abuses of the system had been ameliorated, she wrote on 15 February, 'by Mrs Leith's good sense'. The imposition of expeditions to the town, climbing a high gate, with a birching in prospect if he was caught, and the endless cleaning of candlesticks, tasks expected of Francis alone, were abolished. His tasks were to be divided between four junior boys instead.

Mrs Leith took, Melesina was told, 'all possible care' to protect Francis, when the culprit who had drawn a caricature of the headmaster on the school walls was being sought: 'boys who are not clever enough to excel . . . are fond of bringing others into scrapes and call it sport', she commented.[50] Her intervention over the fagging, so brave and unusual in a mother, was briefly the talk of her social circle. Some, she declared, said 'I am fit to bring about a reform in Parliament since I had power to change any of the established customs of a public school.'[51]

Unfortunately, the 1818 reform in fagging practices at Harrow was short-lived. Notes on Melesina's conversations with her son Philip, who followed Francis and Richard there in the 1820s, indicate how deeply rooted tradition was. Philip himself supported it to his mother's face, confirming that the night fag still went over the wall. It was 'reckoned nothing' if a boy got flogged because a master caught him. Francis, despite his mother's earlier action to save him, was now deeply implicated in Harrow tradition himself.

'There must be fagging you know Mama', Philip maintained, because there were a hundred things in the evening for the older boys, including his brother Francis, to do. But the fag was simply an additional servant, protested Melesina. 'They would not get a servant to do what they make a fag do', laughed Philip. Servants, he was sure, would be afraid of losing their place for illegal purchase of spirits to make punch. It was simply too hard, 'after roughing it', to have no fag in return. 'I stick up for it', Philip told his mother: 'it's very bad at first but very convenient afterwards when you have fags yourself'.[52]

Francis, once a monitor, clearly exercised his authority to the full. He was outraged that junior boys broke the headmaster's windows over successive nights in March 1824, remarking that so far they had 'caught two or three culprits who were well licked'.[53] A campaigner on many social issues, Melesina wrote an essay around this time on fagging and flogging, the 'two deeply rooted evils' of the public school system, so, whatever she thought of the offence, this letter from her son cannot have been easy reading. She was incensed by the regularity with which boys submitted to the birch for the sake of parental reputation. She also resented the pressure exerted on them to do so by school fellows. She knew of a case where a boy, insulted by others over his hesitancy to submit, tried to cut his throat.

Beating children, Melesina argued, was 'a disgusting and degrading punishment as bad for the flogger as the floggee'. Yet, even in her secluded Hampshire life, she encountered deeply objectionable attitudes, exacerbated by class prejudice, among her own circle. She had apologised about local rowdiness to a gentlewoman acquaintance, walking with her in her shrubbery, when they heard village children playing noisily over the fence. 'They should all be well whipped', her companion had asserted.[54]

Melesina Trench could not expect to take on the public school system, the very bedrock of the society that she inhabited. Her pain was the pain of a radical many years ahead of her time. 'We remember her efforts in behalf of the suffering slaves, the suffering sweep chimney boys, the suffering Irish, boys and children suffering from any cruel treatment, boys killed in school fights', wrote her son Francis at her death in 1827.[55] But the liberal principles of her overall argument about how children should and should not be treated, forged in the years from 1807 to 1816 when she had four boys of her own growing up, undoubtedly made an impact, when her treatise on upbringing was published in 1837.

Sometimes, when a boy lacked health and vigour, women were able to modify the fatherly imperative to launch him into boarding school. Some boys seemed, in physique or temperament, unsuited to the rigours of its life. Fathers did not necessarily ride roughshod over this. One such boy was Tommy Verney in 1721. His aunt, Lady Cave, as well as his mother, fussed and worried about him. She accepted that 'his time must not be lost from learning if possible to help it'. She hoped 'a few indulgences and care will enable him to go through it'. The boy spent time at home that autumn, with Lady Cave musing to friends in letters about his 'weak constitution, inferring that he is unable to undergo a school life'. She argued that a winter's good nursing at home would strengthen him for it in the future.[56]

There could also be solace for a mother in knowing that a grandmother was on hand. Sir John Cust, an aspiring Westminster politician who felt bound to make his family home in London, decided, in 1750, on a country prep school for his five-year-old heir Brownlow. He chose one at Stilton, conveniently situated just off the Great North Road, a mere 30 miles from the boy's grand-mother at Grantham. Lady Anne Cust was thrilled at her son's decision, approving, interestingly, of Brownlow's being sent away at only five. So where better to start than this intimate little establishment with 21 boys, all under seven? She would send a man to collect him with the post chaise for the Easter holiday and welcome 'his pretty company'.

During the next year or two, Lady Anne saw Brownlow regularly. 'Thank God the child goes on pure and well', she told his father after the Whitsun holiday in 1757, 'he is very good in every respect; he desires his duty to you and his Mama and love to his sisters'. 'I will do the best I can for your dear little boy', his grandmother avowed. Soon after, she reported his good health and spirits to his mother, noting that, if he was 'a good deal tanned' from time spent out of doors, 'what he loses in beauty he will gain in health and strength'. Brownlow was 'so good and tractable', she found it 'impossible not to be fond of him'. After the rigours of school, the boy undoubtedly found some relaxation under her indulgent grandparental eye.[57]

If grandmothers did not usually challenge the parental line, they could encourage a youngster with gentle, supportive and kind words. Letters from Elizabeth Barne to her grandson Miles in 1754 overflowed with warmth and affection. She hoped to hear that he was 'perfectly well', that he was becoming 'a fine gentleman' with 'sound judgement in all things'. She had heard tell of his new horse and hoped it would prove 'a good servant, no stumbling beast'.[58] She was thrilled to hear about his drawing, Catherine Bromhead told her grandson James at Charterhouse in 1822, 'a delightful accomplishment and you have a natural talent for it'. Where should her parcels be sent? she asked. 'God bless you my dearest grandson', she ended, 'and give you many happy years and grace to walk in His holy commandments.'[59]

Whereas his Uncle Joe simply warned William Young, at Cheam in the 1840s, that this was a little world in which 'the tares and the wheat, the sheep and the goats, the good and the bad' mixed freely, his grandmother sincerely 'wanted his schooldays to be as happy, as those years of childhood that are past'. 'Much of your future happiness', she counselled, 'will now depend upon your own exertions and strictly remembering and putting into practice those excellent precepts and kind advices given you by your dear father and mother, and you will now be able to show your affection for them by your diligence and attention to their wishes.'[60]

There were some mothers who escaped the heavy patriarchal hand through early widowhood. In 1607, Henry Simpson came to live with the Newdigate family at Arbury in Warwickshire as private tutor to John and Richard, who were then respectively seven and five years old. He was a young graduate of Magdalen, Oxford, who gained his MA two years later. When their father died in 1610, Simpson was well established. Lady Anne Newdigate raised his salary by more than two pounds a year in 1614, describing him as 'a most honest, civil, fair-conditioned man, a greater scholar ... and a very good divine'. She made efforts to secure him a living locally, anxious not to lose her tutor, 'now that they are thus forwardly entered by Mr Simpson, to change to one peradventure with a contrary method in teaching'.

Anne Newdigate was determined to see through the education of her boys at home, until they were of 'fit learning and years' to benefit from university. She even provided, in early drafts of her will, for them to be kept together with their tutor at Arbury in the case of her death. She spent heavily on books, purchasing two copies of Ovid's *Metamorphosis* in 1612, the histories of Justinus and Quintus Curtius in 1616 and three volumes of the Stoic philosophy of Marcus Aurelius in 1617. John's sketchy Latin reflections on Ovid at fifteen do not indicate, Vivienne Larminie suggests, any great ability. Nevertheless, Lady Anne pursued her ambition for these boys with the utmost seriousness, achieving the entry of both to Trinity College, Oxford in 1618. They were spared, without disadvantage, the rough and tumble of a seventeenth-century boarding school.[61]

Jane Sacheverell was left a widow in 1692 with a brood of three boys on her hands. She took advice from male relatives about their schooling. She had heard of a master near their home in Derbyshire, Mr Greatrex, she told her brother-in-law John Newton, 'who takes some gentleman's sons and is highly commended'. She was fretting, fearing her boys 'have lost their time too much already'. Newton replied at once, advising a public school rather than this kind of small local establishment. This brought forth the passionate conviction of a mother who had heard too much about the regimes of famous schools:

> I am much persuaded against it, believing it will not suit Will Sacheverell's mild temper so well as a private master, who usually considers a child's disposition more than they do at the great schools and for Jack, though he be of a more brisk and airy temper, yet I know he will do more with a fair word than with severity and Ned I think is of the same temper with Will.

Jane Sacheverell strongly approved of Mr Greatrex, as 'one that studies the temper of his boys and has made many good scholars and his wife so good a manager of children'. A family battle was developing around Jane's notion that she should go and live at this local school herself. Aware that 'my brother Stringer and some others of opinion' opposed this, she declared herself forthrightly: 'if I know myself, I am not one that would prejudice my children by my fondness, though I am sure I love my children as much as any mother can; but my desire is to show it by a care of their future good'. Her boys were 'the greatest comforts I have left in the world'. She hoped she would not be denied 'being with or near them'. But of course she would leave if the master found her in the way, Jane declared, still deferential in her tone.

She would trust her brother-in-law's judgement; if he insisted, the elder boys would go to Eton. But she had her way. Three months later, Jane described the happy pattern of life the family had established. She found Mr Greatrex very mild:

> Yet keeps them strictly to their books for their age . . . and tells me the children are very diligent so that he thinks he never shall have occasion

to chide them for their books. When they have done at school they come into my chamber to make their exercises . . . what they do I see is their own without help, which pleases me well.[62]

Lady Sarah Fitzherbert, recently widowed, corresponded with her Etonian brother William Perrin, in 1793, about her boy Anthony, who was then fourteen. He advised rapid entry to Eton so that Anthony, her eldest and heir to the Tissington estate, could go on to university at seventeen. When she hesitated, he stressed the benefits of a 'public education' for one destined for a landlord's role, mentioning Westminster as an alternative, under a new headmaster. But it was further from Derbyshire. 'New brooms sweep clean', he avowed, but she should not worry about the previous notorious practice of Eton fagging. 'That you know', he insisted, 'is abolished.' The next year, Lady Sarah having opted for neither Eton nor Westminster but for Winchester, Perrin visited Anthony there, found him 'well and satisfied' and offered to accompany him on his journey back to school, after the Easter holiday, as far as Northampton or Oxford.[63]

Henrietta Boughey was at a loss when her husband died in 1823, leaving her with boys already at Eton and at prep school but with little grasp of what future he had planned for them. She leaned heavily on her brother-in-law, for advice about when John should go on to Eton and what kind of career should be set up for Tom, 'whether a mercantile line of life or the army would be most advantageous for him'. As for William, starting at prep school at nine, she threw herself deferentially on his direction. He should say so in 'most open manner if you think I act improperly in any way', for she was 'fully aware of my weakness and want of ability' to handle the duties that had been devolved upon her.[64]

This documentation across two centuries of the trials and tribulations of some mothers whose boys went away to school sheds important light on the workings of patriarchy in England. There were those, like Dorothy Hodges and Georgiana Trench, who enjoyed some confidence in the matter. They lost little sleep about how sons, thrust into the public school system, were faring. There were others, like Melesina Trench, for whom the years of male schooling brought frustration as well as pleasure in boyish achievement.

Having viewed this schooling through both the eyes of fathers and mothers, it is time to assess the record of the public schools in the upbringing of English boys, between 1600 and 1914, overall.

The Public Schools

The public schools were prestigious male institutions which drew their boys from well-to-do families across the whole nation. They were predominantly well-endowed boarding schools. By 1820, seven of them were generally recognised as England's leading schools: Eton, Winchester, Westminster, Harrow, Shrewsbury, Charterhouse and Rugby. In the 1850s and 1860s, many new public schools were founded or promoted in status from old grammar schools. These included Bradfield, Lancing, Haileybury, Marlborough, Radley and Wellington in the south, Uppingham in the Midlands, Sedbergh in the north, to name but a few. The middle and professional classes then colonised an enlarged group of schools that had been the preserve, since 1600, of the aristocracy and gentry. Training the boys who would rule England in parish, county and nation and who would rule the Empire besides, these schools became the fount of English patriarchy. They were men's foremost instrument for the maintenance of class and masculine hegemony. Their importance in the story of boyhood experience between 1600 and 1914 is therefore incalculable.

The public schools provided parenting at one remove. The scandal of excessive brutality, for example the fierce punishment by the monitor Platt of the son of Lord Galloway at Harrow in 1853, brought the occasional critical intervention about practice inside the schools from a father. But the attitude of fathers who sent boys to these schools was overwhelmingly collusive.[1] This collusion between male parents and generations of English schoolmasters rested on an exact match between upper- and middle-class notions of male gender construction and the established practice of upbringing in the schools. The old public schools fostered in English boys a particular form of masculinity, teaching them to internalise a set of characteristics that fathers believed sustained English society and the country's patriotic ideals.

In the period from 1600 to 1850, boys learnt endurance and self-reliance at these schools in an unregulated and competitive environment. The teaching of classics was seen as testing character. Boys were neglected and allowed much freedom beyond academic hours, when fighting and violence between themselves were tolerated pastimes. John Aubrey's account in the 1670s thus serves in outline for generations of English schoolboys, who learnt to hide and contain their emotions in a harsh male environment. 'It is now that he is entered to be of the world, to come from his innocent life, tender care and indulgence of his parents,' he wrote, 'to be beaten by his schoolfellows, to be falsely accused, to be whipped by the master, to understand his tyranny.' ''Tis here he begins to understand the world, the misery, falseness and deceitfulness of it', he went on, ''tis here he begins to understand himself, that he finds others to be his equals and superiors in honour, estate, wit and strength.'[2]

The diaries of Stephen Terry, who was born in 1774, and at Eton from 1783 to 1792, when he became Captain of the School, provide much insight into the unreformed public schools of the eighteenth century. This was the great age of schoolboy fights. When an eleven-year old killed a fifteen-year old, fighting out a quarrel in 1784, the whole school attended the unfortunate loser's funeral. In 1825, a fourteen-year old killed a boy smaller than himself, in a two-and-a-half-hour fight. Stephen Terry was a great fighter. When he fought Jack Musters, the antagonists were so equally matched and handled each other so severely that it was said that, when they shook hands at the close, they were scarcely recognisable.

Stephen's obsession was hunting, of any kind, at any time. He only took to shooting instead at Eton when, after ruining his clothes out drag-hunting with terriers, he was threatened with a flogging on the instruction of his dame. These were the days when an annual levy of five shillings on the boys paid for collection of the birches, from Burnham Beeches in the Chilterns, needed for Eton's disciplinary regime. The flogging feats of the headmasters in Stephen's time, Dr Davies and Dr Heath, bringing huge numbers of boys to the block in one session, were legendary. In the famous revolt against Dr Davies, headmaster until 1792, the rioters broke windows, smashed his furniture and hacked the flogging block to pieces.[3]

In essence nothing changed in the culture of the public schools between the 1000s and 1914. The crucial point, well made by James Mangan, is that 'whereas before 1850 hardship in the schools was largely a product of adult indifference, after this date it was mostly the product of adult calculation'. An ideology of social Darwinism, implicit not explicit at the time, Mangan argues persuasively, came to sustain the Victorian public boarding school system. He cites the case for male teenage privation as it was put in an article in the *Saturday Review* in 1860:

> Boys, like nations, can only attain to the genuine stout self-reliance which is true manliness by battling for themselves against their difficulties and forming their own characters by the light of their own blunders and their own troubles ... The object of the public school is to introduce a boy early to the world, that he may be trained in due time for the struggle that lies before him.

That classic version of the Darwinian argument, published a year after the *Origin of Species*, reflected its purchase on the Victorian mind. The public school world, Mangan notes, 'was often a godless world of cold, hunger, competition and endurance'. Strength, many believed, came through struggle and success was 'the prerogative of the strong'. In identifying 1850 as the date of a shift in the culture of the public schools, Mangan echoed the established view that the critical figure in their history was Thomas Arnold.[4]

Arnold's reforms were seen as making an impact which was carried by others into a new generation of mid-Victorian schools. But a groundbreaking article by Fabrice Neddam has shown how his bid for reform failed. The form of masculinity that Rugby actually inculcated under Arnold, between 1828 and 1842, was in fact the same unofficial one, mediated by the boys themselves, that had always held sway. Boys at public schools still grew up by surviving their physical rough and tumble and bullying, not by imbibing the ideals of the Christian gentleman that Arnold so persuasively set out.

Boys at Rugby confirmed their gender identity by the display, in their own community, of 'manly standards, such as physicality, pluck and aggressiveness'. 'Bullying', writes Neddam, 'must be seen as a gendered practice ... as part of the pressures that boys were under to prove that their own form of masculinity conformed to that expected of them.'[5] When Arnold arrived at Rugby, it was run largely, for lack of enough assistants to the headmaster, by senior boys, who exercised authority over younger boys through an institutionalised system of fagging. This, together with entrenched initiation rituals such as tossing in a blanket, made their first years a frightening ordeal for small boys. John Chandos has described the well-documented fagging and bullying traditions at Eton, Westminster and Winchester, around 1800, in terms which make it justifiable to regard the world of the unreformed public school as one of licensed anarchy. Here, might was right.[6]

Thomas Arnold was obsessed with the evil he found among Rugby boys, mentioning it often in his letters and sermons. He was well aware that he had a battle to fight. Preaching in chapel, he once spoke of a public school as 'a nursery of vice, where a boy unlearns the pure and honest principles which he may have received at home, and gets, in their stead, others which are utterly low and base, and mischievous'. 'I do not think that we have at present a large proportion of clever boys at Rugby', Arnold declared on 25 January 1835, 'and there are many great evils which I have to contend with.' Noting deaths in the school from fever in June 1841, he found these 'as nothing when compared with the existence of any unusual moral evil in the school'.

Arnold had in mind drunkenness and lying, but he knew that bullying was the most intractable of his problems and that this problem was enhanced by what he called the 'bond of evil'. Boys were corrupted and contaminated by the values of the school. The watchword was survival of the strongest. *Tom Brown's Schooldays*, an accurate account of Rugby life, and the memoirs written by boys at Rugby in that period, coincide in showing that bullying was rife.

One boy who started as a fag commented in 1803 that 'the system of bullying seemed to have banished humanity from most of the boys above me'. Several described 'smoking out', an antic which terrified boys and consisted of inserting burning paper into their blocked study doors. George Melly, nicknamed 'hen' in the 1830s, once found his study bereft of furniture, with gravel two inches thick on the floor, chickweed on the walls and perches fixed from wall to wall. A boy called Gover, taught at home to kneel to say his prayers, found himself pelted with slippers and boots when he did so. So much for Arnold's Christianisation. Most brutal of all was 'roasting', the ordeal of holding a boy close to the fire for several minutes. Bullying of many kinds was ineradicable both here and elsewhere across the public school system.

In theory, power and status at Rugby followed academic success. But the chief bullies, those who really held sway, were the losers in the academic stakes. Significantly, a boy at this time noted, they were not 'big boys high up in the school', but idle or unintelligent boys, 'too old for the forms they were in'. They carved out a parallel society with its own set of values, based on physical strength. Arnold saw exactly what was happening. In his scale of excellence, he said in one sermon, moral perfection came first, 'excellence of understanding' second and strength of body third. Yet at Rugby, he found, 'this is just reversed'. The bullies maintained hegemony by coercion, control and force. Theirs was the ruling code of masculinity here and in all the Victorian public schools. Those who failed to achieve and show this physical masculinity or who were blatantly studious, were derided and called, as Tom Brown put it, 'Molly or Jenny or some derogatory feminine nickname'. Bullying, Fabrice Neddam has written, was about 'rejecting what was considered effeminate'.[7]

Arnold could not change Rugby's values, nor the kind of masculinity it inculcated. But public schooling in England, following his headmastership, was revised in ways which, superficially at least, made it look more civilised. There was administrative reform. For many, Arnold was the symbol of a new style of schooling that was more moral, more caring and cleverer. He reassured the professional classes, who had begun to colonise these schools, about their professional standards. But the dominance of physicality, under a veneer of religion, simply became channelled into a new cult of athleticism.

Under the initiative of C.J. Vaughan at Harrow from 1845, G.E.L. Cotton at Marlborough from 1852 and Edward Thring at Uppingham from 1853, games became part of the formal curriculum. No longer were boys left to fill free time exploring the countryside, bird nesting and fishing. Organised games were seen as a moral good and an antidote to indiscipline and lawlessness. Thring, above all, in this generation of headmasters important in supplying the ideological impetus for athleticism, was every inch the muscular Christian.

Fagging was institutionalised in the Victorian public schools as a means of inculcating hierarchy and the principal of servitude on which imperial rule was based. H.J.C. Blake remembered how, during nearly five years of it at Eton, he learnt about how to black shoes, clean knives and grab a stray roll or two from another boy's room for his master's breakfast. He was not averse to fagging: 'I think it is beneficial to a boy for should he in after life experience the fickleness of fortune he is able all the better to rough it.'[8] Etonians throughout the period up to 1914, normally entering at twelve, expected to spend two or three years as a fag while they were in the various divisions of the fourth form.

Upper boys could order lower boys to perform numerous tasks. An anonymous article in the *Edinburgh Review* in 1830 put the case against Eton fagging: 'Corrupting at once and corrupted, the little tyrant riots in the exercise of boundless and unaccountable power; and while he looks back on his servitude is resolved that the sufferings which he inflicts shall be not less than those which he endured.' Fag masters could beat their fags at will. 'A slipper or if the fag master was possessed of that badge of ineffable superiority a cane', wrote Gilbert Coleridge recalling Eton in the 1870s, 'applied smartly to the tight trouser of a bent figure was a sufficient incentive to efficient carrying and cooking.'[9]

The stranglehold of classics remained until well into the twentieth century though, through 'modern sides' and science, the teaching of more relevant subjects was gradually introduced. At Harrow in 1874, there were 21 assistant masters in classics, five in maths, two in modern languages and one in science. But the essence of athleticism was a profound attachment to physical exercise on an unremittingly regular basis and especially to team games, which were seen as developing instrumental and personal skills, in a secular dimension.

Stoicism was the heart of athleticism. Chapel, as religious faith, lost out. John Rae wrote perceptively about the school chapel as 'part of the routine, like lessons, games and field days'. 'It was not so much Christian truth', he observed, that a boy took from compulsory chapel, as 'a longing for atmosphere, for the faces of young friends, for the familiar hymns, above all for a sense of belonging'. As a critique of public school education in the *Dublin Review* noted in 1860, chapel attendance actually focused on keeping up the mask of religion, teaching a boy in practice 'to endure, to suffer, to be patient . . . to take care of himself, to hold his own, to trust to his own best, his own determination, and coolness, and pluck'.

Boys learnt religion in the public schools as a social habit: at its core was unswerving devotion to house and school. The reality, in the later Victorian period, was a kind of boarding school life which distinctly lacked the ideals of Christian piety and kindliness. Secular practice consumed a spiritual ideal. Discipline, from Arnold's days to the First World War, remained overwhelmingly corporal. More English boys were beaten at English boarding schools, more often and more severely, it seems clear, in the late Victorian and Edwardian periods than at any other time in the nation's history. The public schools, at this point, represented the apogee of male parenthood in a solidly patriarchal society. Upper- and middle-class fathers were moulded by them and went on sending sons to them, accepting and knowing well how they would be punished. 'It never did me any harm', they avowed.

Eton set the tone, developing its own particular pathology of discipline, clinging to the block after most schools had switched from the birch to the cane. Eton birches were grotesque instruments, with three feet of handle and nearly two of bush. The headmaster and lower master carried out the floggings of boys 'put in the bill' by their tutors, in public, in the library and schoolroom respectively. The Reverend James Leigh Joynes, lower master from 1878, and Algernon Swinburne's tutor, who handled the birch with an unsparing hand, was the subject of a celebrated caricature in *Vanity Fair* in 1887, showing him pointing grimly to the block. Swinburne's flagellant poems are well-known and his notorious flagellant manuscripts are in the British Library.[10]

Etonians documented their defining experience almost obsessively. They celebrated and gloried in the ordeals and the physical anguish which they believed had made a man of them. The Eton system of flogging, as it was practised well into the twentieth century, emphasised symbolism and ritual, as much as the considerable pain inflicted. The central features were submission, public shame and blood: victims knelt across the block with their naked buttocks at the best angle for the fall of the birch. Two other boys traditionally held them down.

H.J.C. Blake, recalling his first flogging at Eton around 1800, says that the two boys who stood grinning as they held his arms and clothes, got him off with a single stroke, by their whisper that he should call out that it was his first fault.[11] Soon after joining the school in 1857, James Brinsley-Richards remembered the cry 'there's going to be a swishing'. There was a general rush for the upper end of the schoolroom, with clambering on forms and desks for a good view: 'I got a front place', he recounted, 'my heart thumping and seeming to make great leaps within me, as if it were a bird trying to fly away through my throat.' His account conveys well what an Eton birching was like:

> Neville was unbracing his nether garments – next moment, when he knelt on the step of the block and when the Lower Master inflicted upon his person six cuts that sounded like the splashings of so many buckets of water, I turned almost faint. I felt as I have never felt but once since and that was when seeing a man hanged.[12]

An Etonian had real cachet when, after suffering three times at the block, he became eligible for the respected Eton Block Club. Old Etonians stole the block in 1836, so that they could use it as a throne for the Club's president.[13] The day-by-day threat of the birch, H.J.C. Blake argued, created a sense of life's risks. There was a 'relish for adventures of a nobler kind, which was fully proved by the deeds of many who fought and bled'.[14] Stoicism in bearing pain was here the ultimate test of budding manhood. The ritual of the Eton block carries associations of abasement and ignominy, yet for Etonians this was offset by peer group status. Flogging, as one devotee put it in 1846, was a necessary evil for all behaviour 'unbecoming a gentleman'; it answered 'the feeling of the school in general' about misbehaviour; its effects anyway were 'ephemeral'.[15]

In 1856, the *Coventry Herald and Observer* published the correspondence of the previous summer between Morgan Thomas, whose son had been expelled when he refused to submit to a flogging, and the Provost of Eton, Dr Hawtrey. Thomas was then a voice in the wilderness, characterising Eton birching as that 'ignoble and degrading punishment' and that 'filthy and degrading practice'. The *Edinburgh Review* had discussed how boys were hardened by watching others suffer in 1830: 'habit deadens the minds of honourable men to the impropriety and indecorum of such an exhibition'. In 1883, Brinsley-Richards himself commented on how he became hardened, learning to see weakness or flinching under the rod as unmanly, developing a tough hide and stiff upper lip: 'I gradually came to witness the execution in the Lower School not only with indifference but with amusement.' He confessed he could not put aside wholly 'the idea that it was shameful to be whipped' in that way, but when his turn came to kneel at the block, his training in the ritual was complete. 'I rose from my knees', he wrote, 'completely hardened as to any sense of shame in the punishment I had undergone.'

The Juvenile Male Offenders Act of 1862 sought to regularise judicial whippings, forbidding magistrates from imposing them on boys over fourteen and limiting this punishment of younger boys to twelve strokes of the birch, applied to the naked buttocks. MPs, perhaps recalling their own painful school beatings, relented somewhat with regard to national policy, in passing the Children's Act in 1908. They decided that a maximum of six strokes was a decent measure for working-class lads who came before magistrate's courts. Boys over fourteen again escaped.

The Reverend Edward Lyttelton replaced the birch with the cane in Eton's Upper School on his appointment as headmaster in 1905, but Dr Alington, succeeding him in 1916, restored its use. So Eton boys, young and old and aged up to eighteen, were being flogged well into the 1920s, 60 years after boys between fourteen and eighteen years old who appeared before the courts were spared this humiliation. Cyril Connolly related in his autobiography how, arriving at Eton from his prep school in 1917, he found the disgusting old ritual being enforced, with other boys still encouraged to watch. An old college servant now pulled down the victim's trousers and held him down.[16]

The cane replaced the birch from the start in all the new foundations like Wellington and Radley. In 1859, Edward White Benson, Master of the newly opened royal foundation in memory of the Duke of Wellington, was in correspondence with the Prince Consort's Private Secretary, Sir Charles Phipps, who wrote at his direction to question the introduction of fagging and the use by his staff of the cane. Rallying the Victorian establishment behind him, with support from Frederick Temple, who was by then Archbishop of Canterbury, the Master resisted Prince Albert's interference. He oversaw the creation of a highly stratified and organised disciplinary regime at Wellington, with prefects using their powers to cane junior boys for disciplinary offences at will, notifying the school authorities when they had done so.

Widespread use of the cane at Wellington and other new schools enabled traditional flogging with the birch to be largely excluded in a spirit of reform. The cane was both effective and 'free from cruelty and unkindness', Benson told Sir Charles Phipps; it was 'quickly over, breeds no spite, spoils no temper', while every other punishment, he was convinced, did all these. He saw himself as enlightened, replacing the splattering and notorious brutality of the Eton birch with the neat, carefully delivered, strokes of an instrument that any competent colleague, and senior boys as well, could be expected to wield skilfully and sufficiently powerfully.

The basic premise of the public school system remained that many boys needed to be beaten, in their early teens, regularly and effectively. A formidable headmaster, in this scheme of things, while remaining on the sidelines, could thus manipulate an elaborate disciplinary scheme, which touched every boy by its tentacles and was at the same time wholly dependent on boyhood collusion. In 1895, the new master of Wellington, Bertram Pollock, unpopular because he sought to unravel stories about sexual immorality in the school, heard himself hissed at a school assembly. The boys concerned owned up in terror. He required the Head of School, immediately and before this whole company, to cane the culprits, one of whom, a prefect himself, was the Head of School's personal friend. After some minutes of refusal of this public ordeal, those who had hissed submitted. Pollock simply watched the performance.[17]

It was in the period from the 1880s until the 1920s that caning of boys by boys became rife, schools developing their own particular sadistic rituals. At Wellington, the first Master, Edward Benson, was keen to found an effective prefectorial system from the moment that the college opened in 1859. This implied granting senior prefects the liberal use of the cane. The log book of Wellington's Upper School Meeting, from 1859 to 1869, records how punishments grew in severity. The essence of prefectorial power became the demonstration of it by summoning small boys for abasement before them. In 1866, the record runs, 'Browne was caned before the meeting for insubordination to a prefect in his dormitory.' The boy's impertinent demeanour brought him 1,000 lines in addition to the caning. The Upper Ten, a group of senior prefects appointed by the Master, later acquired authority to administer collective beatings for enumerated heinous offences, each boy taking a turn to perform in front of the others.[18]

At Eton, members of the self-elected oligarchy known as Pop, lording it in their coloured waistcoats, could 'cane boys from any house'. Cyril Connolly described the procedure, designed for maximum humiliation: 'the worst part was the suspense, for we might make a mistake the day before and not be beaten for it till the following evening'. Once the chair was out in the middle of the room, the small boys' terror began. Stumbling away afterwards, it was 'wiser to answer' when a sixth former said goodnight:

> we knelt on the chair bottom outwards and gripped the bottom bar with our hands, stretching towards it over the back. Looking round under the chair we could see a monster rushing towards us with a cane in his hand, his face upside down and distorted . . . the pain was acute.[19]

The authenticity of Victorian public school reminiscence is not in doubt. Augustus Hare told tales of Harrow in the 1840s, which show how Melesina Trench's brave intervention had left no real impact. Arriving at thirteen, he was dragged into a crowd and was told to sing to them or, as the penalty for failing to do so, to drink a 'horrible mixture', which was then 'being poured down the throat of another boy'. Passing this first test, he was rewarded with oranges and cakes for his singing. Then came the tossing: 'Up to the ceiling I went and down again but they had no mercy and it was up and down, head over heels, topsy-turvy, till someone called out "satis" – and I was let out very sick and giddy at first.' Augustus was soon in trouble with the prefect for whom he was deputed to fag. Reading a book on duty, he let his fire go out, 'so I got a good licking'. 'He makes me his fag to go errands and do all he bids me and if I don't do it he beats me but I don't mind much', he wrote home. Others, he explained, suffered more than he did: boys who 'did not keep up' at football were made to cut large thorn sticks from the hedges. They were 'flogged with them till the blood poured down outside their jerseys'.[20]

The lesson of Victorian public school life was how to stifle one's emotions. One of the most illuminating commentators on its culture and on his own experience was Edward Carpenter, a boy who realised early in life 'the desire for a passionate attachment' to another male. At Brighton College in the late 1850s, the sea and the Sussex Downs were the two places when he could escape, where he felt at home: 'nature was more to me than any human attachment'. The 'glutinous boy friendships that one formed in classroom or playground staved off a greater hunger but they did not satisfy'. Edward had no experience at this stage of sex; his heart, he said, was 'like an open wound continually bleeding'. Dreaming about them, he worshipped the ground of several older boys.[21]

An autobiographical fragment by the seventh Earl of Shaftesbury, born in 1801, contrasted the 'filth, bullying, neglect and hard treatment' that he received at his prep school with his 'quite different' experience at Harrow, from twelve to fifteen. He learnt little there but was not unhappy or ill-treated: 'I was on the whole idle and fond of amusements.'[22] The school career of Robin Strutt, son of the third Lord Rayleigh of Terling in Essex, is instructive in the same respect. It confirms how it was often Victorian prep school life that was more cruel and miserable than the public school experience that followed. He attended one of the well-known prep schools of the time, the Grange at Hoddesdon in Hertfordshire. 'I was severely drilled in the elements of Latin, Greek, Euclid and Algebra.' But the Reverend Crittenden's regular beatings marked his mind indelibly:

Mistakes in arithmetic or Latin grammar often led to corporal punishment. Mr Crittenden marched out of the schoolroom to his study. A leather strap known as the 'spatter' was produced and applied to the victim's outstretched hands, left and right alternately, something up to ten or more vigorous blows. When he came back to the schoolroom, often with a tearstained face, he held up fingers to his fellows, to signal how many 'cuts' he had received.

Robin's father was a distinguished physicist. He soon developed an interest in science himself, which led to their close companionship in the holidays. As a teenager, he learnt the strength of character to survive Eton, which he entered in 1889 at fourteen. He hated games, which he avoided as much as possible, sometimes instead 'submitting to a fine or caning, sometimes getting excused on grounds of health'. He lived with Miss Evans, the last of the race of Eton dames who ran houses to lodge boys, before the system of house-masters was established. His parents rejected her advice that he should leave, since he was a complete misfit. Sympathetic to him, she recognised the contempt that he was earning from his contemporaries for his failures, as a footballer, cricketer and swimmer.

'Eton science in those days was in a rudimentary stage', Robin recalled in his memoir. But he did work with an outstanding teacher of chemistry, T.C. Porter: 'he admitted me to a great measure of intimacy and I was allowed to come and watch what he was doing in his private laboratory on half-holiday afternoons, when the normal boy was playing games'. Science was not yet on a par with Latin at Eton, or indeed anywhere in the public school system. Practical chemistry at Eton was optional, done at the end of the morning, when most boys in Robin's time played games:

> If a boy was known to be seriously devoting himself to science for example, his tutor often made some attempt to lighten his labours in other directions, e.g. by remitting Latin verses or allowing him to bring a scientific book to read while 'private' was going on in the pupil room.

Robin also learnt 'a good deal' from the physics master, R.H. Whitcombe. He won the physics prize, but since 'no one else went in for it, it is somewhat difficult to assess this achievement'. Above all, though, it was Dr Porter's lessons that he lived for during his Eton years.[23]

Autobiographies of Marlburians, relating to their experience at the school between 1843 and 1916, are bitter. Edward Lockwood's abiding memories in the 1840s were of hunger and brutality. He particularly recalled the 'stale bread washed down by water from the pump' on Wednesdays and Fridays. He used, he said, to scream at beatings, which turned his buttocks 'all the colours of the rainbow', causing horror and indignation when his nurse put him to bed at home. When, however, she heard that the perpetrator was a 'reverend man called to the ministry', she decided that 'I must have deserved every blow I got'. Roland Prothero described the two fires which provided minimum warmth for over a hundred boys, in the upper school at Marlborough in the 1860s. An hour of class with no food preceded breakfast, which was a 'square wad of bread'.

Beverley Nicholls, at Marlborough a little later, recalled windows kept open, and boys sometimes waking under a coverlet of snow inside. There were gymnastic rings in the dormitory for new boys to develop their biceps: 'if we failed we were bent over the bed and given ten strokes in pyjamas in the presence of the rest of the dormitory. If we cried out in pain, the strokes came harder.' The stiff upper lip while being caned, whether privately or publicly, became the very essence of late Victorian and Edwardian public school training. Marlborough seems to have been quite typical.

The reality of public school life was always survival of a harsh and testing ordeal. 'Your character', James Honey wrote, 'was forged like steel in the fire.'[24] There was a tradition of hardening at the heart of English masculinity, which could show itself in macho boyhood behaviour. Francis Place, explaining the severe discipline in his London day school around 1800, noted that 'there was constant emulation among the boys to show how they could bear punishment'. The master beat boys for a range of offences, as well as failures in set exercises, in front of the class, with strokes of the cane on the outstretched hand. Some boys, Place recalled, actually sought this punishment, by disrupting the class until they were called out. They acted in this way, he believed, 'to show how well a large number of strokes on the hand could be taken without wincing'.[25]

'That a version of masculinity, inscribed within values so systematically inculcated over so long a period, and authorized by a dominant class, has until recently been accepted as natural and desirable, is a matter of historical note', wrote Peter Lewis in 1991. His essay, appeared in Michael Roper and John Tosh's groundbreaking investigation of masculinity, which considered it as 'a historical and cultural construct', rather than something 'natural and monolithic'. It explored his own childhood world, as the son of a public school master at Wellington, then as a public schoolboy himself at Sherborne between the 1930s and the 1950s. He reflected upon how the legacy of the period of three hundred years delineated in this book was 'the elimination of feminine characteristics in making boys into men'.

Peter Lewis saw this as 'a sorry preparation for future relationships'. What he remembered, at both Wellington and Sherborne, was 'the policing of experience and the competitive dynamic of a hierarchical system'. Because this structure and set of values faced boys with an emotional vacuum in their teenage lives, they committed themselves to 'team or house or school as a preparation for the world of work'. Lewis inhabited the afterlife of the schooling system that is at the core of this story of boys' experience of growing up in England. These chapters of the book have explored the teenage world that thousands of them endured, more or less cheerfully and resignedly, over three centuries.[26]

Boys at University

Fatherly objectives and intentions in sending boys on from school to university ranged from the completion of social training through a veneer of learning to, at a lower social level, vocational ambition for a boy's ordination. We have seen how leading country gentry, like the Flemings, Smyths and Ishams, chose schools which matched their academic hopes, when they set their sights on Oxford for boys whose destination was life as a landlord. 'I know it's not your intent to have him earn his bread by his books', wrote his son's tutor to Sir Hugh Smyth in the 1620s, 'when you left him here I took upon me the charge of a gentleman, I shall blush to return him you again a mere scholar.'[1] As Sir Daniel Fleming's father put it to him, a spell at Oxford was the time 'to lay the foundation of all accomplishments hereafter'.[2]

The correspondence of Sir John Smyth of Long Aston, so illuminating about the schooling of his boys, is equally helpful in exemplifying how the wheels of patronage could oil the process of Oxford entry and the course of an undergraduate career. Sir John, opening negotiations with Dr Delaune, the President of St John's College at Oxford, in the summer of 1717, at once struck up a sound relationship. 'You may depend upon my particular regard to him', the President wrote, suggesting that a good time to bring him up to be examined and admitted would be August.[3] The tutor he 'pitched upon' for Jack was Dr Meredith, 'a gentleman of learning and prudence and every way qualified to instruct a young gentleman in the course of his study and conduct of life'.[4] This was the crucial step, for the tutorial system, conducted with varying degrees of rigour, was well established by then as the pattern of university work. It involved comprehensive oversight, including supervision of moral behaviour, care of religious education, regulation of expenditure and control and direction of learning by prescribing reading and prepared work.

Sending thanks for the 'favours' Dr Delaune had shown him on his visit, Sir John spoke from his heart to his boy about what an Oxford education should mean that October. He was one of a substantial band of gentleman commoners spread across the colleges. It was good to know, he told him, that Jack was settled 'amongst a society of civil sober gentlemen'. 'I thank God I have no reason to question but that you will use your endeavours to be as bright and virtuous as any of your companions that you may hereafter be an ornament to your country.' His Oxford experience was essentially designed to finish the training in gentlemanly manhood which would fit him for membership of Somerset's squirearchy and a place on its quarter sessions bench.[5] Jack, his only contretemps so far the shortness of breath that he had also suffered at his prep school and Winchester, reported in November that he had been bled for this and settled in well. His tutor, Dr Meredith, presented his service to Sir John; Jack did the same to his sisters at home.[6]

In April 1718, Sir John Smyth recognised his obligation to St John's for their care of Jack, with a generous contribution towards the new altar being erected in the college chapel. In a thank you letter, Dr Delaune assured him that his boy was 'as hopeful a young gentleman as ever adorned our college'. Dr Meredith followed this up, enumerating Jack's virtues that year: his attendance at prayers was 'constant and regular'; his behaviour to all was 'courteous and affable and exactly conformable to the rules and customs of the college'; he was 'willing and ready to be instructed'.

A warm and friendly letter of Oxford news and gossip from Dr Meredith to Jack, in August 1719, shows that he had become well-integrated with his tutor's circle of young gentry: 'all your friends long to see you'. In September, the President was entertained on a social visit to Long Aston, thanking his host afterwards for the 'great civility' he had received. Charmed by the Smyth girls, well bred in London and discovering they had not seen Oxford, he issued an invitation: 'there is a house there which they may call their own'.[7] Astrea and Florence visited Jack in Oxford the following spring. Some banter followed. He wrote teasingly to Florence: 'as to yourself and sister, you have done me immortal honour, in so much that I shall never hear the last of the fine ladies that I showed the university to'.[8]

Sir John's kind letters to Jack about payments to his tutor and for his expenses show the strength of the relationship between father and son, as he worked seriously for three years towards his MA, obtained with congratulations all round in 1720. Dr Meredith, reporting the Congregation in the Sheldonian to Sir John, stressed how Jack's 'virtuous conduct and affable behaviour' had 'universally procured him the esteem of those who know him'. The Public Orator, awarding the degree, had praised his family, mentioning the remembered loyalty of the Smyth family to the Crown 'in the most accursed times'. Jack himself was very well 'and I have reason to believe mightily pleased'.

Jack remained at Oxford a while, seeing his brother Hugh settled in 1722, when, as he explained, things he needed on entry were dearer 'than they were when you entered me'. The general warmth of this family's domestic life radiates from playful correspondence between Jack and his sisters, who, as so often, were the ones to supply male needs from home. When Jack regretted one winter that 'bad weather and worse roads will not suffer me to pass the holidays with you', real affection, more than conventional sibling relations, is apparent. The banter continued: Elizabeth teased with 'I should be glad for to know who was your valentine for my part I had none'; Astrea, when Jack fell silent, wrote 'I hope you will answer this one or else I shall believe you will not be persuaded though one should rise from the dead.'[9]

John Byrom, born in 1691, knew from an early age that his father's ambition was to fit him for ordination. At sixteen, he was writing deferentially and acknowledging his father's support from Merchant Taylors. He strove to practise what his master, who was 'very kind to me and never yet spoke a cross word', preached to him. He should not expect, he was told, to go to university too soon. His father's pressure increased: in 1709, there was much instruction on his theological reading. There was a warning against Locke's *Essay on Human Understanding*, derided by him as Socinian or atheist. Driven hard, John sat and won a scholarship at Cambridge in 1710, but, rather than focus simply on theology, he told his brother and sister that he needed a French dictionary and was about to begin geometry lectures.

John sent his father a report on his studies in February 1710, passing on his duty to his mother and love to his sisters. A stern and demanding lecture reached him soon after this. The stress on his clerical destiny remained intense: 'Good son, look now before you to consider how precious your time is and how to improve yourself to consider the design and end proposed in your education, to fit you for sacred orders, which ought most consistently to be undertaken.' John Byrom senior was satisfied that, with regard to his schooling at Merchant Taylors and the reports of his current tutor, 'God hath given you parts and hitherto you have had nothing wanting in your education'. 'I have no reason to suspect your conversation', his father declared, 'I do but write by way of admonition and caution'; John had 'fine parts', but these 'set upon unprofitable notions will be very impertinent'. The boy's father kept in close touch with his tutor, commenting on items from a report that he had received on the progress of his studies. He forwarded verbatim quotations from one of his tutor's reports. Three years later, the last item in this correspondence shows that John still had his nose down to his books, seeking the loan meanwhile from home, as some kind of diversion, of a spinet and some maps.[10]

Family connection and social clout governed the matriculation of gentlemen commoners at the two universities. They arrived at Oxford, Graham Midgley has written, 'with full purses and ample allowance, able to sustain in their new surroundings a style of living to which they believed themselves entitled, hunting, shooting, fishing, drinking and gambling'.[11] Jack Smyth, achieving his MA, was not typical of the more casual of these young men. A certain level of competence in the classics was required for entry but, once this was achieved, much depended, in the way tutors handled their students, on whether there was the intention to take a degree. Thus Mr Walwyn, tutor to John Filmer at University College, Oxford, wrote to his father, Sir Edward, in April 1735, stating his satisfaction at the boy's initial behaviour. He sought his 'commands in relation to the conduct of his studies'.[12]

Getting in was a question of whom you knew or discovering whom to contact. The widowed Lady Cave told a friend in 1721 about how Sir John Cheshire was helping her over placing her boy Verney, aged sixteen. She had a clear view of the kind of man she wanted for his tutor: 'I wish for a genteelly behaved and bright ingenious man in conversation, which might engage a youth to delight in company and inspire him with noble and honourable thoughts and principles.' Examining the boy, Cheshire had decided he was 'beyond school knowledge' and prompted his schoolmaster to pursue the matter with Balliol, his college. Which particular tutor would he recommend, 'fit for a young gentleman of quality and consequence, that would be a credit to my college, as well as to the school he goes from'? Cheshire offered to carry the boy to Oxford himself in his coach and see him placed there.[13]

University careers were often a source of pride and joy to parents and relatives. Ralph Verney's entry to Merton, Oxford, at seventeen, in 1700, allowed his aged aunt Cary Gardiner to reminisce about her days there, more than 50 years before, in the civil war, when she had attended Henrietta Maria's court in the college. 'I hope my nephew will gain all the advantages you propose for him', she told his father. When his father took Frederick Douglas up to meet the Dean of Christ Church in 1804, they enjoyed a drive round Blenheim Park in his father's open chaise. In the next years, his father's diary records his pleasure at the Dean's and his tutors' accounts of Frederick's progress.[14]

John Pryor swelled with pride when, having seen Fred through Winchester, he entered New College, Oxford in 1841. He saw his rooms, helped him choose furniture and presented him with a fine black riding horse for his journeys to and from Hertfordshire. But he was disappointed when Fred at first rejected his plan that he should enter the church. It was the grief his parents expected to feel, 'if he did not make up his mind positively to apply himself to his studies for that purpose', that eventually swayed him into the career decision that they had set their hearts upon.[15]

The tutorial relationship was the crux of how a young man fared at university. An analysis of the Oxford undergraduate population in the seventeenth century shows that two-thirds had tutors who were young graduates them-selves, under the age of 29. Relatively inexperienced tutors like Dr Meredith were deferential to established country gentlemen who put sons in their charge. Some youths praised their tutors for the support they were given, some were dissatisfied with them, some, especially the scallywags, fell out with them.[16] A critical issue was the company a young man kept. There was a natural tendency for schoolboy alliances to continue. The Master of University College, Thomas Cockman, warned Sir Edward Filmer of the perils before he sent up his son John. Wykhamists included some good and some bad, he opined. It was neces-sary to give firm fatherly advice against being indiscriminate among his school fellows: 'the idle ones will always be about him if he gives them any encouragement', he declared.[17]

The distractions and temptations of the university towns were numerous. The correspondence of the gentleman commoner James Fleming, in the 1690s, reveals a culture of womanising, drink and pleasure. Youths, for the most part, were learning their manhood, rather than engaged in intellectual endeavour.[18] There were lessons available in dancing, fencing and music. John Evelyn, admitted as a gentleman commoner to Balliol in May 1637, noted in his diary the following January his attendance 'into the dancing and vaulting schools'.[19] Physical exercise was taken seriously, with opportunities for archery, tennis and battledore and shuttlecock. But drunkenness, whoring and gambling were always the standard vices. Sir Robert Harley told his boy Ned, in 1640, that Oxford abounded with those who led dissolute lives, dismissing such men, in fine puritan style, as 'such pigs'. A father had advised the Warden of New College in 1623 that he should 'cause a barber to cut off my son's fanciful long hair and locks . . . to take off part of his pride, humble him and make him keep close to his study'.[20]

A tutor's best chance of retaining control over a pupil's pattern of life lay in strict control of his financial resources: fathers were often slow to let their sons off the lead in this respect. It was a matter of some pride to John Evelyn, in April 1638, that his father now trusted him sufficiently to direct 'that I should begin to manage my own expenses which till then my tutor had done'.[21] In 1701 William Ford, tutor to young Edward Filmer, wrote to Sir Robert about how the boy was keeping full accounts under his direction: 'he manages his money very prudently, is very regular in the college and very industrious and therefore is beloved and respected by everybody here'. Thirty years later, Sir Edward, in turn, was setting up arrangements for money to go to his son John's tutor, noting that 'if he behaves prudently you may after trust him with his own money'.[22]

The well-documented career of Jacky Lowther, admitted to Queen's College Oxford as a servitor in 1670, evokes the atmosphere of this period.

After his father's early death, he had come under the wing of his grandfather, the royalist Sir John Lowther, a great man in Cumberland and Westmorland, who designed to bring him up 'in my own way'. This naturally included a period at Sedbergh, the best school in the north, to prepare him for university entrance.[23] Welcoming him to Queen's in April 1670, the Provost, Dr Thomas Barlow, spoke warmly to Sir John of Jacky, as the 'heir and hopes of your ancient and worthy family'. Barlow wrote at length when he actually arrived on 28 June. He appointed a recently arrived fellow, the Reverend Henry Denton, 'a sober person' and a 'good scholar', as the boy's tutor. With no others under his wing, Denton would have plenty of time for 'directing and instructing his pupil in the grounds of religion and good literature': 'I know how much it concerns your family and country that your grandchild be carefully bred to the knowledge and love of learning and civility and it will be my prayer and endeavour that he may be so.'[24]

Young Jacky was considerably in awe of his grandfather, now in his 60s, a crusty figure of huge eminence in the north-west. 'He was a man of rigid virtue, temperate and grave', was the boy's assessment, 'bred from his youth to a great frugality and privacy of living.'[25] His anxious and obsequious first letter, on 22 July, related his expenses on the long journey south, requiring four days' riding and numerous tips, which might make him 'complain of our extravagance'. He believed that Dr Denton, 'accomplished in good manners and famous in good learning', would help him, professing that he was already 'somewhat fixed, knowing in some measure the grounds and methods of study'. He hoped his career would not frustrate his grandfather's expectations, that he would reap comfort to 'your honourable grey hairs' from his experience.

It was the following April that the Provost contacted Sir John to report on Jacky's settling in. They were taking him as an upper commoner, which meant ranking him 'amongst gentlemen of better birth and fortune and so (in reason and probability) of more ingenious breeding and civility'. He would 'read over the grounds of divinity to him' privately himself. But he was not happy at Jacky's having brought a servant from home, since they 'commonly make masters idle'. Instead, his tutor would assign a boy to 'do all little businesses for him'.[26]

Sir John, confident Jacky had found his feet, had given him control of his own money in January 1671. Denton was happy to be relieved of acting for Sir John: 'as I do not distrust his discretion so it will ease me'. 'Your grandson continues his application to his studies not only with diligence but delight', he related in this letter. He confessed, though, that he had just had five days in his chamber after a fight, having sprained his leg 'in jesting with another gentleman'.[27] Worse was soon to come. Jacky was going to pieces as a serious student. He admitted, much later, that his Oxford career from July 1671 to

March 1672 was a disaster. This was his own account: 'My grandfather threw me too soon into the world . . . the rudiments of school learning were planted but not rooted and the indulgence of my tutor at Oxford made me forget all that I had been labouring for the preceding time of my life.'[28]

During the summer of 1671, Sir John heard enough about Jacky's misbehaviour at Oxford to raise his ire. It was the Provost who received this. 'I am heartily sorry his carriage should be such as to cause the displeasure of so good a grandfather', Barlow pleaded in early September, in a letter which carries Sir John's sharp annotation 'not answered'. He vowed he would make Jacky obedient for the future, asking for a little grandfatherly kindness 'to take off that dejection of spirit (at least in part) which will if it continue dispose and disable him to study'. Sir John's rage was leading him to contemplate disinheriting the boy. Seeking to keep Jacky at Oxford, Barlow stressed patriarchal doctrine: 'your name and the best blood of your family must by him as first born be transferred and conveyed down to posterity'.[29]

Then, rather extraordinarily, given Jacky's age of sixteen, Sir John, now an ill man, adopted a new tactic. He would secure the future of the family by finding the boy a bride of his choosing. He would thus create a landed alliance in northern society that would comfort him and outlast his lifetime. He had developed cancer of the scrotum; he took the waters at Tonbridge in early 1671 in hope of a cure and underwent an operation late in the year. He in fact lived another four years, but he was not to know he would be given this lease of life.

During September 1671, Sir John contacted Dr Denton on this issue of marriage. Barlow decided to handle the matter personally, writing at length to him on 28 September, after Jacky's dejection was increased by his tutor telling him that, if he refused the bride his grandfather selected for him, this disobedience might cause 'high displeasure'. Jacky wept that day in the Provost's lodgings. He felt that he faced ruin if the estate was settled on one of his brothers: there were four his grandfather could choose from. He confessed to Barlow that Sir John had been 'a careful and tender father to him' since he lost his own father, that 'all obedience and gratitude' was due to him, that he would only marry with his consent. Yet he hoped not to be importuned, fearing that 'without mutual love marriage was but another word for the greatest misery'.

Barlow, seeking to soften Sir John's anger, took the boy's part. He testified to his 'great parts of body and mind', his civility and his academic progress, despite some misdemeanours. He backed him by arguing that Jacky's consent to a grandfatherly marriage proposal on his behalf was crucial. He reiterated the sacredness of primogeniture, claiming that it should not be forfeited 'for a little fault'. The disinheritance proposed, he declared, would destructively stain the Lowther name.[30]

This was a battle that the Provost lost, since in March 1672, Sir John called Jacky home and sent him off, with his friend Kit Wandesford and a new tutor who they both liked, to study in Paris and make a tour of France, intending he should then go to the Inner Temple. Jacky was idle about learning French, insisting that, since his grandfather was resolved on a country life for him managing the estate, it would be of no use to him. But diligence in the broad tutorial programme set out for him abroad won Jacky a way back into his grandfather's favour: 'during the time that we lie in any place I omit not to give them such masters as may most conduce to polish them as dancing, fencing, singing and the guitar.'[31]

Sir John did have the satisfaction of seeing his rapscallion grandson respectably married, at nineteen, in 1674. It cost him a thousand pounds. Jacky chose a wife 'not out of the rich or high', but 'as I hoped would comply with the privacy of my grandfather's manner of living'. He retained tremendous respect for old Sir John, even if his memoir on his upbringing reflected critically on the mistakes that were made, after he had lost his own father so young. Writing this memoir when he was 33, Jacky regretted that he had forgotten all he learnt at Sedbergh, during those unprofitable eighteen months in Oxford. At his young age, he had lacked a tutor conscientious enough to 'daily improve his school learning', in a manner that was 'friendly and acceptable'.[32]

Mothers feared for their boys in the noisome urban surroundings of Oxford and Cambridge, where they might well be led astray or suffer ill health. The classic account of a cloying and intense mother and son relationship under the strain of this parting, at a time of political tension moreover, is the correspondence of the zealous Lady Brilliana Harley with her son Ned, who was at Magdalen Hall in Oxford in 1640. Brilliana, missing him dreadfully and fretting about Ned's health, sent him presents by the Herefordshire carrier: gammon, dried sweetmeats, apples and a turkey pie. Planning, she wrote, to make a cordial to send him that he should drink in the mornings, she added 'I hope you are careful not to eat too much fish this Lent.' A strict Lent, she had cautioned, was definitely not good for him: 'be careful of your health', she insisted, 'use exercise and a good diet, go to bed betimes and rise early . . . but above all, my dear Ned, look to that precious part of you, your soul; be not wanting to preserve its health, keep it in a spiritual heat by prayer and let the love of your God be the motive of all your obedience'.

Brilliana Harley was abundantly grateful for her son's frequent missives by the Herefordshire carrier. 'Your lines are sweetly welcome to me', she wrote on 8 May 1640, 'it is my joy that you are well'. But as summer wore on, her loneliness increased. 'Dear Ned', she wrote on 4 July, 'I long to see you and I hope I shall with comfort.' She did not forget, but it was in a postscript this time, to 'remember my love to your worthy tutor'.[33]

A letter from Alice Fleming to young Daniel at Oxford in 1651 breathes the motherly commitment which sustained thousands of boys at university over these centuries. 'In the first place fear God', she wrote, 'and then obey your father's advice, and mine which, if you do not doubt but God will so assist your good endeavours that you take in hand, all shall go well with you.' 'Dear son', Alice Fleming added, 'so long ever as I hear your well doing it is my daily comfort and you may assure yourself there shall be nothing wanting in me to perform the part of a loving mother.'[34]

Mary Woodforde's long entry in her diary on 13 October 1687 expresses the same kind of emotions:

> My eldest son Samuel is gone this day towards Cambridge to be a scholar at St John's College. God of his mercy grant that he may do worthily there and bring great honour to his Holy Name and comfort to his parents. And keep him in all ways from sin and danger and the infection of evil company. Make him an example of sobriety and goodness to all his companions.[35]

Jane Sacheverell resisted her boy Will's going to university as fiercely as she had done the entry of her boys to one of the major public schools. It put her on the spot when a Nottingham alderman of her acquaintance offered him a scholarship to Jesus College Cambridge in February 1694. 'I am in great fears to send my son to the university', she wrote to her brother-in-law, 'being a hazardous place for youth as I hear.' She was for keeping him under Mr Greatrix's kindly eye for a while longer 'and let him be his own master after at the Inns of Court'. Will himself was content with this. So Jane prevaricated for more than a year, musing, in March 1695, that her dear husband had spoken of his finishing his education abroad with some time at Utrecht, 'if the times were peaceable'. The outcome is not revealed by her correspondence.[36]

Motherly concern features again, in letters around 1710 to 1712, from his mother to William Bowes, of Gibside in County Durham, studying at Cambridge. Anxiety fills her page in a letter enquiring 'what spa water thou hast drunk':

> I cannot think of your coming down without your tutor along with you. I shall live in hopes. I writ formerly to know how you have come on in your studies but have had no answer. Dear child, you may be assured that it would be a great satisfaction to me to know what books you read though I do not understand them, to enquire after it in way of discourse with other people.

On a later occasion, she fussed about how he would get home, the difficulty of getting horses, and the options of her sending her coach all the way to Cambridge or his taking the stage coach to York, where hers would meet him.[37]

Insight into the kind of life boys lived at Oxford and Cambridge from the Georgian to the Edwardian period can be acquired from letters written by four undergraduates, Richard Cumberland, a nineteen-year old at Magdalene, Cambridge in 1772, John Skinner, arriving at Georgian Oxford to enter Trinity College at eighteen in 1790, Francis Trench, at Oriel from 1825 to 1828 and Reggie Chenevix Trench, who was at Merton in the halcyon days before the Great War. Remarkably little changed across these decades, in an academic society ruled by the privileges of class and by the deeply laid assumptions of hierarchy and service.

Richard Cumberland's account of life in Cambridge, writing to his brother, is closely paralleled by that of John Skinner at Oxford eighteen years later:

> About seven o'clock in the morning the bedmaker comes in, lights the fires, puts on the kettle and sets the room to rights: at half past seven the bell begins to ring, when we immediately get up, dress ourselves and go to Chapel . . . on our return we find everything ready for breakfast and we send to the butler for whatever we choose, at nine o'clock we go to Mr Deighton who gives us a lecture on Euclid . . . we seldom stay longer in the hall than two o'clock, when it is customary to invite one another to drink wine in our rooms . . . we generally form parties for tea, either among ourselves, or from other colleges.[38]

John Skinner delighted in Oxford university's fine buildings in 1790, explaining in a letter to a close friend how he had traversed the ritual of matriculation with friendly help from his tutor, who gave him dinner on his arrival. His scout would put his breeches and great coat neatly by his bed each night. Typically, of a winter morning, he dressed hurriedly and reached the chapel half way through prayers, returning to his room in the hope that a fire would have been lit and water would be boiling for his shave. His scout poured his tea and buttered his breakfast rolls, before he began work on his books at 9.30 a.m., preparing to meet his tutor at 10 o'clock. A walk 'for exercise and air' or skating on the flooded Christ Church meadow was de rigueur in the afternoon. Dinner in hall, arraying fellows, scholars and commoners in hierarchy and order, was followed by dessert and port in his room, with friends sometimes visiting for a social evening, which would end at 9 o'clock when the scout came to clear the bottles and attempt to get his undergraduates to bed.[39]

Francis Trench took his study seriously, as we might expect after his brilliant Harrow career, but he seems to have worked throughout on his own initiative, without a tutor. He ended up with a second class, with which his father was entirely satisfied, deciding in 1827 that he wanted to enter the church. He wished he had made better use of his time after being 'very fairly grounded and prepared'. His mother's death in his second year probably did not help.

Francis's letters suggest that he was a convivial man whose life was typical of Oxford at this time. He enjoyed his college debating society. His college was full of congenial Etonians, Harrovians, Rugbians and Wykhamists. He was keen on the river, joining enthusiastically in the running and cheering of his college boat on the Isis. 'Oxford looks very beautiful . . . the avenue in Christ Church provides a walk of the most perfect shade in the heat', Francis wrote to Melesina Trench on 28 May 1826. He was not averse to shooting parties nearby, though, as he told his father after one of these in October 1827, 'I shot as usual most hopelessly': 'the gamekeepers have reason to be satisfied with me as I don't even wound or touch the birds'.[40]

There were anxious moments about getting in for Reggie Chenevix Trench, who had set his heart on Merton, as his mother knew. He came from Charterhouse to be examined for entry in 1906.[41] The college, its historian Roger Highfield has written, had a sense around that time of 'a small but close-knit family party . . . sustained by sport, especially rowing and cricket, by college "wines" or "smokers" and by clubs like the Myrmidons'.[42] Reggie, an immensely sociable young man at eighteen, when he arrived with his patrician Irish ancestry and Charterhouse behind him, took to the college like a duck to water. He scraped in, only passing his entrance in divinity in his second year.[43] The college's academic demands were a trial and his pass degree was the predictable outcome. 'I am doing a lot of heavy work just at present', he wrote to his sisters on 22 November 1908, in his third year, with an exam coming up, 'it all depends on the next two weeks: my tutor seems fairly hopeful'.

For Reggie, as for all those gentleman commoners through the eighteenth and nineteenth centuries, the Oxford experience was essentially social not academic. Like Jack Smyth in 1720, he had his younger sister Cesca visit in 1907, proudly, in his case, showing her Christ Church, the walk round its meadow and the view of his own college against the old city wall. His November letter to her, in 1908, was dominated by social news, including his activities as secretary of the Myrmidons. He was seeking just then to enhance the facilities of the college's smart dining club, its premises in the High Street adorned with photographs of past members like Max Beerbohm on its walls, by the purchase of a Strohmerger piano, 'on the gradual payment system'. He explained the form about girl friends and dances: 'at two minutes to twelve a great change comes over the room as 90 per cent of the men start running hatless and coatless away to get in by midnight. It is rather amusing'.[44]

Late Stuart Oxford, as the letters of James Fleming in the 1690s indicate, was more riotous and undisciplined than Edwardian Oxford. There were horse races on Port Meadow in those days, the notorious barmaid 'Eastgate Jinny' was being held responsible for spreading syphilis and a coffee house keeper, who consorted with undergraduates, had been 'brought in bed' of a child.[45] Edwardian Oxford was tamer. But, as so often in this story of the English growing up, the basic continuity in terms of the real purposes served by long-established institutions of education is apparent. The universities were as much instruments of English patriarchy, a system of class and gender construction, as the public schools, the Grand Tour, the country house schoolroom and the ritual of coming out.

The Schoolroom

Girls, once out of the nursery, were brought up with their destiny in the marriage market always in the forefront of parental thinking. The watchword, endlessly repeated in the letters and diaries of both parents and the girls themselves, was 'Improvement'. This was moral and spiritual; it was cultural and social; it only omitted the intellectual and academic side of life. Girls were not seen as having minds. Their training was about their carriage and deportment. It focused relentlessly on accomplishments, not learning, skills whether at the piano, with the needle or on the dance floor which would do credit to a gentleman's residence. All elite girls were expected in adulthood to play the role of hostess as well as mother, to grace their husband's home as well as to manage its servant population. This training was therefore both for private and public ends.

Improvement was seen as best served by a scheme of upbringing that was holistic yet also fluid, including at one time or another some or all of these elements: domestic schoolroom education, attendance at a day school or boarding school and periods spent with relatives, in London or a provincial city, that afforded the services of dancing masters and other specialist instructors. England's social elite had its own way of doing these things. There were shared assumptions and principles about this female scheme of training, unspoken because they did not need to be spoken. The manner in which it was pursued with any particular child depended on all sorts of circumstances, especially the availability at particular times and places of the expertise that parents wished to bring into play, but also the age and place of a girl, in relation to siblings in the family on parallel courses in politeness.

Improvement, leading to coming out and a girl's first season, is discussed here over three chapters. We begin with the schoolroom, since this was the foundation of learning for thousands of English girls from the 1770s onwards, whether over a monotonous period of up to twelve years or episodically, with schooling as a break at some point. The census of 1861 listed

24,770 governesses living in England and Wales. The great age of the governess lasted until 1914, as the gentry and wealthier section of the middle class sought the safety of instruction in their own homes, where girls would be immune from bad example. 'As to schools for girls', Thomas Talbot told Mrs Hicks Beach, echoing a new orthodoxy in 1796, 'it is as unserviceable and dangerous as keeping boys at home: the one is liable to be run away with by the dancing master and the other fall in love with the kitchen maid.'[1]

The schoolroom offered personal tuition and guided education in an often cloyingly domestic context. Its trials were as nothing beside the rough and tumble that boys faced in boarding schools. Yet, for girls from six to eighteen who ran this whole course, these were long and deeply formative years, with an intensity of their own. Every schoolroom girl's experience was mediated by the personality and approach of those who took charge of her, adults who, under parental eyes, controlled every waking minute. Governesses, the rulers of this small world, were loved and respected or challenged and disliked, as the case might be.[2]

The schoolroom regime as such had not been invented in Tudor England. But Grace Mildmay's adult recollections of her upbringing provide insight into its essence. She scathingly dismissed the carelessness of parents who simply followed custom and sent daughters to live with relatives. It was her father's niece, Mistress Hamblyn, brought up herself by Grace's mother, who was entrusted with teaching Grace and her sister Ursula. 'She proved very religious, wise and chaste', Grace testified:

> for from her youth she made use of all things that ever she did read, see or hear and observed all companies that ever she came in, good or bad, so that she could give a right answer and true judgement of most things and give wise counsel upon any occasion.

Grace recalled her daily routine at Lacock:

> I delighted so much in her company that I would sit with her all the day in her chamber and by my good will would never go from her, embracing always her rebukes and reproofs. And when she did see me idly disposed, she would set me to cipher with my pen and to cast up and prove great sums and accounts . . . and other times set me to read . . . and other times set me to sing psalms and sometimes set me to curious work.

Mistress Hamblyn counselled Grace to avoid the company of gossiping servants, striking a note about class inviolability, echoed in the training of upper-class girls by governesses and parents across these centuries. Reinforced by the precepts of her parents, she experienced female gender construction in its classic form. 'I should ever carry me with a modest and a chaste ear', Hamblyn insisted, 'a silent tongue and a considerate heart, wary and heedful of myself in all my words and actions.' Her mother taught her 'meditation and prayers by heart and how I should fear and worship God in spirit and truth'. She limited Grace's reading to four books only, which she considered sufficiently pure for a young girl's mind: the Bible, *Common Places*, *The Book of Martyrs* and *Imitatio Christi*. But it was her rigid and authoritarian father's demands that made the deepest impact. He removed unsuitable servants from the household, rather than risk his daughters being corrupted. He:

> could not bear to see a woman unstable or light in her carriage . . . he liked a woman well graced with a constant and settled countenance and good behaviour throughout her whole parts, which presenteth unto all men a good hope of an established mind and virtuous disposition to be in her.[3]

It was after 1770 that the demand for governesses rose, as dissatisfaction with girls' schools increased.[4] This demand coincided with an increase in young unmarried women of respectable background, looking for such a position, and then with a flood of émigrés from France, after the French Revolution of 1789. 'There is a greater choice of French governesses than ever was known', commented Thomas Talbot in 1796, 'possibly of the highest rank, good sense and respectability.'[5] Jane Austen's account of the employment of governesses by Sir Thomas Bartram at Mansfield Park and by the Woodhouse family, who were 'first in consequence' at Hartfield, indicates the normality of domestic teaching for girls in the grander families during the period from 1810 to 1820.[6]

But finding gentlewomen with both the required qualifications and the necessary strength of character was hard. A letter from Catherine Wincle to Lord Bruce illuminates how one governess seeking employment set out her case in 1778. She spoke of her social standing as the widow of an officer in the Coldstream Regiment, listing the aristocratic families for whom she had previously worked. His children would 'always be my companions from the hour of rising till that of retiring to rest', all her time being devoted to 'their internal and external improvement'. She would 'act as tender parent' towards them.[7]

The first governess employed by Mary Fox Strangeways, second Lady Ilchester, at Redlynch in Somerset in 1780, lasted for three years. She was then considered 'unsatisfactory'. For some months thereafter, a writing master visited Redlynch, before Agnes Porter, who stayed for thirteen years, arrived.

In 1783 Elizabeth was ten, Mary was seven and Harriot was five. In the next years, three more girls, Charlotte, Louisa and Susanna came along. This family, with so many girls, really needed a governess and found an exceptional one in Agnes. Her service to the Fox Strangeways family actually stretched, with a break, for over 23 years, because, when the second daughter, Mary, married Thomas Talbot, the squire of Penrice Castle in Glamorgan, and also had girls, she became governess to them, in turn.

Keeping a remarkable journal, Agnes Porter – 'Po' to the children – is the best-documented governess of Georgian England. She was the daughter of a clergyman. She had a 'lively and enquiring mind', notes Joanna Martin, who edited her journal, and her teaching skills were adequate. More importantly, she liked, and was good with, children, the first qualification for a successful governess. Mary Talbot's testimony says it all. She was 'a very naughty sulky child' until Agnes came along, she related to her own daughter Charlotte, born in 1800. But Agnes, meeting her as a seven-year old, had used her 'sweet good sense and discernment of character to charm her out of her obstinacy'.[8]

The recruitment process, Kathryn Hughes has argued, was a 'foretaste of the ambiguities and tensions' that the governess would meet once she started work.[9] The first meeting with her employer brought home the point that the position of a governess, neither quite family nor quite a servant in the family, was an uncertain and fluid one. There were inevitably apprehensions on both sides in the first meeting of a governess with her employer. Mary Cowden Clark was grateful that her first employer, after she had learnt French at Boulogne as a prelude to her career, broke the ice, her first morning in the garden before breakfast, by pressing her to eat an apple that she had picked up and to have one 'whenever I liked'.[10] Georgiana Trench reported positively, to her eldest daughter Haddie, on the arrival at Cangort Park of Mademoiselle Maffey in the 1860s: she 'looks sensible and kind'. She was not much taller than Louey, who she was taking charge of, with her teenage sisters Isabel and Blanche. 'I am favourably impressed on the whole', Georgiana concluded, 'for which I am thankful'.[11]

A relationship between a mistress of the house and her governess could become quite extraordinarily intense, when ill health left a mother feeling needy and isolated. It came to be seen as the 'mark of a genteel family that they were able to stay friends with their governess long after she had left their appointment'.[12] Miss Freestone's relationship with Lady Freda Lorraine, in Victorian Suffolk, proved both intimate and long standing. Yet her 'coming for a kiss' from her employer, in April 1887, crossed the normal boundaries of this relationship, in a remarkable and unusual way that Carole Williams has been able to explain in her acute analysis of the episode.[13]

French Mademoiselles, on short-term contracts while a regular governess was away, sometimes found themselves treated as family, simply because there was less need to keep up formality and distance in these circumstances. 'Yesterday Miss Hugill went away, we're going to have holidays except for a little music with Mademoiselle who is staying for Easter', wrote Eva Knatchbull in her diary for 1874. Next day, 6 April, Mademoiselle was reading to Eva and her sister Kate in the library when dinner was announced: 'Mama said "Now, Papa, will you take in Mademoiselle?" Papa instantly made her a low bow and they went in together.'[14]

When a woman had many daughters, as Lady Maria Stanley did with her seven born between 1797 and 1809, a governess left at home with the little ones bore exceptional responsibility, while their mother launched older girls on London society. The effectiveness of the governess at Alderley with the younger Stanley girls, around 1817 to 1823, is well documented by their well-penned and informative letters to Lady Maria from the schoolroom. Her younger sister Maude had surely 'told almost all the news yesterday', sighed fourteen-year-old Harriott on 15 June 1819, declaring that she felt this letter 'is better written than the last one' and thanking her mother for the drawing book which she was using. The baby of the family, Emmeline, wrote about having measles, insisting that the dog Crab, rather ill, probably had measles too. She explained that the governess was about to start reading her a novel by Sir Walter Scott aloud.[15]

But the hardest situation for a governess was responsibility without parental interest and support. This was Mrs Weeton's fate in her employment with the Armitage family at Huddersfield in 1812. The children's education she wrote, some weeks after taking the post, 'has never, that I recollect, been a subject of conversation'. The Armitage parents, she found with dismay, listened to her weekly account of work in the schoolroom 'with greater indifference than I could wish'. They were 'totally unacquainted with a greater part of what their children learn'. The Armitage children had been much indulged before Mrs Weeton arrived, so she found herself having to 'correct and punish' them 'much more frequently than I could wish'. Mr Armitage baulked at the cost, when Mrs Weeton suggested books she needed for the schoolroom. Mrs Weeton was writing in disillusionment during the early days at Huddersfield when she thought of leaving. As her employers became more conciliatory, she thought better of this drastic course.[16]

Mrs Congreve's letter to her new governess Miss Eyre, in 1817, provides exceptional insight into an appointment in Staffordshire. This letter allows us to reflect on the tensions inherent in a mother's handing over a degree of responsibility to, effectively, a paid assistant in the overwhelmingly important business of motherhood. The previous governess at Burton-on-Trent had been a disaster, as Mrs Congreve had no hesitation in explaining. Miss Hayne had only just left: her 'bare bosom and style altogether' were 'totally disgusting' to Mr Congreve. Neither of them, Mrs Congreve reflected, could have accustomed themselves to Miss Hayne's 'want of decorum and consistency in her dress'. It was unfortunate that she felt degraded by her profession, so that 'out of the schoolroom her constant aim appeared to be, by her conversation and nonchalance to the children, to have it forgotten what was her situation in our family'. The last straw was that her 'weak, silly conduct' had been 'much observed' by the visiting friends of the Congreves.

Mrs Congreve wrote in May and expected Miss Eyre's arrival in September. 'I have family reasons', she explained, 'for apprehending that by that time I shall feel myself a very inactive and inadequate instructress.' Mary Anne was fifteen and Louisa and Jane were in their earlier teens. There may have been boys away at school, she may have been pregnant, she certainly expected to be 'prevented by company' from giving assistance in the schoolroom more than occasionally. Yet she insisted that Mary Anne's piano lessons would be her own concern. The fact was that Mrs Congreve, a dedicated mother with a bad experience behind her, found it difficult to hand the children over again, despite all the trouble that the advice writers took excusing her for doing so.[17]

The extraordinary detail of her instructions and the meticulous approach to Miss Eyre's appointment displayed by Mrs Congreve reflects her concern to ensure that, this time, her governess would not let the family down. Her letter is a potent reminder of just how seriously Georgian women took this delegation, how anxious those most caring among them were about taking this plunge. So much, in academic, social and moral terms, was at stake. Mrs Congreve had required Miss Eyre to send full information about her previous lesson plan, with her single pupil Fanny Trevor. At Burton, she would face a schoolroom of three teenage girls. So she was sending 'a little plan of the management of my children's lessons', Mrs Congreve announced, together with a timetable. 'I think that never less than seven hours in a day should be occupied in study or employment of some kind to do the children any kind of justice', she declared.

The day would begin at seven, or eight at the latest, during the shortest months for daylight, starting with the girls saying their prayers and a bible reading, which Mrs Congreve hoped often to take in person. The habit of early rising was a 'very desirable' one, that she wanted inculcated as a lesson for life. Breakfast was at nine, dinner at two, followed by walks and time outside under supervision, before a final lesson hour from six to seven. Only Sundays varied, when catechising at eight would replace lessons, and should be continued after church with the two younger girls.

Mr and Mrs Congreve's scheme of things put the children firmly in their place, yet it ensured that their parents never became remote. Every day when the children joined them, still under the governessing eye, for dessert, she and they would be tested on their social progress. Bedtimes related to age, with Mary Anne staying up the longest, until about ten o'clock. Mrs Congreve hoped that Miss Eyre would quickly become her partner, though designedly an inferior and dependent one, in promoting the children's 'general improvement and manners also in their conduct and temper'. She was almost obsessive about how one of them should always be watching over them. 'It is impossible', she wrote, 'to define exactly the various little duties that are required in a good mother or next to that a good governess.'

Miss Eyre's relationship with Mary Anne was a special concern that took up a good deal of the letter. Essentially, Mrs Congreve was focusing here on how a governess should conduct a fifteen-year old towards adulthood. She wanted Miss Eyre, for example, to do as she had with her previous pupil, Fanny Trevor, and advise her on tidying up the clothes in her drawers on Saturdays. Mary Anne was 'exceedingly well disposed to love and esteem' her, but she could not, at fifteen, be treated like the other two as a child. She had been her mother's 'constant companion', making her, Mrs Congreve suggested, 'more womanly in her age and ideas than many girls of her standing'.

Thus, to establish 'the sort of respect and deference united with friendship and kind regard that I should wish her to entertain for you', Miss Eyre should invariably use Mary Anne's surname, as a mark of 'some little degree of form and observance' between them. To reiterate the point, the table of lessons referred in turn to 'Miss Congreve, Louisa and Jane'. It was Miss Eyre's daily example that would form Mary Anne's standard of womanhood. So her dress should be 'strictly nice, neat, unattractive and remarkable only for its simplicity and delicacy'. 'Will you forgive me', she wrote, 'if I say at once that I have seen you I think wear your drawers so long in the leg that the flounces of them have made their appearance.' Distaste for what she feared might become a 'general fashion' made Mrs Congreve insist that Miss Eyre's drawers would be 'much better invisible'.[18]

Little changed in the schoolroom curriculum, orchestrated to the age of the children present there and their gradual maturity, over a hundred years. The Congreve template of learning is probably quite exceptional in the detail set out. But the pattern of study between breakfast and dinner, with a period of work on exercises set for the day after tea, was invariable, as was the afternoon spent, if the weather allowed, outside. It was seen as important to balance brainwork with physical exercise, which could be quite boisterous, given the privacy afforded by garden walls. Beyond the estate or within it, the demure daily walk often lasted a couple of hours. The Sitwell girls were expected to be in the fresh air for three to four hours altogether every day in the 1830s.[19]

The schoolroom was generally a world in which the governess ruled and set the curriculum by her own initiative, within a general framework of assumptions about what was suitable for young girls and pre-school boys. At Hagley in Worcestershire, the master and mistress of the house, Lord and Lady Lyttelton, paraded through it to and fro, because the rooms where they worked were at the end of the schoolroom corridor. But the schoolroom was often remote from the main living rooms. It was high on a top floor at Bark Hart in Kent, sliced off the back of the library at Bowen's Court in County Cork and sometimes, as at Lanhydrock, part of a nursery wing. The schoolroom in the fine villa Sir Richard Morrison built for the Trenchs at Cangort Park, complete with its fireplace, was up an attic stair from the girls' bedrooms, looking out over the luxuriant Irish countryside.[20]

Barbara Tasburgh described her unusually grim Northumbrian schoolroom in the 1820s. She remembered no toys, even educational ones, only a barrel organ and a rocking horse. Her sisters insisted on keeping smelly caterpillars in a box on the window sill. Her childhood was overshadowed by her father's sense that, as the third in a line of daughters, she was 'a superfluous addition to the family'. There were few enjoyments, but dinner downstairs with visiting relatives on Christmas Day was 'an unforgettable landmark in our lives'.[21]

The curriculum set out by Mrs Congreve for her girls was a very broad one. There was a great deal of geography and history besides arithmetic, botany, poetry and mythology. While Mary Anne was moving on to beginning Italian, the younger girls were to be set French exercises and translations several days a week. We cannot tell how fully Miss Eyre proved capable of enforcing the demanding academic regime set before her.[22] The Burton-on-Trent scheme encapsulates the central fact that this was usually an extremely intensive kind of education. The days were long, the years must have seemed endless.

The governess was normally expected to teach her girls sewing, knitting and embroidery, besides academic subjects. Numerous samplers, with the names of proud teenagers sewn in, today provide testimony to this tyranny of the needle, the lot of teenage girls from the seventeenth century to the twentieth. Another favourite exercise, involving meticulous attention to detail, and seen as perfect for training the female mind, was 'pasting', or making scrapbooks. One compiled by Louey Trench, at Cangort Park in the 1860s, shows the scope, under the eye of an imaginative governess, for inculcating a feel for intricate patterning, using crests cut off envelopes received by the family and other ephemera. This scrapbook included many photographs of family luminaries, of pets and even of the governess herself. Mademoiselle Maffey appears in a series of poses, grouped demurely with Louey and her sisters Isabel and Blanche. It is a work of art in its neatness and varying page by page design.[23]

At Redlynch, under the tutelage of Agnes Porter, lessons only ended for the elder three girls, Elizabeth, Mary and Harriot, as they were in turn presented at court between 1792 and 1797. The curriculum there included English and French literature, history, geography and classics in translation. Shakespeare featured largely. Regular bible reading was supplemented by catechising on Sundays. Needlework and embroidery were de rigueur. Agnes devoted some afternoons to expeditions in the grounds: 'we made a party to the lodge', she recorded on 7 September 1790, 'where we drank tea with much glee'. Louisa Fox Strangeways described the pattern of a day to her elder sister Mary at eleven years old: 'At nine we breakfast in the square drawing room and at ten begin studying with Po till two. At three we dine and after dinner sometimes we study a little and sometimes ride, walk or work in our gardens. We go to bed about half past eight.'[24]

When she worked at Penrice, her new employer and former pupil Lady Mary Talbot, who acted as co-tutor, encouraged Agnes to broaden the curriculum, so that it included subjects like philosophy, geometry, chemistry and natural history. The Gower peninsular became the Talbot children's schoolroom and playground. Collecting shells and pebbles for sorting, drawing and identification was as important here as arithmetic or French. The children also collected geological specimens, fossils and flints. They were much more broadly educated than most girls in the first years of the nineteenth century.[25]

In her memoir of her life, the Derbyshire girl Elizabeth Bradshawe, born in 1798 and writing at 81, described the regime imposed on her and her pre-teen sisters by Miss Cook, an experienced governess who spent six years with her family. She was 'a first rate governess for children of our age, not a woman who inspired either love or fear, but so decisive no one ever dreamed of disobeying her': 'she was an excellent drilling machine and spared neither herself nor us, especially grounding us in French but in all she taught she did it thoroughly. I think I could repeat the auxiliary verbs now or say the multi-plication tables backwards or forwards.' Prayers with Miss Cook, 'morning and evening when we knelt before her at a form close to the breakfast table side by side', were as much an exercise in deportment as one in religious education. Standing before them, 'she would draw herself up as a hint to us to kneel upright'. 'I wonder God does not strike you dead for poking so', she once solemnly warned Maria.[26]

Mary Williams, born in 1803, provided a brief account of her two governesses in her memoir of childhood in Regency England. The first, Miss Blackburn, was 'a thoroughly religious woman and very clever, her information without being profound was general'. She was a good linguist in French and Italian. 'She was very particular in making me do plain sewing', Mary recalled, 'and I was very proud when I made Willy a shirt all by myself and had a whole shilling as a reward.' Her moral teaching stressed responsibility to the poor, inspiring Mary to give them some of her pocket money each week, besides making baby clothes and flannel petticoats for the village women. Mary also patiently taught Kitty, the housemaid, and John, the schoolroom boy who cleaned the shoes, how to read and write. Miss Price, her teenage governess, read with her 'all the best works in French and in Italian and for the first time Shakespeare and Sir Walter Scott'.[27]

The governess who taught the D'Ewes Coke children, Sophie, Agnes, Emma, Henry and Richard, at Pinxton in Derbyshire, kept a full diary of the year 1818. This illuminates a typical pattern of work with pre-teen boys and girls. Reading, written exercises, spelling and multiplication tables, together with the predictable catechising, absorbed many tedious hours. Yet the interest of this diary is more in what it tells us about discipline, with two boys and three girls interacting in a rowdy schoolroom, than about their learning. The main concern of Mrs D'Ewes Coke, during a Christmas break when the governess was away, had been a running battle with her five-year-old Richard, just out of petticoats and determined not to tie his pinafore. 'The children and servants', Mrs D'Ewes Coke noted, 'are peremptorily forbidden to assist him and he is allowed no breakfast, dinner or supper until he produces a double and single bow in the strings.'

Their mother was annoyed to discover the tales with which servants had frightened her boys: 'I am sorry to find that Henry and Richard are afraid to go even to their own bedrooms in the dark if alone, from the mischievous practice that has prevailed of telling them the chimney sweepers will carry them away.' She was having none of this, punishing Richard, a few days after discovering the problem, by sending him 'to bed in disgrace for being afraid to go upstairs in the dark'.

Richard was a handful, always rioting with his big brother. Papa was a distant presence, but one who Richard looked up to enough for the deprivation of a walk or dinner with him to be a real punishment. The clearest evidence of fatherly authority and the implicit threat that it posed comes in an entry about how Agnes and Henry sought to distract his attention one day at dinner: 'to prevent their Papa observing that they were under punishment', these two, the governess noted, 'keep their meat on their plates till the rest of the party have finished dinner so inaction during pudding time is not obvious'.

When Richard Coke crept into the drawing room before the governess had approved his work on 6 April, 'I followed him', she noted, 'and boxed his ears before the ladies.' This was a case, perhaps unusually, where the parents condoned the governess beating the little boys if need be. When Henry and Richard ran riot in their bedroom, she gave them each 'two or three cuts with a little switch which I keep in the schoolroom both as a preventative and cure to some little irregularities which require correction'. In June, she switched Richard for his 'lie that the gardener gave him the strawberry plant she found in his hand'. On 3 August, she noted 'small flogging for R', after his 'morning face and manner' showed his defiance at lessons. 'It was not till he had felt the cane', she having threatened she would have his Papa use it, 'that he began his morning tasks.' Thereafter, he performed them very well.

Results were achieved by minimal force with Richard. He was also often deprived of his plum pudding for general naughtiness. Agnes suffered more punishments of this non-corporal kind, feeling them keenly. The disgrace of early bed, for careless arithmetic in April, seems to have touched her. Then she became indolent over her needlework. She began, the governess noted, laughing and talking with Emma, 'in my presence as if she was the best girl in the world'. She had her ears boxed for persistent familiarity with the servants. Agnes was at a difficult stage: the summer in 1818 was a long one of early beds and forfeited half holidays. Finally, in September, she was seen to eat blackberries without, as instructed, checking with the governess that they were ripe. This earned her an evening of total isolation, with the others forbidden to speak to her.

Emma was the easiest of the Coke children. Docile and anxious, a silent tear, her governess noted, stole down her cheek on 14 June when, taking their places, Henry reminded her, boasting, that he was now top of the class. But when Sophie joined the schoolroom after a period at boarding school, Emma was quickly led astray, unable to handle her older sister's flattering attachment, which removed her from her companionship with Agnes. The governess reproved her for 'giddiness and lack of concentration'. Sophie, in fact, was a thoroughly disruptive influence, seeking to capture hegemony for herself from the governess. She lost her morning walk when she threw her pinafore round the schoolroom in a fit of temper. But she was cowed quite easily by the grown-up in charge, whose firm words quickly made her burst into tears.[28]

The Countess of Jersey, born in 1849, was another woman who recalled her governess with gratitude in later life, despite all the rote learning that she had endured. Miss Coustade, who ruled the Stoneleigh schoolroom in Warwickshire, as the Countess grew up from age six to fourteen, was 'very good at teaching us to look up information for ourselves'. But, like some others, she felt that she had been imposed upon, not enfolded in kindness: 'she worked too much on my conscience, making me regard trivial faults as actual sins which prevented her from kissing me or showing me affection'. It was her nursery nurse who gave her the security for which she yearned. The Countess remembered the joy for the schoolroom children in 'joining the little ones after tea' with her, when they would 'sit in a circle while she told us fairy tales' or read from novels.[29]

Frances, Countess of Warwick, admired her governess, Miss Blake, portraying her in the rosy glow of her 1930 memoirs in highly positive terms. 'I am thankful for the thoroughness of that early training', she wrote, recalling her introduction to French and German literature, the history she was taught and the love of Scott, Byron and Macaulay that she imbibed. This was a happy childhood, in a family of seven during the 1860s, at Easton Neston in Northamptonshire, with ponies to ride from five years old and kittens, rabbits and dogs around the house.[30]

Evelyn Pocklington was an only child, born in 1886 and brought up by parents far more interested in field sports and country house parties than in she herself. She was looked after, between the ages of six and fourteen, by a governess called Boggie, who found little time for her education, because she was always busy in other roles: 'she ran the chicken incubator, she ran the garden. Above all, she was very good at looking after our dogs.' Her 'schoolroom and bedroom alike were damp, dark and musty', Evelyn recalled in her lively recollections, published by her son under the title *My Mother Told Me*. Evelyn learned to read and then 'proceeded to educate myself', immersing herself in the novels of Harrison Ainsworth, from whom she learned her history. 'Feeling that there were gaps in my education', her laissez-faire father eventually arranged for her to have French lessons twice a week at a convent in Romsey, near their home in Hampshire. While many suffered from too much schoolroom drilling, Evelyn Pocklington described happy teenage years, rearing pheasants for her father's shoot, taking charge of the ferrets and of the stables.[31]

The governess kept order in the Pinxton schoolroom because she had firm parental support and because she used a wide range of punishments, which were broadly condoned. The memoirs of Victorian gentlewomen are full of tales which suggest that the sheer distance between the worlds of the drawing room and schoolroom was the decisive factor in this matter of discipline. Most governesses had considerable discretion. Parental collusion in schoolroom methods of control and keeping noses to the grindstone was the order of the day. In this situation, while governesses did not normally spank schoolroom boys or girls, except when very young, they adopted a range of other punishments which subjected children to real psychological torment and to misery of a kind that would now be seen to be child abuse.

Mary Williams remembered the strictness of Miss Blackburn: 'she used to frighten my wits away'. Starting work at six in summer and seven in winter, Mary 'had to forfeit a penny for every five minutes I was behind time'. When she was stuck in her lesson 'or showed the least sign of rebellion and temper or impatience', Miss Blackburn would shut her up in a closet, 'which I dreaded above everything', making her stay there 'till I could say with a cheerful voice that I was quite good'. Her sister Ellen, 'poor little soul, was forever in the closet'.[32]

Mary Haldane wrote in adulthood about her memory of the sound of the closing door when, as a punishment, she was shut up by her governess in an empty room: 'it was done for good but I question whether it was good'. She suffered, she remembered, from being watched continuously, in the introspectively religious atmosphere of her home. She was a rebel against the monotony of her language work in the mornings, while being made to 'read history aloud', before being questioned on it, in the afternoons.[33]

Lucy Lyttelton has left us a vivid picture of the regimes of five governesses at Hagley Hall, as she matured during the 1840s from a child who, she knew well, was 'horribly naughty, sly obstinate, passionate and very stupid', into a serious and responsible fifteen-year old. She believed, nevertheless, looking back at about sixteen, that her first governess, Miss Nicholson, had been too severe, spanking her 'for obstinacy when I was only dense', letting her see her partiality for her less spirited sisters, Meriel and Lavina, 'and punishing too often'. This left her 'always labouring under a sense of injustice' and suffering 'injured innocence', instead of trying to conquer her faults:

> At Brighton I used to be taken out walking on the parade with my hands tied behind me, terrified out of my wits by Miss Nicholson's declaring it was ten to one we should meet a policeman. At home my usual punishment was being put for a time into a large deep old-fashioned bath, before which hung curtains, so that I was partially in the dark.

If this could happen in the caring and affectionate Lyttelton family, it is no surprise that penalties which, to modern eyes, seem like ill-treatment were widely recorded in other households. How could we tell tales, wrote Mary Carberry in the reminiscence of her childhood, to parents who only saw their governess 'in her charming manners', when she brought them to the drawing room? 'They have no idea of our troubles. They do not know how deplorably artful we are growing; how in our fear we try to propitiate her with flowers, peaches and tender enquiries after her relations. They do not notice how pale and anxious our faces are.'

Severity was not necessarily simply disciplinary. There were governesses who simply drove too hard. In an unusual case in 1795, the twelve-year-old daughter of the Wiltshire nobleman Lord Bruce ran away from home and sought employment as a servant in London. She failed to carry this off, being taken to be of higher rank than she admitted. She confessed 'the imposition of too severe a task by her governess' as the cause of her having escaped. Her parents were contacted and her careful letter of apology to them in copper-plate survives in the Wiltshire Record Office. She asked her Mama to inter-cede with Papa 'and again permit me to have the happiness of passing my evenings with you'.[34]

Children sometimes saw how the land lay. Only when an indulgent parent had made no secret of his or her fondness or a governess was blatantly unrea-sonable, did they dare to be defiant. Muriel Beckwith had no fear of being marched off to her father's study by an enraged Fraulein at Goodwood, because she knew that he would see her bad behaviour as a huge joke. 'You are quite welcome to complain', Mary Bazlinton recorded her pupil Tiney declaring on 10 April 1855, knowing perfectly well she would not be deprived of the family trip to the races that day, because her mother simply did not hold her governess in sufficient respect.[35]

Superb insight into the life of a Victorian governess, who was treated very much as part of a family, comes from a collaborative diary kept by four of the Bowen children in Ireland. 'People who think of Victorian family life as being all repression, superstition and fear, as being a foetid nursery of complexes', Elizabeth Bowen argued, overlook its idyllic side. 'Miss Flavelle took a long walk and crossed the river near the mill, where we had great fun placing step-ping stones', Annie Bowen noted on Good Friday in 1876. 'We brought back a bunch of flowers that the gardener gave to Miss Flavelle', Sarah noted on 3 May, after an expedition in the carriage with her to a nearby property. 'We showed Miss Flavelle the new walks we made when we were last here', wrote Annie on 21 October, the day after she joined them at Camira, the family's second home in County Tipperary. Out with the family in November, their governess gave earrings she bought to Lizzie and shared sweets between her and St John.

Miss Flavelle spent long wet days, we read, in the schoolroom that month with the children, scrapbook-making with pictures Papa had brought them. On 15 November 1876 the Dunhallow Hounds met near Bowen's Court. Mary recorded in the diary driving 'on the mountain road', to see Papa riding with them 'from a great distance'. Robert Cole Bowen was a great rider to hounds, but the teenage girls were not allowed to hunt, so Miss Flavelle took them to the nearby meets on ponies or in the wagonette. Bessie, Sarah and Annie worked under Miss Flavelle's supervision decorating the church that Christmas. All in all, she was fully integrated into the Bowens' family life.[36]

Teenagers could support a governess in trouble with parents, when a warm relationship developed. Sophia Baker became very friendly with Mademoiselle Lanzun, employed to teach her younger sisters and chaperone her on social outings in 1799. On 6 September 1799, she noted 'a dreadful fracas between Mama, William and Mademoiselle Lanzun'. It seems that her brother, now aged 21, had entered the girls' bedroom and the governess, held responsible for this impropriety, was dismissed as a result. Two days later, Sophia noted, 'the dispute happily made up on all sides', without explaining how she had saved Mademoiselle from her mother's wrath. But the companionship she found in this governess is revealed by a reference, heavy with exclamation marks, on 31 August 1800: 'fatal day – my dear Mademoiselle Lanzun left us'.[37]

The 1858 diaries of Constance and Annie Rothschild indicate explicit emotional involvement by young girls in the adult life of a resident governess. Their Mademoiselle came back in mourning for her mother, after a visit to France, in September that year. Constance, at fifteen, became a confidante soon after this, acting as go-between when Mademoiselle, in agitation, confessed that she needed a heart-to-heart with her mother. Later:

> I rushed into the schoolroom and found Mademoiselle with red eyes and an excited air. She kissed me . . . she told me 'It is all done'. Your Mama has promised I am to be married next month . . . she had been quite hysterical with Mama until Mama had begged her to speak . . . and she told Mama everything, all about Mr Goldberg and her mysterious journey to Italy how she rushed in the night over the Mont Cenis . . .

Meeting Mr Goldberg some weeks later, Constance 'was trembling so violently that I could hardly look at him', but she decided that, though decidedly good looking, he was 'not an Adonis'. 'How much one can do for love, I believe I could do as much', she reflected, recording Mademoiselle's story. The girls were distressed that her successor, Mademoiselle Maret, was shy and awkward in comparison. Annie noted derisively how, 'exaggeratedly delicate', she 'skipped every little part about the chansons d'amours' when they read French literature.[38]

The overall impression left by extensive documentation is that the regime of the governess was more often than not benign, that most governesses were dedicated to their charges, patient and caring with them, and that, when there was trouble, young children were often seeking to establish boundaries by

1 Francis Stoll's engraving from the lost portrait by George Romney, *Melesina Trench*, c. 1798. The engraving was commissioned by Melesina's son Richard for the frontispiece to his edition of *The Remains of the Late Mrs Richard Trench* published in 1862. Melesina Trench (1768–1827) was the mother of five sons and one daughter. : Her 'Mourning Journal', written in 1806, reflected upon the death of her son Frederick at three years old. Copies of her *Thoughts on Education by a Parent*, published in 1837 after her death, are very rare.

2 William Hogarth, *The Graham Children*, 1742. The painting shows the children of Dr Daniel Graham, apothecary to George II. Richard plays on his musical box, Anna Maria dances, Henrietta, the eldest, seeks to keep little Thomas, now dead, in the world by holding his hand. (National Gallery, London).

3 Enoch Seeman, *Anne Cust with her Children*, 1743–4. Sir Richard and Lady Anne Cust had six sons and four daughters. The image reinforces dynastic progression, with Anne seated next to her eldest son, Sir John Cust, who holds a miniature depicting his wife and the prospective mother of his successor. Above three daughters, seated with their mother at a tea table, hangs an oval head-and-shoulders portrait of their late father, Sir Richard Cust, as a young boy (Belton House).

4 Sir Joshua Reynolds,
*Lady Cockburn and her
Three Eldest Sons*, 1773
(National Gallery, London).

5 Sir Joshua Reynolds,
*Mrs Thrale and her
Daughter Queenie,* 1781
(Beaverbrook Art Gallery,
Fredericton, NB).

24 C.J. Richardson, *Interior of the Carved Schoolroom of Great Campden House, Kensington, c.* 1840. At this school there was no formal division into classes. Instead, the pupils are dotted around the room, some in small groups gathered around a teacher.

25 Carlo Maratti, *Sir Thomas Isham*, 1677. Sir Thomas was not quite eighteen when he inherited his father's estate at Lamport in Northamptonshire in 1675. His Grand Tour lasted from October 1676 to August 1679. Here he is shown holding a miniature of his mistress in Rome, Gabriella Buoncampagni (Lamport Hall).

26 George Richmond, *Lucy Lyttelton, Lady Frederick Cavendish*, 1864. Lucy was just twenty-two when she sat for this marriage portrait before her wedding to Lord Frederick, the second son of the seventh Duke of Devonshire (Holker Hall).

27 Louisa Bowater, photographed in 1860, aged eighteen. The only daughter of General Sir Edward Bowater, Louisa came to know Lucy Lyttelton when she spent time at court in 1863. She married Sir Rainald Knightley, of Fawsley Park, Northamptonshire in 1869. They had no children. Louisa died in September 1913.

28 Andrew McCullom, *View in Hagley Park*, 1852. The first Lord Lyttelton (1709–73) landscaped the park at Hagley in Worcestershire. He also designed the great Palladian mansion, with its rich rococo decoration.

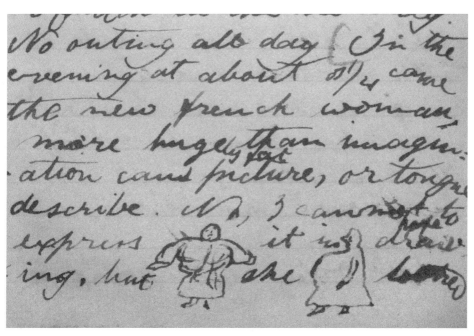

29 Lucy Lyttelton's diary entry on 30 September 1855 reads, 'No outing all day. In the evening about 8 1/4 came the new French woman, more hugely fat than imagination can picture or tongue describe. No, I cannot express it in drawing but she looked just as if an immense pillow had been laid across her chest ... Mama looked a poplar beside her.'

normal displays of naughtiness. Six case studies of schoolrooms across England, between the 1790s and 1900s, sustain this conclusion.

The detailed diaries of Sophia Baker illustrate a child's life, from the age of eleven until she was eighteen, at Bayfordbury in Hertfordshire. Her interactions with four governesses reflected her developing personality and her spirit, as she responded to the demands put upon her through the pre-teen and teenage years. 'Poor dear Miss Laborde went away', wrote Sophia, not yet fourteen, on 1 March 1794, adding a perhaps unique account of a child's feelings about this kind of loss, at the end of this pocket book. This was written, she recorded, four days before the governess left, after her younger sisters Harriet and Charlotte were 'gone to bed', while she was 'looking over her accounts'.

> We were very sorry to part with Miss Laborde, as she was a good governess, minded her duty very particularly and never spake but the truth. She was likewise very neat and clean both in her person and dress, was a remarkably nice workwoman and was very anxious for our going on well, walked out with us in all weathers when Mama wished us and gave us all the little comforts she could think of.

'Oh when shall we get used to another governess', Sophia lamented, her childhood world falling about her.[39]

But her record of the familiar pattern of the days, walks, rides and social visits in the Hertfordshire countryside, with the two governesses who followed – Miss Hoare for a period of months and a French mademoiselle, who stayed nearly a year – show that Sophia managed to accustom herself to each of these new regimes.[40] Things proved different with Miss Allen, who arrived in June 1795, when she was nearly fifteen. A gap in the survival of these annual diaries prevents us from tracking how the relationship deteriorated, but when the 1797 diary opens, she and Miss Allen were already thoroughly at odds.

Numerous entries in her diary for the first half of 1797 refer to Sophia's being 'out of temper' with her mother or her governess. It became habitual for her to record her judgement on the day in terms of her success or failure in controlling her emotions: 'I really behave ill for such trifles that I fear I shall never get the better of this horrid temper', she reflected on 18 January. Poor arithmetic, piano practice and reading aloud all featured, but the problem was much more personal than academic. It was the requirements of social performance that seem to have been alarming Sophia. She found herself expected, as the eldest of the Baker girls, to show visitors her drawings and to play for them on the piano; she was beginning work with dancing and drawing masters while at the family's London home; and she attended her first balls.

Matters came to a head in May 1797, when, a few days after a 'tete a tete dinner' with Mama, Sophia was 'in disgrace all day'. 'Breakfast, dined and supper by myself for my bad bad lesson and for justifying it to Mama' was her summary on 7 May. Miss Allen, together with her mother, saw her through this crisis: 'dear kind Miss Allen in the evening forgave me all my forfeits of every kind', she wrote on 9 May. There was one more crisis in June, when Sophia confessed in her diary that she had 'behaved shockingly to Miss Allen, my best friend', accusing her of severity. 'Very unhappy', she scrawled. Then the clouds began to lift. She seems to have found her confidence. The desperate scrawls of 1797 were followed by neatly written and controlled entries in the diaries for 1798 and 1799, as Sophia was launched on the London social scene.[41]

The Prince Regent's favourite and Private Secretary, Benjamin, Lord Bloomfield, employed a governess, Miss Woodmass, to tutor his elder girls, Harriott and Georgiana, at the Stud House at Hampton Court. She gave Georgiana a sketch book for her tenth birthday on 4 October 1819. Mr Ziegler, a little-known portraitist who later did water-colour portraits of the Bloomfield girls, gave them drawing lessons in their teens. A number of his pencil works, in which he demonstrated the techniques of drawing, including the feel for perspective, survive in this rare drawing master's sketchbook.[42]

When Bloomfield went as ambassador to Sweden in 1823, he left his youngest daughter Charlotte, aged eight, in the charge of a new governess, Susan Ridout. Charlotte's upbringing was deeply evangelical in a devoted family circle, that kept in touch across the North Sea, with presents and letters. Miss Ridout and Charlotte lived in some style, with several staff and family retainers, at the Stud House, the King's grace-and-favour gift to Bloomfield. This remained his English home whilst he was serving in Sweden.

Much time was given in her first schoolroom years to Charlotte's compilation, under Miss Ridout's direction, of a magnificent leather-bound scrapbook. This contains 288 pasted items, including sketches contributed by family friends. Through her painstaking work page by page, with many named black and white drawings of mansions and of landscape scenes from all over England featuring prominently, Charlotte engaged in an extended geography lesson. But the most interesting single entry is a pencil sketch (see opposite), showing little Charlotte as a child held up by her governess from a yapping dog, and a local man: 'look at the dog Miss Charlotte', declares Miss Ridout; 'pauvre chien', replies Charlotte; 'well how I likes to hear French spoken as that was', observes the man.[43]

Charlotte's earliest letters to Miss Ridout, at under ten, are in large copper-plate writing, which exemplifies the care that was being taken over a polite hand. A substantial collection of letters, between 1825 and 1827, provide insight into the kind of child she was, in her close dependence on Miss Ridout and her precociousness. These letters illustrate how correspondence with her governess when she was away could both inculcate the conventions of politeness and confirm the deference expected of a schoolroom pupil. 'Goodbye my dear Miss Ridout', Charlotte ended after two pages of unexceptional news, at ten years old, on 17 November 1825, 'I remain yours affectionately, Charlotte Bloomfield.'[44]

'I hope you no longer feel bilious and goutty', Charlotte wrote to Miss Ridout a few weeks later. She had been given a pincushion 'with a little map of North America on it, so pretty'. 'I have gone on regularly reading my Testament and have now finished the Epistles of St John', she reported in this letter. Her enquiring mind had been stimulated by a story in which Harry taught 'his sister Lucy all that he learns from his father of what occasions the rise of water in a pump, air pumps, steam engines and at last steam packets'. These were familiar to her as the transport her family used across the North Sea.[45]

Charlotte's affectionate and teasing letters to her brother John and her sisters in Sweden, more practice in writing encouraged by Miss Ridout, indicate how she pined for her older siblings. A letter in April 1827, which began 'my own dearest old ferrety eyed sister Georgy', related a dream 'last night that I was showing you my bible which Aunt Norris gave me'. The high seriousness of the Bloomfield upbringing bound the family together. In December 1825, the pious Charlotte was bothered, she told Miss Ridout, about two verses in the Epistle of Jude, which her sister Harriott, on holiday recently with her in Kent, had not been able to explain to her.[46]

In February 1826, again at the seaside, Charlotte confessed, 'I feel that I have not received all the benefit I ought from my last illness.' Miss Ridout had given her a set of questions to test her inner mind and conscience: she vowed to make use of these 'much oftener and shall hope to find myself improve'. She had nearly finished reading Isaiah and was learning verses from the Psalms. The only light relief lay in the news that 'my little canary sings so prettily you cannot think'.[47]

Correspondence with her sisters was almost Charlotte's only solace, in her cloistered life with a kindly but demanding governess. Writing to Georgiana on 1 November 1826, she bemoaned her failure to commiserate over the death of her canary: 'your heart must be turned to an icicle, even more than Miss Ridout you must be changed, little did I think when I saw you leave this house that the coldness of Norway and Sweden would have produced such a change in you'. Miss Ridout had bought her 'two such pretty little new collars'. They were 'such pretty patterns'. She had also helped rearrange the furnishings of Charlotte's room and agreed to finish a needlework bracelet for her, that Harriott had begun when she had been home. She described how her Swedish peasant gloves, a constant reminder of the unity of the family, hung in a different place now. Yet this letter is pervaded by Charlotte's loneliness. She ended with 'best love' to her sisters, brother and to 'dear Papa and Mama'.[48]

Writing to her sisters in January 1827, Charlotte explained that the drawing she had recently sent her father was 'the fruits of a morning's labour while Miss Ridout was in town', so they were mistaken in thinking she had obtained sustained tuition in order to achieve this. She hoped all of them might be together for Harriott's coming of age later that year, adding 'dear Pappy and Mammy how I do long to see them'. A touching letter to Miss Ridout, now affectionately called 'my dear Miss Doutty' and ending 'ever your affectionate little rogue, Chall', in May, contains hints of the illness which was to bring about her early death the next March. It was her elder sister Georgiana who then recorded the last days of this so perfect of childhood deaths, with her family, who had returned to England as she weakened, at her bedside.[49]

Georgina Sitwell's reminiscence of life in the schoolroom at Renishaw in Derbyshire is one of the most evocative accounts we have of this lost world.

Born in 1824, she was the third of five daughters of Sir George and Lady Sitwell. Her father was a keen sportsman, keeping his own hounds, interested in his garden and in ornithology. Her mother ran the Eckington Sunday school and organised its annual feast. The happiest festival of the family year was her parents' wedding day in the summer, when the garden was ablaze with its rhododendrons and flowering shrubs. A ceremony, with presents and drinking of their health, was held each year in a bower in the garden. Later, the servants held an annual dance by moonlight in front of the house.

The schoolroom routine fitted neatly into a time-honoured pattern of household order at Renishaw. How hard they worked, Georgina remembered well, with five governesses in turn living there over her growing years. They were up at six, began at seven, breakfasted at eight, dined in the schoolroom at midday, with lessons again after tea. In the hour before their parents' dinner, schoolroom children joined their mother in the upstairs drawing room, where there was a dolls' house to play with and their father was often resting, after hunting or shooting, in his armchair. 'In white-jacketed frocks with sashes we went to sit at our parents' dinner table during dessert . . . we were never allowed to eat anything however but a plain biscuit.'

Georgina remembered this life as 'a perfect treadmill of learning'. But Sundays at Renishaw were different. As the children became older, they were increasingly expected not just to sit still in the family pew, with the effigies of dead ancestors about them. Georgina knew this pew so well, describing it as 'lined with green baize . . . a little higher than the rest and surrounded with green silk curtains hung on brass rods'. The Sitwell children had to remember and write something down of the sermon; they were put through exercises of chapters of the Bible, psalms, hymns, catechisms, before and after Mattins. Sitwell boys went away to Eton bringing, as Georgina put it, 'an unfailing pleasure to us' when they came home for holidays. Sitwell girls lived out this ritualised life of hierarchy and propriety, conducted in a Derbyshire valley 'as green as an emerald all the year round'. They did this year upon year, from their nursery days to their coming out at eighteen.[50]

Lucy Lyttelton has left us a vivid picture of the regimes of five governesses at Hagley. She had 'a sort of affection for Miss Nicholson', who she found, as we have seen, a rod of iron. Lucy respected her better, however, than her successor, Miss Crump, with her 'broken reed of government'. She hardly coped with six boisterous Lyttelton children in the Hagley schoolroom. Miss Nicholson's harsh punishments were replaced with lines of poetry, set for learning and easily ignored. 'We became untruthful, disobedient and self-conceited', Lucy recorded, yet Miss Crump did make some attempt to instil moral principles. 'We were fond of the gentle affectionate little woman, though we used to wrangle and argue with her', she reflected.

The arrival of Miss Pearson, when Lucy was ten, inaugurated a period of 'almost despairing tears' and 'a good deal of repentance'. But, recognising her need by then 'to have my faults exposed to me with an unsparing hand', she knew that Miss Pearson's regime was the making of her, forging her depth of character and her early maturity, as the second of twelve in this huge family. Her portrait of Miss Pearson is evocative:

> She was a woman of stern and upright mind, with a high and stern standard of duty and little pity for those who did not reach it. Truth and openness were the first of human values with her . . . She quickly won our affection, though it was ever mixed with fear and her influence over me was such that, though I knew her hatred of what was sly, I confessed many things to her . . .

Miss Pearson was a hard taskmaster. Holidays were rare, Lucy recalled, 'and it was seldom we were let off a lesson'. She often worked till bedtime 'and always after tea, finishing what had been left undone'. She particularly recalled Miss Pearson's inculcating her love of poetry, especially Shakespeare and Milton. She described herself, at twelve, as 'a heedless tomboy of a child, the worry of servants and the ruthless destroyer of frocks'. Yet this was also, she understood, when both the deep religious feeling and the emotional warm heartedness, which she prided in her adult character, were born.[51]

A note that Lucy made in her diary in September 1854 suggests contentment with her schoolroom routine. Piano practice at 8.30 a.m. was followed by 'Bible with Papa' and prayers, then lessons through until a 1.30 dinner. The afternoon was for reading or going out, tea at 5.30 p.m. was the schoolroom meal, with a period from 6.30 to 8.0 p.m. for 'lessons not done'. Then she and Meriel, the two eldest, joined their parents at dinner, going up to bed at nine o'clock.

In September 1855, with Lucy just fourteen, the new presence in the Hagley schoolroom was Mademoiselle, 'more hugely fat than imagination can picture or tongue describe . . . Mama looked a poplar beside her'. Lucy watched fascinated, on her arrival, as 'the new French woman' chatted about the Queen, her French Emperor and her mother's brother-in-law, her uncle William Gladstone. She was still 'enlarging herself with some mutton and tea'. Open hearted, Lucy was becoming a connoisseur of governesses. She soon confessed, in the privacy of her diary, that lessons had become 'the very essence of regularity'. 'Fatty does the lessons very very properly I suppose', was her summary. Having shown her the pigs on 2 October, Lucy's initiation of Mademoiselle into Hagley life took the form of what she triumphantly described as a 'wild goose walk', taking her the longest way round the estate:

She made such a rumpus as was never heard about my going the wrong way, my being in the rain, both of us being late for dinner, my not making her know how far off it was etc . . . I was as dry as toast and neither of us were a bit worse so her spirits rose again with dinner.[52]

Mademoiselle only stayed a few months.

Lucy was pleased with her final governess, Miss Smith, who settled in before her fifteenth birthday in June 1856. She was now ready for the intellectual challenge of a wide-ranging curriculum: 'on the 5th came our new governess, a nice real comfortable English one, ladylike and pleasant-looking, she has begun us so well: our week divided into Monday and Thursday for Italian, Tuesday and Friday for French, Wednesday and Saturday for English, with a half-holiday on the latter day.' The initial curriculum was to include, in Italian, conversation, translations and history, in French Racine and dictation, in English arithmetic, Cornwall's geography, Longfellow's poetry and the definition of words. 'We ought to get on', Lucy concluded this diary entry. She was pleased, too, that the younger ones, in the crowded Hagley schoolroom, 'seem to like her'.[53]

When Miss Smith went off for Christmas in December 1856, Lucy reflected on how much she would miss her; her return straight after, she wrote, 'gives one a snug feeling'. Like all schoolroom girls, it was her governess, more than her mother, who was the centre of Lucy's world and of her security, during the prolonged and serious years of growing up.[54] She left the schoolroom when she was seventeen, on 5 September 1858, a few days after beginning a series of visits to country houses which prepared her for coming out.[55]

Louisa Bowater, daughter of a Peninsular War General who fought at Waterloo, had a devoted German governess, Agnes Lentz, from the age of thirteen until she was eighteen, from 1855 to 1860. She lived at Thatched House Lodge in Richmond Park. Their relationship was especially intense because she was an only child. Louisa remained close to her throughout her life, visiting her in Hamburg when she was 65, shortly before Agnes died. She expressed her 'great sorrow', at fourteen, when Agnes took a holiday in June 1856: 'I cried, "God bring her back safe".' She decked the schoolroom, so glad to welcome her back, in August.

At the start of her diary, which she saw as a 'receptacle for interesting conversations with Agnes as well as for daily events', in April 1856, Louisa recorded her fourteenth birthday as 'a day of intense pleasure'. She was collected by Agnes, who had the schoolroom ready early, with 'a little table beautifully adorned with flowers, a large cake in the centre surrounded by four wax lights and four presents', for she was going to London later, to a child's ball at Buckingham Palace. Soon after this, Louisa reciprocated, for Agnes's birthday, noting, 'I had a cake made and put it on a little table near her door surrounded by flowers ... I had a periwinkle and primrose wreath and bouquet for her.'[56]

Written and spoken German naturally dominated Louisa's schoolroom hours. A French Mademoiselle worked with her too. There was arithmetic with her father, scripture with her mother and knitting, pasting, mythology, geography and history, besides German, with Agnes. They took regular walks in the park and her governess encouraged her interest in the natural world. 'I mean to have a book of natural history if I can, prints, drawings of birds, flowers, insects etc', Louisa noted in February 1857. She was grateful, above all, to Agnes Lentz for 'the strong moral and religious principles which she never ceased to impress upon my youthful mind'.[57]

Clare Howard's nature notebook, started in 1904 when she was eleven years old, shows how a competent governess could bind together outdoor and indoor activity in a constructive programme of learning. Afternoon walks in the fields and woods around Bark Hart at Orpington in Kent, then rural countryside, were exercises in observation of agricultural activity and of the seasonal round, besides the recognition of wild flowers. Miss Wall, the governess, pointed out to Clare and her sister Amy in September and October 1904 'a cart carrying away dead strawberry roots' and fields 'being rolled by two horses' and 'hoed by hand'. Clare's record noted 'very pretty colours' in the trees on 5 October 1904, 'especially in the oak, maple, chestnut'. The schoolroom work that followed included watercolour paintings of plants seen on walks, lists of flowers growing wild and of vegetables under cultivation. All this was good practice in spelling and the development of a neat hand.[58]

Girls who spent more than ten years on the schoolroom treadmill of learning, when they recalled it in old age, naturally made little of lesson routines and much of the release that breaks and holidays provided. 'Hip, hip, Hooray!' Lucy Lyttelton would write in her diary, when the boys came home from Eton. Clare Howard, the youngest of a family of six girls and four boys, adored her summer holidays. Then the schoolroom disappeared from her mind and she kept pencil notebook diaries, as the Howard family decamped, in alternate years to Edwardian Brighton 'and some other seaside place'.

At home white cotton pinafores were 'regulation day time wear' for the schoolroom girls, 'a badge of childhood I much resented', Clare remembered. But the morning highlight at Bark Hart was the full hour of freedom outside in the grounds, which her mother insisted upon each day. Freedom from elder sisters issuing reprimands about her drawers or her petticoat showing; 'the freedom of a large garden – trees to climb, birds nesting and going to the farm where there was the interest of a new calf to see or piglings or stolen hen's nests to search'. Even here, though, there were rules, unpoliced but respected nonetheless – half a dozen only each, for instance, from the strawberry and blackcurrant patches.

'Daisy, daisy, give me your answer do', the girls would sing as they roamed, songs they had picked up at the seaside and would not dream of uttering in the presence of their mother, who would denounce them as 'vulgar'. Then there were the special times of the year. Primrosing involved driving in the pony cart to neighbouring woods; haymaking was celebrated with rides on the hay wagon or by leading the pony that pulled the hayrake; blackberrying and mushrooming broke the schoolroom routine with visits to nearby fields.[59]

Schoolroom education, all this documentation shows, always reflected the personality and interests of a particular governess. It was often neither especially coherent nor highly organised, but many young girls found it deeply inspiring. Many benefited from the close attention governesses were able to give to them as individuals. Many flourished under the concentrated tuition of a single adult, learning habits of regularity and self-discipline that they carried through life. Many found firm friends in their governesses, who offered them guidance towards adult responsibility. The schoolroom, we have seen, could be a place of dynamic relationships. It was certainly not all grind. This pattern of domestic education admirably fitted the social and gender conditions of the period from 1770 until 1914. Many hundreds of governesses, in those decades, served many hundreds of children very well indeed.

Girls at School

Most of the schoolroom girls that have been discussed here never went to school. The more aristocratic a family was, the less likely it was that parents would entrust their female offspring to a public establishment, with the uncertainties of tuition by a schoolmistress. But, taking the upper and middle classes as a whole, it is clear that parents trained their girls, in these centuries, through a great mixture of strategies, from hiring a governess, or calling in visiting masters, to using available local schooling and sending girls away for short periods to boarding schools. Whereas boys normally boarded from around seven to well into their teens, girls were seldom away from home at school for more than two years during their teens or pre-teens. The perennial problem was finding teachers who exhibited both appropriate qualities of character and an acceptable balance of learning objectives. The schooling of girls is considered in this chapter firstly through parental eyes, and secondly through records of personal experience.

Henry Oxinden, set on sending his girls Elizabeth and Margaret to school at eleven and twelve respectively in 1647, took advice from a friend who had already patronised Mr Beven's family establishment at Ashford. Mr Beven had support from his wife, 'an excellent good woman', said Unton Dering, and from his daughter, 'a civil well qualified maid'. Dering had found him 'conscienable, discreet and industrious'. His testimonial was well calculated to appeal to any conventional seventeenth-century gentleman:

> And besides the qualities of music both for the virginals and singing (if they have voices) and writing (and to cast account which will be useful to them hereafter), he will be careful also that their behaviour be modest and such as becomes their quality: and that they grow in knowledge and understanding for God and their duty to Him, which is above all.

All this was offered for 30 pounds a year for the two girls which, Unton Dering declared, 'I presume you will think reasonable'.[1]

Parents invariably put much more emphasis on female modesty than on intellectual achievement. There was a firm reaction in the seventeenth century against the classical education of girls, which had been favoured by some at court in the previous century. Yet there were a few further female prodigies, like Lucy Hutchinson, before the civil war.[2] The daughters of Viscount Hutton, recorded around 1698 as being 'good Latin scholars', were by then very much the exception. John Evelyn's eulogy of his daughter Susanna, in 1693, expressed the new orthodoxy, stressing her talents in painting as well as needlework. Evelyn noted that she had 'read most of the Greek and Roman authors', besides learning French, but he pointedly asserted that her use of these intellectual talents was conducted 'with great modesty'.[3]

It is instructive to review the correspondence between Sir Ralph Verney and his godchild Nancy Denton in 1652 in the same context. This intellectual girl's scrawled letter to the royalist exile was audacious:

> I now show my boldness unto you supposing that your goodness is so great that I dare to presume of it . . . I know you and my cousins will outreach me in French, but I am going where I hope I shall outreach you in Hebrew, Greek and Latin, praying you sir, if I may be so bold, as to desire a letter from you.

This to a man who, five years previously in the last year of his own dear child Peg's life, had told his wife, 'being a girl she shall not learn Latin, so will have the more time to learn breeding hereafter and work too'. This is the familiar use of the word 'work' to refer to needlework. Sir Ralph's reply was as much for his friend Dr Denton's ears as the girl's, knowing, as he did, how Denton's view differed from his own. He tried to bring Nancy down to earth:

> I must confess I did not think you had been guilty of so much learning as I see you are . . . Good sweetheart be not so covetous; believe me a bible (with the common prayer) and a good plain catechism in your mother tongue being well read and practised, is well worth all the rest and much more suitable to your sex . . . In French you cannot be too cunning for that language affords many admirable books fit for you as romances, plays, poetry, stories of illustrious (not learned) women, receipts for preserving, making creams and all sorts of cookeries, ordering your gardens and in brief all manner of good husbandry.

Sir Ralph was undoubtedly crusty but Dr Denton, enamoured of his prodigy child, is the one who was really out of line by the 1650s.[4] The belief in French as an ornament of femininity was, of course, deeply enduring. 'How is the child progressing in French?' Blanche Stanley asked, when Nancy Mitford was taken by her mother to see the old lady in 1908. She had not yet begun the language. 'There is nothing so inferior as a gentlewoman who has no French', was Blanche's riposte.[5]

The first girls' boarding schools sprung up around the London suburbs between 1616, when the highly reputed Ladies Hall at Deptford opened, and 1640. These were essentially finishing schools. Hackney, where the schools run by Robert Perwich, Mrs Salmon and Mrs Beckford were particularly patronised by the gentry from a wide area, as well as Chelsea and Putney became favourite locations.[6] Lettice Newdigate, having had a strong beginning in reading and writing from her mother and some teaching from a visiting master, was sent off from Warwickshire to the celebrated Deptford academy in 1616, aged eleven, at the significant cost to her parents of 22 pounds a year.[7] John Evelyn visited Putney 'to see the schools and colleges for young gentlewomen' in 1649.[8] 'That which we went chiefly to see was the young ladies of the schools, whereof there is great store, very pretty', wrote Samuel Pepys, attending Hackney parish church to appraise the girls' looks and breeding on 24 April 1667.[9]

When Giles Moore, rector of Horsted Keynes in Sussex, took in his niece, Martha, in 1667, he set about getting her a term of writing instruction nearby at Rotherfield. He also paid a local goodwife to start her on her needlework. He kept a careful account of the costs of her schooling in London between 1669 and 1671. These included buying her a new gown and petticoat, as well as a primer and Bible, besides the charge for boarding for which he bargained hard. The incidental expenses – clothes, shoes, needles, thread, pocket money – mounted, but in 1673, he felt that the enterprise had paid off, when Martha was married to a local gentleman. He officiated himself at the wedding. Seeing the couple into their new home, Moore was well-satisfied. He gave Martha's spouse a copy of Richard Allestree's *The Whole Duty of Man* as a wedding present.[10]

The expansion of commercial schooling for girls during the eighteenth century, Susan Skedd has argued, 'completely changed the pattern of education in England'. Schools became available in most districts: 'the mixture of useful subjects with polite accomplishments taught at these girls' schools ensured their extraordinary popularity'. Skedd's analysis of provision in Oxfordshire, between 1760 and 1820, revealed 121 schools, either boarding or day, or both, and 32 peripatetic tutors giving lessons for girls. Provision was equally extensive in Sussex. This was a period of public debate about the merits and dangers of boarding schools for girls on moral, social and educational grounds. Just as the curriculum varied considerably, with a trend towards the polite accomplishments of music, dancing and drawing, so did the quality and standards of both kinds of establishment.[11]

Parents relied heavily on advice and local repute in choosing schools. They were prepared to see teenage daughters travel long distances, if they believed a particular school offered the blend they wanted of moral, polite and academic training. John Penrose started looking for a school for his fourteen-year-old daughter while taking the waters at Bath in 1766. He finally picked one there the next year, after consultations with friends back home in Cornwall. The Meins of Devonport sent three girls to a school in Bath in the 1790s, on the advice of the widow of a friend, with whom their father had served during the American War of Independence.

Family connections were often important. Martha Sherwood travelled from her home in Kidderminster to attend Abbey House school in Reading, after her father was much taken with it while visiting a close friend who was headmaster of Reading School. Frances Kemble went at five to a boarding school in Bath kept by her godmother, who was her father's married sister.[12]

There is massive evidence of the thoughtfulness and concern which parents devoted to these schooling arrangements. Most clearly regarded providing daughters with a sound education as a foremost responsibility.[13] Mothers, who were convinced of the benefits of the tuition they themselves could offer or favoured the employment of governesses, at the same time often accepted that the social experience of school, and the regularity of life it inculcated, were considerable benefits. They saw schooling as an ingredient in a rounded upbringing. 'Order and regularity', wrote Hannah Allen's mother to her at boarding school in 1826, 'my dear girl, are important to maintain and will affect us materially in our walk through life.'[14] 'Our reasons for wishing her to go to school', wrote the Victorian novelist Elizabeth Gaskell of her daughter, were 'not to advance her rapidly in any branch of learning . . . but to perfect her habits of obedience, to give her an idea of conquering difficulties by perseverance and to make her apply steadily for a short time.'[15]

Charlotte Papendiek reflected on the determination that she and her husband felt in the 1790s 'that our children should have as good an education as we could possibly manage to give them'. Perhaps she was too severe, she thought, looking back later, but she had been earnest to assist them: 'I was constantly looking after the progress they made, urging them to perseverance and exhorting them against any inclination to indolence, idleness or self-will.' This was where residence in London proved advantageous: 'My desire was that my girls should remain day scholars with Mrs Roach, where they would continue under my guidance . . . knowing at the same time that they were with a woman of strict principle if not altogether of the ornamental manner of good breeding.' For specialist instruction for their girls, the Papendieks found themselves 'surrounded by superior masters in all branches of education'.[16]

When to send a girl to school, where to send her, how long to keep her there: these were the questions parents constantly wrestled with. In some cases, it seemed obvious that the right moment had come, or family circumstances seemed to dictate this moment. Her daughter Sal, Mrs Dickenson reported to Mary Hamilton in 1772, was growing fast and was 'fond of books much more than of the needle'. She therefore proposed sending her to a boarding school the next spring, she explained, 'indeed it is high time for she is almost run wild'.[17]

It was important to define objectives carefully. These were not necessarily primarily social ones. Edward Cutler engaged in correspondence with Richard Stephenson about the education of his daughter, from Tyneside, at a school in Durham in 1759. Unclear about 'what kind of education his girl was intended for', he gathered that Stephenson had in mind her employment in 'clear starching, washing and dressing'. In this case, he advised, the town's boarding school for girls was not suitable, offering tuition in none of the things 'you want to have her qualified for'. But the woman who dressed and clear starched all the linen for the ladies at this boarding school could offer her private tuition three days a week. Mrs Charlton on the Bailey, who took pupils in general needlework, sewing and darning, could take the girl the other three days. 'Your daughter is very well', Cutler told Stephenson that July, having settled her into the vocational pattern of education which her father had opted for.[18]

Thomas Whale noted the problems in his daughter Polly's relationship with her mother, which began before the girl was ten. In 1773, he started her at a school near their home at Shelford in Cambridgeshire, but things did not improve. It was after this that he had to beat her one day, she 'having behaved rudely and impudently to her Mama'. The decision to send her to board came two years later, in view of the long enmity between his wife and Polly: 'the Mama too severe and the daughter somewhat as obstinate and provoking'. He took her to stay with friends in Newmarket, 'till they can enquire out a proper place . . . for her boarding either in a private family or a parlour boarder'. Polly ended up at a school at Great Baddow, with five guineas paid by her father as entrance money and two guineas a quarter allowed her as pin money. Within a short while, her father was involved in negotiation over her marriage. Her difficult start was overcome and a polite boarding education finally brought the result he desired.[19]

Another difficult girl in the eyes of her mother, whose schooling is exceptionally well-documented, was Susanna Thrale. Hester, her mother, sent her to board with her friend Mrs Cumyns, who kept a very well-respected school in Kensington in 1774, before she was four. The child, her mother believed, had acquired 'a habit of self-indulgence, which I do not choose to undertake the breaking through, as I am not partial to her person and might be too rough with her perhaps'. Hester Thrale persuaded herself that sending her child away was almost a kindness. She visited her at intervals, finding Susanna, within four months, 'so altered for the better it quite charms me'. The next January, Hester listed her achievements: she was reading elegantly 'and with an emphasis'; she said her catechism in French and English; she had learnt cursive script; she was neat in her needlework; she also knew the map of Europe and the 'general geography of the globe'. Moreover, Susanna was now reckoned pretty and, 'having learned early to dance, exhibited a mighty graceful carriage'.

In 1776, Hester noted prodigious improvement; in 1777 she commented favourably on Susanna's readiness at translating French into English. Her map sampler was 'a good specimen both of her work and geography'. Yet Hester's view of her daughter's character was unchanged: 'she is special ill-tempered to be sure'. Susanna, it seems, flourished away from her mother and under the influence of Mrs Cumyns. She was never going to acquire the kind of intense relationship with her demanding mother which both made and marred the early life of her elder sister Queeney. But Hester did come to respect her for her looks, her understanding and her knowledge, which was 'extremely copious and uncommon'.[20]

There were a whole series of considerations in the minds of parents. A professional man, intent on seeing a daughter into a high-quality apprentice-ship, like Matthew Flinders, saw the matter very differently from landed families, who simply focused on procuring an advantageous marriage. Flinders's brother-in-law and sister, fortunately, kept a school near Donington, where he sent Susanna at fourteen, to acquire a modicum of breeding. 'We intend her for the millinery business when this term expires', he noted on the payment of eighteen guineas in 1793. Eighteen months later, he took her in the chaise to place her as an apprentice at Boston. Seeing Susanna off, with fifteen pounds of pocket money for her first year, Matthew was then intent on bringing on his younger girl, Hannah. She attended a newly opened dancing school at Donington and went to a local writing master.[21]

When elder girls had led the way, a young sister might be sent to board as early as nine. Lady Anne Cust thought it right to have Dolly join Betty and Jenny at school at Lincoln in 1738, though it left her bereft, with only her little Lucy at home.[22] But more commonly boarding, especially if a school at a fashionable city like Bath was chosen, could effectively smooth the teenage transition from the classroom to public social events. Dolly Penrose was placed at fifteen in one of Bath's many boarding schools in 1767 with this explicit intention. Here she was kitted out in fine clothes, attended the theatre and had her parents visit for occasions like the 'scholar's dance', an annual ball arranged by the city's schools and its dancing masters to show off the skills acquired by teenagers at the fine new Assembly Rooms.[23]

The affectionate father Philip Francis enjoyed visiting the three girls he had at school in 1773, finding them 'healthy and handsome' when he took them out in his carriage. When he left for the East Indies the next year, his directions to his wife in the matter gave her flexibility, whereas, as we have seen, provision for his son's education was specific and precise: 'the girls will fall more particularly under your care. Sally is to come home at Christmas next or at midsummer 1775 at farthest. I leave that and everything relative to the periods of their going to and quitting the school to your own discretion.'

Betsy Francis, seeking to retain the company of some of her five children, decided to end the boarding school regime pretty rapidly. She sent the three girls to a day school in 1774 and had Sally and Betsy complete their schooling altogether, at twelve and eleven respectively, in January 1775. She arranged for dancing and drawing masters to visit their home, instead. Taking advice from her friends, she decided to send little Mary to school, with Harriet, in place of the older girls: 'it is time to send her out from the servants'. This left her and the governess with little Kitty alone. Kitty, she believed, was especially sweet tempered, her 'understanding promises to be strong' and she was 'much admired'.[24] Fond mothers could be reluctant to let their youngest off the apron strings.

James Oakes, at Bury St Edmunds, found it convenient that a governess of whom he thought well, Miss Routh, could teach his girls Maria and Charlotte together, although they were five years apart in age, between 1780 and 1782. It was only when Maria completed her education, at seventeen, that Charlotte, by then twelve, was sent off for a four-year stint at a fashionable London boarding school.[25]

Thomas Moore, visiting his daughter, Anastasia, at school in Bath in 1823, found her in trouble over her alleged inattention in lessons. He felt she was misunderstood, but he reached a satisfactory understanding with the school, enabling him to keep her there for another four years:

> Perceived the schoolmistress had mistaken her disposition, and supposes it is obstinacy prevents the child from answering what she knows; when, in fact, it is the confusion arising from a strong feeling of reproof or disgrace that puts all her ideas to flight and makes her incapable of anything while she is in that state.

It was only when he was alarmed by news from Anastasia about measles in the school, in December 1827, that he sent a chaise and a maid to bring her home at once. He was worrying about 'the unfavourable time of year and the still delicate state of our dear girl's health'. He kept Anastasia at home then, letting her install herself in his library, preparing the parlour as a 'study for me'. [26]

The Papillon girls, Mary and Fanny, settled perfectly happily in their first term at Great Campden House school in Kensington, perhaps because they went there together. When the holidays came, they wrote home on 1 December 1835, they hoped 'you will think us improved'. They had been given rather too many clothes to bring with them, advised the headmistress, 'just enough to wash and wear is all required'. 'We must be temperate in all things', she commented. But the Papillon girls were 'dear loving little things and very good outwardly'. Subsequent bulletins spoke of the gardens they were making, of the worsted material they were working and of work with a visiting French master.[27]

While boys were sent off on long journeys to school and expected to fend for themselves, when a girl left home parents often fussed and cosseted. Georgiana Trench sent her husband several bulletins on the process of settling Georgy, at seventeen, in a school in Wandsworth, when they decided she needed some social training after the schoolroom years. 'They are all so very kind here', she wrote of the atmosphere at the Deanery at Westminster, where her cousin Richard Chenevix Trench provided an English home from home, with daughters much Georgy's age.

Georgiana found it all very emotional, writing 'poor Georgy's day is at last come – she is quite composed and cheery – and slept well – and had no bad dreams'. Describing the handsome house with its seven acres of 'pleasure grounds' and her meeting with some of Georgy's new schoolfellows that evening, she was calmer:

> The sad deed is done and Georgy is at school. I am satisfied however that, if she can make up her mind to bear the trammels, she will be as happy in that establishment as anywhere at any time out of her home . . . Miss Redie is quite a lady – a little stiff but kind and sensible looking. Georgy did not fall in love exactly with her, but at that moment it would have been hard for her to like anything much. She bore up very well.[28]

Isabel Chenevix Trench, widowed in 1900, took her daughters abroad for schooling at Lausanne, but, when they were seventeen and fifteen, she decided that the time had come to exchange excellent progress in French with the broader finishing regimes of English boarding schools. The letters of advice that she showered upon Cesca, when she stayed with relatives and attended Langland School at Malvern, show the primacy she gave to her social and moral education. Isabel saw Cesca's trip to England and Ireland as a fourteen-year old, in 1905, as a prolonged social performance orchestrated, she hoped, through her incessant letters.

The essence was the ideal of unselfishness inculcated by her own mother at Cangort Park: 'I am sure you will try to help anyone who seems to want it darling; be on the look out to do odd jobs for others.' When Cesca stayed with the Bowen family in southern Ireland, she was surely, Isabel reminded her, remembering to open the door for her elders, 'offering them your chair etc'. She 'will be sure to look clean and tidy, darling', Isabel chivvied, and find someone to mend her stockings, 'before the holes are too big'.[29]

At Langland, too, Cesca endured a stream of prescriptions from home. 'Your writing is very much better, darling, I am hoping for a very good report', Isabel declared early in her first term. A reminder was soon needed, however, with the warning that 'it looks so ill-educated to write badly'. 'I want you to work well and hard at the drawing this term, Pet', she urged on 18 January 1907. Success in the French exam was no more than her mother expected. Progress in tennis was commended: 'it will be useful to play fairly well'. Deportment was the absolutely key issue. 'Take great pains', Isabel declared, 'to sit straight darling and to hold yourself properly; so much depends upon it in the future.'[30]

It was Cesca's moral and spiritual progress that was always uppermost in her mother's mind. 'I am so thankful to have two delicious and loving daughters', she wrote to Cesca on 1 February 1907, 'and I pray constantly that God will give you his Grace that you may live as His Soldiers through this very troublesome world, so full of temptations.' 'Be humble-minded; try and take a lowly view of yourself and exalt your neighbours!' she entreated; 'see that you leave a sweet and fragrant remembrance behind you and make people long for your presence', she counselled. Isabel lived Cesca's confirmation at Langland in March 1907 ecstatically. She ordered a silver cross inscribed 'Thine for Ever' for her daughter. Arranging to buy her veil, she told Cesca how pleased she was 'to find it is exactly the shape we always used with dear Father'. She anticipated the thrill she would feel being present to 'put it on your darling head'. 'I remember so well', she wrote, plunging into reminiscence of Cangort Park days, 'my mother writing to me and saying how pleased she was to hear from our governess that I had been trying to be better at my lessons after my confirmation.'[31]

Public education for girls was at a low ebb between 1800 and 1850, but it was transformed by the campaigning efforts of women like Emily Davies,

Dorothea Beale and Frances Buss in the second half of the century.[32] Joyce Pedersen has shown that, in the period from 1850 to 1900, a new type of school for girls was both larger and made a formal commitment, previously lacking, to academic achievement and meritocratic values. Miss Buss's North London Collegiate School led the way in 1850, followed by schools like Roedean in 1885 and Wycombe Abbey in 1896. In that year, there were already 30 schools belonging to the Girls Public Day School Trust. But, as Carol Dyhouse has stressed, the new schools accounted for a minority of girls sent away from home. Nor did the revolt against showy accomplishments mean a change of basic objectives. There was no challenge before 1914 to the sexual division of labour. The schooling of girls remained untouched by social radicalism.[33]

Yet there was a shift of values in the evaluation of femininity. Girls were no longer seen as quite so fragile as they had been. The bicycling craze and the seaside bathing machines permitted upper-class girls to seek fitness in a way previously undreamt of. Exercise, with special attention to rest in periods of menstruation, came to be seen as improving, not endangering, to their health. Above all, the moves by leading boarding schools to appoint games mistresses and acquire playing fields gave teenage girls the beginnings of a new pattern of upbringing. In 1904, the *Girls' Own Paper* carried an article on 'Hockey: A Capital Game for Girls', illustrated by pictures that stressed the speed and vigour of the game. In Edwardian England, the notion of the all-round girl emerged.[34]

At Bark Hart in Orpington, Henry Howard insisted upon all his six girls being taught by a series of governesses, between the 1880s and 1908. Late in Queen Victoria's reign, the two eldest, Edith and Maud, left the schoolroom in preparation for being presented almost immediately at court. But when it came to Clare, this ritual was omitted. At seventeen, as the youngest, keen on cycling, walking, swimming and rowing, she asked her father to let her go to a small boarding school, Effingham House at Bexhill. It was a sign of the times that he agreed.[35]

The experience of girls at day and boarding schools contrasted sharply with that of boys. They were never beaten. In fact, when they recorded their lives at school, they made little reference to punishment of any kind. Real naughtiness and rebellion seemed irrelevant. They were being trained in a different way for a different future from their brothers. They may have been bored at times but, by and large, they were too busy learning to be good and accomplished to be troublemakers.

The diary kept by the unidentified Winchester schoolgirl Emma for the year 1784 reveals the world of a teenager who lived in a shire town, within walking distance of her school. It opens with an extract from John Gregory's recently published conduct book, *A Father's Legacy to his Daughters*. Emma's life included walks, bible reading, catechising, housework and lots of games with her sisters, besides a school routine that appears to have been full but intellectually unchallenging. On a typical weekday, 10 February, she noted a morning of reading and writing in school, followed by needlework there after dinner, after which she 'drank tea' with a neighbour on the way home. Her parents encouraged Emma's accomplishment in music and dancing. Yet she could be recalcitrant. When visitors called on 6 March, she 'was sent for into the parlour to play upon the harpsichord but did not go'.[36]

The schooling for girls available in one city, Chichester, at the turn of the nineteenth century was graphically described by Eliza Fox, in her own words 'a merry, sparkling, curly-haired girl', with a Quaker mother and a dissenting barrister father. She was the first-born of thirteen children. Her evocative account explains how she experienced in turn both the establishments in this city. It was proper she should 'leave off being a tomboy' her Mama remarked, when her father decided, at seven, that it was quite time she went to school and 'learnt to behave like a "young lady"'.

The school she started at, in West Street near her home, 'was kept by two ladies held in high repute on account of the very exemplary manners of the young ladies under their care'. Entering the schoolroom there in 1800, Eliza found 30 girls reading aloud, writing and studying 'the first three rules in arithmetic'. Her mother had sent her with some needlework which, when she was placed in the junior class, where she saw others using their needles, she 'set about doing very demurely'. Children were 'had up to the table' in turns, to read a portion of scripture or a bible story in the mornings; there was history, poetry or biography in the afternoons.

Monday at this school was for history, Tuesday for geography, Wednesday for grammar, Thursday for spelling, Friday for writing of cipher. Saturday was for catechism and collects. The Anglican collects and catechism were seen as pedagogically crucial at this school. They were quite foreign, however, to little Eliza, so 'the children looked askance at me and asked questions'. Her father, seeing the distress this caused her, then moved Eliza to the other Chichester school, in South Street, where the daughters of the Sussex county gentry were educated and 'a greater freedom of opinion was tolerated'.

The headmistress there was committed to a broad social training, taking ten parlour boarders as well as 50 girls able to attend daily. Her drawing room soirées gave the girls, Eliza realised, 'tone to their manners and took away that want of ease so common in young ladies who had been reared in a farmhouse, far removed from fashionable society'. Moreover, this head-mistress took her girls out: to public balls, concerts and lectures. They made a 'goodly appearance', under her charge, in the cathedral on Sundays, where 'the gay bevy of laughing bright eyes attracted many a side glance from the gentlemen'.

Her father, Eliza came to understand, intended her education to be largely one in politeness. He was extremely keen on the stress at the South Street school on deportment. The venerable headmistress was celebrated locally for putting her girls through their paces in the Garland Dance, a 'wonderful display of graceful action'. Because of the importance he attached to them, Eliza kept up her dancing lessons at this school from the age of seven until she was sixteen. When she thought she could 'dance well enough', she asked her father if she could substitute lessons in French, the tuition costing the same as her dancing: four pounds a year. He replied that she could learn that herself, 'by the aid of French dictionary and grammar'. In his eyes, there were some aspects of her studies that he regarded as essential and others that were optional.[37]

Eliza enjoyed life in Chichester, very much a country town in the Regency period. Boys taught her tricks and she went bird's-nesting with them in the fields before breakfast. She gathered violets on the hedge banks, made cowslip balls and daisy chains. Her tomboy ways were not eradicated by her schooling. So her parents decided, at sixteen, that her 'bright and happy girlhood for propriety's sake must be chastened'. Eliza was sent to a London boarding school, to 'bring under discipline', as she put it, this 'high spirited laughing girl', who was now 'removed from the country school to the society of more accomplished ladies'. There were tears at first but Eliza adapted and made new friends.

The new school was strong on geography, which Eliza had long been mad about, on history and chronology. She had drawing, writing, music and dancing masters in London. She began to taste the metropolitan social scene, attending a ball at the Mansion House. Then, after eighteen months, Eliza was called home to help with the younger children. Before dressing to play the polite and respectable daughter, ready to receive the professional men and their wives who made up the social circle of the Fox family, the tamed Eliza tidied the drawing room of a morning and filled the vases with fresh flowers. One of these visitors, who caught her sweeping the drawing room when he paid an early call, engaged in conversation with Eliza about Wordsworth and the *Lyrical Ballads,* which she had been reading the previous evening. 'I must say I don't often meet with a housemaid so lady like and intelligent', he remarked.[38]

In her memoir of her childhood written in 1879, Elizabeth Bradshawe gave vivid accounts of the two stages of her schooling early in the century, sandwiched by six years with Miss Cook as her governess. She was in the 'writing class' at the school kept by Miss Stubbs at Wirksworth, where

neighbouring gentry also sent their older girls, for 'the use of globes, embroidery and a little drawing'. She remembered the breakfasts of 'skimmed milk
with oatmeal thrown in', which came out as 'slimy lumps' and the bread and
cheese for supper. They often finished this 'kneeling in rows on wood
benches' at prayer time, with their faces to a wall which was stained a pale
blue. Elizabeth's finishing school at Doncaster, which she attended with her
sister Maria, was much larger, with 30 or so teenage girls. Their arrival at the
'large handsome house' and their introduction to the formidable Miss
Murphy, where 'my father shortened our very tearful leave taking', was etched
on her mind. 'We were to be in the schoolroom at 7.30 a.m. and there was
great emulation as to who should be first.' The regime was demanding but
this time the food was 'plentiful and wholesome'.

This Doncaster school was attended by many girls from Scotland and
whose parents were in India. Miss Murphy boasted about the breadth of her
curriculum; 'there were masters of every description, probably some from
York, some local, drill and dancing masters'. There were also masters for
piano, harp and guitar, for drawing, writing and flower painting:

> Miss Murphy arrayed us all for our dancing lessons in white, with prim-
> rose coloured sashes, gloves and shoes and was very particular about our
> carriage, especially our way of entering a room. We were to make a
> sweeping curtesy to those assembled, before advancing.

In her second year at this school, Elizabeth Bradshawe was 'suddenly put into
livery of a very effective and expensive style', for Miss Murphy's visits, with
her senior pupils, to the theatre in York. 'We were measured and clothed and
there could be no mistaking Miss Murphy's pupils for those of Mrs Hoare's
more unpretending school'. But she found these social experiences 'a great
pleasure at the time'.[39]

Mary Sewell, daughter of a grocer at Yarmouth in Norfolk, wrote a
scathing account of her brief experience of boarding school at fourteen. All
her learning was by rote and she worked as well with French and dancing
masters. 'I made a small proficiency in copying flowers', she noted. She took
home the embroidery in wool that she had completed, where it was hung up
as all she had to show for her year at school.[40]

There were doubtless stresses and strains for many teenage girls, separated
by the experience of boarding school life from their homes and parents, but it
is unusual to find these so graphically illustrated as they are in a letter from
Jane Heath to her mother, Maria, at fifteen, on 23 November 1820. She had
just begun at Frenchay, some distance from her home at Andover. Jane had
been showered with presents: she thanked her mother for the gingham to

make a dress, biscuits and gingerbread, and nuts 'which were very nice indeed'. She also thanked her father for sending her a hare. 'I relished this', she declared, 'more than anything I have had since I have been here, because it came from home and dear Papa will keep his promise of writing to me very often I hope.' The petticoat they had sent was 'very acceptable in this cold place . . . much colder than dear Andover'.

Feeling bereft, Jane nevertheless gave an interesting account of her days. There was invariably geography, 'with dissected maps', before breakfast, then days were appointed as English or French ones. The English curriculum consisted of geography, grammar, natural history and English history; the French one focused upon grammar, verbs, exercises, translations and ancient chronology. The girls were expected to practise their needlework later in the day and to read aloud in turns.

Jane was evidently very homesick, calling to mind the various members of her family circle in turn. 'Do thank dear governess for her very long and acceptable letter'; 'do give my very dear love to my sisters: kiss them very often for me'; she sent 'dear love' to her grandmother, 'all kind enquiry to friends too numerous to mention' and asked to be remembered 'kindly to the maids'. She pleaded with her mother to write at least once a fortnight, 'the greatest comfort I have', explaining that 'Nancy, the servant here, is very kind such as tucking me up at night and doing any little thing I wish'. This is the paradigmatic schoolchild's letter: 'I am always looking forward to the holidays and am already counting months and weeks . . . how gladly would I shut myself up in this sheet of paper, if possible, and set off home.' The postscript asked for her 'old garden pinafore to be sent for painting', since 'it is very dirty work'.[41]

Yet nearly a hundred years later, for teenage girls with drive and personality, Edwardian sixth-form education, in country boarding schools, could be a thrilling and deeply rewarding time of life. Two positive examples of its experience relate to small and traditional schools: Cesca Chenevix Trench's career at Langland and Clare Howard's at Effingham House, in 1906 to 1908 and 1909 to 1910 respectively.

Cesca's vivid first letter to her sister from Langland made it plain the kind of schoolgirl she was becoming: it set out her candid views on the curriculum, the teachers and the other girls. She quickly took against the headmistress, Miss Farmer, an 'awful bandit', who was rigid and imperious about clothes and hair styles, objecting specifically to Cesca's white shirt and blouse, pink frock and amber beads. 'And then one has to kiss her every night.' Cesca was a ringleader in disrespect for prefects, casting aspersions on them for any lack of the politeness, such as that regarding the sneezing etiquette, in which they were supposed to lead the way. She dismissed traditional needlework out of hand, with the comment that they had to 'sew like good little girls' after lunch for about three quarters of an hour. She was often cheeky and provocative.

But Cesca soon acquired popularity by the speed of her repartee. There were clashes with Miss Leather, the 'ripping' history teacher, about hanging up her dressing gown, tipping up her chair in lessons and displaying too many family photos in her cubicle: 'My dear Miss Leather is it my fault if I have three brothers and a sister?' What really grated with Cesca were the restrictions of a regime bent on imposing physical and moral restraint at every turn. 'It's perfectly horrid being put on one's honour not to do things because one never gets the chance', was her summary.

Each girl said the collect and epistle to Miss Farmer on Sundays. 'She asks if we have transgressed any rules and if so which and why', Cesca explained to her sister Margot, adding that, 'I break all the rules I can.' Yet her spirit was still hampered, she felt, by endless restrictive instruction. She manufactured a wish-fulfilment story, when they were out on the Malvern Hills in a tremendous wind: the teacher with them had been blown away, sending last messages to Miss Farmer about 'where she was blown'.[42]

Clare Howard enjoyed every minute of her two years at Effingham House. Letters to her from her friend Edna in 1909, at home in the middle of term, exemplify the intense and cloying intimacy of this sixth-form world. Edna and another girl, Delia, shared a study with Clare and the fire was always out, 'now that you are not here to keep it up'. One of the younger teachers had banned sixth-formers from 'calling her Darling altogether', difficult, Edna commented, since it had 'got such a habit now'. This was rehearsal for the emotional and sexual life of normal adulthood, directed safely towards teachers of the same sex.[43]

For these senior girls the headmistress, Miss Emily, was a figure of almost mystical honour and eminence. Edna related it, as a major piece of news, that Miss Emily had asked her to put on her new coat and skirt to show her and was wanting her to start putting her hair up. At the same time, these girls were games mad. 'We simply must win', Edna declared, reporting the forthcoming return hockey match against their rivals, the Beehive, 'for Miss Emily's sake more than anything else.'[44]

It was only in the last 50 years before the First World War that schooling became a more positive experience for girls than it had been previously. The tyranny of needlework and the tyranny of rote learning were both measurably reduced in these years. It became possible for girls to enjoy the games field with a little of the pleasure and fulfilment it also brought to boys. But the core of gendered educational tradition had not shifted. Boys were being fitted for the adult world. Girls were only learning to manage and ornament a home.

Training for Society

T he upbringing of upper- and middle-class girls remained extraordinarily consistent over these centuries. The objective was to teach them, as Sir Ralph Verney famously put it to his godchild Nancy's father, Dr Denton, in 1650, 'to live under obedience'.[1] The long-established convention of sending teenage girls away from home was rooted in aspirations for their domestic training and their moral and spiritual upbringing. Parental objectives in sending girls to live with trusted relatives began to be revised in the early eighteenth century, as the obsession with social accomplishments and training in decorum, advocated by the conduct books, took hold. The focus was soon decisively shifted to preparation for the launching of a teenager on society and the marriage market. The process was usually seen, in the eighteenth and nineteenth centuries, as a gradual one, with coming out and a first season of balls as its climax.

Traditional practice is well documented among the Paston, Stonor and Plumpton families in the fifteenth century and the Plantagenet and Bennet families during the 1530s.[2] A letter from Jane Tuttoft to her cousin Nathaniel Bacon of Stiffkey in Norfolk in 1572 summarised customary thinking in the Tudor period:

> I give you hearty thanks for bringing up my daughter in your household. Let her learn to write and read and cast accounts and to wash and brew and to bake and to dress meat and drink and so I trust she will prove herself a great good housewife.[3]

In 1551, Sir Edmund Molineux placed his two daughters with a cousin and his wife, expecting their training 'in virtue, good manners and learning to play the gentlewoman and good housewives, to dress meat and oversee their households'.[4] There were some who became renowned as specialists in the business: 'I know how to breed and govern young gentlewomen', boasted

Lady Catherine Hastings to Sir Julius Caesar in 1618.[5] Lady Joan Barrington took in a god-daughter and the daughter of a brother-in-law in Essex, to be reared alongside her own five girls.[6]

A letter in 1611 from Sir Arthur Capel to his sister about his daughter was wholly traditional:

> Let me entreat you that you will not be wanting to her by your good counsel. She is young and inexperienced in housewifery which I hold one of the best qualities ... stir her up to industry and diligence that idleness, one of the enemies of mankind, may be banished from her. Thus through God's blessing she may be a means to build and maintain the house where she is now planted.[7]

Attitudes among the Sussex gentry were typical. Over a four-year period between her fourteenth and eighteenth birthdays, Nan Pelham spent much of her time far from her home, with her mother's family, the Wilbrahams, in Cheshire. The Busbridges of Etchingham and the Temples of Frankton in Warwickshire, related by marriage, provided reciprocal household training for daughters. Two Temple girls spent time with their married sister in Sussex during the 1630s. 'If her company may be any way comfortable or useful to you', their mother wrote when one of them was there, 'I shall gladly spare her and be thankful to you for her.'

It was the confidence in shared values and loving support for girls away from home for the first time which sustained this scheme of things. When it was Anna Busbridge's turn to send her daughter, Anna, to Warwickshire in 1648, her letters were full of encouragement to the girl to make the most of her opportunity. 'I desire', she wrote on one occasion, 'you may do and receive all the good you can for soul and body, so I could deny myself of my comfort for yours.' 'Take heed', she reiterated later, 'of misspending precious time.'[8] But mothers also worried about their girls when they were away from home. 'Daughter Alice came home from London safely', wrote Mary Woodforde in her diary in June 1689, 'for which blessed be God, may he keep her here in peace.'[9]

There were old-fashioned families in the eighteenth century who believed in this kind of training of girls for adulthood. Early in her teens, Elizabeth Dryden travelled from London to reside with her childless uncle and aunt, Sir John and Lady Elizabeth Dryden, at Canons Ashby in Northamptonshire. 'She is a fine child and we are both mightily pleased with her', Sir John declared in March 1771, promising 'all care' and 'her good consulted in all particulars which are within my power'. The next month he continued to enthuse: 'if I can possibly avoid it I will not spoil her, indeed the girl is so amiable in herself that it is impossible not to be fond of her'. 'Indeed', Sir John wrote, surpassing himself, 'I am as well pleased as if it was a boy.'

Her grandmother, resident at Canons Ashby, took a hand in Elizabeth's upbringing too, updating her mother regularly on her 'health and happiness'. 'She is all day with madam, sir takes her to walk with him in the garden – both are violent fond of her', was her verdict on 4 June. Elizabeth's mother confessed that her 'joy was not to be described' about her daughter settling so well. Her grandmother's next bulletin told of her sitting in her aunt's lap to have two loose teeth drawn 'with some difficulty'. It included a 'natural innocent' letter by the child herself. What was new here was the stress on inculcating social experience. By August 1771, Sir John was confident that his niece had taken Northamptonshire by storm: 'a child after our own hearts, she is admired by all the neighbours for her own merit'. 'Indeed I am very good', added Elizabeth, in a childish scrawl, 'I visit with Aunt wherever she goes.'[10]

The eighteenth century saw increasing parental preoccupation with the physical attributes of their daughters and concern about how these could be most effectively maximised. Assumptions about fashionable feminine beauty settled into a notion of fragility and delicacy, with stress on uprightness of posture and a languid air. Hence John Locke's protests, as early as 1700, against restriction of young bodies by corsets reinforced by metal and whalebone.[11] Parental concern about posture became and remained obsessive. Barbara Tasburgh, born in 1815, remembered that 'to improve our figures we were made to lie for half an hour every day on boards and then to walk up and down the passage with weights on our heads'.[12]

Ironically, much of the criticism of contortion of female bodies in the cause of their adult figures was directed at boarding schools. Emily Shore, being educated at home in 1833, read an article in the *Penny Magazine* on 'the horrible effect of tight-lacing and want of exercise' which, in boarding schools, made the 'whole body diseased'.[13] Yet it is girls who were kept at home that testify most frequently to fearful physical manipulation. When Louisa Trotter, born in 1863, was diagnosed as having curvature of the spine, she was made to lie flat on the floor for twenty minutes at a time, three times a day.[14] Mary Butt, who developed a tendency to stoop with rapid growth as a youngster, was subjected to a back-board, strapped over the shoulders, from the age of six to thirteen. 'Although perfectly straight and well made', recorded Mary Somerville, 'I was enclosed in stiff stays with a steel bust in front, while, above my frock, bands drew my shoulders back till the shoulder-blades met.'

'He says we both have weak spines', Eva Knatchbull recorded the doctor telling her mother about her and her sister Kate in 1875, 'and must lie down for an hour a day.'[15] Deportment, chronicled Angela Forbes, was a distinct element in the schoolroom curriculum. She remembered lessons stretched on a backboard, sitting with straps and 'what-nots' on her shoulders and with her feet in stocks. 'Hold up your head, Miss', was the constant cry that echoed through Lucy Aikin's childhood: 'there were back-boards, iron collars, stocks for the feet and a frightful kind of neck-swing in which we were suspended every morning'.[16]

Such techniques, such straining and contorting of young bodies, may be seen as representing the pathology of gendered upbringing. Yet there is clear evidence, in women's correspondence, of the detail and seriousness with which parents studied and discussed the physical attributes, as well as the characters, of the feminine young, assessing their marriage prospects. For example, Lady Sarah Lennox responded, in a letter on 5 March 1780, to an enquiry from her friend, Lady Susan O'Brien, about 'what sort of girls the Lennoxes are'. Her brother's wife, Lady Louisa Lennox, had, she confessed, 'led a very retired life for some years and I think was a little obstinate about keeping her daughters as children too long'. But Lady Louisa had recently bestirred herself. She 'dresses her daughters as much as anybody, sends them out as much as the country permits of and lets the eldest go to London', Lady Sarah wrote, 'the only thing wanting is her going herself to town with her daughters, as surely it is most proper for all mothers to do'.

Detailed descriptions of the looks and characters of the three Lennox girls followed. Louisa, at nineteen, was 'middle-sized, elegant to the greatest degree in her form and rather plump . . . her nose is like her mother's which is pretty . . . her teeth good'. Lady Sarah found her 'sense quick, strong and steady; her character is reserved and prudent'. 'Her turn is a jolly country life with society', Lady Sarah wrote, 'where walking, working and a flower garden are her chief amusements; she don't love reading, calls everybody wise or affected that is in the least learned.' Louisa was 'feminine to the greatest degree', noted Lady Sarah, which meant that she 'laughs most heartily at a dirty joke but never makes one'.

Lady Sarah's pen portraits indicated her understanding that assuredly looks and personality both mattered in obtaining a husband. The characters of the Lennox girls were 'all three as different as it is in nature to be', she maintained. Emily, at seventeen, was a 'fine, tall large woman', with features marred by an ugly mouth, but 'her countenance very pleasing and all good-ness like her character'. She was very dependent on her elder sister, but lacked some of her 'cultivation', which would 'not be so useful perhaps'. Georgina, at fifteen, by contrast, was 'rather little and strong made', with 'no eyebrows, a long nose, even teeth and the merriest of faces'. Lady Sarah's assessment of her character, showing a liveliness inherited from her mother, was devastatingly candid:

She has all her wit, all her power of satire and all her good nature too, so that if she is not led to give way to the tempting vanity of displaying it she will be delightful, but you know by experience the dangers attending on wit and dear little Georgina I fear will experience them.

She found the manners of this youngest Lennox girl 'more lively or rather less prudent than her sisters'. She concluded, though, that their mother had good reason to be proud of them all and should hasten to 'produce' them.[17]

We have seen how the more prestigious boarding schools for girls in the late eighteenth century sought to combine inculcation of subjects like French, history, geography, English grammar, and music, with manners and deportment. Francis Power Cobbe was told by her mother, who went there, about the famous school run by Mrs Devis in Queen Square, London in the 1790s, where neither 'packing the brains of girls with facts', nor 'teaching their fingers to run over the keys of instruments', were the alpha and omega of education:

> Decorum was the imperative law of a lady's inner life as well as her outer habits: and in Queen Square nothing that was not decorous was for a moment admitted. Every movement of the body in entering and quitting a room, in taking a seat and rising from it, was duly criticised.

This was a school that even kept a carriage available so that pupils could 'practice ascending and descending with calmness and grace, and without any unnecessary display of their ankles'.[18]

An Essex father, George Leathes, made his priorities explicit in a poem that he sent to his daughter at boarding school in 1799 about his hopes for her on her return. His rapture at 'hugging you close to my breast' would be complemented by his wife's pleasure at her politeness: 'Mama too will see, with increasing delight, your address free and easy, your carriage upright.'[19] Diction ranked high, beside deportment, in parental expectations about female graces. An 'easy diction', Jane Heath's father told her in 1819,

> my dear daughter is in my opinion one of the greatest blessings springing from education ... most of thy sex can talk and many of them to good purpose and nearly all of them can write and many of them to good purpose, but from the species of knowledge they possess they find it much easier to puzzle than to instruct generally.[20]

Louisa Trotter's finishing governess in the 1870s drummed deportment into her morning, noon and night: 'she generally looked peevishly down her flat nose but, when required, she could produce an entirely mechanical smile, as when she gave a curtsey lesson.' A letter from Mademoiselle Ravian about Isabel and Blanche Trench, to their mother Georgiana, exemplifies the priority that a governess knew she was expected to give to both the style and deportment of her charges. Georgiana was away from Cangort Park during an exceptionally cold February when her two youngest were in their early to middle teens. The impetuous Blanche, Mademoiselle reported, 'has a little cold but it will not prevent her going out today well wrapped up and I think she is right':

> She is most sweet looking, Mrs Trench, of an evening quite lovely, so elegant and graceful . . . I think they have equal merit. If Isabel is more anxious about study and appears to appreciate all things which occupy the intelligence with greater ardours, Blanche has such lovely harmony in all her thoughts, her character is so sweet and she has much natural esprit, a quality so charming in society. You are most happy and blessed in your children dear Mrs Trench.[21]

The great emphasis on learning dancing reflected the conviction that it revealed gracefulness and therefore governed body language as a whole: bowing, curtseying and proper posture were all in the remit of the dancing master. Lady Strafford was proud about her daughter Lucy's ability on the dance floor, but she worried, writing to her husband in 1734, about another daughter, Harriot, who 'pokes sadly and I tell her of it repeatedly'. 'She 'improves almost as much as she diverts herself here', wrote one mother of her daughter, during a stay at Bath. Relatives who saw parental training in breeding as deficient could be scathing. Lady Frances Hastings found cause to reprove her niece for her Yorkshire accent and dialect, when she offered, in 1730, to cut her 'a bonny flower'. 'There is a great deal of good in her', Elizabeth Montagu noted of Lord Lyttelton's thirteen-year-old daughter in 1758, 'but her virtues are in deshabille, her understanding totally undressed.'[22]

One of the special benefits of time away from home was that teenage girls could be expected to practise and perfect that crucial attribute of their characters, writing the polite letter. Ingrid Tague has noted the characteristics of this literary form in gentry circles as 'the forms of deference, respect and polite enquiries after their recipients' health'. She found young girls, in the Hatton family in the 1690s and the Strafford family in the 1730s, 'mirroring the language and values of adult polite society'. A 'very agreeable' ridotto had been attended by 'all the good company in town' related Anne Wentworth; 'the music is really very pretty', wrote the eighteen-year-old Harriot Wentworth, after going to a new farce at the theatre.[23]

The fact that they were not interested in the training of the female intellect did not mean, Linda Pollock has argued, that parental expectations for their girls were lacking.[24] The sense of these demanding expectations as early as 1655 pervades a touching letter from Katherine Oxinden, aged eight, to her mother. This relates, as a 'register' for her father's approval, her progress in spheres of activity deemed appropriate to her sex: 'I am entering upon two or three gum flowers . . . I am also entering upon the viol the which, together with my dancing and some other necessary things, take of my time from my work . . . I shall endeavour to improve my time for the best.' Katherine, in other words, knew that her needlework was the very essence of her training, yet excused herself from a good deal of time spent on it, since learning other accomplishments crowded it out.[25]

This training in accomplishments really took off after 1700. Correspondence between Lady Elizabeth Smyth and her sister-in-law, Mrs Elizabeth Germon, living near Haymarket in London in around 1710, relates to her daughters Betty and Astrea, who were boarding with her during their schooling there. When they first went up from Somerset, Lady Elizabeth asked her sister-in-law to undertake all the arrangements, including those with private dancing and writing masters. She had her heart in her mouth at this leap in the dark:

> We desire they may have anything that is for their good, only desire they may be bred humble and not too nice to live after our plain way, that they may be easy to live with their home if it please God to bring us to live all together again.

She was worried about the healthiness of the capital, declaring that the children were not to roam from their school. She also had to cope with the tears of her younger boys at the parting with their elder sisters: 'Hugh does cry to part with Astrea that I fear he will do himself harm . . . Sam is as fond of Betty.'

But the reports Lady Elizabeth received were cheering. 'They are as much improved as can be expected for the time and are the prettiest girls in the school', her sister-in-law wrote in February 1711: 'they will be very neat and genteel'. Both girls were making excellent progress in their lessons with one of the best spinet masters in London. Astrea had learnt twelve tunes, Betty nearly as many. That September, Lady Elizabeth, in a rushed emotional letter, declared her obligation for Elizabeth Germon's 'great kindness to my girls', which she hoped they would retain the sense of 'as long as they live'.

She wanted them to practise a variety of kinds of needlework, but this, she insisted, should take a lower priority than the spinet. So they should not, for instance, embark on making stomachers, too lengthy a piece of work; they could begin to make aprons, to see how it was done and then leave off. She hoped for perfection in reading music, since, when she had them home, there was a local organist that she had it in mind who they could play with.[26]

The Smyths' strategy regarding their girls, Betty and Astrea, exemplified the new programme of polite training. A taste of metropolitan ways and society was coming to be seen by many as an essential ingredient in the making of a young lady. Hence parental willingness to spend money on this. Anne Western sent her daughter up to London from Essex, for periods of three to four months each year from 1730 to 1734, lodging her with a French maid in Chelsea. Her expenses included Willelmina's dancing, writing, singing and French masters; her gloves, stockings, frocks, shoes, jewellery and fans; her chair and coach hire and money spent visiting the theatre.[27]

The widow Lady Anne Cust, after giving her girls some local schooling near Grantham, sent them off in turn to live for a period with a trusted relative, Mrs Lucy Woodcock, at Great Marlborough Street in London. Betty, the eldest girl, began there at seventeen in 1741, but Lady Anne brought her home when she found that her health suffered in the capital. Betty herself explained to her brother, Sir John Cust, why she was glad that Jenny had quickly replaced her in London:

> I don't doubt my sister Jenny being greatly improved by having the happiness to be under Mrs Woodcock's direction, who I am sure is quite fit to instruct young people and, as my sister Jenny is so good herself, it will be a great advantage to her and I hope we shall both be better for the change.

Missing her girls as they grew older, Lady Anne was always thrilled when they came home. 'Miss Lucy she has done nothing but laugh ever since she came', she noted in 1746. 'I think her improved and that she will make a genteel woman . . . I trust in God that I shall be as happy in my daughters as in my sons. I think I do them justice in saying they have all good sense and dispositions.'

Sir John himself gradually undertook the oversight of the young Cust girls, ensuring their introduction to the social world of the capital and practise in metropolitan polite behaviour. It was he who then had the main hand in the girls' marriages. Jenny opened her heart to her elder brother about her doubts about marriage to Francis Fane, a much older man than herself, in 1752. 'I never had a dislike of Mr Fane', she wrote, 'but there is something very awful in matrimony and no doubt more so where there is such a disproportion of years, as one may be afraid of oneself, but against that I set his good character which is a very amiable one and his temper, such that I should have a very fair prospect of being happy.' She agreed the following year to marry Mr Fane, telling her brother that she would 'do all in my power to make him happy and not be a discredit to my friends'.[28]

The training of boys and girls took opposite courses. Whereas boys were cloistered away to learn their manhood and eventual rule from boarding school rough and tumble, girls, mothers realised, had to be trained on the actual scene for their polite and accomplished, but ultimately submissive, social destiny. So they were started young in the eighteenth century by being thrown, for practise as teenagers, into the venues of polite urban culture. A dedicated mother, like Frances Boscawen, trained her child through a hectic programme of socialising, which included assemblies, visiting and attendance at court, throughout the teenage years.

Peter Borsay has documented this process, noting François de la Rochefoucauld's observation, in 1784, that, in England, young girls being launched into society 'mix with the company and talk and enjoy themselves with as much freedom as if they were married'. Eleven of 83 people named as attending a London concert in 1765 were titled 'Miss'. Over 1,300 of the 4,000 subscriber tickets for York assemblies, between 1732 and 1737, were assigned to women with the prefix 'Miss'. All these misses can be seen as unmarried searchers after husbands, variously aged in their teens and twenties.

George Lucy was an informative commentator on the family parties, heavily loaded with young girls, to be found visiting Bath. In 1760, he noted the arrival of 'Mr Marat with his family, which consists of his lady, himself, four or five daughters and a son'. In 1763, explaining how the company there was 'much improved', the daughters of Sir Woolstan Dixie caught his eye:

> The two young ladies carry the ball, and the youngest of them I think very deservedly, for surely never did the lily and the rose ever so happily meet, to set off a person, as in the countenance of this young lady, who is said to be about fourteen years of age.

James Harris, of Salisbury, was taking his Gertrude to social events at thirteen and his Louisa to them at a mere ten. The latter, her mother confessed when she was fifteen, was revelling in it all: 'she is always in dining parties, goes perpetually to the opera and whenever we can get a box to comedies'. James Oakes's children and grandchildren, similarly, were attending public balls in Bury St Edmunds by around fifteen.[29]

Yet when mothers tried to start their girls young on courses in metropolitan rather than provincial politeness, they could find them resisting the loss of their country life. Letters from Penelope and Alice Hatton to their father,

Lord Hatton, at Kirby Hall in 1699 and 1700, reveal young teenage girls in a hectic social whirl. Their aunt and uncle, doing their duty, were introducing them to London society, with its shops, balls, operas and plays. Allowing for the deference behind their protestations about the delights of home, it is evident that these girls did at times long for rural Northamptonshire and miss their family there. They struggled to keep their parents informed about the latest fashions, but often confessed themselves bewildered by the gyrations of London and its politics.

One of the dancers at a ball at St James's, Alice Hatton noted, was fitted with one of the huge 'new fashioned periwigs'. To her mind, its 'monstrous bigness with his little face did not look so well'. Their short, scrappy and strained bulletins of news, with the post always just going, suggest that there was an emotional cost to the rapid progress that the Hatton girls made in their social training. Alice returned 'special thanks' for a letter from her father, which emphasised his approving 'of my behaviour here', adding, 'I am sure it shall always be my care never to make your lordship do otherwise'.[30]

Lady Maria Stanley was certainly disappointed when her Rianette and Lucy, at eleven and ten respectively, became unwell under the strain of a first trip to London in January 1808. She tried to juggle this metropolitan initiation with some schooling at home in Cheshire, explaining to the schoolteacher there that she wanted her to receive her girls around April: 'I am quite vexed at their losing so much time with their dancing and also that they have so little pleasure in this long talked of London.'[31]

There were other strategies besides the metropolitan one which proved perfectly sensible in relation to the objective of obtaining favourable marriages for genteel girls. Claver Morris's diary illuminates a West Country pattern of training. He started his daughter Betty on violin and singing, with local tutors in his home town of Wells, at eleven in 1707. She went to Mrs Deer's boarding school at Salisbury the following year, where she was taught by dancing, violin and writing masters. This was a comparatively brief interlude in her programme of training at home, which included attendance at a meeting of a consort of musicians. The culmination was Betty's own ball in February 1710, which lasted until after midnight. She was still only thirteen.

Plans for girls could, of course, go awry. The Catholic Nicholas Blundell, with two daughters to educate, began with nearby teachers in Lancashire and the standard female accomplishments. When Mally was seven, a sewing teacher visited and by eight she was in the hands of a local dancing master. At ten, she went to a children's ball in Liverpool and spent some time away from home with an aunt in Yorkshire. She began quilting and at the same age boarded at a local school. When the girls were eleven and thirteen, Nicholas decided it was time for both of them to go away and, following family tradition, they went to a Benedictine convent in Ghent.

Mally, however, became taken up with the cloistered life, an option denied to Protestant girls. When Nicholas sought to get her home and married, she first pleaded for an extra year and then declared her mind. In 1723, when she was nineteen, Nicholas went himself to bring her home, giving her a tour of all the excitements of the London social scene on the way. He poured out his money on clothes, jewellery and amusements. This was his way of introducing her, he said, to the world, before she made her final decision. Two years later, unconvinced by his eldest daughter's declared vocation as a nun, Nicholas Blundell wrote sadly to a friend that she was still 'no more inclinable to marry than she was':

> I long since told her I would not compel her to marry one she cannot love and so to make her miserable as long as she lives, so leave her entirely to please herself, all I require is that he be a gentleman of a competent estate, one of good character and a catholic.

A disappointed father was biting his lip.[32]

The remarkable 1770s diaries of a motherless Lancaster Quaker girl, Mary Chorley, living from the ages of ten to thirteen with two aunts, the Miss Fords, while her father pursued his business as a merchant in Liverpool, reveal how comprehensive a northern training in polite behaviour could be. Masters visited to give the Chorley girls lessons on six mornings a week: they learned drawing, history and geography, by lesson cards and a globe, together with biology, logic and arithmetic. Mary Chorley's reading included Roman texts in translation, edifying treatises and novels, which she adored. Yet domestic training was not neglected. She learnt from her aunts how to bake, pickle and preserve; her needlework included shirts, shifts and dresses.[33]

The predictable keynote, constantly harped upon by Mary Chorley herself, was her 'improvement', as she acquired, through local travel and her teachers, all the rudiments of gentility on the mere edge of her teens. 'My aunt Mary', she noted on 15 December 1776, 'read to me one of Fordyce's sermons on piety which I admire extremely.'[34] Not only do we know a great deal about what Mary Chorley read, but we can watch her sensibility develop, as her reading went along. Naturally, Mary admired the *Life of William Penn*; she was stirred by the public spirit of Plutarch's hero Publicola, 'the most virtuous citizen and greatest general Rome ever had'; she gasped at the nobility and goodness of Samuel Richardson's *Sir Charles Grandison*. Her identification with the women in Richardson's novel lead her to muse, at twelve years old on 16 February 1779, about how she was put at a loss in her own diary keeping: 'I think if I were to open my heart like Miss Byrom and Miss Jewson the contents would fill a room.'

The essence of all this was Mary's preparation, which she appreciated her father took very seriously, for living the life of a young lady. There is no more compelling vignette, illustrating the training of Georgian girlhood, than Mary Chorley's accounts of her graduation from social visiting as play to practise of the real thing. On 7 July 1776, she noted, when her friends Nell and Maria came, that 'we played at visiting'; on 1 May 1778 she wrote, 'it being my birthday I had many young ladies to drink tea with me'; on 2 June 1780 Mary 'went to Elhill to drink tea'. With three hours of dancing following, this was 'a delightful afternoon'. This social debut, as Amanda Vickery notes, can be seen as 'a treasured performance of female adulthood'.[35]

Abigail Gawthern, daughter of a Nottingham grocer and tallow chandler, recorded in her diary how she learnt to move easily in the town's respectable and professional circles, following her music and dancing lessons there with her first balls in her teens. By nineteen, when she attended the festivities of Assizes week in July 1776, she was thoroughly at home at the Castle Ball in, as she put it, 'my native place'. Her marriage, at 25, to a cousin living in Nottingham and their settling in a home on fashionable Low Pavement, was the intended and entirely predictable outcome of her upbringing.[36]

In some cases, the influence and tuition of a powerful and engaged relative could be the critical determining factor in a youngster's social training. Correspondence from an early age between Maria Holroyd, born in 1771, and her aunt Serena illuminates many years of training in politeness by a fond and devoted overseer. She was only six when Serena started chivvying her on a visit to Bath about 'growing every day more pleasing', by conduct that was 'gentle, good and obliging to everybody'. 'Girls that are not so', Serena warned, 'always pass for vulgar, ill bred children.' Lapping up the child's affection, Serena heard about Maria's first visit to Sadler's Wells in 1782. She reassured her that, back in Bath now aged eleven, she had been reported as being 'very sprightly and polite'.

Visiting her at her home, Sheffield Park, around this time, Serena observed Maria's movements indoors. What mattered, she instructed, was 'a good carriage, a straight slope and genteel person'. These were the qualities, in her view, which 'mark the well educated', seeming to her 'as necessary for a woman of any fashion as to know how to spell'. At fifteen in 1786, Maria found the relative informality of her own home a comfortable setting for acquiring the self-assurance that her aunt had taught her would take her far in society: 'for putting together my rides, my dining and supping downstairs, I feel myself more of a woman there'. But she took her first Haymarket play in her stride that spring and, at her mother's suggestion, her hair was 'turned up'. 'Neatness is elegance and in that your Mama sets you the very best example', Serena advised.

Maria was now reading widely in French, Roman and English literature. Her improvement had been inspired by neither a governess nor schooling but her aunt's determined insistence. She described how she spent a typical day in 1786: she walked in the park before breakfast, played the harpsichord, drew, did translation work and read in the morning, dined at four, played backgammon with her parents after this, ending with needlework or piano practice, before 'a little bit of supper' at ten. When she revisited Bath in August 1787, Serena prepared Maria's mind for her coming out. She knew 'how much you are improved'. 'I only hear', she continued, 'of a certain bad carriage and walk with a little too fast speaking, which I intend should be quite got rid of before winter.' The following January she would be seventeen, so 'you will now in a manner begin the world and make your first appearance as being no longer a child'. This intense correspondence, and Serena's tuition, continued until 1796. Then Maria announced, at 25 years old, that she had accepted the hand in marriage of Mr Stanley. 'I think', she concluded, 'I may be a most happy woman.'[37]

There was much debate in Georgian and Regency England about when the seclusion of proper young girls should end. Launching girls on urban society, we have seen, was usually a gradual process. Jane Austen portrays coming out as typically occurring around fifteen or sixteen. There were different views on how leisurely coming out should be and how it was best conducted. Mrs Delaney argued that eight or nine was not too young for a girl to be launched gradually into the kind of social experiences which would help her to develop poise, graciousness and manners. 'There is a grace and manner', she wrote in 1753, 'which cannot be attained without conversing with a variety of well bred people.' Yet mothers trod a path fraught with risks in managing this sociali-sation. 'For all public places', Mary Delaney warned in 1752, 'till after fifteen (except a play or oratorio) she should not know what they are, and then very rarely.' She believed the new spa towns were especially threatening to female honour.[38]

The pace of social launching depended on thoughtful parental pondering. Nicholas Blundell, as we have seen, sent his daughter Mally to a child's ball in Liverpool at the age of ten in 1714.[39] Fanny Burney recorded in her journal in 1768, aged sixteen, that, though she had never been at a public assembly, she had often been at school balls and 'once at a private ball at an acquain-tance, where I danced till late in the morning'.[40] It was easy for Cornelia Knight to carry things off in Plymouth society as young as thirteen in the 1770s, it was noted, because 'she was so very tall for her age that people tended to treat her like a young lady'.[41]

Annabella Carr, writing to her brother in October 1780, was quite full of herself, at sixteen, about having danced with Robert Williamson, Recorder of Newcastle, at the Assembly Rooms, which she reckoned he might already know of, by 'a former report' that might have reached him:

> This particular attention to your humble servant was noticed by the whole room and people are apt to put wrong constructions on behaviour so public . . . I forgot to tell you that Bowes very politely asked me to dance with him at the last Guild Assembly as did Lord Lindores and Baron Norton . . . I'm in fashion with the Beaux at present.[42]

Two accounts provide unusual detail about the introduction of daughters to society in the 1770s.[43] Entries in Hester Thrale's Children's Book refer to her watchful attention to the progress of the precocious Queenie, on her first steps in society. Confident in her knowledge of languages and her general knowledge, Hester took her to Bath in 1778, at eleven years old. She believed her to be 'very handsome'. She noted that, having been slight, 'she begins now to spread and her breast grows apace'. That autumn, Queenie had a spell in Brighton, causing her imperious mother to note caustically that, 'at every ball . . . she exposed herself; it is amazing that she should dance so vilely with such a figure and so good instruction; but whether it is from bashfulness or naughtiness I know not, or a mixture of both, but she does dance most incomparably ill to be sure.'

In December 1778, Hester and Queenie spent a week in London and 'diverted ourselves with going to plays, operas and other amusements'. The girl 'grows handsomer, taller and fatter and is much admired', her mother commented. But not long after, on her thirteenth birthday, the obsessive Hester was fussing about her looks in a way that reminds us how patriarchal control was often exercised at one remove by older women on young girls: 'she grows long and thin and gangling and her colour is not so high as it was during mere childhood; her extreme shyness is also no friend to her figure, though I think her carriage will be that of a woman of fashion in spite of her.'[44]

The hectic social round continued apace and, a year later, on Queenie's fourteenth birthday, Hester had taken to reflecting upon her lovely figure and cultivated mind, even if her temper was still 'haughty and contemptuous'. 'We kept her birthday merrily', she recorded, 'and she treated the servants with a dance.'[45]

Letters written by Betsy Francis to her husband chronicle the launching of Sally and Betsy in society from 1777 onwards, at fourteen and thirteen respectively. Sally had been out to dine with her mother as early as twelve. The thrill of Ranelagh gardens made an impact on them: 'my girls' surprise was very great indeed at entering the room full of fine company, lights, etc', she wrote, 'they were happy, so was I to see them so'. At the playhouse, they saw 'a very clever comedy'. They attended a ball at Sunbury assembly.

In 1778, Betsy arranged a ball for the girls at their home during the winter season. She also took them to a masquerade. The three of them visited Bath, where they toured the Pump Room and parades, Betsy hiring a fortepiano for the girls to play. 'We don't know a creature', Betsy told her husband, yet Sally's first ball there was a success. They were at Margate in the summer of 1779 and then Tunbridge Wells, where there were lots of balls and the girls' dancing was reportedly 'much admired'. Betsy Francis was doing what she knew was expected of her. She believed that she was making a success of it.[46]

Teenage girls at the highest level of society treated their parents with the same kind of deference that we have observed in boys, but there was often an added touch of obsequiousness and submission. Writing to her father, the Duke of Richmond, in London from Goodwood in the 1740s, Georgina Lennox was heartfelt in gratitude for his permission to go and see the Fleet at Portsmouth, 'for I shall like very much to go'. Such teenagers quickly grasped the realities of their place in both the family and society. Relating the news from London that a friend of her mother's was coming down to Goodwood in 1744, Emily Lennox, at thirteen, said how glad she was, 'for I am afraid my dear Mama finds it a little dull being alone, for as for Papa his hunting takes up most part of his time'. She was delighted at orders she had received to ride regularly herself 'and am vastly obliged to my dear Mama for giving them'.[47] Riding, and sometimes hunting, had become and remained until late Victorian times the only permitted outlet for physical activity. So 'some girls hunted and rode', Leonore Davidoff has observed, 'with a passion that amounted to mania'.[48]

The Georgian marriage market was largely a public one. 'A deal of parental anxiety about public arenas was disingenuous', Amanda Vickery has argued, 'most parents knew full well what they were doing when they towed their prize daughters from assemblies to plays.' But unremitting chaperonage was every young girl's lot. Abigail Gawthern devoted her time in the early nineteenth century to taking her daughter Anna to the Nottingham assize balls, races and plays, to escorting her to Bath and Weymouth and to the London venues of the pleasure gardens, the Opera and British Museum. This was a conscious and explicit matrimonial campaign. She kept a tally of those who Anna danced with and of the proposals of marriage that were mooted or made.

Yet, even as Abigail Gawthern paraded her daughter there, Ranelagh, the most celebrated of the pleasure gardens, was becoming deserted: it was 'now quite forsaken and talked of being taken down', she wrote in 1803. Vauxhall survived for longer, with fashionable galas and firework displays till 1820, but went downhill in the 1840s and was closed in 1859. The tide turned against the promiscuous sociability of the pleasure gardens, despite the best efforts of chaperones to check the vulnerability that threatened young girls at large in such public venues.[49]

By the time Queen Victoria came to the throne in 1837, the upper class was in headlong retreat from pubic socialising into a structured pattern of life, which emphasised exclusiveness, privacy and controlled interaction. The genteel time for dinner was put forward from 2.0 p.m. to the evening, with changing into formal clothes de rigueur and the procession to the dining room, guests appropriately paired off, marking precedence and hierarchy. The hall-marks of the new etiquette were introductions and the ritual of visiting cards. Women carried the burden of this new ritualised social round. Grown-up daughters accompanying mothers while they learnt the ropes, had their names printed on visiting cards underneath their mothers'.[50]

These developments exacerbated the plight of the champing schoolroom girl in her latter years of confinement. She was learning, laboriously and dili-gently, about deference, subordination and obedience. Socialising their daugh-ters, Margaret Hunt has stressed, had long involved mothers instructing them 'on the terms of their subjection to men'.[51] In Victorian England, the tyranny of female improvement and accomplishments, with very limited acceptance, even domestically as a near adult, persisted for most of the teens. Yet for some there was not even a sense of achievement within these rigid conventions. Blanche Wilson, writing to a friend who had been sent to an expensive finishing school in 1861, expostulated:

> I wish I had your chance of improving myself but brothers, howsoever charming they may be, are expensive creatures and take all the money and the sisters have to grow up ignorant and make their own dresses, neither of which processes is pleasant nor am I enamoured of either . . . I shall expect a prodigy of accomplishments, having no brother to swallow up all the money you can stay as long as you like.[52]

Candid expression of inner feelings about gender deprivation by Victorian and Edwardian girls was unusual but not unknown. 'I wanted so much to be a boy', wrote Gwen Raverat, 'that I did not dare to think about it at all, for it made me feel quite desperate to know that it was impossible to be one.'[53] 'I used to long to play cricket and to go out spearing with the boys and ride to hounds', wrote Mary Haldane in a memoir of her long life, published in 1925.[54] 'I see my three long legged uncles coming in from cubbing or setting out to shoot', wrote Mary Carberry of her teenage years in the 1880s:

I want to be one of them, to exchange my silly frock and socks for breeches and gaiters, to have my hair cut short, to feel my face hard and rough, to throw my leg across a horse to ride and ride and ride . . . I pray with all my might to be turned into a boy.

She did hunt, she related, riding side saddle, 'with a manly little hat which I longed to touch, but still I bowed my head like a lady when other hunting people noticed me and touched their hats'.[55]

Emily Lutyens, brought up to the stiff etiquette of well-staffed Knebworth Park in Hertfordshire, was a 'large ungainly girl'. She related poorly to her mother. There was only one punishment, she recalled – early bed: 'if you are naughty you must be ill and bed is the place for you'. When she pulled her little brother from the well fishing for frogs, he was put to bed for falling in, and she was too for pulling him out. She 'bitterly resented my helplessness, my dependence and the fact that so many people in the shape of nurses and grown ups stood between me and my mother and that no child was believed in or treated with respect'. Emily longed to be a boy, recollecting: 'I was always a hero of some kind. Never have I known happier moments than when, sallying forth into the Park, armed with bow and arrows, I pretended to be Robin Hood, Ivanhoe or Richard Coeur de Lion.'[56]

The years before they came out were for many girls a thoroughly awkward and frustrating time. Religious confirmation was perhaps seen as a tactic, at around fifteen, to fill the gap. Parents sought to reconcile daughters to their destiny. 'I fancy that I thought taking the sacrament might make it easier to "be good", though what "being good" actually was became increasingly difficult to understand', wrote Louisa Haldane, 'unless it just meant doing what those "set in authority" over you wished.'[57]

The diaries and letters of Kate Stanley, born in 1842 into the boisterous, argumentative and ebullient Stanley family of Alderley, provide exceptional insight into the experience of one schoolroom girl, whose coming out was on the horizon. The centre of her vigorous intellectual life, from twelve to eighteen, was not her demure governess, Mademoiselle Peyreck, but her lively brother Lyulph, three years her senior. They corresponded incessantly. She had been reading Voltaire on Louis XIV, she told her mother at fourteen, 'I like it very much.' But her parents tried to prohibit the books which they believed would unsettle Kate. At seventeen, she was forbidden later chapters in the Quaker Mary Schimmelpennick's *Life*, because they recorded her religious doubts. The next year, having just finished Macaulay's *Speeches*, she told Lyulph, 'Papa says I may read the two first volumes of *Mill on the Floss* and stop there, Mama has not finished it yet but says I may not read it.' 'I am so sorry', she added, not dreaming of disobeying them. Louisa Haldane could neither understand nor forgive her parents for rationing her reading matter as a young girl, in the belief that much exciting fiction was detrimental to her young mind.[58]

It was hardest to tolerate the control of her life if a girl was herself clever and was brought up in an intellectual milieu. Kate Stanley, a modern girl in the 1850s, quarrelled with her godmother about Jane Austen's 'dreadful' novels, as she saw them. She lived her teenage years to the full, in a much travelled and highly political family, but she was storing up a rude shock for herself. 'We went through five covers before we found a fox', she wrote, describing her first hunt to her Mama, 'when we did . . . Silistria was not herself . . . would be in front and at one time ran with me nearly through a bush after the huntsmen.' 'Tell Papa I like hunting better than going to parties', was Kate's verdict, 'I enjoyed myself excessively'.

She enjoyed herself again at the Naval Review, attended by the family on 23 April 1856: to Waterloo in the brougham at six o'clock in the morning, to Portsmouth by train and home at ten o'clock at night. The Stanleys followed the Queen in the Royal Yacht, on board the Black Eagle. 'A beautiful and majestic sight', she wrote, 'to see those beautiful immense ships pass majestically and slowly along.' Another great day was 2 February 1858 when Kate, now sixteen, went to the opera at Covent Garden: 'you will be quite shocked when I tell you', she related to Mama, 'we went in a cab as it was too slippery for the carriage . . . it was a very large box . . . we saw the *Traviata* it was so beautiful I liked it a great deal better than the *Sonambula* . . . Papa said he thought it dreadful dissipation but did not mind our going'.

Yet Kate was also a very serious girl. On her confirmation day, 1 April 1858, she breakfasted with her mother, read to herself in the morning and went out riding for an hour, before dressing in her muslin skirt, white jacket, white cloak and cap. She was confirmed with 290 others at St James's Piccadilly, an 'imposing ceremony for me and I felt quite sorry when it was over'. A year later she wrote in her diary of her hopes that her communions since then, strengthening her soul, 'may have done me good that I may be a little less sulky and less cold'. 'Help me', was her prayer on Easter Day 1859, 'to be loving, gentle, kind and sympathising and grant me courage to withstand all temptations for Christ's sake.' She was just seventeen.

The shock came the following year at Kate's coming out. She was going to the Duchesse d'Aumale's ball, she related to Lyulph: 'I enjoyed the last ball there so much I think I shall make my London debut at it.' 'I danced all the time', she told him afterwards, 'but I did find the young men so difficult to get on with and so little to say . . . I wish young men were more like you.' A clever girl at ease with her clever brother, it was dawning on Kate that society was an enormous bore. In the next weeks, she was attending lectures by

Professor Owen at the Geological Museum once a week; she was reading John Stuart Mill on *Liberty*; she immersed herself in the debates on Darwin's *Origin of the Species*. All these activities fed her mind. 'I do not think balls quite the perfection of amusement', Kate now confessed to Lyulph, 'I think I should get tired of them and it is so much trouble to talk to silent men.'

Back at Alderley in the summer, Kate was hardly satisfied by the country round of tennis, card games and billiards. She found croquet 'rather amusing but not as engrossing as everybody says it is'. She enjoyed her riding and faced up to the winter season of balls in Cheshire. 'I danced incessantly fourteen times and was very tired', she reported to Lyulph after one of them at Knutsford, 'and I cannot say that I thought it very delightful.' She confessed she had 'got out of the way of talking' and found it 'a trouble and a bore and there was no one interesting there'.

As she began to understand what her subordination meant, Kate struggled to ponder whether she could come to terms with it at all. She was suddenly wildly jealous of Lyulph, in the end writing to him resignedly on 20 November 1860:

> I think that only years settle one's mind . . . you think that we are in the world first and foremost and only to cultivate our intellect, our minds and faculties do you not? but I think that is not the object of life. I think it is to prepare ourselves for another and that it is only a state of trial and waiting.

Lyulph replied quickly, with little sympathy for her tirade. She was glad to receive his long letter, she wrote back to him, 'but I did not like seeing my opinions sent back to me and so commented upon'. Her brother's effortless superiority, confirmed by his Oxford years, had now become insufferable.

Yet Lyulph remained an essential intellectual companion, someone to whom Kate could let off steam. Staying with an aunt in Surrey before her second season in 1861, she told him how inert she found the household, how she longed to poke them all. Aunt Ally 'thinks that everybody's duty is to be quiet and retiring and unobtrusive as possible and contented'. 'I am so thankful I am not destined for this life', she told Lyulph, now brave and defiant.[59]

It probably helped the two exuberant and boisterous Rothschild girls that they had each other to quarrel with, as they went through these teenage years. Their home was at Aston Clinton in Buckinghamshire; from there they often visited their cousins at nearby Mentmore. Their broad education, entirely at home, was based upon visits by a series of tutors, besides the successive resident governesses who have already been mentioned. There was Mr Jeremy their maths teacher, Mr Callow their drawing master, Mrs Chappell, who taught them music, and the fine scholar Dr Kalisch, who instructed them in Hebrew and philosophy, always 'very merry' and affectionately called 'the little Cat'.

Annie, at thirteen, was driven by a desperate rivalry with her older sister, then fifteen, writing in her diary: 'I like to show my superiority in drawing over Connie, my superiority in playing some pieces of brilliancy, my superiority in my little knowledge of Hebrew . . . so difficult do I find it not to exult in the little I know.' Independent and wilful, Annie took immediate offence when Mama ruled that she must inspect all their letters to friends and relatives: 'I went to bed crying with vexation, could not sleep till late.' She told her mother that there would 'always be nonsensical things between young girls which cannot be related to everybody', but Mama refused to listen.

There were battles over how much riding they should do, with Annie making the running and revelling in their first hunt, though Papa was nervous about girls in the field. Constance related how, falling out with her in a German lesson, 'Annie got very rude and in the heat and impetuosity of the moment I gave her a slap on the face.' Then it was she who was in trouble. Mama, seeing her sister's red cheek, forbade Constance to come down that evening, 'when there was to be a little dinner party'.

So the Rothschild girls had their ructions. Their real feelings and sibling rivalry in the tense conditions of their teenage schoolroom are revealed by Annie's and Constance's diaries. Yet they were steadily learning about proper behaviour when it really mattered. The account of an exciting New Year's Day ball at Mentmore in 1859, driving there in the brougham, was ecstatic. Their cousins performed a play for the assembled company before dinner and dancing. 'Our white muslins looked very pretty and simple and I felt very pleased that Mama had ordered white instead of black', wrote Constance. 'We danced away till the end of the ball without sitting down once and returned after a most delightful evening at two o'clock.'[60]

The transition from a private to a public world was inevitably abrupt for a schoolroom girl, whatever measures had been taken to soften it. Restricted through early adolescence, she suddenly found herself expected to socialise and practise polite conversation in an accomplished manner. The metaphor for a girl's launching into the adult world, used over and over again, as Leonore Davidoff has noted, was the butterfly emerging from the chrysalis. All of a sudden, hair was put up and skirts came down. Presentation at court loomed as the mystical event par excellence. Destiny was real.[61]

It is hard now to capture the magic surrounding coming out. A story told by Mary Lucy catches something of its spell. Unwell and aged about fifteen, resting on the schoolroom sofa, she overheard a conversation between an adult visitor and her sisters, all of them believing her to be sleeping. 'How lovely she is. She will eclipse you all when she comes out', said the visitor.[62] Some families made something special of a daughter's seventeenth birthday, to mark the event. Georgina Grenfell of Taplow Court in Buckinghamshire arranged a special last schoolroom tea and a dance after it for her daughter Lina, including 'a lovely cake with her name and seventeen candles burning round it', on 7 November 1870. She had a headache with too much excitement, when it came to her first ball three weeks later. But 'it was partly for children', in her mother's account, 'and not very gay'. At one of the local balls that Christmas, 'Lina was very anxious for one more turn in the cotillon during which she fell down with a great crash'.[63]

One of the Brodrick girls, of Pepper Harrow in Surrey, writing in old age in the 1920s, stressed the dramatic change in life style that coming out involved. Woe betide the schoolroom girl at luncheon with guests, 'if she ventured to say more than "Yes" or "No" to remarks addressed to her – as for a joke of any sort it was unthinkable'. After years of the threat of being frozen into silence in company, suddenly to emerge from the schoolroom, where your word was law to the little ones, into a world where you were 'the youngest and least important personage' felt 'chilly'. But now, as a member of 'Society', it was a girl's duty to contribute her mite to the general pool. Moreover, the new joys of breakfasting at nine not eight, of sitting in the drawing room, of going to bed at the time grown ups did so, of being able to 'talk to who you please', were astonishing.[64]

These coming out seasons were a mad, head-turning, social whirl. 'I have little breathing time to spare from accounts of our perpetual dissipations', wrote Lucy Lyttelton in the midst of her 1859 season.[65] In her first season in 1849, Dorothy Townshend went to 50 balls, 60 parties, 30 dinners and 25 breakfasts.[66] Presented in May 1871, Lina Grenfell thought her first ball, the summer after coming out, 'paradise', according to her mother . She 'looked very nice', yet she hated the Queen's Ball because 'she did not dance', according to this account. By the end of her first season in July 1872, Lina had attended eighteen balls, 'had many other amusements and made some pleasant friends'. She did four seasons in all, marrying eventually at 27 in 1880.[67]

In essence nothing changed in the Victorian and Edwardian period. The social training of girls remained as it had been since 1700, a training in manners and accomplishments with the culmination of marriage in mind. Deportment, dancing, singing, perhaps a little painting, remained the central issues; intellectual interests, for the vast majority of girls, were at a discount. What changed was that, from early in the nineteenth century, house parties and private balls were where the young men and the girls of the upper and professional classes became acquainted, instead of, as previously with the chaperone in tow, at the opera, public concert or pleasure garden.

Clare Howard's Edwardian progress from the Bark Hart schoolroom in Orpington from 1897 to 1908, by way of Effingham House and her captaincy of hockey, to her coming out dance, at home in July 1911, encapsulates a programme of training for society which was by then time-honoured. Except that, in her case, she found her husband immediately. She caught the eye at her coming out dance of a young man from a respectable family that had grown up with hers, when his father was vicar of Orpington.[68] Unusually, a secret engagement, in 1912, was followed by a formal engagement a year later.

Clare found a husband in the normal manner from her own circle, in the last days of that secure and serene traditional world. This world, of tennis parties, weekend house parties and punts on the Thames for the Henley Royal Regatta, never fully recovered from the First World War. Its foundations were an unquestioned and apparently immovable social hierarchy and deeply rooted ideologies of paternalism and deference. At the core of upper-class mentality from 1600 to 1914 were incommensurable patterns of male and female upbringing. Young girls in these centuries, with no choice, learnt to behave in the manner that was expected of them.

PART III

CHILDREN

18

Personal Testimony

In this final section of the book, the meanings that a small number of children brought to five key aspects of their experience and upbringing are explored through their own words. These are unconstrained words. Children have spoken occasionally already in this book, but children always speak, and have always spoken, to parents or adult relatives with the objective of pleasing them. They wanted to satisfy expectations, as they were best able to understand these. Here, child diarists speak in secret to themselves, reflecting upon and pondering their passage through the early stages of life. Correspondence material between siblings, without adult constraint and, in one particular case, letters between sweethearts, with no one else looking over the shoulder, are also used in this final section of the book.

The material presented in the last chapters of this book is raw, powerful and authentic. Would that there was more of it, or that such testimony from the heart had survived from the period before 1750. At least this account may prompt efforts to discover new examples, from the period from 1750 to 1914, of the personal testimony of English teenagers. If the cast list in these final chapters is small, the importance and originality of their testimony is not in doubt.

By and large girls, not boys, kept diaries, as reflective exercises in self scrutiny. A very few exceptions, the male journals used here, can be easily accounted for. Tom Isham, the heir to a fine estate at Lamport in Northamptonshire, kept a diary in Latin for almost two years from 1 November 1671, 'by his father's command'. It is a small, neatly written volume, bound in contemporary leather with a gold border. Sir Justinian Isham had written to him on 21 November 1667, when he was ten years old:

> Tom – I like your writing well and would not have you take it as a trouble upon you, but go on with a line or two most days, setting down ordinary

matters as they happen about the house, garden, town, country or field, nothing can come amiss for you to turn into Latin: even your talk in the nursery which I am sure is not wanting upon several things with your brothers and sisters . . . all that shall come from you will be well taken by your affectionate father.

Young Tom needed a little more prompting to undertake the very prolonged piece of homework that his exacting father had in mind. The offer of a guaranteed six pounds a year in pocket money, as a reward for the labour of Latin diary keeping, besides his having to master the rest of the broad classical learning inculcated by his tutor, finally did the trick.[1]

William Gladstone never wrote about why he kept his laconic Eton journal in 1825 and 1826, but it can be assumed that his avid involvement in his own schooling and the teenage dawn of a deep introspection, which marked his adult character, are explanation enough.[2] Frederick Post, born in 1819 of Quaker parents, kept a diary at his father's prompting from 1832, when he was twelve, until his early death at sixteen. It consisted mainly of religious jottings. Looking it over when he was fourteen, he wondered whether he was 'wiser than when I began it'. His fifteenth birthday, he cogitated, marked an epoch when the pursuits of boyhood would be 'gradually relinquished and verge towards the man'. Frederick's diary, though cut short, approaches the pattern of diaries kept by much more numerous teenage girls, concerned about their souls, but also about their social performance.[3]

Teenage diary keeping among upper-class girls caught on gradually from the middle of the eighteenth century, usually with some parental encouragement. It often became a habit for life. 'I almost from childhood at the request of my father kept a constant journal', wrote Caroline Girle in 1757, beginning the first of what she called her 'annual journals' to have survived, at nineteen years old. It was 'generally allowed', she explained, 'that to acquire an easy manner of writing for the improvement of style nothing can be more beneficial than the frequent exercise of memory and pen'. She was determined to persist with her journalising: 'as some particular events, however trifling to others, one may wish to recollect the period of, I shall in this book set down everything of that kind as places or things'.[4] She then kept her 'annual journals' until 1808, when, after a long marriage to Philip Powys of Hardwick House at Whitchurch in Oxfordshire in 1762, she was 70 years old. Caroline's father encouraged her to keep separate journals when she travelled. Thus, in 1756, copying letters sent to him, she created a concise record of an excursion to Norfolk, at eighteen years old, he desiring her 'to write him an account of our tour and to be particular in my description of places and things that might give me entertainment'.[5]

Another case of fatherly initiative resulted in Harriet Spencer's childish but illuminating journal of the family's travels in Belgium and France on a long continental tour. Lord and Lady Spencer took their girls, Georgina and Harriet, together with the young male heir to Althorp, abroad from 31 July 1772 until the following year, when their return was delayed by her father's illness and an operation at Montpellier. The diary stops on 6 June 1773.[6]

The first diary kept by Sophia Baker, of Bayfordbury in Hertfordshire, was the small vellum-bound *Ladies' New Pocket Companion*, which offered left-hand pages week by week for memoranda and right-hand ones for accounts. Sophia's nicely written autograph on the first page is followed by her record that it was 'the gift of my dear Mama 1 January 1793'. She was eleven years old and began to make entries on some days most weeks. Her diaries, in the West Sussex Record Office, form an exceptional series: eight pocket book ones tell the story of the ups and downs of her teenage life, with just one volume in the mid-teens missing. All were presents from her mother. Her hand, never easy to read, announces the state of her emotions, varying from an expansive but untidy scrawl to a neatly presented orthography. Once the habit of diary keeping was well established, Sophia had no difficulty in continuing it throughout a long life, until she was 77 in 1857. She married, at 30 years old, John Trower of Findon in Sussex.

At nineteen in 1800, Sophia was well and truly launched on fashionable Georgian society, its pattern being richly indicated by her activities that winter. Yet, as two entries show, her diary still remained personal and domestic. On 25 October, in an unusual reference to menstruation, she noted, 'I stayed at home with the fashionable complaint. Papa read original Kit Kat letters and Addison letters.' In December 1800, she contracted pleurisy and charted her illness, mentioning that, when other family members attended a New Year's Eve ball, 'I stayed with Mama and my aunts not being stout enough.'[7]

Emily Shore, who lived from 1819 to 1839, was a compulsive journaliser.[8] Her journal, now published in full, is written throughout in a neat hand. She began it between her eleventh and twelfth birthdays and the original twelve volumes contain almost two thousand pages. It appears to be entirely impromptu.[9]

Lucy Lyttelton of Hagley Hall in Worcestershire is the most prominent of the diarists in this book because her account of her teenage life is so richly rewarding. She completed twelve volumes of her deeply personal diaries, over nearly 28 years, from the age of thirteen up to the assassination of her husband, Lord Frederick Cavendish, in Phoenix Park, Dublin, in 1882. She left them to her brother-in-law John Bailey, their future use being entirely at his discretion. Bailey's publication of an annotated edition, in 1927, brought this remarkable Victorian girl to public attention. Bailey's aim was, by selecting about one-fifth of the long stream of Lucy's diary entries, to exhibit 'her life and personality, both on her ordinary and, so to speak, on her extraordinary days'.[9]

The whole diary now rests, a somewhat intimidating sight on first acquaintance, in a large box at Chatsworth House. It seems doubtful whether anyone has read this whole story of an aristocratic woman's life, her perceptions often so touching and acute, across the central years of Queen Victoria's reign. This book, *Growing Up in England*, would not be quite the same without the teenage Lucy Lyttelton. Much of the original diary has been used here, as well as Bailey's edition. The childish hand and delightful pen and ink sketches of the first volumes turn this source into an archival historian's dream, poignantly revealing the texture and quality of social life in the Victorian past. Wallace Notestein, compiling his charming 'book of characters', under the title *English Folk*, in 1938 made Lucy better known. More recently, she has figured prominently in Sheila Fletcher's study of Lord Lyttelton's daughters, *Victorian Girls*, published in 1997.

Lucy's first diary, known as volume II, is a purple leather-bound volume, with 296 filled pages, begun on 7 August 1854, when she was on the edge of becoming fourteen. There are doodles at the end of the author out riding. The book probably came from her Mama; in the second diary, Lucy made an explicit pencil note, 'Mama gave me this book.' This second diary took her to 27 April 1858, when she was sixteen years and eight months. While she was keeping it, the huge Lyttelton family was at last completed, with the birth of little Alfred, number twelve, on 7 February 1857. The siblings and their birthdays were lovingly inscribed on her last page, by this most family minded of girls. This diary, of 351 pages, and the next one, of 385 pages, took Lucy close to her coming out, at one month off her eighteenth birthday. The next volume was then lost in a cab. Lucy sought to replace it, with a briefer account of the period from December 1860 to June 1862, when she was nearly 21.[11]

Our first hints of the place Lucy's journalising was taking in her developing young mind comes with entries at the end of 1855, which dealt reflectively with the family's Christmas, the sheer safety and security of Hagley life, the events in the Crimea and her feelings about time and eternity. 'There is no feast like Christmas', she wrote, describing how lovely the church across the path from the house looked, 'none that has its peculiar home feeling and kindliness.' 'The little filling-up-chink enjoyments, the mince pies and snap dragons and all the little jollities' rested in her mind. Yet so did the Fall of Sebastopol and every hour of her own life in the year nearly over that had 'been important': 'every day has its record', she noted. 'Will not the Everlasting wings still shield us', Lucy declared, making her first diary entry in a new year, 1856.

We can watch a Victorian teenager becoming emotionally deeper, more thoughtful, more mature with every month of her diary keeping. Lucy's heart was always on her sleeve. At fourteen, she was coming to see her life more and more in terms of a spiritual journey. She read her own attitude into her sister's mind too, remarking on Meriel's sixteenth birthday, 17 June, 'I trust each year will bring her Nearer.' Aunt Coque, Lord Lyttelton's sister, visiting Hagley in August 1856, gave Lucy an advance birthday present: 'a beautiful dark blue enamel locket with on it "Excelsior" and a star above it in diamonds'. 'Such grand thoughts', she meditated that day, 'are connected with the beautiful idea! It shall be my motto for life.'

Then, on 1 September 1856, she wrote, 'well I suppose I must finish off this dear old book . . . brimful of great events'. At home and abroad they ran through her mind: 'glorious Crimea victories, Albert and Nevy to boarding school, my first Queen's Ball and all my other dissipations, the coming of Miss Smith'. Finally, she made a list of the family's events, in her childlike view of the world, which were covered by this diary: 'two deaths (among those near to us), three marriages, two balls, two New Year servants' balls, two Queen's Balls, two birthdays of mine'.[12] Her diary had become precious and compulsive.

Lucy found making that full stop in the record of her life was awesome, so she began her new volume with reference to Aunt Coque's locket:

> Well! I wonder how many things will be in this book when I finish it, if I ever do so. I wonder what length of time will elapse ere I end it. I wonder whether when I end it I shall be able honestly to say that I have mounted Higher, come Nearer. Excelsior! My own motto. I like beginning this book on the first day of my birthday month, though no particular event characterised it beyond a cricket match, which, after a long contest, we lost.[13]

The second oldest of the Lytteltons, Lucy suddenly found new status and responsibility thrust upon her that month, for, with Albert and Nevy back to Eton at twelve and nearly eleven, and Meriel accompanying Papa and Mama on a trip to Wales, she was left as the senior child, in a depleted but massively staffed household. So, reflecting the hierarchy of family and servants, it was she before whom the maids all gathered daily in their clean aprons. 'I shall read prayers in the morning for a month: never have for so long before', her diary entry on 17 September read.

But Lucy had written a much longer entry on 5 September, the day that she was fifteen:

> My birthday again . . . I must think of the long chequered past with its lights and shades, its many sins and its many mercies. I must remember how all its events have been ordained by infinite Love and Wisdom to work together for my good . . . I must set out on my sixteenth year working and praying for he is always with me – whether my life continues one bright stream of blessed happiness or clouds come as they must sooner or later. Either way there will be abundant cause for gratitude, as it is I must wait and pray.[14]

A year later, following her mother's death in August 1857, Lucy read that diary entry and wondered if her faith was now shaken. But she decided that she did have the strength to 'say Amen to my words of trust' last year. It is clear, in this instance, just how important her diary was in this girl's life journey. It represented, by its intimacy and its privacy, a thread of continuity from week to week, month to month. It was sobering, but somehow comforting, to write that 'it might seem as if I had had a presentment'.[15]

Louisa Bowater, who married into the well-known Knightley family of Fawsley in Northamptonshire, kept her diaries from 1856 until a fortnight before her death in 1913. There are 45 volumes of them in the Northamptonshire Record Office. She requested her friend Julia Cartwright to publish extracts, at her discretion, after her death. *The Journals of Lady Knightley of Fawsley* was duly published, under her editorship, in 1915. Cartwright, in her Introduction, painted Louisa's diaries as the 'frankest, most guileless of records'. She noted that she was a woman 'bred in the narrowest of court circles', who 'naturally inherited the strong prejudices and prepossessions of her class'. She explained how Louisa took up her destined role, living a long life as the lady of a Midlands manor, horrified by the advance of democracy, riding to hounds and working for many worthy local causes, such as the education of the poor and the temperance movement.[16]

Louisa Bowater's early diaries are substantial leather-bound volumes. She began the first of them on her fourteenth birthday, 25 April 1856; the fifth took her up to her twentieth birthday in 1862. 'I think one's birthday an excellent day on which to commence any new undertaking', she wrote that first day, 'and today I am going to begin a journal.' She would make it 'a receptacle for interesting conversations', with her governess Agnes Lentz, for 'odds and ends out of books, as well as daily events'. She is the only one of these diarists who recorded ever showing her diary to an adult. Interestingly, this was neither her Mama nor the faithful Agnes.

That first summer of Louisa's regular journalising, Agnes went back to Germany for her holiday. She was briefly replaced by a French Mademoiselle. Sunday 3 August was a typical summer day, filled with attending church and Mademoiselle's lessons, before and after church. Louisa was beginning to feel some confidence in the visiting young Frenchwoman's acceptance of her, after about six weeks in her company every day. She plucked up her courage on a lovely evening: 'after dessert we sat out and I read a bit of my journal aloud'. 'She says it is a good one and I am so glad', Louisa commented.

Louisa had also self-consciously adopted her diary, just as Lucy Lyttelton did at much this time, as an aide memoire for her improvement. This is explicit on 23 August 1856, when she arrived at her grandmother's home, Sotterley Park in Suffolk, for a seaside holiday. Noting that evening that she had just been 'arranging' the room, she wrote out four resolutions about her bedroom, declaring that she asked God to strengthen her in keeping them: 'Never neglect my prayers. Never to do in it what I would not do if Mama or Agnes were there. To make it a place for serious reflection and to make self examination a regular habit. To keep it very tidy.' She signed her fourteen-year old resolutions 'Louisa Mary Bowater'.

Introspection, encouraged by her governess, grew on Louisa, a serious only child. In December 1856, she recorded 'a fit of perverseness', which led to 'a long conversation with Agnes: she says and I feel that she is quite right that I do not think and feel half as much as with the opportunities I enjoy I might about religion'. She was told to make more use of her journal for studied self-reflection and said she was determined to follow this advice. There is, however, little evidence that she did so systematically. At the year's end, her self-assessment was a sober one: 'God grant me to spend 1857 better – more humbly as to my own strength, more courageously towards the world, less selfishly towards my friends.' When this book was full, Louisa spoke of 'parting from an old friend'. 'I flatter myself it has improved of late', she wrote. She planned to exchange her next diary with the one her friend Edith was keeping, 'as a sort of spur to perseverance'.[17] But in April 1858 she was less pleased with herself, even ready to use the diary to berate herself:

> One's sixteenth birthday is no joke. I am no longer a child and not only must my rough childish ways be left off I must strive earnestly to find my work and do it . . . no nonsense now . . . my one bright dawn is over and for anything else time enough. Still be my prayers Lord give me earnestness and courage.

Opening her fourth diary on 3 July 1858, Louisa wrote about making it 'more a criterion of inward progress'. The 'great rush' of her first summer season at sixteen was over. It was a time for preparation for 'that great turning point in life confirmation'. On the first page of this diary she wrote the word 'Excelsior'. Thus two diaries bring together the minds of two young girls who did not then know each other: Lucy and Louisa. 'Excelsior', the notion of going higher, carried a deep religious and moral ring. At the same time, it summarised everything that has been discussed in this book about the training of female teenagers. 'Excelsior' was about self-sacrifice, about dedication of one's life, about being good, about accomplishments as well as earnestness and duty. It spelt out a narrow but compelling form of gender construction that reached its apogee as a Victorian ideology of girlhood.[18]

Emma Trotter began the first of a long series of diaries, expressing preoccupation with her spiritual life, on her eighteenth birthday, 7 September 1859, 'thinking it may be an assistance to me as showing what progress I may make in my journey through life'. For her own eyes alone, she intended that her diary would be 'a means of keeping me humble by showing how fearfully I fail in the smallest duties'.[19] Eva Knatchbull was another Victorian girl prompted into diary keeping. On her twelfth birthday, she began the little notebook now in the Kent Record Office, relating that 'Mama has given me this book to write in it anything that I like which happens to me.'[20]

French teenagers from noble and middle-class families began to write personal diaries during the late eighteenth century, as English ones did. There also, maternal prompting provided the crucial impetus. Colin Heywood suggests that some girls moved from 'initial resentment of maternal pressure' to 'a feeling of true ownership', such as one senses overwhelmingly in reading English diaries by girls like Lucy and Louisa. Yet Heywood, in his study *Growing Up in France,* rejects the French diaries as authentic material for the study of female mentality. He does accept that they 'give a detailed account of efforts made by the girls to assimilate the Catholic model of femininity', but is also convinced that 'apparently mothers and teachers might routinely read such diaries'.[21]

It is not clear how the documentation has led Heywood to this conclusion, but it has precluded the kind of comparative analysis of French and English teenage diaries which might have been informative. It seems as clear as daylight that English teenage diarists opened their hearts, in the privacy of bedrooms, writing journals which they regarded as holding a confessional status. They would never have dreamt of showing a diary to Mama or Papa. When Louisa read a bit of her diary to Mademoiselle that summer evening, she doubtless chose the section she would reveal with care. This was a deliberate approval-seeking tactic, with someone she did not know very well.

Letters from schoolchildren to their parents or adult relatives are taken to be inappropriate to this part of the book, as crafted productions designed to please or placate. But one file of letters that has come to light from the 1770s does seem to fall into a different archival category. These are letters written to young George Lord Bruce at public school from his erstwhile prep school friends. Unconstrained by the adult eye, they do seem to possess a kind of authenticity that other surviving schoolboy letters home seem to lack. They are used here to illuminate the world of Georgian schooling.[22]

Teenage love affairs that ran true as far as marriage, with sexual initiation of some kind along the way, were highly unusual in Georgian, Victorian and Edwardian England. When they occurred, their documentation is unlikely to survive. One such love affair is a story that can be told here. For a whole year Reggie Chenevix Trench, at 24, maintained his secret courtship of the teenager Clare Howard, one of the schoolroom girls discussed above. There is no question of the authenticity, as personal testimony, of the letters through which, by and large, their touching romance in 1912 and 1913 was conducted, under the eye of a conservative Kentish household which held propriety as law.

Clare kept both sides of their correspondence, when she lost her husband, who was killed on the Western Front in 1918. It stayed with her through a long life, taken from home to home, in a tin trunk, which she occasionally opened in old age.[23] She died in 1989. This love story contributes to the epilogue of this book, revealing the mores of country house society on the eve of the Great War in extraordinary and fascinating detail.

19

Home

Around twenty children's diaries used for this book reveal much about the homes in which these children grew up. None tell of deeply unhappy homes; some portray tense and demanding ones, while some suggest relatively relaxed ones, where children developed without undue demands upon them. We learn much here about gendered upbringing. If the foremost figures in children's young lives were their parents, this does not mean that upper-class children saw much of them when they were at home each day. The convention that schoolroom girls attended on Mama downstairs, in the company of their governess, for an hour in the early evening was so well established that diarists never wrote about it. Nor did they describe other routines, taken as read, like morning prayers and lesson time. It was, understandably, the exceptional, the emotional, the exciting or moving events of children's lives that filled diary pages. This is particularly so with regard to domestic life.

The intensity and power of parental authority, the parental presence in the home in itself, structured and made sense of growing up. Diarists invariably wrote of Papa and Mama with respect, sometimes with awe, often with delight, sometimes with disquiet and qualms. Mothers, we have seen, usually elicited great deference and esteem. Mothers and daughters were often close but, special circumstances apart, it was a closeness more taken for granted than needing regular comment. Four relationships between teenagers and fathers, treated in diaries, are especially illuminating.

Correspondence between Sir Justinian Isham, a notable scholar with steadfast ambitions for all his children in learning and his eldest boy Tom, in 1670–1671, just before Tom started his celebrated diary, illuminates their pleasant and mutually respectful relationship. While Tom was studying at home at Lamport, under a tutor, with his brothers Justinian and John, their father spent time in London, where he required regular reports. 'I doubt not but all of you go on in your studies as I directed', he wrote, signing himself 'your affectionate father' on 28 May 1670, 'and shall gladly hear how far you have proceeded'. Tom should not reply 'in haste to spoil your hand which I would have you careful of'. His response, in fact, was immediate, was very neatly penned and fully informative. 'We have almost conquered half the first Iliad, in which although we proceed slowly yet we do it with delight and perfectness', he assured his father. Work on Greek and Latin grammars went on routinely. Their reading matter began to bore the Isham boys, Tom confessed, requesting Tully's longer *Epistles* and some histories of Roman times as fresh material.[1]

Sir Justinian's letters at this time sought to spur his boys on, with the promise that friends of his would shortly be visiting Lamport to try them out. 'You are now bound in reputation to make good what is so largely reported', he insisted on 1 January 1671.[2] While earnestly driving on his sons, Sir Justinian was at the same time a fond father, who worried in each letter, prompting reciprocal effort on the boys' part. 'I hope your continuance of all good healths and that you have an especial care not to overheat yourselves this weather', he wrote on 11 July 1671.[3] The 1661 edition of *Euclid's Elements of Geometry*, with manuscript notes in Sir Justinian's hand, is still in the library at Lamport. This is the book with which he began personally to inculcate the subject in his boys that autumn. 'My father first taught me the way to draw parallel lines and to divide a straight line', Tom noted on 1 November. 'We attacked the fifth proposition of Euclid', was his news of the day just a year later. Sir Justinian also tutored both his boys and girls in arithmetic himself.[4]

The very existence of Tom's diary, kept in Latin, is a monument to his father's dedication to the classics. But its enormous importance, as a document in seventeenth-century social history, rests principally on what it tells us about the training of the heir to a gentleman's estate. At fourteen and fifteen, Tom was often his father's companion in the day-to-day business of managing the estate. Hedges and ditches had to be inspected. Oversight of the planting of apple trees in the sycamore walk was very much the business of the squire and his eldest son. Matter-of-fact narrative entries conceal the boys' constant learning, out and about on and around the estate. Catching partridges together on 20 August, 1672 they 'saw the servants of Sir William Haslewood on the same errand, so we told them not to come any further on our land'. Tom was acquiring the family's values. He was coming to understand his personal role as the eldest in protecting the interests of the Isham family.

His family mattered in Northamptonshire, so Tom's teenage social circle, as the heir, was his father's circle, ranging from the recusant gentleman Ferdinando Poulton at Desborough to the Spensers at Althorp, the Montagus at Boughton and Lord Rockingham at Rockingham. He learnt about his father's local position as a Justice of the Peace and his responsibilities at petty sessions. With Sir Justinian, he visited the newly discovered medicinal spring nearby and patronised the races at Harleston and Rothwell. He imbibed the genteel and patriarchal values of this society almost subconsciously. His mother, hardly mentioned in the diary, only came in to his account as one of the party on social occasions.

Tom was imbibing the gentry's values, for example, when he noted his father's action in letting some men go free on 6 May 1672, who were charged with stealing a tree from his neighbour Sir Edward Nicholls's wood. The joy that Sir Justinian felt on behalf of this friend that day was great, since, after seven daughters, his wife had at last given birth to a son. Nicholls was at first unable to believe the news, such was his despair in the matter. For Sir Justinian, the tree paled into insignificance beside his friend's patriarchal achievement.

Similarly, when Dr Joseph Malden of Northampton requested that 'a couple of rabbits be sent me over', begging 'the Lord to bless you and your honourable Lady and your noble offspring', in January 1673, Tom noted his father's compliance with the request. There was a spirit of *noblesse oblige* which was taken for granted in, and animated, this gentry world.[5]

Mary Chorley's diary, used by Amanda Vickery, is another intimate personal testimony at a time when such documents are rare.[6] She lived, as we have seen, with her aunts the Miss Fords in Lancaster. Beginning her diary after her mother had died just before she was ten, Mary was visited by her father at her home, on 22 January 1776: 'much rejoiced to see my Papa this evening'. His invitation to a dinner guest and inclusion of her and her sister in the party the next day was eagerly remarked, as was his decision, at which she 'much rejoiced', to stay another day on the 29th. He gave her a handsome ten shillings, real wealth to a child then, at his leaving. His letter after a fortnight, in February, mentioning how 'he thinks me improved in my writing', was carefully noted by Mary. Her letter to him in March was consciously motivated by her hopes of more praise on this count. In July, Papa took the girls on an exciting week's holiday in Derbyshire. Beginning to work herself a cap in November, she reflected that she hoped 'to get it done' for his next visit to her Lancaster home.

Mary missed her father badly the next winter, writing of his absence in January and again in February 1778. But she was happy to receive a parcel of oranges and grapes, luxuries that he had the means to obtain in Liverpool. A letter from her papa on 3 March marked her 'unexpressable pleasure', inviting her to Liverpool. 'Found my Papa very well', Mary noted on 11 May. She worried about him when he was ill with gout in June, wishing he lived closer to Lancaster. A long entry recorded her emotions: 'My Papa has given me three guineas as indulgence and encouragement I receive to be a good girl. I wish I may be upon my guard in my behaviour to match the great blessings heaped upon me. Grant that he may long enjoy health and peace.'

Mary Chorley's progress in politeness was the quid pro quo for her father's love and care for her. Her aunts were pleased with her work that summer of 1778, giving her the confidence to bask in her father's approval again on a short visit to Liverpool in November. 'Oh I wish my Papa would come over', she pined on her thirteenth birthday, 1 May 1779. Her yearning was soon relieved by news that he was coming. She was 'so delighted' at his arrival on 4 June, writing the following day, 'this morning went down street with my dear Papa: says he will send me a pair of buckles – a sweet day'. He was as good as his word to his faithful daughter. The buckles arrived on 24 June. 'I think they are the most beautiful ones I ever saw', she noted emotionally. The story breaks off here. Her father had retained her trust, as Mary learnt about growing up mostly in his absence, living in an all-female household run by two aunts, with her sister as company.[7]

Emily Shore, her biographer Barbara Gates has written, was 'a prodigious young polymath'. She kept her diary from 5 July 1831 to 24 June 1839, just before her death at the age of nineteen. 'It offers', Gates concludes, 'the life story of the coming of age of both a young woman and of an early Victorian intellect – one without benefit of formal education.' Emily's father was Thomas Shore, an unbeneficed divine, writer and educator, who taught private pupils at home, alongside his own children. Her sister Arabella testified to the eagerness with which Emily assimilated her father's lessons, making 'her whole existence a happy schoolroom'.[8] Papa is always in the background of a journal that was basically an extraordinary account of a young girl's unslakeable thirst for learning. His daily encouragement, interest and advice, though, was a crucial source of her motivation.

On 31 October 1831, 'Papa took us all to see certain operations in glass, performed by a man who travels about.' He had come to her Bedfordshire town of Potton to exhibit, 'for a day or two', the baskets, candlesticks, birds and horses that he made in glass. Predictably, Emily noted down in detail how he worked, sitting at a table with 'before him a little furnace'. On 16 February 1832, Emily discovered Spenser's poetry, chancing upon an extract from his 'Hymn of Heavenly Love'. 'I went to Papa's study and read the whole poem, which is most exquisitely beautiful and is perhaps equal to anything Milton ever wrote.' Papa's copy of Spenser's works, she noted, was 'a very old edition printed in the time of Queen Elizabeth'.[9] When her father read to her the whole of Shakespeare's *Julius Caesar* during the evening of 28 August 1832, she recorded her response to the play: 'I like it extremely; it is very fine, and the characters remarkably well drawn. Brutus is my favourite; the scene I like best is where he and Cassius quarrel and are reconciled.'

An account in Emily's diary entry for 21 January 1833 shows that both parents were fully involved in a severe household routine at Potton. It was her mother who heard the children on Sundays 'say a hymn of Watts', which we have previously learnt, each saying one verse'. 'I believe none of us are taught anything which is not thoroughly explained', Emily commented, thinking about her mother's catechising, 'and I am afraid this is too unusual.' Reading to Mama, sandwiched between time on her own after dinner and needlework, was a normal part of the weekday routine, as well as Greek or Latin with Papa. At tea time, she, with her brothers and sisters, normally listened to their parents conversing, as they sat by the fire. This was how she imbibed an understanding of the political climate of the day. On 25 January, for example, 'Papa began by condemning the idea that the Duke of Wellington's military prowess ought to exempt him from dislike on account of his political opinions.'

When her mother had a night of intense pain just after this, on 28 January, it seemed that Emily's world might collapse:

> After breakfast Papa called us together and spoke to us at some length . . . he now deemed it proper to inform us that Mama's life was very uncertain and would probably not last long. It is hardly necessary to add that Papa's words made a deep impression on us and that he left us in tears. Indeed I cannot think what we could do without Mama; it seems to be that if she died I should never be happy again. At ten o'clock the doctors came; and at about twelve I went upstairs to see Mama . . . she looked very pale and ill. I kissed her and then left the room and finished hearing the children's lessons, about which I was before employed.

But Emily's alarm decreased, as her mother steadily gained strength over the next weeks. In April, she was reading them Sir Walter Scott's *Lord of the Isles*, her children gathered round her again; in July 1833 she took an evening walk with them on the heath.[10]

Louisa Bowater, unusually for those days an only child, wrote an account of her father, with whom she was very close, in 1908. She was then herself 66 years old. General Sir Edward Bowater, born in 1787, went through the whole Peninsular War and was wounded at Waterloo. One of William IV's equerries in 1830, he was given Thatched House Lodge in Richmond Park by Queen Victoria, when Louisa was one year old in 1843. Looking back through her journals, kept all her life, she felt that her father had dominated her existence and her life story:

In spite of occasional displays of severity, my father was the kindest of men and my happiest hours were spent in his company. He was never tired of recalling his military experiences and telling me stories of Wellington's campaigns. On the 18th of June we always drank in solemn silence to the Great Duke and the heroes of Waterloo.

The rides she took with her father in Richmond Park and on Ham Common on 'Princess', his 'gentle but spirited old mare', stayed in her memory as the 'greatest pleasure' of her teenage years.[11]

When her Papa was home from waiting at court, he would often play bagatelle and chess with Louisa. She thrilled over beating him sometimes. He took her to one of her first dances in the summer of 1856, when she was fourteen. Louisa was 'highly delighted' to receive the invitation at the last minute but she 'did lessons as usual':

Papa approved of my dress and we jumped into the brougham and drove to 36, Charles Street, Berkeley Square. Papa went in with me but only stayed a few minutes. It was fearfully stiff at first but the dancing soon began . . . There were only three boys. I did not dance with any of them. Home at 10.15.

'I told Papa what I had done', she noted, describing the quadrilles, Lancers, Sir Roger and cotillons that she had danced.

A long entry in her diary on 15 September that year recorded Louisa's excitement, when her father joined the family at Sotterley Park in Suffolk, her mother's home, where the family spent holidays with young cousins. She described his present, returning from his vacation shooting in Scotland: 'he has brought us each a complete Scotch costume, dress, petticoat, stockings, scarf and boots'. She felt 'it is very kind of him and I am much pleased'.

Revelling in her Papa's attention those next weeks, she went on long walks with him. She 'poked about on Princess with Papa' on 18 September; she 'got up very early and made Papa's breakfast, as he was going to Norwich', the next morning. On 25 October, she went out shooting under his guidance: 'it was my day and I had great luck, twenty-four rabbits, a hare and a leveret. I shall pocket one pound which is very satisfactory'. When, once only, there was a note of disquiet, this reflected her hurt pride. On 30 October, she put on her Scotch dress to show him: they had a contented outing in the carriage to visit friends. After dessert with her parents as usual, they played backgammon and this was when he spoke harshly about her riding. The scrawled page that night betrayed Louisa's emotions: 'Papa blamed my riding and said some words which cost me bitter tears as soon as I was alone. But he shall retract them before he goes in waiting. I will ride well so it don't signify.' She found their last breakfast together on 17 November, before he left to return to court, upsetting. 'I do not like it at all, nor does he', she summarised.

The General, proud of his teenage daughter, loved taking Louisa out. In her fourth journal for the year 1858, she noted a very special day on 2 August: 'to United Service Institution in Whitehall Place with Papa, who explained the model of the field of Waterloo and showed me where he was wounded'. The Sotterley summers were always glorious: his time there was the highlight of them. On 6 September 1859, Louisa wrote, 'I felt about five o'clock dear Papa's arms round me, his kiss on my brow and his parting charge "take care of Mama" in my ear.' In the next days, she devoted herself to drawing and 'playing duets with Mama'. But her mother never comes alive in her diaries in the same way as her father does.[12]

Two mother and daughter relationships are documented in detail by the diarists Sophia Baker and Lucy Lyttelton, one tempestuous and apparently more placid by turns, the other deep and reverent throughout. Sophia Baker's diaries illuminate her dealings with her mother at intervals, between the ages of eleven and nineteen. The strains which show may relate to expectations placed by an ambitious mother on the eldest of her four daughters, born between two sons who were apples of her eye and four more boys. She launched Sophia on Hertfordshire society with 'a very pleasant ball at home' in January 1793. She was taking her with her on local visits to dine and 'drink tea' that spring, while her Papa was often in London. She attended Montem at Eton, with her parents and brother William, on 21 May.[13] 'I began to dine with Mama and Papa for good', Sophia related with pride on 16 June. Very young for such activities, she seemed to be showing her paces.[14]

Then came the difficult period, in 1796 and 1797, when Sophia's teenage rebellion was in full spate. This was negotiated, it seems, with some patience by Mama, with help from the governess, Miss Allen. 1798 appears to have been a turning point. As Sophia learnt more self-control, her temper tantrums were less prolonged. In January on successive days she was 'dolorosa', was 'in disgrace with Mama for having been out of temper last night' and 'was forgiven by Mama'. Yet the next week the domestic round resumed its normal tempo, with 'a pleasant musical party', drawing and singing.

As she began to appreciate her mother's supportive role as her chaperone, Sophia became more sympathetic to her and less self-absorbed. Left at Bayfordbury with the governess and little ones, she noted on 16 January 1799, 'Mama came down to our joy and surprise as we did not expect her till Monday'. Her father was ill in London, she was relieved at her bringing a 'good account' of him. The birth of an eleventh child in the family on 8 May brought out a protectiveness towards her mother. 'Dear Mama was churched and took an airing', she chronicled on 2 June. But there were tensions again, as we have seen, over Mademoiselle's dismissal and some ructions in her debutante season in 1800.

A remark by Meriel Lyttelton, in the autobiography she wrote in adulthood, summarises the family dynamics at Hagley Hall in the 1850s. The trials of schoolroom life there mattered little, she said, because Sundays were special. The feeling of 'perfect happiness and intimacy with our mother and father' then took hold, 'because we were more with them' than during the week. The Lyttelton children, Meriel asserted, were never ill at ease with their parents. Papa in Meriel's portrait, was 'very stern with himself', a strong Tractarian, never admitting to being tired or missing his meetings. Yet, though she interfered little directly between the children and their governess, Lucy wrote, it was Mama who set the tone of their crowded home: 'there was no fear of getting cowed and spirit-broken while we had that gentle and loving care over us'.[15]

Powerful as the patriarchal figure was, it emerges strikingly from Lucy's diary that in a great house, with a full complement of both sons and daughters, female influence pervaded. This was the case from Lady Lyttelton downwards, through visiting aunts, daughters and governesses who came and went, to the housekeeper Elly. This was essentially a female world, and once boys were off to Eton they knew and felt it as such, as they came and went. From an early age, the children's expectation was of male performance in the world and of care, love and cosseting at home. Lucy quickly fell into this with her 'hip, hip hooray' when the holidays began and her conscientious letter writing in term time. Charles was home from Eton, she noted in December 1854, 'with only a wretched second prize; he has been idle'. 'Boys back to school' was the diary entry, above all others, that punctuated the domestic round and changed the tempo of daily life.[16]

Lucy adored belonging to a large family. How strange, she thought, that some disliked the idea. 'I am sure Papa and Mama are happier with their eleven than many people with their one or two', she wrote in July 1855, reflecting on the 'happy home feeling' that the 'unbroken number of faces beloved and known round one in the same house' provided.[17] The tragedy for the Lyttelton family was that no one felt able to tell Lord Lyttelton about the doctor's firm pronouncement, after Edward was born in 1855, that the strain a twelfth pregnancy would put on on his wife's heart might kill her. It did, in August 1857. Lucy's account, written when she was not quite sixteen, about her mother's failing health, her decline and her early death is a moving record of loving attachment, shown in her last days, by a deeply empathetic second daughter.[18]

Lucy already sensed her mother's physical frailty at the time of Edward's birth. 'Mama went up to London for her eleventh confinement. God bring her safe through it!' she wrote on 22 July 1855.[19] Hearing the bare facts of Papa's announcement, she entreated the maids who sent the news 'to know how Mama was'. 'A thrill of fright came over me and I thought that something had perhaps gone wrong.' When another note arrived, with 'My lady very well' attested, her heart, she wrote in her diary, leapt with relief.[20] Listing the family's 'mercies' after a long period away from Hagley, at their London home on 31 May 1856, Lucy included, 'Mama bearing up so well.' She did not know that Mary was pregnant again.[21]

The birth of Mary Lyttelton's twelfth child, at Hagley on 7 February 1857, required the longest entry Lucy made in her diary in years. Told by a maid, on waking, that the birth was imminent, 'I wrote out a short prayer for the little ones', which they all said before dressing. Seeing the 'small pink scrap with quantities of brown hair', peeping into Mama's room and hearing her 'dear weak voice', Lucy quickly broke down: 'a gushing overpowering sense of thankfulness and relief that made the tears grateful'. In the schoolroom that day, it was Lucy, not Miss Smith, who took charge. Three children not at school, Lavinia, May and Arthur, 'knelt while I read, with such an egg in my throat, some earnest thanksgivings which were great comforts to us'.[22]

Mary Lyttelton's recovery after Alfred's birth was slow and faltering. Back at Hagley after a tour of Sussex and Kent in June, Lucy confided her concern to her diary. Mama, she understood, 'must be kept quiet . . . free from any worry'. She now took charge. Mary responded by letting herself slip into the care of her stalwart fifteen-year old. For so many years, riding out with Mama when she was stronger, or drives with her in the pony carriage, had been times of special delight.[23] Now, Lucy realised that Mary could no longer 'bear the rough jolting of the pony carriage'. She was thrilled, though, with a new light carriage that she started to drive her out in each afternoon. Mama, she noted on 27 June, 'trusts me quite alone to take care of her'.

By the middle of July, Mary's breathlessness meant that she had to be carried upstairs. Spending time alone with Lucy on 19 July, with the others at dinner, 'she looked so piteously at me'. It became impossible for the teenager to face writing her diary as usual, in the weeks of 'nursing' and 'watching' as she called them. But, at intervals, it was a receptacle into which she poured her emotions. On 31 July, she noted her mother's 'serene bright spirit shining through the cloud with patience and peace that passes understanding'.

On 12 August the smile of greeting, Lucy found, as the children came and went from Mary's bedroom, was still constant. She was not looking at, but she now understood, the 'darkening future'. She was carrying the family emotionally, complete as it now was, with all the boys home for the school holidays: 'It wrings my heart bitter by writing all this. The four boys with their entire unrealisation. She sees them continually. They were very good and quiet always in the house but she loved hearing them.'

With the end near, Mary Lyttelton 'kissed all her twelve poor dear children and said goodbye'. Lucy and the elder ones took communion with her. Her mother's death, on 17 August, released a tide of emotion. Lucy found solace in entrusting this to her diary: 'Oh she has gone away. Oh the light of home and life has gone never to see again. Oh my joyous childhood. Oh our bright years . . . It's all over, it's all past, gone quite away and nothing left but the bright track of memory gleaming over the dark sea.'

'I cannot speak of Papa' was all that Lucy said in her diary about her father as she sought to comfort him.[24] For both she and Meriel, thrust the next years into taking on the mantle of mothering boys at school and little ones in the nursery, schoolroom training was cut short. 'God grant that we may act upon the remembrance of that day and service', wrote Meriel in her diary, after her mother's funeral on 24 August.[25] She reckoned, looking back in old age, that she learnt more about life in three years, between this catastrophe and her own marriage at twenty years old, 'than in all the schoolroom years'.[26]

Sophia Baker and Lucy Lyttelton were probably typical of many English girls across these centuries, for whom the happiness of family life rested on the togetherness of aunts and grandparents who visited and of brothers, whether younger than them or older, coming home. This is the constant refrain of both their diaries. Both belonged to large families, families with ten and twelve children respectively. Both were near the top, Lucy merely having Meriel as her senior, and Sophia looking up to William and Edward, respectively two and three years older than she.

Sophia adored her naval brother Ned, close to her in age and sent young to sea. She recorded 'great rejoicings' in October 1793, when both her big boys were home, William on brief respite from Eton and Ned, who had been collected by Papa from Portsmouth. In a few weeks he was off on another voyage. A diary entry the next February spelt out her concern about her brother's well-being: 'dear Papa returned from Portsmouth with the joyful news of dear Ned's being quite well and in good spirits'. After alarm about Papa being detained by fog when he sailed for Plymouth to fetch Ned, his 1794 summer homecoming at Bayfordbury, in June, delighted Sophia. 'What a happy party', she wrote on 30 June. On 2 July there was dressing up, involving 'a great deal of contrivance', to surprise visiting aunts: 'I was Mother Shipton, Charlotte Nobody, little Robert, just breeched, was a Jew and baby Caroline was a flower girl.'

Some of the family visited Ned's ship on his return to Portsmouth. Sophia wrote to him for his birthday in September, anxiously following his progress up the ranks. In November 1795, when he had been at sea a long time and

was expected at Portsmouth, 'our hopes', Sophia noted, were 'cruelly disappointed by letters from dear Ned at St Domingo'. A few days later, Papa sent
on a 'nice long letter' that he had received from Ned in London. It was 'full of
affection for us all'. The terrible news of Ned's having been lost at sea reached
Bayfordbury on 23 January 1797, in a letter describing 'our darling deceased
Edward's death and burial'. His writing box was returned in April. It was
opened in a solemn family ceremony: 'oh how we miss our darling Edward',
wrote Sophia.[27]

It was predictable that William, a year older than Ned and previously less
close to Sophia, should quickly, with the loss of her previously favourite
brother, have replaced him in her affections. Entering the navy on leaving
Eton, his brief visits on leave in 1798 to 1800 lit up her life. 'William rode out
with us,' she wrote on 4 October 1800, the week before he sailed from
Yarmouth to Hamburg: 'Oh how precious is every hour with him now he is
going abroad.' 'Rode with dearest William (our last ride) round the grounds',
was her entry on 11 October.[28]

Four boys in quick succession had followed Lucy Lyttelton at Hagley, the
oldest, Charles, only a year behind her, then Albert and Nevy, the last Spencer
nearly six years younger. The pattern of their boarding school life structured
Lucy's existence. 'The return of the holidays' broke her dull schoolroom
routine.[29] Conversely, the diary entry 'boys back to school' was a marker of the
end of fun and games. Lucy soon understood the strain that prep school and
later Eton put on the boys. Nevy 'is very low as he always is', she noted in
September 1856. 'The poor little boys went.' The day, she declared, 'seemed a
blank'.[30] 'Niobissimus', Lucy wrote on 21 April 1857, employing elegant classical similitude, in the family's slang for persons dissolved in tears. This was
the day that Nevy and Spencer returned to their prep school at Gedington for
the summer term. 'Poor dear old fellows', she lamented.[31]

Lucy applauded the way that her brothers managed their boarding life;
they were always heroes in her eyes. Albert showed 'his usual placid spirits
without even any apparent bathing feel at the impending examination', she
reflected in January 1857. The Eton entrance tests, so fully prepared for by
prep school work, struck her as 'of all awful things the most terrible'. Charles
was 'rather low at the last moment', when the 1857 Easter holidays ended:
'what he hates is going from Hagley'. 'How I miss them', she declared, on the
departure of three brothers to school in April 1858.[32]

When a remarkable innings by Charles in an Eton cricket match earned
mention next day in the *Morning Post*, Lucy related the event, adding three
exclamation marks.[33] By January 1859, there were four Lytteltons in the Eton
phalanx. 'Maximus, major, minor and minimus', Lucy wrote of the brothers
she looked up to and admired, even if they were her juniors in age.[34] She

revelled in a visit on the Fourth of June that year, but was shocked at what she was told about boys getting drunk on the river: 'I'm so glad our boys are dry bobs, in spite of the arrowy boats and brilliant dresses, only I trust cricket will look up under Charles's captaincy and not be everlastingly beaten by Harrow.'[35]

Masculinity, these girls accepted, was all about fending for oneself in the demanding, competitive and sometimes harsh worlds of the navy or of public schools. They glimpsed the world of school for themselves, in their best frocks on high days and holidays, on occasions like Sophia's visit to Montem at Eton in May 1793. Eva Knatchbull visited her brother Ned, then seventeen, at Eton on 6 June 1874, describing the day in her diary. 'He was on his best behaviour all the time', showing her his room, 'a queer little place' where, in bravado, she cut her name on the cupboard door. 'Ned ordered his fag about', she related, 'and made him bring the tea and everything which he did very well.'[36] Girls always hoped for prizes, brought home by boys as evidence of achievement. Lucy Lyttelton mentioned them. They learnt, without questioning their own immunity from it, of male treatment such as beatings, enumerated by their brothers, the evidence of rites of passage triumphantly endured. 'Cecil came home, no prize, has been caned once', was Eva Knatchbull's summary of her younger brother's summer term, at eleven years old in 1874.[37]

The closest and most intimate teenage relationships were undoubtedly not those between parents and children, or even boys and girls, but the friendships formed in the intense atmosphere of the schoolroom, between sisters. Sophia Baker had two sisters, Harriet and Charlotte, who were very close in age and within four years of herself. They naturally did everything together: 'we three' was Sophia's habitual shorthand. On the back leaf of the first of her 1790s pocket book diaries, she made it clear that it was Harriet who claimed her deepest affection. 'Harriet is the sister whom I love most, may she only love me as I love her', she wrote.[38]

Meriel, the Lytteltons' first-born, reticent and staid, could not have been more different from ebullient Lucy, fifteen months her junior, William Gladstone's young niece, who so much enjoyed riding with him at Hawarden. Meriel and Lucy literally grew up together, sharing a bedroom high in that huge gaunt mansion of Hagley, 'catching the eye of each other's noses' whenever they woke, as Lucy once said. The younger children called Meriel, not without affection, the 'Old One'. Lucy, by contrast, game for anything, was always seen as tremendous fun. Lucy recalled her 'perpetual sparring' with Meriel in the nursery. Later, she mostly learnt to control the temptation to be scathing. Lucy was a fearless rider and energetic walker; Meriel was the only one, with Bobbie, of the twelve Lytteltons who did not take to riding.

Lucy adored the company of her little brothers, responding to all their curiosity about life. A long ride with Arthur, in April 1859, had her commenting on how 'delightful ' it had been, 'the child asking all manner of questions about macadamised roads, poor law guardians, fire insurances'. Meriel liked to sit outside; Lucy was all for a walk. Once, on 8 May 1859, leaving her near the house, she could not resist recording the day with the words 'we went eight strong, excluding the most pin-toed Meriel, up Sparry's and Obelisks Hill'.[39]

John Stedman, born in 1744, whose journal as we have seen, illuminates his parenting, wrote also of his boyhood at home. The son of a serving soldier in the War of the Austrian Succession, he spent his years from ten to thirteen at Dunferline, with an uncle and aunt. His aunt's love and care left him with a strong emotional attachment to a woman who was the 'quintessence of humanity': spending a long evening once, he recalled, she combed out of his hair 'a million of vermin'. Giving him silver buttons to treasure, she shed 'abundance of tears' when he left her home. John's school life in Scotland was harsh, but it never broke his spirit, nor did his uncle's power over him. He was fortunate in finding a friend who was as ready as he was for the pranks which he accounted the making of his masculinity. These lived in his memory, bringing him a few beatings, which were as nothing beside the thrill with which he recalled the essence of boyhood adventure:

> breaking into gardens to rob the fruit trees, milking the cows in our hats for the milk, even breaking in the church to steal the parson's pigeons out of the tower ... riding away a whole day with one man's horses and going down the river the next with another man's boat ... being eternally besmirched with blood and dirt, fighting street battles, besides killing cats and dogs and breaking windows.[40]

Few boys kept diaries for any length of time as teenagers, but one who did so was Prince George, nephew of King George III. From twelve to sixteen, home for him, bereft of his mother, who was resident in Hanover, was the royal court. His boyhood diary between 1832 and 1835 is a remarkably candid account of the terrors of a youngster, seeking to prove himself in a formal and largely public society, long before he should have been expected to know all its etiquette. He began it on 7 January 1832, a few months after being separated from his mother, when he was put under a tutor, Mr Wood, who supervised his daily life. His entries that day included, 'I showed some signs of cowardice on horseback, I had a very bad Latin lesson and made many careless mistakes in it, I mean to try all in my power to be better for the future.'

Prince George battled to develop the masculine courage he knew was expected of him. On 18 February 1832, he again berated himself for cowardice out riding. On 9 March, hunting with a cousin, he was at first terrified 'because the horse would not go quietly', then he began to gain in confidence. In the summer of 1834, now fifteen, he was testing himself as a swimmer: 'took several running footers and a hedder for the first time yesterday', he noted on 5 August. Shown his new horse at Ascot that week, he was conscious that he 'showed some signs of fear when mounting him, which at my age is very wrong'. There were several traumatic days for Prince George just then. Activities he had been taught to regard as proof of manliness held great terrors for him. There was a hopeless first shooting expedition on the 14th, with nothing to show for it: 'I had three shots, but, as might be expected, killed nothing. I however at first behaved very ill indeed, and was quite alarmed lest the gun should kick and therefore lost many good opportunities of firing. I feel dreadfully ashamed of what I have done.'

After a fortnight the Prince was able to record some prowess: 'Yesterday I went into the little Park to shoot pigeons and killed five, three sitting on a tree and two flying and I liked it uncommonly. I think I wounded a hare too but could not find it.' Prince George and his friends ended that day, after dinner, by catching more than a dozen sparrows, 'in nets all about the ivy in the Park', which was 'very good fun'. The next test was the leaping exercise of hurdling, which Prince George funked on 28 August: 'so like a baby I was that I felt afterwards very angry with myself and dreadfully ashamed'.

It would have helped the Prince's self-esteem if he had been able to master the requirements of court behaviour. But, visiting his parents in Hanover in early 1834 and under their eye, he soon found the round of court ceremonies and balls there just too much of a strain. He tried to take himself in hand on 6 February: 'yesterday I fear some more bad behaviour showed itself. I have not remembered so many bad days following so soon after each other for some time . . . Yesterday I was violent, hasty and indeed might almost say did everything that was wrong.' George was not pleased to be summoned to return to England in a fortnight by the Queen on 19 February, but, his mother interceding, his vacation at his real home was extended, to cover not only his Papa's birthday on the 24th but his own on 27 March. He needed the reassurance both these events provided very badly indeed. 'First congratulated Papa and gave him my drawing, then played my music for him with my sister.' That night he attended the Hanover ball, staying till half-past one. Generosity to him on his own birthday was a boost: 'received very many pretty presents from various persons'.

Prince George's diary shows a boy desperately attempting to diagnose his weaknesses and to achieve greater self-understanding. It was a 'constant desire to chatter which always brings me into trouble', he decided in February 1834. He returned to the issue the next month: 'Yesterday I again fell into that bad fault of mine to form hasty opinions and speak hastily rather than first thinking them over in my mind and saying my ideas quietly. I am then generally obliged to retract them ... I must really take very great pains to avoid this.'

There is some evidence that the diary proved an effective aide memoire. In January 1835, now almost sixteen, he was working to check his chattering, 'my great defect'. He believed then that he could soon conquer 'my old fault of not liking to leap':

> Yesterday in the riding school, I certainly hesitated taking the bar for a short time, but at length mastered myself and went over. It is indeed of the greatest importance to me to get over this fault, for nothing is so bad as to have the reputation of a coward, which if I do not take care, I fear I shall have.

This was gender indoctrination at its most excruciatingly painful and demanding.[41]

Four more boys who kept brief diaries were George Corrance, John Salter, Frederick Hett and G.R. Scott, the latter hiding his full name under a mask of laconic masculinity. George kept the exercise up over the year 1845, John did so erratically from 1851 to 1859, Frederick did so for ten months in 1859, while Scott wrote a diary over nearly two years in 1867 to 1868. The account these boys give of their school holidays reinforce each other. They exemplify a pattern of youthful manly activity similar to that noted by John Stedman a hundred years previously. Let loose from the parental gaze, these boys found their feet on their own, with brothers, or in male peer groups. Thus George Corrance's winter holiday in 1845 was devoted to setting bird traps in the park and garden, in which he caught two sparrows and two robins; on 9 January he shot a blackbird. When he came home from prep school at Easter, his project was digging a canal. In August, he enjoyed a good deal of fishing. One day he took his guinea pigs out in the park, another he 'hunted the hog on my pony', another he went shooting with 'others round here'.

John Salter, living at the sea in Sussex, caught crabs and winkles in September 1853 and went out shooting with a cross-bow in December, hitting, he boasted, two birds. The next May, he went rook shooting. Yet John was also a family boy. On Good Friday in 1858, he went to church with his parents and sisters 'like good people'; he 'took a ramble with them afterwards' but 'snow made us beat to quarters'. At Mattins on 9 May, 'Jess and Anna took up so much room with their crinolines that I let them have Bank pew to themselves.' He moved away from his sisters, to Arundel's Corporation pew, where there was room to spare.[42]

Frederick's winter activities were typical of others during his 1859 holiday. He mixed backgammon and bagatelle indoors with football, walks, riding and shooting out of doors. On a 'jolly ride' with his friend on 10 January, 'Twigge made fruitless shots at two snipes and a blackbird.' He chronicled another day's shooting on the 18th: 'shot a water-hen and badly wounded a crow, got wet through, had a splendid moonlight ride home'. He no more spared his feelings for wildlife in the North Lincolnshire fields, near Brigg, than George did on his Suffolk estate.

Both, as it happened, had sisters called Louisa and both Louisas, even more coincidentally, sickened and died while these boys were diarists. George helped his little sister with her scrapbook over several days in January 1845. She was not well even then and died in the last week of his spring term. This touched him deeply. 'Came home to this house of mourning', wrote young George Corrance on 20 March; 'Louisa buried', he noted briefly a few days later. Back at school on 23 April, his grief for his sister stood out sharply in a litany of incidents in the 'Doctor's' regime of temper tantrums, which led to beatings suffered by him and his friends: 'this was poor Louisa's birthday' ran a ringed diary entry.[43]

Frederick Hett was concerned about his sister Louisa's ill health in January 1859. He 'felt very uncomfortable about leaving' her to return to school, in Horncastle, on the 22nd. He received news of her death on 4 February and hastened home. 'I have seen dear Louisa's body', he wrote the next night, 'she looks perfectly calm and composed, as well as she did when alive'. He spent a 'melancholy' Sunday, before attending his sister's burial the next day. When 'dear Louisa's birthday' came round in May, Frederick noted how he 'felt somewhat sad in consequence'.[44]

The Winchester schoolboy G.R. Scott spent his holidays at his home on the Quantocks. He was pleased to be admitted to the local cricket team in August 1867, playing for Nether Stowey against Stogursey at cover point. He enjoyed his hunting experience with the staghounds. Contact in those weeks with Mama, her dining with him and joining him to walk in the local woods, was sufficiently exceptional to merit diary comment. Main events of the January holiday, in 1868, were 'a good walk on the hills', with his Aunt Kate and abortive shooting expeditions until 21 January, when he 'at last shot one wretched yellowhammer'. He also chronicled the county ball at Bridgewater and some hare coursing, dismissed as 'not very good sport'.

That summer, Scott played a lot more cricket at home in Somerset. He also undertook a walking tour on Exmoor with a friend. His deep-felt need to distance himself from all things feminine, decisively cutting the apron strings, shows through in a patronising note about his mother's concern at the strenuous walking that he planned. He was, he wrote in his diary, 'deeply impressed by the harrowing fears of our doting Mama that we should knock up before the end of our first day's journey'.[45]

Diaries written by teenage girls are more numerous than ones by boys, providing richer material for an account of the pattern of their family life. Four short Victorian diaries illuminate the domestic round particularly vividly. These were kept by Katherine Neale, daughter of the High Churchman and scholar John Mason Neale, living at East Grinstead in Sussex, in 1865; by Bessy King in Hampshire, in 1871 to 1872; by Eva Knatchbull, whose imposing family home was at Mersham Hatch near Ashford in Kent, from 1873 to 1875, and by Mary Hallward, daughter of the Rector of Frittenden in Kent, in 1878.

Victorian children were adept at a large range of games, played with each other and with visiting families inside and out of doors all the year through. Hide and Seek and Consequences were two of the favourites with the Bowen family at Bowen's Court in the 1870s.[46] Whist, chess, backgammon and croquet were played endlessly by Katherine Neale and her four siblings.[47] The family often played cards in Bessy King's household. Mary Hallward loved Happy Families, Gobang and backgammon, when she was eleven years old. At a party on 14 January 1878, she wrote, 'we enjoyed ourselves very much indeed'. The hostess was 'very kind'. The children that day played Blind Man's Buff, Hunt the Whistle, Musical Chairs, Jane's Hurt Herself and Proverbs.[48]

Patterns of play and leisure were deeply gendered. Eva Knatchbull was organising a dolls' funeral in July 1874, taking it for granted that her elder brother Ned was off shooting that week: 'a black velvet jacket was the pall on which was placed a cloth surrounded by a wreath of white flowers . . . the grave was in a nice little quiet corner, we made a mound which we covered with turf after'.[49] 'We had a ball in the dolls' house', noted Mary Hallward on 5 January 1878, relating the death of one of her rabbits the same week and the acquisition of several more the week after, besides a session she enjoyed with sisters when we 'dressed up'.[50] When Bessy King's cat died after only eight months, she insisted on a full-scale burial of 'darling Lily'; when her dog, 'beloved Vixen', died, only a few months later, she insisted on another one.[51]

Eva Knatchbull's father gave her a pony that she called Birdie, for her twelfth birthday in December 1873. She was thrilled when Birdie was replaced by a new pony, Bopeep, in August 1874, but then desolate when her mother sold this one almost at once, because she kicked and reared: 'I don't know when I shall get another.' It was the next July that she again acquired 'at last a pony' of her own. Meanwhile she tried several, before her parents were satisfied about a sound animal. 'It took me a long time to settle on a name and I am glad I have at last', she wrote, explaining her decision for the name Lady Betty.

Girls wrote incessantly about dolls, pets and people; boys wrote about killing animals and other sorts of manly exercise. When her Aunt Annie, who they were staying with, invited a girl called May to play with her, Eva's dislike of her, she reckoned, was just the kind of thing a diary should contain: 'Now I'll just put about her, she is nine years old, very small, has a thick bush of goldish brownish auburnish fisly fuffy curly hair, brown eyes, a snub nose and small mouth, she is the horridest, selfishest, provokingest little animal I ever saw.' Eva put this down to May's being 'very spoilt'. She herself was, and saw herself as, a spirited girl, keen on skating in the winter and revelling in the sea on holiday at Broadstairs: 'as long as the machines were out we bathed'. She thought it great fun, cheering on Eton on behalf of her brother Ned, at the Eton versus Harrow match at Lords, 'if you see your side winning', to 'chaff the others well' in the stand. Just before she was thirteen, she 'enjoyed my first hunt awfully', though it was not clear what part she took in the field. Recording her thirteenth birthday, with twelve exclamation marks, on 19 December 1874, Eva listed her presents: 'my cake was pretty to look at but was not very nice'.[52]

The highlights of girlhood life were picnics and outings in the summer, dances and parties in the winter. On a picnic in the woods in April 1865, Katherine Neale did some bird's-nesting, finding two thrushes' nests and two hedge sparrows.[53] Bessy King recorded 'good fun' at a picnic in June 1871. Later the same month, she went with her family to a military review in Bushey Park, attended by the Queen and royal family.[54] Noting a long day when the family travelled to London when she was eleven, Mary Hallward chronicled the trip to the station in a fly, visiting the Tower of London and climbing the Monument. 'I was miserably tired', she wrote the following day.[55]

Katherine Neale found a reading of *The Merchant of Venice*, which she attended, 'very jolly'. She used her diary to list humdrum activities, like lengthening her petticoat and helping her mother 'put the study table tidy'. But her longest entries, during the school holidays, were about the dances she attended. 'The conservatory was delightfully cool' for sitting out, she wrote of one dance till after two in the morning, listing her partners. At her own dance in August 1865, the schoolroom came into play, decorated with convolvulus. She danced eight times, including a waltz, a set of Lancers and two sets of Caledonians.[56] Bessy King went to a juvenile ball, given by the mayor in 1872: 'I wore pink tarlatan flounced to the waist.' She noted how much she had enjoyed it.[57]

Eva Knatchbull was thrilled by staying up at thirteen for the traditional servants' dance in January 1875. She 'kept up a whole polka with Cecil', before listening to her mother playing the piano in the drawing room while the band supped. After that, she did a Sir Roger de Coverley. Dancing seven times herself, she concluded 'it went off very well altogether'.[58]

These diaries fully support John Tosh's contentions that Victorian children enjoyed celebration of birthdays 'as never before' and that 'presents between family members became an essential part of the Victorian Christmas'.[59] 'All dined together', noted Eva Knatchbull, listing presents given and received in 1874.[60] Sarah Bowen's account of Christmas Day at Bowen's Court in 1876 is paradigmatic:

> A bright frosty day and the ground covered with snow. We wished every-body a Merry Christmas, then Mama called us all up to the Lobby where we received many pretty presents from our Aunts . . . We did our usual Christmas pieces for Mama and Papa . . . We all went to church . . . We had late dinner with Mama and Papa and plum pudding.[61]

Christmases for Lucy Lyttelton, she wrote at thirteen, recalling early years at Hagley, 'shone out at the end of each year with an indescribable joy of their own: made up of the "bright leaves and red berries" with which the old house was lit up, the joyous home-gathering, the circle of our dear home-faces'. The early waking was exciting: the ritual was that the children sang 'Hark the herald' at all the adult bedroom doors, 'beginning with Mama and Papa, scrambling on to their bed for the kisses and "Merry Christmases"'. The family then assembled in the nurseries, 'to drink coffee and eat tea-cake, surrounded by the admiring maids, with the holly all round the room shining in the firelight'. So the day went on:

> All going to church . . . to hear the dear old hymns. The ecstacy of dining late, the mince pies, the snapdragon, the holiday, the listening to evening carols: and perhaps the dawning of true joy because Christ was born in Bethlehem and it was to His tender love that we owed all our happiness.

'Strong and loving and shining with ever increasing brightness' was how Lucy summarised these memories.[62]

What comes through very strongly in diaries kept by teenage girls is the way that family events structured their existence and held the promise of their future life. In their own marital partnerships, their own homes would literally be that life. In large, close-knit families there were always births and deaths.

In November 1793, Sophia Baker noted the stages of Grandmama's final illness, with a lengthy entry about the 'dreadful day' when she died: 'Dear Grandmama having suffered torments with the patience of a saint and the resignation of an angel expired after having blessed Mama, our four aunts and two uncles.'[63] Grandparents could be important in children's lives. Lucy's 1854 account of her father's mother Sarah, Lady Lyttelton, who had had experience of working with children in the royal nursery, is vivid:

> She always had a charm about her better than beauty. Tall, with great dignity and grace of manner, a sweet smile, a low melodious voice and a power of winning and attracting everyone who knows her . . . I can't do justice on paper to all that is admirable in her mind and character . . . she is full of information, a first-rate teller of stories or reader.

It became Lucy's habit to reflect at the passing of each year about the Lytteltons' fortunes since the previous January began. 'Three births, four deaths, two marriages', she chronicled on 31 December 1854. But when December came in 1857, her heart was full. On the fifteenth, she mentioned 'the little boys home', finding Spencer 'so much improved in looks'. Papa was writing The Record, the account he rather morbidly insisted on compiling of his wife's last days that previous summer. Lucy agreed to read some of it to Winny, May and Arthur. They 'cried piteously', she noted, at Mama's deathbed words about going away, 'touching in their awe and quietness'.

This was inevitably a quiet and sober Christmas at Hagley: 'no more singing at the doors'. This quintessential event had never, Lucy reflected sadly, been a performance with all twelve of them participating in it. That incompleteness tugged at her when she wrote in her diary, on 31 December, 'I wish Baby had been in the carol singing only once'. Alfred had been born just over a month after the last occasion on which the Lyttelton children did their round of singing at the doors. 'Very gently', Lucy declared, closing her story of 1857, 'has His Hand taken our light away sending soothing comfort in the golden memories'.[64]

School

Only a single boy, research for this book suggests, has left really sustained personal testimony in a diary, written regularly over a substantial period, about his schooldays. This was William Ewart Gladstone, who kept a diary of his Eton life from July 1825 to December 1826. He attended the school from September 1821 to December 1827, starting at eleven and leaving just before he was eighteen. These were profoundly formative years in William's life: Eton, his biographer John Morley wrote, 'impressed images that never faded and left traces in heart and mind that the waves of time never effaced'.

For Gladstone, Eton was 'the queen of all schools'; his attachment to the place grew over the years of his adulthood. No one else mentioned in this book lived out an adulthood which is so well known or has been written about by historians so assiduously. What makes Gladstone's Eton diary so fascinating and invaluable is that, as a schoolboy of the 1820s, he wrote a perceptive narrative that yields itself readily to inference. The marks of his adult character are all there. His account of himself makes possible analysis of the mind and emotions of a youth whose destiny, though predictable, was not yet manifest.

William's early life was suffused with the politics of an ambitious father. John Gladstone was a successful Liverpool merchant. He was the Tory MP for Lancaster from 1818, sitting in the 1820s, while William was at Eton, for Woodstock. A childhood memory was George Canning's appearance at his home, when his father managed his election for Liverpool in 1812. Brought up at Seaforth House at the mouth of the Mersey, William attended a small school in the vicarage there. 'I went to Eton in 1821 after a pretty long spell in a very middling state of preparation', he recounted later, 'and wholly without any knowledge or other enthusiasm, unless it were a priggish love of argument which I had begun to develop.'

William joined about 490 boys at Eton, under the wing of an elder brother well established at the school. Starting at an unreformed public school in

1821 was like being thrown into a jungle.[1] His biographer drew on early letters in giving this account:

> He likes his tutor so much that he would not exchange him for any ten. He has various rows with Mrs Shurey, his dame, and it is really a great shame the way they are fed. He and his brother have by far the best room in the dame's house. His captain is very good-natured. Fighting is a favourite diversion, hardly a day passing without one, two, three or even four more or less mortal combats.

William was an ordinary boy, sending home enthusiastic accounts of the daily fights by which boys learnt manhood, fights which, in those days, caused the Windsor and Slough coaches to stop under the wall of the playing fields to watch the slaughter. 'At this time', ran his own summary, 'there was not in me any desire to know or to excel. My first pursuits were football and then cricket; the first I did not long pursue and in the second I never managed to rise above mediocrity.' Until Easter 1822, William, in his own account, was 'stagnant without heart or hope'. He then came under Edward Hawtrey, later an outstanding headmaster, 'who was always on the lookout for any bud he could warm with a little sunshine'. Still a plodder, it was entirely due to Hawtrey 'that I first owed the reception of a spark ... and conceived a dim idea that in some time, manner and degree, I might come to know'.

In the years from 1822 to 1825, before his diary opens, William's intellectual endeavour began to blossom. His Eton life was broadly based and busy. He read widely and immersed himself in work, later praising the accuracy of Eton's teaching of Latin and Greek as 'simply splendid'. He had in fact begun an academic career. He also played chess and cards with his friends. He took up sculling on the Thames. At Montem in 1824, acting the Canningite, he figured 'in all the glories of a Greek patriot'. Gladstone was in the remove between the fourth and fifth forms in 1822, achieving promotion to the fifth form, after moving up sixteen places, in the summer of 1823. This ended his fagging and gave him the blessed power to fag himself.[2]

Before that release from submission to older boys, William experienced the quintessential submissive Eton rite of passage. As praeposter of the remove, leaned upon by three of his friends, 'from kindness or good nature' as he afterwards put it, William was induced to omit them from the list of those to be flogged by Dr Keate one day. Rather implausibly, they simply pleaded the inconvenience of attending the block, since their friends were coming down from London to see them. The master of the remove, hearing what the praeposter had done, roared at him, 'put down your own name on the list'. So it came about that William knelt at the block himself, was held down by his fellows and learnt the agony of the birch, in Keate's next daily session.[3]

The laconic daily entries in his diary between 15 September and 5 December 1825, in M.R.D. Foot's excellent annotated edition, provide the pattern of Gladstone's Eton life at fifteen years old. William had already acquired the drive and determination which was to make possible the unremitting activity of his adult political life. The demands he made upon himself at school emerge strikingly in the diary. Travelling from Gloucester on 15 September, he took the Veteran to Oxford, picking up the Sovereign from Worcester there, and going on to Slough, a twelve-hour journey. His classes next morning, he noted, were 'a good beginning to enure me'. It was his fourth day back before, following much sorting and burning of letters cluttering his room, William declared himself 'settled and comfortable'.

Less than a fortnight into the term, he became introspective: 'today as every day I have wasted much of the time committed to me. May God enable me to make better use for the future.' His urgent evangelical conscience shines through his diary. Thereafter that autumn, his academic life, social life and regular exercise kept him at full stretch. The term left William exhausted. The start of his Christmas holiday was marked by a relentless and ineffective struggle against the need for extra sleep, with a week of references to his rising 'abominably late' and broken resolutions 'about getting up'.

The daily pattern of work consisted of class work and 'private business', which meant preparing work in a small group with his tutor Henry Knapp. There was very extensive homework, based around a weekly Latin essay. William also fitted in regular sessions with a French tutor, with whom he studied the works of Molière and a massive programme of private reading, including daily bible study. Between 4 and 14 October 1825, for example, he went through seven of the ten volumes of Crevier's *History of the Roman Emperors from Augustus to Constantine*.

By this time, William had acquired a boat of his own. He found relaxation in long walks and in sculling the five miles to the inn at Surly Hall, up river, and back. His social life was blossoming, with frequent invitations noted in the diary for boys at his stage in the school to 'mess' with him. His family, with mother and sisters as regular correspondents, was often in his mind. Naval brother John, 'off our coast, to my great surprise and pleasure, safe and well, thank God' on 25 October, visited William in November. He obtained a day's leave 'after eight o'clock school', dined with him at the Castle Inn at Windsor, showed him the sights and took him on the river.

The most exciting and important event in William's school career that autumn of 1825 was undoubtedly his election, on 15 October, to the Eton debating society: 'proposed and received in the Society', he wrote, 'fear they will have a bad bargain in me, attended debate again'. His friend Francis Doyle, later to be his best man, spoke that day, carrying the motion that 'Regulus was a greater patriot than Camillus.' He attended the debate on 22 October on whether Cromwell was more odious than Richard III, but was shocked at the consumption after it of five bottles of wine.

Yet these scruples had to be put aside, for, he knew in his heart, a public speaking career, more compelling to him than Latin or Greek, beckoned. Nervously, William offered to speak himself on 29 October, in favour of a motion recommending education of the poor. The text of this maiden public speech survives. William began with these words:

> In this land of liberty, in this age of increased and gradually increasing civilisation, we shall hope to find few, if indeed any, among the higher classes who are willing to obstruct the moral instruction and mental improvement of their fellow creatures in the humbler walks of life . . . by what argument can they repel, by what pretence can they evade the duty?

Already he was prolix, yet he was at once magnificently persuasive. 'Funked less than I thought I should – by much', concluded his diary entry that night.

The politics of the hour or of the previous 50 years were banned in the Society, but Eton boys could debate historical and moral questions to their hearts' content. At a school impregnated with the spirit of public life, John Morley wrote, 'boys with active minds mimicked the strife of parliament in their debating society'. William adored the Society, cutting his teeth as an orator there with dedicated abandon. He voted aloud for the Marquis of Montrose, for Marcus Aurelius and for the Earl of Clarendon. He changed his mind about Sir Robert Walpole, first voting against him, 'entirely ignorant of the subject', then for him, on 10 February 1827, in his last year at Eton, seeing him by this time as 'the bulwark of the Protestant Succession'.[4]

Made Vice-President of the Debating Society in January 1826, William became increasingly absorbed and preoccupied by its affairs in his two final years at Eton. He became fussy and somewhat authoritarian, given a chance to impose fines for minor infringements of the Society's rules. He fined his friend Francis Doyle, for instance, 'for not filing the papers nor entering the question in time' on 12 February. Later that month, after a 'capital debate on the fall of the Roman Empire', he unsuccessfully opposed providing a chess-board. Nor did he want the rather scurrilous journal *John Bull* to be made available in the Society's rooms. In April, he managed to carry a motion for a new fine of half a crown on members for 'throwing about, striking with or using in any offensive manner' any property of the Society. This seemed to place him in a strong position to check rowdy behaviour. In his office as Vice-President, he was spending a good deal of time in the Society's rooms, seeing to details such as newspapers being kept tidy.

When most of the fellows at his dame's acted a play called *The Captive Princess* in February 1826, William opted out, though agreeing to attend a rehearsal. Nor did he have time any more for the tomfoolery of the traditional procession and pageantry at Montem, Eton's summer day of dressing up and carnival. It offended the intense seriousness of purpose which was coming to dominate his life. Having thought about it, he dressed himself up for Montem day on 16 May, again as a Greek patriot, 'in white fustinelle and embroidered cap'.[5] Two years previously, Lord Byron had died of a fever at Missolonghi, assisting the Greeks in their struggle for independence.

But Montem day, when it came, brought him revulsion. It earned his longest diary entry that year, listing some others he saw in costume, but amounting to a studied diatribe:

> Montem day – did nothing. Day dwindled away and wasted miserably. Hot. Squash excessive in various places. Several fainted. Turn out of men on the whole smart . . . the whole thing a wretched waste of time and money; a most ingenious contrivance to exhibit us as baboons; to most or all of Eton fellows a day of fatigue, smothering, idleness – and – a bore in the full sense of the word.

It was with relief that William 'stowed away my Montem traps' on 17 May 1826; twenty years later Montem was abolished.

William had begun the summer term with his usual resolutions. He did some work on completing his holiday task, tired after the journey from Gloucester on 13 April. Next day, he 'got things in some degree set to rights', the day after he 'became pretty well settled'. But the river allured him that springtime. The second Sunday back he was out in his boat twice. The day after, 25 April, was a whole holiday, with no normal classes, so, letting himself go, he took the boat out twice again, besides doing some work on Boswell's *Life of Johnson*. 'This will not do – again', he chided himself. Yet he was out sculling once or twice almost every day in the next few weeks. He needed this release from his hectic debating and academic life.

With his leading role in the Debating Society, William Gladstone had become someone who mattered in the Etonian world of 1826. He dined with his tutor on 11 March. He recorded on 26 April that 'Trevelyan my fag' had just started with him. Unselfconsciously and confidently assuming the role of command which the Eton training was all about, he recounted that he 'answered very well indeed'. He was now on excellent terms with Keate, promoted from captain of the fifth in October 1826 to the sixth form the next

February. He found that the headmaster spoke to him differently as a senior citizen of the school and treated him better: 'was very civil indeed; told me to take pains etc; to be careful in using my authority etc'.[6]

In due course, Keate had taken to William. The headmaster, with his pathological love of wielding the birch, was always a brooding presence. Only five foot tall, 'by costume, voice, manner (including a little swagger) and character', Gladstone wrote later, 'he made himself in every way the capital figure on the Eton stage'. He was only twice mentioned in William's diary account of 1825 and 1826, both these references relating to his floggings. One of these, when himself a junior, had been enough for Gladstone.

Thereafter, absorbing school gossip and experiencing the regular spectacle of observing fellows suffer at the block, the vagaries of Keate's temper and his ferocity with the birch sometimes preyed on his mind. On 7 November 1825, he noted that Keate's floggings had become 'more savage', after a recent illness. Arriving back at Eton on 19 January 1826, he found a large turnover of servants in Mrs Shurey's establishment, but his dame herself was flourishing. He was shocked, though, at the speed in the new term with which Keate found a crop of victims. 'Keate very savage' was his laconic entry on 20 January.

In 1841, fourteen years after leaving Eton, William attended a special Eton dinner, to celebrate the fourth centenary of the school. He found himself sitting almost opposite Dr Keate. He described the build-up of emotion, as the routine toasts were given. He went on to describe the moment when Keate's name was given to the crowd of Etonians present:

> It is beyond doubt that of the assembled company the vastly preponderating majority had been under his sway . . . any one of them asked how he liked Keate would beyond question have answered 'Keate? Oh I hate him'. It is equally beyond doubt that to the persons of the whole of them, with the rarest exceptions, it had been the case of Keate to administer the salutary correction of the birch. But, upon this occasion, when his name had been announced the scene was indescribable. The roar of cheering had a beginning, but never knew satiety or end . . . we seemed all to have lost our self-possession and to be hardly able to keep our seats.

Victorian Eton, the epitome of England's governing class, that day found the very essence of its being in the memories of sadomasochistic collusion in Keate's brutal, but time honoured, flogging ritual.[7]

Apart from this incomparable schoolboy diary, private diary writing or even correspondence material from schooldays, unalloyed by the requirement of duty to parents, is both rare and scrappy. Boys' experience of being at school in these centuries, even less so that of girls, is hardly susceptible to analytical treatment, on the basis of authentic source material. Yet the subject cannot simply be left with Gladstone. How far is there a personal perspective available to put the dire account of public school brutality in Chapter 13 in context, even to modify its pessimism? Some much shorter diaries, kept with much less consistency, plus a few letters between siblings, do tell us something about what, typically, being at school was really like. Most youngsters, after all, had less rarefied minds than that of the future Prime Minister.

Richard Neville went to Eton at eight years old, in 1758, keeping what he called a scribble book, in which he entered expenses from his pocket money. Tops, marbles, shuttlecocks and cricket balls indicate his diversions. His treats included plumb firmety, sugar candy, caraway comfits, macaroons, raspberry cakes and barley sugar. He noted a feat with his Papa in 1760, when they 'kept up the cock 1834 times' with their battledores. He listed the members of the third form in 1761. Inside the back cover, the egregious Richard recorded an incident which was always graven in his mind, but apparently did him no harm: 5 April 1760 'I swallowed a marble.'[8]

A file of letters received by George Lord Bruce, at Winchester, from his prep school cronies at Wandsworth, after they had gone on their separate ways to different public schools between 1774 and 1778, exhibits them comparing their public schools. 'I am not licked', Edward Kynaston told George, from Harrow, 'and fare better than I did at Wandsworth.' Henry Mount explained why he found his Hackney school to his liking: 'we have almost always a holiday every week and we have a great deal better play places – three fields and a garden'.

He was 'glad you find some sportsmen among the Winchester boys', George Martin told George Bruce in February 1776, 'I hope by this time you are a little more reconciled to the school.' But another friend was still commiserating with the unhappy George at Winchester in early 1777. William Draper wished he had gone on, with him, to Eton and hoped that, if he did find friends at Winchester, they would 'never make you forget your old friends' at Wandsworth.

'I hope you like Winchester now', declared one friend, now already Lord Ancram, anxiously, on 22 February 1777, reporting his own progress with Greek epigrams and Homer. George Bruce did, it seems, belatedly take to Winchester, because the tone of enquiries that year became more positive as well as more specific. 'Have you been flogged since you have been there and for what?' asked Charles Clavering in March. Having repeated this question soon after, George Martin heard that George had so far escaped the Winchester birch. He was 'glad to hear you have not been flogged', explaining that 'the Doctor', his own headmaster at Westminster, had been 'excessive rum' lately. He did not envy George Bruce 'the rum operation of speaking publicly', but he declared, seeking to be comforting, 'in a little time you will get used to it'.

The Westminster crowd stuck together, sometimes having a hard time of it: Clavering might be leaving, Martin explained, since 'the Doctor has not left off beating him and he is at this moment in a great scrape in the waiting room'. The contrast between the holiday life lived by these Georgian boys, discussed in these letters, one of race meetings, balls and trips to Vauxhall pleasure gardens, and the hardships and wretchedness of some of their schooldays is striking. But, equally, these letters show the stoicism and good humour with which a set of boys who, making friends early in their life away from home, corresponded regularly. They sustained each other at their public schools through thick and thin.[9]

George Seymour's 'memoir of my earlier days' provides an account of schooling during the Regency period which may typify the experience of many sons of the gentry. His father was a naval man who took a place near Andover, 'for the sake of his hunting friends in the vicinity'. George's happiness at home stayed in his memory, in contrast to his time at the Reverend Dr Moore's prep school, a building and playground he could hardly ever recall leaving, except for going to church. He was bullied by senior boys and recalled the rigid discipline: 'The rudiments of the language were well taught but I do not remember them with half the vividness that I long did a hard strap of Dr Moore's. It hurt the hand so much. He kept it in vinegar during the holidays.'

George declared in this memoir, written at 50 in 1837, how little it was 'the habits of such schoolboy life' that had developed, in many of the boys there whom he knew afterwards, such 'estimable or agreeable qualities' of character. At Harrow, he was one of the first boarders at Mrs Sophia Smith's house, 'an excellent person very kind to me as since to my son'. His tutor was a 'rough good hearted old fellow'. Harrow, less repressive at ten years old, was 'heaven' after his prep school: 'if a boy learnt a little less it was more willingly and effectively'. The school operated on the principle that 'a boy got a flogging when it was not quite due, he escaped one when it was merited quite as frequently and there was a spirit of generous feeling about the boys and of honourable rectitude about the master which should distinguish a British public school'.[10]

Six short and somewhat scrappy schoolboy diaries provide entry to authentic detail about the emotional lives of Victorian youngsters away from home. Only two of them mention academic matters: Frederick Hett, at school in Horncastle, narrated his beginning Sophocles's *Antigone* and an exam on the first book of Euclid; G.R. Scott listed the order of his school exams in Euclid, divinity, Latin prose and Greek composition. Otherwise, positively, these are accounts of sport, leisure activities and treats. Frederick Hett played hockey and also recorded 'capital' games of football in February 1859. George Corrance noted his first game of cricket in the 1845 season and then a 'great match at cricket' on 29 April. Frederick's diversions included skittles, boating, rowing and long country walks.[11]

John Salter, recounting his time at Mr Grix's boarding school at Littlehampton in the 1850s, filled his diary with the 'jolly sprees', which broke up the tedium of classroom life: 'got a fieldfare stuffed'; 'eel-spearing'; 'bird nesting and ditch jumping'. On the Regatta day, he was 'down on the beach to see the rowing, and then to Wombwell's wild beast show, with which I was very pleased'. Armed with 'great sticks', he set off with a crowd across the Downs near Chichester on 24 August 1853, 'turned up a young hare which we hunted but did not catch'.

His diary for 1858 found John, now a seventeen-year old, boarding at King's College School in London. The longest entries relate to the fights he was in between January and April that year, which he clearly would not have missed for the world, since he could hardly bear to go home:

> Bade farewell to King's College. They devilish near made me blub. With a sigh and a good deal of regret, I turned my back on them and London and some of the jolliest larks and fellows that ever were for – no end of a time. Certainly the thoughts of home consoled me in some measure . . . Found all well at Arundel . . . slept like a top. Nightingales no end singing, ready to split their throats.

John Salter was a tough boy, who revelled in fighting, which brought him great exhilaration. On 1 February, he describes a 'boxing set-to' lasting an hour and a half:

> Never had such a spell before. If he had not dropped his arms I very soon would. I had a good 'un in the throat and gave him some clinkers, finding him tough as Old Harry. He isn't a bad 'un and will stand no end of knocking about.

He was not a boy to be trifled with. When a boy twice wiped his shoes on John's trousers, 'I e'en gave him a lick that he won't forget in a hurry – it sounded all over the room – a deuce of a swipe.' Fights which he took up or watched were highlights of his life. He was disappointed when one rumoured on 26 February 'ended in smoke, one being funky and t'other afraid'. John was never funky. But, in a bout on 9 March, in front of 'all the Upper Sixth', he came a real cropper:

By an unlucky chance just as I was closing he hit me an awful rouster, almost spilling me, though not quite . . . so painful was my nose that I was obliged to get an exeat, saying I had run up against a fellow and pitched my nose in the playground . . . I underwent an inspection from Mrs Cockayne, who prescribed brown paper and vinegar as a cure.[12]

Half holidays and special treats gained particular mentions in several diaries. Young Barrett, son of a Hertfordshire rector at prep school in Eastbourne in 1893, wrote about his football, otherwise confining his entries to outings and the arrival of parcels of tuck from home. He took a steamer to Hastings from the pier at half term. On 5 November, he was allowed out late to see 'the Pope and Guy Fawkes burned' on the sea front. He roamed the Downs with friends, meeting an old shepherd, who handed on 'several dozen battle axes, spearheads, toothpicks and things belonging to a fashionable ancient Briton'.[13]

His longing for the Easter holidays marked George Corrance's account of his spring term in 1845: 'just three weeks' on 27 February, 'just two weeks' on 6 March. But, depressingly, two of these diaries were totally dominated by a litany of punishments and a third, kept by Edward Holland, contained evidence that retribution was swift and harsh, when he was caught at normal schoolboy pranks such as rowdy football: 27 February 1889 'played football in playground – severely licked'.[14]

George Corrance's life at Dr Proctor's school in Brighton in 1845 was punctuated by 'jaws' which frightened him, canings which left him bruised and ritual degradations. He bore all these punishments as best he could, before recording them in his little pocket book. 'Dr gave me a long jaw and compared me to a donkey on a common without a leg' was his pathetic entry on 24 April. 'Dr in a great wax; got caned' occurred at intervals. Adopting a well-worn tactic George noted, on 9 May, 'going to be caned I put a copy book up my back'. In February, awaking Dr Proctor's ire, the day after he had been in a 'towering wax', he had been made by him to 'stand on a form for three hours'.[15]

When G.R. Scott began his Winchester diary in 1867 he had already passed through the days of the licensed tyranny, wielded by prefects in his house, on the bodies of the juniors like himself. The tables would shortly be turned: now in that middle station of school life, largely free of submission himself, he was not yet permitted to demand it of smaller boys. In the summer term, he noted names, naturally surnames, of friends whom he had 'had mess' with; he was still jawed at once 'for shirking off a task'. But returning to Winchester that September, Scott related a new status, with fags now running at his command: 'my pupils are Heggate, Jan and Talbot'.

Scott and Jopp, with whom he had stayed in the summer holidays, now acquired the first stage of prefectorial authority. They could bend juniors over and spank them for minor offences at will. When a boy called Church delivered two letters to him on 8 November, he noticed that they had reached the school three days previously. With no enquiry made, he simply 'spanked Church therefore'. He spanked another boy, next day, 'for not putting up a pint cup'. But Scott still looked up to the rulers of the house, senior prefects, those above him who were permitted to wield the cane.

Scott's autumn story was little more than a catalogue of the house 'tundings', the Winchester reference to prefectorial use of a cane. The new head of the house, Gatty, showed his mettle by caning 'over twenty men for shirking' on 24 October. Thereafter, juniors were variously beaten by prefects for lying, smoking in the mill, failure to watch a school match, besides more shirking. The diary illuminates the world of big boys beating little boys, on which Victorian public school training in masculinity and the stiff upper lip was so explicitly founded, with unusual clarity.[16]

Whereas in their letters to parents, as we have seen, schoolboys concealed much of the real culture of the world that they inhabited away from home, there were occasions when they wrote more unselfconsciously and unguardedly to other relatives. Guardians, from a boy's viewpoint, were usually more lenient than fathers. Tom Boughey enjoyed a highly relaxed relationship, during his Eton years in the 1820s, with his uncle Frank Twenlow, who took on his guardianship following his father's death. He reported 'good sport fishing', then listed the game he had shot, seven partidges, a woodpigeon and a wild duck, during his 1823 summer holidays. Mop was proving 'a capital house dog' and the new bay horse was proving 'quiet with his coach bridle on'. He was delighted, he told his uncle on 24 November, writing from Eton, with the short-eared owl, besides the seagull, that he had been sent for stuffing: 'it looks very nice so these two will make a grand addition to my collection at home'.[17]

A set of nine letters from John Russell to his sister Georgy, beginning soon after he had started at Harrow in April 1857, and taking his life there through to October 1858, illuminates the warmth of a younger brother towards his elder sisters. His dependence on them, away from home after being privately educated, much more strikingly than on his father Earl Russell, a liberal politician, or on his mother, emerges clearly. John was a quiet, sensitive boy, who came in for some bullying. One somewhat frenzied letter explained that he had sought refuge elsewhere, 'my being rather disturbed at fellows squirting water all over my room'.

Georgy's letters were balm: thanking her for sending him a copy of *David Copperfield* on 15 October, he wrote 'you are really the best of sisters, in fact quite a model sister in the way of letter writing'. She kept his wants supplied in the way so many sisters did their brothers at boarding schools. In January 1858, the issue was his india rubber, 'I think in the parlour, having lent it to Mama, which caused me to leave it behind'. John's letter on 11 March 1858 was written with express purpose. At a loss 'how to direct to Laverstoke where' Mama was staying with his aunt, he wrote 'I wish to ask you to do me a favour'. His hands were chapped 'in the most dreadful way', from cold afternoons on the football field; 'a great gap', on the little finger of his right hand, was going to be 'very inconvenient in writing trials'. Could she 'send me a prescription for some glycerine which I can get made up?'.

John was finding his feet in these months. 'Being now in the first shell, I shall only have night fagging', he explained to Georgy, back at Harrow in January 1858, 'but I have not had any yet'. The hard grind of reaching upwards in the boarding school hierarchy, for each stage of respectability, importance and status, comes across powerfully: 'this is my third quarter and I am now entitled to ask names, i.e. to say "What's your name?" when I see a new boy, just as I myself was asked when I first came, and of course I feel highly proud of this new dignity'.

An eager fourteen- and fifteen-year old, John Russell was quickly full of Harrow's rituals and traditions. He regarded the consecration of the refitted school chapel by the Bishop of London 'very interesting and impressing to the youthful minds of the congregation'. The service, including the Bishop's sermon, was 'a fine thing all together', he told Georgy. He worked hard and was full of his academic progress, too. 'I did my last set of verses so very well that Bradby', his housemaster, 'let me off pupil-room from 10 to 11 for correction of verses, there being hardly anything to correct', he boasted in January 1858. He was finding the work he was set easier than he had done the previous year. He was, nevertheless, anxious, he confessed to his sister, about the next 'placing' in his form, since Mama, he knew, would expect news of this. In March, he was so pleased with verses he had written for the assignment of celebrating the brave death of General Havelock in India, winning him six marks out of seven, that he sent them to Georgy verbatim.

These letters shed fascinating light on how John realised that the female members of his family could both strengthen or harm his repute in this overwhelmingly masculine world. Early in 1858, he was mad keen to have Georgy visit with Mama, to see the football teams out on the pitches, 'such a very pretty sight'. Then, when it came to the issue of who might collect him for an exeat in the family's carriage in February, he caught himself with the knowledge that the presence of the mothers of junior boys at the school easily became the subject of ribaldry: 'tell her', he told Georgy, 'I am not afraid of any number of visits and not a word was said about the last. I feel sure no one would laugh at me now, at least, in a way I should at all mind.' If mothers could be an embarrassment, sisters were potentially quite the opposite. Spotted by a Harrow boy walking in Richmond Park with Georgy, the story went round that 'she was very pretty'. He related this to her at once, after the tale came back to him, treasuring the cachet he had acquired.

Yet, fond as he was of his big sisters, John felt bound to tease. This was absolutely obligatory with Victorian young manhood, seeing sisters as cast in a rather threateningly different mould from themselves. 'Poor little Toza! Poor little gay butterfly! Poor little flitting, gadding, laughing bubble of society! What could young men be thinking of not to dance with her!', John commented, hearing that Victoria had endured a ball that failed in her expectations. 'Impudence': his male chivalric nature cried out in defence of his little sister. When big sister, Georgy, was 22 the next week, he could not resist a touch of derision about her being almost on the shelf: 'I shall expect to hear of a marriage before long, seeing twenty-two is rather long to wait anyhow.' Was some 'young swell, at present unknown' to him, currently paying visits to 'the paternal dwelling in Richmond Park'?[18]

The reflections that John Russell wrote in 1860, at eighteen, on leaving Harrow, complement his letters to Georgy in a remarkable way, filling out the picture of those frightening first quarters at the school, three years previously. He remembered the dread with which he had left his 'beloved home', knowing that he was doing so to 'enter on the unknown, the dreadful life of a public school'. He reflected, at the end of running this race, on 'the various changes, temptations and friendships that have occupied that period of my life'. The Earl and Countess Russell delivered John in person, taking him in their open carriage from Richmond to Harrow. 'I was small, very small, I was fourteen however I thought myself rather old':

> It was not a very merry drive . . . the future was to me not only a mystery, but even a very terrible mystery. I knew not what school was: little indeed could I imagine of the wickedness and guilt that I have seen since. I did think though that bullying was triumphant there and that bodily suffering of some sort would surely be my fate.

The housemaster, Mr Bradby, received the Russells in his study where the first shock, an intimation of his new life, was being called Russell, not John. He recalled so well the 'moment of agony' when his parents left: 'I tried to keep in my tears before Mr Bradby but it was not possible. He saw my sorrow and sympathised with me I am sure.' A relationship that gave John confidence in the next months, when he always spoke well of Mr Bradby, was forged that day. 'He spoke most kindly; advising me always to do my duty, to avoid punishment and above all never to forget to pray.'

The second quarter, as John remembered it, was nothing like as bad as the first. He felt older and more experienced in the ways of Harrow, rising academically to the lower form known as the 'shell'. Things became more comfortable for him with the end of his day-time fagging. From the summer of 1858, John found school bearable, above all because he had made friendships that really mattered to him. His was an unremarkable Harrow career, but it hardly mattered that his sole achievement, he felt, was to have played cricket badly in 1859, now that he was sixteen years old. [19]

Another set of schoolboy letters, in this case within a single family, illuminates teenage camaraderie in the context of home and boarding school life, in the years 1874 and 1875. The Grenfell boys wrote much about releasing their spirits in planned holiday adventures. 'Fancy a week hence', wrote Claud from Harrow to Charles at Wellington in July 1874, 'I'll tell you what. We must get some new eel baskets and a casting net. Fancy if we camp out. The holidays will be awfully jolly.' Charles, now eighteen, encouraged Algy, at sixteen, to think big about that summer in March 1875: 'I am looking forward to midsummer like anything so are you I suppose . . . for in midsummer only can you do such deeds of daring as scaling the old kitchen wall . . . then you can go in for manly exercise, rowing . . . or better still slaying fish at the weir.' 'I am very anxious to hear about the pea rifle', wrote Charles to Claud that April, 'it would be so good for potting rabbits in the summer.'

The girls of the Grenfell family were fair game, as sisters often were, for doing up parcels. Like Georgy and Victoria Russell, they were affectionately kept in their place by male demands and teasing. Thus, in October 1875, Algy thanked little Connie, from Harrow, for the hamper, which had arrived damaged, and he asked her to send his rod, reel and line 'immediately', since he very shortly saw a chance of a day's fishing. Charles treated his elder sister Lina, travelling abroad, having come out six years previously, quite witheringly in 1877. It was as if her femininity might contaminate him: 'I hope you will warn us when we are to expect you back because I want to go to Taplow on Saturday and if there is any chance of meeting you I think I shall keep away.'[20]

Female diaries confirm other evidence, cited above, that, in the Victorian and Edwardian periods, the experience of boarding transformed the schooling of girls into something more positive than it had been previously. The Winchester schoolgirl, Emma, for the year 1784 revealed a limited and controlled pattern of life.[21] But Katherine Neale's account of her schooling at Brighton in 1865 concentrated on her many friendships. 'Had great fun at tea and in the evening with Mary Baker', she noted in her second week there; the following week she 'had a very jolly walk' with two new friends, not previously mentioned by name. She was positive about dancing lessons but mentioned one 'very disagreeable music lesson'. There are hints of some emotional involvement with one of the teachers, Miss Buller: on the routine afternoon walk on 9 May, she started out with two of her friends, then 'coming back walked alone with Miss Buller'. She bought birthday presents for her later that month – a dress and an alarm clock. Returning for a new term in August, she was thrilled that 'Miss Buller came to meet me.' On 7 September, after they played rounders, a change from lots of sea bathing which she enjoyed that summer, the girls 'sat in a hollow while Miss Buller read to us'. The emotional spontaneity of Katherine's life in Brighton is abundantly evident.[22]

Katherine Neale's diary contrasts strongly with the inhibited, clipped and unemotional stories told by schoolboys of their lives away from home. It is clear that entirely different cultures made boarding school a much more testing, even frightening, experience for boys than it was for young girls. Yet what is striking is boys' ability to master the conditions they had to bear, the stress of academic examination, the constant threat of punishment which was often imposed upon them, and the inherent bullying. There was nothing soft about English male schooling. Boys tackled it with camaraderie and survived it with determination, because they were taught to see it as the making of their manhood.

21

Travel

There was nothing else that prompted keen journal keeping quite like travel did. The story of the Grand Tour in Europe has been largely reconstructed from the letters and diaries of young men from the ranks of the aristocracy and gentry.[1] More mundanely, even the briefest of teenage manuscript diaries, kept by those without pretensions to the grandeur of travel abroad, usually highlighted trips away from home to see the sights, whether in London, at the seaside or at burgeoning inland centres of manufacture like Cromford or Birmingham. Everyone grew up in those circles with the awareness that, in the decades from 1700 to 1914, the Industrial Revolution was bringing Britain the prestige of ruling the world. Travel was in some sense uniquely formative, feeding the minds and imaginations of youngsters with the substance of an unthinking but ardent patriotism.

London dominated England as few other capitals did a nation, so parents rich enough to travel in the coaching days naturally expected to give teenagers at least a taste of its sights. In the period from 1700 to 1840, Leonard Schwarz has argued, it was the aristocracy, rather than the bourgeoisie, who gathered there for a few months each year, and who 'clearly considered themselves the capital's trend setters'. Ranelagh and Vauxhall, it has been suggested, represented 'a quintessentially eighteenth-century form of refined but not precious amusement'. Moreover, many cheaper pleasure gardens, like Spa Fields and Marylebone, distinguished London from the facilities of all provincial centres, as did its more numerous coffee houses and museums.[2]

Aristocratic patronage of the metropolis remained unwavering, when the London social season, focused upon the court, came to dominate Victorian and Edwardian life. So teenage members of families like the Lytteltons naturally spent time there. Elite spaces now included the restaurants and gentlemen's clubs, which were concentrated along Pall Mall from the 1820s onwards. Hyde Park's Rotten Row remained London's pre-eminent open space, for riding in the mornings and carriage driving in the late afternoon.[3]

The Baker parents began the education of their girls in London sights when Sophia, the eldest, was eleven and her sister Harriet was only eight. Spending a month at their London home, which broke the routine of lessons with the governess at their Hertfordshire mansion, they were out most days in May and June 1793. Mama showed them a 'model temple' off Coventry Street, an exhibition of pictures at Somerset House and an exhibition of 'birds and beasts' at Exeter House. They visited the Tower of London, Sophia noting especially 'the historic gate', Westminster Abbey and Kensington Gardens. In March the following year, 'us three', now including Charlotte, were taken by their aunts to see Manchester House and went walking in Grosvenor Square. On their spring visit in 1794, the Bakers took the girls to Spring Gardens and on their first trip to Covent Garden. In April 1795, now thirteen, Sophia, accompanied by Mama, visited another art exhibition and saw *Macbeth* at Drury Lane.[4]

'We took the coach to London and filled it inside and out', wrote Emily Shore at eleven years old in July 1831, 'with ourselves and our three servants'. The new London Bridge was being built but not completed, outdoing the old bridge. It was 'a heavy ugly fabric', she thought, in its gleaming modernity. Emily admired St Paul's Cathedral 'extremely', considering that everybody below 'looked like dolls or monkeys' from the Whispering Gallery, when her Papa took her up there. She did not have enough time to examine the monuments, some she noted, by John Flaxman. She found the interior of St Stephen's, Wallbrook 'very elegant and beautifully proportioned', though she strongly disapproved of 'an odious little cobbler's stall' which had been allowed, built 'up against the steeple'.[5]

John Salter was taken on trips to London at ten years old in 1853. He visited the British Museum, saw *Whittington and his Cat* at Sadler's Wells and enjoyed 'a capital fish dinner' at the Corn Exchange Tavern in Billingsgate, which cost the family one shilling. On a summer visit, the Salters went to Greenwich Park 'and saw the pensioners'. They also 'looked over Portland Arcade, Soho Bazaar and the Pantheon'. But the highlight was exploring the London docks, 'which we enjoyed very much, especially an American liner of which we went on board, it was very splendid'.[6]

Lucy Lyttelton's early teenage trips to London were usually for great public occasions, which drew from her very extensive diary entries, like the Queen's ball, when she was thirteen. Until 1857, the family kept a house in St James's Square. She stayed around six weeks, with her elder sisters, in March and April 1856, allowing time for sustained courses of music and dancing lessons and for other cultural initiations simply not available in rural Worcestershire. Highlights of this stay were Fanny Kemble's reading of excerpts from *King Lear* and attending a performance with Papa of *The Winter's Tale*, in which

both the Keans appeared on stage. How Lucy hated the 'malice and wicked-
ness' of Goneril and Regan; how she thrilled to 'the beauty of the change to
Cordelia's quiet placidness and touching sorrow or to the broken-down
majestic, agonised old king', in Fanny Kemble's interpretation. Lucy disliked
the Keans' acting, 'so very vulgar, accent, gesture and all', but she 'never imag-
ined, much less saw anything so beautiful and perfect as the scenery' at her
first Shakespearean production.

Another new adventure was riding in London, it seems alone, 'on our old
friend Niger', a horse belonging to the Gladstones that she had previously
ridden at Hawarden: 'I went to Rotten Row and all about there, and home by
Piccadilly and Pall Mall.'[7] Each morning, Lord Lyttelton took the girls to
mattins in Westminster Abbey. That, for this serious girl, represented peace
at the core of a hectic metropolitan world. 'The majestic old hoary Abbey',
Lucy called it, 'whose still, holy, high beauty and grand services are such a
beginning to the day'. She confessed that, amidst a vacation of 'nicenesses of
every kind', to loving these visits to the Abbey 'so exceedingly'. Her eyes
would wander to the monuments, the walls, the roof. 'Oh, solemn beauty in a
church', she reflected, 'so helps one to fix one's thoughts and it is so very nice
in this whirling, busy, happy London life.'[8]

Living in Richmond Park, London was easily accessible by train for Louisa
Bowater, who had many of her drawing and dancing lessons there. One of
her birthday treats, when she was fourteen on 25 April 1856, was going to
the Pantheon and to the Soho bazaars, chaperoned by Agnes Lentz. She
accounted 29 May another 'exciting day', marked by a walk in London 'to see
the illuminations'; a fortnight later, she was taken to the Crystal Palace, with
its ornamental Sydenham Gardens, which had opened two years previously,
after the Great Exhibition had put it permanently on the map.[9]

Louisa's mother arranged a programme of outings as a break from schoolroom work in July 1856. On 15 July after early morning needlework, she put
on her best clothes for a visit to the state apartments at Windsor Castle: 'we
were taken over some rooms not generally seen and oh the pictures there'.
Masterpieces by Claude and Rembrandt, china, vases, the array of portraits
all stuck in her memory. 'Oh what a happy day it was', she ended her
account. By 1858, when Louisa turned sixteen, she was spending a good deal
of time in London, combining the lessons which refined her training in
polite accomplishments with enjoyable shopping expeditions.

It was possible to do a sound day of schoolroom work and also go to town
for the evening. On 27 March 1858, for instance, Louisa noted dressing at
4.45, the journey to London 'in two closed carriages', attending a programme
of three short plays at the Haymarket Theatre and getting home after one in
the morning, to sleep 'like a top'. Her résumé ended, 'altogether I enjoyed it

immensely'. Louisa's interest in art as well as in the shops was burgeoning. In July, Mademoiselle, deputising for Agnes on holiday, accompanied her to an exhibition of French art, following her drawing lesson. In August, she admired Holbeins and Titians, visiting Hampton Court, and spent some of a gift of five shillings from Papa on Longfellow's *Poetical Works*.[10]

Some teenagers had a short fleeting experience of London en route to a seaside holiday. Thus, Frederick Hett was taken to the Pantheon and to Greenwich, where he admired the chapel and the painted hall, travelling through to the Isle of Wight.[11] Those who lived closer to the capital, like Mary Hallward, learnt about it on day trips from home.[12]

The notion of the extended seaside family holiday, with nanny and governess in tow, had caught on with the upper classes by the time Sophia Baker was growing up in inland Hertfordshire. When the Bakers took 'a very nice house' in Ramsgate in August 1795, her diary entries increase in length, with so much to write down. The first day she and others took a walk on the pier and went on the beach. Two days later, she and Harriet, the two eldest, plucked up the courage to bathe for the first time. In the days that followed, they rode round Pegwell Bay, visited the North Foreland lighthouse and took trips to Margate, out to sea and to Dover Castle.[13]

The seaside holiday gained ground in the early years of the nineteenth century.[14] This was when Brighton, quickly England's premier seaside resort, emerged out of the fishing village of Brighthelmstone. A Georgian spa replaced it, when the fishing settlement was lost to the sea, under the patronage of the Prince Regent.[15] There was some time lag before the well-known resorts of the Victorian and Edwardian periods developed all round the coastline, from Scarborough to Blackpool and Morecambe. The creation of the railway system gradually made the seaside accessible to the population as a whole.[16] Between the 1830s and 1914, as the upper and professional classes patronised resorts from Kent to Cornwall, many teenage diarists recorded holidays which hugely enlarged their mental horizons. The importance of travel and of activities pursued away from home in the process of their growing up was incalculable.

After a night at the Spread Eagle in Gracechurch Street, the Shore family party continued their July 1831 journey by coach from London to Broadstairs. Used to the gentle countryside of Bedfordshire, the chalk downs and cliffs of the south-east, which she dismissed as 'odious', came as a shock to Emily. But her first sight of the sea was thrilling. Her diary captures the timeless immediacy of childhood initiation at this point:

> None of us have ever seen the sea before and therefore I at least was much delighted with it. It is a great pleasure to me to sit on the sands

and watch the boats coming out of the harbour . . . I think it is also
extremely amusing to watch a wave rolling on, gradually increasing in
bulk and at last breaking into foam.

A precocious young botanist, Emily found the mignonette on the Broadstairs
rocks, the yellow toad's-flax and a 'splendid' purple scabious. Moving on to
Ramsgate, the family took out a rowing boat, enabling Emily to grasp and
chronicle how crab fishing, with nets close to the shore, was practised there.[17]
The same year that Emily Shore was in Kent, Frederick Post, a serious
introspective boy of Quaker parentage, had a holiday there, travelling more
widely than the Shores did. His favourite occupation, unavailable near his
London home, was taking donkey rides. He and his family hired a two-horse
fly from Tunbridge Wells to Hastings, 'passing through much beautiful
country' and 'luxuriant hop-grounds'. Frederick was alert to and wrote in his
diary about various visits laden with history: entering the dungeons at Battle
Abbey, exploring the Norman castle at Hastings and looking at the recently
built Martello Towers, intended to keep Napoleon at bay.[18]
The watering place laid out at St Leonards in Sussex by James Burton in
1828, still very fashionable three decades later, attracted the patronage of the
Lyttelton family in 1856. They all decamped on 18 February to a small house
on the sea front where, as Lucy put it, they were 'packed delightfully tight'.[19]
They brought five maids with them from Worcestershire. The temporary
schoolroom for four children was 'choked up with table, sofa and armchair
with Mademoiselle's more than portly presence presiding'. After a whole day's
holiday to 'shake down and look about us', Lucy took quickly to a new routine
of 'lessons, outings, reading'. This was 'a very happy time', she wrote on 26
February, following 'a delightful evening with music, dominoes, books etc'.
She loved the rides into the Sussex lanes, in a open wickerwork pony carriage
that the family had hired. Eager for history, she led Mademoiselle up the
steep path to Hastings Castle.
Then, on 7 March, disaster struck: little Arthur had caught scarlet fever
and a fortnight later Bobbie caught it too. Prayers in church, coincidentally,
for those in times of sickness, 'really set me off crying', Lucy confessed to her
diary on 22 March. In early April, the children who were well enjoyed a boat
trip to Fairlight, games in the open air, even time on the beach. There was a
cloud over this prolonged winter and spring holiday, yet Lucy left 'this dear
place unwillingly' on 14 April. Her sick brothers remained behind, with the
family's best nursing care, until they were seen as well enough to travel.
Lucy, at fourteen, reflected upon a 'tiresome' train journey to London, 'as it
was second class with the servants, the two little girls and baby who of course
could not be good all the way'. The experiences of the Sussex seaside,

nevertheless, brought important new dimensions to her life. The exhilaration of being rowed as a passenger able to take it all in, at Brighton in April 1857, shines from her diary account:

> Had the most enchanting boating in a long boat, with four oars, Charles, Albert and two sailors. Herewith we skimmed away briskly; to the Pier in five minutes, a little coasting straight out a mile and a half to sea . . . out to the end of Kemp Town and home in an hour and a half.[20]

It was conventional that at the seaside lessons were shorter and more relaxed but that schoolroom routine, however limited the accommodation, should not be entirely abandoned. The Victorian concern for teenagers' learning order and for the inculcation of formal routines remained overriding. Thus Eva Knatchbull, staying in Brighton with her Mama and sister in 1875, obediently resolved to 'keep my diary all the time I am here'. She described how, after breakfast on their first day, 'we put our books in order and that sort of thing till half past ten'. A cold drive that February morning in an open carriage on the parade was followed by a long afternoon at the Aquarium, where Eva learnt a great deal about porpoises, conger eels, dog fish, spider crabs and seals, 'which amused me very much'.[21]

The Oxford High School girl, Ethel Hatch, spent three months in lodgings with her mother at St Leonards in 1887, after leaving the school just before her eighteenth birthday. She continued with lessons under the supervision of her mother, but enjoyed an expanded life, after years of growing up in an academic circle which included Lewis Carroll.[22] Her diary provides much insight into how Sussex served to release this Oxford girl from the limitations of her warm but very stuffy upbringing. Ethel played with her brother Arthur on the beach and the rocks. She bathed a good deal, played tennis, took lots of walks.

There were experiences in these weeks, Ethel's diary shows, which informed her mind and awoke her imagination. On 19 April, the Hatch family visited Battle Abbey, 'went all over it, saw the spot where Harold fell and the old armour from the battlefield and many other things'; on 30 April, Ethel gathered primroses on the way to Bexhill; on 9 May, she and her Mama had 'a most lovely drive to Winchelsea and dinner in the Inn then went over the beautiful old church'; on 3 June, she 'saw the moon on the sea' and later that month the Hatchs took boat trips to Fairlight and to Eastbourne.[23]

It would be a mistake to assume that, though more Victorian girls than boys wrote thoughtfully about their seaside holidays, boys did not also respond emotionally and with wonder to the English landscape. Frederick

Hett certainly did so. Continuing from London with his father to the unspoilt Isle of Wight in May 1859, he arrived by steamer at Ventnor, enjoying the 'beautiful' coastal scenery from Ryde. 'I never saw any place more beautifully situated than Bonchurch, with trees of all sorts as a background', he noted in his diary. Shanklin Chine also was 'almost perfect in its way'.[24]

Well before the Howards of Orpington, after years of Brighton holidays, began to diversify their summer holiday plans in the Edwardian period, the railways had opened up access to numerous new destinations. In 1907, when Clare at fourteen kept a holiday diary, the family chose Woolacombe, a tiny resort in north Devon, where the magnificent beach afforded excellent bathing. For the Howard girls, set free by revised thinking about the pursuits suitable for females besides riding, such holidays were essentially devoted to sightseeing, fresh air and exercise. It was in the decades from the 1880s to 1900s, Sally Mitchell has written, that 'the age limits for permissible tomboy behaviour rose'.[25]

The previous year at Southbourne in Hampshire, Clare was taught to fish by her brothers and took a turn with the oars when the family went rowing on the River Stour. At Woolacombe, she learnt to bicycle, did long cliff walks and explored Watersmeet. At Westgate-on-Sea in Kent in 1908, a stay from 30 July to 27 August, when she was fifteen, she walked and bicycled like mad. The Howard girls were too impatient to queue for the conveyance into the sea: 'we all waded out to the machines and climbed up by the wheels, as we did not want to wait for the cart'.

Holidays developed teenage curiosity and knowledge. At Margate in August 1908, the Howards investigated the shell cavern discovered about 1840 with, it was reckoned, over a million shells used in its walls and ceiling. They found a ruined medieval castle in the middle of farm buildings on one of their walks. On their major expedition to Canterbury, they paid their two pence to climb the spiral staircase inside the Westgate: 'we saw a figure wearing the actual armour that Oliver Cromwell wore and old guns, chests, flags etc', Clare related.

Venturing further west, the Howards took a house at Perranporth for August 1909, a party of eight led by Clare's grown-up brother Hal and his wife. They took tents, deckchairs and five bicycles on the train down from Paddington. Clare adored the bicycling afforded by quiet Cornish lanes, went prawning and rowing on the Truro river. In the evenings, she practised her prose style in attempts to capture Cornish landscapes at their most entrancing, the sea at Kynance, for instance, 'like a large lake, with the water a beautiful dark green, showing the rocks distinctly below the surface, with occasionally a line of white foam'. She chronicled a memorable month of stifling days, swimming and sunsets.[26]

The tourist attractions of coastal and inland Georgian England, Amanda Vickery has suggested, fell into the categories of exhibitions, fine landscapes, architectural wonders, feats of engineering and impressive institutions. Thus Mary Chorley's introduction to genteel tourism in the 1770s, before her teens, began with Preston and Liverpool docks, a paper factory, a coal pit and a picture gallery. In July 1776 she visited Derbyshire with her aunts and her father: predictably she explored Matlock, with its mills, which she 'admired exceedingly'. At Chatsworth, she commented that 'the water works are very pretty and so is the house'. Twenty years later, Mary's own daughter catalogued her teenage tourism: visits to a furnace, a sugar house, a powder mill, the new Lancaster canal and the aqueducts there and at Preston.[27]

The Sheffield apprentice Richard Holden started his diary in a large leather-bound book, with an account of a trip he took with a friend, at fourteen, to Birmingham in 1835. They were fascinated by the industrial sights, such as Butterley Iron Mills, which they saw en route. His excitement, he noted, rose at their approach to Birmingham: 'the first sight of that large and populous town so celebrated throughout the world for the extensive variety and utility of its manufacture . . . our pulse beat high on our entrance into the town; all seemed life, bustle and motion'.

The resolve to keep his diary returned in 1840, the year that Richard, at eighteen, made a journey, with a horse and gig, conducted by his father, to Manchester and Liverpool. Crossing the Pennines to Glossop, they entered a world quite unfamiliar to him. An acquaintance of his father's showed them round his factory, which employed 500 hands. Richard marvelled at 'nearly all folks wearing clog shoes' and 'women with shawls on their heads not bonnets'. Richard found Manchester 'all in a bustle such as I had never seen before'. He was fascinated by the train journey to Liverpool, where he explored the Mersey, with its docks and ships. He was emotional about leaving his father, who had business to complete in Lancashire:

> I took farewell of father with very sad spirits. We had a fine ride and in a while my thoughts became more composed. I was now on the Sheffield road and on the lookout for every Sheffield face I could see and thinking what news I would have to tell those at home . . . the little ones wanted to know what I had brought 'em.

The next April, given leave by his boss, Richard and a friend undertook a walking tour into Derbyshire. Taking a track across the moors to Bakewell, the young men were given a guided tour at Haddon Hall. Richard was intrigued by its 'old fashioned style', which he described at length. The objective was Matlock. Richard had been there once before. In the park at

Willersley Castle, Sir Richard Arkwright's 1780s residence, 'I found my initials upon one of the seats, which I cut with my knife last time I seated myself upon it.' He was every inch the tourist.[28]

The pious and introspective diarist Emma Trotter embarked on a visit with a friend to Shropshire at nineteen, in 1860, with trepidation: 'it is my first real visit from home and I look to it with much pleasure but some uncertainty how it may fare with my spiritual life'. She felt very worldly, she wrote, in the midst of summer days as a tourist, seeing excavations at Wroxeter, Shrewsbury, 'a pretty town', and Buildwas Abbey. 'The ruins were more beautiful than anything I ever saw', Emma decided, after a picnic at Wenlock Abbey. She described her feelings treading 'the very footsteps of those poor benighted monks', observing 'exquisite beauty crumbling into dust'.[29] Diary accounts of youthful travel show how varying responses to a well-established stock of tourist sites in Georgian and Victorian England was mediated by personal and temperamental make-up.

'As for travelling', argued Lady Polwarth, with regard to the popularity of the Grand Tour, then at its height in 1778, 'it is only eligible from the difficulty of finding employment for a young man not yet of age.' This was the most specifically gendered of all the aspects of English upbringing. Jeremy Black has seen this privileged experience, so blatantly reserved for the male upper class, as being driven by 'belief in foreign travel as a means of education and, particularly, of social finishing'. Until it was, in due course, wrecked by the French Revolution, the Grand Tour prepared the heirs to great estates for a life of landlordism and public service in local government. It introduced young men to the political and constitutional systems of European states, to their art, their language, food and culture.

Thomas Pelham informed his father from Spain that 'visiting other countries is the best indeed the only way of learning how to weigh the perfections and imperfections of our own'.[30] John Skinner wrote more than 340 pages in the series of letters that he sent his mother, memorialising his travels in Holland at sixteen in 1788. His highly cerebral account focuses on landscapes, buildings and antiquities, all described in meticulous detail, accompanied by pen and wash drawings done on the spot.[31]

One of the best documented early Grand Tours was that undertaken by Tom Isham, whom we have encountered through his remarkable teenage diary, in 1676–9. Inheriting his father's baronetcy in March 1675, just before his eighteenth birthday, the young Sir Thomas lived a whole year in Rome, where he spent lavishly on the paintings, cabinets and marble furniture which visitors still admire at his home at Lamport in Northamptonshire. Before leaving England, Sir Peter Lely painted his portrait. In another portrait, done in Rome, Carlo Maratti flattered his fine dark looks, showing him gazing at a miniature of his mistress there, Gabriella Buoncampagni. 'The lemonade wench', wrote one of his friends when he left for Venice, 'with whole floods of tears deplores the loss of her Adonis.' [32]

The Grand Tour was undoubtedly a crucial formative aspect of English upper-class manhood. In Michelle Cohen's argument, it was the rite of passage par excellence, the 'wholesome hardships' of travel testing masculine spirit and endurance.[33] Jeremy Black has shown from letters and journals how youths benefited from a period away from home that finally cut the apron strings. Viscount Lewisham summarised the matter in a letter to his father from Paris in 1775: 'from this account you will certainly be very surprised if you find me in the spring as unlicked a cub as when I left England'.

Yet the growing up that was achieved was more, in most cases, the product of drinking, gaming and whoring than the kind of connoisseurship shown by Sir Thomas Isham. Black has noted how journals, relating the adventures of apparently blameless tourists, on close inspection, often reveal obliterations and tampering with the record. This may relate to an unfavourable public attitude to sexual adventures, influenced by the prevalence abroad of venereal disease. British condoms, designed to prevent young men from contracting the clap or the pox, were given sufficient credit for Louis XV to request a supply. 'He goes to all the bawdy houses he can find and fucks the first whore he meets bare', Edward Digby commented in 1751 about Edward Stevens, hinting at his foolishness.[34]

Female tourism on the Continent, in so far as it occurred at all, was always accompanied by adult family members. We have seen how Lord and Lady Spencer, with their children on a long tour of Europe in 1772 and 1773, insisted that Harriet, aged eleven, should keep a diary. Her narrative is illuminating by its very naivety. She chronicled the 'ice and sweetmeats' at a play in Brussels and the fact that her dress was admired by Princess Charlotte there, 'not being powdered and curled like the little French girls'. Harriet and Georgiana were much fussed over at Spa, where they were applauded for the way they 'danced the Cossack'. A spectator at a hunt, she was then in at the death where, to teach her the distinction between gender roles emphatically, 'Prince Charles jumped off his horse and, just as the boar was striking at a horse with his tusks, plunged his *couteau de chasse* in his side.' At Montpelier, Papa thought, 'as the first English family here', he ought to give a ball on the Queen's birthday. Returning north by Versailles, the Spencers paid court to the royal family: the Dauphiness 'spoke to Mama, kissed my sister and me and gave us flowers'. The Dauphin, she felt, 'looks stupid but good natured and would be handsome if he was not so heavy'.

Harriet learnt a great deal about how even the aristocracy could rough it. At Saintes, with no spare beds at the inn, the girls 'were wrapped up in a blanket and lay on the floor'; at Rouanne they 'lay on the ground wrapped up in great coats'. 'Papa says girls of our age should learn not to make a fuss but sleep anywhere.' As the trip went on, her account became a catalogue of 'shocking sights', since her Papa was determined not to spare her the lessons of French barbarity, to bring home, by contrast Britain's civilised values.

On the road to Toulouse, the Spencers saw executed criminals, 'dead bodies hanging on a wheel'. Their crime was cutting to pieces a pregnant woman. But worse was to come for Harriet while they were staying there. Her Papa tested her courage by taking her alone into a vault full of unburied dead bodies, telling her it was 'foolish and superstitious to be afraid' of seeing them. 'I could hardly help screaming', she wrote in her diary, but Papa, when he 'saw how uncomfortable I was', showed kindness to her: 'it is very awful and I think I shall never forget it . . . there are many children of my age and some younger'. [35]

By the late Victorian and Edwardian period, teenage girls from the upper class, whose predecessors would never have dreamed of travelling in Europe, were taking family holidays in places in Germany and Switzerland that were made possible by long distance and sleeper trains. Clare Howard at eighteen kept a diary, in August 1910, of her first such holiday, with elder sisters and a brother. They were at Kandersteg the morning after leaving Orpington, going on to Arolla. The English had begun to colonise such Swiss resorts, ensuring that there were others to play billiards with in the hotels and get advice from, about the walks that were available on Alpine glaciers and mountains with guides to assist them.

The highlight for Clare, setting out at three in the morning, was an ascent, roped and guided with plenty of crevasses to be jumped, of the Pigne D'Arolla, 12,470 feet, reached at eight o'clock in the morning:

> The guide reined us in like a four-in-hand and we couldn't have got near the edge if we wanted to. We could see the hotels right below us and a glorious panorama of endless snow and rocky mountains but after we had taken two snapshots we started off as it was much too icy to stand still.

When an English teenager, climbing in a long skirt with her alpenstock, could stand on the top of the Pigne D'Arolla, the 'New Girl', we can conclude, had finally arrived.[36] But the society that Clare Howard inhabited remained wholly polarised by gender division. Steadily increasing numbers of

British young people benefited, physically, mentally and culturally, from the expanding opportunities for travel and tourism at home and abroad between 1850 and 1900. Yet, by modern standards, these teenagers grew up in an unbelievably static world.

22

Friendship and Love

A uthentic material about the emotional involvements of teenagers outside their own families is rare. Innocent and platonic friendship between teenage boys or girls was unselfconsciously charted. When such material relates to young men and their girl friends, with the development of an explicitly sexual relationship, documentation occasionally takes the form of surviving secret correspondence. The mores of English upper-class society before 1914 rigidly excluded sexual activity of any kind before formal engagement and marriage. Thus the chastity of young girls was so zealously protected that a few stolen private kisses, each a single momentously overpowering event, could take on enormous significance, as signifiers of passion, love and commitment. This chapter, based upon rare and particular archival material, is about the private lives of a very small number of teenagers, who were touched by and recorded intense friendship or love in their early lives.

Sophia, the eldest girl in the Baker family, was used to doing everything with her younger sisters, Harriet and Charlotte, the 'we three', as we have seen, of numerous diary entries. But the pattern of her life altered when, at twelve, she settled into a routine of working with visiting masters in London. She struck up a close friendship with a girl much her own age, Lucy Strachey, who began joining the Baker girls and their governess, Miss Laborde, for walks in St James's and Hyde Park. It was arranged that they would share dancing lessons with a Mr Jenkins, 'the Scotch dancing master', several times a week. When 'poor dear Lucy' was ill with a 'bad fever' in April, this stayed on Sophia's mind till she was able to note the news, on the tenth, that Lucy was 'mending fast poor thing'.

In June they had an outing together to see the West End illuminations; in July she was writing to her new friend, when the family returned to Bayfordbury for the summer. Back in town the next March, Lucy was quickly round to tea and the friendship resumed. Sophia wrote a note, dating it July

1794, just before she was thirteen, describing candidly what Lucy meant to her: 'Lucy Strachey is my greatest friend and I love her as I do my own self and if I do but have a little neat house with her and dear Mama I shall never wish for anything more.'[1] When Lucy visited the Bakers in the country in 1798, Sophia, aware of their budding womanhood at just seventeen, began referring in her diary to 'dear Miss Strachey'. On 4 September, they enjoyed riding in the park together; next day they rode over to Panshanger so that Sophia could show her visitor the famous oak tree; riding over to Hatfield for her birthday outing on the eleventh, Sophia showed Lucy the House. 'Oh how melancholy', she wrote on 13 September, missing her bosom friend through five teenage years, when she returned to London.[2]

Louisa, the apple of her father Sir Edward Bowater's eye, was a vivacious girl on the lookout for new friends in her teens, after solitary years spent as an only child with a devoted governess. In May 1856, just fourteen, a local friend, Mary, was joining her and her governess for walks in Richmond Park, sometimes with Papa, when he was back from court, coming along too. 'Mary and I hung back and gathered wild flowers and had a nice chat', she wrote in her diary on 20 May. But, more excitingly, she was just then on tenterhooks about a visit by her cousin Edith Barne: 'they are going to ask Edith to come here for a month but my Aunt is sure not to allow it. It is too good to be possible'.

On 3 June, Louisa heard that Edith's visit was a real prospect and on the tenth, she arrived: 'at 4 o'clock my darling Edith arrived and we walked about together till tea which we had in the summerhouse . . . I spent the evening with Edith.' The next day the girls were taken on an outing to Crystal Palace. Crossing the city in two 'ansoms' was a 'regular lark'. Lacking siblings, Louisa was clamping herself to the Barne family, her cousins, whose home was near her grandmother's mansion, which served as her own holiday home, at Sotterley in Suffolk.

Louisa and Edith's bonding was rapid. 'Edith and I agreed to be sisters', she noted on 12 June, 'I hope the boys will join us.' They explored Richmond Park together, gathering wild flowers and revelling in their new-found companionship; they did their daily stints of piano practice and needlework together, too. In the rapture and enchantment of girlish teenage affection, these girls required a home of their own. 'Edith and I sat in our dell and named it Serings Dell', Louisa related on 15 June. The emotional consummation of secret naming followed on the eighteenth: 'Edith and I sat in Serings Dell during all our playtime, in the evening we walked in the Park and heard a band. We arranged that my name is Lily of the Valley or Short May Bell and my cry cuppity and her name Harebell and her cry tabut.'[3]

Next day everything went a little to Louisa's head. Agnes Lentz was on holiday, replaced by a French Mademoiselle. Louisa persuaded her to take them, when she was sent out in the carriage on some errands, and since the rain had stopped, to go on to an outdoor party being held by their neighbours the Fishers. They went 'just as we were', without changing into best frocks. The games, Drop the Handkerchief, The Mulberry Tree and Oranges and Lemons, were enormous fun. There was tea, then a quadrille, a country dance and a reel, 'in which', Louisa recorded, 'I got very hot'. At this point, a note from Mama was brought into the room, summoning the girls home immediately.

Louisa burst into tears in the carriage which Mama had sent for them. A message from Papa directed the delinquents not to appear as usual for dessert. But Mademoiselle, seeing Louisa distraught and realising that she herself was implicated, took them both downstairs herself that evening. 'But when we went to say goodnight Papa said "I will talk to you tomorrow!!!"' The drama quickly blew over.[4]

Blissful June days followed, with lessons from Mademoiselle together in the schoolroom, games of dominoes, retreats to the privacy and intimacy of Serings Dell, high spirits in the park and, finally each day, dessert with Mama and Papa. When visitors called on 24 June, Louisa noted, 'I had to do the honours', but 'when they were gone Edith and I climbed about'. The next day was another tomboy day, when they climbed, both in the morning and 'after dinner, in the Old Oak Tree'. Twenty-nine children came to the tea party for Louisa, arranged by Mama at Thatched House Lodge on 17 July. The games included Blind Man's Buff, Hare and Hounds, Old Soldiers, Hide and Seek and a paper chase, 'which was immense fun': 'Edith and I enjoyed ourselves very much.' On the twentieth, Edith's last day, the girls read together their 'favourite texts and chapters'. Next day, they travelled into London for a 'capital' final dancing lesson together: 'I shall not easily forget the last glimpse I had of my darling at the corner where our roads diverged.'

In the interval before the Bowaters summer in Suffolk began in August, Louisa and Edith were in correspondence. Edith's brothers, spending time at Sotterley then, proved friendly, securing her confidence that she could see them, too, as more than cousins. 'I told St John how pleased I was to have a brother', she mentioned on 4 September. At St John's birthday picnic the next evening, 'Philip was very affectionate and called me sister two or three times.' The relationship with Edith, meanwhile, met a difficult patch. 'I was quite humbled', Louisa wrote, after a letter 'with a humble confession of jealousy the other day.' She wished 'I were as good'.

Later that month, Louisa stayed with Edith for a few days at her home at Dunwich, sharing lesson time with her governess, Miss Bowley. She came to know Edith's parents better, by going down to dessert with her each evening. Left alone in her friend's schoolroom, she took up her diary one day: 'I forgot to say that Edith and I had some very nice conversations yesterday.' She enjoyed the sea views from Dunwich cliff; they read, rode, played, looked over scrapbooks and talked endlessly. This was a happy time. As Louisa said farewell to 1856 she reminded herself that she had 'gained a friend. I trust, for life': 'yes, dear Edith', she chronicled, 'you are my friend and our friendship stands on the sure foundation of complete confidence.'[5]

These two teenagers, approaching the end of their schoolroom years, often shared their feelings about society and its demands. It was Louisa who found herself learning most from the friendship, respecting the wise words of Edith, as the heady days of success on the dance floor prompted her tendency to vanity, which her governess had often warned her about. A diary entry on 10 September 1863, when Louisa was 21, was illuminating:

> Dear Edith has been warning me against an old fault – looking down upon people who are not quite equal to me in refinement and intellect. I know I do and I know I ought not to. I wonder whether there is any sense in struggling against a growing sense of one's own mental superiority?

Edith died the following year. Louisa was devastated at the loss of a deep friendship which had the potential to be a source of joy and strength throughout her life. 'We are parted outwardly', she wrote, 'but for such love as ours there can be no real separation.'[6]

Emma Trotter's deeply introspective diary, started on her eighteenth birthday in 1859, shows a young girl unable to handle going to dances, where male company overwhelmed her with 'the burden of sin'. So she took refuge in an intense female friendship. This troubled her, distracting her from an exacting round of spiritual exercises, as well as lighting up her life. 'My heart has been cold and dead today and my mind wandering' was a typical diary entry. When she tried to come to terms with her feelings about her friend Mary in December that year, she wrote 'I feel I must be disappointed and that a love such as mine is in danger of becoming idolatry.'

In February 1860, Emma's passion had not cooled: 'I think I love her too much', she wrote and 'somehow wrongly'. She used her diary to attempt to make sense of her emotions. 'I have yearned all my life for a real friend, one who could understand me, sympathises with me, cares for what I care for.' Her longing heart had found a resting place. Yet Mary had become an obsession; her 'every thought, action and feeling' seemed connected with her. Emma's parents noticed how her private inner life had taken hold of her, telling her more than once that she was not cheerful enough, 'which I grieve to say is true'. In June, Emma recorded the deep emotional impact of sharing holy communion with Mary for the first time. On her holiday in Shropshire that month, she wrote to her regularly and heard from her in return. But the company of other young people, away from home, did something to alleviate the burdensome intensity of this friendship, which she needed so much and had come to lean upon. New experiences did something to take her mind away from Mary.[7]

The friendships formed by W. E. Gladstone at Eton are an epitome of the role that a public school could play, when the conditions were right, in the formation of character and moral integrity. At Keate's Eton during the 1820s, pupils learnt their budding manhood in a privileged realm of boyhood high seriousness. His biographer, John Morley, described 'the blithe and congenial companionship', through which the mind of the young Gladstone was 'stimulated, opened, strengthened'. Boys like George Selwyn, Francis Doyle and James Gaskell, with formidable careers ahead of them, were of his circle. But perhaps its greatest luminary, two years younger than Gladstone yet precisely on his intellectual and moral wavelength, was his boon companion, the ineffable Arthur Hallam, who died the year after Gladstone entered parliament.

Hallam was the son of the historian Henry Hallam, whose achievement was to lay the foundations of English historical writing. Their home backgrounds were complementary: Hallam's literary and pure Whig, Gladstone's political and Tory.[8] Gladstone's diary records the daily pattern of this friendship: they breakfasted together, took long walks, and drank wine after dinner. They endlessly exercised their razor sharp minds in conversation about the philosophical and political questions of their day. Gladstone, stronger and more sinewy, found great pleasure in sculling the younger boy up the Thames. When they parted on leaving Eton, Hallam on a journey to Italy crucial to his literary growth, and Gladstone entering Oxford, they began an intense correspondence.

This friendship was the zenith of Gladstone's boyhood. He was entirely fascinated by Hallam's tolerance and sweetness of nature. Their affection drew its strength from the nobility each saw in the other. Hallam, to Gladstone, was a model of male virtue, a paragon of goodness. 'His temper was as sweet as his manners were winning', he wrote later, 'his conduct was without a spot or even a speck. He was that rare and blessed creature *anima naturaliter Christiana*. He read largely, and though not superficial with an extraordinary speed. He had no high or exclusive ways.'

'Never since the time when I first knew you', Hallam told Gladstone in June 1830, 'have I ceased to love and respect your character . . . It will be my proudest thought that I may henceforth act worthily of their affection who, like yourself, have influenced my mind for good in the earliest season of its development.' They had been apart for almost three years when Hallam wrote these words, but time could 'never do away with what has been': 'the stamp of each other's minds is on the other. Many a habit of thought in each is modified, many a feeling is associated, which never would have existed in that combination, had it not been for the old familiar days when we lived together.'[9]

Richard Holden, the Sheffield diarist, was a serious young man, brought up a devout Methodist, who attended Carver Street chapel, near the city centre. In an entry on 8 February 1840, he related, with some emotion, how he had felt bound to break off his close friendship with James Wheatcroft, whose family he had come to know, after he had begun courting James's sister. It is not clear what the nature was of the 'very wicked conduct' on James's part, which led Richard to this course of action. Visiting his home, Richard found his erstwhile friend bashful when he returned to him a watch and chain, which James had lent him some while before. In a further entry on 23 March, he made reference to his shock and pity about James making off with some money. If he had shown integrity, they would have remained friends, but now, he wrote, 'I must forget all as well as I can.'

On 31 May, Richard discussed his courtship of Sarah Wheatcroft with his friend Joseph Robinson, saying that he had decided to let the affair drop. So it was upsetting when, in September, he chanced upon her in Manchester. She did not recognise the youth who, as her brother's friend, had visited the Wheatcroft home the previous summer in a sailor's jacket and straw hat. Richard was now taller and in his best dress coat, with a broad-brimmed hat. Then she recognised him, they shook hands and parted, 'perhaps never to meet again on earth'.[10]

That summer, Richard began a new courtship, referring to the girl involved as 'Miss S.' in his diary. In August, he gave her 'a few coloured prints as a token of friendship'. On 5 September, he visited her home, confessing 'a little partiality for her'. He respected her and was proud of her company, but, he reflected, she 'wants too much I fear of her own way'. Yet, when she asked him to write in her album, he responded with a romantic verse. Later that month, Richard took 'Miss S.' to a fireworks display, seeing her safe home and noting that he felt 'as fond as ever'. In October, now past his twentieth birthday, he was writing her poetry.

But Richard was playing it long, noting on 25 November, following a slight tiff when, in a letter, there was a hint that she came to chapel with him mainly so 'that I might take her home', that it felt best to stay simply a friend. The suggestion of a kiss would be a sign of commitment, which made him hesitate: 'I have no doubt, young as I am, if I was to make love to her I should be accepted – but not so – stop a bit, I'll look before I leap.' But, she making the running with 'long and entertaining' letters, by the end of the year, 'Miss S.'

had Richard in confusion. Believing himself proof against 'the mad follies of love', he now found himself 'much softer than I could have believed', yet still found it hard to 'think beyond friendship'.

Plucking up his courage on 11 February 1842, Richard asked for a kiss and was refused: 'I was quite paralysed – did not know what to do.' His passion was aroused, yet he was now, in this rejection, resolved to close the relationship. What unnerved him was that, trying to talk things through, he found 'she was altogether master; there was some talking on both sides but most on hers'. Richard retreated to the company of his family, enjoying 'gipseying' that spring with his brother and sisters in Endcliffe Wood. He found a new girl-friend and was noticed out with her by 'Miss S.' in April. Finally, in a diary entry just before he was 21, he noted 'Miss S. sent a piece of her hair plaited'. The story of this abortive affair illustrates the hesitancy, in courtship at the time, about any kind of sexual contact. This was an age of deference to parental teaching and, especially in nonconformist circles, of moral certitude. There was much broad acceptance of the sublimation of desire until marriage, or, at least, engagement.[11]

This makes the story of the secret courtship and stolen kisses of Reggie Chenevix Trench and Clare Howard, which led to engagement in July 1913, soon after she was twenty, and to marriage in 1915, all the more remarkable. Reggie had not noticed Clare when the Trenchs used to cross the road from the vicarage to play with the Howard children at Bark Hart, the big house in Orpington in the 1890s, because she was the baby of the family. They met again at her coming out dance on 6 July 1911. Small and buxom herself, a sporty girl of eighteen, not long out of boarding school where she had been Captain of Hockey, she always accounted the moment that she saw him at the bottom of the stairs, on a night of palpitations for her, as the moment that she fell in love. Small too, dark and good looking at 23, he was confident, fresh from Merton and training for a career in the City. He fell in love with her that night but he saw no immediate way to pursue his suit.

Their love affair burst into life the following summer, when Reggie was twice invited to Bark Hart house parties. At the first of these, Clare watched his service on the tennis court, the focus of social life there, daring to send him a snapshot complimenting him on it. Her coy but excited note was about the plans for Howards and Trenchs to get together at the Henley Royal Regatta on 5 July. Her photo album has faded images of the Thames, the bridge, punts, boaters and girls in fine dresses that day, also of deck chairs and young people relaxing on the lawn at Bark Hart the day after. This was when Reggie boldly snatched time in private with Clare, taking her on a walk in the woods, where he declared his love for her, she declared hers for him and they promised themselves to each other.[12]

A letter from Reggie on his way to his office on Monday alerted Clare to the dangers of the step that she had so audaciously taken. Responding to the man to whom she was now secretly engaged with the signature 'yours sincerely Clare C. Howard', she added a postscript, 'remember that letters are very public in this house and everyone knows what one gets and wants to hear them'. She had five older sisters, none of them engaged themselves.[13] Reggie invited Clare to dinner at his Chelsea flat, with her brother Walter as chaperone, then set things up for a dance at the Grand Hotel in Folkestone on 27 July, having his unsuspecting mother Isabel invite Clare down there.[14] His brother Arthur and a friend were the chaperones.

Clare's pink dance card survives, with its sharp little pencil attached: all her training told her that she had to accept several different men for the twelve waltzes and twosteps on the card, but she managed four dances, entered simply as 'R', with Reggie.[15] Next day, walking on the Lees together, these young lovers took stock. Reggie had no prospects until he had completed his chartered accountancy exams in June 1913; even then Clare would only be twenty. Clare insisted, desperate to keep the affair secret from her bossy and intruding family, that Reggie could only write to her when she was staying away from home. Mercifully, she was beginning the round of visits to relatives in their country houses, which was normal for a girl who had just come out. A fortnight was planned with her mother's cousins, the Southeys, at Eastleigh Park in Wiltshire. They paraded eligible men before her, who interested her not at all. They took her to demanding events like a garden party for 450 people at Longleat.

During this fortnight at Eastleigh, from 30 July to 12 August, Reggie wrote eleven letters to Clare and she wrote seven to him. Only sixteen of them have survived, since, on strict instructions from the other about letters which poured out their emotions, each destroyed one of them. If the two lost letters were the most crucial in securing this impetuous love affair, entered into in fleeting moments of escape from a tennis party, the letters that do survive prove the couple's manifest intimacy, the teasing of true love and the confidence of caring friendship.

It all quickly become a game. Urged by Reggie to destroy a letter with which she had luxuriated in bed, after the maid brought it with her early morning tea at eight o'clock one morning, Clare hid it instead in her chest of drawers. 'What servant', she declared, 'would suspect a bunch of ties having a letter underneath, but of course I will be cautious.' Reggie went down to Bark Hart for a weekend's tennis amongst the family, while Clare was at Eastleigh: 'it has been quite hard', he related, 'to profess utter ignorance of your movements and to avoid putting my big feet in it again and again'. 'Oh by Jove', he suddenly added, stopping his account, 'you will have to be fearfully careful not to give yourself away when you meet your family again.'

Having accepted that, during the three weeks of the family's holiday in the Pyrenees, there could be no letters either way, the couple hit upon a light-hearted stratagem to fool the stuffy Howards. A letter to Bark Hart, just before they left, would return to the safe ground of the exchange of photographs of Henley, adding entertainment with a family certificate on it, in the form of Reggie's doings with his friend Charlie Pollock at the summer Inns of Court Officers Training Company camp. It should not even begin 'My Dear Clare', he supposed; certainly not, she replied. 'I shall feel such a hypocrite if anyone asks to see your very proper letter', Clare predicted on 10 August. But the ploy worked like a dream. When Clare read out the letter at dinner, Walter and the sisters were much amused by Reggie's account of a kit inspection, with Charlie escaping censure for his trousers 'thrown carelessly over his hut'.

Reggie struggled to control himself, using his sense of honour as a break on the temptation to make sudden dashes to London railway stations when he knew Clare was in town. 'I could have come to Padders to see you off', he wrote to her in Wiltshire, 'only honestly it would not have been the right thing. You might have been seen being seen off by a man and that would have been unfortunate.' He was restless with desire. 'I would give something pretty big', he wrote on 7 August, 'for a long talk but I don't see how it can be managed.' They pondered further chaperoned meetings in London, but recognised how frustrating these were. So they clung to Clare's notion of a final tennis party at Bark Hart, before autumn closed the court in September. Reggie hinted that 'when I go to stay with you it is not very easy either, though perhaps you can arrange something now you see how the land lies with me'. 'I will try and bring off that weekend somehow without being too obviously keen about it', Clare promised on 14 August.[16]

On 21 September, Clare met Reggie at Orpington station; the long parting was over and pent up emotion sought an outlet. A wet Sunday afternoon, with tennis off the programme, gave Clare her chance to ask Reggie if he would teach her to play chess. They climbed the attic stair, but they never got as far as the games box on the billiard room's side table. This was the moment both had dreamed of and longed for: their kisses were immediate and passionate. Their time upstairs that day rocketed the relationship on to another plane. It was too overwhelming for them to stop and think what they were doing. Clare's sexual initiation, at not quite twenty, was brief and partial. Yet here she was, against all the rules and proprieties of this society, letting a man take her in his arms in her own home, well aware that her father, brothers and unmarried sisters were just downstairs.

'They have guessed something and I'm positive Charlie has, but they don't know that I know they've guessed', wrote Clare to Reggie on 28 September. Connivance, even collusion descended upon the Bark Hart household: Clare's brother Walter and his Cambridge friend Charlie, a regular house guest, told themselves that, if something was going on between Reggie and Clare, they were not going to spoil her fun. Father and the spinsterish elder sisters, Edith and Maud, would certainly not approve. Reggie was jocular: 'the family have guessed have they? and Charlie for a cert!' Lunching together that week, he felt Charlie was waiting for confidences but, as he assured Clare, 'he got none'.

Reggie was tying himself in knots on paper to Clare: 'I'm awfully sorry I have made such a mess of things . . . I didn't realise how I was affected – till too late . . . I know I ought not to have shown my feelings so soon and I would have endeavoured not to if I had realised what would happen . . .' They should be good friends for a year and then consider, he suggested: 'I think I should be able to carry it out not to make love to you as I did on Sunday after-noon for a whole year.' 'Don't reproach yourself and think you've made a mess of things', replied Clare, 'you've not. Don't you see that if you had not shown me, I might not have realised anything myself and we should have lost, as it were, a year of mutual knowledge.'[17]

Their passion was aroused. Those few billiard room kisses could not last them through weeks of separation, while Reggie studied hard for his final exams. Their chaste year quickly went by the board. Time in the billiard room became the peak and objective of weekends when Reggie, often with Charlie, was at Bark Hart as a house guest. So, when they were finally able to announce their engagement the following July and end all the secrecy, Charlie, predictably, was ready to tease. Clare had replied to his formal congratulations, coming clean about knowing how he had sought to protect their privacy: 'I am going to send in a claim to Reggie', he replied, 'for the number of times I have broken my shins and injured my lungs going up the billiard room stairs in order to make a sufficient disturbance.' 'I did not mention this in my first letter', he added, 'as some couples prefer to fondly imagine their (shall I say) "antics" are quite unnoticed.'[18]

Reggie and Clare grasped every chance to communicate and meet during a long winter. There was a secret tryst, Reggie escaping from his office, in Oct-ober. 'I felt rather conscience stricken afterwards', Clare reflected, 'although of course there is no actual harm in it, I think it was rather mean to do what I know I shouldn't have been allowed to if my people had known.' Nevertheless, she confessed in this letter that she would steal any opportunity to have him conduct her from station to station, should she be crossing London.[19]

On 11 December, at Reggie's brother Arthur's invitation, they attended the Royal Engineers ball at Woolwich, using a rug to conceal their clutched hands, until he was dropped off for a late train into London. Yet, at Christmas, Clare had a quite prolonged panic, confessed on a walk they snatched together. Reggie was all too aware of his problem about facing her father to request her hand. He realised 'how little I am earning and am likely to earn for a year or two – £105 now which is not only a pretty miserable amount for a Varsity man twenty-four years of age, but poor sort of amount to produce if anyone should ask me what I can provide'. Asking her to wait for him was making him feel 'rather a brute'. For Clare, though, it was not money that mattered. Just past her twentieth birthday, she suddenly felt terribly young to sign her life away, dearly as she loved Reggie. All the conventions and mores of her society warned her against the impetuosity and eagerness of the affair.

Disconsolate at her innocent accounts of a powerful debut in West Country society that winter season, Reggie told Clare he believed that there would be other suitors and 'I know I shall have to make a fight of it some-time'. Clutching at straws, he sought to renegotiate the arrangement about letters to Bark Hart. She temporised, agreeing that she might be able to catch a letter 'before the family came down'; she might even watch for the family's reaction. But she dismissed his invitation to a play in London in March 1913: 'a theatre in Lent would be a violent and unpopular surprise for the family'. No tennis, no dances, no outings: February really was the bottom of the year for secret lovers before the Great War.

It was a weekend with Reggie's ebullient and informal family, including his sister Cesca and brother Herbert, at Folkestone in April that restored the strength and dynamism of this love affair. 'You managed the weekend most beautifully', declared Clare afterwards, 'and I know you know it was thoroughly enjoyed.' Reggie's confidence was boosted: 'I think we saw as much of one another alone that is possible in this state and had a nice end up, travelling up together.' 'Lucky there was a crowd and we didn't have a carriage to ourselves', he bantered. From then on it was really plain sailing for Reggie. He had grasped the importance of wooing the Howard family as a whole. He took Clare, with her sister Violet, to a military parade in London on 28 April; on 17 May Hammond, the Howard's chauffeur, drove Clare, with Violet, Walter and Amy, down to Folkestone for tennis.

Reggie concentrated his mind that summer on launching his career in a manner that would enable him to impress Henry Howard, a retired barrister, Victorian through and through in his attitudes. During a weekend at home in June, he took advice from his widowed mother, who advised him to approach her brother, Uncle Benny, partner in a firm of City stockbrokers, after his exam result. He had introduced Clare to Uncle Benny at one of the dinners in his flat, held to acquaint her with members of his family. 'Oh, she was a very charming girl', Benny told him, when Reggie announced that he wanted to marry her, on the evening he heard he had passed his final accountancy exam. Another family elder statesman, Uncle Charlie, pronounced, peering at a photograph, 'this is obviously a very nice girl'.

The two uncles, cheered by Reggie's stress on the long and close acquaintance of the Howard and Trench families, told him to steam ahead. He could hope for £200 a year as a qualified accountant, Mother would give him £150 a year and he could reasonably hope for another £200 from Clare's father. Clare followed all this with bated breath, finding their present position 'rather impossible'. She added that it was 'almost as difficult when we meet as when we are apart'.

Clare advised Reggie, as a final step, to consult her eldest brother Hal, a stockbroker who had made the family's finances his business. She believed that he would be 'terribly pleased'. So Walter took him to meet Hal and his family at Cobham. He had to undergo the trials of an afternoon of tennis, 'two ripping "men's fours"' as he put it, before confiding his plan to approach Henry Howard, once the ladies had left the dinner table that night. No longer nervous, he seemed to be 'in for a cheery half hour', he told Clare on 13 July.

On Tuesday 15 July 1913, Clare waited on tenterhooks, while Reggie asked permission to marry her in the library. Henry Howard cannot have expected, after long years of waiting to see all the six girls he had launched on to Edwardian society wed, that it would be little Clare whose hand was sought first. Listening to the figures that Reggie presented, he quickly approved the match. At 6.25 exactly the next day, looking at a clock in the King's Road, Reggie could hardly believe that it was 24 hours since their long embrace in the hall at Bark Hart: 'Priceless person', he wrote to Clare, 'and then that hour, a very short hour, in the billiard room that was dreamland'. Clare wrote immediately after seeing him off at Orpington station: 'Oh Reggie darling, isn't this all quite too perfect? I simply cannot grasp it. All I know is that there is nothing on earth like it.' Signing herself 'ever yours Clare', she ran the pen from the capital C to her postscript, which read 'The happiest girl in the world.' She was not quite seven months out of her teens.[20]

Reggie and Clare's wedding was delayed by the outbreak of war in August 1914 and the deaths of Clare's father, Henry Howard, and her sister Edith in October. They married on 28 January 1915. Reggie went to the Western Front in February 1917 and was killed in battle on 21 March 1918. His daughter Delle had been born on 4 November 1915.

23

Identity: Class, Nation and Gender

At the heart of all the reflection in diaries kept by English teenagers, thousands of words written by them in the quiet of evenings, are firm assumptions, attitudes and principles, about themselves as individuals and about their place in society. The diary, as we have seen, could become interactive with the self. It was a dear friend. It could assist a teenage girl to realise and construct identity. Upper-class girls believed that they were born to a place and to a position in a hierarchical society, whatever language they might use to define it. They never spoke explicitly about it, but class was always with them.[1] They also took their British patriotism entirely for granted. Their gender, finally, was the very essence of their being, given, unalterable, structuring and constraining the pattern of their lives. It is appropriate to conclude the book by exploring identity, as this is revealed by diarists in their private moments.

But this is where boys let us down. Diaries kept by schoolboys were few in number and, as we have seen, laconic in style. Even Tom Isham's or Gladstone's diary, though kept much more regularly than most that have been used here, conceal the inner lives of their subjects and have to be read by inference. Boys, by and large, defy the historian who is seeking to reconstruct the process of their gender construction and to understand their emotional lives. Diaries present these lives as a blank, which they can never have been. Yet, as we have seen, schoolboy diaries are a form of historical source material, which tell their own story of control and denial, of constraint, inhibition and repression. No schoolboy between 1600 and 1914 really poured out his feelings on paper: this was simply not possible for a boy in the way that girls could do so.

Becoming a man was about physicality and virility. It was a cerebral training, denying the emotions. How else would boys have coped with the struggle to keep their end up, to retain respect and to conform, which was what their schooling, their whole upbringing indeed, was about? We have seen that schoolboys fought to prove themselves, that bullying was rife in English boarding schools from 1600 to 1914, that punishment regimes involved codes of endurance and survival and then, in Victorian and Edwardian England, rituals in addition of dominance and submission, through the permitted beating of younger boys by their senior peers.

In their holidays killing animals was the routine male pastime, as boys learnt to hunt with their fathers and indulged in myriad forms of destruction of rural wildlife. Emotional rapport between boys and their mothers was severely limited during teenage years. As a substitute, it was permitted, within limits, with sisters, who provided some of the caring sustenance, the unselfish and loving support, which was often badly missing in a demanding parental relationship.

We can begin this survey of female teenage identity with class. William Baker brought up ten children in the 1790s on his extensive estate, in quiet country close to London, at Bayfordbury in Hertfordshire. Squire of the village of Bayford, he was influential in nearby Hertford, where he made a traditional appearance with his older teenagers at the winter ball. Sophia and her brothers and sisters never left the estate on foot and did not normally go out, in the coach, the phaeton, or the chaise, without their governess or Mama. 'I drove Charlotte in the cabriolet to pick sweet peas and roses', Sophia noted with pride on 15 July 1797, allowed, at sixteen, to take charge of her twelve-year-old sister. Travel was an expression of privilege and its mode expressed the family's separation from the people.

Summer picnics, which Sophia loved, were expeditions to the farm, some way from the mansion but within the estate, where the servants always served the family with syllabub. On 21 August 1798, Sophia recorded a harvest home at the farm: 'we sang "The Sons of England" in chorus'. Next day was a half holiday from schoolroom work, 'to glean which we did all morning'.[2] At such events, with its drinking and singing, or at the traditional gleaning after the corn had been brought in, the landlord's family, tenants and farm workers came together. Yet these were performances. The ranking of each person remained; all the rituals of social hierarchy were respected.

Teenage girls like Sophia also took a full part in the *noblesse oblige* of caring for and visiting the local poor, especially in the midst of winter. On successive days in January 1798, she noted, 'we saw the soup given away to the Bayford poor' and 'we took advantage of a frosty day to walk to Bayford and see all the poor'.[3]

Hagley Hall and Park, at the end of the lane through the original estate village, is a supreme achievement of Georgian architecture and landscape planning. A memoir in later life written by her brother Edward, Meriel's autobiography in 1913 and Sheila Fletcher's book on Lord Lyttleton's daughters, besides Lucy's diary, make it possible to describe its world. Hagley became a powerful representation of the Victorian class system and its society in miniature. A hundred years had passed since the house was built when Lucy Lyttelton, her brothers and sisters, grew up there. Her brother Edward came, on reflection, to marvel at the loyalty and length of service of the Hagley servants and their pride in the family, all this consistent with, and involving no questioning of, 'the deepest gulf between the two groups of human beings'.

Elly, Mrs Ellis the housekeeper, in her black silk dress and close white cap, was manager of Hagley from the day that Lord Lyttelton married Mary Glynne, always sitting up until all were in bed, checking the doors with her great mastiff Otto. Lucy's adored Newmany was nurse to all Mary Lyttelton's dozen, for 37 years, from 1840 to 1877. She crops in and out of Lucy's diary all through her teens: a 'loving, sensible, humorous good woman as ever was', Meriel called her. John Daphne, the coachman, was on equally intimate terms with the children, teaching them all to ride at an early age. His wife was the village schoolmistress, in this most feudal of estate schools. Clarke, the pompous house steward, Meriel remembered, pronounced, in his most patronising style, when she and Lucy were sixteen and fifteen respectively, that they were 'very fine young women', who 'at least will command rectors'.

A dozen or so indoor servants, together with the groom, gardener and forester out of doors, besides the coachman, kept the wheels of Hagley turning. 'We used to meet the maids on Sundays', wrote Meriel in her recollections, for this was the day of the week that the children would carry up plates of plum pudding and beer to their attic bedrooms, with stone floors and no fireplaces. Children of the house shared with the maids a style of plain living, which bore no comparison to the rich fare served in the dining room, where the sculptor Vassalli's carefree Rococo ceiling and festoons of plasterwork entranced the family's visitors. Meriel recorded the occasional egg, 'allowed on journey days', to replace the bread and butter which was normal at schoolroom breakfast and tea.[4]

To Lucy, every member of this tight little community was a person in their own right, however indelibly marked as a servant, a sibling or a relative. Class was always present and never questioned. So, when she heard about the death of a servant, 'where he was fond of sitting' in the saddle room on 11 April 1855, she wrote a sensitive brief memoir in her diary, remembering one who, in the wide sense, was of her family. He 'just quietly slept himself away apparently painlessly'. 'Oh how one'll miss him', she reflected, 'at sheep shearing, hay making etc.'[5]

When a village girl was found to be pregnant, having 'been led into evil', as she put it, Lucy reflected on the tight moral control that the Lytteltons exercised in their estate village. It was 'such a rare thing in this parish that it is extra horrible'. She was devastated by the disgrace suffered by her little sisters' Swiss maid, Henriette, arrested for thieving and sentenced to fourteen days of prison and hard labour in 1861. Lucy, entering another world, declared herself much edified by a visit to Worcester gaol, where the girl, who cried after seeing her, was at her needlework: 'the prisoners looked subdued but not sullen, all busy at something or other, everything as clean as it's possible to be and beautifully ordered'.[6]

When Granny read *Adam Bede* to the children, Lucy pondered the 'irrevocableness of sin' as well as the fact of poverty. In her teens, she learnt that, even at feudal Hagley, sin was all around them. She recorded a talk about parish matters with Aunt Emmy, the rector's wife, who knew all about these things: 'Six people prayed for: four expecting babies, three of whom are anxious cases . . . little Wright children with disgraced father, mad mother and no money; little Shilcocks ill with dregs of scarlet fever . . . a bewildering bother about Annie Farmer, who we trusted was off our hands.'[7]

Teenage responsibility in the local Sunday schools was a deep-rooted expression of social paternalism. 'I had a class of little girls on Sundays from eleven till I married', recorded Meriel in her autobiography. Lucy had one, likewise. 'We both take our classes a walk', she noted on an October Sunday in 1856, 'mine into the garden.'[8] Status stood in for age and physical maturity, as a source of authority, with village children.

Then there were the regular events through which the family expressed their largesse and the local community its deference. Within the house, this was the function of the annual servants' ball in January, with country dances and Sir Roger de Coverley, an evening that always thrilled Lucy. In August, by tradition, the Sunday school children were feasted at the big house: 'the children sung before the house and dispersed cheering at about 6.30', Lucy wrote in her diary on 31 August 1854. She noted the event enthusiastically again in 1856, proud that several of her class had won prizes that year.[9]

Meriel testified to how the Lytteltons prided themselves on taking 'immense interest in all the village life and events'. 'We were always allowed and encouraged to visit in the cottages', she explained, 'after taking the people vegetables from our own gardens.'[10] In the autumn of 1856, Lucy was regularly visiting and reading to an old man in the village, George Rowe, who was in failing health, as well as calling upon a poor old woman at Clent.[11]

Louisa Bowater described her reception at Sotterley's harvest home in September 1861, following her London coming out that year:

> it was a pretty sight to see the labourers come in wearing their different badges . . . I found them all seated in the very prettily decorated barn

and worked hard distributing plum pudding etc . . . then came sports and tea, in the middle of which they insisted on cheering me and I could not resist thanking them in a few short broken sentences.[12]

Whereas on the Hagley estate, or staying with her Uncle William Gladstone at Hawarden, Lucy felt very safe indeed, outside the security of the family's own land, like all upper-class girls, she was vulnerable. She was a fearless rider on her own ground.[13] But, taking the pony carriage through her nearest market town on her thirteenth birthday, she knew she was a sight to behold in her fine clothes, causing 'the great amusement of all the little Stourbridge scugs who were dirtier and ruder than ever'.

Left as the senior figure at Hagley for a whole month in 1858, when she was still only seventeen, Lucy was anxious when her parents and Meriel were an hour late on the day that they came home. She reflected, 'I am never comfortable till a railway journey is safely over, they are never to be trusted.'[14] Not that travel by coach was necessarily preferable. After the journey to London in the open britzka for her first season in May 1859, Lucy found 'Papa the complexion of a stoker, having faced wind rain and dirt on the box'. She had not fared much better: she had herself begged off dining with Lady Wenlock on their arrival, 'being the colour of a turkey-cock from having to wash my face with cold water'.[15]

Emily Shore described a journey by the Regent coach to Stamford at thirteen, more than twenty years earlier than this, in the same sort of terms of disdain. Meeting the coach at Tempsford, they found the Wheatsheaf Inn there 'a horrid little place tainted with a vile smell of tobacco', so they 'resolved to walk about the churchyard'. When the coach arrived, they considered themselves 'very lucky' in securing the whole inside to themselves. They were pleased to find it extremely clean. But Emily mentioned a distasteful incident en route: 'someone tossed into the coach, through the window, a nasty dirty cloth, which rolled down my knee and fell on the floor'. Beyond home and the park gates, there was never complete safety for the upper class and the genteel, easily bothered by intrusive plebian and vulgar ways.

The teenagers in this book carried their class prejudices around with them unashamedly. It never crossed their minds that there was any other kind of structure for human society than the one they knew. Thus, in their diary writing, class could intrude quite unexpectedly and unselfconsciously. Thrust into her first London dancing lesson as she prepared for Queen Charlotte's Ball in 1856, Lucy commented, with aristocratic hauteur, that the twenty others were 'all remarkably plain vulgar girls, I suppose merchants' or tradesmen's daughters'.[16]

Among Protestant Ascendancy families in Ireland, class and colonialism, taken together, produced the insouciant attitude to cheap labour displayed by Louey Gore-Booth, born a Trench of Cangort Park, writing to her husband, stationed at Woolwich, in 1875. She was about to interview four Irish girls for a new nursemaid, reckoning, if she took one of them on, 'they would not want so much going out as people from about Woolwich'. 'Irish nurses if they are at all good certainly have more heart than English, this everyone agrees to', Louey insisted. 'If I can get one that is not vulgar and otherwise what one wants it will be a mercy', she concluded.[17]

What is striking about these diarists, as commentators on the class system, is their total confidence in a social order buttressed by many decades of gentry rule. This only began to be shattered by the cataclysm of 1914 and the First World War. Nowhere is this triumphant belief in the benevolence of current social realities more complete than in a diary that Caroline Girle wrote, on her trip into Norfolk in 1756. 'Never did landlord seem more beloved or indeed deserve to be so', she declared, visiting Weasenham Hall. 'Real benevolence', she concluded, was best exhibited 'in a family at their country seat'. At Weasenham 'nothing but death ever makes a servant leave them'. The housekeeper had served the family for 51 years, the butler for 32: ''tis really a pleasure to see them all so happy', she noted. Tenants dined at the Hall in turn. The glory of rural paternalism was the sense that it conveyed, and that many teenagers absorbed, of immutability, a sense that all was right with the world.[18]

Teenagers who were especially conscientious in their diary keeping, like Sophia Baker and Lucy Lyttelton, punctuated their domestic accounts with reference to a wider world, where, as Britons, they experienced, with others around them, the emotional ups and downs of ruling Brittania and of Imperial destiny. Sophia's Bayfordbury estate shared the horror which swept across England at the outbreak of the French Revolution, especially the execution of Louis XIV in January 1793. It was on 24 January, three days after the guillotine had fallen in Paris, that 'Mama had a letter from Papa saying that poor Louis was put to death.' 'About this time war was declared against France', she inscribed in February. Later that year, she heard about the progress of the Terror, mentioning on 26 October that 'the unfortunate Queen of France was guillotined after a mock trial' and a period of imprisonment.[19]

The war against France impinged on Sophia's consciousness several times in 1797 and 1798. In February 1797, she heard a story that 1,200 Frenchmen had landed in Wales. In June, she noted the third anniversary of the 1794 victory over the French fleet off Brest, quickly known as the Glorious First of June. In October, she chronicled the defeat of the Dutch at the battle of

Camperdown. In April 1798, Sophia was concerned at several accounts reaching her home of landings in Ireland and of civil war there: 'Oh Lord deliver us', she wrote emotionally.

Then Nelson's annihilation of the French fleet at the Battle of the Nile raised Sophia's spirits. This victory, she believed, was 'more complete than any since the Spanish Armada'. On 4 June 1799, the 'dear King's birthday', Sophia described his review of 13,000 volunteers in Hyde Park, 'the grandest sight of the kind ever seen', she was told. But her royalist loyalty was jolted the following May, when, in London herself at the time, 'at the play the king was shot at from the pit, providentially not hurt'. There was satisfaction in being able to conclude that 'the wretch was taken'.[20]

When Allied troops under Lord Raglan landed in the Crimea in September 1854, Lucy Lyttelton followed the course of the subsequent war avidly, reading Russell's despatches in *The Times*. She wrote three pages about Raglan's victory at Alma, six days after landing. 'I have been talking of nothing but the war lately and not mentioning home concerns', she noted on 2 November, 'we are leading a quiet life'. But the next week she filled six whole pages with the Crimea, such was the intensity of her involvement, describing the charge of the Light Brigade at Balaclava on 29 October: 'The slaughter was prodigious . . . The glorious fellows! On they rushed to certain, or almost certain, death, and flinched no more than if they were exercising in Hyde Park. They never paused in that fearful charge, that sent so many to Eternity.' Lucy attended the ceremony of presentation of medals in the Mall on 18 May 1855, illustrating it in her diary with pencil sketches of the arrival of the royal carriage and the Queen, who gave out the medals. It all seemed to her 'inexpressibly grand'. Everything that day, the file of wounded soldiers, the Queen's manner, the bands playing *Rule Britannia* and *Hearts of Oak*, thrilled her to the core. This was the apogee of Empire. When, at last, the long drawn-out siege of Sebastopol ended in September 1855, the words SEBASTOPOL HAS FALLEN won capital letters in the diary. Such 'grand news', declared Lucy, 'thank God at last He has sent this much prayed for blessing'.[21]

The Crimean War was only just over when Louisa Bowater began her diary. As the daughter of a Peninsular War general, who had doubtless followed its course with intense interest, she felt the same patriotic dedication to the Allied cause as Lucy. Visiting a panorama of Sebastopol in April 1856, she recorded enjoying it very much, because it gave 'such a clear idea of what happened'. In June, she gave a full account of her day out inspecting the Scutari Monument, 'erected to the officers and soldiers who fell in the late war'.[22] In 1857 Louisa spent an evening reading aloud to her Papa and Mama the account they had received of the siege of Lucknow: 'thrilling indeed', she wrote in her diary, 'are these hurried unvarnished notes which tell of their terrible experiences of death and starvation staring them in the face'.[23]

Socially conservative and royalist to the core of her being, Lucy found Queen Victoria's early widowhood hard to bear. Because she knew the Queen, having been introduced several times by then, she felt hugely concerned at her plight. Reflecting on her life on her own in the year 1861, the year she, Lucy, was twenty, she saw Prince Albert's death as 'the greatest grief of all'. Lucy was overwhelmed with the 'thought of our Queen now setting out on the untried sea of loneliness and affliction'. Papa, she noted in January 1862, as Lord Lieutenant, 'wrote a beautiful address of condolence for the county'.[24]

We end with gender. Our principal female diarists, Sophia Baker in the 1790s, and Lucy Lyttelton and Louisa Bowater in the 1850s, lived their gender daily through their emotions and, as their adult social life began, the rigours of their femininity became fully apparent. They are our most vivid and informative witnesses. Everything led up to their coming out. So what fundamentally, given this context of class and patriotism, do their accounts of themselves reveal in this respect?

They had been trained to be good, to speak and to move well, to be accomplished, to secure a husband with as much money and standing in society as their efforts in all these directions could possibly muster. The story is left untold here only in the sense that although all of these three girls married, none of them did so within our time scale, as teenagers.

During the last schoolroom years, we have seen that teenage girls faced intensifying pressure: the fashioning of them as polite and respectable young ladies jostled with the traditional exercises, such as their needlework and the pasting of scrapbooks. It was from around twelve or thirteen to seventeen that they were led into new accomplishments, into the broader knowledge acquired by historical and cultural tourism and into their apprenticeship in socially refined behaviour, on private visits or at public balls and assemblies. They had not yet actually come out but adult society was firmly on the horizon.

We have seen Sophia Baker experiencing the London sights, theatres and exhibitions, as early as eleven, twelve and thirteen. As the eldest girl in the family, her social education was already being taken seriously in 1793 to 1795. Her governess took her out visiting in the neighbourhood. She went out for the evening with her parents to see local friends on 21 October 1793, remaining upstairs with their child, 'while the rest were at dinner and stayed till nine o'clock'. It was in February 1794 that Sophia's schoolroom regime was first leavened by periods in London, focused upon frequent and intensive lessons, with new dancing, drawing and music masters, who visited the Bakers' home. 'Oh dear', she wrote, chronicling a six-hour day of these new lessons on 22 February. On the 1795 trip, there was one new master to get to know and more work with Mr Jenkins, Sophia's Scottish dancing master, who now took her out to show her off on the floor at a small salon. That April, she dined out alone with her Aunt Tilly.[25]

The frequent temper tantrums confessed by Sophia in her 1797 diary presumably reflected the cumulative impact upon her of parental pressure to perform. When visitors called at Bayfordbury on 12 January, Sophia was called upon to show them some of the drawings she had recently done, under the tuition of her London drawing master. She 'played on the piano and danced to the organ', when more visitors called on 16 January. Although much of her ill behaviour that year showed Sophia simply kicking out at her siblings, her governess and her Mama, some diary entries suggest a pattern of deliberate heel dragging. This expressed general protest at the expectations of her. She was 'out of temper' after Miss Allen's reprimands about not doing her piano practice and about the maid's disquiet, when she failed to have her pins put ready for her to be dressed. She cried when Miss Allen gave her 'ten lines to learn for not being dressed soon enough' on 20 January.[26]

Sophia's emotions were stirred almost daily with her struggle to behave properly and her many failings in this respect. In the midst of this difficult time came her confirmation, fixed on 28 March for a fortnight hence: 'Oh may I be deserving of so great an indulgence. I and Mama dined tete a tete and she gave me a little book on the confirmation.' A few days later, Sophia recorded that her Mama had cancelled all her lessons with her visiting masters, for 'more time to prepare for confirmation'. She recorded the event itself, on 11 April, as 'a great and solemn day with me'. She regretted answering Mama back on 13 April, but at least felt able to congratulate herself that she had 'behaved well' at the time of her first communions, on Good Friday and Easter Day that week.

The special imperative to be better as a confirmed Christian caused Sophia to abandon taking communion on the following Sunday: 'unfortunately angry with Charlotte and by that means prevented myself'. In the lonely presence of her diary, the fifteen-year old recorded the daily struggle to be good with total candour. In the following months, her testimony to the progress of her demanding social education was punctuated by notes on her devotions. For example, on 18 March 1798, Sophia 'received the sacrament with dear Mama' and on 25 March, she 'heard a lovely sermon at Mayfair on a timely repentance'.[27]

'Began with masters', Sophia had noted on 22 February 1797, signifying another gruelling round of training for the dance floor. The cotillon and scotch steps were now on the agenda. 'Did not do my lesson very perfectly with the dancing master', Sophia confessed on 20 March, but there were other days when it went very well. Mama was now regularly taking her out visiting. On 13 March, for example, we 'put on our new bonnets and suspenders and went with Mama to Mrs Stuart's . . . saw her baby linen and I took my basket to Lady Clayton . . . saw Miss Blackwell's painting'. That spring, Sophia was handling reels and country dances confidently at a series of balls; she was increasingly enjoying time spent in the London shops; she acquired a new master to teach her the tambourine. Yet the self-control she needed was only coming slowly. In May 1797, there were tears at her marching lesson, Mama found fault with her reading and 23 May was inscribed as a 'good day except telling Miss Allen I would not do what she told me'.

At home in the country the following January, guests at Bayfordbury 'came to see us dance': 'we made up country dances afterwards'. Now approaching seventeen, with younger sisters joining her course in politeness, they were soon back at the round of work with their masters. 'Dear Mama says she will allow Harriet and I to learn on the harp', chronicled Sophia on 20 February, adding that the same day they had 'bought our bonnets and purses'. Four days later, Madame Meriel appeared to start them on this new accomplishment. More demanding and sophisticated pursuits than previously were now filling Sophia's life, like attendance at the Lent lectures by the Bishop of London on St Matthew's gospel and an oratorio. A landmark came on 4 April: 'I drank tea sole at Mrs Hammersley's, saw the whole family and had a good deal of music.' Shopping lists began to appear in the diary.

At her debut at the Hertford Ball that December, Sophia danced eight dances. During 1799, besides accompanying her parents on social occasions more frequently than previously, she continued work with her singing, dancing and Italian masters, began serious work in watercolours and tackled some demanding reading. The diary mentions Molière's *Tartuffe* and Shakespeare's *Richard II* that autumn. It was in 1800, when she was rising nineteen, that Sophia was finally launched on society.[28]

Sophia Baker wrote of the early months of that year as a time of tea parties and evening socialising, with visits to the ballet and opera. In January, planning the season ahead, she recorded Mama's gift of 'a pair of topaz earings'. Lady Banks, who it was planned would present her to Queen Charlotte, died suddenly of an apoplectic fit just before her great day. A long entry described her presentation on 13 February: 'I was presented by Mama . . . I was dressed in white with a festoon of roses, three yellow feathers and a gold chain in my hair, a set of topaz earings, clasp and locket, all kind presents . . . The Queen was very gracious and good humoured . . . Mama was in purple velvet.' Sophia's first London season lasted until August. She was at court again on 20 February and also on 4 June, a 'very crowded and brilliant' occasion marking the King's sixty-second birthday.

Sophia kept up a hectic programme of public appearances with the opera, assemblies and balls, accompanied throughout, of course, by her mother as her chaperone. At Lady Salisbury's assembly on 13 March, she saw the Prince of Wales and Mrs Fitzherbert for the first time. She was 'much amused' by her first masquerade on 1 May, when she, her mother and her aunt all went as 'nuns in white veils'. Several assemblies were recorded as 'very dull' or even 'odious'. But she enjoyed Ranelagh, walked in the Temple Gardens and Kew Gardens and was at a gala at Vauxhall, 'the first time I had seen it'.

Mother and daughter did not see entirely eye to eye during this exhausting spring and summer. They had a 'fracas' on 3 July and, back in Hertfordshire, quarrelled in August, when her mother called her debutante girl, now almost nineteen, a 'blowsy brute'. But suitors gathered. Sophia's fondness for a Mr Methicke, often mentioned in these weeks, was betrayed by her comment on the Hertford ball, in the local winter season that followed on 3 November, when she confessed that he was 'much missed'.[29]

At thirteen and fourteen, Lucy Lyttelton's Worcestershire life still remained fundamentally domestic. Learning that turnips from the garden boiled better cut up and feeding and cleaning out her rabbits were typical activities outside schoolroom hours. But she was beginning to glimpse her future. She found the girls in the Fortescue family she had to entertain in September 1854, when their parents and hers were socialising, 'not pretty but nice'. One of them, in her view, talked 'too much, too fast and not of interesting enough subjects'. Piano practice was a daily chore. When more visitors arrived, she had to play her duets three times: 'I learnt today the tiresomeness of boring people with one's company uninvited from twelve to five.'

In April 1856, when Lucy was not yet fifteen, Meriel, Lucy and Lavinia had a concentrated set of dancing lessons to prepare them for the Queen's ball. Lucy found them long and dull. They were encouraged to take their clothes and hair very seriously. 'Poor Win', Lucy related, 'is to have her hair curl-papered every night till the great day to make it look a little less Irish and wild.' They were alike for the ball, 'in tarlatan frocks, trimmed with white ruches, twined round with some pretty pink trimmings'. They wore 'wreaths of pink roses' in their hair.

Lucy's posture became an issue. 'I groan under fearful inquisitory exercises', she wrote in January 1857, 'for the wrenching my shoulder blades into shape.' Meanwhile, her cultural knowledge and experience increased. She followed visits to *King Lear* and *The Winter's Tale* in 1856 with Handel's *Messiah*, 'wonderfully done', in 1857. There were trips to Oxford and Eton that March: 'we saw the boys' rooms, with characteristic differences between Charles' and Willy's'. In these years, still a schoolroom girl at home, Lucy was at the same time on the edge of society, learning how to behave, being moulded in bearing, in conversation and in her poise.[30]

Lucy's confirmation took place during a lovely visit to Falconhurst in Kent, the home of the Lytteltons' widowed family friend Catherine Talbot, in June 1857. The lush garden there was a paradise for bird's-nesting. Witherby the butler showed Lucy 'a darling linnet's nest, with five birdlings in it', besides teaching her how to fish for carp in the pond. Such diversions were a release from the confirmation classes held by Mr Hunt the vicar. Her parents had chosen to take her there because the Archbishop of Canterbury was holding a confirmation service, at Penshurst nearby. Her diary account well summarises the emotional impact of the actual confirmation on a serious and sensitive young girl:

> I had Papa on one side, Mama on the other . . . I went up and knelt on the altar step, feeling the strangest thrill as I did so for the first time . . . I know that I shall never forget the touch of the hand on my head . . . and then I went back and knelt down. The crying came then . . . And the new life has begun.[31]

Lucy marked her subsequent first communion with a long diary entry on her spiritual state of mind.[32]

Lucy recounted her coming out with all the feeling which makes her diary so remarkable an account of a Victorian girlhood. The process in her case was very gradual. On 9 May 1858, 'we met the three eldest Miss Fortescues . . . the third is just out'. Her older sister Meriel had preceded her, so at a party at the Gladstones on 26 May, while she appeared '*en qualite* of child', Meriel was a 'grown-up young lady'. A fortnight later, out to dinner with her widower father Lord Lyttelton, 'for the first time I was bowed at to leave the room . . . I didn't know if I was on my head or my heels'. Still aged sixteen, she ordered dinner at Hagley 'for the very first time in my life', reflecting on this in a note which summarised her feelings with the overawed words 'Oh dear.' Yet Lucy could not wait for her freedom. 'Can you imagine me writing in the gallery, having breakfasted with the "grown-ups", with my time in my own hands?', she asked her Aunt Pussy on the day after her seventeenth birthday:

> I mean to read a good deal – such a number of books that one ought to know, and in this way I hope to learn more than I could in the school-room with those repeated lessons . . . Then it will be nice being more *au fait* of everything, from hearing the talk at breakfast . . . Altogether I look forward greatly to my out life.

Lucy formally left the schoolroom on 5 September 1858, her seven-teenth birthday. 'Oh the deep sadness of the flying years', she wrote. The next stage of dress rehearsal for the aristocratic social world was the autumn round of house party visits. 'I am exhausted with behaving prop-erly', she noted after two days on the first of these to Alderley in Cheshire. She soon learnt it was not all fun: 'I am amused at everything, dullness and all, and in part it has been very pleasant.' 'I enjoyed it greatly and kept clear of all scrapes', Lucy reasoned, after time with cousins in North Yorkshire, where 'for the first time in my life I played for money'. 'I never saw finer country or more perfect and beautiful Early English ruins', she related after a 60-mile drive in a four-in-hand. There was a good deal of gambling and riding, as well as shooting, to watch and country house concerts to enjoy, before her return to Hagley, with 'a very happy launch into the world' behind her.

A trip by train with Meriel to see leading families in Cornwall, like the Robartes's at Lanhydrock and the Carew Poles at Antony, came next. Lucy loved a day out on Plymouth Sound, getting drenched up to the knees climbing to a lighthouse. She was awed by Tintagel, on an 80-mile exped-ition there in a post-chaise and two. But Christmas at home, blowing bubbles with the boys and playing draughts, whist and backgammon came as a merciful release from all this formal performance. On 30 December, Lucy 'much enjoyed' her first local ball at Stourbridge, chaperoned by Papa: 'we were not in bed till past three, nor up next morning till eleven-thirty! It felt so dissipated'.[33]

Meriel and Lucy's formal social initiation, in the season of 1859, was orchestrated, in place of their mother, in a manner that Meriel remem-bered as 'scrambling, casual and unarranged', by Mary Gladstone, their supportive Aunt Pussy. She was bringing out her own eldest daughter Agnes too, from 11, Carlton House Terrace in London. The season began with Madame de Persigny's ball, a brilliant one, as Lucy remarked, 'for them as danced'. Lord Lyttelton had made his rules clear: 'two balls a week', Lucy told her Aunt Emy, 'while some people go to two a night'. No waltzing was allowed, because Lord Lyttelton saw it as threatening to his daughters' inviolability and chastity, which brought Lucy intense frus-tration and meant some 'eventless' balls. The Lyttelton girls could only go to the opera when it did not include the ballet. Lucy's diary that summer was written up in snatched moments or by the light of dawn, after long nights out.

Royalty was the heart of it all. Lucy recorded 'frightful bathing-feel', the family's term taken from nervous anticipation of childhood sea dipping, at coming up to Queen Victoria, when she was presented at court on 7 June:

The look of interest and kindliness in the dear little Queen's face . . . the way she gave her hand to me to be kissed filled me with pleasure that I can't describe and that I wasn't prepared for . . . I feel as if I could do anything for her. She said to Aunt Pussy 'you have brought your nieces to me', with great feeling . . . so touching of her for no doubt she was thinking of our having no Mama to bring us.

In the next weeks there was much to learn, as Lucy swooned at meeting the King of France, or the Comte de Paris as this young man was called, and then kept failing in her aim of dancing with him, though she did manage to converse with him in her best French. This first season was a time for chaste but romantic encounters. 'Low was my curtsey, most gracious was his bow' ran her account of her introduction to the Duc d'Aumale. 'Well, dear Auntie', Lucy wrote to Lord Lyttelton's sister Emy on 27 May, 'I quite agree with what you say about society . . . only I do hope very earnestly that it may do me good in many ways – teaching one carefulness in talk, giving one opportunities to avoid silliness . . . and then the perpetual need of self-control.' Her mother had found her a handful in London in 1855: 'such want of stability', she commented then. Coming out in the way her mother would have wished, Lucy finally put aside her tomboyish ways. She had rolled in the grass in St James's Square when Mary Gladstone called there once. Now she took on the mantle of a young lady.

The climax, thrilling her to the core, came with an Ashridge 'breakfast', an elaborate entertainment, dancing combined with a garden party, on 9 July 1859. Travelling by train, the Lytteltons arrived at seven and got home, 'feeling wicked' because it was by then Sunday, at two in the morning. Her hopes of a quadrille with the Comte de Paris had not previously come off, but at Ashridge they danced the Lancers together. Entranced with his 'beautiful old French courtesy', Lucy confided to her diary the feelings that this romantic encounter produced: 'what with awe, respect, compassion and gratitude I was nearly out of my mind'.

Yet by this time she needed a break. 'Thank heaven', Lucy wrote on 29 July, 'we came safely home to the dear bright snug quietness of green summer Hagley.'[34] Her next years would inevitably be one long social performance, until that day when she accepted a hand in marriage, a Cavendish one, as it turned out, creating her potential destiny as mistress of Chatsworth. Lucy moved in the highest social and political circles of the land: 'Uncle William in rollicking spirits over his Budget', she wrote at nineteen, 'and very kind to me.'

Constrained by endless chaperoning, Lucy occasionally had to break free. She found it was somewhat easier to escape adult oversight when the family was away from home. 'I walked alone on the pier, which it suddenly struck me was scampish', Lucy confided to her diary in April 1861. A couple of days later, attending evensong at a church near their hotel, she found herself walking back alone. She reacted instinctively: 'I pretended to belong to two elderly ladies in succession, who I don't think found out that they were escorting me.'[35]

Louisa Bowater wrote an account of the stages of her launching into society, beginning with the Queen's juvenile ball at age twelve on 1 May 1854. 'My frock', she wrote vividly, recalling the event in old age, 'was white tarlatan over silk with a silver band and a streamer of flowers on the upper skirt and I wore a white acacia wreath in my hair.' 'How my heart beat', was her memory, 'as we went up the great staircase.' She never forgot her social gaffe that night: 'at supper I made a dreadful mistake. I went up to the top of one table where the Queen was going not knowing it was the top. The Queen asked me who I was and what I would like.' The same note mentions her first play, her first country house visits, in Warwickshire in January 1854, and her first wedding that May. At her first concert that month, given by the German Choral Singers, 'they sang Rule Britannia and God save the Queen into the bargain which were most inspiring'.[36]

Louisa began serious dancing lessons in Kingston at around her fourteenth birthday in 1856, soon graduating to a London dancing master. She really enjoyed them, describing her lesson on 17 May as 'great fun' and one on 14 July as 'a capital lesson, especially a splendid lancers and waltz'. Her mother and governess added to her practice on the dance floor with solid doses of cultural and historical visits that summer to develop Louisa's mind and conversation. By the end of July, she was seen as fit to be let loose in company. So, after lessons on 30 July she put on her best clothes and walked, on a 'horribly hot' afternoon, with Mademoiselle across the Park at Richmond, to take tea with a girl a little younger than herself. But she was taller, Louisa noted. This was a competitive and staged teenage social performance: 'she plays most admirably, a great great deal better than I do. Between speaking English and German together and French to the governess, we ended by not knowing which language we were speaking.'

Although Louisa was still only fourteen when the Bowaters travelled to Suffolk for their summer holiday in 1856, she was given a personal maid to take care of her clothes and coiffeur. On 25 August, her maid Mellish, she wrote, 'took an immense time at my head', perfecting her hair. On an expedition to Southwold in the chariot, her governess travelled inside with Mama and Grandmama, while she rode with Mellish, between her two male cousins. This relaxed family time was also practice in the rituals that Louisa needed to master for her appearances on the national social stage. A trip in the little carriage on her own, but accompanied by Mellish, was the next stage in October. Friends nearby had a child to be baptised. 'I felt rather shy about it', Louisa chronicled, relapsing into plain narrative, 'but was most kindly received. Mother was churched and then all the friends went to the font. We walked back to the house, had tea, went up and saw the baby and drove home.'

This intermediate stage of life is still evident in Louisa's diary for 1857, when she turned fifteen. Every now and then, the chrysalis was expected briefly to open her wings. Her detailed account of a country house weekend, early in 1857, indicates her response to a new test: arrival and tea, dressing for dessert the first evening; a piano performance to accompany her hostess next day; a drawing room evening with the Saxon reel, 'a merry dance made up of Lancers, quadrille and reel'; then the predictable Sir Roger de Coverley's, before bed at 11.30. The next day there was snowballing and Hare and Hounds, in a party of ten or so, then 'a frantic Lancers and waltz interspersed with tea'.[37]

Well before her confirmation day, as we have seen, Louisa had adopted her diary as the crucial aide memoire of her spiritual progress.[38] The heady impact of social success was threatening her equilibrium in 1857, with a June ball in Berkeley Square which turned her head in a way she was not prepared for. She danced the whole evening, which was 'much pleasanter than I expected'. 'I really enjoyed it very much', she confessed. At a garden party on 6 July, four days before her confirmation, Louisa had a long conversation with a chaplain of the Brigade of Guards about 'the world and its pleasures, how sad to see people entirely engrossed by them and fine intellects wasted upon trifles'. Louisa was amazed to find herself having 'a conversation of such depth and earnestness in society . . . with such an entire stranger'.

On 9 July, Louisa rode in Richmond Park with her Papa: 'Princess very bumptious and it was capital fun.' Predictably she made much of her confirmation the next day. She was a little over sixteen. Her long journal account stressed, more than parental involvement, how she leaned on her governess, being comforted by Agnes Lentz, who 'read to me and talked with me'. She summarised her feelings as follows:

> I never was so intensely and purely happy in my life as while dressing with my eyes fixed upon the 'blue ethereal sky' . . . I felt nothing but the infinite love of God to me personally and a high resolution, an earnest eager longing, to dedicate myself heart and soul to him.[39]

Back at Suffolk in March 1859 Louisa luxuriated in estate life. The blossom was on the apricot tree, the elms were in full leaf, wood pigeons, rooks and robins were nesting. 'Was there ever anything so lovely, or was any place in the world as this dear old Sotterley', the grandparental home where she had always spent holidays, she mused. Her mind was opening. A visit to the historian Agnes Strickland, who she found surrounded by books at her home near Southwold, was one of the 'red letter days of my girlhood'.

In the autumn of 1859, now seventeen, Louisa left the schoolroom and attended two balls in Norwich. At the first, on 19 October, 'I wore white tarlatan with lilies of the valley and danced ten dances never sitting down once.' In a dazzling social whirl quite new to her, she did not hear governess Agnes Lentz, who had always warned her about vanity. Three days afterwards she collected herself in a long diary entry:

> One can tell oneself that one is a little goose for thinking any more of the attention paid one or imagining one has anything personally to do with success one has had (for I certainly consider it a success to dance all night at one's first ball). It is always pleasant to be good natured and I had every advantage in point of Papa and Mama knowing people, going with a party and being all but in one's own county. But I did forget rather and it has taken me three days to find out that I was vain. The thought Agnes would say it was all fudge did cross my mind . . . but it was as she said – in that brilliant scene it all seemed true and her words distant and faint.

That autumn was a crisis in Louisa's emotional life, as she sought to escape from the trammels of her governess's training. She struggled with the precepts about modesty that Agnes had inculcated. Her diary became the agent of her emerging self, as she immersed herself once and for all in society and began to adopt its values.

In a wildly enthusiastic account of her second public ball on 1 December, Louisa concluded that 'it was a most capital ball that everyone agreed'. 'I danced to my very heart's content no less than fourteen times and only sat down once.' Salving any conscience remaining, Louisa listed her partners, reminding herself of the safety in numbers and reflecting, 'I don't know that one man was more interesting or a better partner than another for on the whole they were all pleasant.' The account this time continues:

> And now for the serious side. I know I was vain this time – it was about my waltzing. I was complimented and sought after and I was disappointed when I sat down one Lancers. Oh, fie, am I as single-hearted, as simple and earnest as I ought to be? I fear not . . . I did not pray so anxiously beforehand. Agnes's words sounded fainter than before. Much, though very much, comes to me now which she said and

proves itself often too true. We did not come away till the last dance, were very merry over supper and did not get to bed till 5.0. However I enjoyed it tremendously and would fain be thankful for the granted pleasure.[40]

In her first full London season at nineteen in 1861, Louisa, revelled in her mastery of the waltz. Taking the floor repeatedly by storm, she was a brilliant success. Her presentation to the Queen went well. 'I think Papa, the person I was most anxious to please', she wrote, 'was really gratified at the reception I met with and the way I got through it.' Predictably, she replicated Lucy's nerves two years previously when, at her presentation, she began to feel 'very pit-a-pat', as we 'began to make our way into the Presence'.[41]

This is the place to leave these girls, whose diaries are so wonderfully candid. Their experience of childhood reached its climax with their coming out; adulthood now beckoned. Both, the waltzing Louisa and the fretful Lucy, so tried by her father's forbidding her to waltz, duly found partners in marriage and became the mistresses of great houses.[42] Neither, strangely, ever had children of her own. Both had been taught to 'live under obedience', the watchwords of female growing up from 1600, across three centuries and more, until 1914. Boys, we have seen, were, in many respects, brought up more harshly than girls, but girls faced much greater constraints on themselves and on their emotions. The insistent and demanding imperative for them was learning the practice of total self-control.

Abbreviations

BL	British Library
NA	National Archives
ODNB	*Oxford Dictionary of National Biography*
RO	Record Office
TRHS	*Transactions of the Royal Historical Society*

Notes

Introduction

1. Wrightson, in Barry and Brooks, eds, *The Middling Sort of People*, pp. 28–51.
2. Langton, in Clark, ed., *Cambridge Urban History of Britain*, II, pp. 453–90; Hunt, *The Middling Sort*.
3. Cannadine, *Class in Britain*, pp. 24–105.
4. Langford, *A Polite and Commercial People*, p. 116.
5. Shore, *Journal*, pp. 1–2; *ODNB*.
6. Davidoff and Hall, *Family Fortunes*, p. 13.
7. Scott, 'Gender: A Useful Category of Historical Analysis', pp. 42–4.
8. Willes, *Memories of Childhood*, pp. 8, 18; Pevsner and Radcliffe, *Cornwall*, p. 89.
9. K. and M. Fawday, *Pollock's History of English Dolls and Toys*, pp. 170, 186–7.
10. Plumb, 'New World of Children', in McKendrick, Brewer and Plumb, eds, *The Birth of a Consumer Society*, p. 310; cited in Fawday, *Pollock's History of English Dolls and Toys*, p. 151.
11. Willes, *Memories of Childhood*, pp. 34–5.
12. Willes, *Memories of Childhood*, pp. 38–9.
13. Pickering, *John Locke and Children's Books in Eighteenth-Century England*, pp. 104–37.
14. Plumb, 'New World of Children', in McKendrick, Brewer and Plumb, eds, *The Birth of a Consumer Society: The Commercialisation of Eighteenth-Century England*, pp. 300–10; Jackson, *Engines of Instruction, Mischief and Magic*, pp. 71–99.
15. Willes, *Memories of Childhood*, pp. 40–43; Ricketts, *The Unforgiving Minute*, pp. 289–94.
16. Plate.
17. Plate.
18. Willes, *Memories of Childhood*, pp. 26–7; plate.
19. Willes, *Memories of Childhood*, pp. 22, 26–38.

Chapter 1: Childhood

1. Thomas, 'Age and Authority in Early Modern England', *Proceedings of the British Academy*, 52 (1976), p. 218; MacDonald, *Mystical Bedlam*, p. 43.
2. Cited in Fildes, ed., *Women as Mothers*, p. 117.
3. Cited in Fletcher, 'Prescription and Practice', in Wood ed., *The Church and Childhood*, p. 326.
4. Schnucker, 'Puritan Attitudes towards Childhood Discipline', in Fildes, ed., *Women as Mothers*, 108–21; Schucking, *Puritan Family*, p. 74.

5. Cunningham, *Children and Childhood in Western Society*, pp. 49–51.
6. Houlbrooke, *English Family Life*, p. 158.
7. Cited in Cliffe, *The Puritan Gentry*, p. 69.
8. Hill, *Society and Puritanism*, pp. 443–81.
9. Gouge, *Domestical Duties*, appendix of prayers. I am grateful for this quotation to Patrick Collinson.
10. Guy, *Piety's Pillar, a Sermon Preached at the Funeral of Mistress Gouge* (1626).
11. Fletcher in Wood, ed., *The Church and Childhood*, pp. 327–9.
12. Fletcher, 'The Expansion of Education in Berkshire and Oxfordshire 1500–1670', *British Journal of Educational Studies*, XV (1967), pp. 51–9.
13. Fletcher in Wood, ed., *The Church and Childhood*, pp. 335–8.
14. Cited in Thomas, *Rule and Misrule in the Schools of Early Modern England*, pp. 8–9.
15. Fletcher in Wood, ed., *The Church and Childhood*, p. 338; Fletcher, *Gender, Sex, and Subordination*, pp. 300–3.
16. Childs, 'Prescriptions for Manners in English Courtesy Literature 1690–1760 and their Social Implications', Oxford D.Phil thesis, 1984, pp. 267–8; *ODNB*.
17. Fletcher, *Gender, Sex and Subordination*, pp. 331, 384–9; Shoemaker, *Gender in English Society*, p. 32.
18. Bayne-Powell, *The English Child in the Eighteenth Century*, pp. 46–7; *ODNB*.
19. Cited in Summerfield, *Fantasy and Reason: Children's Literature in the Eighteenth Century*, p. 2.
20. Citations from Cunningham, *Children and Childhood in Western Society*, pp. 62–4.
21. I am grateful for discussion of this point with Professor Julia Briggs.
22. Calvert, *Children in the House*, p. 59.
23. Plumb, *The Pursuit of Happiness*, pp. 59, 123; Retford, *Art of Domestic Life*, pp. 83–148.
24. Citations from Cunningham, *Children and Childhood in Western Society*, p. 66.
25. Coveney, *The Image of Childhood*, p. 46.
26. Langford, *A Polite and Commercial People: England 1727–1783*, p. 501.
27. Jackson, *Engines of Instruction, Mischief and Magic*, pp. 71–168.
28. More, *Strictures on the Modern System of Female Education* (1799), I, 57.
29. Cunningham, *Children and Childhood in Western Society*, pp. 70–2.
30. Morgan, *Manners, Morals and Class in England 1774–1858*, pp. 12–15.
31. Morgan, *Manners, Morals and Class*, pp. 15–18.
32. Fletcher, *Gender, Sex and Subordination*, pp. 401–8.
33. Shoemaker, *Gender in English Society*, p. 42; Sulloway, *Jane Austen and the Province of Womanhood*; Morgan, *Sisters in Time: Imagining Gender in Nineteenth-Century British Fiction*.
34. Shoemaker, *Gender in English Society*, pp. 42–3.
35. Girouard, *The Return to Camelot: Chivalry and the English Gentleman*; Newsome, *Godliness and Good Learning*; Shoemaker, *Gender in English Society*, p. 43.
36. Cunningham, *Children and Childhood in Western Society*, pp. 73–5; Davidoff *et al.*, *The Family Story*, pp. 65–6.
37. Cited in Morgan, *Manners, Morals and Class in England*, p. 18.
38. Morgan, *Manners, Morals and Class in England*, pp. 19–31.
39. Curtin, *Propriety and Position: A Study of Victorian Manners*, p. 38.

Chapter 2: Boyhood

1. Roper and Tosh, eds, *Manful Assertions*, p. 18.
2. Elyot, *The Boke named the Governor*, ed., D.W. Rude, I, xxi, 93.
3. Shoemaker, *Gender in English Society*, pp. 25–6, 29.
4. Cogan, *The Haven of Health*, p. 241.

5. Collinson, *The Religion of Protestants: The Church in English Society 1559–1625*, pp. 227–9; Hitchcock, *English Sexualities 1700–1800*, especially chapter 3.
6. Gowing, *Domestic Dangers: Women, Words and Sex in Early Modern London*, pp. 121–2. See also T. Meldrum, 'A Women's Court in London: Defamation at the Bishop of London's Consistory Court 1700–1745, *London Journal*, 19 (1994), pp. 10–11.
7. Tosh, *A Man's Place*, pp. 107–8, 130; Tosh, 'The Old Adam and the New Man: Emerging Themes in the History of English Masculinities 1750–1850', in Hitchcock and Cohen, eds, *English Masculinities*, pp. 224–5.
8. Farmington, Lewis Walpole Library, Hanbury Williams papers, vol. 68, fols 110, 146. See also Fletcher, *Gender, Sex and Subordination*, pp. 342–3.
9. Gillis, 'Servants, Sexual Relations and the Risks of Illegitimacy in London 1801–1900', in Newton, *et al.*, eds, *Sex and Class in Women's History*, pp. 114–45.
10. Cited in Barber, '"Stolen Goods": The Sexual Harassment of Female Servants in West Wales during the Nineteenth Century', *Rural History* 4 (1993), p. 132.
11. Citations from Foyster, 'Boys Will Be Boys? Manhood and Aggression, 1660–1800', in Hitchcock and Cohen, eds, *English Masculinities*, p. 151.
12. Shepard, *Meanings of Manhood*, pp. 93–151; Roper, *Oedipus and the Devil*, p. 107.
13. Spufford, *Small Books and Pleasant Histories*, pp. 225–32.
14. Huntington Library, San Marino, California, STT 1943.
15. Fletcher, *Gender, Sex and Subordination*, pp. 129–30.
16. Amussen, '"The Part of a Christian Man": The Cultural Politics of Manhood in Early Modern England', in Amussen and Kishlansky, eds, *Political Culture and Cultural Politics in Early Modern England*, pp. 220, 227.
17. Cited in Thomas, 'Age and Authority in Early Modern England', *Proceedings of the British Academy* 52 (1976), p. 218.
18. Allestree, *The Gentleman's Calling*, p. 21.
19. Foyster in Hitchcock and Cohen, eds, *English Masculinities*, pp. 154, 159.
20. Cited in Brauer, *The Education of a Gentleman*, p. 20.
21. Brauer, *The Education of a Gentleman*, pp. 15–16.
22. Citations from Fletcher, *Gender, Sex and Subordination*, p. 132; Brauer, *The Education of a Gentleman*, p. 25.
23. Martyn, *Youth's Instructions*, pp. 16, 31–2, 52, 68–9.
24. Henry Lord Delamere, Earl of Warrington, *Advice to his Children*, p. 16.
25. Scott, *A Father's Instructions to his Son*, pp. 13–14, 16, 23–4, 27.
26. Gailhard, *The Compleat Gentleman*, I, pp. 79–80.
27. Locke, 'Some Thoughts Concerning Education', in Axtell, ed., *The Educational Writings of John Locke*, pp. 114, 121–2.
28. Fletcher, *Gender, Sex and Subordination*, pp. 87–8, 297–8.
29. Tosh, *A Man's Place*, pp. 103–4.
30. Fletcher, *Gender, Sex and Subordination*, p. 305.
31. For hospitality see Heal, *Hospitality in Early Modern England*, especially chapters 2 and 4.
32. Tosh, *A Man's Place*, p. 111.
33. Citation from Brauer, *The Education of a Gentleman*, pp. 110–20.
34. Bryson, *From Courtesy to Civility*, pp. 276–83.
35. Bryson, *From Courtesy to Civility*, pp. 8–25.
36. Bryson, *From Courtesy to Civility*, pp. 31–6, 54–7.
37. Cleland, *The Institution of a Young Nobleman*, p. 65.
38. Martyn, *Youth's Instruction*, p. 79.
39. Allestree, *The Gentleman's Calling*, p. 26.
40. Ellis, *The Gentle Sinner*, pp. 108–9.
41. Walker, *Of Education, Especially of Young Gentlemen*, part 2, chapter 3.
42. Gailhard, *Compleat Gentleman*, I, pp. 89–90.

43. Martyn, *Youth's Instructions*, p. 99.
44. Bryson, *From Courtesy to Civility*, pp. 161–4.
45. Allestree, *The Gentleman's Calling*, p. 26.
46. Gailhard, *Compleat Gentleman*, I, pp. 89–90.
47. Bryson, *From Courtesy to Civility*, pp. 183–7.
48. Henry, Lord Delamere, *The Earl of Warrington's Advice to his Children*, p. 20.
49. Ellis, *Gentle Sinner*, pp. 114–15.
50. Gailhard, *Compleat Gentleman*, I, p. 57.
51. Lacqueur, *Making Sex*; Fletcher, *Gender, Sex and Subordination*, pp. 283–97, 322–46, 376–400; Shoemaker, *Gender in English Society*, pp. 31–5, 85, 313–14; Fissell. 'Gender and Generation: Representing Reproduction in Early Modern England', *Gender and History*, 7 (1995), pp. 433–56.
52. Harvey, *Reading Sex in the Eighteenth Century*, pp. 78–145.
53. Cited in Childs, 'Prescription for Manners in English Courtesy Literature 1690–1760 and their Social Implications', Oxford D.Phil thesis, 1984, p. 98.
54. Klein, *Shaftesbury and the Culture of Politeness: Moral Discourse and Cultural Politics in Early Eighteenth-Century England*; Klein 'Liberty, Manners and Politeness in early Eighteenth-Century England', *Historical Journal* 32 (1989), pp. 583–605.
55. Cohen, *Fashioning Masculinity: National Identity and Language in the Eighteenth Century*, especially pp. 42–3. See also Cohen 'Manliness, Effeminacy and the French: Gender and the Construction of National Character in Eighteenth-Century England', in Hitchcock and Cohen, eds, *English Masculinities*, pp. 44–62.
56. Berger, 'Maxims of Conduct into Literature: Jonathan Swift and Polite Conversation', in Carré, ed., *The Crisis of Courtesy* (1994), pp. 83–9.
57. Carter, 'Men about Town: Representations of Foppery and Masculinity in Early Eighteenth-Century Urban Society', in Barker and Chalus, eds, *Gender in Eighteenth-Century England: Roles, Representations and Responsibilities*, pp. 49–50.
58. Lamoine, 'Lord Chesterfield's "Letters" as Conduct Books', in Carré, ed., *The Crisis of Courtesy* (1994), pp. 105–17; Fletcher, *Gender, Sex and Subordination*, pp. 336–8.
59. Carter, *Men and the Emergence of Polite Society*, pp. 78–80, 88–9.
60. Carter, 'An "Effeminate" or "Efficient" Nation? Masculinity and Eighteenth-Century Social Documentary', *Textual Practice* 11 (1997), 436–43.
61. Cohen, *Fashioning Masculinity*, pp. 43–50.
62. Carter, *Men and the Emergence of Polite Society*, pp. 124–63.
63. Alexander, *The History of Women from the Earliest Antiquity to the Present Time*, I, p. 314.
64. Gisborne, *An Enquiry into the Duties of the Female Sex*, p. 58.
65. Cohen, *Fashioning Masculinity*, pp. 109–10.
66. Langford, *A Polite and Commercial People*, p. 586.
67. Fordyce, *Addresses to Young Men*, p. 16.
68. Davidoff and Hall, *Family Fortunes*, pp. 108–13.
69. Taylor, *Advice to the Teens: or Practical Helps towards the Formation of One's Own Character*, p. 93; Tosh in Hitchcock and Cohen, eds, *English Masculinities*, pp. 234–6.
70. Neddam, 'Constructing Masculinities under Thomas Arnold of Rugby (1828–1842): Gender, Educational Policy and School Life in an Early-Victorian Public School', in *Gender and Education* 16 (2004), pp. 303–26.
71. Mangan, 'Social Darwinism and Upper Class education in Late Victorian and Edwardian England', in Mangan and Walvin eds, *Manliness and Morality*, pp. 137–8.
72. Girouard, *Life in the English Country House*, pp. 292–8.
73. Tosh, 'The Old Adam and the New Man: Emerging Themes in the History of English Masculinities 1750–1850', in Hitchcock and Cohen, eds, *English Masculinities*, pp. 216–19.
74. Fletcher, *Gender, Sex and Subordination*, pp. 101–53.
75. Tosh in Hitchcock and Cohen, eds, *English Masculinities*, p. 231.

Chapter 3: Girlhood

1. Whately, *The Bride Bush*, p. 97.
2. Citations from Childs, 'Prescriptions for Manners', pp. 265, 267.
3. Sommerville, *Sex and Subjection: Attitudes to Women in Early Modern Society*, pp. 8–34; Fletcher, *Gender, Sex and Subordination*, pp. 30–59.
4. Fletcher, *Gender, Sex and Subordination*, pp. 60–82.
5. Schiebinger, *The Mind Has No Sex? Women and the Origins of Modern Science*, p. 2.
6. Barker-Benfield, *Culture of Sensibility*, pp. 1–36; Schiebinger, *Mind Has No Sex?*, pp. 190–261; Fletcher, *Gender, Sex and Subordination*, pp. 291–3, 390.
7. Moscucci, *The Science of Woman: Gynaecology and Gender in England 1800–1929*, p. 15.
8. Digby, 'Women's Biological Straitjacket', in Mendus and Rendall, eds, *Sexuality and Subordination*, pp. 192–220.
9. Jordanova, *Sexual Visions: Images of Gender in Science and Medicine Between the Eighteenth and Twentieth Centuries*.
10. Fletcher, *Gender, Sex and Subordination*, pp. 3–43, 60–82; Fletcher, 'Men's Dilemma: The Future of Patriarchy in England 1560–1660', *TRHS*, IV (1994); Foyster, 'A Laughing Matter? Marital Discord and Gender Control in Seventeenth-Century England', *Rural History: Economy, Society, Culture*, 4 (1993), pp. 5–21.
11. Fletcher, 'The Protestant Idea of Marriage in Early Modern England', in Fletcher and Roberts, eds, *Religion, Culture and Society in Early Modern Britain*, pp. 161–81; Hull, *Chaste, Silent and Obedient: English Books for Women 1475–1640*; Henderson and McManus, eds, *Half Humankind: Contexts and Texts of the Controversy about Women* in England 1540–1640; Fletcher, *Gender, Sex and Subordination*, pp. 377–83.
12. For example, Pollock, *With Faith and Physic: The Life of a Tudor Gentlewoman Lady Grace Mildmay 1552–1620*, pp. 25–30.
13. Pollock, '"Teach Her to Live Under Obedience": The Making of Women in the Upper Ranks of Early Modern England', *Continuity and Change* 4 (1989), pp. 231–58.
14. Fletcher, *Gender, Sex and Subordination*, pp. 378–400.
15. George Saville, Marquess of Halifax, 'The Lady's New Year Gift or Advice to a Daughter' (1688), in Jones, ed., *Women in the Eighteenth Century: Constructions of Femininity*, p. 18.
16. Fletcher, *Gender, Sex and Subordination*, pp. 385, 390–1.
17. Mandeville, *The Fable of the Bees* (1724), I, pp. 60–1, cited in Hill, *Eighteenth-Century Women: An Anthology* (1984), p. 28.
18. Fielding, *Tom Jones*, I, 16–17 cited in Hill, *Eighteenth-Century Women*, p. 29.
19. Wilkes, *A Letter of Genteel and Moral Advice*, p. 77; for masturbation see Hitchcock, *English Sexualities 1700–1800*, p. 29.
20. Citations from Fletcher, *Gender, Sex and Subordination*, pp. 380, 386.
21. Shoemaker, *Gender in English Society*, pp. 62–5.
22. Barker-Benfield, *Culture of Sensibility*, p. 147.
23. Fordyce, *Sermons to Young Women*, p. 147.
24. Richardson, *Clarissa* (1748), cited in B. Hill, *Eighteenth-Century Women*, p. 32; see also Jones, 'The Seductions of Conduct: Pleasure and Conduct Literature', in Porter and Roberts, eds, *Pleasure in the Eighteenth Century*, pp. 119, 122–4.
25. Fletcher, *Gender, Sex and Subordination*, pp. 393–4.
26. Cited in Pollock in '"Teach Her to Live Under Obedience", in *Continuity and Change* 4, 1989, p. 245.
27. Pollock, *A Lasting Relationship*, pp. 249–50; Fletcher, *Gender, Sex and Subordination*, pp. 378, 381, 385.
28. For example, Steele, *The Ladies Library* (1714) I, pp. 43–5.
29. Steele, *Ladies Library*, III, pp. 47–8.
30. Gregory, *A Father's Legacy to his Daughters* (1774), pp. 10, 13–15.

31. Langford, *Polite and Commercial People*, pp. 606–7.
32. Pennington, *An Unfortunate Mother's Advice to her Absent Daughters in a Letter to Miss Pennington* (1761), p. 19.
33. Gisborne, *An Enquiry into the Duties of the Female Sex* (1798), p. 43.
34. Ellis, *The Women of England, their Social Duties and Domestic Habits* (1850), p. 29, cited in Shoemaker, *Gender in English Society*, p. 24.
35. Davidoff and Hall, *Family Fortunes*, p. 89; Girouard, *Life in the English Country House*, pp. 270–1; Tosh, *A Man's Place*, pp. 36–7, 83–4.
36. Sandford, *Woman in her Social and Domestic Character* (1831), pp. 135–6.
37. Gorham, *The Victorian Girl and the Feminine Ideal*, pp. 78–9.
38. Langford, *Polite and Commercial People*, pp. 59–122; Brewer, *The Pleasures of the Imagination*.
39. Fletcher, *Gender, Sex and Subordination*, pp. 19–20.
40. Braithwaite, *The English Gentlewoman*, p. 297.
41. Price, *The Virtuous Wife is the Glory of her Husband* (1667), pp. 12–13.
42. Langford, *Polite and Commercial People*, p. 109.
43. Tague, *Women of Quality*, pp. 162–6.
44. Vickery, *The Gentleman's Daughter: Women's Lives in Georgian England*, pp. 225–72, 279–80.
45. Borsay, *The English Urban Renaissance*, pp. 257–83.
46. Vickery, *Gentleman's Daughter*, pp. 276–9.
47. Davidoff, *The Best Circles: Society, Etiquette and the Season*, pp. 20–53.
48. Dyhouse, *Girls Growing Up in Late Victorian and Edwardian England*, pp. 23–4.
49. Ellis, *Daughters of England* (1842), p. 255.
50. Dyhouse, *Girls Growing Up*, pp. 25–6.
51. Braithwaite, *English Gentlemen*, p. 293.
52. Essex, *The Young Ladies Conduct* (1722), pp. 80–2, 90–3.
53. Wilkes, *A Letter of Genteel and Moral Advice to a Young Lady* (1780), pp. 123, 126; Steele, *Ladies Library*, I, p. 63.
54. Citations from Pollock, *Continuity and Change* 4 (1989), pp. 238–9.
55. Allestree, *Lady's Calling*, part II, p. 8; Pollock, '"Teach Her to Live Under Obedience": The Making of Women in the Upper Ranks of Modern England', in *Continuity and Change* 4 (1989), p. 240.
56. Pennington, *An Unfortunate Mother's Advice*, pp. 23–4.
57. Fordyce, *Sermons to Young Women*, p. 25.
58. Jenyns, *The Modern Fine Lady* (1717).
59. Chapone, *Letters on the Improvement of the Mind* (1793), cited in Jones, ed., *Women in the Eighteenth Century*, p. 105.
60. Sandford, *Woman in her Social and Domestic Character*, p. 124.
61. Cited in Pollock, *Lasting Relationship*, p. 222.
62. Cited in Ezell, *The Patriarch's Wife: Literary Evidence and the History of the Family*, p. 15, who gives other examples.
63. Cited by Pollock, *Continuity and Change* 4 (1989), p. 240.
64. Braithwaite, *English Gentlewoman*, cited by Cahn, *Industry of Devotion: The Transformation of Women's Work in England 1550–1660*, p. 114.
65. Pollock, *A Lasting Relationship*, p. 226.
66. Smith, *Reason's Disciples*, pp. 117–39, 151–201; Rogers, *Feminism in Eighteenth-Century England*, 72–4, 89–113; Shoemaker, *Gender in English Society*, pp. 47–52.
67. Gisborne, *An Enquiry into the Duties of the Female Sex* (1798), especially p. 62.
68. Steele, *Ladies Library* I, pp. 21–8, 438–44; Fletcher, *Gender, Sex and Subordination*, p. 398.
69. Essex, *Young Ladies Conduct*, pp. 39–40.

70. Wilkes, *A Letter of Genteel and Moral Advice*, pp. 96–7; Fletcher, *Gender, Sex and Subordination*, p. 398.
71. Chapone, *Letters on the Improvement of the Mind*, pp. 3–8; Francis and Keary, eds, *Francis Letters*, p. 203.
72. Fordyce, *Sermons to Young Women* I, pp. 269–88.
73. Pennington, *An Unfortunate Mother's Advice*, p. 24.
74. Gisborne, *Enquiry into the Duties of the Female Sex*, p. 62.
75. Citations from Fletcher, *Gender, Sex and Subordination*, pp. 385–7, 396–400.
76. Retford, *Art of Domestic Life*, p. 83.
77. Vickery, *Gentleman's Daughter*, pp. 8–9, 225–84.
78. Marriott, *Female Conduct being an Essay on the Art of Pleasing* (1759), pp. xvii–xix, xxv–xxviii.
79. Tosh, *A Man's Place*, pp. 27–59; Flint, *The Woman Reader 1837–1914* , p. 71.
80. John Ruskin, *Sesame and Lilies*, p.145, cited in Davidoff, *Worlds Between*, p. 52.
81. Poovey, *The Proper Lady and the Woman Writer: Ideology and Style in the Works of Mary Wollstonecraft, Mary Shelley and Jane Austen*; Armstrong, *Desire and Domestic Fiction: A Political History of the Novel*.
82. Hobby, *Virtue of Necessity: English Women's Writings 1649–1688*, p. 8.
83. Austen, *Pride and Prejudice*, p. 113; Jones, 'The Seduction of Conduct', in Porter and Roberts, eds, *Pleasure in the Eighteenth Century*, pp. 130–2.
84. Twycross-Martin, 'Woman Supportive or Woman Manipulative? The "Mrs Ellis" Woman', in C.C. Orr, ed., *Wollstonecraft's Daughters: Womanhood in England and France 1780–1920*, pp. 109–20.

Chapter 4: Parenthood

1. Collinson, *Birthpangs of Protestant England*, p. 78.
2. Martyn, *Youth's Instructions*.
3. Huntingdon Library, San Marino, California, STT 1943.
4. Leigh, *The Mother's Blessing* (1616), sig A2; Pollock, *Lasting Relationship*, p. 174.
5. Joceline, *A Mother's Legacy* (1624), pp. 1–4.
6. Crawford, 'Women's Published Writings 1600–1700', in Prior, ed. *Women in English Society 1500–1800*, pp. 221–2.
7. Cited in Pollock, *Lasting Relationship*, pp. 227–8.
8. Heywood, *A Curtain Lecture* (1637) , pp. 92–3. I am grateful to Elizabeth Foyster for this reference.
9. Fletcher, *Gender, Sex and Subordination*, p. 297.
10. Allestree, *Lady's Calling*, pp. 41–60.
11. Dod and Cleaver, *Godly Form of Household Government* (1614), sigs Q1, R3.
12. Gouge, *Domestical Duties*, pp. 565–6.
13. Dod and Cleaver, *Godly Form of Household Government*, sig T1; see also Fletcher, 'Prescription and Practice: Protestantism and the Upbringing of Children 1560–1700', in Wood, ed., *The Church and Childhood*, pp. 326–30.
14. Gardiner, *The Oxinden and Peyton Letters*, p. 128, cited in Pollock, *Continuity and Change*, 4 (1989), p. 245.
15. Marriott, *Female Conduct*, pp. xvii–xviii.
16. Cohen, *Fashioning Masculinity*, pp. 52–3.
17. Citations from Cohen, *Fashioning Masculinity*, pp. 57–8; Cunningham, *Children and Childhood in Western Society*, p. 64.
18. Bowers, *Politics of Motherhood*, pp. 156–67.
19. Essex, *Young Ladies Conduct*, p. 129.
20. Kenrick, *Whole Duty of Woman*, p. 78.

21. Gisborne, *Enquiry into the Duties of the Female Sex*, pp. 12, 102–3.
22. Essex, *Young Ladies Conduct*, p. 129.
23. Retford, *Art of Domestic Life*, pp. 83–92, plate 82.
24. Wotton, *An Essay on the Education of Children in the First Rudiments of Learning* (1753), especially p. 39.
25. Pennington, *An Unfortunate Mother's Advice*, p. 36; Pollock, *Lasting Relationship*, pp. 66, 77, 86.
26. Nelson, *An Essay on the Government of Children* (1763), pp. 124–5, 141–6, 152, 170, 189, 263–76, 239.
27. Carter, *Men and the Emergence of Polite Society*, pp. 96–100.
28. Percival, *A Father's Instructions Consisting of Moral Tales, Fables and Reflections*, (1781), p. xi and passim.
29. Moir, *Female Tuition or an Address to Mothers on the Education of Daughters* (1800), pp. 31, 37, 124.
30. More, *Strictures on the Modern System of Female Education* (1799), pp. 57, 89.
31. Myers, *The Bluestocking Circle* (1990).
32. Kitteridge, 'Melesina Chenevix St George Trench (1768–1827)', *The Female Spectator*, 10 (2006), p. 5.
33. *ODNB*: Melesina Trench; see below, pp. 189–92.
34. Trench, *The Remains of the Late Mrs Trench*, pp. 3–5; Pollock, *Forgotten Children*, p. 170.
35. Hampshire RO, 23/M/93/10: Austen Leigh Mss. I am grateful to Diana Fletcher for this reference.
36. Melesina Trench to Charles St George, April 1816. I am grateful to Lucy Trench for lending me this letter.
37. Trench, *Thoughts on Education by a Parent*, pp. 1–11.
38. *ODNB*: Richard Chenevix Trench; Fletcher, *Richard Chenevix Trench and his Legacy* (privately printed, 2007).
39. Trench, *Thoughts on Education by a Parent*, pp. 12–27.
40. Jackson, *Engines of Instruction, Mischief and Magic*, pp. 129–68; Cunningham, *Children and Childhood in Western Society*, p. 71; Summerfield, *Fantasy and Reason*, pp. 100–110.
41. Trench, *Thoughts on Education by a Parent*, pp. 32–48, 53–8.
42. Pollock, *Forgotten Children*, p. 163.
43. Trench, *Thoughts on Education by a Parent*, pp. 49–52, 57–8.
44. Pollock, *Lasting Relationship*, pp. 297, 304, 308.
45. *Extracts from the Journal of Margaret Woods* (1829), pp. 205–6, 428; Pollock, *Lasting Relationship*, pp. 169–70, 187.
46. Pollock, *Lasting Relationship*, pp. 150–1, 212–13, 238–9.
47. Pollock, *Lasting Relationship*, pp. 173, 240–1.
48. Pollock, *Lasting Relationship*, pp. 180–1.
49. Tosh, *A Man's Place*, pp. 4–5.
50. Davidoff, *Worlds Between*, pp. 50–3.
51. Davidoff, *Worlds Between*, p. 60.
52. Taylor, *Advice to the Teens or Practical Helps towards the Formation of One's own Character* (1818), pp. 60, 75.
53. Howard, *Reminiscences of My Children* (1831) I, pp. 32–6, 39.
54. Gorham, *Victorian Girl and the Feminine Ideal*, pp. 47–51, 70–3, 86–95.
55. Mitchell, *The New Girl: Girls' Culture in England 1880–1915*.
56. Sewell, *Principles of Education* (1865), pp. 75, 90–2, 213.
57. Citations from Tosh, 'Authority and Nurture in Middle-Class Fatherhood: the Case of Early and Mid-Victorian England', *Gender and History* 8 (1996), p. 52.
58. Tosh, in *Gender and History* 8 (1996), p. 56.
59. Hughes, *Victorian Governess*, p. 13.

60. Cited in Tosh, *A Man's Place*, p. 85.
61. Tosh, *A Man's Place*, pp. 117–19; Tosh, in *Gender and History* 8 (1996), pp. 48–64.
62. Thompson, *Rise of Respectable Society*, p. 145.
63. Tosh, *A Man's Place*, pp. 183–4.
64. Tosh, *A Man's Place*, pp. 95–6; Hammerton, *Cruelty and Companionship*, pp. 89–94, 127–8.
65. Gorham, *Victorian Girl and the Feminine Ideal*, pp. 27–48.
66. Cunningham, *Children and Childhood in Western Society*, p. 197.

Chapter 5: Care and Affection

1. Schnucker in Fildes, ed., *Women as Mothers*, p. 115.
2. For the doctrine of providence in the seventeenth century see Thomas, *Religion and the Decline of Magic*, pp. 78–113.
3. Houlbrooke, ed., *English Family Life*, p. 144; *ODNB*.
4. Citations from Wrightson, *English Society 1580–1680*, pp. 114–15; *ODNB*.
5. *Diary of Lady Willoughby* (1845), pp. 8, 13, 23, 31–2.
6. Pollock, *Lasting Relationship*, p. 62; *ODNB*.
7. Townshend, *Life and Letters of Mr Endymion Porter*, p. 92.
8. Houlbrooke, ed., *English Family Life*, p. 166.
9. Pollock, *Lasting Relationship*, p. 57.
10. Cited in Mack, *Visionary Women: Ecstatic Prophecy in Seventeenth-Century England*, p. 359.
11. Bristol RO, Smyth of Long Ashton Mss, AC/C86/2: Lady Elizabeth Smyth to Mrs Elizabeth Germon, 24 September 1711.
12. Townshend, *Life and Letters*, p. 68; Pollock, *Lasting Relationship*, p. 142.
13. Fletcher, *A County Community in Peace and War: Sussex 1600–1660*, p. 34.
14. Larminie, *Wealth, Kinship and Culture*, p. 100.
15. Clifford, ed., *Diaries of Lady Anne Clifford*, pp. 48–9; Houlbrooke, ed., *English Family Life*, p. 139.
16. Macfarlane, ed., *Diary of Ralph Josselin*, pp. 27, 40–1; Beier, *Sufferers and Healers: the Experience of Illness in Seventeenth-Century England*, p. 191.
17. Beier, *Sufferers and Healers*; Fletcher, *A County Community in Peace and War*, p. 41.
18. Pollock, *Forgotten Children*, p. 126.
19. Macfarlane, ed., *Diary of Ralph Josselin*, p. 447.
20. Houlbrooke, *English Family Life*, pp. 154–5; *ODNB*.
21. Thomas, *Religion and the Decline of Magic*, pp. 78–112.
22. Williams, 'Women's Experience', p. 223.
23. Macfarlane, ed., *Diary of Ralph Josselin*, pp. 113, 156, 433, 473.
24. Houlbrooke, ed., *English Family Life*, pp. 167–8.
25. Houlbrooke, ed., *English Family Life*, pp. 147–8, 155–6, 167, 169.
26. Houlbrooke, ed., *English Family Life*, pp. 148, 157, 167–8.
27. Houlbrooke, ed., *English Family Life*, pp. 138, 148.
28. Houlbrooke, ed., *English Family Life*, pp. 151, 154; *ODNB*.
29. Fletcher, *Gender, Sex and Subordination*, pp. 233–5; Pollock, *With Faith and Physic*, pp. 97–109; Beier, *Sufferers and Healers*, p. 172; Pollock, *Lasting Relationship*, pp. 100–102.
30. Pollock, *Lasting Relationship*, p. 100.
31. Vickery, *Gentleman's Daughter*, p. 117.
32. Citations in Pollock, *Forgotten Children*, p. 130.
33. Porter, *Disease, Medicine and Society in England 1550–1860*, pp. 23–31.
34. Blundell, ed., *Blundell's Diary and Letter Book*, pp. 65–8.
35. Fiske, ed., *Oakes Diaries*, I, p. 188.

36. Parkinson, ed., *Private Journal of John Bryon*, pp. 356, 389–90; Pollock, *Lasting Relationship*, pp. 111–14.
37. Thompson, ed., *Journal of John Gabriel Stedman 1744–97*, p. 324.
38. Doe, ed., *The Diary of James Clegg of Chapel-en-le-Frith 1708–1755*, p. 94.
39. Houlbrooke, *Death, Religion and the Family*, p. 359.
40. Margaret Lady Verney, ed., *Verney Letters of the Eighteenth Century*, II, p. 68; Pollock, *Forgotten Children*, pp. 231–2. For a full account, see Miller, *The Adoption of Inoculation for Smallpox in England and France* (Philadelphia, 1957); see also Trumbach, *The Rise of the Egalitarian Family*, pp. 193–7.
41. Pollock, *Forgotten Children*, pp. 233–4.
42. Pollock, *Lasting Relationship*, p. 102.
43. Pollock, *Lasting Relationship*, p. 102; Pollock, *Forgotten Children*, p. 233; *ODNB*.
44. I owe this point to Helen Berry.
45. Pollock, *Lasting Relationship*, pp. 118–19; *ODNB*.
46. Pollock, *Lasting Relationship*, p. 105.
47. Perry, 'Colonising the Breast: Sexuality and Maternity in Eighteenth-Century England', *Eighteenth-Century Life* 16 (1992), 185–213.
48. Perry, *Novel Relations*, pp. 224–9.
49. 'At Home in Renaissance Italy', Exhibition at the V and A, October 2006–January 2007.
50. Thomas, 'Art and Iconoclasm in Early Modern England', in Fincham and Lake, eds, *Religious Politics in Post-Reformation England*, p. 34.
51. Retford, *Art of Domestic Life*, pp. 6–7; Stone, *Family, Sex and Marriage in England*; Perry, *Novel Relations*.

Chapter 6: Marital Partnership

1. See especially Bailey, *Unquiet Lives*.
2. *The Private Correspondence of Lady Jane Cornwallis*, pp. 84, 92–3, 99, 105, 108, 140, 165.
3. Eales, *Puritans and Roundheads*, pp. 21–7; Fletcher, *Gender, Sex and Subordination*, pp. 157–60; *ODNB*.
4. Citations in Cliffe, *The Puritan Gentry*, pp. 74, 77–8; *ODNB*.
5. Verney, ed., *Memoirs of the Verney Family*, II, pp. 292–3; Pollock, *Lasting Relationship*, p. 56.
6. Slater, *Family Life in the Seventeenth Century*, pp. 126, 195.
7. Slater, *Family Life in the Seventeenth Century*, pp. 136–7; *ODNB*.
8. Charlton, *Women, Religion and Education in Early Modern England*, pp. 140–1.
9. Cited in Wrightson, *English Society 1580–1680*, p. 111.
10. Macfarlane, *The Family Life of Ralph Josselin*, pp. 82–102.
11. Trappes-Lomax, ed., *The Diary and Letter Book of Rev. Thomas Brockbank 1679–1709*, pp. 3–45.
12. Warwickshire RO, CR 1368, I, 1–42: Pollock, *Lasting Relationship*, p. 143.
13. Tillyard, *Aristocrats*, p. 34.
14. Tillyard, *Aristocrats*, pp. 28–9, 86–7; *ODNB*.
15. Cited in Tillyard, *Aristocrats*, p. 92.
16. Tillyard, *Aristocrats*, pp. 87–8.
17. Tillyard, *Aristocrats*, pp. 238–9.
18. Trumbach, *The Rise of the Egalitarian Family*, pp. 210–11.
19. Cited in Stone, *Family, Sex and Marriage*, p. 436.
20. Tillyard, *Aristocrats*, pp. 295–6; *ODNB*.
21. Pollock, *Lasting Relationship*, p. 35.
22. Christie, ed., *Diary of Reverend William Jones 1777–1821*, pp. 77, 98, 103–4, 168; Pollock, *Lasting Relationship*, pp. 58–9.

23. Christie, ed., *Diary of Reverend William Jones*, pp. 102, 104, 106; Pollock, *Lasting Relationship*, pp. 170–1.
24. Christie, ed., *Diary of William Jones*, pp. 103, 107–9, 169, 181, 210–13, 227.
25. Derbyshire RO, Fitzherbert MSS, D 239/F6555–6563.
26. Derbyshire RO, Fitzherbert MSS, D4061/3/1–9, 17/6–8.
27. Bailey, ed., *Diary of Lady Frederick Cavendish*, I, p. 13.
28. Cited in Fletcher, *Victorian Girls*, p. 5.
29. Fletcher, *Victorian Girls*, pp. 2–5, 25–36; *ODNB*.
30. Bailey, ed., *Diary of Lady Frederick Cavendish*, I, pp. 13–15.
31. Fletcher, *Victorian Girls*, pp. 37–120.
32. Chenevix Trench, *Story of Orpington*, pp. 16–18.
33. Gerard, *Country House Life*, pp. 162–89.
34. I owe this to my mother, Delle Fletcher.
35. National Archives, Census Enumerators Returns, Orpington, Kent, 1891, 1901. I am grateful to Diana Fletcher for transcripts of these returns.
36. Trench Archive, Ellen Howard's notebook.
37. Trench Archive, 1889 programme; information from Delle Fletcher.
38. Trench Archive, The Bark Hart Gazette, 2 August 1890.
39. Trench Archive, programme, 6 July 1893; Edith Howard to Maud Howard, 15 July 1896.
40. Trench Archive, Clare Howard's diary, 1903.
41. Trench Archive, Maud Howard to Clare Howard, undated.
42. Trench Archive, Ellen Howard to Clare Howard, 3 undated letters; Maud Howard to Clare Howard, 25 September 1905.
43. Trench, ed., *Remains of the Late Mrs Richard Trench*, pp. 1–13.
44. Melesina Chenevix to Mrs Gervais, 7 January 1778. I am grateful for the loan of this letter to Lucy Trench.

Chapter 7: Children who Died

1. Jalland, *Death in the Victorian Family*, pp. 119–20.
2. Mendelson, *The Mental World of Stuart Women: Three Studies*, p. 88.
3. Cited in Crawford, 'The Construction and Experience of Maternity in Seventeenth-Century England', in Fildes, ed., *Women as Mothers*, p. 23.
4. Macdonald, *Mystical Bedlam*, p. 82.
5. See, for example, for the eighteenth century, Vickery, *Gentleman's Daughter*, pp. 124–5.
6. Pollock, *Lasting Relationship*, p. 124.
7. Pollock, *Lasting Relationship*, p. 123.
8. Lincolnshire RO, Flinders MSS, 1–3.
9. Trench, ed., *The Remains of the Late Mrs Richard Trench*, pp. 199–206.
10. Pollock, *Lasting Relationship*, p. 130.
11. Macfarlane, ed., *The Diary of Ralph Josselin*, pp. 110–13, 201–7, Houlbrooke, ed., *English Family Life*, pp. 113–16.
12. Pollock, *Lasting Relationship*, pp. 123–4; Houlbrooke, ed., *English Family Life*, p. 153.
13. Houlbrooke, ed., *English Family Life*, p. 128, cited in Martin, *Wives and Daughters*, p. 187.
14. Houlbrooke, ed., *English Family Life*, p. 152.
15. Thomas-Stanford, ed., *The Private Memorandums of William Roe*, 1, pp. 21–4.
16. Houlbrooke, ed., *English Family Life*, p. 142; Seaver, *Wallington's World: A Puritan Artisan in Seventeenth-Century London*, p. 87.
17. Verney, *Memoirs of the Verney Family*, II, 296; Slater, *Family Life in the Seventeenth Century*, pp. 118–23.
18. Verney, *Memoirs of the Verney Family*, II, 293–302; Slater, *Family Life*, pp. 118–23.

19. Macfarlane, ed., *Diary of Ralph Josselin*, pp. 201–3.
20. Loftis, ed., *Memoirs of Anne Lady Halkett and anne Lady Fanshaw*, p. 84.
21. Citations from Houlbrooke, *Death, Religion and the Family in England 1480–1570*, pp. 236–7.
22. Lord John Russell, ed., *Memoirs, Journal and Correspondence of Thomas Moore*, V, pp. 236, 278, 304, 311; VI, pp. 18–22.
23. Vickery, *Gentleman's Daughter*, pp. 124–5; Jalland, *Death in the Victorian Family*, pp. 122–39.
24. Larminie, *Wealth, Kinship and Culture*, pp. 97–8.
25. Cited in Vickery, *Gentleman's Daughter*, p. 124.
26. BL, Loan MS 29/202. I am grateful to Jacqueline Eales for this reference.
27. Larminie, *Wealth, Kinship and Culture*, pp. 97–8.
28. Matthews, ed., *Elizabeth Mascall: Remnants of a Life*, p. 22; Russell, ed., *Memoirs of Thomas Moore*, VI, p. 22.
29. Freemantle, ed., *The Wynne Diaries*, p. 326.
30. Seaver, *Wallington's World*, pp. 85–9; Pollock, *Lasting Relationship*, p. 123; Houlbrooke, ed., *English Family Life*, pp. 141–6.
31. Citations from Williams, 'Women's Experience', pp. 223–4.
32. Trench, *Letters and Memorials*, I, p. 255.
33. Jalland, *Death in the Victorian Family*, p. 139; see also, Newsome, *Godliness and Good Learning: Four Studies on a Victorian Ideal*, pp. 148–93; Tosh, *A Man's Place*, pp. 119–20.
34. Marquess of Anglesey, *The Capel Letters 1814–17*, pp. 140–3.
35. Bloomfield Archive, Charlotte Bloomfield's book of prayers.
36. Bloomfield Archive, letters from Charlotte Bloomfield to Harriott and Georgiana Bloomfield, 1825–7.
37. Bloomfield Archive, Georgiana Bloomfield's account of the death of her sister Charlotte. For a fuller version of this account, see Fletcher, 'Beyond the Church: Women's Spiritual Experience at Home and in the Community 1600–1900', in Swanson, ed., *Gender and Christian Religion*, pp. 199–200.
38. Warwickshire RO, CR 2017/TP 625.
39. Jalland, *Death in the Victorian Family*, pp. 298–9.
40. Bristol Record Office, Smyth of Ashton Court MS AC/C97/2–8.
41. Houlbrooke, ed., *English Family Life*, pp. 116, 146.
42. Fiske, ed., *Oakes Diaries*, I, pp. 188–91.
43. Pollock, *Lasting Relationship*, p. 127; *ODNB*.
44. Trench, *Remains of the Late Mrs Richard Trench*, pp. 199–200.
45. Pollock, *Lasting Relationship*, pp. 128–9.
46. Toynbee, ed., *Diaries of William Charles Macready*, II, 99; Pollock, *Forgotten Children*, p. 138.
47. Cited in Tosh, *Man's Place*, p. 100.
48. Christie, *Diary of Reverend William Jones*, pp. 210–11.
49. Cited in Davidoff and Hall, *Family Fortunes*, p. 331.
50. Jalland, *Death in the Victorian Family*, pp. 127–42.
51. Jalland, *Death in the Victorian Family*, p. 193.

Chapter 8: Maternity

1. Citations from P. Crawford, 'The Construction and Experience of Maternity in Seventeenth-Century England', in Fildes, ed., *Women as Mothers*, p. 28.
2. Williams, 'Women's Experience', p. 151.
3. Cited in Wrightson, *English Society*, p. 104.

4. Citations from Williams, 'Women's Experience', p. 189.
5. L.A. Pollock, 'Embarking on a Rough Passage: The Experience of Pregnancy in Early Modern Society', in Fildes, ed., *Women as Mothers*, pp. 39, 46: Vickery, *Gentleman's Daughter*, pp. 99–100.
6. Cited in Slater, *Family Life in the Seventeenth Century*, p. 125.
7. Pollock in Fildes, *Women as Mothers*, pp. 48–9.
8. A. Wilson, 'The Ceremony of Childbirth and its Interpretation', in Fildes, ed., *Women as Mothers*, p. 68: Williams, 'Women's Experience', pp. 162–8.
9. Citations from P. Crawford, 'The Construction and Experience of Maternity in Seventeenth-century England', in Fildes, ed., *Women as Mothers in Pre-Industrial England*, pp. 19–20, 35. See also Slater, *Family Life in the Seventeenth Century*, pp. 82–3; Mendelson and Crawford, *Women in Early Modern England*, pp. 80–1.
10. Vickery, *Gentleman's Daughter*, pp. 102–4.
11. I owe this suggestion to Helen Berry.
12. Trench, ed., *Remains of Late Mrs Richard Trench*, p. 16.
13. Williams, 'Women's Experience', pp. 165, 168–9.
14. P. Crawford, 'The Sucking Child: Adult Attitudes to Child Care in the First Year of Life in Seventeenth-Century England', *Continuity and Change*, 1 (1986), pp. 31–2.; Fildes, *Breasts, Babies and Bottles*, pp. 98–134, 398–401.
15. Vickery, *Gentleman's Daughter*, pp. 107–10.
16. Williams, 'Women's Experience', p. 174.
17. Retford, *Art of Domestic Life*, p. 88; Davidoff and Hall, *Family Fortunes*, p. 322.
18. Williams explores the remarkably detailed and honest account Frederica Orlebar wrote in 'Women's Experience', pp. 172–80.
19. Davidoff and Hall, *Family Fortunes*, pp. 338–9.
20. Vickery, *Gentleman's Daughter*, p. 114–15.
21. Vickery, *Gentleman's Daughter*, pp. 110–13.
22. Cited in Williams, 'Women's Experience', p. 199.
23. Northants RO, Matilda Bosworth's diary, 31 August 1886.
24. Williams, 'Women's Experience', pp. 181–8.
25. Cooper, *Houses of the Gentry 1480–1680*, p. 306.
26. Warwickshire RO, CR 1368, Vol 1, 99.
27. Citations from Charlton, *Women, Religion and Education in Early Modern England*, pp. 205–16; *ODNB*.
28. North, *Lives of the Norths*, p. 4.
29. Jenkins, *The Making of a Ruling Class*, p. 262.
30. Adeane, ed., *The Early Married Life of Maria Josepha, Lady Stanley*, pp. 195, 208, 212, 300.
31. Hanbury, *Life of Mrs Albert Head*, pp. 107–9; Pollock, *Lasting Relationship*, p. 152.
32. Freemantle, ed., *Wynne Diaries*, III, p. 65.
33. Staffordshire RO, D4216/ E/ 2/112, Anastasia Fletcher to Elizabeth Twenlow, *c*.1818.
34. Northants RO, Diary of Matilda Bosworth, March 1884.
35. Cited in Mendelson and Crawford, *Women in Early Modern England*, p. 81.
36. Watkin, ed., *A Kingston Lacy Childhood*, pp. 7–9, 118–24.
37. Pollock, *Forgotten Children*, pp. 144–88.
38. Carberry, *Happy World*, p. 61.
39. Sadler, ed., *Diary, Reminiscences and Correspondence of Henry Crabb Robinson*, pp. 6–9.
40. Fairfax-Lucy, *Mistress of Charlecote*, p. 20.
41. Davidoff and Hall, *Family Fortunes*, p. 340.
42. Allen, *A Beloved Mother*, p. 93.
43. Bailey, ed., *Diary of Lady Frederick Cavendish*, I, p. 7.

44. Williams, 'Women's Experience', pp. 203, 205–6, 212–13; Williams, 'Illness and Impact: the Mistress of the House and the Governess', in Harvey, ed., *The Kiss in History*, p. 149.
45. Pollock, *Lasting Relationship*, pp. 81–2.
46. Houlbrooke, ed., *English Family Life*, p. 150.
47. Macfarlane, *Diary of Ralph Josselin*, p. 407.
48. Freemantle, ed., *Wynne Diaries*, III, p. 37.
49. Tosh, *A Man's Place*, p. 103.
50. Barker-Benfield, *Culture of Sensibility*, pp. 280–1.
51. Vickery, *Gentleman's Daughter*, p. 114.
52. Retford, *Art of Domestic Life*, p. 103, plate 82.
53. Lilly Library, Indiana University, Elisabeth Ball Collection, Jane Johnson's Nursery Library.
54. Durham RO, Pease Mss: D/Pe/5/11–12.
55. Martin, *Wives and Daughters*, pp. 227–9.
56. Cited in Stone, *The Family, Sex and Marriage*, p. 456.
57. Citations from Stone, *The Family, Sex and Marriage*, pp. 457–8.
58. Trench, *Remains of the Late Mrs Richard Trench*, pp. 484–5.
59. Allen, *A Beloved Mother* (ed., her daughter), p. 31.
60. Pollock, *Lasting Relationship*, p. 90.

Chapter 9: Motherly Performance

1. Tinniswood, *Belton House* (1992), pp. 18–20; Retford, *Art of Domestic Life*, pp.108–9.
2. Cust, *Records of the Cust Family*, II, pp. 234–75; *ODNB*.
3. Leicestershire Record Office, Hastings MS 14 D 32, pp. 66–78; *ODNB*.
4. Aspinall-Oglander, ed., *Admiral's Wife*, pp. 180, 192; Stone, *The Family, Sex and Marriage*, p. 457.
5. Pollock, *Lasting Relationship*, p. 150.
6. Pollock, *Forgotten Children*, p. 118.
7. *ODNB*, Edward Boscawen.
8. Aspinall-Oglander, ed., *Admiral's Wife*, p. 68.
9. Pollock, *Lasting Relationship*, p.112.
10. Pollock, *Lasting Relationship*, pp. 149–50; Aspinall-Oglander, ed., *Admiral's Wife*, p. 179.
11. For breeching see Fletcher, *Gender, Sex and Subordination*, p. 297.
12. Pollock, *Lasting Relationship*, pp. 57, 83; Aspinall-Oglander, ed., *Admiral's Wife*, p. 28.
13. Aspinall-Oglander, ed., *Admiral's Wife*, p. 73.
14. Aspinall-Oglander, ed., *Admiral's Wife*, pp. 179–80, 229, 282.
15. Aspinall-Oglander, ed., *Admiral's Wife*, pp. 68, 73, 92–8, 117–18, 123, 179–93; Pollock, *Lasting Relationship*, p.186.
16. Balderston, ed., *Thraliana: The Diary of Mrs Hester Lynch Thrale 1776–1809*, p. 321.
17. This is printed in full in M. Hyde *The Thrales of Steatham Park*, pp. 21–218.
18. Pollock, *Forgotten Children*, p. 247; Stone, *The Family, Sex and Marriage*, pp. 458–9
19. Cited in Stone, *The Family , Sex and Marriage*, p. 459.
20. Hyde, *Thrales of Streatham Park*, pp. 21, 24, 39, 75, 105–6; Balderston, ed., *Thraliana*, p. 321.
21. Hyde, *Thrales of Streatham Park*, pp. 45, 49, 80, 112–13, 143–4; Stone, *The Family , Sex and Marriage*, p. 460.
22. Hyde, *Thrales of Streatham Park*, pp. 34, 45, 55, 62, 86, 112, 127–8, 148, 163, 182, 188; Stone, *The Family, Sex and Marriage*, pp. 460–3.
23. Francis and Keary, *Francis Letters*, pp. 151–9, Stone, *The Family, Sex and Marriage*, pp. 372–3.

24. For the social education of the Francis girls, see below pp. 272–3.
25. Francis and Keary, eds, *The Francis Letters*, pp. 162–339.
26. Stone, *The Family, Sex and Marriage*, p. 373.
27. Palgrave, ed., *Francis Thomas Palgrave*, pp. 2–3.
28. Palgrave, ed., *Francis Turner Palgrave*, pp. 2–16; also see above page.
29. Williams, 'Women's Experience', pp. 157, 184, 189, 192, 199.
30. Williams, 'Women's Experience', pp. 208–11, 218–9, 228–9.
31. Pollock, *Lasting Relationship*, pp. 151, 188–9, 239–40.
32. *Memoirs and Letters of Sara Coleridge* (ed. her daughter), p. 126.
33. Stone, *The Family, Sex and Marriage*, p. 458.
34. Mitford, ed., *The Ladies of Alderley* (1938), pp. 12, 87, 128, 133, 143, 146, 195–7, 280. *ODNB*: Henrietta Maria, Lady Stanley.
35. Mitford, ed., *The Ladies of Alderley*, pp. 128, 280; Mitford, ed., *The Stanleys of Alderley*, pp. 177–90
36. See below, pp. 275–7.
37. Buckinghamshire RO, D/X 1174: Grenfell Mss, The Children's Journal. fols 1– 20.
38. Gurney, ed., *Isabel Mrs Gurney*, p. 41.
39. Gurney, ed., *Isabel Mrs Gurney*, pp. 38–9, 41, 112–13; Pollock, *Forgotten Children*, pp. 80–1, 108.
40. Northants RO, Diary of Matilda Bosworth (unpaginated).
41. Mary T. Ryan, 'The First Lord Bloomfield', *Newport News*, 1990, pp. 99–102. I am grateful to Keith Robbins for this reference; *ODNB*: Benjamin, First Lord Bloomfield.
42. Bloomfield Archive, Benjamin Lord Bloomfield to the Hon. Georgiana Bloomfield, 1 January, 23 April, 11 June 1830.
43. Trench Archive, Georgiana Trench to Harriott Trench, c. 1863.
44. Trench Archive, Georgiana Trench to Harriott Trench, undated.
45. Trench Archive, Georgiana Trench to Harriott Trench, 10, 19 August 1864.
46. Trench Archive, Isabel Trench to Georgiana Trench, undated.
47. Coffey Archive, Isabel Trench to Harriott Trench, 27 January 1898.
48. Coffey Archive, Isabel Trench to Margot Trench, undated 1899.

Chapter 10: Fatherly Performance

1. Cliffe, *Puritan Gentry*, pp. 69–70; Stone, *The Family, Sex and Marriage*, p. 155; Richardson, *Puritanism in North-West England*, pp. 91–2; *ODNB*.
2. Citations from Cliffe, *Puritan Gentry*, pp. 73–4.
3. Cited in Charlton, *Women, Religion and Education in Early Modern England*, p. 98.
4. *Athenian Mercury*, 19 (2), 2 November, 1695. I am grateful to Helen Berry for this reference.
5. Cited in Fletcher 'Prescription and Practice: Protestantism and the Upbringing of Children, 1560–1700', in Wood, ed., *The Church and Childhood*, p. 333; Gosse, *Father and Son*, p. 53; *ODNB*.
6. Citations from Stone, *Family, Sex and Marriage*, p. 171; *ODNB*.
7. North, *Lives of the Norths*, pp. 1–4.
8. Carter, *Men and the Emergence of Polite Society*, pp. 96–100.
9. J. Bailey, 'Reassessing Parenting in Eighteenth-Century England', in Berry and Foyster, eds, *The Family in Early Modern England*, pp. 213–19.
10. Cliffe, *Puritan Gentry*, pp. 36, 252.
11. Haigh, ed., *Cambridge Historical Encyclopedia of Great Britain and Ireland*, p. 231.
12. Retford, *Art of Domestic Life*, pp. 100, 105–7, 117, 127.
13. Retford, *Art of Domestic Life*, pp. 115–117, Fig. 2; *ODNB*.
14. Stone, *The Family, Sex and Marriage*, p. 453; *ODNB*.

15. Citations from Vickery, *Gentleman's Daughter*, p. 123.
16. Fiske, ed., *Oakes Diaries*, I, pp. 165–6, 170–2, 189–91, 359–60.
17. Staffordshire RO, D4468/B/2/1–4.
18. Davidoff and Hall, *Family Fortunes*, p. 330.
19. Pollock, *Lasting Relationship*, p. 171; *ODNB*.
20. Richard Chenevix Trench to his sons Charlie and Arthur, 1 October 1848. I am grateful to Lucy Trench for lending me this letter; *ODNB*.
21. M. Trench, ed., *Letters and Memorials of Archbishop Richard Cheneuix Trench*, I, 298–9. I am grateful to The Hon. Roderick Trench for showing me Barney Trench's record of this story, told him by Francie.
22. Davidoff and Hall, *Family Fortunes*, p. 330.
23. Forbes, *Memories and Bare Details*, pp. 13–14.
24. Gerard, *Country House Life*, p. 73.
25. Williams 'Illness and Impact: The Mistress of the House and the Governess', in Harvey, ed., *The Kiss in History*, pp. 150–1.
26. Citations from Tosh, *A Man's Place*, pp. 88–9.
27. J. Tosh, 'Authority and Nurture in Middle Class Manhood: the Case of Early and Mid-Victorian England', *Gender and History*, 8 (1996), pp. 53–4.
28. Cumbria RO, D/Lons/C1/1/12; *ODNB*.
29. Gray, ed., *Papers and Diaries of a York Family 1764–1839*, pp. 20–25.
30. Thompson, ed., *Journal of John Gabriel Stedman*, pp. 318–76; Pollock, *Lasting Relationship*, p. 126.
31. This paragraph is based upon Lincolnshire Record Office, Flinders 1, 2, 3.
32. Thomas-Stanford, ed., *The Private Memorandums of William Roe*, 1, pp. 4–70.
33. Berry, 'Sense and Singularity: the Social Experiences of John Marsh and Thomas Stutterd in Late-Georgian England', in French and Barry, eds, *Identity and Agency in England*, p. 190.
34. Citations from Tosh, 'Authority and Nurture in Middle Class Manhood: The Case of Early and Mid-Victorian England', in *Gender and History*, 8, p. 55.
35. Bickley, ed., *Diaries of Sylvester Douglas*, II, 68.
36. Pollock, *Lasting Relationship*, pp. 176–7.
37. Tosh, *A Man's Place*, pp. 97–8, 102–22.
38. Freemantle, ed., *Wynne's Diaries*, III, p. 99. I am grateful to Helen Berry for her comment here.
39. King-Hall, ed., *Sea Saga*, pp. 79–89.
40. Berkshire RO, D/Ebp F17: Diary of Sidney Pusey.
41. Bowen, *Bowen's Court and Seven Winters*, pp. 314–24; *ODNB*.
42. Pollock, *Lasting Relationship*, pp. 190–1.
43. Pollock, *Lasting Relationship*, pp. 192, 244.
44. Trench Archive, see plate X. For the Anglo-Irish see McConville, *Ascendancy to Oblivion*.
45. Trench Archive, David McCready to Harriot Trench, 16 March 1881.
46. Trench Archive, Georgiana to Harriot Trench, 5 May 1881.
47. MacMahon, *In the Shadow of the Fairy Hill*, pp. 122, 131, 134.
48. Trench Archive, memorandum by David McCready, 10 June 1881.
49. Vickery, *Gentleman's Daughter*, p. 272; Fletcher, *A County Community in Peace and War: Sussex 1600–1660*, pp. 28–30.
50. West Sussex RO, Goodwood MSS 102, nos 40–58.
51. Warwicks RO, Seymour Papers, CR114A/646: Francis Seymour's record of family events.
52. Oxley Parker, *The Oxley Parker Papers*, pp. 243, 248.
53. Jones, *A Victorian Boyhood*, p. 87.
54. Chenevix Trench, *My Mother Told Me*, pp. 2, 7–8
55. Carberry, *Happy World*, pp. 36–8.

56. Roberts, 'The Pater familias of the Victorian Governing Classes', in Wohl, ed. *The Victorian Family* (1978), pp. 59–65.
57. Gurney, ed., *Isabel Mrs Gurney*, pp. 34, 39; Gillis, *A World of Their Own Making: A History of Myth and Ritual in Family Life*, pp. 81–108.
58. Roberts, 'The Pater Familias of the Victorian Governing Classes', in Wohl, ed., *Victorian Family*, pp. 61–3.
59. Tosh, *A Man's World*, pp. 93–5.
60. Tosh, *A Man's Place*, pp. 97–8; Newsome, *History of Wellington College*, pp. 156–7.
61. Trench Archive, Clare Howard's holiday diaries; Henry Howard to Amy Howard, 13 August 1910.
62. Trench Archive, Clare Howard manuscript reminiscences.
63. Trench Archive, Clare Howard to Reggie Chenevix Trench, 7 October 1914.
64. Trench Archive, Clare Howard to Reggie Chenevix Trench, 12, 13, 14 October 1914.
65. Trench Archive, Clare Howard to Reggie Chenevix Trench, 15 October 1914.
66. Trench Archive, Will of Henry Howard, 7 November 1913.
67. Trench Archive, Clare Howard to Reggie Chenevix Trench, 17 October 1914.
68. Beckwith, *When I Remember*, pp. 13–14.
69. Fletcher, 'Patriotism, Identity and Commemoration: New Light on the Great War from the Papers of Major Reggie Chenevix Trench', *History*, 90, 2005, pp. 532–49.

Chapter 11: Fathers and Educating Boys

1. Bamford, ed., *A Royalist's Notebook*, pp. 249–50; *ODNB*.
2. Roberts, 'The Pater Familias of the Victorian Governing Classes', in Wohl, ed., *Victorian Family*, pp. 61–3.
3. Elyot, *The Book Named the Governor*, p. 19; Pollock, *Forgotten Children*, pp. 188–90.
4. Cohen, *Fashioning Masculinity*, pp. 50–2.
5. Bowers, *The Politics of Motherhood*, pp. 158–9; *ODNB*.
6. *ODNB*. See below, pp. 292–4.
7. Isham, ed., *The Diary of Thomas Isham of Lamport*, pp. 60–1, 147–9, 173, 189.
8. Pollock, *Lasting Relationship*, pp. 237–8.
9. Adeane, ed., *Early Married Life of Maria Josepha, Lady Stanley*, pp. viii, 2–53.
10. Lincolnshire RO, Flinders 1.
11. Cowden-Clarke, *My Long Life*, p. 7.
12. Fletcher, *Gender, Sex and Subordination*, pp. 303–4; Bristol RO, Smyth MS/AC/C/97/1–14.
13. Kent RO, U 120, C46/1–5, C49.
14. Kent RO, U 120, C25/20, 23, 29, C46/6–28, 32, 40–1.
15. Kent RO, U 120, C50/1–18, C51/1–8.
16. Cliffe, *The Puritan Gentry*, p. 81.
17. Whale, *My Grandfather's Pocket Book*, pp. 158–9.
18. Warwickshire RO, CR 114A/716/1; Lincolnshire RO, Monson MSS 7/13/140, 7/14/8.
19. Gardiner, ed., *The Oxinden and Peyton Letters*, pp. 126–7, 132.
20. These two paragraphs are based on East Sussex RO, Sayer MSS, 1510–67, 1570–1628, 2270.
21. For the London pleasure gardens, see Vickery, *Gentleman's Daughter*, pp. 244–50.
22. Ingram, *Leaves from a Family Tree*, pp. 78–99.
23. Lincolnshire RO, Flinders 2, 3 Jan 1785, 14 August 1786, 31 December 1787.
24. West Sussex RO, Goodwood MS 102, nos 40–58; Tillyard, *Aristocrats*, pp. 50, 83–4.
25. Hertfordshire RO, D/EX 83/21.
26. Warwickshire RO, C2017/C 359/1: Rudolf Fielding to the Earl of Denbigh, 1831.

27. Hampshire RO, 31M 57/957: letters from James and William Wiggett to their father, 1807–11.
28. Trench Archive, William Trench to Georgiana Trench, 30 January 1861.
29. Trench Archive, William Trench to Henry Trench, 5 February 1861.
30. Trench Archive, William Trench to Henry Trench, 10 February 1861.
31. Trench Archive, Benjamin Trench to Georgiana Trench, 2 March 1859.
32. Trench Archive, Henry Trench to Benjamin Trench, 15 June, 10 July 1859.
33. Trench Archive, Henry Trench to Benjamin Trench, 10 July 1859.
34. Trench Archive, Henry Trench to Benjamin Trench, 27 May 1860.
35. Trench Archive, Oscar Browning to Henry Trench, 20 December 1860.
36. Trench Archive, Benjamin Trench to Henry Trench, 28 October 1862.
37. Wiltshire RO, 9/35/331: letters from Samuel and Charlotte Devis to Lord Bruce.
38. Warwickshire RO, CR 114A/716/1; *ODNB*.
39. Warwickshire RO, CR 114A/718/1.
40. Warwickshire RO, CR 114A/718/3, 4.
41. Pollock, *Lasting Relationship*, p. 238; Lord John Russell, ed., *Memoirs, Journal and Correspondence of Thomas Moore*, V, p. 270.
42. Pollock, *Lasting Relationship*, p. 232.
43. Thomas-Stanford, ed., *The Private Memorandums of William Roe*, p. 52.
44. Curtis, *A Chronicle of Small Beer*, pp. 25, 36.
45. Thomas-Stanford, ed., *The Private Memorandums of William Roe*, p. 52.
46. Bickley, ed., *Diaries of Sylvester Douglas*, I, 188, 191, 213; Pollock, *Forgotten Children*, p. 246.
47. Gisborne, *A Brief Memoir of his Life*, pp. 107, 126.
48. B. and P. Russell, eds, *The Amberley Papers*, pp. 163–75; *ODNB*.
49. Oxley Parker, *Oxley Parker Papers*, pp. 239–42.
50. Trench Archive, Georgiana Trench to Henry Trench, c. 1863; Bromley, *Man of Ten Talents*, p. 18.
51. Cartwright, *Sachrissa*, pp. 26–7.
52. Sterry, *Annals of Eton College*, p. 132.
53. Blundell, ed., *Blundell's Diary and Letter Book*, p. x.
54. Verney, ed., *Verney Letters*, I, p. 92.
55. Cumbria RO, D/Hud/B, 1.
56. Pollock, *Lasting Relationship*, p. 211.
57. Alford, ed., *Life, Journals and Letters of Henry Alford*, pp. 4, 17; see also Pollock, *Lasting Relationship*, p. 141.
58. Bickley, ed., *Diaries of Sylvester Douglas*, pp. 213, 257, 311.
59. Curtis, *A Chronicle of Small Beer*, pp. 36–40.
60. Richard Chenevix Trench to his son Charles, undated. I am grateful to Lucy Trench for the loan of this letter.
61. Suffolk RO, HA 408/F3/2.
62. Leicestershire RO, 14D 32/1–24.
63. Warner, ed., *Epistolary Curiosities*, pp. 163–4; Pollock, *Lasting Relationship*, p. 148; Fletcher, *Gender, Sex and Subordination*, pp. 306–7.
64. Northamptonshire RO, Isham letters 1641, 3308, 4077, 4079,4202; Sir Gyles Isham, 'A Rugby Headmaster's Letters to a Parent in the Early Eighteenth Century', *Northamptonshire Past and Present*, I (1952), pp. 1–8; H.I. Longden, 'The Diaries (Home and Foreign) of Sir Justinian Isham 1704–1736', *TRHS*, third series I (1907), pp. 182–3; *ODNB*.
65. Hobhouse, ed., *Diary of a West Country Physician*, pp. 33, 103; Pollock, *Lasting Relationship*, p. 195.
66. Fletcher, *Gender, Sex and Subordination*, p. 304.

67. Mitford, ed., *The Stanleys of Alderley*, pp. 25–6, 28–32; for Vaughan see Chandos, *Boys Together*, pp. 240–4, 306; *ODNB*.
68. Pollock, *Forgotten Children*, p. 192.
69. Hampshire RO, 10M 52/ 7/2: Thomas Bishop to his cousin, undated.

Chapter 12: Mothers and Educating Boys

1. A.A. Wace, *The Story of Wadhurst* (1923), pp. 117–18. I am grateful to The Hon. Roderick Trench for this reference.
2. Trench Archive, Georgiana Trench to Benjamin Trench, undated summer 1860.
3. Verney, ed., *Verney Letters*, II, 131–3.
4. Bessborough, ed., *Journal of Charlotte Guest*, pp. 164–5; Pollock, *Forgotten Children*, p. 197; Pollock, *Lasting Relationship*, p. 200.
5. Williams, 'Women's Experience', p. 215.
6. Wiltshire RO, 634/2: letters from Frances Duke to her son Robert, c. 1740; Pevsner, *Wiltshire*, p. 576.
7. Woodforde, ed., *Woodforde Papers and Diaries*, p. 15.
8. Aspinall-Oglander, *Admiral's Wife*, p. 192.
9. E. and F. Anson, eds, *Mary Hamilton*, pp. 7–9.
10. Kent RO, U49, Twisden Mss, C13/96, 104–38.
11. Chandos, *Boys Together*, pp. 304–5.
12. Warwickshire RO, CR 1635/33/3.
13. Warwickshire RO, CR 1635/33/ 5–14.
14. Bickley, ed., *Diaries of Sylvester Douglas*, I, 188; Pollock, *Forgotten Children*, p. 246.
15. Freemantle, ed., *The Wynne Diaries*, III, p. 203.
16. Durham RO, Beal letters.
17. Allen, *A Beloved Mother: Life of Hannah Allen*, pp. 107, 111.
18. Sheppard, ed., *George Duke of Cambridge*, pp. 5–19.
19. Buckinghamshire RO, D/RA/A/3C/1: John Ramsden to his mother, February 1842.
20. Suffolk RO, HA 408/ F3/2: letters from Edmund Holland to his mother.
21. Cited in Fletcher, *Victorian Girls*, p. 43.
22. Leicestershire RO. Hastings Mss 14D 32/79–149; above p. 111.
23. Chandos, *Boys Together*, pp. 176–84.
24. Cheshire RO, DSA/45: letters from Edward Stanley to Lady Maria Stanley.
25. Cheshire RO, DSA/45: letters from Edward Stanley to Lady Maria Stanley; Chandos, *Boys Together*, pp. 211–12.
26. Above, p. 159.
27. Warwickshire RO, C 2017/C 394: Rudolf Fielding to the Countess of Denbigh, 8 November 1831; Pevsner, *Warwickshire*, p. 357.
28. Buckinghamshire RO, D/RA/A/3C/I: letters from John Ramsden to Lady Ramsden 1844–8; D/RA/A/3C/5: letters from John Ramsden's tutors to Lady Ramsden, 1845–8.
29. Cheshire RO, Stanley Mss, DSA 102/1: letters from Lyulph Stanley to Lord Edward and Lady Henrietta Stanley 1856–6.
30. Kent RO, U840: Pratt Mss, John Pratt to Lady Clementine Pratt, 26 Sept. 1855.
31. Trench Archive, Benjamin Trench to Georgiana Trench, 2 March, 27 October, 3 November 1859.
32. Trench Archive, Benjamin Trench to Georgiana Trench, 28 November, 2 December 1859.
33. Trench Archive, Benjamin Trench to Georgiana Trench, 14 May 1860; Georgiana Trench to Benjamin Trench, 3 June 1860.
34. Trench Archive, Georgiana Trench to Benjamin Trench, undated summer 1860.
35. West Sussex RO, Goodwood Mss 102, no. 40.

36. Kent RO, Twisden Mss, U49 C13/96.
37. Cited in Fletcher, *Gender, Sex and Subordination in England*, pp. 309–10
38. Woodforde, ed., *Woodforde Papers and Diaries*, p. 15; Pollock, *Lasting Relationship*, p. 193.
39. Francis and Keary, eds, *Francis Letters*, pp. 163, 320.
40. Chandos, *Boys Together*, p. 294.
41. Francis and Keary, eds, *Francis Letters*, pp. 327, 331, 374.
42. I am grateful for this reference to Jo Bowler.
43. Hampshire RO, 23M/93/14/1/A: Austen Leigh Mss. I am grateful to Diana Fletcher for this reference.
44. Hampshire RO, 23/M/93/134. I am grateful to Diana Fletcher for this reference; Trench, *A Few Notes from Past Life*, p. 15.
45. Richard Trench to Charles St George, 25 July 1819. I am grateful to Lucy Trench for lending me this letter.
46. Trench, *A Few Notes from Past Life*, pp. 9–28. I am grateful to The Hon. Roderick Trench for the loan of this book.
47. Trench, *A Few Notes from Past Life*, pp. 29–31.
48. Hampshire RO, Austen Leigh Mss. I am grateful to Diana Fletcher for this reference.
49. Trench, *A Few Notes from Past Life*, pp. 43–9.
50. Trench, *A Few Notes from Past Life*, pp. 6–7.
51. Citations from Cooke–Trench, *A Memoir of the Trench Family*, pp. 118–19.
52. Hampshire RO, 23/M/93/7: Austen Leigh Mss.
53. Trench, *A Few Notes from Past Life*, pp. 40–1.
54. Hampshire RO, 23/M/93/41: Austen Leigh Mss.
55. Trench, *A Few Notes from Past Life*, pp. 117–18.
56. Verney, ed., *Verney Letters*, I, 71, 137.
57. Cust, ed., *Records of the Cust Family*, I, pp. 271–2.
58. Suffolk RO, HA 53: Barne Mss, Elizabeth Barne to Miles Barne, 1754.
59. Essex RO, D/DR2/ C3: Catherine Bromhead to James Edwards, 18 January 1822.
60. Suffolk RO, HA 18/HF: Long of Saxmundham letters, 3, 17.
61. Larminie, *Wealth, Kinship and Culture*, pp. 109–11.
62. Lincolnshire RO, Monson Mss 7/13/187, 188 14/61.
63. Derbyshire RO, D 239. Fitzherbert Mss, F 6568, 6570, 6585–8: William Perrin to Lady Sarah Fitzherbert, 23 August 1793–27 April 1794.
64. Staffordshire RO, D4216/E/2/226, Henrietta Boughey to Frank Twenlow, 17 July 1823.

Chapter 13: The Public Schools

1. Chandos, *Boys Together*, pp. 239–40.
2. Cited in Fletcher, *Gender, Sex and Subordination*, p. 307.
3. Stirling, ed., *The Diaries of Dummer*, pp. 1–73; Chandos, *Boys Together*, pp. 137–54.
4. J.A. Mangan, 'Social Darwinism and Upper Class Education in Late Victorian and Edwardian England', in Mangan and Walvin, eds, *Manliness and Morality*, p. 143; *ODNB*.
5. Neddam, 'Constructing Masculinities under Thomas Arnold of Rugby (1828–1842): Gender, Educational Policy and School Life in an Early-Victorian Public School', in *Gender and Education*, 16 (2004), pp. 303–26.
6. Chandos, *Boys Together*, pp. 63–109.
7. Citations from Neddam in *Gender and Education*, 16 (2004), pp. 308–16.
8. Blake, *Reminiscences of an Etonian*, pp. 65–6.
9. Citations from Gibson, *The English Vice*, pp. 117–19.
10. Gibson, *The English Vice*, pp. 119–35; for Victorian flagellation see Pearsall, *Worm in the Bud*, pp. 328–43.

11. H.J.C. Blake, *Reminiscences of an Etonian* (1831), pp. 32–3.
12. Cited in Gibson, *The English Vice*, p. 102 ; Pearsall, *The Worm in the Bud*, p. 330.
13. Pearsall, *The Worm in the Bud*, p. 328.
14. Blake, *Reminiscences of an Etonian*, p. 51.
15. I.E.M., *The Confessions of an Etonian* (1846), p. 51.
16. Gibson, *The English Vice*, pp. 107–12, 137–8, 146–7; *ODNB*.
17. Newsome, *History of Wellington College*, pp. 114–17, 156–8, 241–3.
18. Newsome, *History of Wellington College*, pp. 162, 186.
19. Cited in Gibson. *The English Vice*, pp. 138–9.
20. Hare, *The Years with Mother*, pp. 49–53; *ODNB*.
21. Carpenter, *My Days and Dreams*, pp. 24–30.
22. Hodder, *Life and Work of the seventh Earl of Shaftesbury*, I. pp. 50–2; *ODNB*.
23. Strutt, ed., *The Strutt Family of Terling*, pp. 77–82.
24. J.A. Mangan, 'Social Darwinism and Upper Class Education in Late Victorian and Edwardian England', in Mangan and Walvin, eds, *Manliness and Morality*, pp. 142–52.
25. Thale, ed., *Autobiography of Francis Place*, pp. 41–2.
26. Lewis, 'Mummy, Matron and the Maids: Feminine Presence and Absence in Male Institutions, 1934–63', in Roper and Tosh, eds, *Manful Assertions*, pp. 168–89.

Chapter 14: Boys at University

1. Cited in S. Porter, 'The University and Society', in Tyacke, ed., *History of the University of Oxford*, IV, p. 68.
2. Cited in Fletcher, *Gender, Sex and Subordination*, p. 313.
3. For examination and admittance of undergraduates to Merton in this period see Martin and Highfield, *A History of Merton College*, pp. 270–5.
4. Bristol RO, Smyth of Ashton Court Mss, AC/C95/1.
5. Bristol RO, Smyth of Ashton Court Mss, AC/C94/1; Landau, *The Justices of the Peace 1679–1760*, pp. 333–66.
6. Bristol RO, Smyth of Ashton Court Mss, AC/C98/1.
7. Below, pp. 265–6.
8. Bristol RO, Smyth of Ashton Court Mss, AC/C95/2,3, AC/C98/1, AC/C99/1.
9. Bristol RO, Smyth of Ashton Court Mss, AC/C94/1–13, AC/C96/1–3; AC/C98/4,AC/C100/1–14.
10. Parkinson, ed., *Journal of John Byrom*, I, part 1, pp. 1–20.
11. Midgley, *University Life in Eighteenth-Century Oxford*, p. 2.
12. Kent RO, U120/C48.
13. Verney, *Verney Letters*, II, pp. 68–70.
14. Verney, *Verney Letters*, I, p. 94; Bickley, ed., *Diaries of Sylvester Douglas*, I, p. 397, II, p. 26.
15. Curtis, *Chronicle of Small Beer*, pp. 40–5.
16. Porter, 'University and Society' in Tyacke, ed., *History of the University of Oxford*, IV, pp. 65–9.
17. Kent RO, U120/C48.
18. Fletcher, *Gender, Sex and Subordination*, pp. 313–5: Midgley, *University Life in Eighteenth-Century Oxford*, pp. 61–157.
19. Bray, ed., *Diary and Correspondence of John Evelyn*, I, p. 9.
20. Citations from Tyacke, ed., *History of the University of Oxford*, IV, pp. 72–3.
21. Bray, ed., *Diary and Correspondence of John Evelyn*, I, p. 11.
22. Kent RO, U120, C19, C48.
23. Owen, *The Lowther Family*, pp. 175–89.
24. Cumbria RO, D/Lons/ L1/ 22/1–2; *ODNB*.

25. Owen, *The Lowther Family*, p. 177.
26. Cumbria RO, D/Lons/ L1/ 22/4–5.
27. Cumbria RO, D/Lons/ L1/22/6.
28. Owen, *The Lowther Family*, pp. 188–9.
29. Cumbria RO, D/Lons/L1/22/7.
30. Cumbria RO, D/Lons/L1/22/8.
31. Cumbria RO, D/Lons/L1/22/10–25.
32. Cumbria RO, D/Lons/L3/1/5: Sir John Lowther's advice, 1688, fols 243–4; Owen, *The Lowther Family*, pp. 187–9.
33. Lewis, *Letters of Lady Brilliana Harley*, pp. 82–3, 85, 93, 99–100.
34. McGrath, *The Flemings in Oxford*, I, p. 13.
35. Woodforde, ed., *Woodforde's Papers and Diaries*, p. 16.
36. Lincolnshire RO, Monson Mss 7/13/194–8.
37. Durham RO, D/ST/C1/2/90(4), (14), (16); Bowes Papers.
38. Pollock, *Lasting Relationship*, p. 137.
39. BL, Add Mss 33634, fols 4–44; *ODNB*: John Skinner.
40. Trench, *A Few Notes from Past Life*, pp. 81, 88–9, 92–3, 107–8, 114–16, 118–19, 122, 128, 132–6.
41. Coffey Archive, Isabel Chenevix Trench to Cesca Chenevix Trench, 9 October 1906.
42. Martin and Highfield, *A History of Merton College*, p. 314.
43. I am grateful to Roger Highfield for details of Reggie's academic career.
44. Coffey Archive, Cesca Chenevix Trench diary 1907; Reggie Chenevix Trench to Margot and Cesca Chenevix Trench, 22 November 1908.
45. McGrath, *The Flemings at Oxford*, III, pp. 217–21 228–34; cited in Fletcher, *Gender, Sex and Subordination*, pp. 314–15.

Chapter 15: The Schoolroom

1. Cited in Martin, ed., *A Governess in the Age of Jane Austen*, p. 52.
2. Hughes, *The Victorian Governess*, pp. 22, 59.
3. Pollock, *With Faith and Physic: The Life of a Tudor Gentlewoman: Lady Grace Mildmay 1552–1620*, pp. 6, 25–8; see also Fletcher, *Gender, Sex and Subordination*, pp. 370–1.
4. Kamm, *Hope Deferred*, pp. 112–51; Skedd, 'Women Teachers and the Expansion of Girls' Schooling in England *c.* 1760–1820', in Barker and Challus, eds, *Gender in Eighteenth-Century England*, p. 125.
5. Martin, ed., *A Governess in the Age of Jane Austen*, pp. 52–3.
6. Martin, ed., *A Governess in the Age of Jane Austen*, p. 54.
7. Wiltshire RO, Bruce MSS 9/35/329/7: Catherine Wincle to Lord Bruce, 30 September 1778.
8. Martin, *Wives and Daughters*, pp. 219–21.
9. Hughes, *Victorian Governess*, p. 42.
10. Broughton and Symes, *The Governess*, pp. 35–7.
11. Trench Archive, Georgiana Trench to Harriott Trench, undated.
12. Hughes, *Victorian Governess*, p. 173.
13. Williams, 'Illness and Impact: The Mistress of the House and the Governess', in Harvey, ed., *The Kiss in History*, pp. 148–65.
14. Kent RO, U951 F30/1: Diary of Eva Knatchbull, p. 5.
15. Cheshire RO, DSA 54: Stanley Papers.
16. Hall, ed., *Mrs Weeton's Journal of a Governess*, pp. 67–75.
17. Hughes, *The Victorian Governess*, pp. 55–7.
18. Staffordshire RO, D1057/M/R.
19. Hughes, *Victorian Governess*, pp. 71, 219.

20. Bowen, *Bowen's Court and Seven Winters*, p. 323. I am grateful to Mr and Mrs Brendan Smith for showing me the schoolroom at Cangort Park.
21. Charlton, ed., *Recollections of a Northumbrian Lady*, pp. 28–9.
22. Staffordshire RO, D1057/M/R.
23. Trench Archive, Louey Trench's scrapbook.
24. Martin, *Wives and Daughters*, p. 221; Martin, *A Governess in the Age of Jane Austen*, p. 56.
25. Martin, *A Governess in the Age of Jane Austen*, pp. 62–3.
26. Derbyshire RO, D1491 M/Z1: Elizabeth Bradshawe's notes on 'a part of my life for those who care to read it'.
27. Fairfax-Lucy, ed., *Mistress of Charlecote*, pp. 18–24.
28. These paragraphs are based upon Derbyshire RO, D'Ewes Coke of Pinxton diary, 1818.
29. Countess of Jersey, *Fifty-one Years of Victorian Life*, pp. 6–9.
30. Frances, Countess of Warwick, *Life's Ebb and Flow*, pp. 17–27.
31. Chenevix Trench, *My Mother Told Me*, pp. 11–13, 30–1, 33.
32. Fairfax-Lucy, ed., *Mistress of Charlecote*, pp. 16–17.
33. Haldane, *Record of a Hundred Years*, pp. 43–5, 63, 75; Pollock, *Lasting Relationship*, pp. 199–200.
34. Wiltshire RO, Bruce Mss, 9/35/329/ 10/2. 9/35/329/1033.
35. Citations from Hughes, *Victorian Governess*, pp. 67–70.
36. Bowen, *Bowen's Court and Seven Winters*, pp. 325–47.
37. West Sussex RO, Add MSS, 7467, 6 September 1799; Add MSS 7468, 31 August 1800.
38. Cohen, *Lady Rothschild and Her Daughters*, pp. 81–5.
39. West Sussex RO, Add MS 7463, 1 March 1794, end page.
40. West Sussex RO, Add MS 7463, 7464.
41. West Sussex RO, Add MS 7465–7467. Fletcher, 'Courses in Politeness: The Upbringing and Experiences of Five Teenage Diarists, 1671–1860', in *TRHS*, 12 (2002), pp. 421–3.
42. Trench Archive, Georgiana Bloomfield's sketchbook, 1819.
43. Trench Archive, Charlotte Bloomfield's scrapbook; for her death see Fletcher, 'Beyond the Church: Women's Spiritual Experience at Home and in the Community 1660–1900', in Swanson, ed., *Gender and Christian Religion*, pp. 199–200 and above pp. 289–91.
44. Trench Archive, Charlotte Bloomfield to Miss Ridout, 17 November 1825.
45. Trench Archive, Charlotte Bloomfield to Miss Ridout, 15 December 1825.
46. Trench Archive, Charlotte Bloomfield to Miss Ridout, 20 December 1825; Charlotte Bloomfield to Georgiana Bloomfield, 9 April 1827.
47. Trench Archive, Charlotte Bloomfield to Miss Ridout, 2 February 1826.
48. Trench Archive, Charlotte Bloomfield to Georgiana Bloomfield, 1 November 1826.
49. Trench Archive, Charlotte Bloomfield to Harriott and Georgiana Bloomfield, 23 January 1827; Charlotte Bloomfield to Miss Ridout, 3 May 1827.
50. Sitwell, ed., *Two Generations*, pp. 1–68; *ODNB*.
51. Bailey, ed., *Diary of Lady Frederick Cavendish*, I, pp. 3–12.
52. Bailey, ed., *Diary of Lady Frederick Cavendish*, I, p. 28; Chatsworth House, Lucy Lyttleton's Diary, 18 September 1854, 1–4 October 1855.
53. Bailey, ed., *Diary of Lady Frederick Cavendish*, pp. I, 36–7; Chatsworth House, Lucy Lyttleton's Diary, 5 June 1856.
54. Chatsworth House, Lucy Lyttleton's Diary, 8, 30 December 1856.
55. Bailey, ed., *Diary of Lady Frederick Cavendish*, I, p. 65.
56. Cartwright. ed., *Journals of Lady Knightley*, pp. 1–4; Northants RO, K 2876, Louisa Bowater's Diary, 25 April, 4 May 1856.
57. Fletcher, 'Courses in Politeness: The Upbringing and Experiences of Five Teenage Diarists, 1671–1860', in *TRHS*, 12 (2002), pp. 424–7.
58. Trench Archive, Clare Howard's nature notebook, 1904.
59. Trench Archive, Clare Howard's notes for a talk on 'A Victorian Childhood'.

Chapter 16: Girls at School

1. Pollock, *Lasting Relationship*, p. 223.
2. Fletcher, *Gender, Sex and Subordination*, pp. 366–7.
3. Citations in Pollock, '"Teach Her to Live Under Obedience": The Making of Women in the Upper Ranks of Early Modern England', *Continuity and Change*, 4 (1989), pp. 239–40.
4. Verney, ed., *Memoirs of the Verney Family*, III, pp. 72–4; Pollock, *Lasting Relationship*, p. 226.
5. Mitford, ed., *The Stanleys of Alderley*, p. xvii.
6. O'Day, *Education and Society*, pp. 186–9; Charlton, *Women, Religion and Education in Early Modern England*, pp. 131–41.
7. Larminie, *Wealth, Kinship and Culture*, p. 120.
8. De Beer, ed., *Diary of John Evelyn*, II, p. 555.
9. Pepys, *Diary*, VIII, pp. 174; see also Fletcher, *Gender, Sex and Subordination*, pp. 369–70.
10. Bird, ed., *The Journal of Giles Moore*, pp. 70–81; Charlton, *Women, Religion and Education in Early Modern England*, p. 141.
11. S. Skedd, 'Women Teachers and the Expansion of Girls' Schooling in England, *c.* 1760–1820', in Barker and Challus, eds, *Gender in Eighteenth-Century England*, pp. 101–4, 125; J. Caffyn, *Sussex Schools in the Eighteenth Century*, pp. 6–17.
12. Citations from Barker and Challus, eds, *Gender in Eighteenth-Century England*, pp. 105–7.
13. For examples, see Pollock, *Forgotten Children*, pp. 239–49.
14. Allen, *A Beloved Mother*, p. 16.
15. Cited in Pollock, *Forgotten Children*, p. 248; *ODNB*.
16. Pollock, *Lasting Relationship*, pp. 236–7.
17. E. and F. Anson, eds, *Mary Hamilton at Court and at Home*, pp. 10–11.
18. Durham RO, D/St/c2/3/100, nos 15–17.
19. Whale, *My Grandfather's Pocket Book*, pp. 168, 174–86; Pollock, *Lasting Relationship*, pp. 273–4.
20. Hyde, *Thrales of Streatham Park*, pp. 86, 112, 146, 178–9, 188, 196–7.
21. Lincolnshire RO, Flinders 2, July 1793, January 1795, September 1797, March 1798, August 1798. For girls in service, see Mendelson and Crawford, *Women in Early Modern England*, pp. 92–108.
22. Cust, ed., *Records of the Cust Family* II, pp. 239, 21.
23. Borsay, 'Children, Adolescents and Fashionable Urban Society in Eighteenth-Century England', in Muller, ed., *Fashioning Childhood in the Eighteenth Century*, pp. 53–62.
24. Francis and Keary, eds, *Francis Letters*, pp. 151, 163, 196, 211, 237–8.
25. Fiske, ed., *Oakes Diaries*, I, pp. 175–6.
26. Russell, ed., *Memoirs, Journal and Correspondence of Thomas Moore*, IV, p. 132, V, pp. 236, 274; Pollock, *Forgotten Children*, p. 192.
27. Kent RO, U1015/C127/1–14.
28. Trench Archive, Georgiana Trench to Henry Trench, undated c. 1862.
29. Coffey Archive, Isabel Trench to Cesca Trench, 17, 27 July, 4 August 1905; Elizabeth Bowen, *Bowens Court*, pp. 20–6, 405–15.
30. Coffey Archive, Isabel Trench to Cesca Trench, 9, 11, undated October 1906, 18 January, 3 June and undated 1907.
31. Coffey Archive, 1 February, 4, 14 and undated March 1907.
32. Kamm, *Hope Deferred*, pp. 166–98.
33. Dyhouse, *Girls Growing Up in Late Victorian and Edwardian England*, pp. 55–9.
34. Mitchell, *New Girl*, pp. 2, 106–8.
35. Dyhouse, *Girls Growing Up in Late Victorian and Edwardian England*, pp. 40–73.
36. Hampshire RO, 29M69/1: Diary of a Schoolgirl.

37. Fox, ed., *Memoir of Mrs Eliza Fox*, pp. 1–11.
38. Fox, ed., *Memoir of Mrs Eliza Fox*, pp. 12–20.
39. Derbyshire RO, D 1491 M/Z1.
40. Sewell, *Life and Letters of Mrs Sewell*, p. 44.
41. Hants RO, 12M 58/2.
42. Coffey Archive, CCT to MCT, undated October, November 1906.
43. M. Garber, *Bisexuality and the Eroticism of Everyday Life*, chapter 4. I am grateful to Helen Berry for this reference and for discussion of this issue.
44. Trench Archve, Edna to Clare Howard, 22, 24, 26 February 1909.

Chapter 17: Training for Society

1. Cited by Pollock, '"Teach Her to Live Under Obedience": The Making of Women in the Upper Ranks of Early Modern England', *Continuity and Change*, 4 (1989), p. 245.
2. Orme, *From Childhood to Chivalry: The Education of Kings and Aristocrats 1066–1530*, pp. 58–60; Charlton, *Women, Religion and Education in Early Modern England*, pp. 126–31.
3. Hassell-Smith *et al.*, eds, *The Papers of Nathaniel Bacon of Stiffkey*, I, 1566–77, pp. 24, 39.
4. Cited in O'Day, *Education and Society 1500–1600*, p. 184.
5. Cited in Charlton, *Women, Religion and Education in Early Modern England*, p. 129.
6. Hassell-Smith *et al.*, eds, *The Papers of Nathaniel Bacon of Stiffkey*, I, 1566–77, pp. 24, 39.
7. Essex RO, D/DRb/ 214.
8. Fletcher, *County Community in Peace and War*, pp. 22, 38.
9. Woodforde, ed., *Woodforde Papers and Diaries*, p. 21.
10. Northamptonshire RO, Dryden MSS, D (CA), 1030–7.
11. Axtell, ed., *The Educational Writings of John Locke*, p. 123.
12. Charlton, ed., *Recollections of a Northumbrian Lady* pp. 29–30.
13. Gates, ed., *Journal of Emily Shore*, p. 38.
14. Haldane, *Friends and Kindred*, p. 58.
15. Kent RO, U951 F30/1: Diary of Eva Knatchbull, p. 119.
16. Angela Forbes, *Memories and Base Details*, p. 14; citations from Stone, *Family, Sex and Marriage*, pp. 445–7.
17. Countess of Illchester and Lord Stavordale, *Life and Letters of Lady Sarah Lennox*, I, pp. 304–7; Tillyard, *Aristocrats*, p. 332.
18. Cited in Martin, *Wives and Daughters*, pp. 226–7.
19. Essex RO, Acc C1032.
20. Hampshire RO, 12M 58/1.
21. Haldane, *Friends and Kindred*, p. 78; Trench Archive, Mademoiselle Ravian to Georgiana Trench, undated.
22. Citations from Tague, *Women of Quality*, pp. 169–72.
23. Tague, *Women of Quality*, pp. 173–4.
24. Pollock '"Teach Her to Live Under Obedience": The Making of Women in the Upper Ranks of Early Modern England', in *Continuity and Change*, 4 (1989), pp. 240–1.
25. The letter appears in facsimile and verbatim in Pollock, *Lasting Relationship*, pp. 138–9.
26. Bristol RO, Smyth of Ashton Court MSS, C86/1,2; C86/8,9,11.
27. Essex RO, D/DU 77/1, pp. 29–33.
28. Cust, ed., *Records of the Cust Family*, pp. 234–83.

29. Borsay, 'Children, Adolescents and Fashionable Urban Society in Eighteenth-Century England', in Muller, ed., *Fashioning Childhood in the Eighteenth Century*, pp. 53–62.
30. BL, ADD Mss 29575, especially 351r, 379r, 391; Tague, *Women of Quality*, p. 173.
31. Cheshire RO, DSA 61: Lady Maria Stanley to Mrs Butler, 30 January 1808.
32. Houlbrooke, ed., *English Family Life*, pp. 167–70; Hobhouse, ed., *Diary of a West Country Physician*, pp. 31–2; Blundell, ed., *Blundell's Diary and Letter Book*, pp. 69–70, 144–7, 156–8, 179, 206–7, 210–14, 222, 256–7. See also Pollock, *Lasting Relationship*, p. 271.
33. Vickery, *Gentleman's Daughter*, pp. 156, 343, 378.
34. Lancaster Public Library, 8752: Mary Chorley's Diary, 15 December 1776.
35. Vickery, *Gentleman's Daughter*, pp. 7, 71, 209, 259.
36. Henstock, ed., *Diary of Abigail Gawthern*, pp. 25–32.
37. Adenne, ed., *Girlhood of Maria Josepha Holroyd*, pp. xvi–37, 207, 209, 316, 375.
38. Cited in Vickery, *Gentleman's Daughter*, p. 267; Tague, *Women of Quality*, pp. 167–8; *ODNB*.
39. Blundell, ed., *Blundell's Diary and Letter Book*, p. 70.
40. Troide, ed., *The Early Journals and Letters of Frances Burney*, I, pp. 25–6.
41. Cited in Vickery, *Gentleman's Daughter*, p. 345.
42. Cited in H. Berry, 'Creating Polite Space: The Organisation and Social Function of the Newcastle Assembly Rooms', in Berry and Gregory, eds, *Creating and Consuming Culture in North-East England, 1660–1830*, p. 135.
43. For general background, see Langford, *Polite and Commercial People*, pp. 59–122; Borsay, *English Urban Renaissance*, pp. 115–9, 257–83; Vickery, *Gentleman's Daughter*, pp. 225–84.
44. I am grateful for this point to Helen Berry.
45. Hyde, *Thrales of Streatham Park*, pp. 164–5, 170, 188–9, 209.
46. Francis and Keary, eds, *Francis Letters*, pp. 243, 292–3, 297, 301, 318, 322, 333–5.
47. West Sussex RO, Goodwood MS 102, 43, 46.
48. Davidoff, *The Best Circles*, p. 29.
49. Vickery, *Gentleman's Daughter*, pp. 277–80, 347–8.
50. Davidoff, *The Best Circles*, pp. 41–9.
51. Hunt, *Middling Sort*, p. 84.
52. Pollock, *Lasting Relationship*, p. 241.
53. Cited in Mitchell, *The New Girl*, p. 103.
54. Pollock, *Lasting Relationship*, p. 157.
55. Carberry, *Happy World*, pp 48–51.
56. Lutyens, *A Blessed Girl*, pp. 7–10., 41; Mitchell, *The New Girl*, p. 103.
57. Cited in Davidoff, *The Best Circles*, p. 51.
58. Haldane, *Friends and Kindred*, p. 69.
59. B. and R. Russell, eds, *Amberley Papers*, pp. 13–137.
60. Cohen, *Lady de Rothschild and her Daughters*, pp. 76–97.
61. Davidoff, *Best Circles*, pp. 41–58.
62. Fairfax-Lucy, ed., *Mistress of Charlecote*, p. 22.
63. Buckinghamshire RO, DX 1174 /1: Grenfell Mss, Children's Journal, fol. 21v.
64. The Hon. Mrs Gell, *Under Three Reigns 1860–1920*, pp. 48–9; cited in Davidoff, *The Best Circles*, p. 52.
65. Fletcher, 'Courses in Politeness: The Upbringing and Experiences of Five Teenage Diarists, 1671–1860', in *TRHS*, 12 (2002) pp. 423–30.
66. Neville, ed., *Reminiscences of Lady Dorothy Neville*, p. 50.
67. Buckinghamshire RO, D/X 1174/1, fols 22V–23r.
68. Trench Archive, photographs and letters by Clare Howard.

Chapter 18: Personal Testimony

1. Isham, ed., *Diary of Thomas Isham*, pp. 10–11, 61; Fletcher, 'Courses in Politeness: The Upbringing and Experiences of Five Teenage Diarists, 1671–1860', in *TRHS* 12 (2002), pp. 417–19.
2. Foot, ed., *Gladstone Diaries*, I, pp. 1–91.
3. Post, *Extracts from his Diary*, pp. xii, 78, 86.
4. BL, Add Mss 42160, fols 1–2.
5. BL, Add Mss 42160–42162, 42163, fol.1.
6. Bessborough, ed., *Lady Bessborough and her Family Circle*, pp. 18–30.
7. West Sussex RO, Add Mss 7468.
8. *ODNB*: Emily Shore.
9. Gates, ed., *Journal of Emily Shore*.
10. Bailey, ed., *The Diary of Lady Frederick Cavendish*, 2 vols.
11. Bailey, ed., *Diary of Lady Frederick Cavendish*, I, pp. 17–18. Chatsworth, Lucy Lyttelton's diary, II, III, IV, V.
12. Chatsworth, Lucy Lyttelton's diary, II.
13. Bailey, ed., *Diary of Lady Frederick Cavendish*, I, p. 45.
14. Chatsworth, Lucy Lyttelton's diary, 5–17 September 1856.
15. Chatsworth, Lucy Lyttelton's diary, 5 September 1857.
16. Cartwright, ed., *The Journals of Lady Knightley*, pp. xiv–xviii.
17. Northamptonshire RO, K 2879.
18. Northamptonshire RO, K 2881, 2882.
19. Hertfordshire RO, D/ECK F6.
20. Kent RO, U951 F 30/1, p. 4.
21. Heywood, *Growing Up in France*, pp. 18–20.
22. Wiltshire RO, Bruce Mss 9/35/335.
23. Trench Archive. Letters 1911–1915

Chapter 19: Home

1. Isham, ed., *The Diary of Thomas Isham*, pp. 15–16
2. Isham, ed., *The Diary of Thomas Isham*, pp. 90–2.
3. Northants RO, Isham Correspondence, 734, Sir Justinian Isham to his son Thomas, 11 July 1671.
4. Isham, ed., *Diary of Thomas Isham*, pp. 60–1, 83, 112, 171–3.
5. Isham, ed., *Diary of Thomas Isham*, pp. 67, 105, 109, 133, 143, 167, 177, 183, 191, 213, 225; Fletcher, 'Courses in Politeness: The Upbringing and Experiences of Five Teenage Diarists, 1671–1860', in *TRHS*, 12 (2002), pp. 417–19.
6. Vickery, *Gentleman's Daughter*, pp. 7, 71, 156, 209, 218, 237, 259, 343–4, 378.
7. Lancaster Public Library, MS 8752, 8753, 8754.
8. *ODNB*, Emily Shore.
9. Gates, ed., *Journal of Emily Shore*, pp. 8, 12.
10. Gates, ed., *Journal*, pp. 22, 31–3, 42, 61.
11. Cartwright, ed., *Journals of Lady Knightley*, pp. 1–6.
12. Northants RO, K2879, 13, 16, 18 May, 27 June, 31 July, 1 August, 15–19 September, 23, 30 October, 2, 5, 17 November 1856; K2882, 2 August 1858; K2883, 6 September 1859.
13. For Montem see Chandos, *Boys Together*, pp. 206–10.
14. West Sussex RO, Add Mss 7462, 5 January, 3 March, 21 May, 16 June.
15. Kent RO, U1612 F 104: Autobiography of Meriel Lyttelton, 1913; Bailey, ed., *Diary of Lady Frederick Cavendish*, I, p. 11.

16. Chatsworth, Lucy Lyttelton's diary, 3–14 December 1854, 17–21 April 1855.
17. Chatsworth, Lucy Lyttelton's diary, 23 July 1855.
18. Fletcher, *Victorian Girls*, pp. 34–6.
19. Bailey, ed., *Diary of Lady Frederick Cavendish*, I, p. 28.
20. Chatsworth, Lucy Lyttelton's diary, 23 July 1855.
21. Chatsworth, Lucy Lyttelton's diary, 31 May 1856.
22. Bailey, ed., *Diary of Lady Frederick Cavendish*, I, pp. 47–9.
23. Bailey, ed., *Diary of Lady Frederick Cavendish*, I, p. 15.
24. Chatsworth, Lucy Lyttelton's diary, 13 June–31 August 1857; Bailey, ed., *Diary of Lady Frederick Cavendish*, I, p. 57.
25. Kent RO, U1612 F105: Meriel Lyttelton's diary, 1857.
26. Kent RO, U1612 F104: Autobiography of Meriel Lyttelton; Fletcher, *Victorian Girls*, pp. 37–77.
27. West Sussex RO, Add Mss 7462, 3 February, 5 October, 9 November 1793: 7463, 14 Feb., 23 June–2 July, 18–28 August 1794; 7464, 18–19 Jan., 11–13 Nov. 1795; 7467, 23 Jan. 6 April 1797.
28. West Sussex RO, Add Mss 7467–7468.
29. Bailey, ed., *Diary of Lady Frederick Cavendish,* I, p. 14.
30. Chatsworth, Lucy Lyttelton's diary, 3–16 September 1856.
31. Bailey, ed., *Diary of Lady Frederick Cavendish*, I, pp. 52, 341.
32. Chatsworth, Lucy Lyttelton's diary, 14 January, 30 April 1857, 13–14 January 1858.
33. Bailey, *Diary of Lady Frederick Cavendish*, I, p. 70.
34. Fletcher, *Victorian Girls*, p. 55.
35. Bailey, ed., *Diary of Lady Frederick Cavendish*, I, p. 86.
36. West Sussex RO, Add Mss 7462, 21 May 1793; Kent RO, U951 F30/1: Diary of Eva Knatchbull, pp. 28–30.
37. Chatsworth, Lucy Lyttelton's diary, 14 December 1854; Kent RO, U951 F30/1, p. 46.
38. West Sussex RO, Add Mss 7464, back leaf.
39. Chatsworth, Lucy Lyttelton's diary, 7 April, 8 May 1859; Fletcher, *Victorian Girls*, p. 47.
40. Thompson, ed., *Journal of John Gabriel Stedman*, pp. 10–17.
41. Sheppard, ed., *George Duke of Cambridge*, pp. 11–21.
42. Thompson, ed., *Dr Salter: His Diary and Reminiscences*, pp. 3–12.
43. Suffolk RO, HD384/1: Diary of George Corrance.
44. Lincolnshire RO, Hett Mss 2/1/5.
45. Bodleian Library, Top Hants e 9: Diary of a Winchester schoolboy.
46. Bowen, *Bowen's Court*, pp. 330, 341.
47. West Sussex RO, Add Mss 19765, pp. 6, 11 Jan., 25 April 1865.
48. Hampshire RO, 1110M88W/1, fol. 5v.; Kent RO, U1291 F1/1, pp. 1–4.
49. Kent RO, U951 F 30/1, p. 41.
50. Kent RO, U1291, pp. 1–2.
51. Hampshire RO, 1110M88W/1, fols 7v–8.
52. Kent RO, U951 F30/1, pp. 48, 89, 93. 185; P. Rowsby, Extracts from the diary of Eva Knatchbull (typescript).
53. West Sussex RO, Add Mss 19765, 22 April 1865.
54. Hampshire RO, 1110M 88W/1, 2, 30 June 1871.
55. Kent RO, U1291, pp. 13–14.
56. West Sussex RO, Add Mass 19765, 7 Jan., 17 April, 15 July, 7 August 1865.
57. Hampshire RO, 110M 88W/1, 25 Jan., 1872.
58. Kent RO, U 951 F 30/1, p. 102.
59. Tosh, *A Man's Place*, p. 82.
60. Kent RO, U951 F30/1, p. 98.
61. Bowen, *Bowen's Court*, p. 341.

62. Bailey, ed., *Diary of Lady Frederick Cavendish*, I, pp. 13–4.
63. West Sussex RO, Add Mss 7462, 21–6 November, 1793.
64. Bailey, ed., *Diary of Lady Frederick Cavendish*, I, pp. 16–17; Chatsworth, Lucy Lyttleton's diary, 31 December 1854, 6–31 December 1857.

Chapter 20: School

1. Chandos, *Boys Together*, pp. 63–205.
2. Morley, *The Life of Gladstone*, I, pp. 7–34.
3. Morley, *The Life of Gladstone*, I, p. 32, footnote, citing *Daily Telegraph*, 20 May, 1898.
4. Foot, ed., *The Gladstone Diaries*, I, pp. 1–26; Morley, *Life of Gladstone*, I, pp. 34–7.
5. Chandos, *Boys Together*, pp. 205–8.
6. Foot, ed., *The Gladstone Diaries*, I, pp. 28–88; Morley, *Life of Gladstone*, I, pp. 32–4.
7. Foot, ed., *The Gladstone Diaries*, I, pp. 17, 29; Morley, *Life of Gladstone*, I, pp. 44–6
8. Edwards, ed., *The Scribble Book of an Eton Boy, 1758–67*, pp. 18–20, 25, 37.
9. Wiltshire RO, Bruce Mss: 9/35/335/ 879–905, 1613–17, 2032, 3152–75.
10. Warwicks RO, Seymour Mss, CR 114A/382: George Seymour's 'memoir of my earlier days', 1837.
11. Bodleian, Top Hants e 9: Winchester schoolboy diary 1867, p. 77; Lincolnshire RO, Hett Mss 2/1/5; Suffolk RO, HD 384/1: diary of George Corrance.
12. Thompson, ed., *Dr Salter his Diary and Reminiscences*, pp. 3–11.
13. Hertfordshire RO, D/P15/25/22: Barrett diary.
14. Suffolk RO, HA 408/f3/1: diary of Edmund Holland, p. 34.
15. Suffolk RO, HD 384/1: diary of George Corrance, pp. 93–8, 103–5.
16. Bodleian, Top Hants e 9: Winchester schoolboy diary 1867, pp. 76–89.
17. Staffordshire RO, D4216/E/2/227, 230, 234–5.
18. B. and P., eds, *The Amberley Papers*, pp. 164–75.
19. B. and P., eds, *The Amberley Papers*, pp. 199–203.
20. Buckinghamshire RO, Grenfell Mss: D/X 1174/2/ 23–35.
21. Hampshire RO, 29M69/1: Diary of a Schoolgirl; above, pp. 253–4.
22. West Sussex RO, Add Mss 19765.

Chapter 21: Travel

1. Black, *The British Abroad: The Grand Tour in the Eighteenth Century*.
2. Schwarz, 'London 1700–1840' in Clark, ed., *Cambridge Urban History of Britain*, II, pp. 655–8.
3. Dennis, 'Modern London' in Daunton, ed., *Cambridge Urban History of Britain*, III, pp. 120–1; Davidoff, *The Best Circles*, pp. 28–32.
4. West Sussex RO, Add Mss 7462–7464.
5. Gates, ed., *Journal of Emily Shore*, pp. 2–3.
6. Thompson, ed., *Dr Salter his Diary and Reminiscences*, pp. 3–5.
7. Bailey, ed., *The Diary of Lady Frederick Cavendish*, I, pp. 25–8, 30–6.
8. Chatsworth, Lucy Lyttelton's diary, 2–16 May 1856.
9. Reid, 'Playing and Praying', in Daunton, ed., *Cambridge Urban History of Britain*, III, pp. 765, 769–70.
10. Northants RO, K 2879–2883: journals of Louisa Bowater.
11. Lincolnshire RO, Hett Mss 2/1/5: diary of Frederick Hett, 4 May 1869.
12. See above, p. 309.
13. West Sussex RO, Add Mss 7464: diary of Sophia Baker, 18 August–21 September 1795.

14. Vickery, *Gentleman's Daughter*, p. 344n.
15. Nairn and Pevsner, *Sussex*, pp. 426–7, 438–42.
16. Walton, *The English Seaside Resort*; Walton, 'Towns and Consumerism'; and Reid, 'Playing and Praying', in Daunton, ed., *Cambridge Urban History of Britain*, pp. 715–807.
17. Gates, ed., *Journal*, pp. 2–7.
18. Post, *Extracts from his Diary*, pp. 170–3.
19. Nairn and Pevsner, *Sussex*, pp. 527–9.
20. Bailey, ed., *The Diary of Lady Frederick Cavendish*, I, pp. 29–30, 52: Chatsworth, Lucy Lyttleton's diary, 18 February–14 April 1856.
21. Kent RO, P. Rowsby, Extracts from the Diary of Eva Knatchbull (typescript), 3 February 1875.
22. Ethel Hatch, 'Some Reminiscences of Oxford', *Oxford Magazine*, 14 June 1956.
23. Oxfordshire RO, P/284/1J/2: diary of Ethel Hatch, 13 April–11 July 1887.
24. Lincolnshire RO, Hett Mss 2/1/5: diary of Frederick Hett, 1859.
25. Mitchell, *The New Girl*, p. 104.
26. Trench Archive, Clare Howard's diaries, 1906–9.
27. Vickery, *Gentleman's Daughter*, p. 252; Lancaster Public Library, 8572: Mary Chorley's diary, 17–30 July 1776.
28. Sheffield City RO, MD 1761: diary of Richard Holden, 1835–41.
29. Hertfordshire RO, D/ECK F6: diary of Emma Trotter, 17 June–9 July 1860.
30. Black, *The British Aboard: the Grand Tour in the Eighteenth Century*, especially, pp. 301–3.
31. BL, Add Mss 33633: John Skinner's journal 1788–9.
32. Northamptonshire RO, IC 975-1197. I am grateful to George Drye for showing me Sir Thomas's purchases and relevant documentation at Lamport.
33. Cohen, 'The Grand Tour: Constructing the English Gentleman in Eighteenth-century France', *History of Education* 21 (1992), pp. 241–57; Fletcher, *Gender, Sex and Subordination*, pp. 317–21.
34. Black, *The British Abroad*, pp. 189–204.
35. Bessborough, ed., *Lady Bessborough and her Family Circle*, pp. 18–29.
36. Trench Archive, Clare Howard's diaries 1909–12.

Chapter 22: Friendship and Love

1. West Sussex RO, Add Mss 7462–7464: Sophia Baker's diary, 1793, 20 January–8 April, 10 May–13 June, 7 July , 15 September–29 October 1794, endnote.
2. West Sussex RO, Add Mss 7466, Sophia Baker's diary, 4–13 September 1798.
3. Northamptonshire RO, K 2879: Louisa Bowater's diary, April 1856–February 1857, 18–20 May, 3, 10–18 June 1856.
4. Northamptonshire RO, K 2879: Louisa Bowater's diary, 19 June 1856; Cartwright, ed., *Journals of Lady Knightley*, p. 5; Fletcher, 'Courses in Politeness: The Upbringing and Experiences of Five Teenage Diarists, 1671–1860', in *TRHS*, 12 (2002), pp. 425–6.
5. Northamptonshire RO, K 2879: Louisa Bowater's diary , 20 June–31 December 1856.
6. Cartwright, ed., *Journals of Lady Knightley*, pp. 62–3, 73.
7. Hertfordshire RO, D/ECK F6: Emma Trotter's diary.
8. Magnus, *Gladstone*, pp. 1–8; *ODNB*: Henry and Arthur Hallam.
9. Morley, *The Life of William Ewart Gladstone*, I, pp. 34–42; Foot, ed., *The Gladstone Diaries*, I, pp. 1–91; Fletcher, 'Courses in Politeness: The Upbringing and Experiences of Five Teenage Diarists, 1671–1860', in *TRHS*, 12 (2002), pp. 420–1.

10. Sheffield City RO, MD 1761: diary of Richard Holden, 8 Feb., 23 March, 31 May, 30 Sept. 1840.
11. Sheffield City RO, MD 1761: diary of Richard Holden, 28 August 1841–15 September 1842.
12. Trench Archive, Clare Howard to Reggie Chenevix Trench, 19 June 1912; Clare's photo album, 1912.
13. Trench Archive, Clare Howard to Reggie Chenevix Trench, 11 July 1912.
14. Trench Archive, Reggie Chenevix Trench to Clare Howard, 13, 17 July 1912.
15. Trench Archive, Clare Howard's dance card, The Grand, Folkestone, 27 July 1912.
16. Trench Archive, Clare Howard to Reggie Chenevix Trench, 31 July–14 August 1912; Reggie Chenevix Trench to Clare Howard, 1–10 August 1912.
17. Trench Archive, Clare Howard to Reggie Chenevix Trench, 28, 30 September 1912; Reggie Chenevix Trench to Clare Howard, 29 September 1912.
18. Trench Archive, Charles Pollock to Clare Howard, 23 July 1913.
19. Trench Archive, Clare Howard to Reggie Chenevix Trench, 31 October 1912.
20. Trench Archive, Reggie Chenevix Trench to Clare Howard, 16 December 1912–16 July 1913; Clare Howard to Reggie Chenevix Trench, 14 December 1912–16 July 1913.
21. Fletcher, 'An Officer on the Western Front', *History Today*, 54 (August 2004), pp. 31–7.

Chapter 23: Identity: Class, Nation and Gender

1. For a general account and analysis of class across this period see Cannadine, *Class In Britain*.
2. West Sussex RO, Add Mss 7465, 15 July 1797, 7466, 21–2 August 1798.
3. West Sussex RO, Add Mss 7466, 25–6 January 1798.
4. Kent RO, U1612 F104: autobiography of Meriel Lyttelton; Fletcher, *Victorian Girls*, pp. 26–7.
5. Chatsworth, Lucy Lyttelton's diary, 11 April 1855.
6. Bailey, ed., *The Diary of Lady Frederick Cavendish*, I, pp. 83, 117–18.
7. Cited in Notestein, *English Folk*, p. 63
8. Kent RO, U1612 F104: autobiography of Meriel Lyttelton; Chatsworth, Lucy Lyttelton's autobiography, 26 October 1856.
9. Chatsworth, Lucy Lyttelton's diary, 31 August 1854, 2–4 January, 26 August 1856.
10. Kent RO, U1612 F104: autobiography of Meriel Lyttelton.
11. Chatsworth, Lucy Lyttelton's diary, 24 September–9 October 1856.
12. Cartwright, ed., *Journals of Lady Knightley*, p. 23.
13. Bailey, ed., *The Diary of Lady Frederick Cavendish*, I, p. 351.
14. Chatsworth, Lucy Lyttelton's diary, 5 September 1854, 14 April 1856, 16 October 1858.
15. Bailey, ed., *The Diary of Lady Frederick Cavendish*, I, p. 83.
16. Chatsworth, Lucy Lyttelton's diary, 15 April 1856.
17. Trench Archive, Louey Gore Booth to James Gore Booth, September 1875.
18. BL, Add Mss 42163, fol.7.
19. West Sussex RO, Add Mss 7462.
20. West Sussex RO, Add Mss 7465–7468.
21. Bailey, ed., *The Diary of Lady Frederick Cavendish*, I, pp. 24, 27–8; Chatsworth, Lucy Lyttelton's diary, 16 October–10 November 1854.
22. Northants RO, K2879: Louisa Bowater's diary, 26 April, 11 June 1856.
23. Cartwright, ed., *Journals of Lady Knightley*, p. 10.
24. Bailey, ed., *The Diary of Lady Frederick Cavendish*, I, p. 121.

25. West Sussex RO, Add Mss 7462–7464: Sophia Baker's diary, 19, 22 February 1794, 24 March 1795.
26. West Sussex RO, Add Mss 7465; Fletcher, 'Courses in Politeness: The Upbringing and Experiences of Five Teenage Diarists, 1671–1860', in *TRHS*, 12 (2002), p. 422.
27. West Sussex RO, Add Mss 7462–7517.
28. West Sussex RO, Add Mss 7466–7.
29. West Sussex RO, Add Mss 7468.
30. Bailey, ed., *The Diary of Lady Frederick Cavendish*, I, pp. 31–4, 50–1; Chatsworth, diary of Lucy Lyttelton, 14–16 September 1854, 26 January 1855, 17–22 April 1856, 9 January 1857.
31. Bailey, ed., *The Diary of Lady Frederick Cavendish*, I, pp. 52–7. For the Talbots see Fletcher, *Victorian Girls*, pp. 38–43.
32. Chatsworth, Lucy Lyttlelton's diary, 7 June 1857.
33. Bailey, ed., *The Diary of Lady Frederick Cavendish*, I, pp. 65–79.
34. Bailey, ed., *The Diary of Lady Frederick Cavendish*, I, pp. 94–101; Fletcher, *Victorian Girls*, pp. 49–53; Fletcher, 'Courses in Politeness: The Upbringing and Experiences of Five Teenage Diarists, 1671–1860', in *TRHS*, 12 (2002), pp. 428–9.
35. Bailey, ed., *The Diary of Lady Frederick Cavendish*, I, pp. 113, 115.
36. Northants RO, K2826, Louisa Bowater's 'Account of my First Ball'.
37. Northants RO, K2879: Louisa Bowater's diary, 17 May, 14 July, 30 July, 25, 27 August, 5 September, 26 October 1856; K2880, 29 January–1 February 1857.
38. Above, pp. 288–90.
39. Northants RO, K2882: Louisa Bowater's diary, 10 July 1858.
40. Northamptonshire RO, K2883; Cartwright, *The Journals of Lady Knightley*, p. 14.
41. Cartwright, ed., *Journals of Lady Knightley*, p. 19.
42. *ODNB*, Frederick Cavendish, Sir Rainald Knightley.

Bibliography

Manuscripts Collections

Manuscripts: International

Huntington Library, San Marino, USA

Temple Papers

Lewis Walpole Library, Farmington, USA

Hanbury Williams papers

Manuscripts: National

Bodleian Library

Diary of G.R. Scott
Diary of a Winchester schoolboy

British Library

Add Mss 29575: Hatton Papers
Add Mss 33633–4: Diary of John Skinner
Add Mss 42160–42163: Diaries of Caroline Girle
Loan 29: Harley Papers

Manuscripts: Local

Berkshire Record Office

Pusey Papers

Bristol Record Office

Smyth of Ashton Court Papers

Buckinghamshire Record Office

Grenfell Papers
Ramsden Papers

Chatsworth House
Diary of Lady Frederick Cavendish

Cheshire Record Office
Stanley Papers

Cumbria Record Office
Heber Papers
Lowther Papers

Derbyshire Record Office
Memoir of Elizabeth Bagshawe
Bradshawe Papers
Fitzherbert Papers

Durham Record Office
Beal Papers
Bowes Papers
Pease Papers
Stephenson Papers

East Sussex Record Office
Sayer Papers

Essex Record Office
Bromhead Papers
Capel Papers
Leathes Papers
Western Papers

Hampshire Record Office
Austen–Leigh Papers
Bishop Papers
Heath Papers
Diary of Bessy King
Wiggett Papers
Diary of a Schoolgirl

Hertfordshire Record Office
Barrett Diary
Rugeley Papers
Diaries of Emma Trotter

Kent Record Office

Filmer Papers
Diary of Mary Hallward
Diary of Eva Knatchbull
Autobiography of Meriel Lyttelton
Diary of Meriel Lyttelton
Papillon Papers
Pratt Papers
Twisden Papers

Lancaster Public Library

Diary of Mary Chorley

Leicestershire Record Office

Hastings Papers

Lincolnshire Record Office

Flinders Papers
Diary of Frederick Hett
Monson Papers

Northants Record Office

Diary of Matilda Bosworth
Diary of Lady Louisa Knightley
Dryden Papers
Isham Papers

Sheffield Record Office

Diary of Richard Holden

Staffordshire Record Office

Congreve Papers
Eyre Papers
Fletcher Papers
Twenlow Papers

Suffolk Record Office

Barne Papers
Diary of George Corrance
Diary of Edmund Holland
Holland Papers
Long Papers

Warwickshire Record Office

Fielding Papers
Mordaunt Papers
Seymour Papers
Warriner Papers

West Sussex Record Office

Diary of Sophia Baker
Goodwood Papers
Diary of Katherine Neale

Wiltshire Record Office

Bruce Papers

Manuscripts: In Private Hands

Bloomfield Archive
Coffey Archive
Loughton Archive
Trench Archive

Printed Primary Sources

J.H. Adeane (ed.), *The Early Married Life of Maria Josepha, Lady Stanley* (1897)
J.H. Adeane (ed.), *The Girlhood of Maria Josepha Holroyd* (1896)
W. Alexander, *The History of Women from the Earliest Antiquity to the Present Time* (1779)
F. Alford (ed.), *Life, Journals and Letters of Henry Alford* (1873)
H. Allen, *A Beloved Mother: Life of Hannah Allen* (1889)
R. Allestree, *The Gentleman's Calling* (1660)
R. Allestree, *The Lady's Calling* (1673)
Marquess of Anglesey (ed.), *The Capel Letters, Being the Correspondence of Lady Caroline Capel and her Daughters with the Dowager Countess of Uxbridge 1814–17* (1955)
E. and F. Anson (eds), *Mary Hamilton: At Court and at Home* (1925)
C. Aspinall-Oglander (ed.), *Admiral's Wife: Life and Letters of Fanny Boscawen 1719–1761* (1940)
J.L. Axtell, *The Educational Writings of John Locke* (Cambridge, 1969)
J. Bailey (ed.), *The Diary of Lady Frederick Cavendish*, 2 vols (1927)
K.C. Balderston (ed.), *Thraliana: the Diary of Mrs Hester Lynch Thrale 1776–1809* (1951)
F. Bamford (ed.), *A Royalist's Notebook* (1936)
A. Barbauld, *Lessons for Children* (1778)
Lady Muriel Beckwith, *When I Remember* (1936)
Earl of Bessborough (ed.), *Lady Bessborough and Her Family Circle* (1940)
Earl of Bessborough (ed.), *Extracts from the Journal of Lady Charlotte Guest 1832–52* (1950)
F. Bickley (ed.), *Diaries of Sylvester Douglas*, 2 vols (1928)
R. Bird (ed.), *The Journal of Giles Moore* (Sussex Record Society, LXIII, 1971)
H.J.C. Blake, *Reminiscences of an Etonian* (1831)
N. Blundell (ed.), *Blundell's Diary and Letter Book 1702–28* (Liverpool, 1952)
R. Braithwaite, *The English Gentleman* (1628)
R. Braithwaite, *The English Gentlewoman* (1631)

W. Bray (ed.), *Diary and Correspondence of John Evelyn*, 2 vols (1850–2)

T. Broughton and R. Symes (eds), *The Governess: An Anthology* (1997)

J. Caffyn, *Sussex Schools in the Eighteenth Century* (Sussex Record Society, LXXXI, 1998)

M. Carberry, *Happy World: The Story of a Victorian Childhood* (1941)

E. Carpenter, *My Days and Dreams* (1916)

J. Cartwright, *Sacharissa: Some Account of Dorothy Sidney, Countess of Sunderland 1617–84* (1893)

J. Cartwright (ed.), *The Journals of Lady Knightley of Fawsley 1856–1884* (1915)

H. Chapone, *Letters on the Improvement of the Mind Addressed to a Young Lady* (1773)

L.E.O. Charlton, *Recollections of a Northumbrian Lady* (1949)

O.F. Christie (ed.), *The Diary of Reverend William Jones 1777–1821* (1929)

J. Cleland, *The Institution of a Young Nobleman* (1607)

D.J.H. Clifford (ed.), *The Diaries of Lady Anne Clifford* (1990)

T. Cogan, *The Haven of Health* (1596)

L. Cohen, *Lady de Rothschild and her Daughters 1821–1931* (1935)

Memoirs and Letters of Sara Coleridge (1873)

T.R.F. Cooke-Trench, *A Memoir of the Trench Family* (1897)

The Private Correspondence of Lady Jane Cornwallis (1842)

M. Cowden-Clarke, *My Long Life* (1896)

G. Curtis, *A Chronicle of Small Beer: The Early Victorian Diary of a Hertfordshire Brewer* (1970)

Lady Elizabeth Cust (ed.), *Records of the Cust Family* (1898)

E. De Beer (ed.), *Diary of John Evelyn* (1955)

Henry, Lord Delaware, Earl of Warrington, *Advice to his Children* (1696)

J. Dod and R. Cleaver, *A Godly Form of Household Government* (1614)

V. Doe (ed.), *The Diary of James Clegg of Chapel-en-le-Frith 1708–1755, Part I* (Derbyshire Record Society, II, 1978)

C. Ellis, *The Gentle Sinner or England's Brave Gentleman* (1660)

S. Ellis, *Daughters of England* (1842)

S. Ellis, *The Women of England, their Social Duties and Domestic Habits* (1850)

T. Elyot, *The Book Named the Governor* (1531)

J. Essex, *The Young Ladies Conduct* (1722)

A. Fairfax-Lucy (ed.), *Mistress of Charlecote: The Memoirs of Mary Elizabeth Lucy* (1983)

J. Fiske (ed.), *The Oakes Diaries: Business, Politics and the Family in Bury St Edmonds 1778–1827*, 2 vols (Suffolk Records Society, 1990)

M.R.D. Foot (ed.), *The Gladstone Diaries*, Vol I, 1825–1832 (1968)

Lady Angela Forbes, *Memories and Base Details* (1921)

J. Fordyce, *Sermons to Young Women* (1766)

J. Fordyce, *Addresses to Young Men* (1777)

W.J. Fox (ed.), *Memoir of Mrs Eliza Fox* (1869)

B. Francis and E. Keary (eds), *The Francis Letters* (1901)

A. Freemantle (ed.), *The Wynne Diaries* (1940)

J. Gailhard, *The Compleat Gentleman: or Directions for the Education of Youth as to their Breeding at home and Travelling abroad* (1678)

D. Gardiner (ed.), *The Oxinden and Peyton Letters 1642–1670* (1937)

B.T. Gates (ed.), *Journal of Emily Shore (1991)*

The Hon. Mrs Gell, *Under Three Reigns 1860–1920* (1927)

J. Gisborne, *A Brief Memoir of his Life* (1852)

T. Gisborne, *An Enquiry into the Duties of Men* (1794)

T. Gisborne, *An Enquiry into the Duties of the Female Sex* (1798)

E. Gosse, *Father and Son* (1907)

W. Gouge, *Domestical Duties* (1622)

E. Gray (ed.), *Papers and Diaries of a York Family 1764–1839* (1927)

J. Gregory, *A Father's Legacy to his Daughters* (1774)

S. Gurney (ed.), *Isabel Mrs Gurney* (1935)

N. Guy, *Piety's Pillar, a Sermon Preached at the Funeral of Mistress Gouge* (1626)

L.K. Haldane, *Friends and Kindred: Memoirs* (1961)

M.E. Haldane, *Record of a Hundred Years 1825–1925* (1925)

Marquess of Halifax, George Saville, *The Lady's New Year Gift or Advice to a Daughter* (1688)

E. Hall (ed.), *Miss Weeton's Journal of a Governess* (Newton Abbott, 1969)

C. Hanbury, *Life of Mrs Albert Head* (1905)

A.J.C. Hare, *The Years with Mother* (1952)

A. Hassell-Smith, *et al.* (eds), *The Papers of Nathaniel Bacon of Stiffkey* (1979)

A. Henstock (ed.), *Diary of Abigail Gawthern of Nottingham* (Thoroton Society, 33, 1980)

T. Heywood, *A Curtain Lecture* (1637)

E. Hobhouse (ed.), *The Diary of a West Country Physician* (Rochester, 1934)

E. Hodder, *The Life and Work of the Seventh Earl of Shaftesbury*, vol. I, (1886)

C.M. Howard, *Reminiscences of my Children*, 2 vols (1831)

I.E.M., *The Confessions of an Etonian* (1846)

Countess of Ilchester and Lord Stavordale (eds), *Life and Letters of Lady Sarah Lennox, 1745–1826* (1902)

M.E. Ingram, *Leaves from a Family Tree* (Hull, 1957)

Sir G. Isham (ed.), *The Diary of Thomas Isham of Lamport* (1971)

S. Jenyns, *The Modern Fine Lady* (1717)

Countess of Jersey, *Fifty-one Years of Victorian Life* (1922)

L.E. Jones, *A Victorian Boyhood* (1955)

E. Joceline, *A Mother's Legacy to her Unborn Child* (1624)

W. Kenrick, *The Whole Duty of Woman* (1753)

L. King-Hall, *Sea Saga: the Naval Diaries of Four Generations of the King-Hall Family* (1935)

R.C. Latham (ed.), *Diary of Samual Pepys*, 12 vols (1970–7)

D. Leigh, *The Mother's Blessing* (1616)

T. Lewis (ed.), *Letters of the Lady Brilliana Harley* (1854)

J. Loftis (ed.), *The Memoirs of Anne Lady Halkett and Anne Lady Fanshawe* (1979)

Lady Emily Lutyens, *A Blessed Girl* (1989)

A. Macfarlane (ed.), *The Diary of Ralph Josselin 1616–1683* (1976)

J.M. Magrath (ed.), *The Flemings in Oxford: Documents selected from the Rydal Papers*, vol. I, 1650–1680 (Oxford Historical Society, 1904)

Bernard Mandeville, *The Fable of the Bees* (1724)

T. Marriott, *Female Conduct being an Essay on the Art of Pleasing* (1759)

J. Martin (ed.), *A Governess in the Age of Jane Austen: The Journal and Letters of Agnes Porter* (1998)

W. Martyn, *Youth's Instruction* (1613)

N. Mitford (ed.), *The Ladies of Alderley: Letters between Maria Josepha and her daughter-in-law Henrietta Maria* (1938)

N. Mitford (ed.), *The Stanleys of Alderley* (1939)

J. Moir, *Female Tuition or an Address to Mothers on the Education of Daughters* (1800)

H. More, *Strictures on the Modern System of Female Education* (1799)

J. Nelson, *An Essay on the Government of Children* (1763)

R. Neville (ed.), *The Reminiscences of Lady Dorothy Neville* (1909)

R. North, *The Lives of the Norths* (1890)

J. Oxley Parker, *The Oxley Parker Papers* (Colchester, 1964)

G. Palgrave (ed.), *Francis Turner Palgrave: His Journals and Memories of his Life* (1899)

R. Parkinson (ed.), *The Private Journal and Literary Remains of John Byrom* (Chetham Society, vols 32, 34, 40, 1854)

S. Pennington, *An Unfortunate Mother's Advice to her Absent Daughters in a Letter to Mrs Pennington* (1761)

T. Percival, *A Father's Instructions Consisting of Moral Tales, Fables and Reflections* (1781)

F.J. Post, *Extracts from his Diary and other Manuscripts* (1838)

L. Price, *The Virtuous Wife is the Glory of her Husband* (1667)

J.R. Richards, *Seven Years at Eton 1857–1864* (1883)

J.-J. Rousseau, *Emile* (1762)

B. and P. Russell (eds), *The Amberley Papers: The Letters and Diaries of Lord and Lady Amberley* (1937)

Lord John Russell (ed.), *Memoirs, Journal and Correspondence of Thomas Moore* (1853)

T. Sadler (ed.), *Diary, Reminiscences and Correspondence of Henry Crabb Robinson* (1869)

M. St Clare Byrne (ed.), *The Lisle Letters* (1982)

E. Sandford, *Woman in her Social and Domestic Character* (1831)

T. Scott, *A Father's Instructions to his Son* (1620)

E. Sewell, *Principles of Education* (1865)

M. Sewell, *The Life and Letters of Mrs Sewell* (1869)

E. Sheppard (ed.), *George Duke of Cambridge: A Memoir of his Private Life*, vol I, 1819–1871, (1906)

O. Sitwell (ed.), *Two Generations* (1940)

R. Steele, *The Ladies Library* (1714)

P. Sterry, *Annals of Eton College* (1898)

A.M.W. Stirling (ed.), *The Diaries of Drummer* (1934)

A. Strutt (ed.), *The Strutt Family of Terling 1845–1973* (1980)

I. Taylor, *Advice to the Teens or Practical Helps Towards the Formation of One's Own Character* (1818)

M. Thale (ed.), *Autobiography of Francis Place 1771–1854* (1972)

C. Thomas-Stanford (ed.), *The Private Memorandums of William Roe 1775–1809* (1928)

J.O. Thompson (ed.), *Dr Salter: His Diary and Reminiscences 1849–1932* (1933)

S. Thompson (ed.), *The Journal of John Gabriel Stedman 1744–97* (1962)

D. Townshend, *The Life and Letters of Mr Endymion Porter* (1897)

W. Toynbee (ed.), *The Diaries of William Charles Macready 1833–51* (1912)

R. Trappes-Lomax (ed.), *The Diary and Letter Book of Reverend Thomas Brockbank 1679–1709* (1930)

F. Trench, *A Few Notes From Past Life 1818–1832 Edited From Correspondence* (1862)

M. Trench, *Thoughts on Education by a Parent* (1837)

M. Trench (ed.), *Letters and Memorials of Archbishop Richard Chenevix Trench* (1888)

R.C. Trench, *The Remains of the Late Mrs Richard Trench* (1862)

L.E. Troide (ed.), *The Early Journals and Letters of Fanny Burney*, I, 1768–1773 (1988)

F.P. Verney (ed.), *The Memoirs of the Verney Family*, 4 vols (1970)

Margaret Lady Verney, *Verney Letters of the Eighteenth Century from the MSS at Claydon House* (1930)

O. Walker, *Of Education, Especially of Young Gentlemen* (1673)

R. Warner (ed.), *Epistolary Curiosities* (1818)

Earl of Warrington, *Advice to his Children* (1696)

Frances, Countess of Warwick, *Life's Ebb and Flow* (1930)

P. Watkin (ed.), *A Kingston Lacy Childhood: Reminiscences of Viola Banks* (1986)

A. Weight Matthews (ed.), *Elizabeth Mascall: Remnants of a Life* (1902)

H.J. Whale (ed.), *My Grandfather's Pocket Book* (1883)

W. Whateley, *The Bride Bush* (1623)

W. Wilkes, *A Letter of Genteel and Moral Advice to a Young Lady* (1780)

Diary of Lady Willoughby (1845)

D. Woodforde (ed.), *Woodforde Papers and Diaries* (1932)

Extracts from the Journal of Margaret Woods (1829)

H. Wotton, *An Essay on the Education of Children in the First Rudiments of Learning* (1753)
J.W. and J.S. Yolton, *Works of John Locke* (1989)

Printed Secondary Sources: Books

N. Armstrong, *Desire and Domestic Fiction: A Political History of the Novel* (1987)
J. Bailey, *Unquiet Lives: Marriage and Marriage Breakdown in England 1660–1800* (2003)
G.J. Barker-Benfield, *The Culture of Sensibility: Sex and Society in Eighteenth-Century Britain* (1992)
J. Barry and C. Brooks, *The Middling Sort of People: Culture, Society and Politics in England, 1550–1800* (1994)
R. Bayne-Powell, *The English Child in the Eighteenth Century* (1939)
L. McC.Beier, *Sufferers and Healers: The Experience of Illness in Seventeenth-Century England* (1987)
J. Black, *The British Abroad: The Grand Tour in the Eighteenth Century* (1992)
P. Borsay, *The English Urban Renaissance: Culture and Society in the Provincial Town, 1660–1770* (1989)
E. Bowen, *Bowen's Court and Seven Winters* (1999)
T. Bowers, *The Politics of Motherhood: British Writing and Culture, 1680–1760* (1996)
G.C. Brauer, *The Education of a Gentleman: Theories of Gentlemanly Education in England* (1959)
J. Brewer, *The Pleasures of the Imagination: English Culture in the Eighteenth Century* (1997)
J. Bromley, *The Man of Ten Talents: A Portrait of Richard Chenevix Trench 1807–86* (1959)
A. Bryson, *From Courtesy to Civility: Changing Codes of Conduct in Early Modern England* (1998)
S. Cahn, *Industry of Devotion: The Transformation of Women's Work in England* (1987)
K. Calvert, *Children in the House: The Material Culture of Early Childhood 1600–1900* (1992)
D. Cannadine, *Class in Britain* (1998)
P. Carter, *Men and the Emergence of Polite Society* (2001)
J. Chandos, *Boys Together: English Public Schools 1800–1864* (1984)
K. Charlton, *Women, Religion and Education in Early Modern England* (1999)
C. Chenevix Trench, *My Mother Told Me* (1958)
F. Chenevix Trench, *The Story of Orpington* (1898)
P. Clark (ed.), *The Cambridge Urban History of Britain*, II, 1540–1840 (2000)
J.T. Cliffe, *The Puritan Gentry: The Great Puritan Families of Early Stuart England* (1984)
M. Cohen, *Fashioning Masculinity: National Identity and Language in the Eighteenth Century* (1996)
P. Collinson, *The Religion of Protestants: The Church in English Society 1559–1625* (1982)
P. Collinson, *The Birthpangs of Protestant England: Religious and Cultural Change in the Sixteenth and Seventeenth Centuries* (1988)
N. Cooper, *Houses of the Gentry 1480–1680* (1999)
P. Coveney, *The Image of Childhood* (1957)
H. Cunningham, *Children and Childhood in Western Society* (1995)
M. Curtin, *Propriety and Position: A Study of Victorian Manners* (1987)
M. Daunton (ed.), *The Cambridge Urban History of Britain*, III 1840–1950 (2000)
L. Davidoff, *The Best Circles: 'Society', Etiquette and the Season* (1986)
L. Davidoff, *Worlds Between: Historical Perspectives on Gender and Class* (1995)
L. Davidoff and C. Hall, *Family Fortunes: Men and Women of the English Middle Class 1780–1850* (1987)
L. Davidoff, M. Doolittle, J. Fink, K. Holden, *The Family Story: Blood, Contract and Intimacy 1830–1960* (1999)
C. Dyhouse, *Girls Growing Up in Late Victorian and Edwardian England* (1981)

J. Eales, *Puritans and Roundheads: The Harleys of Brampton Bryan and the Outbreak of the English Civil War* (1990)

A.C. Edwards, *The Scribble Book of an Eton Boy 1758–67* (1952)

M.J.M. Ezell, *The Patriarch's Wife: Literary Evidence and the History of the Family* (1987)

K. and M. Fawday, *Pollock's History of English Dolls and Toys* (1962)

V.A. Fildes, *Breasts, Babies and Bottles* (1986)

V.A. Fildes (ed.) *Women as Mothers in Pre-Industrial England* (1990)

A.J. Fletcher, *A County Community in Peace and War: Sussex 1600–1660* (1975)

A.J. Fletcher, *Gender, Sex and Subordination in England 1500–1800* (1995)

A.J. Fletcher, *Richard Chenevix Trench and his Legacy* (2007)

S. Fletcher, *Victorian Girls: Lord Lyttelton's Daughters* (1997)

M. Garber, *Bisexuality and the Eroticism of Everyday Life* (2000)

I. Gibson, *The English Vice: Beating, Sex and Shame in Victorian England and After* (1978)

J.R. Gillis, *A World of their Own Making: A History of Myth and Ritual in Family Life* (1997)

K. Flint, *The Woman Reader 1837–1914* (1993)

J. Gerard, *Country House Life: Family and Servants 1815–1914* (1994)

M. Girouard, *Life in the English Country House: A Social and Architectural History* (1978)

M. Girouard, *The Return to Camelot: Chivalry and the English Gentleman* (1981)

D. Gorham, *The Victorian Girl and the Feminine Ideal* (1982)

L. Gowing, *Domestic Dangers: Women, Words and Sex in Early Modern London* (1996)

C. Haigh (ed.), *Cambridge Historical Encyclopedia of Great Britain and Ireland* (1985)

A.J. Hammerton, *Cruelty and Companionship: Conflict in Nineteenth-Century Married Life* (1992)

K. Harvey, *Reading Sex in the Eighteenth Century* (2004)

F. Heal, *Hospitality in Early Modern England* (1990)

K.U. Henderson and B.F. McManus, *Half Humankind: Contexts and Texts of the Controversy about Women in England, 1540–1640* (1985)

C. Heywood, *Growing Up in France: From the Ancien Régime to the Third Republic* (2007)

B. Hill, *Eighteenth-Century Women: An Anthology* (1984)

C. Hill, *Society and Puritanism in Pre-Revolutionary England* (1964)

T. Hitchcock, *English Sexualities 1700–1800* (1997)

E. Hobby, *Virtue of Necessity: English Women's Writings 1649–1688* (1988)

R. Houlbrooke (ed.), *English Family Life 1576–1716: An Anthology from Diaries* (Oxford, 1989)

R. Houlbrooke, *Death, Religion and the Family in England 1480–1750* (1998)

K. Hughes, *The Victorian Governess* (1993)

S.W. Hull, *Chaste, Silent and Obedient: English Books for Women 1475–1640* (1982)

M.R. Hunt, *The Middling Sort: Commerce, Gender and the Family in England 1680–1780* (1996)

M. Hyde, *The Thrales of Streatham Park* (1976)

M.V. Jackson, *Engines of Instruction, Mischief and Magic: Children's Literature in England from its Beginnings to 1839* (1989)

P. Jalland, *Death in the Victorian Family* (1996)

P. Jenkins, *The Making of a Ruling Class: The Glamorgan Gentry 1640–1790* (1983)

V. Jones (ed.), *Women in the Eighteenth Century: Constructions of Femininity* (1990)

L. Jordanova, *Sexual Visions: Images of Gender in Science and Medicine Between the Eighteenth and Twentieth Centuries* (1989)

J. Kamm, *Hope Deferred: Girls' Education in English History* (1965)

L. Klein, *Shaftesbury and the Culture of Politeness: Moral Discourse and Cultural Politics in Early Eighteenth-Century England* (1994)

N. Landau, *The Justices of the Peace 1679–1760* (1984)

P. Langford, *A Polite and Commercial People: England 1727–1783* (1992)

T. Laqueur, *Making Sex: Body and Gender from the Greeks to Freud* (1990)

V. Larminie, *Wealth, Kinship and Culture: The Seventeenth-Century Newdigates of Arbury and their World* (1995)

N. McKendrick, J. Brewer and J.H. Plumb, *The Birth of a Consumer Society: The Commercialisation of Eighteenth-Century England* (1983)

M. McConville, *Ascendancy to Oblivion: The Story of the Anglo-Irish* (1986)

M. Macdonald, *Mystical Bedlam: Madness, Anxiety and Healing in Seventeenth-Century England* (1981)

A. Macfarlane, *The Family Life of Ralph Josselin: A Seventeenth-Century Clergyman* (1970)

P. Mack, *Visionary Women: Ecstatic Prophecy in Seventeenth-Century England* (1992)

N. MacMahon, *In the Shadow of Fairy Hill* (1998)

P. Magnus, *Gladstone* (1954)

G.H. Martin and J.R.L. Highfield, *A History of Merton College, Oxford* (1997)

J. Martin, *Wives and Daughters: Women and Children in the Georgian Country House* (2004)

S.H. Mendelson, *The Mental World of Stuart Women: Three Studies* (1987)

S.H. Mendelson and P. Crawford, *Women in Early Modern England* (1998)

G. Midgley, *University Life in Eighteenth-Century Oxford* (1996)

G. Miller, *The Adoption of Inoculation for Smallpox in England and France* (1957)

S. Mitchell, *The New Girl: Girls' Culture in England 1880–1915* (1995)

M. Morgan, *Manners, Morals and Class in England* (1994)

S. Morgan, *Sisters in Time: Imagining Gender in Nineteenth-Century British Fiction* (1989)

J. Morley, *The Life of Gladstone* (1903)

O. Moscucci, *The Science of Woman: Gynaecology and Gender in England 1800–1929* (1990)

S.H. Myers, *The Bluestocking Circle: Women, Friendship and the Life of the Mind in Eighteenth-Century England* (1990)

D.H. Newsome, *A History of Wellington College 1859–1959* (1959)

D.H. Newsome, *Godliness and Good Learning: Four Studies on a Victorian Ideal* (1961)

W. Notestein, *English Folk: A Book of Characters* (1938)

R. O'Day, *Education and Society 1500–1800: The Social Foundations of Education in Early Modern Britain* (1982)

N. Orme, *From Childhood to Chivalry: The Education of Kings and Aristocrats 1066–1530* (1984)

H. Owen, *The Lowther Family* (1990)

R. Pearsall, *The Worm in the Bud: The World of Victorian Sexuality* (1993)

R. Perry, *Novel Relations: The Transformation of Kinship in English Literature and Culture, 1748–1818* (2004)

S.F. Pickering, *John Locke and Children's Books in Eighteenth-Century England* (1981)

J.H. Plumb, *The Pursuit of Happiness: A View of Life in Georgian England* (1977)

L.A. Pollock, *Forgotten Children: Parent-Child Relations from 1500 to 1900* (1983)

L.A. Pollock, *A Lasting Relationship: Parents and Children over Three Centuries* (1987)

L.A. Pollock, *With Faith and Physic: the Life of a Tudor Gentlewoman Lady Grace Mildmay 1552–1620* (1993)

M. Poovey, *The Proper Lady and the Woman Writer: Ideology as Style in the Works of Mary Wollstonecraft, Mary Shelley and Jane Austen* (1984)

R. Porter, *Disease, Medicine and Society in England 1550–1860* (1987)

K. Retford, *The Art of Domestic Life: Family Portraiture in Eighteenth-Century England* (2006)

R.C. Richardson, *Puritanism in North-West England* (1972)

H. Ricketts, *The Unforgiving Minute: A Life of Rudyard Kipling* (2000)

P. Rogers, *Feminism in Eighteenth-Century England* (1956)

L. Roper, *Oedipus and the Devil: Witchcraft, Sexuality and Religion in Early Modern Europe* (1994)

M. Roper and J. Tosh (eds), *Manful Assertions: Masculinities in Britain since 1800* (1991)

L. Schiebinger, *The Mind Has No Sex?: Women in the Origins of Modern Science* (1989)

L.L. Schucking, *The Puritan Family: A Social Study from Literary Sources* (1969)

P.S. Seaver, *Wallington's World: A Puritan Artisan in Seventeenth-Century London* (1985)

A. Shepard, *Meanings of Manhood in Early Modern England* (2003)

R.E. Shoemaker, *Gender in English Society: The Emergence of Separate Spheres?* (1998)

M. Slater, *Family Life in the Seventeenth Century: The Verneys of Claydon House* (1984)

H. Smith, *Reason's Disciples* (1982)

M.R. Sommerville, *Sex and Subjection: Attitudes to Women in Early Modern Society* (1995)

M. Spufford, *Small Books and Pleasant Histories* (1981)

L. Stone, *The Family, Sex and Marriage in England 1500–1800* (1977)

A.G. Sulloway, *Jane Austen and the Province of Womanhood* (1989)

G. Summerfield, *Fantasy and Reason: Children's Literature in the Eighteenth Century* (1984)

I.H. Tague, *Women of Quality: Accepting and Contesting Ideals of Femininity in England, 1890–1760* (2002)

K.V. Thomas, *Religion and the Decline of Magic* (1971)

K.V. Thomas, *Rule and Misrule in the Schools of Early Modern England* (1976)

F.M.L. Thompson, *The Rise of Respectable Society: A Social History of Victorian Britain* (1988)

S. Tillyard, *Aristocrats: Caroline, Emily, Louisa and Sarah Lennox 1740–1832* (1994)

A. Tinniswood, *Belton House* (1992)

J. Tosh, *A Man's Place: Masculinity and the Middle-Class Home in Victorian England* (1999)

R. Trumbach, *The Rise of the Egalitarian Family* (1978)

A. Vickery, *The Gentleman's Daughter: Women's Lives in Georgian England* (1998)

A.A. Wace, *The Story of Wadhurst* (1923)

M. Willes, *Memories of Childhood* (National Trust, 1997)

K. Wrightson, *English Society 1580–1680* (1982)

Printed Secondary Sources: Articles and Essays

S.D. Amussen, '"The Part of a Christian Man": The Cultural Politics of Manhood in Early Modern England', in S.D. Amussen and M.A. Kishlansky (eds), *Political Culture and Cultural Politics in Early Modern England: Essays Presented to David Underdown* (1995)

J. Bailey, 'Reassessing Parenting in Eighteenth-Century England', in H. Berry and E. Foyster (eds), *The Family in Early Modern England* (2007)

J. Barber, '"Stolen Goods": The Sexual Harassment of Female Servants in West Wales during the Nineteenth Century', *Rural History*, 4 (1993)

D. Berger, 'Maxims of Conduct into Literature: Jonathan Swift and Polite Conversation', in J. Carre (ed.), *The Crisis of Courtesy* (1994)

H. Berry, 'Creating Polite Space: The Organisation and Social Function of the Newcastle Assembly Rooms', in H. Berry and J. Gregory (eds), *Creating and Consuming Culture in North-East England, 1660–1830* (2004)

H. Berry, 'Sense and Singularity: The Social Experiences of John Marsh and Thomas Stutterd in Late-Georgian England', in H. French and J. Barry (eds), *Identity and Agency in England 1500–1800* (2004)

P. Borsay, 'Children, Adolescents and Fashionable Urban Society in Eighteenth-Century England', in A. Muller (ed.), *Fashioning Children in the Eighteenth Century* (2006)

P. Carter, 'Men about Town: Representations of Foppery and Masculinity in early Eighteenth-century Urban Society', in H. Barker and E. Challus (eds), *Gender in Eighteenth-Century England: Roles, Representations and Responsibilities* (1997)

P. Carter, 'An "Effeminate" or an "Efficient" Nation? Masculinity and Eighteenth-Century Documentary', *Textual Practice*, 11 (1997)

M. Cohen, 'The Grand Tour: Constructing the English Gentleman in Eighteenth-Century France', *History of Education*, 21 (1992)

M. Cohen, 'Manliness, Effeminacy and the French: Gender and the Construction of National Character in Eighteenth-Century England', in T. Hitchcock and M. Cohen (eds), *English Masculinities 1660–1800* (1999)

P. Crawford, 'Women's Published Writings 1600–1700', in M. Prior (ed.), *Women in English Society* (1985)

P. Crawford, 'The Sucking Child: Adult Attitudes to Child Care in the First Year of Life in Seventeenth-Century England', *Continuity and Change*, 1 (1986)

P. Crawford, 'The Construction and Experience of Maternity in Seventeenth-Century England', in V. Fildes (ed.), *Women as Mothers in Pre-Industrial England: Essays in Memory of Dorothy McLaren* (1990)

A. Digby, 'Women's Biological Straitjacket', in S. Mendus and J. Rendall, *Sexuality and Subordination: Interdisciplinary Studies of Gender in the Nineteenth Century* (1989)

M. Fissell, 'Gender and Generation: Representing Reproduction in Early Modern England', *Gender and History*, 7 (1995)

A.J. Fletcher, 'The Expansion of Education in Berkshire and Oxfordshire 1500–1670', *British Journal of Educational Studies*, XV (1967)

A.J. Fletcher, 'Men's Dilemma: The Future of Patriarchy in England 1560–1660', *TRHS*, IV (1994)

A.J. Fletcher, 'The Protestant Idea of Marriage in Early Modern England', in A.J. Fletcher and P.R. Roberts (eds) *Religion, Culture and Society in Early Modern England: Essays in Honour of Patrick Collinson* (1994)

A.J. Fletcher, 'Prescription and Practice: Protestantism and the Upbringing of Children, 1560–1700', in D. Wood (ed.), *The Church and Childhood*, Studies in Church History, 31 (1994)

A.J. Fletcher, 'Beyond the Church: Women's Spiritual Experience at Home and in the Community 1600–1900', in R.W. Swanson (ed.), *Gender and Christian Religion*, Studies in Church History, 34 (1998)

A.J. Fletcher, 'Courses in Politeness: The Upbringing and Experiences of Five Teenage Diarists, 1671–1860', *TRHS* 12 (2002)

A.J. Fletcher, 'An Officer on the Western Front', *History Today*, 54 (2004)

A.J. Fletcher, 'Patriotism, Identity and Commemoration: New Light on the Great War from the Papers of Major Reggie Chenevix Trench', *History*, 90 (2005)

E. Foyster, 'A Laughing Matter? Marital Discord and Gender Control in Seventeenth-Century England', *Rural History: Economy, Society, Culture,* 4 (1993)

E. Foyster, 'Boys will be boys? Manhood and Aggression, 1660–1800', in T. Hitchcock and M. Cohen (eds), *English Masculinities 1660–1800* (1999)

J.R. Gillis, 'Servants, Sexual Relations and the Risks of Illegitimacy in London 1801–1900', in J.L. Newton, *et al.*, *Sex and Class in Women's History* (1983)

E. Hatch, 'Some Reminiscences of Oxford', *Oxford Magazine* (14 June, 1956)

V. Jones, 'The Seduction of Conduct: Pleasure and Conduct Literature', in R. Porter and M.M. Roberts (eds), *Pleasure in the Eighteenth Century* (1996)

K. Kitteridge, 'Melesina Chenevix St George Trench (1768–1827)', *The Female Spectator*, 10 (2006)

L. Klein, 'Liberty, Manners and Politeness in early Eighteenth-Century England', *Historical Journal*, 32 (1989)

G. Lamoine, 'Lord Chesterfield's "Letters" as Conduct Books', in J. Carre (ed.) *The Crisis of Courtesy* (1994)

P.M. Lewis, 'Mummy, Matron and the Maids: Feminine Presence and Absence in Male Institutions 1934–1963', in M. Roper and J. Tosh (eds), *Manful Assertions: Masculinities in Britain since 1800* (1991)

H.I. Longden, 'The Diaries (Home and Foreign) of Sir Justinian Isham 1704–1736', *TRHS* (1907)

J.A. Mangan, 'Social Darwinism and Upper Class Education in Late Victorian and Edwardian England', in J.A. Mangan and J. Walvin, *Manliness and Morality: Middle-class Masculinity in Britain and America, 1800–1940* (1987)

T. Meldrum, 'A Women's Court in London: Defamation at the Bishop of London's Consistory Court 1700–1745', *London Journal*, 19 (1994)

F. Neddam, 'Constructing Masculinities under Thomas Arnold of Rugby (1828–1842): Gender, Educational Policy and School Life in an Early-Victorian Public School', *Gender and Education*, 16 (2004)

R. Perry, 'Colonising the Breast: Sexuality and Maternity in Eighteenth-Century England', *Eighteenth-Century Life*, 16 (1992)

J.H. Plumb, 'The New World of Children', *Past and Present*, 67 (1975)

L.A. Pollock, '"Teach Her to Live Under Obedience": The Making of Women in the Upper Ranks of Early Modern England', *Continuity and Change*, 4 (1989)

L.A. Pollock, 'Embarking on a Rough Passage: the Experience of Pregnancy in Early Modern Society', in V. Fildes (ed.), *Women as Mothers in Pre-Industrial England: Essays in Memory of Dorothy McLaren* (1990)

S. Porter, 'The University and Society', in N.R.N. Tyacke (ed.), *The History of the University of Oxford*, vol. IV

D. Roberts, 'The Paterfamilias of the Victorian Governing Classes', in A.S. Wohl (ed.), *The Victorian Family* (1978)

M.T. Ryan, 'The First Lord Bloomfield', *Newport News* (1990)

R.V. Schnucker, 'Puritan Attitudes Towards Childhood Discipline', in V. Fildes (ed.), *Women as Mothers in Pre-Industrial England: Essays in Memory of Dorothy McLaren* (1990)

J.W. Scott, 'Gender: A Useful Category of Historical Analysis', in J.W. Scott, *Gender and the Politics of History* (1988)

S. Skedd, 'Women Teachers and the Expansion of Girls' Schooling in England, c. 1760–1820', in H. Barker and E. Challus (eds), *Gender in Eighteenth-century England: Roles, Representations and Responsibilities* (1997)

K.V. Thomas, 'Age and Authority in Early Modern England', *Proceedings of the British Academy*, 52 (1976)

K.V. Thomas, 'Art and Iconoclasm in Early Modern England', in K. Fincham and P. Lake (eds), *Religious Politics in Post-Reformation England: Essays in Honour of Nicholas Tyacke* (2006)

J. Tosh, 'Authority and Nurture in Middle Class Fatherhood: the Case of Early and Mid-Victorian England', *Gender and History*, 8 (1996)

J. Tosh, 'The Old Adam and the New Man: Emerging Themes in the History of English Masculinities, 1750–1850' , in T. Hitchcock and M. Cohen (eds), *English Masculinities 1660–1800* (1999)

H. Twycross-Martin, 'Woman Supportive or Woman Manipulative? The "Mrs Ellis" Woman', in C.C. Orr (ed.), *Wollstonecraft's Daughters: Womanhood in England and France 1780–1920* (1996)

C. Williams, 'Illness and Impact: The Mistress of the House and the Governess', in K. Harvey (ed.), *The Kiss in History* (2005)

A. Wilson, 'The Ceremony of Childbirth and its Interpretation', in V. Fildes (ed.), *Women as Mothers in Pre-Industrial England: Essays in Memory of Dorothy McLaren* (1990)

Unpublished Theses

F.A. Childs, 'Prescriptions for Manners in English Courtesy Literature 1690–1760 and their Social Implications', DPhil thesis, Oxford University (1984)

C. Williams, 'Ideology and Identity: Married Women's Experience c. 1800–1900', PhD thesis, Essex University (2005)

Index

428